UNIX® for Programmers and Users

Second Edition

Graham Glass
ObjectSpace

King Ables
Hewlett-Packard Company

Prentice Hall
Upper Saddle River, New Jersey 07458

Library of Congress Cataloging-in-Publication Data

Glass, Graham.
    UNIX for programmers and users / Graham Glass and King Ables. —
    p. cm.
  Includes bibliographical references and index.
  ISBN 0-13-681685-1
  1. UNIX (Computer file) 2. Operating Systems.
  I. Ables, King. II. Title
  QA76.76.063G583   1999
  005.4'3--dc21   98-44439
                                                   CIP

Publisher: **ALAN APT**
Acquisitions editor: **LAURA STEELE**
Editor-in-chief: **MARCIA HORTON**
Production editor: **IRWIN ZUCKER**
Managing editor: **EILEEN CLARK**
Manufacturing buyer: **PAT BROWN**

Director of production and manufacturing: **DAVID W. RICCARDI**
Cover art director: **ANN FRANCE**
Cover designer: **JAYNE CONTE**
Cover illustration: **ROLANDO CORUJO, JOHN CHRISTIANA**
Twister art on cover: **DON MARTINETTI, DM GRAPHICS, INC.**
Editorial assistant: **TONI HOLM**

Printed in the United States of America

10 9 8 7 6 5

ISBN   0-13-681685-1

Prentice-Hall International (UK) Limited, London
Prentice-Hall of Australia Pty. Limited, Sydney
Prentice-Hall Canada Inc., Toronto
Prentice-Hall Hispanoamericana, S.A., Mexico
Prentice-Hall of India Private Limited, New Delhi
Prentice-Hall of Japan, Inc., Tokyo
Pearson Education Asia Pte. Ltd., Singapore
Editora Prentice-Hall do Brasil, Ltda., Rio de Janeiro

To Truth and Beauty,
wherever they are found.

Preface

ABOUT THE AUTHOR OF THE FIRST EDITION

My name is Graham Glass. I graduated from the University of Southampton, England, with a Bachelor's degree in computer science and mathematics in 1983. After getting this degree, I emigrated to the United States and obtained my Master's degree in computer science from the University of Texas at Dallas in 1985. Next, I worked in industry as a UNIX/C systems analyst and became heavily involved in research in neural networks and parallel distributed processing. Interested in becoming a professor, I then began teaching at the University of Texas at Dallas, covering a wide variety of subjects, including UNIX, C, assembly language, programming languages, C++, and Smalltalk. After some time spent teaching, I branched out into industry and cofounded a corporation called ObjectSpace, and I currently train and consult for companies, including DSC Corporation, Texas Instruments, Northern Telecom, J.C. Penney, and Bell Northern Research. I am using my knowledge of OOP and parallel systems to design and build a parallel object-oriented computer system and language based on the new Inmos T9000 transputer chip. In my spare time, I write music, scuba dive, ski, and occasionally sleep.

ABOUT THE AUTHOR OF THE SECOND EDITION

My name is King Ables. I earned my Bachelor-of-Arts degree in computer science from the University of Texas at Austin in 1982. I've been a UNIX user, developer, and systems administrator since 1979, and I've worked at both small start-up companies and large corporations. While working at the Microelectronics and Computer Technology Corporation (MCC) in Austin, I became interested in parallel processing and distributed systems and later joined a research group in which we developed several prototypes of distributed network database systems. In the mid-1990s, I operated my own consulting company for UNIX-related issues in Austin before finally succumbing to the "bug" to move to Colorado. I am currently employed by the Hewlett-Packard Company in Fort Collins, where I am part of a small group that is developing tools for electronic commerce.

ABOUT THIS BOOK

One of my (Glass') jobs before writing this book was to teach UNIX to a variety of individuals, including university students, industry C hackers, and occasionally friends and colleagues. During that time, I acquired a large amount of knowledge, stored both in my head and a substantial library, and I often thought that it would be good to put all of this knowledge into book form. When I began preparing my university lecture series about UNIX, I found that none of the available textbooks on UNIX suited my purpose—they were either too unstructured, too specialized, or lacking in suitable exercises and projects for my students. In response to this situation, I wrote the first version of this book. After a couple of years of use, I then completely rewrote it, giving careful thought to the organization of the new material. I decided to group the information based on the various typical kinds of UNIX users, allowing the book to be used by a wide range of people without the material completely going over anyone's head or being overly simplistic. One tricky decision concerned the level of detail to include about subjects like utilities and system calls. Most of these items have a large number of specialized options and features that are rarely used, and to document them all and still cover the range of topics that I had targeted would result in a book about two-feet thick. Because of this limitation, I've included information only about the most common and useful features of utilities, shells, and system calls; however, I include page references to other commercially available books for the less useful details. I believe that this hybrid-book approach is a good compromise; I hope that you agree.

ADDITIONAL INFORMATION ABOUT THE SECOND EDITION

Graham's company ObjectSpace, which he mentioned previously, has done very well—so well, in fact, that he did not have time to update this book for a second edition. So, his publisher approached me about doing the work. Every author approaches a project differently, and every author has a different style. As I read the original manuscript, I noticed how different our two styles are. (Neither style is wrong, simply different from the other style.) I have strived simply to update and add information and remain as true to the original style as possible. At this point, I would like to apologize in advance for any continuity problems or stylistic changes you may encounter that cause confusion.

In the past twenty years, I've seen many changes in the world of UNIX. Even since the first edition of this book was printed, many things have changed, but in all of these changes, the basic tenets and philosophies of UNIX remain constant; thus, most of the original text is still applicable. I've added chapters on windowing systems (specifically, the X Window System for UNIX) and the Internet. Also, I've made many smaller updates to the existing text to reflect the changes in versions of UNIX that have occurred since the first edition was published. I have also reworked the last chapter, in which Graham examined the possibilities of UNIX in the future. As many of his ideas proved to be accurate, the last chapter now examines the next steps in the evolution of UNIX.

THE LAYOUT OF THE BOOK

UNIX is a big thing. To describe it fully requires an explanation of many different topics from several different angles, which is exactly what I've done in this text. This book is split into several sections, each designed for a particular kind of user:

1. What is UNIX?
2. UNIX for Nonprogrammers
3. The UNIX Shells
4. The Bourne Shell
5. The Korn Shell
6. The C Shell
7. Utilities
8. Networking
9. The Internet
10. Windowing Systems
11. C Programming Tools
12. Systems Programming
13. UNIX Internals
14. System Administration
15. The Future
    Appendix
    Bibliography

I recommend that various types of users read certain chapters, according to the table that follows:

Category of User	Chapters
Day-to-day casual users	1, 2
Advanced users	1, 2, 3, 7, 8, 9, 10
Programmers	1 through 12, 15
System analysts	1 through 13, 15
Wizards	Everything (of course!)

LAYOUT OF THE CHAPTERS

Every chapter in this book has a standard prologue that is divided into the sections that follow:

Motivation
Why it is useful to learn the material in the chapter.

Prerequisites
What the reader should know in order to successfully negotiate the chapter.

Objectives
A list of the topics that are presented in the chapter.

Presentation
A description of the method by which the topics are presented.

Utilities
A list of the utilities that are covered in the chapter (when appropriate).

System calls
A list of the system calls that are covered in the chapter when appropriate).

Shell commands
A list of the shell commands that are covered in the chapter (when appropriate).

In addition, every chapter ends with a review section that contains the following sections:

Checklist
A recap of the topics.

Quiz
A quick self-test.

Exercises
A list of exercises, rated *easy*, *medium*, or *hard*.

Projects
One or more related projects, rated *easy*, *medium*, or *hard*.

A GUIDE FOR TEACHERS

As mentioned previously, this book was originally written for an audience of undergraduate and graduate students. I suggest that a lecture series based on this book could be designed as follows:

- If the students do not know the C language, then a medium-paced course could begin with Chapters 1, 2, 3, and 11. The lecturer could then introduce the students to the C language and use the contents of Chapter 12 for class exercises and projects.
- If the students already know the C language, then a medium-paced course could include Chapters 1, 2, 3, 6, 11, 12, and 13. Projects focusing on parallel processing and interprocess communication will ensure that the students end up with a good knowledge of UNIX fundamentals.
- If the students know the C language and are enthusiastic, I suggest that all of the chapters, with the exception of Chapters 4, 5, and 7, can be covered in one semester. I know that such a course is possible, as I've taught it that way!

NOMENCLATURE

There are references throughout this book to UNIX utilities, shell commands, and system calls. It's quite easy to confuse these three things, so I have adopted a consistent way to differentiate them:

- UNIX utilities are always written in boldface, as in the following sentence: "The **mkdir** utility makes a directory."
- System calls are always followed by parentheses, as in the following sentence: "The fork () system call duplicates a process."
- Shell commands are always written in italics, as in the following sentence: "The *history* command lists your previous commands."

Formal descriptions of utilities, system calls, and shell commands are supplied in a box, using a Backus–Naur notation that is modified for UNIX. The conventions of this notation are fairly simple and are fully described in the appendix. As an example, a description of the UNIX **man** utility follows:

Utility: **man** [*chapter*] *word*
   man -k *keyword*

The first usage of **man** displays the manual entry associated with *word*. If no chapter number is specified, the first entry found is displayed. The second usage of **man** displays a list of all of the manual entries that contain *keyword*.

All utilities, system calls, and shell commands are fully cross-referenced in the appendix, including the page numbers of the scripts and programs that use them.

Sample UNIX sessions are presented in a courier font. Keyboard input from a user is always displayed in italics, and annotations are always preceded by ellipses (. . .). An example of these notations is as follows:

```
$ ls                    . . . generate a directory listing.
myfile.txt  yourfile.txt
$ whoami
glass
$ _                     . . . a new prompt is displayed.
```

REFERENCES TO OTHER BOOKS

For the same reason that it is good to reuse existing code in a new program, it is also good to use other peoples' reference material in a book when this material does not interfere with the natural flow of the presentation of the text. Information that I consider to be too specialized for this book is referenced by a pair of numbers such as in the following sentence: "For information concerning a port of UNIX to a 68030 processor, see [14,426]." The first number in brackets indicates a reference in the bibliography section in the back of this book. In this case, book #14 is titled *UNIX*

Papers. The second number, if present, is the page number of the reference. It is always possible that the pages of future reprints of these books will be numbered differently. In these cases, the reference will hopefully still remain reasonably close to the quoted page number.

AVAILABILITY OF SOURCE CODE ON-LINE

Examples of source code used in the second edition of this book are now available on-line so that you do not have to waste your time retyping them. Short examples are not included, but examples of any significant length can be found on Prentice Hall's Web site at http://www.prenhall.com/books/esm_0136816851.html.

ACKNOWLEDGMENTS FOR THE FIRST EDITION

I'd like to thank the following people for reviewing my manuscript: James F. Peters, III, Kansas State University; Fadi Deek, New Jersey Institute of Technology; Dr. William Burns, University of Texas at Dallas; and Richard Newman-Wolfe, University of Florida.

I'd also like to thank the following lifeforms for technical and emotional support during the writing of this book: Laura, Mum, Dad, Blair, Beauty, Ross, Agatha, Tim, Howard, Jeff, Tom, Nemo, Danielle, David, Gwen, Bill, Jennifer, and Mike.

ACKNOWLEDGMENTS FOR THE SECOND EDITION

Again, many people were involved in helping bring this project to completion. First and foremost, I must thank Graham Glass for having the confidence in me to allow me to modify his original work. Other authors might have resisted such an arrangement or may have wanted to be involved in every detail of the project, but after a few initial consultations about ideas and directions, Graham basically said, "Go for it."

Special thanks go to David Carver for his detailed reviewing that went above and beyond the call of duty. Bill Tepfenhart, Stephen Rago, and Mark Ellis also provided valuable insights into early versions of the text. Chuck Morse, Marianne Jeffries, and Martin Fink gave me encouragement and indulgence, which I really appreciate. As usual, the folks at Prentice Hall have been nothing but supportive and helpful, especially Alan Apt and Laura Steele.

And a special thank you to Dee for putting up with endless weekends of my being a geek (and missing some skiing) to help make this edition happen.

Graham Glass
King Ables

Contents

4   THE BOURNE SHELL   *110*

What Is UNIX?

Motivation

UNIX is a popular operating system in the engineering world and has lately been growing in popularity in the business world. Knowledge of its functions and purpose will help you to understand why so many people choose to use it and will make your own use of UNIX more effective.

Prerequisites

To fully understand this chapter, you should have a little experience using a computer and a familiarity with basic computer terms such as *program, file,* and *CPU.*

Objectives

In this chapter, I describe the basic components of a computer system, define the term *operating system,* and explain why UNIX is so successful. I also present UNIX from several different perspectives, ranging from that of a nonprogrammer to that of an advanced systems programmer.

Presentation

To begin with, I describe the main bits and pieces that make up a typical computer system. I then show how a special program called an *operating system* is needed to control these pieces effectively, and present a short list of the facilities of an operating system. Following this list is a description of the basic philosophy of UNIX that acts as a framework for the information presented in the rest of this book. Finally, I present a short history of UNIX and a glimpse of where I believe UNIX is heading.

COMPUTER SYSTEMS

A typical single-user computer system is built out of many parts, including a central processing unit (CPU), memory, disks, a monitor, and a keyboard. Such small systems may be connected together to form larger computer networks, enabling tasks to be distributed among individual computers. Fig. 1.1 is an illustration of such a network.

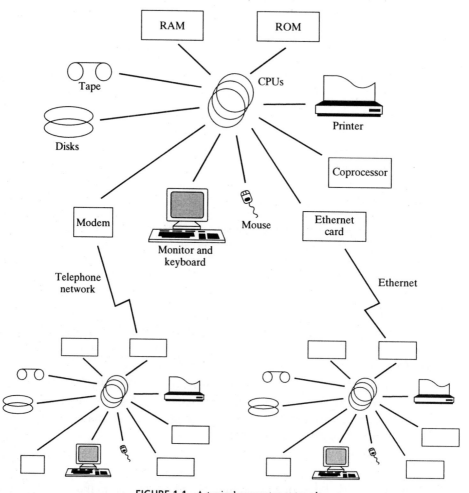

FIGURE 1.1 A typical computer network

The hardware that makes up a computer network is only half of the story; the software that runs on the computers is equally important. Let's take a closer look at the various hardware and software components of a computer system.

HARDWARE

Computer systems, whether large or small, multiuser or single user, expensive or cheap, include most of the following pieces of hardware:

Central processing unit (CPU)

This piece of hardware reads machine code (instructions in a form that a computer can understand) from memory and executes it. A CPU is often thought of as the "brain" of a computer.

Random-access memory (RAM)

This component holds the machine code and data that are accessed by the CPU. RAM normally forgets everything it holds when the power to the computer is turned off.

Read-only memory (ROM)

This component holds both machine code and data. Its contents may not be changed and are remembered even when the power to the computer is turned off.

Disk

This component holds large amounts of data and code on a magnetic or optical medium and remembers it all even when the power to the computer is turned off. Floppy disks are generally removable from the computer, whereas hard disks are not. Hard disks can hold a lot more information than floppy disks can.

CD-ROM drive

This piece of hardware allows digitally published information on a compact disc to be read by the computer. The information may be in a data stream or may make up a file system that the operating system can read as if it were on a hard-disk drive.

Monitor

This piece of hardware displays information and comes in two types: monochrome and color. Monochrome monitors are rare in newer computer systems.

Graphics card

This component allows the CPU to display information on a monitor. Some graphics cards can display characters only, whereas others can support graphics.

Keyboard

This piece of hardware allows a user to enter alphanumeric information. There are several different kinds of keyboards available, partly depending on the language of the user. For example, Japanese keyboards are much larger than keyboards to be used by speakers of western languages, as the Japanese alphabet is much larger. The keyboards for speakers of western languages are often referred to as QWERTY keyboards, as these letters are the first six letters on the upper left-hand side of the keyboard.

Mouse

This component allows a user easily to position cursors, icons, graphics, text, and other items on the screen by using short movements of the hand. Most mice have "tails" that connect them to the computer, but some have radio or infrared connections that make the tail unnecessary. I recommend some form of cordless mouse to anyone who has a cat, as cats tend to get tangled up in a mouse cord very easily.

Printer

This piece of hardware allows a user to obtain hard copies of information. Some printers print characters only, whereas others can print graphics.

Tape

This component is generally used for making backup copies of information stored on disks. Tapes are slower than disks, but store large amounts of data in a fairly cheap way.

Modem

A modem allows the user to communicate with other computers across a telephone line. Different modems allow different rates of communication. Most modems even correct for errors that occur due to a poor telephone connection.

Ethernet interface

An Ethernet is a medium (typically, it is made up of some wires) that allows computers to communicate at high speeds. Computers attach to an Ethernet by a special piece of hardware called an *Ethernet interface.*

Other peripherals

There are many other kinds of peripherals that computer systems can support, including graphics tablets, optical scanners, array processors, sound cards, voice-recognition cards, and synthesizers, to name a few.

You cannot just connect these pieces of hardware together and have a working computer system; you must also have some software that controls and coordinates it all. The ability to share peripherals, to share memory, to communicate between machines, and to run more than one program at a time is made possible by a special kind of program called an *operating system.* You may think of an operating system as a "super program" that allows all of the other programs to operate. Let's take a closer look at operating systems.

OPERATING SYSTEMS

As previously mentioned, a computer system cannot function without an operating system. There are many different operating systems that are available for PCs, mini-computers, and mainframes; the most common ones are Windows, OS/2, VMS, MacOS, and UNIX. OS/2 is only available for PCs, VMS is only available for mini-computers and mainframes, and UNIX is available for all platforms. This aspect is one of the advantages of UNIX—it is available for just about any machine. Of the operating systems listed previously, only UNIX and VMS allow more than one user to use the computer system at a time, which is an obvious requirement for systems for businesses. Many businesses buy a powerful minicomputer with twenty or more terminals and then use UNIX as the operating system that shares the CPUs, memory, and disks among the users.

If it is assumed that we have picked UNIX as the operating system for our computer system, what can we do with it? Let's now take a look at the software side of things.

SOFTWARE

One way to describe the software of a computer system is that it provides a framework for executing programs and storing files. The kinds of programs that run on UNIX platforms vary widely in size and complexity, but tend to share certain common characteristics. Here is a list of useful facts concerning UNIX programs and files:

- A *file* is a collection of data that is usually stored on disk, although some files are stored on tape. UNIX treats peripherals as special files so that terminals, printers, and other devices are accessible in the same way as disk-based files.
- A *program* is a collection of bytes representing code and data that is stored in a file.
- When a program is started, it is loaded from disk into RAM. (Actually, only parts of it are loaded, but we'll come to that detail later.) When a program is running, it is called a *process*.
- Most processes read and write data from files.
- Processes and files have an *owner* and may be protected against unauthorized access.
- UNIX supports a hierarchical directory structure.
- Files and processes have a "location" within the hierarchy of a directory. A process may change its own location and/or the location of a file.
- UNIX provides services for the creation, modification, and destruction of programs, processes, and files.

Here is an illustration of a tiny UNIX directory hierarchy that contains four files and a process running the "sort" utility:

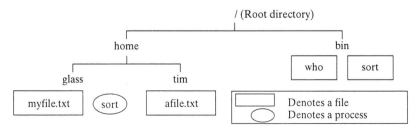

FIGURE 1.2   Directory hierarchy

SHARING RESOURCES

Another operating-system function that UNIX provides is the sharing of limited resources among competing processes. Limited resources in a typical computer system include CPUs, memory, disk space, and peripherals such as printers. Here is a brief outline of how these resources are shared:

- UNIX shares *CPUs* among processes by dividing each second of CPU time into equal-sized "slices" (typically 1/10 second) and then allocating the slices to processes based on a priority scheme. Important processes are allocated more slices than are others.
- UNIX shares *memory* among processes by dividing RAM up into thousands of equal-sized "pages" of memory and then allocating the pages to processes based on a priority scheme. Only those portions of a process that actually need to be in RAM are ever loaded from disk. Pages of RAM that are not accessed for a while are saved back to disk so that the memory may be reallocated to other processes.
- UNIX shares *disk space* among users by dividing the disks into thousands of equal-sized "blocks" and then allocating the blocks to users based on a quota system. A single file is built out of one or more blocks.

Chapter 13 contains more details on how these sharing mechanisms are implemented. We've now looked at every major role that UNIX plays as an operating system except one—as a medium for communication.

COMMUNICATION

The components of a computer system cannot achieve very much when they work in isolation; for example:

- A process may need to talk to a graphics card to display output.
- A process may need to talk to a keyboard to get input.
- A network mail system needs to talk to other computers to send and receive mail.
- Two processes need to talk to each other in order to collaborate on a single problem.

UNIX provides several different ways for processes and peripherals to talk to each other, depending on the type and the speed of the communication. For example, one way that a process can talk to another process is via an interprocess communication mechanism called a "pipe." A pipe is a one-way medium-speed data channel that allows two processes on the same machine to talk. If the processes are on different machines connected by a network, then a mechanism called a "socket" may be used instead. A socket is a two-way high-speed data channel.

It is becoming quite common nowadays for different pieces of a problem to be tackled by different processes on different machines. For example, there is a graphics system called the X Window System that works by using something termed a "client–server" model. One computer (the X "server") is used to control a graphics terminal and to draw the various lines, circles, and windows, while another computer (the X "client") generates the data that is to be displayed. Such arrangements are examples of distributed processing, where the burden of computation is spread among many computers. In fact, a single X server may service many X clients. Here's an illustration of an X-based system:

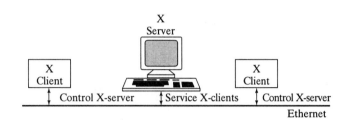

FIGURE 1.3 X client/server arrangement

We will discuss the X Window System further in Chapter 10.

UTILITIES

Even the most powerful operating system isn't worth too much to the average user unless there is a good chunk of useful software that is available for it. Due to the relatively old age of UNIX and its perceived market value, there is no shortage of good utilities for it. Standard UNIX comes complete with at least 200 small utility programs, usually including a couple of editors, a C compiler, a sorting utility, a graphical user interface, some shells, and some text-processing tools. Popular packages like spreadsheets, compilers, and desktop-publishing tools are also commercially available. There is also plenty of free software that is available from computer sites all over the world via the Internet, which we examine in Chapter 9.

PROGRAMMER SUPPORT

UNIX caters very well to programmers. It is an example of an "open" system, which means that the internal software architecture is well documented and available in source-code form for a relatively small fee. Features of UNIX such as parallel processing, interprocess communication, and file handling are all easily accessible from a programming language such as C via a set of library routines known as system calls. Many facilities that were difficult to use on older operating systems are now within the reach of every systems programmer.

STANDARDS

UNIX is a fairly standard operating system, with two main versions that are slowly merging into one. As you'll see shortly, UNIX was created in AT&T's Bell Laboratories and evolved from that genesis into what is currently known as "System V" UNIX. The University of California at Berkeley obtained a copy of

UNIX early on in its development and spawned another major version, known as BSD (Berkeley Standard Distribution) UNIX. Both System V and BSD UNIX have their own strengths and weaknesses, as well as a large amount of commonality. Two consortiums of leading computer manufacturers gathered behind these two versions of UNIX, each believing its own version to be the best. UNIX International, headed by AT&T and Sun Microsystems, backed the latest version of System V UNIX, called System V Release 4. The "Open Software Foundation" (OSF), headed by IBM, Digital Equipment Corporation, and Hewlett-Packard, attempted to create a successor to BSD UNIX, called OSF/1. Both groups tried to comply with a set of standards set by the POSIX (Portable Operating System Interface) committee and other such organizations. The OSF project has fallen by the wayside in recent years, leaving System V as the apparent winner of the "UNIX wars." However, this designation is actually misleading, since most of the best features of BSD UNIX have been rolled into most System V-based versions of UNIX. Hence, Solaris (from Sun Microsystems), HP-UX (from Hewlett-Packard), AIX (from IBM), and IRIX (from Silicon Graphics, Inc.), while all System V based, also include most of the different features of BSD UNIX at varying levels of completeness. While this evolution is not complete, it is further along than it was before and will continue.

UNIX is mostly written in the C language, which makes it relatively easy to port to different platforms. This feature is an important benefit and has contributed a great deal to the proliferation and success of UNIX.

LIST OF UNIX FEATURES (A RECAP)

Here is a recap of the features that UNIX provides:

- It allows many users to access a computer system at the same time.
- It supports the creation, modification, and destruction of programs, processes, and files.
- It provides a directory hierarchy that gives a location to processes and files.
- It shares CPUs, memory, and disk space in a fair and efficient manner between competing processes.
- It allows processes and peripherals to talk to each other, even if they're on different machines.
- It comes complete with a large number of standard utilities.
- There are plenty of high-quality, commercial software packages available for most versions.
- It allows programmers to easily access operating features via a well-defined set of system calls, which are analogous to library routines.
- It is a portable operating system and is thus available on a wide variety of platforms.

Now that we've covered the main features of UNIX, it's time to examine some of the philosophies behind UNIX and to explore both its past and its future.

PHILOSOPHIES OF UNIX

The original UNIX system was lean and mean. It had a very small number of utilities and virtually no network or security functionality. The original designers of UNIX had some pretty strong notions about how utilities should be written: A program should do one thing and do it well, and combining these small utilities should accomplish more complex tasks. To this end, they built a special mechanism called a "pipe" into the heart of UNIX to support their vision. A pipe allows a user to specify that the output of one process is to be used as the input to another process. Two or more processes may be connected in this fashion, resulting in a "pipeline" of data flowing from the first process through to the last:

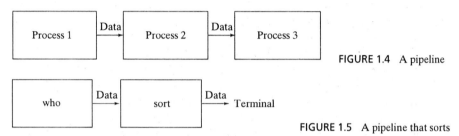

FIGURE 1.4   A pipeline

FIGURE 1.5   A pipeline that sorts

The nice thing about pipelines is that many problems can be solved by such an arrangement of processes. Each process in the pipeline performs a set of operations upon the data and then passes the results on to the next process for further processing. For example, imagine that you wish to obtain a sorted list of all of the users on a UNIX system. There is a utility called **who** that outputs an unsorted list of the users, and there is another utility called **sort** that outputs a sorted version of its input. These two utilities may be connected together with a pipe so that the output from **who** passes directly into **sort,** resulting in a sorted list of users.

This method is a more powerful approach to solving problems than writing a fresh program from scratch every time a new problem arises or using two programs such that the intermediate data has to be stored in a temporary file in order for the next program to have access to it.

Thus, the UNIX philosophy for solving problems can be stated as:

- If you can solve the problem by combining multiple existing utilities using pipes, do it; *otherwise*
- . . . ask people on the network if they know how to solve it. If they do, great; *otherwise*
- . . . if you could solve the problem with the aid of some other hand-written utilities, write the utilities yourself and add them into the UNIX repertoire. Design each utility to do one thing well and one thing only so that each utility may be reused to solve other problems. If more utilities won't do the trick, then
- . . . write a program (typically in C or C++) to solve the problem.

Inside UNIX is hidden another more subtle philosophy that is slowly eroding. The original system was designed by guys who liked to have the power to access data or code anywhere in the system, regardless of who owns it. To support this notion, they built the concept of a "super-user" into UNIX, which meant that certain privileged individuals could have special access rights. For example, the system administrator of a UNIX system always has the capability to become a super-user so that he/she may perform clean-up tasks such as terminating rogue processes or removing unwanted users from the system. However, the concept of a super-user has security implications that are a little frightening. Anyone with the right password to become a super-user could potentially wipe out an entire system or extract top-security data with relative ease. Some of the research versions of UNIX do away entirely with the super-user concept and instead subdivide privileged tasks among several different "slightly super" users.

UNIX YESTERDAY

A computer scientist named Ken Thompson at Bell Laboratories built the first version of UNIX. Ken was interested in building a video game called "Space Wars" that required a fairly fast response time. The operating system that he was using, "MULTICS," didn't give him the performance that he needed, so he decided to build his own operating system. He called it UNIX because the "UNI" part of the name implied that it would do one thing well, as opposed to the "MULTI" part of the "MULTICS" which he felt tried to do many things without much success. He wrote it in assembly language, and the first version was very primitive; it was only a single-user system, it had no network capability, and it had a poor memory-management system for sharing memory between processes. However, it was efficient, compact, and fast, which was exactly what he wanted.

A few years later, a colleague of Ken's, Dennis Ritchie, suggested that they rewrite UNIX using the C language, which Dennis had recently developed from a language called B. The idea that an operating system could be written in a high-level language was an unusual approach at that time. Most people felt that assembly language was the only language fast enough for such an important component of a computer system. Fortunately, C was slick enough that the conversion was successful, and the UNIX system suddenly had a huge advantage over other operating systems—its source code was understandable. Only a small percentage of the original source code remained in assembly language, which meant that porting the operating system to a different machine was quite easy. As long as the target machine had a C compiler, most of the operating system would work with no changes; only the assembly-language component had to be translated by hand.

Bell Laboratories started using this prototype version of UNIX in its patent department, primarily for text processing, and a number of UNIX utilities that are found in modern UNIX systems were originally designed during this time period. Examples of these utilities are **nroff** and **troff.** Bell Laboratories allowed universities to obtain a free copy of the UNIX source code, hoping that enterprising students would enhance the system and further its progress into the marketplace. Indeed, graduate students at the University of California at Berkeley took the task to heart and made some huge improvements over the years, including the first good memory-management system and the first real networking capability. The University started to market its own version of UNIX, called BSD (Berkeley

Standard Distribution) UNIX, to the general public. The differences in the implementation of the Bell Labs UNIX and the BSD UNIX remain to this day.

UNIX TODAY

The currently commercially available versions of UNIX include, but are not limited to, offerings from AT&T, DEC®, IBM®, Hewlett-Packard, Silicon Graphics, Inc., and Sun Microsystems. A more recent entry into the UNIX world is Linux, a free version of UNIX written by a student in Finland and now marketed and supported by several different companies. The older versions of UNIX are derived from either System V or BSD 4.3, whereas the newer versions tend to contain features from both. Here is an abbreviated genealogy of UNIX:

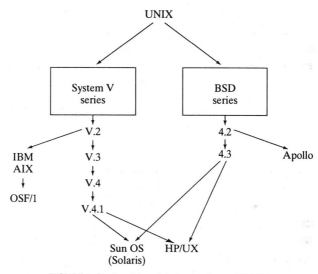

FIGURE 1.6   An abbreviated genealogy of UNIX

For more information on which versions of UNIX are available for various hardware platforms, please see Chapter 15.

UNIX TOMORROW

It is likely that the future versions of UNIX will follow a philosophy similar to that of the present UNIX systems—for example, the idea that you can build an application from a collection of interconnected utilities. Additionally, UNIX will need to embrace some of the newer trends in computing, such as parallel processing and object-oriented programming. We'll take a look at some of these future issues in Chapter 15.

THE REST OF THIS BOOK

As you can probably tell by now, UNIX is a fairly substantial topic and can only be properly digested in small portions. In order to aid this process and to allow individual readers to focus on the subjects that they find to be most applicable, I decided to write this book's chapters based on the different kinds of UNIX users. These users tend to fall into one of several categories:

- *Nonprogrammers,* who occasionally want to perform simple tasks like sending and receiving electronic mail, using a spreadsheet, or doing some word processing.
- *Shell users,* who use background processing and write small scripts from within a convenient interface.
- *Advanced nonprogrammers,* who use more complex facilities like file encryption, stream editors, and file processing.
- *Advanced shell users,* who write programs in a high-level shell language (a little like JCL) for performing useful tasks such as enacting automatic backups, monitoring disk usage, and performing software installations.
- *Programmers,* who write programs in a general-purpose language such as C for speed and efficiency.
- *System programmers,* who write programs that require a good knowledge of the underlying computer system, including network communications and advanced file access.
- *System architects,* who invent better computer systems. These people provide a vision and a framework for the future.
- *System administrators,* who make sure that the computer system runs smoothly and that the users are generally satisfied.

To begin with, read the chapters that interest you the most. Then go back and fill in the gaps when you have the time. If you're unsure of which chapters are most appropriate for your skill level, read the introductory section "About This Book" for some hints.

CHAPTER REVIEW

Checklist

In this chapter, I mentioned:

- the main hardware components of a computer system
- the purpose of an operating system
- the meaning of the terms *program, process,* and *file*
- the layout of a hierarchical directory structure
- that UNIX shares CPUs, memory, and disk space among competing processes
- that UNIX supports communication between processes and peripherals

- that UNIX comes complete with a multitude of standard utilities
- that most major software packages are available on UNIX systems
- that UNIX is an "open" system
- that UNIX has a rosy future

Quiz

1. What are the two main versions of UNIX, and how did each begin?
2. Write down five main functions of an operating system.
3. What is the difference between a *process* and a *program?*
4. What is the UNIX philosophy?
5. Who created UNIX?
6. What makes UNIX an "open" system?

Projects

1. Investigate the MULTICS system and find the similarities and differences between it and the UNIX system. [level: *medium*]
2. Obtain a list of the other currently popular operating systems and determine whether any of them could be serious contenders to UNIX. [level: *medium*]

CHAPTER 2

UNIX For Nonprogrammers

Motivation

This section contains theabsolute basics that you really need to know in order to be able to do anything useful with UNIX.

Prerequisites

In order to understand this chapter, you must have already read Chapter 1. It also helps if you have access to a UNIX system so that you can try out the various UNIX features that I discuss.

Objectives

In this chapter, I'll show you how to log on and off a UNIX system, how to change your password, how to get on-line help when you're stuck, how to stop a program, and how to use the file system. I'll also introduce you to the mail system so that you can enter the world of computer networking.

Presentation

The information in this section is presented in the form of a couple of sample UNIX sessions. If you don't have access to a UNIX account, read through the sessions anyway and try them out later.

Utilities

This section introduces the following utilities, listed in alphabetical order:

cancel	head	passwd
cat	lp	pwd
chgrp	lpstat	rm
chmod	ls	rmdir
chown	mail	stty
clear	man	tail
cp	mkdir	tset
date	more	vi

emacs	mv	wc
file	newgrp	
groups	page	

Shell command

This section introduces the following shell command:

cd

OBTAINING AN ACCOUNT

This part might be tricky. If you can't just go buy your own UNIX computer, then you'll need to get an account on someone else's. If you're a student, the best way to get access to a UNIX account is to enroll in a UNIX course or beg for an account from a professor. If you're a professional, it's likely that your company already has some UNIX facilities, in which case it's a matter of contacting either the training staff or a suitable manager. If you have a little cash and a PC, you can download one of several distributions of Linux or buy it at many computer stores. If you have more cash, you could buy a commercial version of UNIX from a company like the Santa Cruz Operation, which markets a very nice version of UNIX called SCO UNIX, or Sun Microsystems, which sells its Solaris for Intel-based platforms. The good thing about having your own version of UNIX is that you can be a super-user, since you're the one who owns the system. Most companies won't let a nonguru near the super-user password.

LOGGING IN

In order to use a UNIX system, you must first log in with a suitable username. A username is a unique name that distinguishes you from the other users of the system. For example, my own username is "glass". Your username and initial password are assigned to you by the system administrator or set to something standard if you bought your own UNIX system. It's sometimes necessary to press the *Enter* key (also known as the *Return* key) a couple of times to make the system give you a login prompt. This action effectively tells UNIX that somebody's waiting to log in. UNIX first asks you for your username by prompting you with the line "login:" and then asks for your password. When you enter your password, the letters that you type are not displayed on your terminal for security reasons. UNIX is case sensitive, so make sure that the case of the letters is matched exactly to those of your password. Depending on how your system is set up, you should then see either a $ or a % prompt. Here's an example login:

```
UNIX(r) System V Release 4.0
login: glass
Password:                    ...what I typed here is secret and doesn't show.
Last login: Sun Feb 15 18:33:26 from dialin
$ _
```

It's quite common for the system to immediately ask you which kind of terminal you're using. It asks this question so that it can set special characters like the backspace and cursor movement keys to their correct values for your particular terminal. You are usually allowed to press the *Enter* key for the default terminal setting, and I suggest that you do so when you log in for the first time. I'll show you later how to change the terminal type if necessary. Other possible events that might occur when you log in are as follows:

- A help system recognizes that you're a first-time user and asks you whether you'd like a guided tour of UNIX.
- The "news of the day" messages are displayed to your screen, informing you of scheduled maintenance times and other useful information.

Here's an example of a slightly more complex login sequence that asked me what my terminal type was. I pressed the *Enter* key to select the default terminal type, which is vt100:

```
UNIX(r) System V Release 4.0

login: glass
Password:                                            ...secret.
Last login: Sun Feb 15 21:26:13 from dialin
You have mail                    ....the system tells me I have mail waiting.
TERM = (vt100)                                  ...I pressed Enter.
$ _
```

SHELLS

The $ or % prompt that you see when you first log in is displayed by a special kind of program called a *shell*. A shell is a program that acts as a middleman between you and the raw UNIX operating system. It lets you run programs, build pipelines of processes, save output to files, and run more than one program at the same time. A shell executes all of the commands that you enter. The three most popular shells are:

- the Bourne shell
- the Korn shell
- the C shell

All three of these shells share a similar set of core functionality, together with some specialized properties. The Korn shell is a superset of the Bourne shell, and thus users typically choose either the C shell or the Korn shell to work with. I personally favor the Korn shell, as it's easy to program with and has the best command-line interface. This book contains information on how to use all three shells, separated into four chapters. Chapter 3 describes the core functionality of the three shells and Chapters 4 through 6 describe the specialized features of each shell.

Each shell has its own programming language. One reasonable question to ask is: Why would you write a program in a shell language rather than a language like C? The answer is that the shell languages are tailored to manipulating files and processes in the UNIX system, which makes them more convenient in many situations. In this chapter, the only shell facilities that I use are the abilities to run utilities and to save the output of a process to a file. Let's go ahead and run a few simple UNIX utilities.

RUNNING A UTILITY

To run a utility, simply enter its name at the prompt and press the *Enter* key. From now on, when I mention that you should enter a particular bit of text, I also implicitly mean that you should press the *Enter* key after typing the text. Pressing the *Enter* key tells UNIX that you've entered the command and that you wish it to be executed.

Not all systems have exactly the same utilities, so if a particular example doesn't work, don't be flustered. I'll try to point out the utilities that vary a lot from system to system. One utility that every system has is called **date,** which displays the current date and time:

```
$ date                        ...run the date utility.
Thu Mar 12 10:41:50 MST 1998
$ _
```

Whenever I introduce a new utility, I'll write a small synopsis of its typical operation in the format shown in the box below. The format is self-explanatory, as you can see. I use a modified-for-UNIX BNF (Backus–Naur Form) notation for the syntax description, which is fully documented in the appendix.

Please note that I do not list every different kind of option or present a particularly detailed description of each utility—this task is best left to the manual pages for your particular version of UNIX and books that focus almost entirely on UNIX utilities.

Utility: **date** [*yymmddhhmm* [*.ss*]]

Without any arguments, **date** displays the current date and time. If arguments are provided, **date** sets the date to the supplied setting, where *yy* is the last two digits of the year, the first *mm* is the number of the month, *dd* is the number of the day, *hh* is the number of hours (using the 24-hour clock), and the last *mm* is the number of minutes. The optional *ss* is the number of seconds. Only a super-user may set the date.

Another useful utility is **clear**, which clears your screen.

Utility: **clear**

This utility clears your screen.

OBTAINING ON-LINE HELP: MAN

There are bound to be many times when you're at your terminal and you can't quite remember how to use a particular utility. Alternatively, you may know what a utility does, but don't remember what it's called. You may also want to look up an argument that is not described in this text or that differs slightly between different versions of UNIX. All UNIX systems have a utility called **man** (short for manual page) that puts this information at your fingertips. **man** works as follows:

Utility: **man** [*-s section*] *word*
     man *-k keyword*

The manual pages are on-line copies of the original UNIX documentation, which is usually divided into eight sections. They contain information about utilities, system calls, file formats, and shells. When **man** displays help about a given utility, it indicates in which section the entry appears.

The first usage of **man** displays the manual entry associated with *word*. If no section number is specified, the first entry that it finds is displayed. The second usage of **man** displays a list of all the manual entries that contain *keyword*.

The typical division of topics in manual page sections is as follows:

1. Commands and Application Programs
2. System Calls
3. Library Functions
4. Special Files
5. File Formats
6. Games
7. Miscellaneous
8. System Administration Utilities

There is sometimes more than one manual entry for a particular word. For example, there is a utility called **chmod** and a system call called chmod (), and there are manual pages for both (in sections 1 and 2). By default, **man** displays the manual pages for the first entry that it finds, so it will display the manual page for the **chmod** utility. In the case that other entries exist, the manual page of the first entry will state, "SEE ALSO . . . ," with a list of the other entries, followed by their section numbers.

Here's an example of **man** in action:

```
$ man -k mode        ...search for keyword "mode".
chmod (1V)                - change the permissions mode of a file
chmod, fchmod (2V)        - change mode of file
getty (8)                 - set terminal mode
ieeeflags (3M)            - mode and status function
umask (2V)                - set file creation mode mask
$ man chmod          ...select the first manual entry.
CHMOD(1V)              USER COMMANDSCHMOD (1V)
NAME
      chmod - change the permissions mode of a file
SYNOPSIS
      chmod C -fR V mode filename ...
...the description of chmod goes here.
SEE ALSO
      csh(1), ls(1V), sh(1), chmod(2V), chown(8)
$ man -s 2 chmod ...select the manual entry from section 2.
CHMOD(2V)   SYSTEM CALLS   CHMOD(2V)
NAME
      chmod, fchmod - change mode of file
SYNOPSIS
      #include <sys/stat.h>
      int chmod(path, mode)
      char *path;
      mode_t mode;
...the description of chmod () goes here.
SEE ALSO
      chown(2V), open(2V), stat(2V), sticky(8)
$ _
```

SPECIAL CHARACTERS

Some characters are interpreted specially when typed at a UNIX terminal. These characters are sometimes called *metacharacters* and may be listed by using the **stty** utility with the **-a** (all) option. The **stty** utility is discussed fully at the end of this chapter. Here's an example of the use of the **stty** utility for listing metacharacters:

```
$ stty -a                    ...obtain a list of terminal metacharacters
speed 38400 baud; -parity hupcl
rows = 24; columns = 80; ypixels = 0; xpixels = 0;
```

```
-inpck -istrip ixoff imaxbel
crt tostop iexten
erase  kill    werase rprnt   flush   lnext   susp    intr   quit  stop   eof
H      ^U      ^W     ^R      ^O      ^V      ^Z/^Y ^C   ^\      ^S/^Q ^D
```

The carat (^) in front of each letter means that the *Control* key must be pressed at the same time as the letter. The default meaning of each option is as follows:

Option	Meaning
erase	Backspace one character.
kill	Erase all of the current line.
werase	Erase the last word.
rprnt	Reprint the line.
flush	Ignore any pending input and reprint the line.
lnext	Don't treat the next character specially.
susp	Suspend the process for a future awakening.
intr	Terminate (interrupt) the foreground job with no core dump.
quit	Terminate the foreground job and generate a core dump.
stop	Stop/restart terminal output.
eof	End of input.

Some of these characters won't mean much to you until you read some more chapters of this book, but there are a few worth mentioning immediately: *Control*-C, *Control*-S, *Control*-Q, and *Control*-D.

Terminating A Process: *Control-C*

There are often times when you run a program and then wish to stop it before it's finished. The standard way to execute this action in UNIX is to press the keyboard sequence *Control*-C. Although there are a few programs that are immune to this form of process termination, most processes are immediately killed and your shell prompt is returned. Here's an example of the use of *Control*-C:

```
$ man chmod
CHMOD(1V)     USER COMMANDS       CHMOD(1V)
NAME
        chmod - change the permissions mode of a file
SYNOPSIS
^C     ...terminate the job and go back to the shell.
$ _
```

Pausing Output: *Control-S/Control-Q*

If the output of a process starts to rapidly scroll up the screen, you may pause it by pressing *Control*-S. To resume the output, you may either press *Control*-S again or press *Control*-Q. This sequence of control characters is sometimes called XON/XOFF protocol. Here's an example of its use:

```
$ man chmod
CHMOD(1V)     USER COMMANDS   CHMOD(1V)
NAME
      chmod - change the permissions mode of a file
^S    ...suspend terminal output.
^Q    ...resume terminal output.
SYNOPSIS
      chmod C -fR V mode filename ...
...the rest of the manual page is displayed here.
SEE ALSO
      csh(1), ls(1V), sh(1), chmod(2V), chown(8)
$ _
```

End Of Input: *Control-D*

Many UNIX utilities may take their input from either a file or the keyboard. If you instruct a utility to do the latter, you must tell the utility when the input from the keyboard is finished. To do so, press *Control*-D on a line of its own after the last line of input. *Control*-D signifies the end of input. For example, the **mail** utility allows you to send mail from the keyboard to a named user:

```
$ mail tim   ...send mail to my friend tim.
Hi Tim,      ...input is entered from the keyboard.
I hope you get this piece of mail. How about building a country one of
these days?

- with best wishes from Graham
^D             ...tell the terminal that there's no more input.
$ _
```

The **mail** utility is fully described later in this chapter.

SETTING YOUR PASSWORD: PASSWD

After you first log in to a UNIX system, it's a good idea to change your initial password. (Someone set it, so you know that at least one other person knows it.) Passwords should generally be at least six letters long and *should not* be words from a dictionary or proper nouns because it's quite easy for someone to set up a computer program that runs through all of the words in a standard dictionary and tries each as your password. I know this problem firsthand, as I've had someone break into my account using the very same technique. My password is now a mixed expression of letters and numbers, like "GWK145W." Get the idea?

To set your password, use the **passwd** utility, which works as follows:

Utility: **passwd**

passwd allows you to change your password. You are prompted for your old password and then twice for the new one. (Since what you type isn't shown on the screen, you would not know if you made a typo; if the two instances of your new password don't match, you will be asked to retype the new password because you made a mistake typing it in one of the times.) The new password may be stored in an encrypted form in the password file "/etc/passwd" or in a "shadow" file (for more security), depending on your version of UNIX. Your particular version may store the password in a remote database as well.

Below is an example of changing a password, with the passwords shown. Note that you wouldn't normally be able to see the passwords, as UNIX turns off the keyboard echo when you enter them.

```
$ passwd
Current password: penguin
New password (? For help): GWK145W
New password (again): GWK145W
Password changed for glass
$ _
```

If you forget your password, the only thing to do is to contact your system administrator and ask for a new password.

LOGGING OUT

To leave the UNIX system, press the keyboard sequence *Control*-D at your shell prompt.[1] This comand tells your login shell that there is no more input for it to process, causing it to disconnect you from the UNIX system. Most systems then display a "login:" prompt and wait for another user to log in. Here's an example of a logout sequence:

```
$ ^D          ...I'm done!

UNIX(r) System V Release 4.0

login:        ...wait for another user to log in.
```

---

[1]The C shell can be set to ignore ^D for logout, since you might type it by accident. In this case, you must type "logout" at the prompt instead in order to log out.

Congratulations! You've now seen how you can log into a UNIX system, execute a few simple utilities, change your password, and then log out. In the next few sections, I'll describe some more utilities that allow you to explore the directory hierarchy and manipulate files.

POETRY IN MOTION: EXPLORING THE FILE SYSTEM

I decided that the best way to illustrate some common UNIX utilities is to describe a session that uses them in a natural fashion. One of my hobbies is to compose music, and I often use the UNIX system to write lyrics for my songs. The next few sections of this chapter are a running commentary on the UNIX utilities that I used to create a final version of the lyrics of one of my songs, called "Heart To Heart." Here is the approximate series of events that took place, together with the utility that I used at each stage:

Action	Utility
I displayed my current working directory.	pwd
I wrote the first draft and stored it in a file called "heart".	cat
I listed the directory contents to see the size of the file.	ls
I displayed the "heart" file using several utilities.	cat, more, page, head, tail
I renamed the first draft "heart.ver1".	mv
I made a directory called "lyrics" to store the first draft.	mkdir
I moved "heart.ver1" into the "lyrics" directory.	mv
I made a copy of "heart.ver1" called "heart.ver2".	cp
I edited the "heart.ver2" file.	vi
I moved back to my home directory.	cd
I made a directory called "lyrics.final".	mkdir
I renamed the "lyrics" directory to "lyrics.draft".	mv
I copied the "heart.ver5" file from "lyrics.draft" to "lyrics.final", renaming the file "heart.final".	cp
I removed all the files from the "lyrics.draft" directory.	rm
I removed the "lyrics.draft" directory.	rmdir
I moved into the "lyrics.final" directory.	cd
I printed the "heart.final" file.	lpr
I counted the words in "heart.final".	wc
I listed the file attributes of "heart.final".	ls
I looked at the file type of "heart.final".	file
I obtained a list of my groups.	groups
I changed the group of "heart.final".	chgrp
I changed the permissions of "heart.final."	chmod

PRINTING YOUR SHELL'S CURRENT WORKING DIRECTORY: PWD

Every UNIX process has a location in the directory hierarchy, termed its *current working directory*. When you log into a UNIX system, your shell starts off in a particular directory called your *home directory*. In general, every user has a different home directory, which often begins with the prefix "/home". For example, my own home directory is called "/home/glass". The system administrator assigns these home-directory values. To display your shell's current working directory, use the **pwd** utility, which works like this:

Utility: **pwd**

Prints the current working directory.

To illustrate this utility, I will now show you what happened when I logged into UNIX to start work on my song's lyrics:

```
UNIX(r) System V Release 4.0

login: glass
Password: ...secret.

$ pwd
/home/glass
$ _
```

Here's a diagram that indicates the location of my login Korn shell in the directory hierarchy:

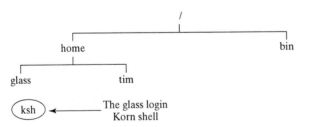

FIGURE 2.1 The login shell starts at the user's home directory

ABSOLUTE AND RELATIVE PATHNAMES

Before I continue with the sample UNIX session, it's important to introduce to you to the idea of *pathnames*.

Two files in the same directory may not have the same name, although it's perfectly OK for several files in *different* directories to have the same name. For example, here's a small hierarchy that contains a "ksh" process and three files called "myFile":

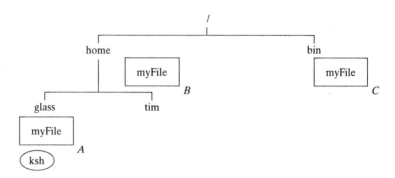

FIGURE 2.2   Different files may have the same name

Although these files have the same name, they may be unambiguously specified by their *pathname* relative to "/", the root of the directory hierarchy. A pathname is a sequence of directory names that leads you through the hierarchy from a starting directory to a target file. A pathname relative to the root directory is often termed an *absolute,* or *full,* pathname. Here are the absolute pathnames of the "A," "B," and "C" instances of "myFile":

File	Absolute Pathname
A	/home/glass/myFile
B	/home/myFile
C	/bin/myFile

A process may also unambiguously specify a file by using a pathname *relative* to its current working directory. The UNIX file system supports the following special fields that may be used when supplying a relative pathname:

Field	Meaning
.	current directory
..	parent directory

For example, here are the pathnames of the three instances of "myFile" relative to the "ksh" process located in the "/home/glass" directory:

File	Relative Pathname
A	myFile
B	../myFile
C	../../bin/myFile

Note that the pathname "myFile" is equivalent to "./myFile," although the second form is rarely used because the leading "." is redundant.

CREATING A FILE

I already had an idea of what the first draft of my song's lyrics would look like, so I decided to store them in a file called "heart." Ordinarily, I would use a UNIX editor such as **vi** or **emacs** to create the file, but since this chapter is for beginners, I used a simpler utility called **cat** to achieve the same result. Here's how **cat** works:

Utility: **cat** -n {*fileName*}*

The **cat** utility takes its input from standard input or from a list of files and displays them to standard output. The **-n** option adds line numbers to the output. **cat** is short for "catenate" which means "to connect in a series of links."

By default, the *standard input* of a process is from the keyboard and the *standard output* is to the screen. We can send the standard output of a process to a file instead of to the screen by making use of a shell facility called *output redirection*. If you follow a command by a ">" character and the name of a file, the output from the command is saved to the file. If the file doesn't already exist, it is created; otherwise, its previous contents are overwritten. Right now, use this feature without worrying how it works; Chapter 3 explains it all in detail. To create the first draft of my lyrics, I entered the following text at the shell prompt:

```
$ cat > heart      ...store keyboard input into a file called "heart".
I hear her breathing,
I'm surrounded by the sound.
Floating in this secret place,
I never shall be found.
^D      ...tell cat that the end of input has been reached.
$ _
```

LISTING THE CONTENTS OF A DIRECTORY: ls

Once the "heart" file was created, I wanted to confirm its existence in my home directory and see how many bytes of storage it used. To do so, I used the **ls** utility, which lists information about a file or a directory. **ls** works like this:

Utility: **ls** -adglsFR { *fileName* }* { *directoryName* }*

With no arguments at all, **ls** lists all of the files in the current working directory in alphabetical order, excluding files whose names start with a period. The **-a** option causes such files to be included in the listing. Files that begin with a period are sometimes known as *hidden files*. The **-d** option causes the details of the directories themselves to be listed, rather than their contents. The **-g** option lists a file's group. The **-l** option generates a long listing, including permission flags, the file's owner, and the last modification time. The **-s** option causes the number of disk blocks that the file occupies to be included in the listing. (A block is typically between 512 and 4K bytes.) The **-F** option causes a character to be placed after the file's name to indicate the type of the file: * means an executable file, / means a directory file, @ means a symbolic link, and = means a socket. The **-R** option recursively lists the contents of a directory and its subdirectories. To obtain a listing of directories other than the current directory, place their names after the options. To obtain listings of specific files, place their names after the options.

Some of the **ls** options described above won't mean a lot right now, but will become increasingly relevant as this book progresses.

Here's an example of the use of **ls**:

```
$ ls                ...list all files in current directory.
heart
$ ls -l heart       ...long listing of "heart."
-rw-r--r--  1     glass      106    Jan 30 19:46    heart
$ _
```

I'll describe the exact meaning of each field in the long directory listing later in this chapter, but for now I'll give you a brief overview:

Field #	Field value	Meaning
1	-rw-r--r--	the type and permission mode of the file, which indicates who can read, write, and execute the file
2	1	the hard-link count (discussed in Chapter 7)
3	glass	the username of the owner of the file
4	106	the size of the file, in bytes
5	Jan 30 19:46	the time that the file was last modified
6	heart	the name of the file

You may obtain even more information by using additional options:

```
$ ls -algFs        ...extra-long listing of current dir.
total 3            ...total number of blocks of storage.
1 drwxr-xr-x  3   glass    cs    512   Jan 30 22:52 ./
1 drwxr-xr-x 12   root     cs   1024   Jan 30 19:45 ../
1 -rw-r--r--  1   glass    cs    106   Jan 30 19:46 heart
$ _
```

The **-s** option generates an extra first field, which tells you how many disk blocks the file occupies. On my UNIX system, each disk block is 1024 bytes long, which implies that my 106-byte file actually takes up 1024 bytes of physical storage. This situation is a result of the physical implementation of the file system, which is described in Chapter 13.

LISTING A FILE: cat, more, page, head, and tail

To check the contents of the "heart" file that I had created in my home directory "/home/glass", I listed its contents to the screen using the **cat** utility. Notice that I supplied **cat** with the name of the file that I wanted to display:

```
$ cat heart      ...list the contents of the "heart" file.
I hear her breathing,
I'm surrounded by the sound.
Floating in this secret place,
I never shall be found.
$ _
```

cat can actually take any number of files as arguments, in which case the contents of the files are listed together, one following the other. **cat** is good for listing the contents of small files, but it doesn't pause between full screens of output. The **more** and **page** utilities are better suited for listing the contents of larger files and contain advanced facilities such as the ability to scroll backward through the listing of a file. Here are some notes on each utility for listing the contents of a file:

Utility: **more** -f [+*lineNumber*] { *fileName* }*

The **more** utility allows you to scroll through a list of files, one page at a time. By default, each file is displayed starting at line 1, although the + option may be used to specify the starting line number. The -f option tells **more** not to fold (or wrap) long lines. After each page is displayed, **more** displays the message "-- More --" to indicate that it's waiting for a command. To list the next page, press the space bar. To list the next line, press the *Enter* key. To quit from **more**, press the "q" key. To obtain help on the multitude of other commands you could issue at this point, press the "h" key.

Utility: **page** -f [+*lineNumber*] { *fileName* }*

The **page** utility works just like **more**, except that it clears the screen before displaying each page. This feature sometimes makes the listing a little quicker.

While we're on the topic of listing files, there are a couple of handy utilities called **head** and **tail** that allow you to peek at the start and end of a file, respectively. Here's how they work:

Utility: **head** -n { *fileName* }*

The **head** utility displays the first *n* lines of a file. If *n* is not specified, it defaults to 10. If more than one file is specified, a small header identifying each file is displayed before its contents.

Utility: **tail** -n { *fileName* }*

The **tail** utility displays the last *n* lines of a file. If *n* is not specified, it defaults to 10. If more than one file is specified, a small header identifying each file is displayed before its contents.

In the following example, I displayed the first two lines and last two lines of my "heart" file:

```
$ head -2 heart          ...list the first two lines.
I hear her breathing,
I'm surrounded by the sound.
$ tail -2 heart          ...list the last two lines.
Floating in this secret place,
I never shall be found.
$ _
```

RENAMING A FILE: mv

Now that I had created the first draft of my lyrics, I wanted to create a few more experimental versions. To indicate that the file "heart" was really the first generation of many versions to come, I decided to rename it "heart.ver1" by using the **mv** utility, which works as follows:

Utility: **mv** -i *oldFileName newFileName*
       mv -i {*fileName*}* *directoryName*
       mv -i *oldDirectoryName newDirectoryName*

The first form of **mv** renames *oldFileName* as *newFileName*. If the label *newFileName* already exists, the contents of that file are replaced by the contents of *oldFileName*. The second form allows you to move a collection of files to a directory, and the third form allows you to move an entire directory. None of these options actually moves the physical contents of a file if the destination location is within the same filesystem as the original; instead, they just move labels around the hierarchy. **mv** is, therefore, a very fast utility. The **-i** option prompts you for confirmation if *newFileName* already exists so that you do not accidently replace its contents.

Here's how I renamed the file using the first form of the **mv** utility:

```
$ mv heart heart.ver1    ...rename to "heart.ver1".
$ ls
heart.ver1
$ _
```

The second and third forms of the **mv** utility are illustrated later in this chapter.

MAKING A DIRECTORY: mkdir

Rather than clog up my home directory with the many versions of "heart," I decided to create a subdirectory called "lyrics" in which to keep them all. To do so, I used the **mkdir** utility, which works like this:

Utility: **mkdir** -p *newDirectoryName*

The **mkdir** utility creates a directory. The **-p** option creates any parent directories in the *newDirectoryName* pathname that do not already exist. If *newDirectoryName* already exists, an error message is displayed and the existing file is not altered in any way.

Here's how I created the subdirectory "lyrics":

```
$ mkdir lyrics    ...create a directory called "lyrics".
$ ls -lF          ...check the directory listing in order to confirm the
                  ...existence of the new directory.
-rw-r--r--  1 glass   106 Jan 30 23:28    heart.ver1
drwxr-xr-x  2 glass   512 Jan 30 19:49    lyrics/
$ _
```

The letter "d" at the start of the permission flags of "lyrics" indicates that it's a directory file.

In general, you should keep related files in their own separate directory. If you name your directories sensibly, it'll make it easy to track down files weeks, or even years, after you create them.

Once the "lyrics" directory was created, the next step was to move the "heart.ver1" file into its new location. To do so, I used **mv** and confirmed the operation using **ls**:

```
$ mv heart.ver1 lyrics   ...move into "lyrics".
$ ls                     ...list the current directory.
lyrics/                  ..."heart.ver1" has gone.
$ ls lyrics              ...list the "lyrics" directory.
heart.ver1               ..."heart.ver1" has moved.
$ _
```

MOVING TO A DIRECTORY: cd

Although I could remain in my home directory and access the various versions of my "lyric" files by preceding them with the prefix "lyrics/", doing so would be rather inconvenient. For example, to edit the file "heart.ver1" with the UNIX **vi** editor, I'd have to issue the following command:

```
$ vi lyrics/heart.ver1 ...invoke the vi editor.
```

In general, it's a good idea to move your shell into a directory if you intend to do a lot of work there. To do so, use the *cd* command. *cd* isn't actually a UNIX utility, but instead is an example of a shell built-in command. Your shell recognizes it as a special keyword and executes it directly. Notice that I write shell commands using italics, in adherence to the nomenclature that I described at the start of this book. Here's how *cd* works:

Shell Command: **cd** [*directoryName*]

The *cd* shell command changes a shell's current working directory to be *directoryName*. If the *directoryName* argument is omitted, the shell is moved to its owner's home directory.

The following example shows how I moved into the "lyrics" directory and confirmed my new location using **pwd**:

```
$ pwd                   ...display where I am.
/home/glass
$ cd lyrics             ...move into the "lyrics" directory.
$ pwd                   ...display where I am now.
/home/glass/lyrics
$ _
```

Here's an illustration of the shell movement caused by the previous *cd* command:

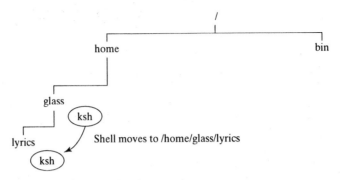

FIGURE 2.3   *cd* moves a shell

Since "." and ".." refer to your shell's current working directory and parent directory, respectively, you may move up one directory level by typing "cd ..". Here's an example:

```
$ pwd          ...display current position.
/home/glass/lyrics
$ cd ..         ...move up one level.
$ pwd          ...display new position.
/home/glass
$ _
```

COPYING A FILE: cp

After moving into the "lyrics" directory, I decided to work on a second version of my lyrics. I wanted to keep the first version for posterity, so I copied "heart.ver1" into a new file called "heart.ver2" and then edited the new file. To copy the file, I used the **cp** utility, which works as follows:

Utility: **cp** -i *oldFileName newFileName*
    cp -ir { *fileName* }* *directoryName*

The first form of **cp** copies the contents of *oldFileName* to *newFileName*. If the label *newFileName* already exists, its contents are replaced by the contents of *oldFileName*. The -i option prompts you for confirmation if *newFileName* already exists so that you do not accidentally overwrite its contents. The second form of **cp** copies a list of files into *directoryName*. The -**r** option causes any source files that are directories to be recursively copied, thus copying the entire directory structure.

---

cp actually does two things:

- It makes a physical copy of the original file's contents.
- It creates a new label in the directory hierarchy that points to the copied file.

The new copy of the original file can therefore be edited, removed, and otherwise manipulated without having any effect on the original file. Here's how I copied the "heart.ver1" file:

```
$ cp heart.ver1 heart.ver2    ...copy to "heart.ver2".
$ ls -l heart.ver1 heart.ver2 ...confirm the existence of both files.
-rw-r--r--  1     glass    106   Jan 30  23:28 heart.ver1
-rw-r--r--  1     glass    106   Jan 31  00:12 heart.ver2
$ _
```

EDITING A FILE: vi

At this point, I edited the "heart.ver2" file using a UNIX editor called **vi**. The way that the **vi** editor works is described later in this chapter, together with information about another editor called **emacs**. For the time being, assume that I edited "heart.ver2" to look like this:

```
$ vi heart.ver2                      ...edit the file.
...editing session takes place here.
$ cat heart.ver2                     ...list the file.
I hear her breathing,
I'm surrounded by the sound.
Floating in this secret place,
I never shall be found.

She pushed me into the daylight,
I had to leave my home.
But I am a survivor,
And I'll make it on my own.
$ _
```

After creating five versions of my song's lyrics, my work was done. I moved back to my home directory and created a subdirectory called "lyrics.final" in which to store the final version of my lyrics. I also renamed the original "lyrics" directory to "lyrics.draft", which I felt was a better name. I accomplished these tasks using the following commands:

```
$ cd                       ...move back to my home directory.
$ mkdir lyrics.final ...make the final lyrics directory.
$ mv lyrics lyrics.draft   ...rename the old lyrics dir.
$ _
```

The final version of my lyrics was stored in a file called "heart.ver5" in the "lyrics.draft" directory, which I then copied into a file called "heart.final" in the "lyrics.final" directory:

```
$ cp lyrics.draft/heart.ver5 lyrics.final/heart.final
$ _
```

DELETING A DIRECTORY: rmdir

Although posterity is a good reason for keeping old things around, it can interfere with your disk usage in a multiuser system. I therefore decided to remove the "lyrics.draft" directory to avoid exceeding my modest disk quota. Before I removed it, I archived its contents using the **cpio** utility, which is described in Chapter 7. To remove the directory, I used the **rmdir** utility, which works like this:

Utility: **rmdir** { *directoryName* }+

The **rmdir** utility removes all of the directories in the list of directory names provided in the command. A directory must be empty before it can be removed. To recursively remove a directory and all of its contents, use the **rm** utility with the **-r** option, described in the next section.

I tried to remove the "lyrics.draft" directory while it still contained the draft versions, and received the following error message:

```
$ rmdir lyrics.draft
rmdir: lyrics.draft: Directory not empty
$ _
```

To remove the files from the "lyrics.draft" directory, I made use of the **rm** utility, described next.

DELETING A FILE: rm

The **rm** utility allows you to remove a file's label from the hierarchy. When no more labels reference a file, UNIX removes the file itself. In most cases, every file has only one label, so the act of removing the label causes the file's physical contents to be deallocated. However, in Chapter 7, I'll show you some occasions for which a single file has more than one label. In these cases, a label may be removed without affecting the file that it refers to. Here's a description of **rm**:

Utility: **rm** -fir {*fileName*} *

The **rm** utility removes a file's label from the directory hierarchy. If the filename doesn't exist, an error message is displayed. The **-i** option prompts the user for confirmation before deleting a filename; press **y** to confirm and **n** otherwise. If *fileName* is a directory, the -r option causes all of its contents, including subdirectories, to be recursively deleted. The **-f** option inhibits all error messages and prompts.

To remove every file in the "lyrics.draft" directory, I moved into the "lyrics.draft" directory and used **rm**:

```
$ cd lyrics.draft        ...move to "lyrics.draft" directory.
$ rm heart.ver1 heart.ver2 heart.ver3 heart.ver4 heart.ver5
$ ls                     ...nothing remains.
$ _
```

Now that all of the files were erased, I moved back to my home directory and erased the draft directory:

```
$ cd                     ...move to my home directory.
$ rmdir lyrics.draft     ...this time it works.
$ _
```

As you'll see in Chapter 3, there's a much easier way to erase a collection of files when you're using a shell. I could have issued the following commands instead:

```
$ cd lyrics.draft   ...move into "lyrics.draft" directory.
$ rm *              ...erase all files in the current directory.
```

Even better, I could have used the more advanced **-r** option of **rm** to delete the "lyrics.draft" directory and all of its contents with just one command:

```
$ cd                     ...move to my home directory.
$ rm -r lyrics.draft   ...recursively delete directory.
$ _
```

PRINTING A FILE: lp, lpstat, and cancel

Now that the hard work was done, I wanted to obtain a printout of my lyrics from which to sing. I used the UNIX print utility called **lp**, which works like this:

Utility: **lp** [-d *destination*] [-n *copies*] { *fileName* }*

lp prints the named file(s) to the printer specified by the -**d** option. If no files are specified, standard input is printed instead. By default, one copy of each file is printed, although this default may be overridden by using the **-n** option to specify the number of copies.

---

lp causes a numbered print job to be started for the specified files. You may find the status of a particular job and/or printer by using the **lpstat** utility, which works as follows:

Utility: **lpstat** [*destination*]

lpstat displays the status of all print jobs sent to any printer with the **lp** command. If a printer destination is specified, **lpstat** reports queue information for that printer only. **lpstat** displays information about the user, the name and size of the job, and a print-request ID.

If, for some reason, you wish to cancel a print job, you may do so by using the **cancel** utility (note that you will need the request ID displayed by **lpstat** and given to you when you ordered the print job):

Utility: **cancel** { *request-ID* }+

cancel removes all of the specified jobs from the printer queue. If you're a super-user, then you may cancel any queued job, even if it was ordered by someone else.

You may obtain a list of the printers on your system from your system administrator.

In the next example, I started by ordering a printout of "heart.final" from the "lwcs" printer. I then decided to order two more copies, and I obtained a printer status. Finally, I changed my mind and canceled the last print job.

```
$ lp -d lwcs heart.final                          ...order a printout.
request id is lwcs-37 (1 file)
$ lpstat lwcs                              ...look at the printer status.
printer queue for lwcs
lwcs-36         ables       priority 0  Mar 18 17:02 on lwcs
        inventory.txt                       457 bytes
lwcs-37         glass       priority 0  Mar 18 17:04 on lwcs
        heart.final                         213 bytes
$ lp -n 2 -d lwcs heart.final                    ...order two more copies.
request id is lwcs-38 (1 file)
$ lpstat lwcs                         ...look at the printer status again.
printer queue for lwcs
lwcs-37         glass       priority 0  Mar 18 17:04 on lwcs
        heart.final                         213 bytes
lwcs-38         glass       priority 0  Mar 18 17:05 on lwcs
        heart.final     2 copies            213 bytes
$ cancel lwcs-38                                 ...remove the last job.
request "lwcs-38" cancelled
$ _
```

In the following example, I used the keyboard to compose a quick message for the printer:

```
$ lp -d lwcs                              ...print from standard input.
Hi there,
This is a test of the print facility.
- Graham
^D                                                ...end of input.
request id is lwcs-42 (standard input)
$ mail                            ...wait a little and then read my mail.
Mail version SMI 4.0 Sat Oct 13 20:32:29 PDT 1990 Type ? for help.
>N 1 daemon@utdallas.edu Fri Jan 31 16:59  15/502  printer job
& 1                                     ...read the first mail message.
From: daemon@utdallas.edu
To: glass@utdallas.edu
Subject: printer job
Date: Wed, 18 Mar 1998 17:59:17 -0600

printer request lwcs-42 has been printed on printer lwcs
& q                               ...quit out of mail.
$ _
```

COUNTING THE WORDS IN A FILE: wc

I was quite interested to find out how many characters, words, and lines were in the "heart.final" file (even though printing it gave me a byte count). To do so, I used the **wc** utility, which works as follows:

Utility: **wc** −lwc { *fileName* }*

The **wc** utility counts the number of lines, words, and/or characters in a
list of files. If no files are specified, standard input is used instead. The **-l**
option requests a line count, the **-w** option requests a word count, and
the **-c** option requests a character count. If no options are specified, then
all three counts are displayed. A word is defined by a sequence of characters surrounded by tabs, spaces, or new lines.

Here's an example of the use of **wc**:

```
$ wc heart.final       ...obtain a count of the number of lines, words,
                       ...and characters.
        9        43    213 heart.final
$ _
```

FILE ATTRIBUTES

Now that I've introduced you to some of the common file-oriented utilities, it's time
to look at the various file attributes. I used **ls** to obtain a long listing of "heart.final"
and got the following output:

```
$ ls -lgsF heart.final
1 -rw-r--r--   1  glass cs  213  Jan 31 00:12  heart.final
$ _
```

Each field is the value of a file attribute, described by the following table:

Field #	Field value	Meaning
1	1	the number of blocks of physical storage occupied by the file
2	-rw-r--r--	the type and permission mode of the file, which indicates who can read, write, and execute the file
3	1	the hard-link count (discussed in Chapter 7)
4	glass	the username of the owner of the file
5	cs	the group name of the file
6	213	the size of the file, in bytes
7	Jan 31 00:12	the time that the file was last modified
8	heart.final	the name of the file

The next few sections describe the meaning of the individual fields, in increasing order of difficulty.

File Storage

The number of blocks of physical storage taken up by the file is shown in field 1 and is useful if you want to know how much actual disk space a file is using. It's possible to create sparse files that seem to be very large in terms of the value displayed in field 6, but that actually take up very little physical storage. Sparse files are discussed in detail in Chapter 12.

Filenames

The name of the file is shown in field 8. A UNIX filename may be up to 255 characters in length. You may use any printable[2] characters you want in a filename except the slash (/), although I recommend that you avoid the use of any character that is special to a shell (like <, >, *, ?, or the tab) as these characters can confuse both the user and the shell. Unlike in some operating systems, there's no requirement in UNIX that a filename end in an extension such as ".c" and ".h", although many UNIX utilities such as the C compiler will only accept files that end with a particular suffix. Thus, the filenames "heart" and "heart.final" are both perfectly legal. The only filenames that you definitely *can't* choose are "." and "..", as these names are predefined filenames that correspond to your current working directory and its parent directory, respectively.

Time of Last File Modification

Field 7 shows the time that the file was last modified and is used by several utilities. For example, the **make** utility, described in Chapter 11, uses the last modification time of files to control its dependency checker. The **find** utility, described in Chapter 7, may be used to find files based on their last modification time.

File Owner

Field 3 tells you the owner of the file. Every UNIX process has an owner, which is typically the same as the username of the person who started it. For example, my login shell is owned by "glass", which is my username. Whenever a process creates a file, the file's owner is set to the process' owner. This procedure means that every file that I create from my shell is owned by "glass", the owner of the shell itself. Chapter 12 contains more information on processes and ownership.

Note that while the string of text known as the username is typically how we refer to a user, UNIX represents this identity internally as an integer known as the *user ID*. The username is easier for humans to understand than a numeric ID.

---

[2]Some nonprintable characters are valid in filenames, but can result in unexpected behavior when displayed or used, so their use is discouraged.

Therefore, I will refer to the textual name as *username,* while using *user ID* when I am referring to the numeric value itself.

File Group

Field 5 shows the file's group. Every UNIX user is a member of a group. This membership is initially assigned by the system administrator and is used as part of the UNIX security mechanism. For example, my group name is "cs". Every UNIX process also belongs to a specific group, usually the same as that of the user that started the process. My login shell belongs to the group name "cs". Because a file created by a process is assigned to the same group as that of the creating process, every file that I create from my shell has the group name "cs". Chapter 12 contains more information on processes and groups. The use of groups in relation to the UNIX security mechanism is described in the next few sections.

As with the username, the group is usually referenced by the text string of the name, but is represented internally as an integer value called the *group ID.* Therefore I will refer to the textual name as *group name,* while using *group ID* when I am referring to the numeric value itself.

File Types

Field 2 describes the file's type and permission settings. For convenience, let's look at the output from the previous **ls** example again:

```
1 -rw-r--r--  1  glass cs  213   Jan 31 00:12 heart.final
```

The first character of field 2 indicates the type of file, which is encoded as follows:

Character	File type
-	regular file
d	directory file
b	buffered special file (such as a disk drive)
c	unbuffered special file (such as a terminal)
l	symbolic link
p	pipe
s	socket

In our example, the type of "heart.final" is indicated as a regular file. You'll encounter symbolic links in Chapter 7, pipes and sockets in Chapter 12, and buffered and unbuffered special files in Chapter 13.

A file's type can often be determined by using the **file** utility, which works like this:

Utility: **file** { *fileName* }+

The **file** utility attempts[3] to describe the contents of the *fileName* argument(s), including the language in which any of the text is written. When **file** is used on a symbolic-link file, **file** reports on the file that the link is pointing to, rather than on, the link itself.

For example, when I ran **file** on "heart.final," I saw this result:

```
$ file heart.final                    ...determine the file type.
heart.final: ascii text
$ _
```

File Permissions

The next nine characters of field 2 indicate the file's permission settings. In the current example, the permission settings are "rw-r--r--":

```
1 -rw-r--r--  1 glass cs  213  Jan 31 00:12 heart.final
```

These nine characters should be thought of as being arranged in three groups of three characters, such as follows:

User (owner)	Group	Others
rw-	r--	r--

Each cluster of three letters has the same format:

Read permission	Write permission	Execute permission
r	w	x

---

[3]While **file** is quite useful, it is not 100% accurate and can be fooled by some file formats.

If a dash occurs instead of a letter, then that permission is denied. The meaning of the read, write, and execute permissions depends on the type of file:

	Regular file	Directory file	Special file
Read	The process may change the contents.	The process may read the directory (i.e., list the names of the files that it contains).	The process may read from the file using the read () system call.
Write	The process may change the contents.	The process may add or remove files to/from the directory.	The process may write to the file using the write () system calls.
Execute	The process may execute the file, which only makes sense if the file is a program.	The process may access files in the directory or any of its subdirectories.	No meaning.

When a process executes, it has four values related to file permissions:

1. a *real* user ID
2. an *effective* user ID
3. a *real* group ID
4. an *effective* group ID

When you log in, your login shell process has its real and effective user IDs set to your own user ID and its real and effective group IDs set to your group ID. When a process runs, the file permissions apply as follows:

- If the process' effective user ID is the same as the owner of the file, the **User** permissions apply.
- If the process' effective user ID is different from the owner of the file, but its effective group ID matches the file's group ID, then the **Group** permissions apply.
- If neither the process' effective user ID nor the process' effective group ID matches the owner of the file and the file's group ID, respectively, the **Others** permissions apply.

The permission system is therefore a three-tier arrangement that allows you to protect your files from general users, but at the same time allows access to the files by certain groups. Later on in this chapter, I'll illustrate the use of permission settings to good effect and describe the utilities that are used to alter them.

Note that only a process' effective user and group IDs affect its permissions; its real user and group IDs are only used for accounting purposes. Note also that a process' access rights depend ordinarily on who *executes* the process and not on who *owns* the executable. There are some occasions for which this attribute is undesirable. For example, there is a game called "rogue" that comes with some UNIX systems that maintains a file of the best scores of previous players. Obviously, the "rogue" process must have permission to alter this file when it is executing, but the player that executes "rogue" should not. Meeting this requirement seems impossible, however, based on the permission rules that I just described. To get around this problem, the designers of UNIX added two special file permissions called *set user*

ID and *set group ID*. When an executable with "set user ID" permission is executed, the process' effective user ID becomes that of the executable. Similarly, when an executable with "set group ID" permission is executed, the process' effective group ID becomes that of the executable. In both cases, the real user or group ID is unaffected. In the case of the "rogue" game, the executable and the score file are both owned by the user "rogue," and the "rogue" executable has "set user ID" permission. The score file has write permission only for its owner, thus preventing general users from modifying it. When a player executes "rogue", the player process executes with the effective user ID of "rogue" and thus is able to modify the score file.

"Set user ID" and "set group ID" permissions are indicated by an "s" instead of an "x" in the user and group clusters, respectively. They may be set using the **chmod** utility, described shortly, and by the chmod () system call, described in Chapter 12.

Here are a few other notes relating to file permissions:

- When a process creates a file, the default permissions given to that file are modified by a special value called the *umask*. The umask value is usually set to a sensible default, so we will wait until Chapter 3 to discuss it further.
- The super-user automatically has all access rights, regardless of whether they're specifically granted to the super-user or not.
- It's perfectly possible, although unusual, for the owner of a file to have fewer permissions than the group or anyone else.

Hard-Link Count

Field 3 shows the file's hard-link count, which indicates how many labels in the hierarchy are pointing to the same physical file. Hard links are rather advanced and are discussed in conjunction with the **ln** utility in Chapter 7.

GROUPS

Now that you've read about file permissions, it's time to see how they can come in handy. Recall that the "heart.final" file's user and group names were "glass" and "cs," respectively, inherited from my login shell:

```
$ ls -lg heart.final
-rw-r--r--  1  glass  cs  213  Jan 31 00:12 heart.final
$ _
```

The original permission flags allow anyone to read the file, but only the owner to write it. What I really wanted to do was to set up a new group called "music" and allow anyone in the "music" group to read my work. I, the owner, would retain read and write permissions, and anyone else would be denied all access rights.

The only way to create a new group is to ask the system administrator to add it. The actual way in which a new group is added is described in Chapter 14. After a new group is added, any user who wants to be a part of that group must also ask the system administrator. At this time, I e-mailed a request to the system administrator for the creation of a new "music" group and asked for myself and my friend Tim to be added to the group. When I received a confirmation of the request, it was time to update my file attributes.

LISTING YOUR GROUPS: groups

Before changing my file's group setting, I wanted to confirm that I was now an official member of the "music" group. The **groups** utility allows you to list all of the groups that you're a member of, and it works like this:

Utility: **groups** [*userId*]

When invoked with no arguments, the **groups** utility displays a list of all of the groups that you are a member of. If the name of a user is specified, a list of the groups to which that user belongs are displayed.

Here's what I saw when I executed the **groups** utility:

```
$ groups                         ...list my groups.
cs    music
$ _
```

CHANGING A FILE'S GROUP: chgrp

The first step toward protecting my lyrics was to change the group name of "heart.final" from "cs" to "music". I did so by using the **chgrp** utility, which works as follows:

Utility: **chgrp** -R *groupname* { *fileName* }*

The **chgrp** utility allows a user to change the group of files that he/she owns. A super-user can change the group of any file. All of the files that follow the *groupname* argument are affected. The **-R** option recursively changes the group of the files in a directory.

I used **chgrp** like this:

```
$ ls -lg heart.final
-rw-r--r-- 1 glass  cs    213 Jan 31 00:12 heart.final
$ chgrp music heart.final       ...change the group.
$ ls -lg heart.final            ...confirm it changed.
-rw-r--r-- 1 glass  music 213 Jan 31 00:12 heart.final
$ _
```

You may also use the **chgrp** utility to change the group of a directory.

CHANGING A FILE'S PERMISSIONS: chmod

Now that the file's group was changed, it was necessary to update its permissions to deny all access rights to general users. To do so, I used the **chmod** utility, which works as follows:

Utility: **chmod** −R *change* { , *change* }*{ *fileName* }+

The **chmod** utility changes the modes of the specified files according to the *change* parameters, which may take the following forms:

clusterSelection+newPermissions   (add permissions)
clusterSelection−newPermissions   (subtract permissions)
clusterSelection=newPermissions   (assign permissions absolutely)

where *clusterSelection* is any combination of:

- u (user/owner)
- g (group)
- o (others)
- a (all)

and *newPermissions* is any combination of

- r (read)
- w (write)
- x (execute)
- s (set user ID/set group ID)

The **-R** option recursively changes the modes of the files in directories. Please see the next set of text for examples. Note that changing a directory's permission settings doesn't change the settings of the files that it contains.

To remove read permission from others, I used **chmod** as follows:

```
$ ls -lg heart.final          ...to view the settings before the change.
-rw-r--r-- 1 glass     music 213 Jan 31 00:12 heart.final
$ chmod o-r heart.final       ...remove read permission for others.
$ ls -lg heart.final          ...to view the settings after the change.
-rw-r----- 1 glass     music 213 Jan 31 00:12 heart.final
$ _
```

Here are some other examples of the use of **chmod**:

Requirement	Change parameters
Add group write permission.	g+w
Remove user read and write permission.	u—rw
Add execute permission for user, group, and others.	a+x
Give the group read permission only.	g=r
Add write permission for user, and remove group read permission.	u+w, g—r

I recommend that you protect your login directory from unauthorized access by not granting write permission for anyone but yourself and by restricting read and execute permission to yourself and members of your group. Here's an example of how to set these permissions:

```
$ cd                      ...change to home directory.
$ ls -ld .                ...list attributes of home directory.
drwxr-xr-x 45 glass       4096 Apr 29 14:35 .
$ chmod o-rx              ....update permissions.
$ ls -ld .                ....confirm.
drwxr-x--- 45 glass       4096 Apr 29 14:35 .
$ _
```

Note that I used the **-d** option of **ls** to ensure that the attributes of my home directory were displayed, rather than the attributes of its files.

The **chmod** utility allows you to specify the new permission setting of a file as an octal number. Each octal digit represents a permission triplet. For example, if you wanted a file to have the permission settings of

```
rwxr-x--
```

then the octal permission setting would be 750, calculated as follows:

	User	Group	Others
setting	rwx	r-x	--
binary	111	101	000
octal	7	5	0

The octal permission setting would be supplied to **chmod** as follows:

```
$ chmod 750 .             ...update permissions.
$ ls -ld                  ....confirm.
drwxr-x--- 45 glass       4096 Apr 29 14:35 .
$ _
```

CHANGING A FILE'S OWNER: chown

If, for some reason, you ever want to relinquish ownership of a file, you may do so by using the **chown** utility, which works as follows:

Utility: **chown** -R *newUserId* { *fileName* }+

The **chown** utility allows a super-user to change the ownership of files. All of the files that follow the *newUserId* argument are affected. The **-R** option recursively changes the owner of the files in directories.

Some versions of UNIX allow only a super-user to change the ownership of a file, while some allow the owner of the file to reassign ownership to another user. The latter is generally not allowed on a system for which disk quotas (the limitation of disk space per user) are in effect. Several occasions for which the system administrator needs to use **chown** are described in Chapter 14.

If I was a super-user, I could have executed the following sequence of commands to change the ownership of "heart.final" to "tim" and then back to "glass" again:

```
$ ls -lg heart.final       ...to view the owner before the change.
-rw-r-----  1  glass  music 213  Jan 31 00:12 heart.final
$ chown tim heart.final    ...change the owner to "tim".
$ ls -lg heart.final       ...to view the ownership after the change.
-rw-r-----  1  tim    music 213  Jan 31 00:12 heart.final
$ chown glass heart.final  ...change the owner back to "glass".
$ _
```

CHANGING GROUPS: newgrp

If you're a member of several groups and you create a file, to which group does the file belong? Well, although you may be a member of several groups, only one of them is your *effective* group at any given time. When a process creates a file, the group ID of the file is set to the process' *effective* group ID, which means that when you create a file from a shell, the group ID of the file is set to the effective group ID of your shell. In this example session, I was a member of the "cs" and "music" groups, and my login shell's effective group name was "cs".

The system administrator is the one who chooses which one of your groups is used as your login shell's effective group ID. The only way to permanently alter your login shell's effective group ID is to ask the system administrator to change it.

However, you may create a shell with a different effective group ID by using the **newgrp** utility, which works like this:

Utility: **newgrp** [-] [*groupname*]

The **newgrp** utility, when invoked with a group name as an argument, creates a new shell with an effective group ID corresponding to the group name. The old shell sleeps until you exit the newly created shell. You must be a member of the group that you specify. If you use a dash (-) instead of a group name as the argument, a shell is created with the same settings as those of the shell that was created when you logged into the system.

In the next example, I created a file called "test1" from my login shell, which had an effective group of "cs". I then created a temporary shell with an effective group of "music" and then created a file called "test2". I then terminated the temporary shell and went back to the original shell, where I obtained a long listing of both files:

```
$ date > test1              ...create from a "cs" group shell.
$ newgrp music              ...create a "music" group shell.
$ date > test2              ...create from a "music" group shell.
^D                          ...terminate the new shell.
$ ls -lg test1 test2  ...look at each file's attributes.
-rw-r--r--   1   glass  cs     29 Jan 31 22:57  test1
-rw-r--r--   1   glass  music  29 Jan 31 22:57  test2
$ _
```

POETRY IN MOTION: EPILOGUE

This section concludes the "Poetry In Motion" series of examples. During this series, you were introduced to many useful UNIX concepts and utilities. I thoroughly recommend that you try them out before progressing further through this book, as doing so will help you retain and understand the basics of UNIX. The remainder of this chapter covers the two most popular UNIX editors and explains how you can alter your terminal settings so that they work correctly. It also contains some information on using the UNIX e-mail system.

DETERMINING YOUR TERMINAL'S TYPE: tset

Several UNIX utilities, including the two standard editors **vi** and **emacs**, need to know what kind of terminal you're using so that they can control the screen correctly. The type of your terminal is stored by your shell in something called an *environment variable*. Environment variables are described in more detail in Chapter 3. You may think of them as being rather like global variables that hold strings. Before

vi or **emacs** can work correctly, your shell's TERM environment variable must be set to your terminal type. Common settings for this variable include "vt100" and "vt52". There are several ways that this variable can be set:

- Your shell startup file, described in the next section, can set TERM directly by containing a line of the form: "setenv TERM vt100" (C shell) or "TERM= vt100 ; export TERM" (Bourne and Korn shells). This method is only practical if you know the type of your terminal in advance and you always log into the same terminal.
- Your shell startup file can invoke the **tset** utility, which looks at the communications port that you're connected to and then examines a special file called "/etc/ttytab", which contains a table of port/terminal mappings. In most cases, **tset** can find out what kind of terminal you're using from this table and set TERM accordingly. If **tset** can't find the terminal type, it can be told to prompt you for the terminal type when you log in.
- You can manually set TERM from a shell.

The rest of this section describes the operation of **tset**. Before using **vi** or **emacs**, you should also be sure to read the next section, which describes the operation of a related utility called **stty**.

The best way to set TERM is to use **tset** from your login shell. **tset** works as follows:

Utility: **tset** -s [-ec] [-ic] {-m *portId*:[?]*terminalType*}*

tset is a utility that tries to determine your terminal's type and then resets it for standard operation.

If the -s option is not used, **tset** assumes that your terminal type is already stored in the TERM environment variable and resets it using terminal-capability information stored in "/etc/termcap" or the *terminfo* database, depending on your version of UNIX.

If you use the -s option, **tset** examines the "/etc/ttytab" file and tries to map your terminal's port to a terminal type. If the terminal type is found, the utility initializes your terminal with an appropriate initialization sequence from the "/etc/termcap" file. The -s option also causes **tset** to generate shell commands to standard output that, when executed, cause the TERM and TERMCAP environment variables to be set properly. **tset** uses the contents of the SHELL environment variable to determine which kind of shell commands to generate. Filename expansion must be temporarily inhibited during the execution of the command sequence that **tset** generates, since there could be special characters that might be misinterpreted by the shell. Examples of this situation are exhibited shortly.

The -**e** option sets the terminal's erase character to *c* instead of the default *Control*-H setting. Control characters may be indicated either by typing the character directly or by preceding the character by a carat (^) (i.e., use "^h" to indicate *Control*-H).

> The **-i** option sets the terminal's interrupt character to *c* instead of the default *Control*-C setting. Control characters may be indicated as described in the previous paragraph.
>
> The "/etc/ttytab" mappings may be overridden or supplemented by using the **-m** option. The sequence "-m pp:tt" tells **tset** that if the terminal's port type is "pp", then it should assume that the terminal is of type "tt". If a question mark (?) is placed after the colon (:), **tset** displays "tt" and asks the user to either press the *Enter* key to confirm that the terminal type is indeed "tt" or to enter the actual terminal type that **tset** should use.

The "/etc/ttytab" file contains lines of the following form:

```
tty0f  "usr/etc getty std.9600"     vt100      off local
ttyp0  none                         network    off secure
ttyp1  none                         network    off secure
```

The first field contains the names of ports, and the third field contains the names of terminal types. For example, if I were logged on via port tty0f, my terminal type would be read from this file as vt100. In environments where terminals are *hardwired* (directly connected to a specific port), this method works nicely, since the terminal is always on the same port. In a network environment, this method doesn't work very well, as we will see shortly. In the following example, I found out my actual port name by using the **tty** utility (described in Chapter 7) and then examined the output from the **tset** command:

```
$ tty                    ...display my terminal's port ID.
/dev/ttyp0
$ tset -s               ...call tset.
set noglob;             ...shell commands generated by tset.
TERM = network;
export TERM;
TERMCAP = 'sa;cent;network:li#24:co#80:am:do=^J: ';
export TERMCAP;
unset noglob;
Erase is Ctrl-H
$ _
```

The previous example is provided only to illustrate how **tset** does its stuff. To actually make **tset** change the TERM and TERMCAP variables, which, after all, is the reason for using it in the first place, you must "eval" its output. The *eval* shell command is described fully in the next chapter. Here's a more realistic example of the use of **tset**:

```
$ set noglob            ...temporarily inhibit filename expansion.
$ eval `tset -s`        ...evaluate output from tset.
Erase is Backspace      ...message from tset.
$ unset noglob          ...re-enable filename expansion.
```

```
$ echo $TERM          ...look at the new value of TERM.
network               ...the terminal type that tset found.
$ _
```

Unfortunately, the terminal type "network" is not very useful, as it assumes that my terminal has almost no capabilities at all. The **tset** command may be presented with a rule that tells it, "if the terminal type is discovered to be 'network', assume that the terminal is a vt100 and prompt the user for confirmation." Here is the variation of **tset** that does this task:

```
$ set noglob          ...disable filename expansion.
$ eval `tset -s -m 'network:vt100'` ...provide rule.
TERM = (vt100) <Enter>  ...I pressed the Enter key.
Erase is Backspace
$ unset noglob        ...re-enable filename expansion.
$ echo $TERM          ...display new TERM setting.
vt100                 ...this is the terminal type that tset used.
$ _
```

In summary, it's wise to contain a command in your shell's startup file that calls **tset** to set your terminal type. Shell startup files are described in Chapter 3. The simplest form of **tset** is the following set of commands:

C shell

```
setenv TERM vt100
tset
```

Bourne/Korn shell

```
TERM=vt100; export TERM
tset
```

The more sophisticated form of **tset** searches the "/etc/ttytab" file for your terminal type, and it should look somewhat like this:

C shell

```
set noglob
eval `tset -s -m 'network:?vt100'`
unset noglob
```

Bourne/Korn shell

```
eval `tset -s -m 'network:?vt100'`
```

CHANGING A TERMINAL'S CHARACTERISTICS: stty

All terminals have the ability to process certain characters in a special manner; these characters are called *metacharacters*. Examples of metacharacters include the backspace character and the *Control*-C sequence, which is used to terminate programs. The default metacharacter settings may be overridden using the **stty** utility, which works as follows:

Utility: **stty** -a { *option* }* { *metacharacterString <value>*} *

The **stty** utility allows you to examine and set a terminal's characteristics. **stty** supports the modification of over 100 different settings, so I've only listed the most common ones here. Consult **man** for more details. To list a terminal's current settings, use the -**a** option. To alter a particular setting, supply one or more of the following options:

Option	Meaning
-echo	Don't echo typed characters.
echo	Echo typed characters.
-raw	Enable the special meaning of metacharacters.
raw	Disable the special meaning of metacharacters.
-tostop	Allow background jobs to send output to the terminal.
tostop	Stop background jobs that try to send output to the terminal.
sane	Set the terminal characteristics to sensible default values.

You may also set the mappings of a metacharacter by following the name of its corresponding string with its new value. A control character may be indicated by preceding the character with a carat (^) or by typing a backslash (\) followed by the actual control character itself. Here are the common metacharacter strings, together with their respective meanings:

Option	Meaning
erase	Backspace one character.
kill	Erase all of the current line.
lnext	Don't treat the next character specially.
susp	Suspend the process for a future awakening.
intr	Terminate (interrupt) the foreground job with no core dump.
quit	Terminate the foreground job with a core dump.
stop	Stop/restart terminal output.
eof	End of input (or end of file).

Here's an example of **stty** in action:

```
$ stty -a                   ...display current terminal settings.
speed 38400 baud, 24 rows, 80 columns
parenb -parodd cs7 -cstopb -hupcl cread -clocal -crtscts
-ignbrk brkint ignpar -parmrk -inpck istrip -inlcr -igncr icrnl -iuclc
ixon -ixany -ixoff imaxbel
isig iexten icanon -xcase echo echoe echok -echonl -noflsh -tostop
echoctl -echoprt echoke
opost -olcuc onlcr -ocrnl -onocr -onlret -ofill -ofdel
erase  kill  werase  rprnt  flush  lnext  susp  intr  quit  stop  eof
^H     ^U    ^W      ^R     ^O     ^V     ^Z/^Y ^C    ^\    ^S/^Q ^D
$ stty erase ^b        ...set erase key to Control-B.
$ stty erase ^h        ...set erase key to Control-H.
$ _
```

Invoke **stty** from your shell's startup file if your favorite metacharacter mappings differ from the norm. **stty** is useful when you are building shells that need to turn keyboard echoing on and off; an example of such a script is included in Chapter 6. Here's an example that uses **stty** to turn off keyboard echoing:

```
$ stty -echo      ...turn echoing off.
$ stty echo       ...turn echoing back on again.
$ _
```

Note that the last line of input (*stty echo*) would not ordinarily be visible on the screen, due to the inhibition of echoing caused by the preceding line! However, I have included it here so that you can see what I typed.

Now that you've seen how to set your terminal type and alter its settings, it's time to take a look at the two most popular UNIX editors: **vi** and **emacs**.

EDITING A FILE: vi

The two most popular UNIX text editors are called **vi** and **emacs**. It's handy to be reasonably proficient in **vi**, as it is found on nearly every version of UNIX, while **emacs** is not shipped with every version (although it is available for almost every version). This section and the next section contain enough information about each editor to allow you to perform essential editing tasks. They also contain references to other books for obtaining more advanced information.

Starting vi

The **vi** editor was originally developed for BSD UNIX by Bill Joy of the University of California at Berkeley (and later, of Sun Microsystems, Inc.). **vi** proved so popular in the UNIX world that it later was adopted as a standard utility for System V and most other versions of UNIX. Today, **vi** is found on virtually every UNIX system. **vi** stands for "**visual editor**."

To start **vi** with a blank slate, enter the command **vi** without any parameters at the UNIX prompt. To edit an existing file, supply the name of the file as a command-line parameter. When your screen is initialized, blank lines are indicated by tilde (~) characters. **vi** then enters *command mode* and awaits instructions. To conserve space, the screens shown in this text are only six lines long. For example, when I executed **vi** with no parameters, I saw this:

Command mode is one of the two modes that **vi** may be in; the other mode is called *text-entry mode*. Since it's easier to describe command mode when there's some text on the screen, I'll start by describing text-entry mode.

Text-Entry Mode

To enter text-entry mode from command mode, press one of the keys in the table below. Each key enters you into text-entry mode in a slightly different way:

Key	Action
i	Text is inserted in front of the cursor.
I	Text is inserted at the beginning of the current line.
a	Text is added after the cursor.
A	Text is added to the end of the current line.
o	Text is added after the current line.
O	Text is inserted before the current line.
R	Text is replaced (overwritten).

Any text that you enter at this point will be displayed on the screen. To move to the next line, press the *Enter* key. You may use the backspace key to delete the last character that you entered. *You may not move the cursor around the screen using the cursor, or arrow, keys when you're in text-entry mode.* In text-entry mode, cursor keys are interpreted as regular ASCII characters, and their control codes are entered as normal text. This feature takes many users by surprise, so beware.

To go from command mode to text-entry mode, press the *Esc,* or *Escape,* key.

To enter a short four-line poem, I pressed the "a" key to add characters in text-entry mode, entered the text of the poem, and then pressed the *Esc* key to return to command mode. Here's what I entered into the **vi** editor:

```
I always remember standing in the rains,
On a cold and damp september,
Brown Autumn leaves were falling softly to the ground,
Like the dreams of a life as they slide away.
~
~
```

The next section describes the editing features of **vi** that allowed me to change this poem to something a little more appealing.

Command Mode

To edit text, you must enter command mode. To travel from text-entry mode to command mode, press the *Esc* key. If you accidentally press the *Esc* key when in command mode, nothing bad happens. (Depending on your terminal settings, you may hear a beep or bell that tells you that you are already in command mode).

vi's editing features are selected by pressing special character sequences. For example, to erase a single word, position the cursor at the beginning of the word and press the "d" key followed by the "w" key ("delete word").

Some editing features require parameters and are accessed by pressing the colon (:) key, followed by the command sequence, followed by the *Enter* key. When the colon key is pressed, the remainder of the command sequence is displayed at the bottom of the screen. In the following example as well as throughout this book, the *Enter* key is indicated as <Enter>. The "<" and ">" characters act as delimiters and should not be entered. For example, to delete lines one through three, you'd enter the following command sequence:

```
:1,3d<Enter>
```

Some editing features, such as the block-delete command that I just described, act upon a range of lines. **vi** accepts a couple of formats for a line range:

- To select a single line, state its line number.
- To select a block of lines, state the first and last line numbers inclusively, separated by a comma.

vi allows you to use the "$" to denote the line number of the last line in the file and the "." to denote the line number of the line currently containing the cursor. **vi** also allows you to use arithmetic expressions when stating line numbers. For example, the sequence

```
:.,.+2d<Enter>
```

would delete the current line and the two lines that follow it. Here are some other examples of commands for line ranges:

Range	Selects
1,$	all of the lines in the file
1,.	all of the lines from the start of the file to the current line, inclusive
.,$	all of the lines from the current line to the end of the file, inclusive
.-2	the single line that's two lines before the current line

In the text that follows, the term *<range>* indicates a range of lines in the format described above.

Common Editing Features

The most common **vi** editing features can be grouped into the following categories:

- cursor movement
- deleting text
- replacing text
- pasting text
- searching text
- search/replacing text
- saving/loading files
- miscellaneous (including how to quit **vi**)

These categories are described and illustrated in the next set of subsections, using the text of the sample poem that I entered at the start of this section.

Cursor Movement

Here is a table of the common cursor-movement commands:

Movement	Key sequence
Up one line	<cursor up> or the "k" key
Down one line	<cursor down> or the "j" key
Right one character	<cursor right> or the "l" key (will not wrap around)
Left one character	<cursor left> or the "h" key (will not wrap around)
To start of line	^
To end of line	$
Back one word	the "b" key
Forward one word	the "w" key
Down a half screen	*Control*-D
Forward one screen	*Control*-F
Up a half screen	*Control*-U
Back one screen	*Control*-B
To line *nn*	:*nn*<*Enter*> (*nn*G also works)

For example, to insert the word "Just" before the word "Like" on the fourth line of the poem, I moved the cursor to the fourth line, pressed the "i" key to enter text-entry mode, entered the text, and pressed the *Esc* key to return to command mode. To move the cursor to the fourth line, I used the key sequence :4<*Enter*> (or, instead, I could have used the key sequence 4G).

Deleting Text

Here is a table of the common text-deletion commands:

Item to delete	Key sequence
Character	Position the cursor over the character and then press the "x" key.
Word	Position the cursor at the start of word and then type the two characters "dw".
Line	Position the cursor anywhere on the line and then type the two characters "dd" (Typing a number ahead of "dd" will cause **vi** to delete the specified number of lines beginning with the current line.)
Current position to end of current line	Press the "D" key.
Block of lines	:<*range*>d<*Enter*>

For example, to delete the word "always", I typed :1<*Enter*> to move to the start of line one, pressed the "w" key to move forward one word, and then typed the two letters "dw". To delete the trailing "s" on the end of "rains" on the first line, I moved my cursor over the letter "s" and then pressed the "x" key. My poem now looked like this:

```
    I remember standing in the rain,
    On a cold and damp september,
    Brown Autumn leaves were falling softly to the ground,
    Just Like the dreams of a life as they slide away.
    ~
    ~
```

Replacing Text

Following is a table of the common text-replacement commands:

Item to replace	Key sequence
Character	Position the cursor over the character, press the "r" key, and then type the replacement character.
Word	Position the cursor at start of word, type the two characters "cw", type the replacement text, and press the *Esc* key.
Line	Position the cursor anywhere on the line, type the two characters "cc", type the replacement text, and press the *Esc* key.

For example, to replace the word "standing" with "walking", I moved to the start of the word and then typed the letters "cw". I then typed the word "walking" and pressed the *Esc* key. To replace the lowercase "s" of "september" by an uppercase "S", I positioned the cursor over the "s", pressed the "r" key, and then pressed the "S" key.

I then performed a few more tidy-up operations, replacing "damp" with "dark", "slide" with "slip", and the "L" of "like" with "l". Here's the final version of the poem:

```
    I remember walking in the rain,
    On a cold and dark September,
    Brown Autumn leaves were falling softly to the ground,
    Just like the dreams of a life as they slip away.
    ~
    ~
```

Pasting Text

vi maintains a paste buffer that may be used for copying and pasting text between areas of a file. Here is a table of the most common pasting operations:

Action	Key sequence
Copy (yank) lines into paste buffer.	*:<range>*y*<Enter>*
Insert (put) paste buffer after current line.	p or :pu*<Enter>* (contents of paste buffer are unchanged)
Insert paste buffer after line *nn*.	*:nn*pu*<Enter>* (contents of paste buffer are unchanged)

For example, to copy the first two lines of the poem into the paste buffer and then paste them after the third line, I entered the following two commands:

```
:1,2y
:3pu
```

The poem then looked like this:

I remember walking in the rain,
On a cold and dark September,
Brown Autumn leaves were falling softly to the ground,
I remember walking in the rain,
On a cold and dark September,
Just like the dreams of a life as they slip away.

To restore the poem as it was before this change, I typed :4,5d*<Enter>*.

Searching

vi allows you to search forward and backward through a file, relative to the current line, for a particular substring. Here is a table of the most common search operations:

Action	Key sequence
Search forward from current position for string *sss*.	/*sss*/*<Enter>*
Search backward from current position for string *sss*.	?*sss*?*<Enter>*
Repeat last search.	n
Repeat last search in the opposite direction.	N

The trailing "/" and "?" in the first two searches are optional. **vi** figures out what you mean when you press the *Enter* key, but it's a good habit to include these optional characters, since you can add other commands after them, rather than simply hitting *Enter*.

For example, I searched for the substring "ark" in line one of the poem by entering the following commands:

```
:1<Enter>
/ark/<Enter>
```

vi positioned the cursor at the start of the substring "ark" located in the word "dark" on the second line:

```
I remember walking in the rain,
On a cold and dark September,
Brown Autumn leaves were falling softly to the ground,
Just like the dreams of a life as they slip away.
~
~
```

Search/Replacing

You may perform global search-and-replace operations by using the following commands:

Action	Key sequence
Replace the first occurrence of *sss* on each line with *ttt*.	*:<range>*s/ *sss*/ *ttt*/*<Enter>*
Relace every occurrence of *sss* on each line with *ttt* (global replace).	*:<range>*s/ *sss*/ *ttt*/g*<Enter>*

For example, to replace every occurrence of the substring "re" with "XXX", I entered the command displayed below:

```
I XXXmember walking in the rain,
On a cold and dark September,
Brown Autumn leaves weXXX falling softly to the ground,
Just like the dXXXams of a life as they slip away.
~
:1,$s/re/XXX/g
```

Saving/Loading Files

Here is a table of the most common save/load file commands:

Action	Key sequence
Save file as *<name>*.	:w *<name>* *<Enter>*
Save file with current name.	:w*<Enter>*
Save only certain lines to another file.	:*<range>* w *<name>* *<Enter>*
Read in contents of another file at current position.	:r *<name>* *<Enter>*
Edit file *<name>* instead of current file.	:e *<name>* *<Enter>*
Edit next file on initial command line.	:n *<Enter>*

For example, I saved the poem in a file called "rain.doc" by entering the command displayed below:

```
I remember walking in the rain,
On a cold and dark September,
Brown Autumn leaves were falling softly to the ground,
Just like the dreams of a life as they slip away.
~
:w rain.doc
```

vi tells you how many bytes a file occupies when you save it and won't let you accidentally quit **vi** without saving the current file.

If you place more than one filename on the command line when you first invoke **vi**, **vi** starts by loading up the first file. You may edit the next file by using the key sequence :n.

Miscellaneous

Here's a list of the most common miscellaneous commands, including the commands for quitting **vi**:

Action	Key sequence
Redraw screen.	*Control*-L
Execute *command* in a subshell and then return to **vi**.	:!*<command>* *<Enter>*
Execute *command* in a subshell and read its output into the edit buffer at the current position.	:r !*<command>* *<Enter>*
Quit **vi** if work is saved.	:q*<Enter>*
Quit **vi** and discard unsaved work.	:q!*<Enter>*

Control-L is particularly useful for refreshing the screen when a message pops up and messes up your screen or when some static interferes with your modem connection during a **vi** session.

To finally quit **vi** after saving the final version of the poem, I typed the command illustrated below:

```
I remember walking in the rain,
On a cold and dark September,
Brown Autumn leaves were falling softly to the ground,
Just like the dreams of a life as they slip away.
~
:q
```

For More Information

For more information about **vi**, I recommend *The UNIX Operating System,* second edition [8].

EDITING A FILE: emacs

emacs is a popular editor that is often found on many UNIX systems (and for those for which it is not included in the distribution, a version is probably available via download on the Internet). **emacs** had its start in the Lisp-based artificial-intelligence community. In 1975, Richard Stallman and Guy Steele wrote the original version, which has evolved into the version that is now distributed for free and in source-code form through the Free Software Foundation (FSF). Stallman formed the FSF because of his objection to copyright and patent laws and his belief that all software should be free. **emacs** stands for "editor **mac**ros."

Starting emacs

To start **emacs** with a blank file, enter the command **emacs** with no parameters. To edit an existing file, specify its name as a command-line parameter. Assuming that you supply no parameters, your screen will initially look something like the one that follows, depending on your version of **emacs**:

```
GNU Emacs 18.58.1
Copyright (C) 1990 Free Software Foundation, Inc.
Type C-h for help, C-x u to undo changes ('C'- means use CTRL-key)
--- Emacs:  *scratch*        (Fundamental)   ---  All  -----------
```

I'll draw screens that are only six lines long to conserve space. The line that is second from the bottom is called the *mode line*, and it contains information in the following left-to-right order:

- If the first three dashes contain a "**", it means that the current file has been modified.
- The name that follows "Emacs:" is the name of the current file. If no file is currently loaded, the name "*scratch*" is used instead.
- The current editing mode is shown between parentheses. In this case, it's *Fundamental*, which is the standard editing mode.
- The last entry indicates your relative position in the file as a percentage. If the file is very small and fits completely on the screen, then *All* is displayed. If you're at the top or the bottom of a file, then *Top* or *Bot* are displayed, respectively.

emacs Commands

Unlike **vi**, **emacs** doesn't distinguish between text-entry mode and command mode. To enter text, simply start typing. The initial **emacs** welcome banner automatically disappears when you type the first letter. Long lines are not automatically broken, so you must press the *Enter* key when you wish to start a new line. Lines longer than the screen width are indicated by a "\" character at the end of the screen, and the remainder of the line is "wrapped" onto the next line:

```
This is a very long line that illustrates the way that unbroken lines a \
re displayed.
This is a much shorter line.
--- Emacs:  *scratch*(Fundamental)   ---   All   -----------
```

emacs's editing features are accessed via either a control sequence or a meta-sequence. I'll indicate control sequences by preceding the name of the key with the prefix *Control-*. For example, the sequence

```
Control-H t
```

means "press and hold the *Control* key and then press the "H" key. (For control sequences, it doesn't matter whether you use uppercase or lowercase, so I suggest that you use lowercase, as it's easier.) Then release both keys and press the "t" key on its own." Similarly, metasequences use the *Esc* key. For example, the sequence

```
Esc x
```

means "press the Esc key (but don't hold it) and then press the "x" key." The next few sections contain many examples of **emacs** command sequences. If you ever accidentally press *Esc* twice, **emacs** warns you that you're trying to do something advanced and suggests that you press the "n" key to continue. Unless you're a seasoned **emacs** user, it's good advice.

Getting Out of Trouble

Whenever you're learning a new editor, it's quite easy to get lost and confused. Here are a couple of useful command sequences to return you to a sane state:

- The command sequence *Control*-G terminates any **emacs** command, even if it's only partially entered, and returns **emacs** to the state at which it's waiting for a new command.
- The command sequence *Control*-X 1 closes all **emacs** windows except your main file window. This sequence is useful, as several **emacs** options create a new window to display information, and it's important to know how to close them once you've read their contents.

Getting Help

There are several ways to obtain help information about **emacs**. One of the best ways to get started with **emacs** is to read the self-describing help tutorial. I suggest that you do so before anything else. To read the tutorial, use the command sequence Control-*H* t. The tutorial will appear and give you directions on how to proceed.

Leaving emacs

To leave **emacs** and save your file, use the command sequence *Control*-X *Control*-C. If you haven't saved your file since it was last modified, you'll be asked whether you want to save it.

emacs Modes

emacs supports several different modes for entering text, including Fundamental, Lisp Interaction, and C. Each mode supports special features that are customized for the particular kind of text that you're editing. **emacs** starts in Fundamental mode by default, which is the mode that I'll be using during my description of **emacs**. For more information about modes, consult the **emacs** tutorial.

Entering Text

To enter text, simply start typing. For example, here's a short four-line poem:

> There is no need for fear in the night,
> You know that your Mommy is there,
> To watch over her babies and hold them tight,
> When you are in her arms you can feel her sigh all night.
> --- Emacs: *scratch*   (Fundamental)   ---   All   ------------

The next section describes the editing features of **emacs** that allowed me to change this poem to something a little better.

Common Editing Features

The most common **emacs** editing features can be grouped into the following categories:

- cursor movement
- deleting, pasting, and undoing text
- searching text
- search/replacing text
- saving/loading files
- miscellaneous

These categories are described and illustrated in the next set of subsections, using the sample poem that I entered at the start of this section.

Moving the Cursor

Here's a table of the common cursor-movement commands:

Movement	Key sequence
Up one line	*Control*-P (previous)
Down one line	*Control*-N (next)
Right one character	*Control*-F (forward, wraps around)
Left one character	*Control*-B (backward, wraps around)
To start of line	*Control*-A (a is first letter)
To end of line	*Control*-E (end)
Back one word	*Esc* b (back)
Forward one word	*Esc* f (forward)
Down one screen	*Control*-V
Up one screen	*Esc* v
Start of file	*Esc*<
End of file	*Esc*>

For example, to insert the words "worry or" before the word "fear" on the first line, I moved the cursor to the first line of the file by typing *Esc* < and then moved forward several words by using the *Esc* f sequence. I then typed in the words, which were automatically inserted at the current cursor position.

Deleting, Pasting, and Undoing

Here is a table of the common deletion commands:

Item to delete	Key sequence
Character before cursor	*Delete* key
Character after cursor	*Control*-D
Word before cursor	*Esc Delete* key
Word after cursor	*Esc* d
To end of current line	*Control*-K
Sentence	*Esc* k

Whenever an item is deleted, **emacs** remembers it in an individual "kill buffer." A list of kill buffers is maintained so that deleted items may be retrieved long after they have been removed from the display. To retrieve the last killed item, press *Control*-Y. After you have pressed *Control*-Y, you may press *Esc* y to replace the retrieved item with the previously deleted item. Every time you press *Esc* y, the retrieved item moves one step back through the kill-buffer list.

You may append the next deleted item onto the end of the last kill buffer rather than create a new one by pressing *Esc Control*-W immediately prior to executing the delete command. This feature is useful if you wish to cut different bits and pieces out of a file and then paste them all together back into one place.

You may undo editing actions one at a time by typing *Control*-X u for each action that you wish to undo.

Here is a summary of the kill-buffer and undo commands:

Action	Key sequence
Insert last kill buffer.	*Control*-Y
Retrieve previous kill.	*Esc* y
Append next kill.	*Esc Control*-W
Undo.	*Control*-X u

Searching

emacs allows you to perform something called an *incremental search*. To search forward from your current cursor position for a particular sequence of letters, type *Control*-S. The prompt "I-search:" is displayed on the bottom line of the screen, indicating that **emacs** wants you to enter the string that you wish to search for. As you enter the character sequence, **emacs** searches to find the first string from your initial cursor position that matches what you've entered so far; in other words, partial substrings are found as you enter the full string. To terminate the search and leave your cursor at its current position, press *Esc*. If you delete characters in the full string before pressing the *Esc* key, **emacs** moves back to the first match of the remaining substring. To repeat a search, don't press *Esc*, but instead press *Control*-S to search forward or *Control*-R to search backward. Here is a summary of the searching commands:

Action	Key sequence
Search foward for *str.*	*Control*-S *str*
Search backward for *str.*	*Control*-R *str*
Repeat last search forward.	*Control*-S
Repeat last search backward.	*Control*-R
Leave search mode.	*Esc*

Search/Replacing

To perform a global search/replace procedure, press *Esc* x, followed by the string "repl s" followed by the *Enter* key. **emacs** then prompts you for the string to be replaced. Enter the string and press *Enter.* **emacs** then prompts you for the replacement string. Enter the string and press *Enter.* **emacs** then performs the global text substitution.

Saving/Loading Files

To save your current work to a file, press *Control*-X *Control*-S. If your work hasn't been associated with a filename yet, you will be prompted for a filename. Your work is then saved into its associated file.

To edit another file, press *Control*-X *Control*-F. You will be prompted for the new filename. If the file already exists, its contents are loaded into **emacs**; otherwise, the file is created.

To save your file and then quit out of **emacs**, press *Control*-X *Control*-C.

Here's a summary of the saving and loading commands:

Action	Key sequence
Save current work.	*Control*-X *Control*-S
Edit another file.	*Control*-X *Control*-F
Save work and then quit.	*Control*-X *Control*-C

Miscellaneous

To redraw the screen, press *Control*-L. To place **emacs** into auto-wrap mode, which automatically inserts line breaks when words flow past the end of a line, type "*Esc* **x** auto-fill-mode" and press *Enter.* To leave this mode, repeat the command again.

For More Information

For more information about **emacs,** I recommend "UNIX Desktop Guide to emacs" [19].

ELECTRONIC MAIL: mail and mailx

This section is the last section of this chapter, and it contains information about how to use the UNIX electronic-mail system. It's handy to be able to use **mail** when you first start to use UNIX, as it's a convenient way to ask the system administrator and other seasoned users questions about UNIX. The name of this electronic-mail system is **mail** on some versions of UNIX and **mailx** on others. For the purposes of this section, I shall refer to both of them as **mail.**

mail has a large number of features, so in accordance with the initial aim of this book, I shall only describe those features that I consider to be the most useful; consult **man** for more information. Here's a description of **mail**:

Utility: **mail** -H [-f *fileName*] { *userID*}*

mail allows you to send and read electronic mail. If a list of usernames is supplied, mail reads standard input, mails it to the specified users, and then terminates. Usernames can be a combination of the following forms:

- a local user name (i.e., login name)
- an Internet address of the form name@hostname.domain
- a filename
- a mail group

Internet addresses are described in Chapter 8, and mail groups are described shortly.

If no usernames are specified, **mail** assumes that you wish to read mail from a mail folder. The folder "/var/mail/<username>", where <username> is your own username, is read by default, although this default may be overridden by using the **-f** option. **mail** prompts you with an ampersand (&) prompt and then awaits commands. The **-H** option causes **mail** to list the headers from your mail folder without entering the command mode. A list of the most useful command-mode options is contained in the next few pages.

When **mail** is invoked, it begins by reading the contents of the mail startup file, which may contain statements that customize the **mail** utility. By default, mail reads the file ".mailrc" in your home directory, although the name of this file may be overridden by setting the environment variable MAILRC. Environment variables are discussed in Chapter 3.

There are a large number of customizable options. The most important option is the ability to define mail groups (also sometimes called aliases), which are variables that denote a group of users. To specify a mail group, place a line of the form

```
group name {userId}+
```

into the **mail** startup file. You may then use *name* as an alias for the specified list of users, either on the command line or in command mode.

Here is a list of the most useful **mail** commands that are available from command mode:

Command	Meaning
?	Display help.
copy [*mesgList*] [*fileName*]	Copy messages into *fileName* without marking them as "saved."
delete [*mesgList*]	Delete specified messages from system mailbox.
file [*fileName*]	Read mail from mailbox *fileName*. If no filename is given, display the name of the current mailbox together with the number of bytes and messages that it contains.
headers [*message*]	Display page of message headers that include *message*.
mail { *userId* }+	Send mail to specified users.
print [*mesgList*]	Display specified messages using **more**.
quit	Exit **mail**.
reply [*mesgList*]	Mail response back to senders of message list.
save [*mesgList*] [*fileName*]	Save specified messages to *fileName*. If no filename is given, save them in a file called "mbox" in your home directory by default.

mesgList describes a collection of one or more mail messages using the following syntax:

Syntax	Meaning
	current message
nn	message number *nn*
^	first undeleted message
$	last message
*	all messages
nn-mm	messages numbered *nn* through *mm*, inclusive
user	all messages from *user*

As you'll see in the next set of examples, these **mail** commands may be invoked by their first letter; for example, you can use "p" instead of "print".

Sending Mail

The easiest way to send mail is to enter the mail directly from the keyboard and terminate the message by pressing *Control*-D on a line of its own:

```
$ mail tim      ...send some mail to the local user tim.
Subject: Mail Test     ...enter the subject of the mail.
Hi Tim,
 How is Amanda doing?
- with best regards from Graham
^D               ...end of input; standard input is sent as mail.
$ _
```

I wanted to create a mail group called "music" that would allow me to send mail to all of the people in my band. To do so, I created a file called ".mailrc" in my home directory with this line of code:

```
group music jeff richard kelly bev
```

This line of code allowed me to send mail to all four band members as follows:

```
$ mail music  ...send mail to each member of the group.
Subject: Music
Hi guys,
How about a jam sometime?

- with best regards from Graham.
^D                ...end of input.
$ _
```

For mail messages that are more than just a few lines long, it's a good idea to compose the message using a text editor, save it in a named file, and then, as in the following command, redirect the input of **mail** to be from the file:

```
$ mail music < jam.txt      ...send jam.txt as mail.
$ _
```

To send mail to users on the Internet, use the standard Internet-addressing scheme described in Chapter 8:

```
$ mail glass@utdallas.edu < mesg.txt      ...send mesg.txt.
$ _
```

Reading Mail

When mail is sent to you, it is stored in a file called "/var/mail/<username>", where <username> is your login name. Files that hold mail are termed "mail folders." For

example, my own incoming mail is held in the mail folder "/var/mail/glass". To read
a mail folder, type "mail", followed by an optional folder specifier. You are notified
if no mail is currently present:

```
$ mail        ...try reading my mail from the default folder.
No mail for glass
$ _
```

If mail is present, **mail** displays a list of the incoming mail headers and then prompts
you with an ampersand (&). Press *Enter* to read each message in order, and press
"q" (quit) to exit **mail**. The mail that you read is appended by default to the mail
folder "mbox" in your home directory; mail in this folder may be read at a later time
by typing the following in your home directory:

```
$ mail -f mbox      ...read mail saved in the mbox folder.
```

In the next set of examples, I've deleted some of **mail**'s verbose information so that
the output fits in a reasonable amount of space. In the following example, I read two
pieces of mail from my friend Tim and then exited **mail**:

```
$ ls -l /var/mail/glass              ...see if mail is present.
-rw-------  1 glass              758 May 2 14:32 /var/mail/glass
$ mail                               ...read mail from default folder.
Mail version SMI 4.0 Thu Oct 11 12:59:09 PDT 1990  Type ? for help.
"/var/mail/glass": 2 messages 2 unread
>U  1 tim@utdallas.edu Sat May  2 14:32 11/382  Mail test
 U  2 tim@utdallas.edu Sat May  2 14:32 11/376  Another
& <Enter>                            ...press Enter to read message #1.
From tim@utdallas.edu Sat Mar 14 14:32:33 1998
To: glass@utdallas.edu
Subject: Mail test
hi there
& <Enter>                            ...press Enter to read message #2.
From tim@utdallas.edu Sat Mar 14 14:32:33 1998
To: glass@utdallas.edu
Subject: Another
hi there again
& <Enter>                            ...press Enter to read next message.
At EOF                               ...there are no more messages!
& q                                  ...quit mail.
Saved 2 messages in /home/glass/mbox
$ _
```

To see the headers of the messages in your mail folder without entering mail's command mode, use the **-H** option:

```
$ mail -H          ...peek at my mail folder.
>U  1 tim@utdallas.edu Sat May  2 14:32 11/382  Mail test
 U  2 tim@utdallas.edu Sat May  2 14:32 11/376  Another
$ _
```

To respond to a message after reading it, use the "r" (reply) option. To save a message to a file, use the "s" (save) option. If you don't specify a message list, **mail** selects the current message by default. Here's an example:

```
& 15                             ...read message #15.
From ssmith@utdallas.edu Tue Mar 17 23:27:11 1998
To: glass@utdallas.edu
Subject: Re: come to a party
The SIGGRAPH party begins Thursday NIGHT at 10:00 PM!!
Hope you don't have to teach Thursday night.
& r                              ...reply to ssmith.
To: ssmith@utdallas.edu
Subject: Re: come to a party
Thanks for the invitation.
- see you there
^D                               ...end of input.
& s ssmith.party                 ...save the message from ssmith.
"ssmith.party" [New file] 27/1097
& q                              ...quit from mail.
$ _
```

Caution: Some mailers default that "r" replies to the sender and "R" replies to the sender and everyone who received the original message. Other mailers are the other way around, where "R" replies to the sender and "r" replies to everyone who received the original message. Until you know which way your mailer works, be careful with your replies so that you don't annoy everyone on a public distribution list, or worse, say something you didn't intend for public disclosure!

It's quite possible that you'll receive quite a bit of junk mail; to delete messages that aren't worth reading, use the "d" (delete) option:

```
& d1-15     ...delete messages 1 thru 15, inclusive.
& d*        ...delete all remaining messages.
```

Contacting the System Administrator

The system administrator's mailing address is usually *root*, or possibly *sysadmin*. In general, the alias *postmaster* will direct mail to the person in charge of e-mail-related issues.

CHAPTER REVIEW

Checklist

In this chapter, I described:

- how to obtain a UNIX account
- how to log in and out of a UNIX system
- the importance of changing your password
- the function of a shell
- how to run a utility

- how to obtain on-line help
- the special terminal metacharacters
- the most common file-oriented utilities
- two UNIX editors
- how to set up your terminal correctly
- how to send electronic mail

Quiz

1. What is one way in which hackers try to break UNIX security?
2. What's the best kind of password?
3. Is UNIX case sensitive?
4. Name the three most common shells.
5. Why are shells better suited than C programs for some tasks?
6. How do you terminate a process?
7. How do you indicate the end of input when entering text from the keyboard?
8. How do you terminate a shell?
9. What term is given to the current location of a process?
10. What attributes does every file have?
11. What is the purpose of groups?
12. How do permission flags relate to directories?
13. Who may change the ownership of a file?
14. What does "case sensitive" mean?

Exercises

1. Design a file-security mechanism that alleviates the need for the "set user ID" feature. [level: *hard*]
2. Explain why a process may have only one current group? [level: *medium*]
3. Even seemingly trivial inventions such as a flashing cursor and a scrolling window have been granted patents, and many software designers construct programs only to find that they have unintentionally reinvented someone else's patented invention. Do you think that patents are fair, and if not, can you think of a better philosophy? [level: *hard*]
4. Obtain the Internet mailing address of an acquaintance in another country and send him or her e-mail. How long does the e-mail take to get there? Does the travel time seem reasonable? [level: *easy*]

Project

Send e-mail to the system administrator and set up two new groups for yourself. Experiment with the group-related utilities and explore the permissions system. [level: *easy*]

CHAPTER 3

The UNIX Shells

Motivation

A shell is a program that sits between you and the raw UNIX operating system. There are three shells that are commonly supported by UNIX vendors: the Bourne shell (sh), the Korn shell (ksh), and the C shell (csh).[1] All three of these shells share a common core set of operations that make life in the UNIX system a little easier. For example, all three shells allow the output of a process to be stored in a file or to be "piped" to another process. They also allow the use of wildcards in filenames, so it's easy to make commands like "list all of the files whose name ends with the suffix '.c'." This chapter describes all of the common core-shell facilities, whereas Chapters 4 through 6 describe the special features of each individual shell.

Prerequisites

In order to understand this chapter, you must already have read Chapters 1 and 2. Some of the utilities that I mention in this chapter are described fully in Chapter 7. It also helps if you have access to a UNIX system so that you can try out the various UNIX features that I discuss.

Objectives

In this chapter, I'll explain and demonstrate the common shell features, including I/O redirection, piping, command substitution, and simple job control.

Presentation

The information in this section is presented in the form of several sample UNIX sessions. If you don't have access to a UNIX account, march through the sessions anyway, and hopefully you'll be able to try them out later.

_____

[1] In terms of the myriad of lesser known shells that are available, some will claim that the lack of a discussion of the so-called Born Again shell (bash) amounts to a serious omission. Because it is so closely related to the C shell and it is not included in many distributions of UNIX, we will draw the line there with apologies to bash fans.

Utilities

This section introduces the following utilities, listed in alphabetical order:

chsh	kill	ps
echo	nohup	sleep

Shell Commands

This section introduces the following shell commands, listed in alphabetical order:

echo	kill	umask
eval	login	wait
exec	shift	
exit	tee	

INTRODUCTION

A shell is a program that is an interface between a user and the raw operating system. It makes basic facilities such as multitasking and piping easy to use, and it adds useful file-specific features such as wildcards and I/O redirection. There are three common shells in use:

- the Bourne shell
- the Korn shell
- the C shell

Your decision on which shell to use is a matter of taste, power, compatibility, and availability. For example, the C shell is better than the Bourne shell for interactive work, but slightly worse in some respects for script programming. The Korn shell was designed to be upwardly compatible with the Bourne shell, and it incorporates the best features of the Bourne and C shells, plus some more of its own. Unfortunately, it's not available on absolutely every version of UNIX, as the other two are. (Well, there might be a version somewhere that lacks the C shell, but I doubt it.) If you don't have much time to learn a particular shell, I'd recommend starting with the Bourne shell and then upgrading to the Korn shell when you can. I personally use the Korn shell.

SHELL FUNCTIONALITY

This chapter describes the common core of functionality that all three shells provide. Here is a diagram that illustrates the relationship among the three shells:

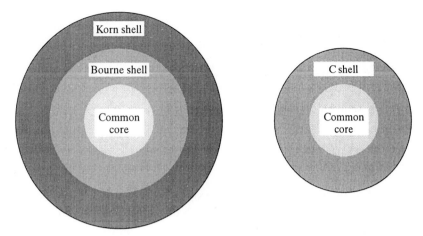

FIGURE 3.1   The relationship of shell functionality

A hierarchy diagram is a useful way to illustrate the features shared by the three shells—so nice, in fact, that I use the same kind of hierarchy chart throughout the rest of this book:

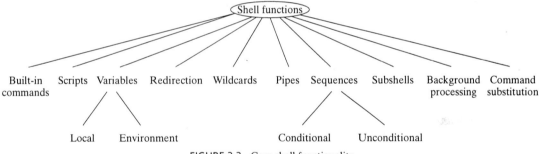

FIGURE 3.2   Core shell functionality

The rest of this chapter describes each component of the hierarchy in detail.

SELECTING A SHELL

When you are provided with a UNIX account, the system administrator chooses a shell for you. To find out which shell was chosen for you, look at your prompt. If you have a $ prompt, you're probably in a Bourne shell or a Korn shell. If you have a % prompt, you're probably in a C shell. When I wrote this chapter, I used a Bourne shell, but it really doesn't matter, since the facilities that I'm about to describe are common to all three shells. However, in later chapters, you will want to select the particular shell that the chapter is about.

Utility: **chsh**

chsh allows you to change your default login shell. It prompts you for the full pathname of the new shell, which is then used as your shell for subsequent logins.

To change your default login shell, use the **chsh** utility, which works as follows: In order to use **chsh**, you must know the full pathnames of the three shells. Here they are:

Shell	Full pathname
Bourne	/bin/sh
Korn	/bin/ksh
C	/bin/csh

In the following example, I changed my default login shell from a Bourne shell to a Korn shell:

```
$ chsh                        ...change the login shell from sh to ksh.
Changing login shell for glass
Old shell: /bin/sh            ...pathname of old shell is displayed.
New shell: /bin/ksh           ...enter full pathname of new shell.
$ ^D                          ...terminate login shell.
login: glass                  ...log back in again.
Password:                     ...secret.
$ _                           ...this time I'm in a Korn shell.
```

Another way to find out the full pathname of your login shell is to type the following:

```
$ echo $SHELL    ...display the name of my login shell.
/bin/ksh         ...full pathname of the Korn shell.
$ _
```

This example illustrated the *echo* shell command and a shell variable called SHELL. Both of these new facilities—echoing and variables—are discussed later in this chapter.

SHELL OPERATIONS

When a shell is invoked, either automatically during a login or manually from a keyboard or script, it follows a preset sequence:

1. It reads a special startup file, typically located in the user's home directory, that contains some initialization information. Each shell's startup sequence is different, so I'll leave the specific details to later chapters.
2. It displays a prompt and waits for a user command.
3. If the user enters a *Control*-D character on a line of its own, this command is interpreted by the shell as meaning "end of input", and it causes the shell to terminate; otherwise, the shell executes the user's command and returns to step 2.

Commands range from simple utility invocations like:

```
$ ls
```

to complex-looking pipeline sequences like:

```
$ ps -ef | sort | ul -tdumb | lp
```

If you ever need to enter a command that is longer than a line on your terminal, you may terminate a portion of a command by a backslash (\) character, and the shell will allow you to continue the command on the next line:

```
$ echo this is a very long shell command and needs to \
be extended with the line-continuation character. Note \
that a single command may be extended for several lines.
this is a very long shell command and needs to be extended with the line-
continuation character. Note that a single command may be extended for
several lines.
$ _
```

EXECUTABLE FILES VERSUS BUILT-IN COMMANDS

Most UNIX commands invoke utility programs that are stored in the directory hierarchy. Utilities are stored in files that have execute permission. For example, when you type

```
$ ls
```

the shell locates the executable program called "ls", which is typically found in the "/bin" directory, and executes it. The way that the shell finds a utility is described later in this chapter. In addition to its ability to locate and execute utilities, the shell contains several built-in commands, which it recognizes and executes internally. I'll describe two of the most useful ones now: *echo* and *cd*.

Displaying Information: *echo*

The built-in *echo* command displays its arguments to standard output and works like this:

Shell Command: echo {arg}*

echo is a built-in shell command that displays all of its arguments to standard output. By default, it appends a new line to the output.

All of the shells we will see contain this built-in function, but you may also invoke the utility called **echo** (usually found in /bin) instead. This utility is sometimes useful, as some arguments and subtle behavior may vary between the different built-in shell commands, and it can be confusing if you write scripts in more than one of these shells. We'll look at writing shell scripts shortly.

Changing Directories: *cd*

The built-in *cd* command changes the current working directory of the shell to a new location and was described fully in Chapter 2.

METACHARACTERS

Some characters are processed specially by a shell and are known as *metacharacters*. All three shells share a core set of common metacharacters, whose meanings are as follows:

Symbol	Meaning
>	Output redirection; writes standard output to a file.
>>	Output redirection; appends standard output to a file.
<	Input redirection; reads standard input from a file.
*	File-substitution wildcard; matches zero or more characters.
?	File-substitution wildcard; matches any single character.
[...]	File-substitution wildcard; matches any character between the brackets.
`command`	Command substitution; replaced by the output from *command*.
|	Pipe symbol; sends the output of one process to the input of another.

Symbol	Meaning
;	Used to sequence commands.
||	Conditional execution; executes a command if the previous one fails.
&&	Conditional execution; executes a command if the previous one succeeds.
(...)	Groups commands.
&	Runs a command in the background.
#	All characters that follow up to a new line are ignored by the shell and programs (i.e., used for a comment).
$	Expands the value of a variable.
\	Prevents special interpretation of the next character.
<< *tok*	Input redirection; reads standard input from script up to *tok*.

When you enter a command, the shell scans it for metacharacters and processes them specially. When all metacharacters have been processed, the command is finally executed. To turn off the special meaning of a metacharacter, precede it by a backslash (\) character. Here's an example:

```
$ echo hi > file          ...store output of echo in "file".
$ cat file                ...look at the contents of "file".
hi
$ echo hi \> file         ...inhibit > metacharacter.
$ cat file                ...look at the file again.
hi > file                 ...> is treated like other characters.
$ _
```

This chapter describes the meaning of each metacharacter in the order that it was listed in the preceding table.

REDIRECTION

The shell redirection facility allows you to:

- store the output of a process to a file (*output redirection*)
- use the contents of a file as input to a process (*input redirection*)

Let's have a look at each facility, in turn.

Output Redirection

Output redirection is handy because it allows you to save a process' output into a file so that it can be listed, printed, edited, or used as input to a future process. To redirect output, use either the ">" or ;">>" metacharacters. The sequence

```
$ command > fileName
```

sends the standard output of *command* to the file with name *fileName*. The shell creates the file with name *fileName* if it doesn't already exist or overwrites its previous contents if it does already exist. If the file already exists but doesn't have write permission, an error occurs. In the next example, I created a file called "alice.txt" by redirecting the output of the **cat** utility. Without parameters, **cat** simply copies its standard input—which, in this case, is from the keyboard—to its standard output.

```
$ cat > alice.txt                        ...create a text file.
In my dreams that fill the night,
I see your eyes,
^D                                       ...end of input.
$ cat alice.txt                          ...look at its contents.
In my dreams that fill the night,
I see your eyes,
$ _
```

The sequence

```
$ command >> fileName
```

appends the standard output of *command* to the file with name *fileName*. The shell creates the file with name *fileName* if it doesn't already exist. In the following example, I appended some text to the existing "alice.txt" file:

```
$ cat >> alice.txt              ...append to the file.
And I fall into them,
Like Alice fell into Wonderland.
^D                              ...end of input.
$ cat alice.txt                 ...look at the new contents.
In my dreams that fill the night,
I see your eyes,
And I fall into them,
Like Alice fell into Wonderland.
$ _
```

By default, both forms of output redirection leave the standard error channel connected to the terminal. However, all shells have variations of output redirection that allow them to redirect the standard error channel. The C and Korn shells also provide protection against accidental overwriting of a file due to output redirection. These facilities are described in later chapters.

Input Redirection

Input redirection is useful because it allows you to prepare a process' input beforehand and store it in a file for later use. To redirect input, use either the "<" or "<<" metacharacters. The sequence

```
$ command < fileName
```

executes *command* using the contents of the file *fileName* as its standard input. If
the file doesn't exist or doesn't have read permission, an error occurs. In the following example, I sent myself the contents of "alice.txt" via the **mail** utility:

```
$ mail glass < alice.txt                          ...send myself mail.
$ mail                                            ...look at my mail.
Mail version SMI 4.0 Sat Oct 13 20:32:29 PDT 1990 Type ? for help.
>N 1 glass@utdallas.edu Mon Feb 2 13:29 17/550
& 1                                               ...read message #1.
From: Graham Glass <glass@utdallas.edu>
To: glass@utdallas.edu
In my dreams that fill the night,
I see your eyes,
And I fall into them,
Like Alice fell into Wonderland
& q                                               ...quit mail.
$ _
```

When the shell encounters a sequence of the form

```
$ command << word
```

it copies its standard input up to, but not including, the line starting with *word* into a
buffer and then executes *command* using the contents of the buffer as its standard
input. This facility is used almost exclusively to allow shell programs (*scripts*) to supply the standard input to other commands as in-line text, and it is revisited in more
detail later on in this chapter.

FILENAME SUBSTITUTION (WILDCARDS)

All shells support a wildcard facility that allows you to select files that satisfy a
particular name pattern from the file system. Any word on the command line that
contains at least one of the wildcard metacharacters is treated as a pattern and is
replaced by an alphabetically sorted list of all of the matching filenames. This act
of pattern replacement is called *globbing*. The wildcards and their meanings are
as follows:

Wildcard	Meaning
*	Matches any string, including the empty string.
?	Matches any single character.
[..]	Matches any one of the characters between the brackets. A range of characters may be specified by separating a pair of characters by a hyphen.

You may prevent the shell from processing the wildcards in a string by surrounding the string with single quotes (apostrophes) or double quotes. See the section on quoting later in this chapter for more details. A backslash (/) character in a filename must be matched explicitly. Here are some examples of wildcards in action:

```
$ ls -FR                ...recursively list my current directory.
a.c      b.c      cc.c      dir1/     dir2/

dir1:
d.c      e.e

dir2:
f.d      g.c
$ ls *.c                ...list any text ending in ".c".
a.c      b.c      cc.c
$ ls ?.c                ...list text for which one character is followed
                        ...by ".c".
a.c      b.c
$ ls [ac]*              ...list any string beginning with "a" or "c".
a.c      cc.c
$ ls [A-Za-z]*          ...list any string beginning with a letter.
a.c      b.c      cc.c
$ ls dir*/*.c           ...list all files ending in ".c" files in "dir*"
                        ...directories (that is, in any directories beginning
                        ...with "dir").
dir1/    d.c      dir2/g.c
$ ls */*.c              ...list all files ending in ".c" in any subdirectory.
dir1/    d.c      dir2/g.c
$ ls list/* 2/?.? ?.?   ...list all files with extensions in "2*" directories and
                        ...current directory
a.c      b.c      dir2/f.d      dir2/g.c
$ _
```

The result of a pattern that has no matches is shell specific. Also, some shells have a mechanism for turning off wildcard replacement.

PIPES

Shells allow you to use the standard output of one process as the standard input of another process by connecting the processes together using the pipe (|) metacharacter. The sequence

```
$ command1 | command2
```

causes the standard output of *command1* to "flow through" to the standard input of *command2*. Any number of commands may be connected by pipes. A sequence of commands chained together in this way is called a *pipeline*.

Pipelines support one of the basic UNIX philosophies, which is that large problems can often be solved by a chain of smaller processes, each performed by a relatively small, reusable utility.

The standard error channel is not piped through a standard pipeline, although some shells support this capability.

In the next example, I piped the output of the **ls** utility to the input of the **wc** utility in order to count the number of files in the current directory. See Chapter 2 for a description of the **wc** utility.

```
$ ls                          ...list the current directory.
a.c b.c cc.c dir1 dir2
$ ls | wc -w                  ...count the entries.
   5
$ _
```

Here's an illustration of the pipeline I just used:

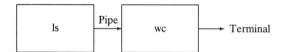

FIGURE 3.3   A simple pipeline

In the next example, I piped the contents of the "/etc/passwd" file into the **awk** utility to extract the first field of each line. The output of **awk** was then piped to the sort utility, which sorted the lines alphabetically. The result was a sorted list of every user on the system. The **awk** utility is described fully in Chapter 7.

```
$ head -4 /etc/passwd       ...look at the password file.
root:eJ2S1OrVe8mCg:0:1:Operator:/:/bin/csh
nobody:*:65534:65534::/:
daemon:*:1:1::/:
sys:*:2:2::/:/bin/csh
$ cat /etc/passwd | awk -F: '{ print $1 }' | sort
audit
bin
daemon
glass
ingres
news
nobody
root
sync
sys
tim
uucp
$ _
```

Here's an illustration of the pipeline that I just used:

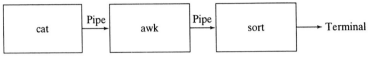

FIGURE 3.4   A pipeline that sorts

There's a very handy utility called **tee** that allows you to copy the output of a pipe to a file while still allowing it to flow down the pipeline. As you might have guessed, the name of this utility comes from the "T" connections that plumbers use. Here's how **tee** works:

Utility: **tee** -ia -{fileName}+

The **tee** utility copies its standard input to the specified files and to its standard output. The -a option causes the input to be appended to the files rather than overwriting them. The -i option causes interrupts to be ignored.

In the following example, I copied the output of **who** to a file called "who.capture" and also let it pass through to **sort**:

```
$ who | tee who.capture | sort
ables      ttyp6    May   3  17:54   (waterloo.com)
glass      ttyp0    May   3  18:49   (bridge05.utdalla)
posey      ttyp2    Apr  23  17:44   (blackfoot.utdall)
posey      ttyp4    Apr  23  17:44   (blackfoot.utdall)
$ cat who.capture    ...look at the captured data.
glass      ttyp0    May   3  18:49   (bridge05.utdalla)
posey      ttyp2    Apr  23  17:44   (blackfoot.utdall)
posey      ttyp4    Apr  23  17:44   (blackfoot.utdall)
ables      ttyp6    May   3  17:54   (waterloo.com)
$_
```

Notice that the output captured is directly from the **who** utility and reflects the list before it was sorted.

COMMAND SUBSTITUTION

A command surrounded by grave accents (`) is executed, and its standard output is inserted in the command's place in the entire command line. Any new lines in the output are replaced by spaces. For example:

```
$ echo the date today is `date`
```

```
the date today is Mon Feb 2 00:41:55 CST 1998
$ _
```

It's possible to do some crafty things by combining pipes and command substitution. For example, the **who** utility, described in Chapter 8, outputs a list of all of the users on the system, and the **wc** utility, described in Chapter 2, counts the number of words or lines in its input. By piping the output of **who** to the **wc** utility, it's possible to count the number of users on the system:

```
$ who              ...look at the output of who.
posey          ttyp0    Jan 22   15:31   (blackfoot:0.0)
glass          ttyp3    Feb  3   00:41   (bridge05.utdalla)
huynh          ttyp5    Jan 10   10:39   (atlas.utdallas.e)
$ echo there are `who | wc -l` users on the system
there are 3 users on the system
$ _
```

The result of command substitution may also be used as part of another command. For example, the **vi** utility allows you to specify a list of files to be edited on the command line, which are then visited by the editor one after the other. The **grep** utility, described in Chapter 7, has a **-l** option that returns a list of all of the files on the command line that contain a specified pattern. For example, by combining these two features using command substitution, it's possible, using a single command, to specify that **vi** be invoked upon all files ending in ".c" that contain the pattern "debug":

```
$ vi `grep -l debug *.c`
```

SEQUENCES

If you enter a series of simple commands or pipelines separated by semicolons, the shell will execute them in sequence, from left to right. This facility is useful for type-ahead (and think-ahead) addicts who like to specify an entire sequence of actions at once. Here's an example:

```
$ date; pwd; ls     ...execute three commands in sequence.
Mon Feb 2 00:11:10 CST 1998
/home/glass/wild
a.c     b.c     cc.c    dir1    dir2
$ _
```

Each command in a sequence may be individually I/O redirected as well:

```
$ date > date.txt; ls; pwd > pwd.txt
a.c           b.c           cc.c        date.txt   dir1        dir2
$ cat date.txt                ...look at output of date.
Mon Feb 2 00:12:16 CST 1998
$ cat pwd.txt                 ...look at output of pwd.
/home/glass
$ _
```

Conditional Sequences

Every UNIX process terminates with an exit value. By convention, an exit value of 0 means that the process completed successfully, and a nonzero exit value indicates failure. All built-in shell commands return a value of 1 if they fail. You may construct sequences that make use of this exit value:

- If you specify a series of commands separated by "&&" tokens, the next command is executed only if the previous command returns an exit code of 0.
- If you specify a series of commands separated by "||" tokens, the next command is executed only if the previous command returns a nonzero exit code.

The && and || metacharacters therefore mirror the operation of their counterpart C operators.

For example, if the C compiler **cc** compiles a program without fatal errors, it creates an executable program called "a.out" and returns an exit code of 0; otherwise, it returns a nonzero exit code. The following conditional sequence compiles a program called "myprog.c" and only executes the "a.out" file if the compilation succeeds:

```
$ cc myprog.c && a.out
```

On the other hand, the following example compiles a program called "myprog.c" and displays an error message if the compilation fails:

```
$ cc myprog.c || echo compilation failed.
```

Exit codes are discussed in more detail toward the end of this chapter.

GROUPING COMMANDS

Commands may be grouped by placing them between parentheses, which causes them to be executed by a child shell (*subshell*). The group of commands shares the same standard input, standard output, and standard error channels and may be redirected and piped as if it were a simple command. Here are some examples:

```
$ date; ls; pwd > out.txt        ...execute a sequence.
Mon Feb 2 00:33:12 CST 1998      ...output from date.
a.c          b.c                 ...output from ls.
$ cat out.txt                    ...only pwd was redirected.
/home/glass
$ (date; ls; pwd) > out.txt      ...group and then redirect.
$ cat out.txt                    ...all output was redirected.
Mon Feb 2 00:33:28 CST 1998
a.c            b.c
/home/glass
$ _
```

BACKGROUND PROCESSING

If you follow a simple command, pipeline, sequence of pipelines, or group of commands by the "&" metacharacter, a subshell is created to execute the commands as a background process. The background process runs concurrently with the parent shell and does not take control of the keyboard. Background processing is therefore very useful for performing several tasks simultaneously, as long as the background tasks do not require input from the keyboard. In windowed environments, it's more common to run each command within its own window than to run many commands in one window using the background facility. When a background process is created, the shell displays some information that may be used to control the process at a later stage. The exact format of this information is shell specific.

In the next example, I executed a **find** command in the foreground to locate the file called "a.c". This command took quite a while to execute, so I decided to run the next **find** command in the background. The shell displayed the background process' unique process ID number and then immediately gave me another prompt, allowing me to continue my work. Note that the output of the background process continued to be displayed at my terminal, which was inconvenient. In the next few sections, I'll show you how you can use the process ID number to control the background process and how to prevent background processes from messing up your terminal.

```
$ find . -name a.c -print       ...search for "a.c".
./wild/a.c
./reverse/tmp/a.c
$ find . -name b.c -print &      ...search in the background.
27174                            ...process ID number
$ date                           ...run "date" in the foreground.
./wild/b.c                       ...output from background "find".
Mon Feb 2 18:10:42 CST 1998      ...output from date.
$ ./reverse/tmp/b.c              ...more output from background "find"
        ...came after we got the shell prompt, but we don't
        ...get another prompt
```

You may specify several background commands on a single line by separating each command by an ampersand:

```
$ date & pwd &      ...create two background processes.
27310                            ...process ID of "date".
27311                            ...process ID of "pwd".
/home/glass                      ...output from "pwd".
$ Mon Feb 2 18:37:22 CST 1998    ...output from "date".
$ _
```

REDIRECTING BACKGROUND PROCESSES

Redirecting Output

To prevent the output from a background process from arriving at your terminal, redirect its output to a file. In the following example, I redirected the standard output of the **find** command to a file called "find.txt". As the command was executing, I watched it grow using the **ls** command:

```
$ find . -name a.c -print > find.txt &
27188                          ...process ID of "find".
$ ls -l find.txt               ...look at "find.txt".
-rw-r--r-- 1 glass      0 Feb 3 18:11 find.txt
$ ls -l find.txt               ...watch it grow.
-rw-r--r-- 1 glass     29 Feb 3 18:11 find.txt
$ cat find.txt                 ...list "find.txt".
./wild/a.c
./reverse/tmp/a.c
$ _
```

Another alternative is to mail the output of the background process to yourself:

```
$ find . -name a.c -print | mail glass &
27193
$ cc program.c ...do other useful work.
$ mail            ...read my mail.
Mail version SMI 4.0 Sat Oct 13 20:32:29 PDT 1990 Type ? for help.
>N 1 glass@utdallas.edu Mon Feb 3 18:12 10/346
& 1
From: Graham Glass <glass@utdallas.edu>
To: glass@utdallas.edu
./wild/a.c        ...the output from "find".
./reverse/tmp/a.c
& q
$ _
```

Some utilities also produce output on the standard error channel, which must be redirected *in addition* to standard output. The next chapter describes in detail how this task is done, but I'll supply an example of how it is done in the Bourne and Korn shells now, just in case you're interested:

```
$ man ps > ps.txt &    ...save documentation in background.
27203
$ Reformatting page. Wait    ...shell prompt comes here, followed by
                             ...standard error messages.
done
man ps > ps.txt 2>&1 &      ...redirect error channel too.
27212
$ _                         ...all output is redirected.
```

Redirecting Input

When a background process attempts to read from a terminal, the terminal automatically sends it an error signal that causes it to terminate. In the following example, I ran the **chsh** utility in the background. It immediately issued the "Login shell unchanged" message and terminated, never bothering to wait for any input. I then ran the **mail** utility in the background, which similarly issued the message "No message !?!":

```
$ chsh &                              ...run "chsh" in background.
27201
$ Changing NIS login shell for glass on csservrl.
Old shell: /bin/sh
New shell: Login shell unchanged.     ...didn't wait for my input.

mail glass &                          ...run "mail" in background.
27202
$ No message !?!                      ...didn't wait for keyboard input.
```

SHELL PROGRAMS: SCRIPTS

Any series of shell commands may be stored inside a regular text file for later execution. A file that contains shell commands is called a *script.* Before you can run a script, you must give it execute permission by using the **chmod** utility. Then, to run it, you need only to type its name. Scripts are useful for storing commonly used sequences of commands, and they range in complexity from simple one-liners to fully blown programs. The control structures supported by the languages built into the shells are sufficiently powerful to enable scripts to perform a wide variety of tasks. System administrators find scripts particularly useful for automating repetitive administrative tasks such as warning users when their disk usage goes beyond a certain limit.

When a script is run, the system determines which shell the script was written for and then executes the shell using the script as its standard input. The system decides which shell the script is written for by examining the first line of the script. Here are the rules that it uses to make this decision:

- If the first line of the script is just a pound sign (#), then the script is interpreted by the shell from which you executed this script as a command.
- If the first line of the script is of the form #! *pathName*, then the executable program *pathName* is used to interpret the script.
- If neither rule 1 nor rule 2 applies, then the script is interpreted by a Bourne shell.

If a pound sign (#) appears on any other line apart from the first line, all characters up to the end of that line are treated as a comment and are therefore not executed. Scripts should be liberally commented in the interests of maintainability.

When you write your own scripts, I recommend that you use the #!*pathName* form to specify which shell the script is designed for, as it's completely unambiguous and doesn't require the reader to be aware of the default rules.

Here is an example that illustrates the construction and execution of two scripts, one for the C shell and the other for the Korn shell:

```
$ cat > script.csh           ...create the C-shell script.
#!/bin/csh
# This is a sample C-shell script.
echo -n the date today is      # in csh, -n omits new line
date  # output today's date.
^D                             ...end of input.
$ cat > script.ksh             ...create the Korn-shell script.
#!/bin/ksh
```

```
# This is a sample Korn shell script.
echo "the date today is \c"   # in ksh, \c omits the new line
date            # output today's date.
^D                                    ...end of input.
$ chmod +x script.csh script.ksh      ...make the scripts executable.
$ ls -lF script.csh script.ksh        ...look at the attributes of the
                                      ...scripts.
-rwxr-xr-x 1 glass         138 Feb 1 19:46 script.csh*
-rwxr-xr-x 1 glass         142 Feb 1 19:47 script.ksh*
$ script.csh                  ...execute the C-shell script.
the date today is Sun Feb 1 19:50:00 CST 1998
$ script.ksh                  ...execute the Korn-shell script.
the date today is Sun Feb 1 19:50:05 CST 1998
$ _
```

The ".csh" and ".ksh" extensions of my scripts are used only for clarity; scripts can be called absolutely anything and don't even require an extension.

Note the usage of "\c" and "-n" in the previous examples of the **echo** command. Different versions of "/bin/echo" use one or the other to omit the new line. The difference may also depend on the shell being used. If the shell has a built-in *echo* function, then the specifics of "/bin/echo" won't matter. You'll want to experiment with your particular shell and echo combination; it isn't quite as simple as I implied in the previous comments.

SUBSHELLS

When you log into a UNIX system, you execute an initial login shell. This initial shell executes any simple commands that you enter. However, there are several circumstances for which your current (*parent*) shell creates a new (*child*) shell to perform some tasks:

- When a grouped command, such as (ls; pwd; date), is executed, the parent shell creates a child shell to execute the grouped commands. If the command is not executed in the background, the parent shell sleeps until the child shell terminates.
- When a script is executed, the parent shell creates a child shell to execute the commands in the script. If the script is not executed in the background, the parent shell sleeps until the child shell terminates.
- When a background job is executed, the parent shell creates a child shell to execute the background commands. The parent shell continues to run concurrently with the child shell.

A child shell is called a *subshell*. Just like any other UNIX process, a subshell has its own current working directory; thus *cd* commands executed in a subshell do not affect the working directory of the parent shell:

```
$ pwd   ...display my login shell's current directory.
/home/glass
```

```
$ (cd /; pwd)   ...the subshell moves and executes pwd.
/               ...output comes from the subshell.
$ pwd           ...my login shell never moved.
/home/glass
$ _
```

Every shell contains two data areas: an environment space and a local-variable space. A child shell inherits a copy of its parent's environment space and a clean local-variable space:

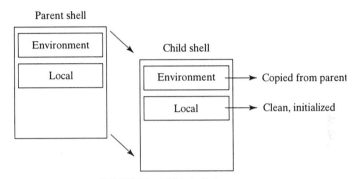

FIGURE 3.5   Child-shell data spaces

VARIABLES

A shell supports two kinds of variables: *local* and *environment* variables. Both kinds of variables hold data in a string format. The main difference between them is that when a shell invokes a subshell, the child shell gets a copy of its parent shell's environment variables, but not its local variables. Environment variables are therefore used for transmitting useful information between parent shells and their children.

Every shell has a set of predefined environment variables that are usually initialized by the startup files described in later chapters. Similarly, every shell has a set of predefined local variables that have special meanings to the shell. Other environment and local variables may be created as needed and are particularly useful for writing scripts. Here is a list of the predefined environment variables that are common to all shells:

Name	Meaning
$HOME	the full pathname of your home directory
$PATH	a list of directories to search for commands
$MAIL	the full pathname of your mailbox
$USER	your username
$SHELL	the full pathname of your login shell
$TERM	the type of your terminal

The syntax for assigning variables differs between shells, but the way that you access the variables is the same: If you precede the name of a variable with a $, this token sequence is replaced by the shell with the value of the named varable.

To create a variable, simply assign it a value; variables do not have to be declared. The details of how variables are assigned are left to the chapters on specific shells, but for now it's enough to know that the syntax for assigning a variable in the Bourne and Korn shells is as follows:

```
variableName=value          ...place no spaces around the =.
```

or

```
variableName = "value"      ...here, spacing doesn't matter.
```

In the following example, I displayed the values of some common shell environment variables:

```
$ echo HOME = $HOME, PATH = $PATH              ...list two variables.
HOME = /home/glass, PATH = /bin:/usr/bin:/usr/sbin
$ echo MAIL = $MAIL                            ...list another.
MAIL = /var/mail/glass
$ echo USER = $USER, SHELL = $SHELL, TERM=$TERM
USER = glass, SHELL = /bin/sh, TERM=vt100
$ _
```

The next example illustrates the difference between local and environment variables. I assigned values to two local variables and then made one of them an environment variable by using the Bourne shell *export* command, described fully in Chapter 4. I then created a child Bourne shell and displayed the values of the variables that I had assigned in the parent shell. Note that the value of the environment variable was copied into the child shell, but the value of the local variable was not. Finally, I pressed *Control*-D to terminate the child shell and restart the parent shell, and then I displayed the original variables:

```
$ firstname=Graham              ...set a local variable.
$ lastname=Glass                ...set another local variable.
$ echo $firstname $lastname     ...display their values.
Graham Glass
$ export lastname               ...make "lastname" an environment variable.
$ sh                            ...start a child shell; the parent sleeps.
$ echo $firstname $lastname     ...display values again.
Glass                           ...note that firstname wasn't copied.
$ ^D                            ...terminate child; the parent awakens.
$ echo $firstname $lastname     ...they remain unchanged.
Graham Glass
$ _
```

There are several common built-in variables that have special meanings:

Name	Meaning
$$	The process ID of the shell.
$0	The name of the shell script (if applicable).
$1..$9	$n refers to the nth command line argument (if applicable).
$*	A list of all the command-line arguments.

The first special variable is especially useful for creating temporary filenames, and the rest are handy for accessing command-line arguments in shell scripts. Here's an example of a script that illustrates all of the common special variables:

```
$ cat script.sh                              ...list the script.
echo the name of this script is $0
echo the first argument is $1
echo a list of all the arguments is $*
echo this script places the date into a temporary file
echo called $1.$$
date > $1.$$    # redirect the output of date.
ls $1.$$        # list the file.
rm $1.$$        # remove the file.
$ script.sh paul ringo george john          ...execute the script.
the name of this script is script.sh
the first argument is paul
a list of all the arguments is paul ringo george john
this script places the date into a temporary file
called paul.24321
paul.24321
$ _
```

QUOTING

There are often times when you want to inhibit the shell's wildcard-replacement, variable-substitution, and/or command-substitution mechanisms. The shell's quoting system allows you to do just that. Here's the way that it works:

- Single quotes (') inhibit wildcard replacement, variable substitution, and command substitution.
- Double quotes (") inhibit wildcard replacement only.
- When quotes are nested, it's only the outer quotes that have any effect.

The following example illustrates the difference between the two different kinds of quotes:

```
$ echo 3 * 4 = 12      ...remember, * is a wildcard.
3 a.c b b.c c.c 4 = 12
```

```
$ echo "3 * 4 = 12"    ...double quotes inhibit wildcards.
3 * 4 = 12
$ echo '3 * 4 = 12'    ...single quotes inhibit wildcards.
3 * 4 = 12
$ name=Graham
```

By using single quotes (apostrophes) around the text, we inhibit all wildcarding and variable and command substitutions:

```
$ echo 'my name is $name - date is `date`'
my name is $name=date is `date`
```

By using double quotes around the text, we inhibit wildcarding, but allow variable and command substitutions:

```
$ echo "my name is $name - date is `date`"
my name is Graham - date is Mon Feb 2 23:14:56 CST 1998
$ _
```

HERE DOCUMENTS

Earlier in the chapter, I briefly mentioned the "<<" metacharacter. I delayed its full description until now, as it's really only used in conjunction with scripts and variables. When the shell encounters a sequence of the form

```
$ command << word
```

it copies its own standard input up to, but not including, the line starting with *word* into a shell buffer and then executes *command* using the contents of the buffer as its standard input. Obviously, you should choose a sensible value for *word* that is unusual enough not to occur naturally in the text that follows. If no line containing only *word* is encountered, the Bourne and Korn shells stop copying input when they reach the end of the script, whereas the C shell issues an error message. All references to shell variables in the copied text are replaced by their values. The most common use of the "<<" metacharacter is to allow scripts to supply the standard input of other commands as in-line text, rather than having to use auxiliary files. Scripts that use "<<" are sometimes called *here documents*. Here's an example of a here document:

```
$ cat here.sh          ...look at an example of a "here" document.
mail $1 << ENDOFTEXT
Dear $1,
Please see me regarding some exciting news!
- $USER
ENDOFTEXT
echo mail sent to $1
```

```
$ here.sh glass              ...send mail to myself using the script.
mail sent to glass
$ mail                       ...look at my mail.
Mail version SMI 4.0 Sat Oct 13 20:32:29 PDT 1990 Type ? for help.
>N 1 glass@utdallas.edu Mon Feb 2 13:34 12/384
& 1                          ...read message #1.
From: Graham Glass <glass@utdallas.edu>
To: glass@utdallas.edu

Dear glass,
Please see me regarding some exciting news!

- glass

& q                          ...quit out of mail.
$ _
```

JOB CONTROL

Convenient multitasking is one of UNIX's best features, so it's important to be able to obtain a listing of your current processes and to control their behavior. There are two utilities and one built-in command that allow you to do so:

- **ps**, which generates a list of processes and their attributes, including their names, process ID numbers, controlling terminals and owners
- **kill**, which allows you to terminate a process based on its ID number
- **wait**, which allows a shell to wait for one of its child processes to terminate

The next few sections describe these facilities in more detail.

Process Status: ps

The **ps** utility allows you to monitor the status of processes and works as follows:

Utility: **ps** -efl

ps generates a listing of process-status information. By default, the output is limited to processes created by your current shell. The **-e** option instructs **ps** to include all running processes. The **-f** option causes **ps** to generate a full listing. The **-l** option generates a long listing. The meaning of each **ps** column is described in the upcoming text.

In the next example, I made use of the **sleep** utility to delay a simple echo statement and placed the command in the background. I then executed the **ps** utility to obtain a list of my shell's associated processes. Each "sh" process was a Bourne-shell process; one of them was my login shell, and the other one was the subshell created to execute the command group.

```
$ (sleep 10; echo done) &          ...delayed echo in background.
27387                              ...the process ID number.
$ ps                              ...obtain a process status list.
PID TTY  TIME CMD
27355 pts/3 0:00 -sh              ...the login shell.
27387 pts/3 0:00 -sh              ...the subshell.
27388 pts/3 0:00 sleep 10         ...the sleep.
27389 pts/3 0:00 ps               ...the ps command itself!
$ done          ...the output from the background process.
```

For the record, here's a description of the **sleep** utility:

Utility: **sleep** *seconds*

The **sleep** utility sleeps for the specified number of seconds and then terminates.

The meanings of the common column headings of **ps** output are as follows:

Column	Meaning
S	the state of the process
UID	the effective user ID of the process
PID	the ID of the process
PPID	the ID of the parent process
C	the percentage of CPU time that the process used in the last minute
PRI	the priority of the process
SZ	the size of the process' data and stack, in kilobytes
STIME	the time the process was created, or the date, if the process was created before the current day
TTY	the controlling terminal
TIME	the amount of CPU time used so far (MM:SS)
CMD	the name of the command

The S field encodes the state of the process as follows:

Letter	Meaning
O	running on a processor
R	runable
S	sleeping
T	suspended
Z	zombie process

The meanings of most of these terms are described later in the book; only the R and S fields will make sense right now. Here's an example of some user-oriented output from **ps**:

```
$ (sleep 10; echo done) &
27462
$ ps -f          ...request user-oriented output.
     UID    PID  PPID  C     STIME TTY    TIME CMD
    glass   731   728  0  21:48:46 pts/5  0:01 -ksh
    glass   831   830  1  22:27:06 pts/5  0:00 sleep 10
    glass   830   731  0  22:27:06 pts/5  0:00 -ksh
$ done           ...output from previous command
```

If you're interested in tracking the movements of other users on your system, try the **-e** and **-f** options of **ps**:

```
$ ps -ef         ...list all users' processes.
  UID    PID PPID C    STIME  TTY TIME CMD
  root     0    0 0 18:58:16  ?   0:01 sched
  root     1    0 0 18:58:19  ?   0:01 /etc/init -
  root     2    0 0 18:58:19  ?   0:00 pageout
  root     3    0 1 18:58:19  ?   0:53 fsflush
  root   198    1 0 18:59:38  ?   0:00 /usr/sbin/nscd
  root   178    1 0 18:59:35  ?   0:00 /usr/sbin/syslogd
  root   302    1 0 18:59:58  ?   0:00 /usr/lib/saf/sac
  root   125    1 0 18:59:14  ?   0:00 /usr/sbin/rpcbind
  root   152    1 0 18:59:29  ?   0:01 /usr/sbin/inetd -s
  root   115    1 0 18:59:13  ?   0:00 /usr/sbin/in.routed -q
  root   127    1 0 18:59:15  ?   0:00 /usr/sbin/keyserv
  root   174    1 0 18:59:34  ?   0:00 /etc/automountd
  glass  731  728 0 21:48:46  p5  0:01 -ksh
$ _
```

In Chapter 5, I describe a utility called "track" that makes use of this option to monitor other users.

The Bourne and Korn shells automatically terminate background processes when you log out, whereas the C shell allows them to continue. If you're using a Bourne or Korn shell and you want to make a background process immune to this effect, use the **nohup** utility to protect it. **nohup** works like this:

Utility: **nohup** *command*

The **nohup** utility executes *command* and makes it immune to the hangup (HUP) and terminate (TERM) signals. The standard output and error channels of *command* are automatically redirected to a file called "nohup.out," and the process' priority value is increased by 5, thereby reducing its priority. This utility is ideal for ensuring that background processes are not terminated when your login shell is exited.

If you execute a command using **nohup**, log out, and then log back in again, you won't see the command listed in the output of a regular **ps**. This situation occurs because a process loses its control terminal when you log out and continues to execute without it. To include a list of all of the current processes without control terminals in a **ps** output, use the **-x** option. Here's an example of this effect:

```
$ nohup sleep 10000 &                    ...nohup a background process.
27406
Sending output to 'nohup.out'           ...message from "nohup".
$ ps                                     ...look at processes.
PID TT STAT TIME COMMAND
27399 p3 S       0:00 -sh (sh)
27406 p3 S N     0:00 sleep 10000
27407 p3 R       0:00 ps
$ ^D                                     ...log out.

UNIX(r) System V Release 4.0
login: glass                            ...log back in.
Password:                               ...secret.
$ ps                                     ...the background process is not
                                         ...listed.
PID TT STAT TIME COMMAND
27409 p3 S       0:00 -sh (sh)
27411 p3 R       0:00 ps
$ ps -x                                  ...the background process is listed.
PID     TT    STAT   TIME    COMMAND
27406   ?     IN     0:00    sleep 10000
27409   p3    S      0:00    -sh (sh)
27412   p3    R      0:00    ps -x
$ _
```

For more information about control terminals, consult Chapter 12.

Signaling Processes: kill

If you wish to terminate a process before it completes, use the **kill** command. The Korn and C shells contain a built-in command called **kill**, whereas the Bourne shell invokes the standard utility instead. Both versions of **kill** support the following functionality:

Utility/Shell Command: **kill** [-signalId] {pid }+
   kill -l

kill sends the signal with code signalId to the list of numbered processes. signalId may be the number or name of a signal. By default, **kill** sends a TERM signal (number 15), which causes the receiving processes to terminate. To obtain a list of the legal signal names, use the **-l** option. To send a signal to a process, you must either own it or be a super-user. For more information about signals, refer to Chapter 12.

Processes may protect themselves from all signals except for the KILL signal (number 9). Therefore, to ensure a kill, send signal number 9. (Note that sending a KILL signal will not allow a process to clean up and terminate normally as many programs do when they receive a TERM signal.)

The **kill** utility (as opposed to the Korn and C shell built-in shell commands) allows you to specify 0 as the *pid*, which causes all of the processes associated with the shell to be terminated. Chapter 5 contains information on the advanced features of the built-in *kill* command.

In the following example, I created a background process and then killed it. To confirm the termination, I obtained a **ps** listing:

```
$ (sleep 10; echo done) &          ...create background process.
27390                              ...process ID number.
$ kill 27390                       ...kill the process.
$ ps                               ...it's gone!
PID TT STAT TIME COMMAND
27355 p3 S      0:00  -sh (sh)
27394 p3 R      0:00  ps
$ _
```

The next example illustrates the use of the **-l** option and a named signal. The signal names are listed in numerical order, starting with signal #1.

```
$ kill -l                          ...list the signal names.
HUP INT QUIT ILL TRAP ABRT EMT FPE KILL BUS SEGV SYS PIPE ALRM TERM URG
STOP TSTP CONT CHLD TTIN TTOU IO XCPU XFSZ VTALRM PROF WINCH LOST USR1
USR2
```

```
$ (sleep 10; echo done) &
27490                    ...process ID number.
$ kill -KILL 27490       ...kill the process with signal #9.
$ _
```

Finally, here's an example of the **kill** utility's ability to kill all of the processes associated with the current shell:

```
$ sleep 30 & sleep 30 & sleep 30 &          ...create three processes.
27429
27430
27431
$ kill 0                                     ...kill them all.
27431 Terminated
27430 Terminated
27429 Terminated
$ _
```

Waiting For Child Processes: wait

A shell may *wait* for one or more of its child processes to terminate by executing the built-in wait command, which works as follows:

Shell Command: wait [*pid*]

wait causes the shell to suspend until the child process with the specified process ID number terminates. If no arguments are supplied, the shell waits for all of its child processes.

In the following example, the shell waited until both background child processes had terminated before continuing:

```
$ (sleep 30; echo done 1) &        ...create a child process.
24193
$ (sleep 30; echo done 2) &        ...create a child process.
24195
$ echo done 3; wait; echo done 4   ...wait for children.
done 3
done 1                             ...output from first child.
done 2                             ...output from second child.
done 4
$ _
```

This facility is generally useful only in advanced shell scripts.

FINDING A COMMAND: $PATH

When a shell processes a command, it first checks to see whether it's a built-in comand; if it is, the shell executes it directly. *echo* is an example of a built-in shell command:

```
$ echo some commands are executed directly by the shell
some commands are executed directly by the shell
$ _
```

If the command isn't a built-in command, the shell looks to see if the command begins with a slash (/) character. If it does, it assumes that the first token is the absolute pathname of a command and tries to execute the file with the stated name. If the file doesn't exist or isn't an executable, an errors occurs:

```
$ /bin/ls                    ...full pathname of the ls utility.
script.csh script.ksh
$ /bin/nsx                   ...a nonexistent filename.
/bin/nsx: not found
$ /etc/passwd                ...the name of the password file.
/etc/passwd: Permission denied  ...it's not executable.
$ _
```

If the command isn't a built-in command or a full pathname, the shell searches the directories whose names are stored in the PATH environment variable. Each directory in the PATH variable is searched, from left to right, for an executable matching the command name. If a match is found, the file is executed. If a match isn't found in any of the directories or if the file that matches is not executable, an error occurs. If PATH is not set or is equal to the empty string, then only the current directory is searched. The contents of the PATH variable may be changed using the methods described in later chapters, thereby allowing you to tailor the search path to your needs. The original search path is usually initialized by the shell's startup file and typically includes all of the standard UNIX directories that contain executable utilities. Here are some examples:

```
$ echo $PATH
/bin:/usr/bin:/usr/sbin      ...directories searched.
$ ls                         ...located in "/bin".
script.csh script.ksh
$ nsx                        ...not located anywhere.
nsx: not found
$ _
```

OVERLOADING STANDARD UTILITIES

Users often create a "bin" subdirectory in their home directory and place this subdirectory *before* the traditional "bin" directories in their PATH setting. This feature allows the users to overload default UNIX utilities with their own "homebrewed" versions, since these versions will be located by the search process ahead of their standard counterparts. If you choose to do so, you should take great care, as scripts run from a shell expect to use standard utilities and might be confused by the non-standard utilities that actually get executed. In the following example, I inserted my own "bin" directory into the search-path sequence and then overrode the standard **ls** utility with my own version:

```
$ mkdir bin      ...make my own personal "bin" directory.
$ cd bin         ...move into the new directory.
$ cat > ls       ...create a script called "ls".
echo my ls
^D       ...end of input.
$ chmod +x ls  ...make it executable.
$ echo $PATH   ...look at the current PATH setting.
/bin:/usr/bin:/usr/sbin
$ echo $HOME    ...get pathname of my home directory.
/home/glass
$ PATH=/home/glass/bin:$PATH  ...update.
$ ls              ...call "ls".
my ls             ...my own version overrides "/bin/ls".
$ _
```

Note that only this shell and its child shells would be affected by the change to PATH; all other shells would be unaffected.

TERMINATION AND EXIT CODES

Every UNIX process terminates with an exit value. By convention, an exit value of 0 means that the process completed successfully, and a nonzero exit value indicates failure. All built-in commands return an exit value of 1 if they fail. In the Bourne and Korn shells, the special shell variable $? always contains the value of the previous command's exit code. In the C shell, the $status variable holds the exit code. In the following example, the **date** utility succeeded, whereas the **cc** and **awk** utilities failed:

```
$ date                       ...date succeeds.
Mon Feb 2 22:13:38 CST 1998
$ echo $?                    ...display its exit value.
0                            ...indicates success.
$ cc prog.c        ...compile a nonexistent program.
cpp: Unable to open source file 'prog.c'.
$ echo $?                    ...display its exit value.
1                            ...indicates failure.
$ awk                        ...use awk illegally.
awk: Usage: awk [-Fc] [-f source | 'cmds'] [files]
$ echo $?                    ...display its exit value.
2                            ...indicates failure.
$ _
```

Any script that you write should always explicitly return an exit code. To terminate a script, use the built-in *exit* command, which works as follows:

Shell Command: **exit** *number*

exit terminates the shell and returns the exit value *number* to its parent process. If *number* is omitted, the exit value of the previous command is used.

If a shell doesn't include an explicit *exit* statement, the exit value of the last command is returned by default. The script in the following example returned an exit value of 3:

```
$ cat script.sh              ...look at the script.
echo this script returns an exit code of 3
exit 3
$ script.sh                  ...execute the script.
this script returns an exit code of 3
$ echo $?                    ...look at the exit value.
3
$ _
```

The next chapter contains some examples of scripts that make use of a command's exit value.

COMMON CORE BUILT-IN COMMANDS

There are a large number of built-in commands that are supported by the three shells, of which only a few commands are common to all three shells. This section describes the most useful common core built-in commands.

eval

Shell Command: **eval** *command*

The *eval* shell command executes the output of *command* as a regular shell command. It is useful for processing the output of utilities that generate shell commands (e.g., **tset**).

In the following example, I executed the result of the *echo* command, which caused the variable *x* to be set:

```
$ echo x=5              ...first execute an echo directly.
x=5
$ eval `echo x=5` ...execute the result of the echo.
$ echo $x                   ...confirm that x was set to 5.
5
$ _
```

For a more complex example, see the description of **tset** in Chapter 2.

exec

Shell Command: **exec** *command*

The *exec* shell command causes the shell's image to be replaced with *command* in the process' memory space. If *command* is successfully executed, the shell that performed the *exec* ceases to exist. If this shell was a login shell, then the login session is terminated when *command* terminates.

In the following example, I exec'ed the **date** command from my login shell, which caused the **date** utility to run and then my login process to terminate:

```
$ exec date                             ...replace shell process by date process.
Sun Feb 1 18:55:01 CDT 1998             ...output from date.
login: _                                ...login shell is terminated and starts anew
                                        ...for the next user.
```

shift

Shell Command: **shift**

The *shift* shell command causes all of the positional parameters $2..$n to be renamed $1..$(n-1), and $1 to be lost. It's particularly handy in shell scripts when cycling through a series of command-line parameters. If there are no positional arguments left to shift, an error message is displayed.

In the following example, I wrote a C-shell script to display its arguments before and after a shift.

```
$ cat shift.csh                    ...list the script.
#!/bin/csh
echo first argument is $1, all args are $*
shift
echo first argument is $1, all args are $*
$ shift.csh a b c d                ...run with four arguments.
first argument is a, all args are a b c d
first argument is b, all args are b c d
$ shift.csh a                      ...run with one argument.
first argument is a, all args are a
first argument is , all args are
$ shift.csh                        ...run with no arguments.
first argument is , all args are
shift: No more words               ...error message.
$ _
```

umask

When a C program creates a file, it supplies the file's original permission settings as an octal parameter to the system call open (). For example, to create a file with read and write permission for the owner, group, and others, it would execute a system call like this:

```
fd = open ("myFile", OCREAT | ORDWR, 0666);
```

For information on the encoding of permissions as octal numbers, see Chapter 2. For information on the open() system call, see Chapter 12. When the shell performs redirection using the ">" character, it uses a system call sequence similar to the one shown above to construct a file with octal permission 666. However, if you try creating a file using the ">" character, you'll probably end up with a file that has a permission setting of 644 octal:

```
$ date > date.txt
$ ls -l date.txt
-rw-r--r-- 1 glass      29 May 3 18:56 date.txt
$ _
```

The reason for this difference is that every UNIX process contains a special quantity called a *umask* value, which is used to restrict the permission settings that it requests when a file is created. The default umask value of a shell is 022 octal. The set bits of a umask value mask out the set bits of a requested permission setting. In the previous example, the requested permission 666 was masked with 022 to produce the final permission 644:

	r	w	x	r	w	x	r	w	x
original	1	1	0	1	1	0	1	1	0
mask	0	0	0	0	1	0	0	1	0
final	1	1	0	1	0	0	1	0	0

If a file already exists before it is redirected to, the original file's permission values are retained and the umask value is ignored.

Here's how the *umask* command may be used to manipulate the umask value:

Shell Command: **umask** [*octalValue*]

The *umask* shell command sets the shell's umask value to the specified octal number or displays the current umask value if the argument is omitted. A shell's umask value is retained until changed. Child processes inherit their umask values from their parent shells.

In the following example, I changed the umask value to 0 and then created a new file to illustrate its effect:

```
$ umask                   ...display current umask value.
22            ...mask write permission of group/others.
$ umask 0                 ...set umask value to 0.
$ date > date2.txt        ...create a new file.
$ ls -l date2.txt
-rw-rw-rw- 1 glass       29 May 3 18:56 date2.txt
$ _
```

CHAPTER REVIEW

Checklist

In this chapter, I described:

- the common functionality of the three major shells
- the common shell metacharacters
- output and input redirection
- filename substitution
- pipes
- command substitution
- command sequences
- grouped commands

- the construction of scripts
- the difference between local and environment variables
- the two different kinds of quotes
- basic job control
- the mechanism that the shell uses to find commands
- several core built-in commands

Quiz

1. Can you change your default shell?
2. How can you enter commands that are longer than one line?
3. What is the difference between a built-in command and a utility?
4. How can you make a script executable?
5. What is the strange term that is sometimes given to filename substitution?
6. Describe a common use for command substitution.
7. Describe the meaning of the terms *parent shell*, *child shell*, and *subshell*.
8. How do you think the **kill** command got its name?
9. Describe a way to override a standard utility.
10. What is a good *umask* value and why?

Exercises

1. Write a script that prints the current date, your user name, and the name of your login shell. [level: *easy*]
2. Experiment with the *exec* command by writing a series of three shell scripts called "a.sh", "b.sh", and "c.sh" that each display their name, execute **ps**, and then *exec* the next script in the sequence. Observe what happens when you start the first script by executing *exec* a.sh. [level: *medium*]
3. Why is the file that is created in the following session unaffected by the umask value? [level: *medium*]

```
$ ls -l date.txt
-rw-rw-rw- 1 glass 29 Aug 20 21:04 date.txt
$ umask 0077
$ date > date.txt
$ ls -l date.txt
-rw-rw-rw- 1 glass 29 Aug 20 21:04 date.txt
$ _
```

4. Write a script that creates three background processes, waits for them all to complete, and then displays a simple message. [level: *medium*]

Project

Compare and contrast the UNIX shell features against the graphical shells available on Windows. Which type of shell do you think is better? [level: *medium*]

# CHAPTER 4

The Bourne Shell

Motivation

The Bourne shell, written by Stephen Bourne, was the first popular UNIX shell and is available on all UNIX systems. It supports a fairly versatile programming language and is a subset of the more powerful Korn shell that is described in Chapter 5. Knowledge of the Bourne shell will therefore allow you to understand the operation of many scripts that have already been written for UNIX, as well as prepare you for the more advanced Korn shell.

Prerequisites

You should already have read Chapter 3 and experimented with some of the core-shell facilities.

Objectives

In this chapter, I'll explain and demonstrate the Bourne-specific facilities, including the use of environment and local variables, the built-in programming language, and advanced I/O redirection.

Presentation

The information in this section is presented in the form of several sample UNIX sessions.

Utilities

This section introduces the following utilities, listed in alphabetical order:

expr   test

Shell Commands

This section introduces the following shell commands, listed in alphabetical order:

break   for..in..do..done   set

case..in..esac	if..then..elif..fi	trap
continue	read	while..do..done
export	readonly	

INTRODUCTION

The Bourne shell supports all of the core-shell facilities described in Chapter 3, plus the following new facilities:

- several ways to set and access variables
- a built-in programming language that supports conditional branching, looping, and interrupt handling
- extensions to the existing redirection and command-sequence operations
- several new built-in commands

These new facilities are described by this chapter and are illustrated by the following hierarchy diagram:

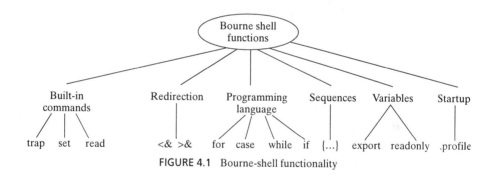

FIGURE 4.1   Bourne-shell functionality

STARTUP

The Bourne shell is a regular C program whose executable file is stored as "/bin/sh." If your chosen shell is "/bin/sh," an interactive Bourne shell is invoked automatically when you log into UNIX. You may also invoke a Bourne shell manually from a script or from a terminal by using the command **sh**. **sh** has several command-line options that are described at the end of this chapter.

When an interactive Bourne shell is started, it searches for a file called ".profile" in the user's home directory. If it finds the file, it executes all of the shell commands that it contains. Then, regardless of whether ".profile" was found or not, an interactive Bourne shell displays its prompt and awaits user commands. The standard Bourne shell prompt is $, although it may be changed by setting the local variable PS1 described later in this chapter. Noninteractive Bourne shells do not read any startup files.

One common use of ".profile" is to initialize environment variables such as TERM, which contains the type of your terminal, and PATH, which tells the shell where to search for executable files. Here's an example of a Bourne-shell ".profile" startup file:

```
TERM=vt100                          # Set terminal type.
export TERM                         # Copy to environment.
# Set path and metacharacters
stty erase "^?" kill "^U" intr "^C" eof "^D"
PATH='.:$HOME/bin:/bin:/usr/sbin:/usr/bin:/usr/local/bin'
```

VARIABLES

The Bourne shell can perform the following variable-related operations:

- simple assignment and access
- testing a variable for existence
- reading a variable from standard input
- making a variable read only
- exporting a local variable to the environment

The Bourne shell also defines several local and environment variables in addition to those mentioned in Chapter 3.

The next few sections describe each feature in turn.

Creating/Assigning a Variable

The Bourne-shell syntax for assigning a value to a variable is:

```
{name=value}+
```

If a variable being assigned doesn't already exist, it is implicitly created; otherwise, its previous value is overwritten. A newly created variable is always local, although it may be turned into an environment variable using a method that I'll describe shortly. To assign a value that contains spaces, surround the value by quotes. Here's an example of variable creation and assignment:

```
$ firstName=Graham lastName=Glass age=29     ...assign variables.
$ echo $firstName $lastName is $age
Graham Glass is 29                           ...simple access.
$ name=Graham Glass                          ...syntax error.
Glass: not found
$ name="Graham Glass"     ...use quotes to built strings.
$ echo $name                                 ...now it works.
Graham Glass
$ _
```

Accessing a Variable

The Bourne shell supports the following access methods:

Syntax	Action
$*name*	Replaced by the value of *name*.
${*name*}	Replaced by the value of *name*. This form is useful if the expression is immediately followed by an alphanumeric expression that would otherwise be interpreted as part of the variable name.
${*name—word*}	Replaced by the value of *name* if set, and *word* otherwise.
${*name+word*}	Replaced by *word* if *name* is set, and nothing otherwise.
${*name=word*}	Assigns *word* to the variable *name* if *name* is not already set and then is replaced by the value of *name*.
${*name?word*}	Replaced by *name* if *name* is set. If *name* is not set, *word* is displayed to the standard error channel and the shell is exited. If *word* is omitted, then a standard error message is displayed instead.

If a variable is accessed before it is assigned a value, it returns a null string.

I personally find these variable-access techniques to be "hack" methods of dealing with certain conditions, and I hardly ever use them. However, it's good to be able to understand code that uses them. The next set of examples illustrate each access method. In the first example, I used braces to append a string to the value of a variable:

```
$ verb=sing              ...assign a variable.
$ echo I like $verbing   ...there's no variable "verbing".
I like
$ echo I like ${verb}ing  ...now it works.
I like singing
$ _
```

Here's an example that uses command substitution to set the variable *startDate* to the current date if it's not already set:

```
$ startDate=${startDate-`date`}   ...if not set, run date.
$ echo $startDate                 ...look at its value.
Tue Wed 4 06:56:51 CST 1998
$ _
```

In the next example, I set the variable *x* to a default value and printed its value, both at the same time:

```
$ echo x = ${x=10}   ...assign a default value.
x = 10
$ echo $x            ...confirm the variable was set.
10
$ _
```

In the following example, I displayed messages based on whether certain variables were set or not:

```
$ flag=1                            ...assign a variable.
$ echo ${flag+'flag is set'}        ...conditional message #1.
flag is set
$ echo ${flag2+'flag2 is set'}      ...conditional message #2.
                                    ...result is null
$ _
```

In the next example, I tried to access an undefined variable called *grandTotal* and received an error message instead:

```
$ total=10                          ...assign a variable.
$ value=${total?'total not set'}    ...accessed OK.
$ echo $value                       ...look at its value.
10
$ value=${grandTotal?'grand total not set'}    ...not set.
grandTotal: grand total not set
$ _
```

In the final example, I ran a script that used the same access method as the previous example. Note that the script terminated when the access error occurred:

```
$ cat script.sh                     ...look at the script.
value=${grandTotal?'grand total is not set'}
echo done       # this line is never executed.
$ script.sh                         ...run the script.
script.sh: grandTotal: grand total is not set
$ _
```

Reading a Variable from Standard Input

The *read* command allows you to read variables from standard input and works like this:

Shell Command: **read** { *variable* }+

read reads one line from standard input and then assigns successive words from the line to the specified variables. Any words that are left over are assigned to the last named variable.

If you specify just one variable, the entire line is stored in the variable. Here's an example script that prompts a user for his or her full name:

```
$ cat script.sh                     ...list the script.
echo "Please enter your name: \c"
read name                    # read just one variable.
echo your name is $name      # display the variable.
$ script.sh                         ...run the script.
Please enter your name: Graham Walker Glass
your name is Graham Walker Glass       ...the whole line was read.
$ _
```

Here's an example that illustrates what happens when you specify more than one variable:

```
$ cat script.sh                     ...list the script.
echo "Please enter your name: \c"
read firstName lastName      # read two variables.
echo your first name is $firstName
echo your last name is $lastName
$ script.sh     ...run the script.
Please enter your name: Graham Walker Glass
your first name is Graham              ...first word.
your last name is Walker Glass         ...the rest.
$ script.sh    ...run it again.
Please enter your name: Graham
your first name is Graham              ...first word.
your last name is                      ...only one word was entered.
$ _
```

Exporting Variables

The *export* command allows you to mark local variables for export to the environment and works as follows:

Shell Command: export { *variable* }+

export marks the specified variables for export to the environment. If no variables are specified, a list of all of the variables marked for export during the shell session is displayed.

Although it's not necessary, I tend to use uppercase letters to name environment variables. The **env** utility allows you to modify and list environment variables:

Utility: **env** { *variable=value* }* [*command*]

env assigns values to specified environment variables and then executes an optional command using the new environment. If no variable or command is specified, a list of the current environment is displayed.

In the next example, I created a local variable called DATABASE, which I then marked for export. When I created a subshell, a copy of the environment variable was inherited:

```
$ export              ...list my current exports.
export TERM           ...set in my ".profile" startup file.
$ DATABASE=/dbase/db  ...create a local variable.
$ export DATABASE     ...mark it for export.
$ export              ...note that it's been added.
export DATABASE
export TERM
$ env                 ...list the environment.
DATABASE=/dbase/db
HOME=/home/glass
LOGNAME=glass
PATH=:/usr/ucb:/bin:/usr/bin
SHELL=/bin/sh
TERM=vt100
USER=glass
$ sh                  ...create a subshell.
$ echo $DATABASE      ...a copy was inherited.
/dbase/db
$ ^D                  ...terminate subshell.
$ _
```

Read-Only Variables

The *readonly* command allows you to protect variables against modification and works like this:

Shell Command: *readonly* { *variable* }*

readonly makes the specified variables readonly, protecting them against future modification. If no variables are specified, a list of the current read-only variables is displayed. Copies of exported read-only variables do not inherit the read-only status of the originals.

In the following example, I protected a local variable from modification. I then exported the variable and showed that its copy did not inherit the read-only status:

```
$ password=Shazam            ...assign a local variable.
$ echo $password             ...display its value.
Shazam
$ readonly password          ...protect it.
$ readonly                    ...list all readonly variables.
readonly password
$ password=Phoombah          ...try to modify it.
password: is read only
$ export password            ...export the variable.
$ password=Phoombah          ...try to modify it.
password: is read only
$ sh    ...create a subshell.
$ readonly                    ...the exported password is not listed as
        ...readonly.
$ echo $password             ...its value was copied correctly.
Shazam
$ password=Alacazar          ...but its value may be changed.
$ echo $password             ...echo its value.
Alacazar
$ ^D    ...terminate the subshell.
$ echo $password             ...echo original value.
Shazam
$ _
```

Predefined Local Variables

In addition to the core predefined local variables, the Bourne shell defines the following local variables:

Name	Value
$@	an individually quoted list of all of the positional parameters
$#	the number of positional parameters
$?	the exit value of the last command
$!	the process ID of the last background command
$-	the current shell options assigned from the command line or by the built-in *set* command, which is discussed later
$$	the process ID of this shell

Here's a small shell script that illustrates the first three variables. In this example, the C compiler (**cc**) was invoked on a file that didn't exist and therefore returned a failure exit code.

```
$ cat script.sh                       ...list the script.
echo there are $# command line arguments: $@
cc $1                     # compile the first argument.
echo the last exit value was $?     # display exit code.
$ script.sh nofile tmpfile           ...execute the script.
there are 2 command line arguments:  nofile tmpfile
cc: Warning: File with unknown suffix (nofile) passed to ld
ld: nofile: No such file or directory
the last exit value was 4              ...cc errored.
$ _
```

The next example illustrates how $! may be used to kill the last background process:

```
$ sleep 1000 &     ...create a background process.
29455              ...process ID of background process.
$ kill $!          ...kill it!
29455 Terminated
$ echo $!          ...the process ID is still remembered.
29455
$ _
```

Predefined Environment Variables

In addition to the core predefined environment variables (listed in Chapter 2), the Bourne shell defines the following environment variables:

Name	Value
$IFS	When the shell tokenizes a command line prior to its execution, it uses the characters in this variable as delimiters. IFS usually contains a space, a tab, and a new line character.
$PS1	This variable contains the value of the command-line prompt and is $ by default. To change the command-line prompt, simply set PS1 to a new value.
$PS2	This variable contains the value of the secondary command-line prompt that is displayed when more input is required by the shell and is > by default. To change the prompt, set PS2 to a new value.
$SHENV	If this variable is not set, the shell searches the user's home directory for the ".profile" startup file when a new shell is created. If this variable is set, then the shell searches the directory specified by SHENV.

Here's a small example that illustrates the first three predefined environment variables. I set my prompt to something different by assigning a new value to PS1 and changed the delimiter character to a colon, saving the previous value in a local variable. Finally, I set PS2 to a new value and illustrated an occasion for which the secondary prompt is displayed.

```
$ PS1="sh? "              ...set a new primary prompt.
 sh? oldIFS=$IFS          ...remember the old value of IFS.
sh? IFS=":"               ...change the word delimiter to a colon.
sh? ls:*.c                ...this command executes OK!
badguy.c  number.c  open.c   trunc.c  writer.c
fact2.c  number2.c reader.c  who.c
sh? IFS=$oldIFS           ...restore the old value of IFS.
sh? string="a long\       ...assign a string of over 2 lines
> string"                 ...">" is the secondary prompt.
sh? echo $string          ...look at the value of "string".
a long string
sh? PS2="???"             ...change the secondary prompt.
sh? string="a long\       ...assign a long string.
??? string"               ..."???" is the new secondary prompt.
sh? echo $string          ...look at the value of /"string".
a long string
sh? _
```

ARITHMETIC

Although the Bourne shell doesn't directly support arithmetic, it may be performed by using the **expr** utility, which works like this:

Utility: **expr** *expression*

expr evaluates *expression* and sends the result to standard output. All of the components of *expression* must be separated by blanks, and all of the shell metacharacters must be escaped by a backslash (\). *expression* may yield a numeric or string result, depending on the operators that it contains. The result of *expression* may be assigned to a shell variable by the appropriate use of command substitution.

expression may be constructed by applying the following binary operators to integer operands, grouped in decreasing order of precedence:

OPERATOR	RESPECTIVE MEANING
* / %	multiplication, division, remainder
+ −	addition, subtraction
= > >= < <= !=	comparison operators
&	logical and
|	logical or

Parentheses may be used to explicitly control the order of evaluation (and also must be escaped using the backslash). **expr** also supports a few string operators:

OPERATOR	MEANING
string : regularExpression **match** *string regularExpression*	Both forms return the length of string if both sides match and 0 otherwise.
substr *string start length*	Returns the substring of *string* starting from index *start* and consisting of *length* characters.
index *string charList*	Returns the index of the first character in *string* that appears in *charList*.
length *string*	Returns the length of *string*.

The format of *regularExpression* is defined in the appendix.

The following example illustrates some of the functions of **expr** and makes plentiful use of command substitution:

```
$ x=1                                       ...initial value of x.
$ x=`expr $x + 1`                           ...increment x.
$ echo $x
2
$ x=`expr 2 + 3 \* 5`                        ...* is conducted before +.
$ echo $x
17
$ echo `expr \( 2 + 3 \) \* 5`              ...regroup.
25
$ echo `expr length "cat"`                   ...find length of "cat".
3
$ echo `expr substr "donkey" 4 3`           ...extract a substring.
key
$ echo `expr index "donkey" "ke"`           ...locate a substring.
4
$ echo `expr match "smalltalk" '.*lk'`      ...attempt a match.
9
$ echo `expr match "transputer" '*.lk'`     ...attempt match.
0
$ echo `expr "transputer" : '*.lk'`         ...attempt a match.
0
$ echo `expr \( 4 \> 5 \)`                   ...is 4 > 5 ?
0                                           ...0 for false.
$ echo `expr \( 4 \> 5 \) \| \( 6 \< 7 \)`  ...4>5 or 6<7?
1                                           ...1 for true.
$ _
```

CONDITIONAL EXPRESSIONS

The control structures described in the next section often branch based on the value of a logical expression—that is, an expression that evaluates to true or false. The **test** utility supports a substantial set of UNIX-oriented expressions suitable for most occasions and works like this:

Utility: **test** *expression*
    [*expression*] (equivalent form on some UNIX systems)

test returns a zero exit code if *expression* evaluates to true; otherwise, it returns a nonzero exit status. The exit status is typically used by shell control structures for branching purposes.
    Some Bourne shells support **test** as a built-in command, in which case they support the second form of evaluation as well. The brackets of the second form must be surrounded by spaces in order for it to work.
    See the next set of text for a description of the syntax of *expression*.

A **test** expression may take the following forms:

Form	Meaning
−b *filename*	True if *filename* exists as a block special file.
−c *filename*	True if *filename* exists as a character special file.
−d *filename*	True if *filename* exists as a directory.
−f *filename*	True if *filename* exists as a nondirectory.
−g *filename*	True if *filename* exists as a "set group ID" file.
−h *filename*	True if *filename* exists as a symbolic link.
−k *filename*	True if *filename* exists and has its sticky bit set.
−l *string*	True if length of *string* is nonzero.
−n *string*	True if *string* contains at least one character.
−p *filename*	True if *filename* exists as a named pipe.
−r *filename*	True if *filename* exists as a readable file.
−s *filename*	True if *filename* contains at least one character.
−t *fd*	True if file descriptor *fd* is associated with a terminal.
−u *filename*	True if *filename* exists as a "set user ID" file.
−w *filename*	True if *filename* exists as a writeable file.
−x *filename*	True if *filename* exists as an executable file.
−z *string*	True if *string* contains no characters.
str1 = *str2*	True if *str1* is equal to *str2*.

Form	Meaning
str1 != *str2*	True if *str1* is not equal to *str2*.
string	True if *string* is not null.
int1 −eq *int2*	True if integer *int1* is equal to integer *int2*.
int1 −ne *int2*	True if integer *int1* is not equal to integer *int2*.
int1 −gt *int2*	True if integer *int1* is greater than integer *int2*.
int1 −ge *int2*	True if integer *int1* is greater than or equal to integer *int2*.
int1 −lt *int2*	True if integer *int1* is less than integer *int2*.
int1 −le *int2*	True if integer *int1* is less than or equal to integer *int2*.
! *expr*	True if *expr* is false.
expr1 −a *expr2*	True if *expr1* and *expr2* are both true.
expr1 −o *expr2*	True if *expr1* or *expr2* is true.
\(*expr* \)	Escaped parentheses are used for grouping expressions.

test is very picky about the syntax of expressions; the spaces shown in this table are *not* optional. For examples of the use of **test**, please consult the next section, which uses them in a natural context.

CONTROL STRUCTURES

The Bourne shell supports a wide range of control structures that make it suitable as a high-level programming tool. Shell programs are usually stored in scripts and are commonly used to automate maintenance and installation tasks. The next few subsections describe the control structures in alphabetical order. They assume that you are already familiar with at least one high-level programming language.

case .. in .. esac

The *case* command supports multiway branching based on the value of a single string and has the following syntax:

```
case expression in
pattern { | pattern }* )
list
;;
esac
```

expression is an expression that evaluates to a string, *pattern* may include wild-cards, and *list* is a list of one or more shell commands. You may include as many pattern/list associations as you wish. The shell evaluates *expression* and then compares it to each pattern in turn, from top to bottom. When the first matching pattern is found, its associated list of commands is executed and then the shell skips to the matching **esac**. A series of patterns separated by "or" symbols (|) are all associated with the same list. If no match is found, then the shell skips to the matching **esac**.

Here's an example of a script called "menu.sh" that makes use of a *case* control structure:

```
#! /bin/sh
echo menu test program
stop=0                     # reset loop-termination flag.
while test $stop -eq 0     # loop until done.
do
 cat << ENDOFMENU                   # display menu.
 1      : print the date.
 2, 3   : print the current working directory.
 4      : exit
ENDOFMENU
 echo
 echo 'your choice? \c'    # prompt.
 read reply                # read response.
 echo
 case $reply in            # process response.
  "1")
    date                   # display date.
    ;;
  "2"|"3")
    pwd                    # display working directory.
    ;;
  "4")
    stop=1                 # set loop termination flag.
    ;;
  *)                       # default.
    echo illegal choice    # error.
    ;;
 esac
done
```

Here's the output from a sample run of the "menu.sh" script:

```
$ menu.sh
menu test program
 1      : print the date.
 2, 3   : print the current working directory.
 4      : exit
your choice? 1
```

```
Thu Feb 5 07:09:13 CST 1998
 1      : print the date.
 2, 3   : print the current working directory.
 4      : exit
your choice? 2
/home/glass
 1      : print the date.
 2, 3   : print the current working directory.
 4      : exit
your choice? 5
illegal choice
 1      : print the date.
 2, 3   : print the current working directory.
 4      : exit
your choice? 4
$ _
```

for .. do .. done

The *for* command allows a list of commands to be executed several times, using a different value of the loop variable during each iteration. Here's its syntax:

---

for name [*in* { *word* } *]
do
  list
done

The *for* command loops the value of the variable *name* through each *word* in the word list, evaluating the commands in *list* after each iteration. If no word list is supplied, $@ ($1..) is used instead. A *break* command causes the loop to immediately end, and a *continue* command causes the loop to immediately jump to the next iteration. Here's an example of a script that uses a *for* control structure:

```
$ cat for.sh                   ...list the script.
for color in red yellow green blue
do
 echo one color is $color
done
$ for.sh                       ...execute the script.
one color is red
one color is yellow
one color is green
one color is blue
$ _
```

if .. then .. fi

The *if* command supports nested conditional branches and has the following syntax:

---

if list1
then
   list2
elif list3   ...optional, the *elif* part may be repeated several times.
then
   list4
else   ...optional, the *else* part may occur zero times or one time.
   list5
fi

The *if* command works as follows:

- The commands in *list1* are executed.
- If the last command in *list1* succeeds, the commands in *list2* are executed.
- If the last command in *list1* fails and there are one or more *elif* components, then a successful command list following an *elif* causes the commands following the associated *then* to be executed.
- If no successful lists are found and there is an *else* component, the commands following the *else* are executed.

Here's an example of a script that uses an *if* control structure:

```
$ cat if.sh                    ...list the script.
echo 'enter a number: \c'
read number
if [ $number -lt 0 ]
then
 echo negative
elif [ $number -eq 0 ]
then
 echo zero
else
 echo positive
fi
$ if.sh                        ...run the script.
enter a number: 1
positive
$ if.sh                        ...run the script again.
enter a number: -1
negative
$ _
```

trap

The *trap* command allows you to specify a command that should be executed when the shell receives a signal of a particular value. Here's its syntax:

---

trap [[*command*] { *signal* } +]

The *trap* command instructs the shell to execute *command* whenever any of the numbered signals *signal* are received. If several signals are received, they are trapped in numeric order. If a signal value of 0 is specified, then *command* is executed when the shell terminates. If *command* is omitted, then the traps of the numbered signals are reset to their original values. If *command* is an empty string, then the numbered signals are ignored. If *trap* is executed with no arguments, a list of all of the signals and their *trap* settings are displayed. For more information on signals and their default actions, see Chapter 12.

Here's an example of a script that uses the *trap* control structure. When Control-C was pressed, the shell executed the *echo* command followed by the exit command:

```
$ cat trap.sh                    ...list the script.
trap 'echo Control-C; exit 1' 2  # trap Control-C (signal #2)
while 1
do
 echo infinite loop
 sleep 2                         # sleep for two seconds.
done
$ trap.sh                        ...execute the script.
infinite loop
infinite loop
^C                     ...I typed a Control-C here.
Control-C              ...displayed by the echo command.
$ _
```

until .. do .. done

The *until* command executes one series of commands as long as another series of commands fails and has the following syntax:

---

until list1
do
    list2
done

The *until* command executes the commands in *list1* and ends if the last command in *list1* succeeds; otherwise, the commands in *list2* are executed and the process is repeated. If *list2* is empty, the *do* keyword should be omitted. A *break* command causes the loop to immediately end, and a *continue* command causes the loop to immediately jump to the next iteration.

Here's an example of a script that uses an *until* control structure:

```
$ cat until.sh                    ...list the script.
x=1
until [ $x -gt 3 ]
do
 echo x = $x
 x=`expr $x + 1`
done
$ until.sh                ...execute the script.
x = 1
x = 2
x = 3
$ _
```

while .. done

The *while* command executes one series of commands as long as another series of commands succeeds. Here's its syntax:

```
while list1
do
  list2
done
```

The *while* command executes the commands in *list1* and ends if the last command in *list1* fails; otherwise, the commands in *list2* are executed and the process is repeated. If *list2* is empty, the *do* keyword should be omitted. A *break* command causes the loop to end immediately, and a *continue* command causes the loop to immediately jump to the next iteration.

Here's an example of a script that uses a *while* control structure to generate a small multiplication table:

```
$ cat multi.sh                        ...list the script.
if [ "$1" -eq " " ]; then
   echo "Usage: multi number"
   exit
fi
x=1                             # set outer-loop value
while [ $x -le $1 ]             # outer loop
```

```
do
  y=1                                  # set inner-loop value
  while [ $y -le $1 ]
  do                                   # generate one table entry
    echo `expr $x \* $y`  "  \c"
    y=`expr $y + 1`                    # update inner-loop count
  done
  echo                                 # blank line
  x=`expr $x + 1`                      # update outer-loop count
done
$ multi.sh 7                           ...execute the script.
1        2        3        4        5        6        7
2        4        6        8        10       12       14
3        6        9        12       15       18       21
4        8        12       16       20       24       28
5        10       15       20       25       30       35
6        12       18       24       30       36       42
7        14       21       28       35       42       49
$ _
```

SAMPLE PROJECT: TRACK

To illustrate a good percentage of the Bourne-shell capabilities, I'll present a small project that I call "track." This script tracks a user's logins and logouts, generating a simple report of their sessions. It uses the following utilities:

- **who**, which displays a listing of the current users of the system
- **grep**, which filters text for lines that match a specified pattern
- **diff**, which displays the differences between two files
- **sort**, which sorts a text file
- **sed**, which performs preprogrammed edits on a file
- **expr**, which evaluates an expression
- **cat**, which lists a file
- **date**, which displays the current time and date
- **rm**, which removes a file
- **mv**, which moves a file
- **sleep**, which pauses for a specified number of seconds

grep, **diff**, **sort**, and **sed** are described in Chapter 7. **who** is described in Chapter 8. The usage of **track** is as follows:

Script: **track** [-n*count*] [-t*pause*] *userId*

track monitors the specified user's login and logout sessions. Every *pause* number of seconds, **track** scans the system and makes a note of who is currently logged on. If the specified user has logged on or logged off since the last scan, this information is displayed to standard output. **track** operates until *count* scans have completed. By default, *pause* is 20 seconds and *count* is 10,000 scans. **track** is usually executed in the background with its standard output redirected.

Here's an example of **track** at work:

```
$ track -n3 ivor -t200     ...track ivor's sessions.
track report for ivor:     ...initial output.
login          ivor        ttyp3    Feb 5 06:53
track report for ivor:     ...ivor logged out.
logout         ivor        ttyp3    Feb 5 06:55
^C                         ...terminate program using Control-C.
stop tracking              ...termination message.
$ _
```

The implementation of **track** consists of three files:

- "track", the main Bourne-shell script
- "track.sed", a **sed** script for editing the output of the **diff** utility
- "track.cleanup", a small script that cleans up temporary files at the end

The operation of **track** may be divided into three pieces:

- It parses the command line and sets the values of three local variables: *user*, *pause*, and *loopCount*. If any errors occur, a usage message is displayed and the script terminates.
- It then sets two traps: one to trap the script's termination and the other to trap an INT (*Control-C*) or QUIT (*Control-*) signal. The latter trap invokes the former trap by executing an explicit exit so that the cleanup script always gets called regardless of how the script terminates. The cleanup script takes the process ID of the main script as its single argument and removes the temporary files that **track** uses for its operation.
- The script then loops the specified number of times, storing a filtered list of the current users in a temporary file called ".track.new.$$", where $$ is the process ID of the script itself. This file is then compared against the last version of the same output, stored in ".track.old.$$". If a line is in the first file but not the second, the user must have logged in, and if a line is in the second file but not the first, the user must have logged out. If the output file from **diff** is of a nonzero length, it is massaged into a suitable form by **sed** and then displayed. The script then pauses for the specified number of seconds and continues to loop.

The output from two *diff*ed **who** outputs is illustrated by the following session:

```
$ cat track.new.1112          ...the new output from who.
```

```
glass                ttyp0           Feb    4  23:04
glass                ttyp2           Feb    4  23:04
$ cat track.old.1112                          ...the old output from who.
glass                ttyp0           Feb    4  23:04
glass                ttyp1           Feb    4  23:06
$ diff track.new.1112 track.old.1112          ...the changes.
2c2
< glass              ttyp2           Feb    4  23:04
- - -
> glass              ttyp1           Feb    4  23:06
$ _
```

The **sed** script "track.sed" removes all lines that start with a digit or "- - -" and then substitutes "<" for login and ">" for logout. Here is a listing of the three source files:

track.sed

```
/^[0-9].*/d
/^---/d
s/^</login/
s/^>/logout/
```

track.cleanup

```
echo stop tracking
rm -f .track.old.$1 .track.new.$1 .track.report.$1
```

track

```
pause=20         # default pause between scans
loopCount=10000  # default scan count
error=0          # error flag
for arg in $*    # parse command-line arguments
do
 case $arg in
  -t*)           # time
   pause=`expr substr $arg 3 10`        # extract number
   ;;
  -n*)           # scan count
   loopCount=`expr substr $arg 3 10`    # extract number
   ;;
  *)
   user=$arg                            # user name
   ;;
 esac
done
if [ ! "$user" ]         # check if a user ID was found
then
 error=1
fi
if [ $error -eq 1 ]      # display error if error(s) found
```

```
then
 cat << ENDOFERROR          # display usage message
usage: track [-n#] [-t#] userId
ENDOFERROR
 exit 1# terminate shell
fi
trap 'track.cleanup $$; exit $exitCode' 0 # trap on exit
trap 'exitCode=1; exit' 2 3              # trap on INT/QUIT
> .track.old.$$              # zero the old track file
count=0                      # number of scans so far
while [ $count -lt $loopCount ]
do
 who | grep $user | sort > .track.new.$$  # scan system
 diff .track.new.$$ .track.old.$$ | \
       sed -f track.sed > .track.report.$$
 if [ -s .track.report.$$ ]           # only report changes
 then                                 # display report
  echo track report for ${user}:
  cat .track.report.$$
 fi
 mv .track.new.$$ .track.old.$$    # remember current state
 sleep $pause                      # wait a while
 count=`expr $count + 1`           # update scan count
done
exitCode=0                         # set exit code
```

MISCELLANEOUS BUILT-IN COMMANDS

The Bourne shell supports several specialized built-in commands. I described several of them in other sections of this chapter, such as those related to control structures and job control. This section contains an alphabetical list of the rest, together with a brief description of each command.

Read Command: .

To execute the contents of a text file from within a shell's environment (i.e., not by starting a subshell, as you do when executing a shell script), use a period followed by the name of the file. The file does not have to have execute permission. This command is handy if you make modifications to your ".profile" file and wish to re-execute it.

```
$ cat .profile    ...assume that ".profile" was just edited.
TERM=vt100
export TERM
$ . .profile   ...reexecute it.
$ _
```

Note that since a subshell is not created to execute the contents of the file, any local variables that the file sets are those of the current shell.

The *null* Command

The *null* command is usually used in conjunction with the control structures listed earlier in this chapter, and it performs no operation. It is often used in case structures to denote an empty set of statements associated with a particular switch.

Shell Command: **null**

The *null* command performs no operation.

Setting Shell Options: *set*

The *set* command allows you to control several shell options:

Shell Command: **set** -ekntuvx { *arg* }*

set allows you to choose the shell options that are displayed in the table below. Any remaining arguments are assigned to the positional parameters $1, $2, etc., overwriting their current values.

Here is a list of the *set* options:

Option	Meaning
-e	If the shell is not executing commands from a terminal or a startup file and a command fails, then execute an ERR trap and exit.
-n	Accept, but do not execute, commands. This flag does not affect interactive shells.
-t	Execute the next command and then exit.
-u	Generate an error when an unset variable is encountered.
-v	Echo shell commands as they are read.
-x	Echo shell commands as they are executed.
-	Turn off the **-x** and **-v** flags and treat further "-" characters as arguments.

Here's a small example of a script that makes use of these options. The **-x** and **-v** options are very useful when debugging a shell script, as they cause the shell to display lines before and after the variable, wildcard, and command-substitution metacharacters are processed. I recommend that you always use these options when testing scripts. Here's an example:

```
$ cat script.sh                        ...look at the script.
set -vx a.c        # set debug trace and overwrite $1.
ls $1              # access first positional parameter.
set -              # turn off trace.
echo goodbye $USER
echo $notset
set -u        # unset variables will generate an error now.
echo $notset       # generate an error.
$ script.sh b.c                        ...execute the script.
ls $1                                  ...output by -v option.
+ ls a.c                               ...output by -x option.
a.c                                    ...regular output.
set -                                  ...output by -v option.
+ set -                                ...output by -x option.
goodbye glass                          ...regular output.
script.sh: notset: parameter not set   ...unset variable.
$ _
```

ENHANCEMENTS

In addition to the new facilities that have already been described, the Bourne shell also enhances the following areas of the common core:

- redirection
- sequenced commands

This section describes each enhancement.

Redirection

In addition to the common core redirection facilities, the Bourne shell allows you to duplicate, close, and redirect arbitrary I/O channels. You may associate the standard-input file descriptor (0) with file descriptor *n* by using the following syntax:

```
$ command <& n   ...associate standard input.
```

Similarly, you may associate the standard-output file descriptor (1) with file descriptor *n* by using the following syntax:

```
$ command >& n   ... associate standard output.
```

To close the standard input and output channels, use the following syntax:

```
$ command <&-   ...close stdin and execute command.
$ command >&-   ...close stdout and execute command.
```

You may precede any redirection metacharacters, including the Bourne-specific ones described above, by a digit to indicate the file descriptor that should be used instead of 0 (for input redirection) or 1 (for output redirection). It's fairly common to redirect file descriptor 2, which corresponds to the standard error channel.

The next example illustrates the use of these redirection facilities. The **man** utility always writes a couple of lines to the standard error channel: It writes "Reformatting page. Wait" when it begins and "done" when it ends. If you only redirect standard output, these messages are seen on the terminal. To redirect the standard error channel to a separate file, use the "2>" redirection sequence, and to send it to the same place as standard output, use the "2>&1" sequence.

```
$ man ls > ls.txt                       ...send standard output to
                                        ..."ls.txt".

Reformatting page. Wait... done         ...from standard error.
$ man ls > ls.txt 2> err.txt            ...send error to "err.txt".
$ cat err.txt                           ...look at the file.
Reformatting page. Wait... done
$ man ls > ls.txt 2>&1                   ...associate stderr with stdout.
$ head -1 ls.txt                        ...look at first line of
                                        ..."ls.txt".

Reformatting page.
$ _
```

Sequenced Commands

When a group of commands is placed between parentheses, they are executed by a subshell. The Bourne shell also lets you group commands by placing them between braces, in which case they are still redirectable and "pipeable" as a group, but are executed directly by the parent shell. A space must be left after the opening brace, and a semicolon must precede the closing brace.

In the following example, the first *cd* command didn't affect the current working directory of my login shell, since it executed inside a subshell, but the second *cd* command did:

```
$ pwd                                   ...display current working directory.
/home/glass
$ (cd /; pwd; ls | wc -l)               ...count files with subshell.
/
    22
$ pwd                                   ...my shell didn't move.
/home/glass
```

```
$ { cd /; pwd; ls | wc -l; }          ...count files with shell.
/
   22
$ pwd                                 ...my shell moved.
/
$ _
```

COMMAND-LINE OPTIONS

The Bourne shell supports several command line options:

Option	Meaning
-c *string*	Create a shell to execute the command *string*.
-s	Create a shell that reads commands from standard input and sends shell messages to the standard error channel.
-i	Create an interactive shell; like the -s option except that the SIGTERM, SIGINT, and SIGQUIT signals are all ignored. For information about signals, consult Chapter 12.

CHAPTER REVIEW

Checklist

In this chapter, I described:

- the creation of a Bourne-shell startup file
- the creation and access of shell variables
- arithmetic
- conditional expressions
- six control structures
- a sample project for tracking user login sessions
- some miscellaneous built-in commands
- several enhancements to the core facilities

Quiz

1. Who wrote the Bourne shell?
2. Describe a common use of the built-in variable $$.
3. What is the easiest way to re-execute your ".profile" file?
4. What debugging features does the Bourne shell provide?

Exercises

1. Write a utility called **junk** that satisfies the following specification:

Utility: **junk** -lp { *fileName* }*

junk is a replacement for the **rm** utility. Rather than removing files, it moves them into the subdirectory ".junk" in your home directory. If ".junk" doesn't exist, it is automatically created. The **-l** option lists the current contents of the ".junk" directory, and the **-p** option purges ".junk".

Here's an example of junk at work:

```
$ ls -l reader.c              ...list existing file.
-rw-r--r-- 1 glass       2580 May 4 19:17 reader.c
$ junk reader.c               ...junk it!
$ ls -l reader.c              ...confirm that it was moved.
reader.c not found
$ junk badguy.c               ...junk another file.
$ junk -l                     ...list the contents of "junk" directory.
-rw-r--r-- 1 glass         57 May 4 19:17 badguy.c
-rw-r--r-- 1 glass       2580 May 4 19:17 reader.c
$ junk -p                     ...purge junk.
$ junk -l                     ...list junk.
$ _
```

Remember to comment your script liberally. [level: *medium*]

2. Modify the **junk** script to be menu driven. [level: *easy*]

3. Write a **shhelp** utility that works as follows:

Utility: **shhelp** -k { *command* }*

shhelp lists help about the specified Bourne-shell command. The **-k** option lists every command that **shhelp** knows about.

Here's an example of **shhelp** in action:

```
$ shhelp null       ...ask for help about null.
The null command performs no operation.
$ _
```

Make sure that your utility displays a suitable error message if *command* is not a legal command. I suggest that the text of each command's help message is kept in a separate file, rather than stored inside the **shhelp** script. If you do decide to place it all inside a script, try using the here-document facility. [level: *easy*]

4. Write a crafty script called **ghoul** that is difficult to kill: When it receives a SIGINT (from a *Control*-C), it should create a copy of itself before dying. Thus, every time an unwary user tries to kill a **ghoul**, another **ghoul** is created to take its place! Of course, **ghoul** can still be killed by a SIGKILL (-9) signal. [level: *medium*]

Projects

1. Build a phonebook utility that allows you to access and modify an alphabetical list of names, addresses, and telephone numbers. Use the utilities described in Chapter 7, such as **awk** and **sed**, to maintain and edit the file of phonebook information. [level: *hard*]

2. Build a process-management utility that allows you to kill processes based on their CPU usage, user ID, total elapsed time, etc. This kind of utility is especially useful to system administrators. (See Chapter 14.) [level: *hard*]

CHAPTER 5

The Korn Shell

Motivation

The Korn shell, written by David Korn, is a powerful superset of the Bourne shell, and it offers improvements over the Bourne shell in job control, command-line editing, and programming features. It's rapidly becoming the industry favorite and looks likely to be the UNIX shell of choice for many years to come.

Prerequisites

You should already have read Chapter 4 and experimented with the Bourne shell.

Objectives

In this chapter, I explain and demonstrate the Korn-specific facilities.

Presentation

The information in this section is presented in the form of several sample UNIX sessions.

Shell Commands

This section introduces the following shell commands, listed in alphabetical order:

alias	jobs	select
bg	kill	typeset
fc	let	unalias
fg	print	
function	return	

INTRODUCTION

The Korn shell supports all of the Bourne shell facilities described in Chapter 4, plus the following new features:

- command customization using aliases
- access to previous commands via a history mechanism (through vi-like and emacs-like command-line editing features)

- functions
- advanced job control
- several new built-in commands and several enhancements to existing commands

These new facilities are described by this chapter and are illustrated by the following hierarchy diagram:

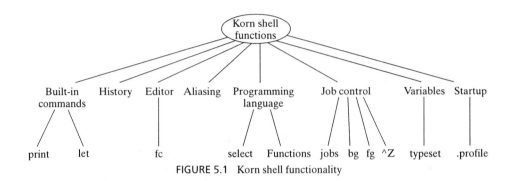

FIGURE 5.1   Korn shell functionality

START-UP

The Korn shell is a regular C program whose executable file is stored as "/bin/ksh". If your chosen shell is "/bin/ksh", an interactive Korn shell is invoked automatically when you log into UNIX. You may also invoke a Korn shell manually from a script or from a terminal by using the command "ksh". "ksh" has several command-line options that are described at the end of this chapter.

When a Korn shell is invoked, the start-up sequence is different for interactive shells and noninteractive shells:

Step	Shell Type	Action
1	interactive only	Execute commands in "/etc/profile" if it exists.
2	interactive only	Execute commands in "$HOME/.profile" if it exists.
3	both	Execute commands in $ENV if it exists.

The value $ENV is usually set to "$HOME/.kshrc" in the "$HOME/.profile" script. After reading the startup files, an interactive Korn shell then displays its prompt and awaits user commands. The standard Korn shell prompt is a dollar sign ($), although it may be changed by setting the local variable PS1, described in the previous chapter. Here's an example of a Korn shell ".profile" script that is executed exactly once at the start of every login session:

```
TERM=vt100; export TERM              # my terminal type.
ENV=~/.kshrc; export ENV             # environment filename.
HISTSIZE=100; export HISTSIZE        # remember 100 commands.
```

```
MAILCHECK=60; export MAILCHECK          # seconds between checks.
set -o ignoreeof                        # don't let Control-D log me out.
set -o trackall                         # speed up file searches.
stty erase '^H'                         # set backspace character.
tset                                    # set terminal.
```

Some of these commands won't mean much to you right now, but their meaning will become clear as the chapter progresses.

Here's an example of a Korn-shell ".kshrc" script that contains useful Korn-shell-specific information required by all shells, including those that are created purely to execute scripts:

```
PATH='.:~/bin:/bin:/usr/bin:/usr/local/bin:/gnuemacs'
PS1='! $ ';export PS1     # put command number in prompt.
alias h="fc -l"           # set up useful aliases.
alias ll="ls -l"
alias rm="rm -i"
alias cd="cdx"
alias up="cdx .."
alias dir="/bin/ls"
alias ls="ls -aF"
alias env="printenv|sort"
function cdx              # function to display path and directory when
                           moving.
{
 if 'cd' "$@"
 then
   echo $PWD
   ls -aF
 fi
}
```

Every Korn shell, including all subshells, executes this script when it begins.

ALIASES

The Korn shell allows you to create and customize your own commands by using the *alias* command, which works like this:

Shell Command: alias [-tx] [*word* [=*string*]]

alias supports a simple form of command-line customization. If you alias *word* to be equal to *string* and then later enter a command beginning with *word*, the first occurrence of *word* is replaced by *string* and then the command is reprocessed. If you don't supply *word* or *string* in the shell command, a list of all of the current shell aliases is displayed. If you only supply *word*, then the string currently associated with the alias *word* is displayed. If you supply *word* and *string*, the shell adds the specified alias to its collection of aliases. If an alias already exists for *word*, it is replaced by the one provided in the shell command. If the replacement string begins with *word*, it is not reprocessed for aliases in order to prevent infinite loops. If the replacement string ends with a space, then the first word that follows it in a command is processed for aliases.

Here's an example of *alias* in action:

```
$ alias dir='ls -aF'       ...register an alias.
$ dir                      ...same as typing "ls -aF".
./          main2.c    p.reverse.c        reverse.h
../         main2.o    palindrome.c       reverse.old
$ dir *.c                  ...same as typing "ls -aF *.c".
main2.c                p.reverse.c palindrome.c
$ alias dir                ...definition of "dir".
dir=ls -aF
$ _
```

In the following example, I defined a command in terms of itself:

```
$ alias ls='ls -aF'        ...no problem.
$ ls *.c                   ...same as typing "ls -aF *.c".
main2.c         p.reverse.c        palindrome.c
$ alias dir='ls'           ...define "dir" in terms of "ls".
$ dir                      ...same as typing "ls -aF".
./          main2.c    p.reverse.c        reverse.h
../         main2.o    palindrome.c       reverse.old
$ _
```

Aliasing Built-In Commands

All built-in commands may be aliased except for the following: *case, do, done, elif, else, esac, fi, for, function, if, select, then, time, until, while, {, }*.

Removing an Alias

To remove an alias, use the *unalias* command, which works as follows:

Shell Command: unalias {word} +

unalias removes all of the specified aliases.

Here's an example of the use of *unalias*:

```
$ alias dir            ...look at an existing alias.
dir=ls
$ unalias dir          ...remove the alias.
$ alias dir            ...try looking at the alias again.
dir alias not found
$ _
```

Predefined Aliases

For convenience, the Korn shell predefines the following aliases:

Alias	Value
false	let 0
functions	typeset -f
history	fc -l
integer	typeset -i
nohup	nohup
r	fc -e -
true	:
type	whence -v
hash	alias -t

The uses of these aliases will become more apparent as the chapter progresses. For example, the "r" alias is particularly useful, as it allows you to recall previous commands without having to use the tedious sequence "fc -e -".

Some Useful Aliases

Here's a grab bag of useful aliases that I've gathered from various sources:

Alias	Value
rm	rm -i This alias causes the rm command to prompt for confirmation.
mv	mv -i This alias causes the mv command to prompt for confirmation.
ls	ls -aF This alias causes the ls command to display more information.
env	printenv | sort This alias displays a sorted list of the environment variables.
ll	ls -l This alias allows you to obtain a long directory listing more conveniently.

For some other interesting aliases, please see the "Aliases" section in Chapter 6.

Tracked Aliases

One common use of aliases is as a shorthand for full pathnames in order to avoid the lookup penalty of the standard search mechanism as it scans the directories specified by $PATH. You may arrange for the full-pathname replacement to occur automatically by making use of the *tracked alias* facility. All aliases listed with the "-t" option are flagged as tracked aliases, and the standard search mechanism is used to set their initial values. From then on, a tracked alias is replaced by its value, thereby avoiding the search time. If no aliases follow the "-t" option, a list of all of the currently tracked aliases is displayed. An example of the use of the "-t" option is as follows:

```
$ alias -t page        ...define a tracked alias for "page".
$ alias -t             ...look at all tracked aliases.
page=/usr/ucb/page     ...its full pathname is stored.
$ _
```

The "-o trackall" option of the *set* command (described later in this chapter) tells the shell to track all commands automatically:

```
$ set -o trackall      ...all commands are now tracked.
$ date                 ...execute date.
Fri Feb 6 00:54:44 CST 1998
$ alias -t             ...look at all tracked aliases.
date=/bin/date         ...date is now tracked as well.
page=/usr/ucb/page
$ _
```

Since the value of a tracked alias is dependent on the value of $PATH, the values of all tracked aliases are reevaluated every time the $PATH variable is changed. If $PATH is unset, the values of all tracked aliases are set to null, but remain tracked.

Sharing Aliases

To make an alias available to a child shell, you must mark it as an *export alias* by using the "-x" option of *alias*. All aliases listed with the "-x" option are flagged as export aliases. If no aliases follow the "-x" option, a list of all currently exported aliases is displayed. Note that if the value of an alias is changed in a child shell, it does not affect the value of the original alias in the parent shell. An example of the use of the "x" option is as follows (note that parts of the session have been edited out because they are irrelevant to the current lesson and would take up too much space if displayed):

```
$ alias -x mroe='more'  ...add an export alias.
$ alias -x              ...list exported aliases.
autoload=typeset -fu    ...a standard alias.
...                     ...other aliases are listed here.
ls=ls -F
```

```
mroe=more                    ...the alias I just added.
...                          ...other aliases are listed here.
type=whence -v
vi=/usr/ucb/vi
$ cat test.ksh               ...a script using the new alias.
mroe main2.c
$ test.ksh...run the script. mroe works!
/* MAIN2.C */
#include #stdio.h,
#include "palindrome.h"
main ()
{
 printf ("palindrome (\"cat\") = %d\n",
      palindrome ("cat"));
 printf ("palindrome (\"noon\") = %d\n",
      palindrome ("noon"));
}
$ _
```

HISTORY

The Korn shell keeps a record of commands entered from the keyboard so that they may be edited and reexecuted at a later stage. This facility is known as a *history* mechanism. The built-in command *fc* (which stands for the "fix command") gives you access to your command history. There are two forms of *fc*. The first, simpler form allows you to reexecute a specified set of previous commands, and the second, more complex form allows you to edit them before reexecution.

Numbered Commands

When you're using history, it's very handy to arrange for your prompt to contain the "number" of the command that you're about to enter. To do so, set the primary prompt variable (PS1) to contain a "!" character:

```
$ PS1='! $ '        ...set PS1 to contain a "!".
103 $ _             ...prompt for command #103.
```

Storage of Commands

The Korn shell records the last *$HISTSIZE* commands in the file "$HISTFILE". If the environment variable $HISTSIZE is not set, a default value of 128 is used. If $HISTFILE is not set or the named file is not writeable, then the file "$HOME/.sh_history" is used by default. All of the Korn shells that specify the same history file will share it. Therefore, as long as you don't change the value of $HISTFILE during a login session, the commands entered during that session are available as history at the next session. In the following example, I examined the history file where commands are stored:

```
$ echo $HISTSIZE                        ...set in ".profile".
100
$ echo $HISTFILE                        ...not set previously.
$ tail -3 $HOME/.sh_history       ...display last 3 commands.
echo $HISTSIZE
echo $HISTFILE
tail -3 $HOME/.sh_history
$ _
```

Command Reexecution

The *fc* command allows you to reexecute previous commands. The first, simpler form of *fc* works as follows:

Shell Command: fc -e - [*old* = *new*] *prefix*

This form of the *fc* command reexecutes the last command beginning with *prefix* after optionally replacing the first occurrence of the string *old* by the string *new*. *prefix* may be a number, in which case the numbered event is reexecuted.

Here's an example of *fc* in action:

```
360 $ fc -e - ech               ...last command starting with "ech".
echo $HISTFILE
361 $ fc -e - FILE=SIZE ech      ...replace "FILE" by "SIZE".
echo $HISTSIZE
100
362 $ fc -e - 360                ...execute command #360.
echo $HISTFILE
363 $ _
```

The token "r" is a predefined alias for "fc -e -", that allows for a more convenient way to reexecute commands:

```
364 $ alias r          ...look at "r"'s alias.
r=fc -e 365
365 $ r 364            ...execute command #364.
alias r
r=fc -e -
366 $ _
```

Editing Commands

The Korn shell allows you to preedit commands before they are reexecuted by using a more advanced form of the *fc* command, which works as follows:

Shell Command: fc [-e editor] [-nlr] [start] [end]

This form of *fc* invokes the editor called *editor* upon the specified range of commands. When the editor is exited, the edited range of commands is then executed. If *editor* is not specified, then the editor whose pathname is stored in the environment variable $FCEDIT is used. The value $FCEDIT is "/bin/ed" by default, and I *don't* recommend that you use this default. I personally prefer "/usr/ucb/vi" (the full pathname of the **vi** editor on my system), as I'm most familiar with the UNIX **vi** editor. If no other options are specified, the editor is invoked upon the last command.

When you enter the editor, you may edit the command(s) as you wish and then save the text. When you exit the editor, the Korn shell automatically echoes and executes the saved version of the command(s).

To specify a particular command either by its index or by its prefix, supply the number or the prefix as the value of *start,* but don't supply a value for *end.* To specify a range of commands, set the value of *start* to select the first command in the series, and set the value of *end* to select the last command in the series. If a negative number is supplied, it's interpreted as an offset to the current command.

The **-l** option causes the selected commands to be displayed, but not executed. In this case, if no command series is specified, the last sixteen commands are listed. The **-r** option reverses the order of the selected commands, and the **-n** option inhibits the generation of command numbers when they are listed.

The following example illustrates the method of editing and reexecution (note that parts of this procedure are summarized rather than fully displayed in order to save space):

```
371 $ whence vi          ...find the location of "vi".
/usr/ucb/vi
372 $ FCEDIT=/usr/ucb/vi   ...set FCEDIT to full path of vi.
373 $ fc 371              ...edit command #371.
...enter vi, edit the command to say "whence ls", save, and quit vi
whence ls                ...display edited command.
/bin/ls                  ...output from edited command.
374 $ fc 371 373         ...edit commands #371 through 373.
...enter vi and edit a list of the last three commands.
...assume that I deleted the first line, changed the remaining lines
```

```
...to read "echo -n hi" and "echo there", respectively, and then quit.
echo -n "hi "              ...display edited commands.
echo there
hi there                  ...output from edited commands.
$ _
```

Here's an example of the use of the "-l" option:

```
376 $ fc -l 371 373       ...list commands with numbers.
371 $ whence vi
372 $ FCEDIT=/usr/ucb/vi
373 $ fc 371
377 $ fc -6               ...edit command six before current (#371).
...edit command to say "whence ls" and then quit.
whence ls                 ...display edited command.
/bin/ls                   ...output by command.
$ _
```

EDITING COMMANDS

The Korn shell contains simplified built-in versions of the **vi**, **gmacs**, and **emacs** editors that may be used to edit the current command or previous commands. To select one of these built-in editors, set either the VISUAL or the EDITOR variable to a string that ends in the name of one of these editors. In the following example, I selected the **vi** editor:

```
380 $ VISUAL=vi    ...select the built-in "vi" editor.
381 $ _
```

Each built-in editor is now described separately.

The Built-In vi Editor

This description assumes that you are familiar with the **vi** editor. If you're not, please consult the description of the **vi** editor in Chapter 2.

To edit the current line, press the *Esc* key to enter the built-in **vi** editor's control mode and make the required changes. To enter append or insert mode from control mode, press the "a" key or the "i" key, respectively. To go back to control mode from either of these modes, press the *Esc* key. To reexecute the command, press the *Enter* key. Be warned that if you press *Control*-D inside the editor, it terminates the shell, not just the editor.

When in control mode, key sequences fall into one of several categories:

- standard **vi** key sequences (described in Chapter 2).
- additional movement.
- additional searching.
- filename completion.
- alias replacement.

The last four categories of key sequences are described in the next set of subsections.

Additional Movement   The cursor-up (the "k" or "-" key) and cursor-down (the "j" or "+" key) keys select the previous and next commands in the history list, respectively. These keys allow you easily to access history from within the built-in editor. To load a command with a particular number, enter command mode and then enter the number of the command, followed by the "G" key. Here's an example of the use of these options:

```
125 $ echo line 1
line 1
126 $ echo line 2
line 2
127 $ ...at this point, I pressed the Esc key followed by the
      ..."k" key twice (up, up). This sequence loaded command #125 onto
      ...the command line, and I then executed the command by
      ...pressing the Enter key.
line 1
128 $ ...at this point, I pressed the Esc key and then typed "125G".
      ...This sequence loaded command #125 onto the command line, and
      ...I then executed the command by pressing the Enter key.
line 1
129 $ _
```

Additional Searching   The standard search mechanisms /*string* and ?*string* search backward and forward through history, respectively. Here's an example of the use of these options:

```
127 $ echo line 1
line 1
128 $ echo line 2
line 2
129 $ ...at this point, I pressed the Esc key and then typed
      ..."/ech", which loaded the last command
      ...containing the string "ech" onto the command-line.
      ...Then I pressed the "n" key to continue the search to
      ...the next command that matched. Finally, I
      ...pressed the Enter key to execute that command.
line 1
130 $ _
```

Filename Completion   If you type an asterisk (*) in control mode, the asterisk is appended to the word that the cursor is over and then processed as if it were a wildcard by the filename-substitution mechanism. If no match for the wildcarded filename is found, a beep is sounded; otherwise, the word is replaced by an alphabetical list of all of the matching filenames, and the editor enters input mode automatically. Here's an example of the use of this option:

```
$ ls m*
m          m3          main.c      mbox
m1         madness.c   main.o      mon.out
```

```
m2           main         makefile              myFile
115 $ ls ma  ...at this point, I pressed the Esc key,
             ...the "*" key, and then the Enter key.
115 $ ls madness.c main main.c main.o makefile
madness.c    main.c              makefile
main         main.o
$ _
```

If you type an equals sign (=) in control mode, the editor displays a numbered list of all of the files that have the current word that you are typing as a prefix and then redraws the command-line:

```
116 $ ls ma        ...at this point, I pressed the Esc key
                   ...and then the "=" key.
madness.c
main
main.c
main.o
makefile
116 $ ls ma_       ...back to the original command-line.
```

If you type a backlash (\) in control mode, the editor attempts to complete the current filename in an unambiguous way. If a completed pathname matches a directory, a slash (/) is appended; otherwise, a space is appended. Here's an example of the use of this option:

```
116 $ ls ma   ...at this point, I pressed the Esc key
              ...and then the "\" key.
              ...No completion was performed, since "ma"
              ...is a prefix of more than one file.
116 $ ls mak  ...at this point, I pressed the Esc key
              ...and then the "\" key. The editor
              ...completed the name to be "makefile".
116 $ ls makefile _
```

Alias Replacement   If you find yourself typing the same pattern again and again from the editor, you can make good use of the alias-replacement mechanism. If you give _letter an alias of *word*, the sequence @*letter* is replaced by *word* when you're in command mode. In the following example, the letter "i" at the start of the alias causes the built-in editor to go into insert mode, and the literal *Esc* at the end of the string causes it to leave **vi** mode:

```
123 $ alias _c='icommon text^['      ...^[ represents the key sequence Control-V
                                     ...followed by Esc.
124 $ echo   ...at this point I pressed the Esc followed by "@c."
124 $ echo common text_
```

The Built-In emacs/gmacs Editor

This description assumes that you are familiar with the **emacs** editor. If you're not, please consult the description of the **emacs** editor in Chapter 2.

Most of the **emacs** key sequences are supported in its built-in counterpart. You may move the cursor and manipulate text using the standard **emacs** key sequences. To reexecute the command, press the *Enter* key.

The main difference between the built-in editor and standard **emacs** is that the cursor-up, cursor-down, search-forward, and search-backward key sequences operate on the history list. For example, the cursor-up key sequence, *Control*-P, displays the previous command on the command line. Similarly, the search-backward key sequence, *Control*-R *string*, displays the last command that contains *string*.

ARITHMETIC

The *let* command allows you to perform arithmetic and works like this:

Shell Command: *let expression*

The *let* command performs double-precision integer arithmetic and supports all of the basic math operators using the standard precedence rules. Here are the operators, grouped in descending order of precedence, and their respective meanings:

OPERATOR	MEANING
-	unary minus
!	logical negation
*, /, %	multiplication, division, remainder
+, −	addition, subtraction
<=, >=, <, >	relational operators
==, !=	equality, inequality
=	assignment

All of the operators associate from left to right, except for the assignment operator. Expressions may be placed between parentheses to modify the order of evaluation. The shell doesn't check for overflow, so beware! Operands may be integer constants or variables. When a variable is encountered, it is replaced by its value, which in turn may contain other variables. You may explicitly override the default base (10) of a constant by using the format *base#number,* where *base* is a number between 2 and 36. You must not put spaces or tabs between the operands or operators, and you must not place a dollar sign ($) in front of variables that are part of an expression.

Here are some examples of the use of the *let* command:

```
$ let x = 2 + 2         ...expression contains spaces.
ksh: =: syntax error    ...no spaces or tabs allowed!
$ let x=2+2             ...OK.
$ echo $x
4
$ let y=x*4             ...don't place "$" before variables.
$ echo $y
16
$ let x=2#100+2#100     ...add two numbers in base 2.
$ echo $x
4                       ...number is displayed in base 10.
$ _
```

Preventing Metacharacter Interpretation

Unfortunately, the shell interprets several of the standard operators such as "<", ">", and "*" as metacharacters, so they must be quoted or preceded by a backslash (\) to inhibit their special meaning. To avoid this inconvenience, there is an equivalent form of *let* that automatically treats all of the tokens as if they were surrounded by double quotes and allows you to use spaces around tokens. For example, the token sequence

```
((list))
```

is equivalent to

```
let " list "
```

Note that double quotes do not prevent the expansion of variables. I personally *always* use the (( )) syntax instead of *let*. Here's an example of the use of this syntax:

```
$ ((x = 4))         ...spaces are OK.
$ ((y = x * 4))
$ echo $y
16
$ _
```

Return Codes

If an expression evaluates to zero, its return code is unity; otherwise, the return code is zero. The return code may be used by decision-making control structures, such as an *if* statement:

```
$ ((x = 4))         ...assign x to 4.
$ if ((x > 0))      ...OK to use in a control structure.
> then
> echo x is positive
> fi
x is positive       ...output from control structure.
$ _
```

For simple arithmetic tests, I recommend using ((..)) instead of *test* expressions.

TILDE SUBSTITUTION

Any token of the form ~*user* is subject to *tilde substitution*. In tilde substitution, the shell checks the password file to see if *user* is a valid username, and if it is, the shell replaces the ~*user* sequence with the full pathname of the user's home directory. If *user* isn't a valid username, the ~*user* sequence is left unchanged. Tilde substitution occurs *after* aliases are processed. Here's a table of all of the tilde substitutions, including the special cases ~+ and ~—:

Tilde sequence	Replaced by
~	$HOME
~*user*	home directory of *user*
~/*pathname*	$HOME/*pathname*
~+	$PWD (current working directory)
~—	$OLDPWD (previous working directory)

The predefined local variables $PWD and $OLDPWD are described later in this chapter. Here are some examples of tilde substitution:

```
$ pwd
/home/glass          ...current working directory.
$ echo ~
/home/glass          ...my home directory.
$ cd /                ...change to root directory.
$ echo ~+
/                    ...current working directory.
$ echo ~-
/home/glass          ...previous working directory.
$ echo ~dcox
/home/dcox           ...another user's home directory.
$ _
```

MENUS: *SELECT*

The *select* command allows you to create simple menus and has the following syntax:

select name [*in* {*word*}+]
do
list
done

The *select* command displays a numbered list of the words specified by the *in* clause to the standard error channel, displays the prompt stored in the special variable PS3, and then waits for a line of user input. When the user enters a line, it's stored in the predefined variable REPLY, and then one of three things occurs:

- If the user entered one of the listed numbers, *name* is set to that number, the commands in *list* are executed, and then the user is prompted for another choice.
- If the user entered a blank line, the selection is displayed again.
- If the user entered an illegal choice, *name* is set to null, the commands in *list* are executed, and then the user is prompted for another choice.

The next example is a recoding of the example on menu selection from the chapter on the Bourne shell. It replaces the *while* loop and termination logic with a simpler *select* command.

```
$ cat menu.ksh              ...list the script.
echo menu test program
select reply in "date" "pwd" "pwd" "exit"
do
 case $reply in
   "date")
     date
     ;;
   "pwd")
     pwd
     ;;
   "exit")
     break
     ;;
   *)
     echo illegal choice
     ;;
 esac
done
$ menu.ksh                  ...execute the script.
menu test program
1) date
2) pwd
3) pwd
4) exit
#? 1
Fri Feb 6 21:49:33 CST 1998
#? 5
illegal choice
#? 4
$ _
```

FUNCTIONS

The Korn shell allows you to define functions that may be invoked as shell commands. Parameters passed to functions are accessible via the standard positional-parameter mechanism. Functions must be defined before they are used. There are two ways to define a function:

function name
{
list
}
list is a list of commands.

or

name()
{
list
}
list is a list of commands.

I personally favor the second form because it looks more like the language of C. To invoke a function, supply its name followed by the appropriate parameters. For obvious reasons, the shell does not check the number or type of the parameters.

Here's an example of a script that defines and uses a function that takes no parameters:

```
$ cat func1.ksh            ...list the script.
message ()  # a no-parameter function.
{
  echo hi
  echo there
}
i=1
while (( i <= 3 ))
do
  message # call the function.
  let i=i+1 # increment loop count.
done
```

```
$ func1.ksh              ...execute the script.
hi
there
hi
there
hi
there
$ _
```

Using Parameters

As I mentioned previously, parameters are accessible via the standard positional-parameter mechanism. Here's an example of a script that passes parameters to a function:

```
$ cat func2.ksh              ...list the script.
f ()
{
echo parameter 1 = $1        # display first parameter.
echo parameter list = $*     # display entire list.
}
# main program.
f 1                          # call with 1 parameter.
f cat dog goat               # call with 3 parameters.
$ func2.ksh                  ...execute the script.
parameter 1 = 1
parameter list = 1
parameter 1 = cat
parameter list = cat dog goat
$ _
```

Returning from a Function

The *return* command returns the flow of control back to the caller and has the following syntax:

---

return [*value*]

When *return* is used without an argument, the function call returns immediately with the exit code of the last command that was executed in the function; otherwise, it returns with it's exit code set to *value*. If a *return* command is executed from the main script, it is equivalent to an *exit* command. The exit code is accessible from the caller via the $? variable. Here's an example of a function that multiplies its arguments and returns the result:

```
$ cat func3.ksh          ...list the script.
f ()  # two-parameter function.
{
 ((returnValue = $1 * $2))
 return $returnValue
}
# main program.
f 3 4                    # call function.
result=$?                # save exit code.
echo return value from function was $result
$ func3.ksh              ...execute the script.
return value from function was 12
$ _
```

Context

A function executes in the same context as that of the process that calls it, which means that they share the same variables, current working directory, and traps. The only exception to this rule is the "trap on exit"; a function's "trap on exit" executes when the function returns.

Local Variables

The *typeset* command (described in more detail later in this chapter) has some special function-oriented facilities. Specifically, a variable created using the *typeset* command is limited in scope to the function in which it's created and all of the functions that the defining function calls. If a variable of the same name already exists, its value is overwritten and replaced when the function returns. This property is similar, but not identical, to the scoping rules in most traditional high-level languages. Here's an example of a function that declares a local variable using *typeset*:

```
$ cat func4.ksh          ...list the script.
f ()                     # two-parameter function.
{
 typeset x               # declare local variable.
 ((x = $1 * $2))         # set local variable.
 echo local x = $x
 return $x
}
# main program.
x=1                      # set global variable.
echo global x = $x       # display value of global variable before function call.
f 3 4                    # call function.
result=$?                # save exit code.
echo return value from function was $result
echo global x = $x       # value of global after function.
$ func4.ksh              ...execute the script.
global x = 1
local x = 12
return value from function was 12
global x = 1
$ _
```

Recursion

With careful thought, it's perfectly possible to write recursive functions. Here are two example scripts that implement a recursive version of "factorial ()". The first uses the exit code to return the result, and the second uses standard output to echo the result.

Recursive Factorial Using Exit Code

```
factorial ()                    # one-parameter function
{
 if (($1 <= 1))
 then
    return 1                     # return result in exit code.
 else
    typeset tmp                  # declare two local variables.
    typeset result
    ((tmp = $1 - 1))
    factorial $tmp               # call recursively.
    ((result = $? * $1))
    return $result               # return result in exit code.
 fi
}
# main program.
factorial 5                      # call function
echo factorial 5 = $?            # display exit code.
```

Recursive Factorial Using Standard Output

```
factorial ()                            # one-parameter function
{
 if (($1 <= 1))
 then
    echo 1                              # echo result to standard output.
 else
    typeset tmp                         # declare two local variables.
    typeset result
    ((tmp = $1 - 1))
    ((result = `factorial $tmp` * $1))
    echo $result                        # echo result to standard output.
 fi
}
#
echo factorial 5 = `factorial 5`     # display result.
```

Sharing Functions

To share the source code of a function between several scripts, place it in a separate file and then read it using the "." built-in command at the beginning of the scripts that use the function. In the following example, assume that the source code of one of the previous factorial scripts was saved in a file called "fact.ksh":

```
$ cat func6.ksh                  ...list the script.
. fact.ksh                       # read the source code of the function.
```

```
echo factorial 5 = `factorial 5`    # call the function.
$ func6.ksh                         ...execute the script.
factorial 5 = 120
$ _
```

ENHANCED JOB CONTROL

In addition to the job-control facilities of the Bourne shell, the Korn shell supports the following commands:

Command	Function
jobs	lists your jobs
bg	places a specified job into the background
fg	places a specified job into the foreground
kill	sends an arbitrary signal to a process or job

These facilities are only available on UNIX systems that support job control. The next few sections contain a description of each job-control facility and examples of its use. The job-control features of the Korn shell that are about to be described are identical to those of the C shell.

Jobs

Shell Command: jobs [-l]

jobs displays a list of all of the shell's jobs. When *jobs* used with the **-l** option, process IDs are added to the listing. The syntax of each line of output is

job# [+\−] PID status command
where a "+" means that the job was the last job to be placed into the background and a "-" means that it was the second-to-last job to be placed into the background. *status* may be one of the following:

- Running
- Stopped (suspended)
- Terminated (killed by a signal)
- Done (zero exit code)
- Exit (nonzero exit code)

The only real significance of the "+" and "-" is that they may be used when specifying the job in a later command. (See the section "Specifying a Job.")

Here's an example of *jobs* in action:

```
$ jobs                                  ...no jobs right now.
$ sleep 1000 &                          ...start a background job.
[1] 27128
$ man ls | ul -tdumb > ls.txt &         ...another background job.
[2] 27129
$ jobs -l                               ...list current jobs.
[2] + 27129 Running     man ls | ul -tdumb > ls.txt &
[1] - 27128 Running     sleep 1000 &
$ _
```

Specifying a Job

The *bg, fg,* and *kill* commands that I'm about to describe allow you to specify a job using one of several forms:

Form	Specifies
%*integer*	the job number *integer*
%*prefix*	the job whose name starts with *prefix*
%+	the job that was last referenced
%%	same as "%+"
%−	the job that was referenced second to last

The next set of descriptions contains examples of job specification.

bg

> *Shell Command*: bg [%*job*]
>
> *bg* resumes the specified job as a background process. If no job is specified, the last referenced job is resumed.

In the next example, I started a foreground job and then decided it would be better to run it in the background. I suspended the job using *Control*-Z and then resumed it in the background.

```
$ man ksh | ul -tdumb > ksh.txt          ...start in foreground.
^Z                                       ...suspend it.
[1] + Stopped  man ksh | ul -tdumb > ksh.txt
$ bg %1                                   ...resume it in background.
```

```
[1] man ksh | ul -tdumb > ksh.txt&
$ jobs                                  ...list current jobs.
[1] + Running  man ksh | ul -tdumb > ksh.txt
$ _
```

fg

```
┌─────────────────────────────────────────────────────────────────┐
│                                                                   │
│                                                                   │
│    Shell Command: fg [%job]                                       │
│                                                                   │
│    fg resumes the specified job as the foreground process. If no job is speci-  │
│    fied, the last referenced job is resumed. The value of job may be the job    │
│    number or any unique abbreviation of the command text.                       │
│                                                                   │
└─────────────────────────────────────────────────────────────────┘
```

In the following example, I brought a background job into the foreground using *fg*:

```
$ sleep 1000 &                     ...start a background job.
[1]    27143
$ man ksh | ul -tdumb > ksh.txt &  ...start another background job.
[2]    27144
$ jobs                             ...list the current jobs.
[2] + Running          man ksh | ul -tdumb > ksh.txt &
[1] - Running          sleep 1000 &
$ fg %ma                           ...bring job to foreground.
man ksh | ul -tdumb > ksh.txt      ...command is redisplayed.
$ _
```

kill

```
┌─────────────────────────────────────────────────────────────────┐
│                                                                   │
│                                                                   │
│    Shell Command: kill [-l] [-signal] {process|%job}+             │
│                                                                   │
│    kill sends the specified signal to the specified job or processes. A process │
│    is specified by its PID number. A signal may be specified either by its      │
│    number or symbolically by removing the "SIG" prefix from its symbolic        │
│    constant in "/usr/include/sys/signal.h". To obtain a list of the signal      │
│    names, use the -l option. If no signal is specified, the TERM signal is       │
│    sent. If the TERM or HUP signals are sent to a suspended process, the         │
│    process is sent the CONT signal, which causes it to resume.                   │
│                                                                   │
└─────────────────────────────────────────────────────────────────┘
```

The following example contains a couple of *kill* commands:

```
$ kill -l                                    ...list all kill signals.
1) HUP           12) SYS              23) STOP
2) INT           13) PIPE             24) TSTP
3) QUIT          14) ALRM             25) CONT
4) ILL           15) TERM             26) TTIN
5) TRAP          16) USR1             27) TTOU
6) ABRT          17) USR2             28) VTALRM
7) EMT           18) CHLD             29) PROF
8) FPE           19) PWR              30) XCPU
9) KILL          20) WINCH            31) XFSZ
10) BUS          21) URG
11) SEGV         22) POLL
$ man ksh | ul -tdumb > ksh.txt &        ...start a background job.
[1]   27160
$ kill -9 %1                             ...kill it via a job specifier.
[1] + Killed          man ksh | ul -tdumb > ksh.txt &
$ man ksh | ul -tdumb > ksh.txt &        ...start another background job.
[1]   27164
$ kill -KILL 27164                       ...kill it via a process ID.
[1] + Killed          man ksh | ul -tdumb > ksh.txt &
$ _
```

ENHANCEMENTS

In addition to the new facilities that have already been described, the Korn shell also offers some enhancements to the Bourne shell in the following areas:

- redirection
- pipes
- command substitution
- variable access
- extra built-in commands

This section describes each enhancement.

Redirection

The Korn shell supplies a minor extra redirection facility: the ability to strip leading tabs off of here documents. Here is the augmented syntax for this facility:

---

command <<- word

If *word* is preceded by a "-", then leading tabs are removed from the lines of input that follow. Here's an example:

```
$ cat <<- ENDOFTEXT
>              this input contains
>      some leading tabs
> ^D
this input contains
some leading tabs
$ _
```

This facility allows here-document text in a script to be indented to match the nearby shell commands without affecting how the text is used.

Pipes

The "|&" operator supports a simple form of concurrent processing. When a command is followed by "|&", it runs as a background process whose standard input and output channels are connected to the original parent shell via a two-way pipe. When the original shell generates output using a *print -p* command (discussed later in this chapter), it is sent to the child shell's standard input channel. When the original shell reads input using a *read -p* command (also discussed later in this chapter), it is taken from the child shell's standard output channel. Here's an example of the use of this facility:

```
$ date |&                        ...start child process.
[1] 8311
$ read -p theDate  ...read from standard output of child.
[1] + Done     date |&           ...child process terminates.
$ echo $theDate                  ...display the result.
Sun May 10 21:36:57 CDT 1998
$ _
```

Command Substitution

In addition to the older method of command substitution—surrounding the command with grave accents—the Korn shell also allows you to perform command substitution using the following syntax:

```
$(command)
```

Note that the "$" that immediately precedes the open parentheses is part of the syntax and is *not* a prompt. Here's an example of the use of this form of command substitution:

```
$ echo there are $(who | wc -l) users on the system
there are 6 users on the system
$ _
```

To substitute the contents of a file into a shell command, you may use the command "$(<file)" as a faster form of the command "$(cat file)".

Variables

The Korn shell supports the following additional variable facilities:

- more flexible access methods
- more predefined local variables
- more predefined environment variables
- simple arrays
- a *typeset* command for formatting the output of variables

The next few subsections describe each feature.

Flexible Access Methods   In addition to the variable-access methods supported by the Bourne shell, the Korn shell supports some more complex access methods, as follows:

Syntax	Action
${#name}	Replaced by the length of the value of *name*.
${#name[*]}	Replaced by the number of elements in the array *name*.
${name: + word} ${name: = word} ${name:?word} ${name: + word}	Work like their counterparts that do not contain a ":", except that *name* must be set *and* nonnull instead of just set.
${name#pattern} ${name##pattern}	Remove a leading *pattern* from *name*. The expression is replaced by the value of *name* if *name* doesn't begin with *pattern* and with the remaining suffix if it does. The first form removes the smallest matching pattern, and the second form removes the largest matching pattern.
${name%pattern} ${name%%pattern}	Remove a trailing *pattern* from *name*. The expression is replaced by the value of *name* if *name* doesn't end with *pattern* and with the remaining suffix if it does. The first form removes the smallest matching pattern, and the second form removes the largest matching pattern.

Here are some examples of the use of these features:

```
$ fish='smoked salmon'          ...set a variable.
$ echo ${#fish}                 ...display the length of the value.
13
$ cd dir1                       ...move to directory.
$ echo $PWD                     ...display the current working directory.
/home/glass/dir1
$ echo $HOME
/home/glass
$ echo ${PWD#$HOME/}            ...remove leading $HOME/
```

```
dir1
$ fileName=menu.ksh          ...set a variable.
$ echo ${fileName%.ksh}.bak  ...remove trailing ".ksh" and add ".bak".
menu.bak
$ _
```

Predefined Local Variables In addition to the common predefined local variables, the Korn shell supports the following predefined local variables:

Name	Value
$_	The last parameter of the previous command.
$PPID	The process ID number of the shell's parent.
$PWD	The current working directory of the shell.
$OLDPWD	The previous working directory of the shell.
$RANDOM	A random integer.
$REPLY	Set by a *select* command.
$SECONDS	The number of seconds since the shell was invoked.
$CDPATH	Used by the *cd* command.
$COLUMNS	Sets the width of the edit window for the built-in editors.
$EDITOR	Selects the built-in editor type.
$ENV	Selects the name of the Korn-shell startup file.
$FCEDIT	Defines the editor that is invoked by the *fc* command.
$HISTFILE	The name of the history file.
$HISTSIZE	The number of history lines to remember.
$LINES	Used by *select* to determine how to display the selections.
$MAILCHECK	Tells the shell how many seconds to wait between mail checks. The default value is 600 seconds (10 minutes).
$MAILPATH	This variable should be set to a list of filenames separated by colons. The shell checks these files for modification every $MAILCHECK seconds.
$PS3	The prompt used by the *select* command, "#?" by default.
$TMOUT	If $TMOUT is set to a number greater than zero and more than $TMOUT seconds elapse between commands, the shell terminates.
$VISUAL	Selects the built-in editor type.

Here are some examples of the use of these predefined variables:

```
$ echo hi there    ...display a message to demonstrate $_.
hi there
$ echo $_          ...display the last argument of the previous command.
there
$ echo $PWD        ...display the current working directory.
/home/glass
```

```
$ echo $PPID          ...display the process ID of the shell's parent.
27709
$ cd /                ...move to the root directory.
$ echo $OLDPWD        ...display last working directory.
/home/glass
$ echo $PWD           ...display current working directory.
/
$ echo $RANDOM $RANDOM   ...display two random numbers.
32561 8323
$ echo $SECONDS       ...display the number of seconds since the shell began.
918
$ echo $TMOUT         ...display the timeout value.
0                     ...no timeout selected.
$ _
```

One-Dimensional Arrays   The Korn shell supports simple one-dimensional arrays. To create an array, simply assign a value to a variable name using a subscript between 0 and 511 in brackets. The syntax for this assignment is as follows:

---

name[*subscript*]=*value*

Array elements are created when needed. To access an array element, use the following syntax:

${*name*[*subscript*]}

If you omit *subscript*, the value of 0 is used by default. Here's an example that uses a script to display the squares of the numbers between zero and nine:

```
$ cat squares.ksh                    ...list the script.
i=0
while ((i < 10))
do
((squares[$i] = i * i))   ...assign individual element.
((i = i + 1))              ...increment loop counter.
done
echo 5 squared is ${squares[5]}    ...display one element.
echo list of all squares is ${squares[*]}   ...display all elements.
$ squares.ksh                        ...execute the script.
5 squared is 25
list of all squares is 0 1 4 9 16 25 36 49 64 81
$ _
```

typeset

Shell Command: typeset {- HLRZfilrtux [value] [name [=word]]}*

typeset allows the creation and manipulation of variables. It allows variables to be formatted, converted to an internal integer representation for speedier arithmetic, made read only, made exportable, and switched between lowercase and uppercase.

Every variable has an associated set of flags that determine its properties. For example, if a variable has its "uppercase" flag set, it will always map its contents to uppercase, *even when they are changed.* The options to *typeset* operate by setting and resetting the various flags associated with named variables. When an option is preceded by a "-", it causes the appropriate flag to be turned on. To turn a flag off and reverse the sense of the option, precede the option by a "+" instead of a "-".

The next set of subsections contain a list of the options for *typeset* with illustrations of their usage. I've split the descriptions up into related sections to make the explanations a little easier to follow.

FORMATTING   In all of the formatting options, the field width of *name* is set to *value* if present; otherwise, it is set to the width of *word*.

Option	Meaning
-L	Turn the "L" flag on and turn the "R" flag off. Left justify *word* and remove leading spaces. If the width of *word* is less than the field width of *name*, then pad it with trailing spaces. If the width of *word* is greater than the field width of *name*, then truncate its end to fit. If the "Z" flag is set, leading zeros are also removed.
-R	Turn the "R" flag on and turn the "L" flag off. Right justify *word* and remove trailing spaces. If the width of *word* is less than the field width of *name*, then pad it with leading spaces. If the width of *word* is greater than the field width of *name*, then truncate its end to fit.
-Z	Right justify *word* and pad it with zeros if the first character that is not a space is a digit and the "L" flag is off.

CASE

Option	Meaning
-l	Turn the "l" flag on and turn the "u" flag off. Convert *word* to lowercase.
-u	Turn the "u" flag on and turn the "l" flag off. Convert *word* to uppercase.

Here's an example of a script that left justifies all of the elements in an array and then displays them in uppercase:

```
$ cat justify.ksh        ...list the script.
wordList[0]='jeff'       # set three elements.
wordList[1]='john'
wordList[2]='ellen'
typeset -uL7 wordList    # typeset all elements in array.
echo ${wordList[*]}      # beware! shell removes nonquoted spaces.
echo "${wordList[*]}"    # preserve spacing.
$ justify.ksh            ...execute the script.
JEFF JOHN ELLEN
JEFF    JOHN    ELLEN
$ _
```

TYPE

Option	Meaning
-i	Store *name* internally as an integer for arithmetic speed. Set the output base to *value* if specified; otherwise, use the base of *word*.
-r	Flag the named variables as read only.
-x	Flag the named variables as exportable.

In the following example, I modified a previous example by declaring the array of the squares of numbers to be an array of integers, making the script run faster:

```
$ cat squares.ksh        ...list the script.
typeset -i squares       # declare array as integers (for speed).
i=0
while ((i < 10))
do
 ((squares[$i] = i * i))
 ((i = i + 1))
done
echo 5 squared is ${squares[5]}
echo list of all squares is ${squares[*]}
$ squares.ksh            ...execute the script.
5 squared is 25
list of all squares is 0 1 4 9 16 25 36 49 64 81
$ _
```

MISCELLANEOUS

Option	Meaning
-f	The only flags that are allowed in conjunction with this option are "t", which sets the trace option for the named functions, and "x", which displays all functions with the "x" attribute set.
-t	Tags name with the token *word*.

In the following example, I selected the function "factorial ()" to be traced using the "f" and "t" options and then ran the script:

```
$ cat func5.ksh          ...list the script.
factorial ()             # one-parameter function.
{
  if (($1 <= 1))
  then
    return 1
  else
    typeset tmp
    typeset result
    ((tmp = $1 - 1))
    factorial $tmp
    ((result = $? * $1))
    return $result
    fi
}
#
typeset -ft factorial    ...select a function trace.
factorial 3
echo factorial 3 = $?
$ func5.ksh              ...execute the script.
+ let 3 <= 1            ...debugging information.
+ typeset tmp
+ typeset result
+ let  tmp = 3 - 1
+ factorial 2
+ let  2 <= 1
+ typeset tmp
+ typeset result
+ let  tmp = 2 - 1
+ factorial 1
+ let  1 <= 1
+ return 1
+ let  result = 1 * 2
+ return 2
+ let  result = 2 * 3
+ return 6
factorial 3 = 6
$ _
```

TYPESET WITH NO NAMED VARIABLES. If no variables are named, then the names of all of the parameters that have the specified flags set are listed. If no flags are specified, then a list of all of the parameters and their flag settings are listed. Here's an example of these options (note that parts of the listings are omitted due to space considerations):

```
$ typeset       ...display a list of all typeset variables.
export NODEID
export PATH
...
```

```
leftjust 7 t
export integer MAILCHECK
$ typeset -i   ...display list of integer typeset variables.
LINENO=1
MAILCHECK=60
...
$ _
```

Built-In Commands

The Korn shell enhances the following built-in commands:

- *cd*
- *set*
- *print* (an enhancement of the Bourne-shell *echo* command)
- *read*
- *test*
- *trap*

The next few subsections contain a description of each built-in command:

cd   The Korn-shell's version of *cd* supports several new features and works like this:

Shell Command: cd {name}
             cd oldName newName

The first form of the *cd* command is processed as follows:

- If *name* is omitted, the shell moves to the home directory specified by $HOME.
- If *name* is equal to "-", the shell moves to the previous working directory that is kept in $OLDPWD.
- If *name* begins with a slash (/), the shell moves to the directory whose full name is *name*.
- If *name* begins with anything else, the shell searches through the directory sequence specified by $CDPATH for a match and moves the shell to the matching directory. The default value of $CDPATH is null, which causes *cd* to search only the current directory.

If the second form of *cd* is used, the shell replaces the first occurrence of the token *oldName* by the token *newName* in the current directory's full pathname and then attempts to change to the new pathname. The shell always stores the full pathname of the current directory in the variable $PWD. The current value of $PWD may be displayed by using the built-in command *pwd*.

Here's an example of *cd* in action:

```
$ CDPATH=.:/usr   ...set my CDPATH.
$ cd dir1         ...move to "dir1", located under ".".
$ pwd
/home/glass/dir1
$ cd include      ...move to "include", located in "/usr".
$ pwd             ...display the current working directory.
/usr/include
$ cd -            ...move to my previous directory.
$ pwd             ...display the current working directory.
/home/glass/dir1
$ _
```

set   The *set* command allows you to set and unset flags that control shell-wide characteristics:

Shell Command: *set* [+-aefhkmnpstuvx] [+-o *option*] {*arg*} *

The Korn-shell version of *set* supports all of the *set* features of the Bourne shell, plus a few more. The various features of *set* do not fall naturally into categories, so I have just listed each one together with a brief description in the table below. An option preceded by a "+" instead of a "-" reverses the sense of the description.

Here is a list of some of the options of *set*:

Option	Meaning
a	All variables that are created are automatically flagged for export.
f	Disable filename substitution.
h	All non-built-in commands are automatically flagged as tracked aliases.
m	Place all background jobs in their own unique process group and display notification of completion. This flag is automatically set for interactive shells.
n	Accept, but do not execute, commands. This flag has no effect on interactive shells.
o	This option is described separately below.
p	Set $PATH to its default value, cause the startup sequence to ignore the "$HOME/.profile" file, and read "/etc/suid_profile" instead of the "$ENV" file. This flag is set automatically whenever a shell is executed by a process in "set user ID" or "set group ID" mode. For more information on "set user ID" processes, consult Chapter 12.
s	Sort the positional parameters.
--	Do not change any flags. If no arguments follow, all of the positional parameters are unset.

THE "O" OPTION   The "o" option of *set* takes an argument. The argument frequently has the same effect as one of the other flags of *set*. If no argument is supplied, the current settings are displayed. Here is a list of the valid arguments and their meanings:

Option	Meaning
allexport	Equivalent to the "a" flag.
bgnice	Background processes are executed at a lower priority.
emacs	Invokes the built-in **emacs** editor.
errexit	Equivalent to the "e" flag.
gmacs	Invokes the built-in **gmacs** editor.
ignoreeof	Don't exit on *Control*-D. *exit* must be used instead.
keyword	Equivalent to the "k" flag.
markdirs	Append trailing "/" to directories generated by filename substitution.
monitor	Equivalent to the "m" flag.
noclobber	Prevents redirection from truncating existing files.
noexec	Equivalent to the "n" flag.
noglob	Equivalent to the "f" flag.
nolog	Do not save function definitions in history file.
nounset	Equivalent to the "u" flag.
privileged	Equivalent to the "p" flag.
verbose	Equivalent to the "v" flag.
trackall	Equivalent to the "h" flag.
vi	Invokes the built-in **vi** editor.
viraw	Characters are processed as they are typed in **vi** mode.
xtrace	Equivalent to the "x" flag.

I set the "ignoreeof" option in my ".profile" script to protect myself against accidental *Control*-D logouts:

```
$ set -o ignoreeof
$ _
```

print   The *print* command is a more sophisticated version of *echo* and allows you to send output to an arbitrary file descriptor. It works like this:

Shell Command: print -npsuR [*n*] {*arg*}*

By default, *print* displays its arguments to standard output, followed by a new line. The **-n** option inhibits the new line, and the **-u** option allows you to specify a single-digit file descriptor *n* for the output channel. The

-s option causes the output to be appended to the history file instead of an output channel. The -p option causes the output to be sent to the shell's two-way pipe channel. The -R option causes all further words to be interpreted as arguments.

Here's an example of the use of the *print* command:

```
121 $ print -u2 hi there        ...send output to the standard error channel.
hi there
122 $ print -s echo hi there    ...append to history.
124 $ r 123                     ...recall command #123.
echo hi there
hi there
125 $ print -R -s hi there      ...treat "-s" as an argument.
-s hi there
126 $ _
```

read The Korn shell's *read* command is a superset of the Bourne shell's *read* command and works like this:

Shell Command: read -prsu [n] [name?prompt] {name}*

The Korn shell's *read* works just like the Bourne shell's *read*, except for the following new features:

- The -p option causes the input line to be read from the shell's two-way pipe.
- The -u option causes the file descriptor *n* to be used for input.

If the first argument contains a "?", the remainder of the argument is used as a prompt.

Here's an example of the use of the *read* command:

```
$ read 'name?enter your name '
enter your name Graham
$ echo $name
Graham
$ _
```

test The Korn shell's version of *test* accepts several new operators:

Operator	Meaning
-L *fileName*	Return true if *fileName* is a symbolic link.
file1 -nt *file2*	Return true if *file1* is newer than *file2*.
file1 -ot *file2*	Return true if *file1* is older than *file2*.
file1 -ef *file2*	Return true if *file1* is the same file as *file2*.

The Korn shell also supports a more convenient syntax for *test*:

[[*testExpression*]]

is equivalent to

test textExpression

I prefer the more modern form of *test*—the one that uses the double brackets—as it allows me to write more readable programs. Here's an example of this newer form of *test* in action:

```
$ cat test.ksh          ...list the script.
i=1
while [[i -le 4]]
do
echo $i
((i = i + 1))
done
$ test.ksh              ...execute the script.
1
2
3
4
$ _
```

trap   The Korn shell's *trap* command is a superset of the Bourne shell's *trap* command and works as follows:

Shell Command: trap [command] [signal]

The Korn shell's *trap* command works just like the Bourne shell's *trap* command, except for the following features:

- If the argument is "-", then all of the specified signal actions are reset to their initial values.
- If an EXIT or zero signal value is given to a *trap* inside a function, then *command* is executed when the function is exited.

In the following example, I set the EXIT trap inside a function to demonstrate local function traps:

```
$ cat trap.ksh                    ...list the script.
f ()
{
echo 'enter f ()'
trap 'echo leaving f...' EXIT    # set a local trap.
echo 'exit f ()'
}
# main program.
trap 'echo exit shell' EXIT      # set a global trap.
f                                # invoke the function "f ()".
$ trap.ksh                        ...execute the script.
enter f ()
exit f ()
leaving f...                     ...local EXIT is trapped.
exit shell                       ...global EXIT is trapped.
$ _
```

SAMPLE PROJECT: JUNK

To illustrate some of the Korn shell's capabilities, I now present a Korn-shell version of the "junk" script project that was suggested at the end of the chapter on the Bourne shell. Here's the definition of the **junk** utility about to be described using the Korn shell:

Utility: **junk** -lp {*fileName*}*

junk is a replacement for the **rm** utility. Rather than removing files, it moves them into the subdirectory ".junk" in your home directory. If ".junk" doesn't exist, it is automatically created. The **-l** option lists the current contents of the ".junk" directory, and the **-p** option purges ".junk".

The Korn-shell script that is listed below uses a function to process error messages and uses an array to store filenames. The rest of the functionality should be pretty easy to follow from the embedded comments.

junk

```ksh
#! /bin/ksh
# junk script
# Korn-shell version
# author: Graham Glass
# 9/25/91
#
# Initialize variables
#
fileCount=0        # the number of files specified.
listFlag=0         # 1 if list option (-l) is used.
purgeFlag=0        # 1 if purge option (-p) is used.
fileFlag=0         # 1 if at least one file is specified.
junk=~/.junk       # the name of the junk directory.
#
error ()
{
#
# Display error message and quit.
#
cat << ENDOFTEXT
Dear $USER, the usage of junk is as follows:
  junk -p means "purge all files"
  junk -l means "list junked files"
  junk <list of files> to junk them
ENDOFTEXT
exit 1
}
#
# Parse command line.
#
for arg in $*
do
  case $arg in
    "-p")
      purgeFlag=1
      ;;
    "-l")
      listFlag=1
      ;;
    -*)
      echo $arg is an illegal option
      ;;
    *)
      fileFlag=1
      fileList[$fileCount]=$arg # append to list.
```

```
        let fileCount=fileCount+1
        ;;
    esac
done
#
# Check for too many options.
#
let total=$listFlag+$purgeFlag+$fileFlag
if (( total != 1 ))
then
 error
fi
#
# If junk directory doesn't exist, create it.
#
if [[ ! (-d $junk)]]
then
 'mkdir' $junk                    # quoted just in case it's aliased.
fi
#
# Process options.
#
if (( listFlag == 1 ))
then
 'ls' -lgF $junk                  # list junk directory.
 exit 0
fi
#
if (( purgeFlag == 1 ))
then
 'rm' $junk/*                     # remove files in junk directory.
 exit 0
fi
#
if ((fileFlag == 1))
then
 'mv' ${fileList[*]} $junk    # move files to junk directory.
 exit 0
fi
#
exit 0
```

Here's some sample output from **junk**:

```
$ ls *.ksh                      ...list some files to junk.
fact.ksh* func5.ksh*            test.ksh* trap.ksh*
func4.ksh* squares.ksh*         track.ksh*
$ junk func5.ksh func4.ksh      ...junk a couple of files.
$ junk -l                       ...list my junk.
total 2
-rwxr-xr-x 1 gglass apollocl  205 Feb 6 22:44 func4.ksh*
```

```
-rwxr-xr-x 1 gglass apollocl  274 Feb 7 21:02 func5.ksh*
$ junk -p                     ...purge my junk.
$ junk -z                     ...try a nonexistent option.
-z is an illegal option
Dear glass, the usage of junk is as follows:
  junk -p means "purge all files"
  junk -l means "list junked files"
  junk <list of files> to junk them
$ _
```

THE RESTRICTED SHELL

There is a variation of the Korn shell called the *restricted Korn shell* that provides every Korn-shell feature except for the following:

- You may not change directory.
- You may not redirect output using ">" or ">>".
- You may not set the $SHELL, $ENV, or $PATH environment variables.
- You may not use absolute pathnames.

These restrictions only become active *after* the shell's ".profile" and "$ENV" files have been executed. Any scripts executed by the restricted Korn shell are interpreted by their associated shell and are not restricted in any way.

The restricted Korn shell is a regular C program whose executable file is stored as "/bin/rksh". If your chosen shell is "/bin/rksh", an interactive restricted Korn shell is invoked automatically when you log into UNIX. You may also invoke a restricted Korn shell manually from a script or from a terminal by using the command "rksh".

System administrators use the restricted Korn shell to provide users with limited access to UNIX features as follows:

- They write a series of regular Korn-shell scripts that provide access to the features that the particular restricted user wishes to use.
- They place these scripts into a read-only directory, typically called something like "/usr/local/rbin".
- They set up the restricted user's ".profile" file so that $PATH contains only "/usr/local/rbin" and a few other select directories.
- They change the user's entry in the password file (discussed in Chapter 14) so that the user's login shell is "/bin/rksh".

COMMAND-LINE OPTIONS

If the first command-line argument is a "-", the Korn shell is started as a login shell. In addition to this feature, the Korn shell supports the Bourne-shell command-line options, the flags of the built-in *set* command (including "-x" and "-v"), and the following:

Option	Meaning
-r	Make the Korn shell a restricted Korn shell.
fileName	Execute the shell commands in *fileName* if the "-s" option is not used. *fileName* is "$0" within the *fileName* script.

CHAPTER REVIEW

Checklist

In this chapter, I described:

- the creation of a Korn-shell start-up file
- aliases and the history mechanism
- the built-in **vi** and **emacs** line editors
- arithmetic
- functions
- advanced job control
- several enhancements of inherited Bourne-shell commands

Quiz

1. Who wrote the Korn shell?
2. Why is the alias mechanism useful?
3. How can you reedit and reexecute previous commands?
4. Does the Korn shell support recursive functions?
5. Describe the modern syntax of the *test* command.

Exercises

1. Rewrite the **junk** script of this chapter to be menu driven. Use the *select* command. [level: *easy*]
2. Write a function called "dateToDays" that takes three parameters—a month string, such as "Sep"; a day number, such as 18; and a year number, such as 1962—and returns the number of days from January 1, 1900 to the entered date. [level: *medium*]
3. Write a set of functions that emulate the directory stack facilities of the C shell (described in the next chapter). Use environment variables to hold the stack and its size. [level: *medium*]
4. Build a script called "pulse" that takes two parameters: the name of a script and an integer. "pulse" should execute the specified script for the specified number of seconds, suspend it for the same number of seconds, and continue this cycle until the specified script is finished.

Projects

1. Write an alias-manager script that allows you to choose DOS emulation, VMS emulation, or none. [level: *medium*]

2. Write a script that allows system-administration tasks to be performed automatically from a menu-driven interface. Useful tasks to automate include:

- automatic deletion of core files
- automatic warnings to users that use a lot of CPU time or disk space
- automatic archiving

[level: *hard*]

C H A P T E R   6

The C Shell

Motivation

The C shell was written after the Bourne shell and adheres more closely to the syntax and control structures of the C language. The C shell was the first shell to support advanced job control and became a favorite of early UNIX developers. Many C-shell users are changing over to the Korn shell due to the Korn shell's more powerful command editor, but the C shell still remains popular.

Prerequisites

You should already have read Chapter 3 and experimented with some of the core-shell facilities.

Objectives

In this chapter, I explain and demonstrate the facilities specific to the C shell.

Presentation

The information in this section is presented in the form of several sample UNIX sessions and a small project.

Shell Commands

This section introduces the following shell commands, listed in alphabetical order:

alias	nice	source
chdir	nohup	stop
dirs	notify	suspend
foreach..end	onintr	switch..case..endsw
glob	popd	unalias
goto	pushd	unhash
hashstat	rehash	unset

history	repeat	unsetenv
if..then..else..endif	set	while..end
logout	setenv	

INTRODUCTION

The C shell supports all of the core shell facilities described in Chapter 3, plus the following new features:

- several ways to set and access variables
- a built-in programming language that supports conditional branching, looping, and interrupt handling
- command customization using aliases
- access to previous commands via a history mechanism
- advanced job control
- several new built-in commands and several enhancements to existing commands

These new facilities are described in this chapter and are illustrated by the following hierarchy diagram:

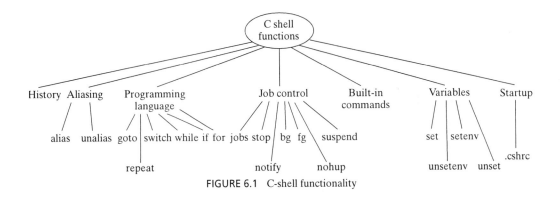

FIGURE 6.1   C-shell functionality

START-UP

The C shell is a regular C program whose executable file is stored as "/bin/csh". If your chosen shell is "/bin/csh", an interactive C shell is invoked automatically when you log into UNIX. You may also invoke a C shell manually from a script or from a terminal by using the command "csh". "csh" has several command-line options that are described at the end of this chapter.

When a C shell is started as a login shell, a global login initialization file which applies to all users may also be executed, if present. This file is useful for setting up environment variables (such as $PATH) to contain information about the local environment. The name of this file varies from one version of UNIX to another, but it is generally something like "/.login" or "/etc/login".

When a C shell is invoked, the startup sequence is different for login shells and nonlogin shells:

Step	Shell Type	Action
1	both	Execute commands in "$HOME/.cshrc" if it exists.
2	login only	Execute commands in global login initialization file if it exists.
3	login only	Execute commands in "$HOME/.login" if it exists.

Note that the ".cshrc" file is run before either type of login initialization file. This aspect may seem counterintuitive and has been the cause of much unexpected behavior when users are crafting their initialization files. The way to keep this situation straight is to remember that the C shell always runs its own initialization file immediately upon starting and then determines if the shell is a login shell that would require running the other initialization files.

Once an interactive shell finishes running all of the appropriate initialization files, it displays its prompt and awaits user commands. The standard C-shell prompt is "%", although it may be changed by setting the local variable $prompt, described shortly.

The ".login" file typically contains commands that set environment variables such as $TERM, which contains the type of your terminal, and $PATH, which tells the shell where to search for executable files. Put commands in your ".login" file that only need to be set once (e.g., environment variables whose values are inherited by other shells) or that only make sense for an interactive session (like specifying terminal settings). Here's an example of a ".login" file:

```
echo -n "Enter your terminal type (default is vt100): "
set termtype = $<
set term = vt100
if ("$termtype" != "") set term = "$termtype"
unset termtype
set path=(. /bin /usr/bin /usr/local/bin )
stty erase "^?" kill "^U" intr "^C" eof "^D" crt crterase
set cdpath = (~)
set history = 40
set notify
set prompt = "! % "
set savehist = 32
```

The ".cshrc" file generally contains commands that set common aliases (discussed later) or anything else that applies only to the current shell. The "rc" suffix of ".cshrc" stands for "run commands." Here's an example of a ".cshrc" file:

```
alias emacs /usr/local/emacs
alias h history
alias ll ls -l
alias print prf -pr pbl-2236-lp3
```

```
alias ls ls -F
alias rm rm -i
alias t more
```

VARIABLES

The C shell supports local and environment variables. A local variable may hold either one value, in which case it's called a *simple* variable, or more than one value, in which case it's termed a *list*. This section describes the C-shell facilities that support variables.

Creating/Assigning Simple Variables

To assign a value to a simple variable, use the built-in *set* command as follows:

---

set {name [=word]}*

If no arguments are supplied, a list of all of the local variables is displayed. If *word* is not supplied, *name* is set to a null string. If the variable *name* doesn't exist, it is implicitly created. Here are some examples of the use of the *set* command:

```
% set flag                  ...set "flag" to a null string.
% echo $flag                ...nothing is printed, as it's null.

% set color = red           ...set the variable "color" to the string "red".
% echo $color
red
% set name = Graham Glass   ...Beware! You must use quotes to include the part
                            ...of the string after the space.
% echo $name                ...only the first string was assigned.
Graham
% set name = "Graham Glass"  ...now it will work as expected.
% echo $name
Graham Glass
% set                       ...display a list of all local variables.
argv           ()
cdpath         /home/glass
color          red
cwd            /home/glass
flag
...edited out for space considerations.
name           Graham Glass
term           vt100
user           glass
% _
```

Accessing a Simple Variable

In addition to the simple syntax for accessing a variable (*name*), the C shell supports the following complex access methods:

Syntax	Action
${*name*}	Replaced by the value of *name*. This form is useful if the expression is immediately followed by an alphanumeric expression that would otherwise be interpreted as part of the variable's name.
${?*name*}	Replaced by 1 if *name* is set and 0 otherwise.

Here are some examples that illustrate these access methods. In the first example, I used braces to append a string to the value of a variable:

```
% set verb = sing
% echo I like $verbing
verbing: Undefined variable.
% echo I like ${verb}ing
I like singing
% _
```

In the following example, I used a variable as a simple flag in a conditional expression:

```
% cat flag.csh          ...list the script.
#
set flag                ...set "flag" to a null string.
if (${?flag}) then      ...branch if "flag" is set.
echo flag is set
endif
% flag.csh              ...execute the script.
flag is set
% _
```

Creating/Assigning List Variables

To assign a list of values to a variable, use the built-in *set* command with the following syntax:

set {name = ({ word}) }*

If the named variable doesn't exist, it is implicitly created. The named variable is assigned to a copy of the specified list of words. Here's an example of the use of this feature:

```
% set colors = ( red yellow green )      ...set to a list.
% echo $colors                           ...display entire list.
red yellow green
% _
```

Accessing a List Variable

The C shell supports a couple of ways to access a list variable. Both of these methods have two forms, the second of which is surrounded by braces. The second form is useful if the expression is immediately followed by an alphanumeric expression that would otherwise be interpreted as part of the variable's name. Here is a description of the access methods:

Syntax	Action
$name[selector] ${name[selector]}	Both forms are replaced by the element of *name* whose index is specified by the value of *selector*. *selector* may be either a single number, a range of numbers in the format *start-end*, or an asterisk (*). If *start* is omitted, the index of the first element is assumed. If *end* is omitted, the index of the last element is assumed. If an asterisk (*) is supplied, then all of the elements are selected. The first element of a list has an index of 1.
$#name ${#name}	Both forms are replaced by the number of elements in *name*.

Here are some examples of the use of these access methods:

```
% set colors = ( red yellow green )   ...set to a list.
% echo $colors[1]                     ...display first element.
red
% echo $colors[2-3]                   ...display second and third elements.
yellow green
% echo $colors[4]                     ...illegal selector.
Subscript out of range.
% echo $#colors                       ...display size of list.
3
% _
```

Building Lists

To add an element onto the end of a list, set the original list equal to itself plus the new element and surround both the list and the item together by parentheses; if you try to assign the new element directly, you'll get an error message. The following example illustrates some list manipulations:

```
% set colors = ( red yellow green )   ...set to a list.
% set colors[4] = pink                ...try to set the fourth element.
Subscript out of range.
% set colors = ( $colors blue )       ...add to the list.
% echo $colors                        ...it works!
```

```
red yellow green blue
% set colors[4] = pink              ...OK to do, since the fourth element already
                                    ...exists.
% echo $colors                      ...the original fourth element has been
                                    ...replaced.
red yellow green pink
% set colors = $colors black        ...don't forget to use parentheses.
% echo $colors                      ...only the first element was set because
                                    ...there were no parentheses.
red
$ set girls = ( sally georgia )     ...build one list.
$ set boys = ( harry blair )        ...build another list.
$ set both = ( $girls $boys )       ...add the lists.
$ echo $both                        ...display the result.
sally georgia harry blair
% _
```

Predefined Local Variables

In addition to the common predefined local variables, the C shell defines the following local variables:

Name	Value
$?0	1 if the shell is executing commands from a named file and 0 otherwise.
$<	The next line of standard input, fully quoted.
$argv	A list that contains all of the positional parameters; $argv[1] is equal to $1.
$cdpath	The list of alternative directories that *chdir* uses for searching purposes.
$cwd	The current working directory.
$echo	Set if the "-x" command-line option is active.
$histchars	May be used to override the default history metacharacters. The first character is used in place of "!" for history substitutions, and the second character is used in place of "^" for quick command reexecution.
$history	The size of the history list.
$home	The shell's home directory.
$ignoreeof	Prevents the shell from terminating when *Control*-D is pressed.
$mail	A list of the files to check for mail. By default, the shell checks for mail every 600 seconds (10 minutes). If the first word of $mail is a number, the shell uses this value instead.
$noclobber	Prevents existing files from being overridden by ">", and nonexistent files from being appended to by ">>".
$noglob	Prevents wildcard expansion.
$nonomatch	Prevents an error from occurring if no files match a wildcard filename.
$notify	By default, the shell notifies you of changes in job status just before a new prompt is displayed. If $notify is set, the status change is displayed immediately when it occurs.
$path	Used by the shell for locating executable files.

Name	Value
$prompt	The shell prompt.
$savehist	The number of commands to save in the history file.
$shell	The full pathname of the login shell.
$status	The exit code of the last command.
$time	If this variable is set, any process that takes more than this number of seconds will cause a message to be displayed that indicates process statistics.
$verbose	Set if the "-v" command-line option is used.

Here's a small shell script that uses the "$<" variable to obtain a user response:

```
% cat var5.csh                              ...list the script.
#
echo -n "please enter your name: "
set name = $<                               # take a line of input.
echo hi $name, your current directory is $cwd
% var5.csh                                  ...execute the script.
please enter your name: Graham
hi Graham, your current directory is /home/glass
% _
```

Creating/Assigning Environment Variables

To assign a value to an environment variable, use the built-in command *setenv* as follows:

setenv name word

If the named variable doesn't exist, it is implicitly created; otherwise, its current value is overwritten. Note that environment variables always hold exactly one value; there is no such thing as an environment list. Here's an example of the use of *setenv*:

```
% setenv TERM vt52        ...set my terminal type.
% echo $TERM              ...confirm.
vt52
% _
```

Predefined Environment Variables

In addition to the common predefined environment variables, the C shell supports the following predefined environment variable:

Name	Value
$LOGNAME	the shell owner's user ID

EXPRESSIONS

The C shell supports string, arithmetic, and file-oriented expressions. Let's take a look at each kind of expression.

String Expressions

The C shell supports the following string operators:

Operator	Meaning
==	Return true if the string operands are exactly equal.
!=	Return true if the string operands are unequal.
=~	Like "==", except that the right operand may contain wildcards.
!~	Like "!=", except that the right operand may contain wildcards.

If either operand is a list, then the first element of the list is used for the comparison. The script in the following example uses the string-matching technique to infer a user's response:

```
% cat expr1.csh                    ...list the script.
#
echo -n "do you like the C shell? "  # prompt.
set reply = $<                       # get a line of input.
if ($reply == "yes") then            # check for exact match.
echo you entered yes
else if ($reply =~ y*) then          # check for inexact match.
echo I assume you mean yes
endif
% expr1.csh                          ...execute the script.
do you like the C shell? yeah
I assume you mean yes
% _
```

Arithmetic Expressions

The C shell supports the following arithmetic operators, listed in descending order of precedence with their respective meanings:

Operator(s)	Meaning
−	unary minus
!	logical negation
*, /, %	multiplication, division, remainder
+, −	addition, subtraction
<<, >>	bitwise left shift, bitwise right shift
<=, >=, < >	relational operators
==, !=	equality, inequality
&, ^, |	bitwise "and", bitwise "xor", bitwise "or"
|, &&	logical "or", logical "and"

These operators work just like their standard counterparts in C, except that they can operate only on integers. Expressions may be surrounded by parentheses in order to control the order of evaluation. When an arithmetic expression is evaluated, a null string is equivalent to zero. Any expression that uses the "&", "&&", "‖", "‖", "<", ">", "<<", or ">>" operators must be surrounded by parentheses to prevent the shell from interpreting these characters specially. Here's a sample script that uses a couple of operators:

```
% cat expr3.csh                    ...list the script.
#
set a = 3
set b = 5
if ($a > 2 && $b > 4) then
 echo expression evaluation seems to work
endif
% expr3.csh                        ...execute the script.
expression evaluation seems to work
% _
```

To assign the result of an expression to a variable, you may not use the *set* command. Instead, use the built-in "@" command, which has the following forms, where *op* is "=", "+=", "−=", "*=", or "/=". Here are some examples of the use of the "@" command:

@	List all of the shell variables.
@ variable op expression	Set *variable* to *expression*.
@ variable[index] op expression	Set *index*th element of *variable* to *expression*.

```
% set a = 2 * 2                    ...you can't use set for assignment.
set: Syntax error.
% @ a = 2 * 2                      ...use "@" instead.
```

```
% echo $a
4
% @ a = $a + $a          ...add two variables.
% echo $a
8
% set flag = 1
% @ b = ($a && $flag)    ...need parentheses because of "&&".
% echo $b
1
% _
```

You may also increment or decrement a variable by using "++" or "−−". For example:

```
% set value = 1
% @ value ++
% echo $value
2
% _
```

File-Oriented Expressions

To make file-oriented decisions a little easier to program, the C shell supports several file-specific expressions. Each expression is of the form

-option fileName

where 1 (true) is returned if the selected option is true and 0 (false) is returned otherwise. If *fileName* does not exist or is inaccessible, all options return 0. Here is a description of each option:

Option	Meaning
r	Shell has read permission for *fileName*.
w	Shell has write permission for *fileName*.
x	Shell has execute permission for *fileName*.
e	*fileName* exists.
o	*fileName* is owned by the same user as that of the shell process.
z	*fileName* exists and is zero bytes in size.
f	*fileName* is a regular file (not a directory or special file).
d	*fileName* is a directory file (not a regular or special file).

Here's an example script that uses the "-w" option to determine whether a file is writeable or not:

```
% cat expr4.csh      ...list the script.
#
echo -n "enter the name of the file you wish to erase: "
set filename = $<  # get a line of input.
if (! (-w "$filename")) then # check that I have access.
echo you do not have permission to erase that file.
else
rm $filename
echo file erased
endif
% expr4.csh          ...execute the script.
enter the name of the file you wish to erase: /
you do not have permission to erase that file.
% _
```

FILENAME COMPLETION

Like the Korn shell, most C shells provide a way for you to avoid typing a long filename on a command line. (This feature was introduced during the evolution of the C shell, so older versions may not provide this functionality.)

To turn on the filename-completion function, you need to set the "filec" variable:

```
% set filec
```

Now, whenever you type part of a filename, you can press the *Escape* key and if the part of the filename you have typed so far uniquely identifies a file, the rest of the name will be added automatically. If the text does not uniquely identify a file, no text will be modified and you may hear a beep or tone. You can also type an asterisk (*) to see a list of the filenames that currently match the part of the name you have typed. For example:

```
% ls -al .log*         ...I pressed the Escape key; nothing, so I typed an
                       ...asterisk (*).
.login    .logout
% ls -al .login        ...shell retyped; I added "i" and pressed
                       ...the Escape key, and the "n" was added automatically.
```

ALIASES

The C shell allows you to create and customize your own commands by using the built-in command *alias*, which works like this:

Shell Command: alias [*word* [*string*]]

alias supports a simple form of command-line customization. If you alias *word* to be equal to *string* and then later enter a command beginning with *word*, the first occurrence of *word* is replaced by *string* and then the command is reprocessed.

If you don't supply *word* or *string*, a list of all of the aliases of the current shell is displayed. If you only supply *word*, then the string currently associated with the alias *word* is displayed. If you supply both *word* and *string,* the shell adds the specified alias to its collection of aliases. If an alias already exists for *word*, it is replaced with the new value.

If the replacement string begins with *word*, it is not reprocessed for aliases in order to prevent infinite loops. If the replacement string contains *word* elsewhere (as a command), an error message is displayed when the alias is executed.

Here's an example of *alias* in action:

```
% alias dir 'ls -aF'          ...register an alias.
% dir                         ...same as typing "ls -aF".
./      main2.c      p.reverse.c        reverse.h
../      main2.o      palindrome.c      reverse.old
% dir *.c                     ...same as typing "ls -aF *.c".
main2.c      p.reverse.c      palindrome.c
% alias dir                   ...look at the value associated with "dir".
ls -aF
% _
```

In the following example, I aliased a word in terms of itself:

```
% alias ls "ls -aF'          ...define "ls" in terms of itself.
% ls *.c                      ...same as typing "ls -aF *.c".
main2.c      p.reverse.c      palindrome.c
% alias dir 'ls'              ...define "dir" in terms of "ls".
% dir                         ...same as typing "ls -aF".
./          main2.c      p.reverse.c        reverse.h
../          main2.o      palindrome.c      reverse.old
% alias who 'date; who'       ...infinite-loop problem.
% who
Alias loop.
% alias who 'date; /bin/who'  ...full path avoids error.
% who                         ...works fine now.
Fri Feb 13 23:33:37 CST 1998
glass              ttyp0        Feb 13 23:30    (xyplex2)
% _
```

Removing an Alias

To remove an alias, use the built-in command *unalias*, which works as follows:

Shell Command: *unalias pattern*

unalias removes all of the aliases that match *pattern*. If *pattern* is an asterisk (*), then all aliases are removed.

Useful Aliases

Here's a list of the useful aliases that I keep in my ".cshrc" file, together with a brief description of each:

Alias	Value
cd	cd \!*; set prompt = "$cwd \! > "; ls This alias changes your prompt to contain both the current working directory and the latest command number. (See the history section for more details.)
ls	ls -F This alias causes "ls" to include extra file information.
rm	rm -i This alias causes "rm" to ask for confirmation.
rm	mv \!* ~/tomb This alias causes "rm" to move files into a special "tomb" directory instead of removing them.
h	history This alias allows you to obtain history information by typing just one letter.
vi	(mesg n; /bin/vi \!*; mesg y) This alias stops people from sending you messages while you're in the vi editor.
mroe	more This alias corrects a common spelling error.
ls-l	ls -l This alias corrects a common spelling error.
ll	ls -l This alias allows you to obtain a long directory listing more conveniently.

Sharing Aliases

To make an alias available to a subshell, place its definition in the shell's ".cshrc" file.

Parameterized Aliases

An alias may refer to arguments in the original prealiased command by using the history mechanism that is described in the next section. The prealiased command is treated as if it were the previous command. The useful alias for *cd* that I mentioned in the previous section makes good use of this facility; the "\!*" part of the alias is replaced by all of the arguments in the prealiased command. The "!" is preceded by a "\" to inhibit its special meaning during the assignment of the alias:

```
alias cd 'cd \!*; set prompt = "$cwd \! > "; ls'
```

HISTORY

The C shell keeps a record of the commands that you enter from the keyboard so that they may be edited and reexecuted at a later stage. This facility is sometimes known as a *history mechanism*. The "!" metacharacter gives you access to history.

Numbered Commands

When you're using history, it's very handy to arrange for your prompt to contain the "number" of the command that you're about to enter. To do so, insert the "\!" character sequence into your prompt:

```
% set prompt = '\! % '    ...include event number in prompt.
1 % echo Genesis          ...this command is event #1.
Genesis
2 % _                     ...the next command will be event #2.
```

Storage of Commands

The C shell records the last $history commands during a particular session. If $history is not set, a default value of 1 is used. If you want these commands to be accessible from the next session, set the $savehist variable. If you do so, the last $savehist commands are maintained in the file specified by the $HISTFILE variable (usually defaults to "$HOME/.history", but may vary with versions of UNIX). A history file is shared by all of the interactive C shells created by the same user unless $HISTFILE is purposely set to a unique value in each different shell. In the following example, I instructed my shell to remember the last 40 commands in my history list and to store the last 32 commands between sessions:

```
2 % set history = 40     ...remember the last 40 commands.
40
3 % set savehist = 32    ...save the last 32 commands between sessions.
32
4 % _
```

Reading History

To obtain a listing of a shell's history, use the built-in command *history*, which works like this:

Shell Command: *history* [-rh] [*number*]

history allows you to access a shell's history list. If no parameters are supplied, this command lists the last $history commands. The **-r** option causes the history list to be listed in reverse order, and the **-h** option inhibits the display of event numbers. The command "history" is usually aliased to "h" for speed.

Here's an example of the use of the *history* command:

```
4 % alias h history        ...make a useful alias.
5 % h                      ...list current history.
  1 echo Genesis
  2 set history = 40
  3 set savehist = 32
  4 alias h history
  5 h
6 % h -r 3   ...list the last three commands in reverse order.
  6 h -r 3
  5 h
  4 alias h history
7 % _
```

Command Reexecution

To reexecute a previous command, use the "!" metacharacter in one of the following forms:

Form	Action
!!	Replaced with the text of the last command.
!*number*	Replaced with the text of the command with the specified event number.
!*prefix*	Replaced with the text of the last command that started with *prefix*.
!?*substring?*	Replaced with the text of the last command that contained *substring*.

These sequences may be used anywhere in a command line, although they're usually used in isolation. The recalled command is echoed to the terminal before it is executed. The value of *prefix* or *substring* may not contain a space. The special meaning of "!" is not inhibited by any kind of quote, but may be inhibited by preceding it with a space, tab, "=", "(", or "\". Here are some examples of the use of the "!" meta-character to reexecute commands:

```
41 % echo event 41        ...a simple echo.
event 41
42 % echo event 42        ...another simple echo.
event 42
43 % !!                    ...reexecute last command.
echo event 42             ...command is echoed before reexecution.
event 42
44 % !41                   ...reexecute command #41.
echo event 41             ...command is echoed before reexecution.
event 41
45 % !ec                   ...reexecute the first command starting with "ec".
echo event 41             ...command is echoed before reexecution.
event 41
46 % _
```

Accessing Pieces of History

You may access a portion of a previous command by using *history modifiers*. These modifiers are a collection of options that may immediately follow an event specifier. Each modifier returns a single token or range of tokens from the specified event. Here is a list of the modifiers:

Modifier	Token(s) returned
:0	first
:number	(number + 1)th
:start-end	(*start* + 1)th through to (*end* + 1)th
:^	first
:$	last
:*	second through to last

The colon before the "^", "$", and "*" options is optional. To use one of these modifiers on the previous command, you may precede the modifier by "!!" or just "!". Here are some examples of the use of these modifiers:

```
48 % echo I like horseback riding      ...original line.
I like horseback riding
49 % !!:0 !!:1 !!:2 !!:4               ...access specified arguments.
echo I like riding
I like riding
50 % echo !48:1-$                       ...access range of arguments.
echo I like horseback riding
I like horseback riding
51 % _
```

Accessing Portions of Filenames

If a history modifier refers to a filename, it may be further modified in order to access a particular portion of the filename. The previously described modifiers may be followed immediately by the following filename modifiers:

Modifier	Part of file	Portion of the specified filename that is returned
:h	head	the filename minus the trailing pathname
:r	root	the filename minus the trailing suffix following a "."
:e	extension	the trailing suffix following a "."
:t	tail	the filename minus the leading directory path

In the following example, I accessed various portions of the original filename by using this filename-access facility:

```
53 % ls /usr/include/stdio.h        ...the original filename.
/usr/include/stdio.h
54 % echo !53:1:h                   ...access head.
echo /usr/include
/usr/include
55 % echo !53:1:r                   ...access root.
echo /usr/include/stdio
/usr/include/stdio
56 % echo !53:1:e                   ...access extension.
echo h
h
57 % echo !53:1:t                   ...access tail.
echo stdio.h
stdio.h
% _
```

History Substitution

In order to substitute a new pattern for part of a previous event, the substitution modifier is used. The substitution modifier is replaced by the specified portion of a previous event after a textual substitution is performed. Here is the syntax for history substitution:

!event:s/pat1/pat2/

This sequence is replaced by the specified event after the first occurrence of *pat1* is replaced by *pat2*. Here's an example of the use of the substitution modifier:

```
58 % ls /usr/include/stdio.h          ...the original command.
/usr/include/stdio.h
58 % echo !58:1:s/stdio/signal/       ...perform substitution.
echo /usr/include/signal.h
/usr/include/signal.h
59 % _
```

CONTROL STRUCTURES

The C shell supports a wide range of control structures that make it suitable as a high-level programming tool. Shell programs are usually stored in scripts and are commonly used to automate maintenance and installation tasks.

Several of the control structures require several lines on which to be entered. If such a control structure is entered from the keyboard, the shell prompts you with a "?" for each additional line until the control structure is ended, at which point it executes.

Next is a description, in alphabetical order, of each control structure. I made the C-shell examples correspond closely to the Bourne-shell examples so that you can compare and contrast the two shells.

foreach .. end

The *foreach .. end* command allows a list of commands to be repeatedly executed, each time using a different value for a named variable. Here's its syntax:

---

foreach name (wordList)

commandList
end

The *foreach .. end* command iterates the value of *name* through each variable in *wordList*, executing the list of commands *commandList* after each assignment. A *break* command causes the loop to end immediately, and a *continue* command causes the loop to jump immediately to the next iteration. Here's an example of a script that uses a *foreach .. end* control structure:

```
% cat foreach.csh                     ...list the script.
#
foreach color (red yellow green blue) # four colors.
  echo one color is $color
end
% foreach.csh                         ...execute the script.
one color is red
one color is yellow
```

```
one color is green
one color is blue
% _
```

goto

The *goto* command allows you to jump unconditionally to a named label. The label may precede or follow the *goto* statement, even if the command is entered from the keyboard. To declare a label, simply start a line with the name of the label, followed immediately by a colon. Here's the syntax of a *goto* command:

> *goto name*

Here's the syntax of a label:

> *name:*

Use *goto*s sparingly in order to avoid nasty spaghetti-like code (even if you like spaghetti). Here's an example of a simple *goto*:

```
% cat goto.csh              ...list the script.
#
echo gotta jump
goto endOfScript  # jump
echo I will never echo this
endOfScript:    # label
echo the end
% goto.csh                  ...execute the script.
gotta jump
the end
% _
```

if .. then .. else .. endif

There are two forms of the *if* command. The first form supports a simple one-way branch and has the following syntax:

> *if (expr) command*

This form of the *if* command evaluates *expr* and, if it is true (nonzero), executes *command*:

```
% if (5 > 3) echo five is greater than 3
five is greater than three
% _
```

The second form of the *if* command supports alternative branching. Here's its general syntax:

```
if (expr1) then

    list1

else if (expr2) then

    list2

else

    list3

endif
```

The *else* and *else if* portions of this command are optional, but the terminating *endif* is not. The second form of the *if* command works as follows:

- *expr1* is executed.
- If *expr1* is true, the commands in *list1* are executed and the *if* command is done.
- If *expr1* is false and there are one or more *else if* components, then a true expression following an *else if* causes the commands following the associated *then* to be executed and the *if* command to finish.
- If no true expressions are found and there is an *else* component, the commands following the *else* are executed.

Here's an example of the use of this sequence:

```
% cat if.csh                 ...list the script.
#
echo -n 'enter a number: '   # prompt user.
set number = $<              # read a line of input.
if ($number < 0) then
  echo negative
```

```
else if ($number == 0) then
 echo zero
else
 echo positive
endif
% if.csh                        ...execute the script.
enter a number: -1
negative
% _
```

onintr

The *onintr* command allows you to specify a label that should be jumped to when the shell receives a SIGINT signal. This signal is typically generated by a *Control-C* from the keyboard and is described in more detail in Chapter 12. Here's the syntax of the *onintr* command:

---

onintr [- | *label*]

The *onintr* command instructs the shell to jump to *label* when SIGINT is received. If the "-" option is used, SIGINTs are ignored. If no options are supplied, the command restores the shell's original SIGINT handler. Here's an example of the use of the *onintr* command:

```
% cat onintr.csh          ...list the script.
#
onintr controlC           # set Control-C trap.
while (1)
 echo infinite loop
 sleep 2
end
controlC:
echo control C detected
% onintr.csh              ...execute the script.
infinite loop
infinite loop
^C                        ...press Control-C.
control C detected
% _
```

repeat

The *repeat* command allows you to execute a single command a specified number of times. Here's its syntax:

---

repeat expr command

The *repeat* command evaluates *expr* and then executes *command* the resultant number of times:

```
% repeat 2 echo hi there        ...display two lines.
hi there
hi there
% _
```

switch .. case .. endsw

The *switch* command supports multiway branching based on the value of a single expression. Here's the general form of a *switch* construct:

```
switch (expr)
  case pattern1:
    list
    breaksw
  case pattern2:
  case pattern3:
    list2
    breaksw
  default:
    defaultList
endsw
```

---

expr is an expression that evaluates to a string; *pattern1*, *pattern2*, and *pattern3* may include wildcards; and *list1*, *list2*, and *defaultList* are lists of one or more shell commands. The shell evaluates *expr* and then compares it to each pattern in turn, from top to bottom. When the first matching pattern is found, its associated list of commands is executed and then the shell skips to the matching *endsw*. If no match is found and a default condition is supplied, then *defaultList* is executed. If no match is found and no default condition exists, then execution continues from after the matching *endsw*.

Here's a script called "menu.csh" that makes use of a *switch* control structure:

```
#
echo menu test program
set stop = 0                      # reset loop-termination flag.
while ($stop == 0)                # loop until done.
 cat << ENDOFMENU                 # display menu.
 1  : print the date.
 2, 3: print the current working directory
 4  : exit
ENDOFMENU
 echo
 echo -n 'your choice? '          # prompt.
 set reply = $<                   # read response.
 echo ""
 switch ($reply)                  # process response.
   case "1":
     date                         # display date.
     breaksw
   case "2":
   case "3":
     pwd                          # display working directory.
     breaksw
   case "4":
     set stop = 1                 # set loop-termination flag.
     breaksw
   default:                       # default.
     echo illegal choice          # error.
     breaksw
 endsw
end
```

Here's the output from the "menu.csh" script:

```
% menu.csh
menu test program
 1  : print the date.
 2, 3: print the current working directory
 4  : exit
your choice? 1
Sat Feb 14 00:50:26 CST 1998
 1  : print the date.
 2, 3: print the current working directory
 4  : exit
your choice? 2
/home/glass
 1  : print the date.
 2, 3: print the current working directory
 4  : exit
```

```
your choice? 5
illegal choice
 1  : print the date.
 2, 3: print the current working directory
 4  : exit
your choice? 4

% _
```

while .. end

The built-in *while .. end* command allows a list of commands to be repeatedly executed as long as a specified expression evaluates to true (nonzero). Here's its syntax:

```
while ( expr )
   commandlist
end
```

The *while* command evalutes the expression *expr* and, if it is true, proceeds to execute every command in *commandlist* and then repeats the process. If *expr* is false, the while loop terminates and the script continues to execute from the command following the *end*. A *break* command causes the loop to end immediately, and a *continue* command causes the loop to jump immediately to the next iteration.

Here's an example of a script that uses a *while .. end* control structure to generate a small multiplication table:

```
% cat multi.csh              ...list the script.
#
 set x = 1                   # set outer-loop value.
 while ($x <= $1)            # outer loop.
   set y = 1                 # set inner-loop value.
   while ($y <= $1)          # inner loop.
     @ v = $x * $y           # calculate entry.
     echo -n $v " "          # display entry.
     @ y ++                  # update inner-loop counter.
 end
 echo ""                     # print a new line.
 @ x ++                      # update outer-loop counter.
end
% multi.csh 7                ...execute the script.
1       2       3       4       5       6       7
2       4       6       8       10      12      14
3       6       9       12      15      18      21
4       8       12      16      20      24      28
```

5	10	15	20	25	30	35
6	12	18	24	30	36	42
7	14	21	28	35	42	49

% _

SAMPLE PROJECT: JUNK

To illustrate some of the C shell's capabilities, I now present a C-shell version of the "junk" script project that was suggested at the end of the chapter on the Bourne shell. Here's the definition of the **junk** utility about to be described:

Utility: junk -lp { fileName }*

junk is a replacement for the **rm** utility. Rather than removing files, it moves them into the subdirectory ".junk" in your home directory. If ".junk" doesn't exist, it is automatically created. The **-l** option lists the current contents of the ".junk" directory, and the **-p** option purges ".junk".

The C-shell script that is listed below uses a list variable to store filenames. The rest of the functionality should be pretty easy to follow from the embedded comments.

junk

```csh
#! /bin/csh
# junk script
# author: Graham Glass
# 9/25/91
#
# Initialize variables
#
set fileList = ()          # a list of all specified files.
set listFlag = 0           # set to 1 if "-l" option is specified.
set purgeFlag = 0          # 1 if "-p" option is specified.
set fileFlag = 0           # 1 if at least one file is specified.
set junk = ~/.junk         # the junk directory.
#
# Parse command-line.
#
foreach arg ($*)
 switch ($arg)
   case "-p":
     set purgeFlag = 1
     breaksw
```

```
    case "-l":
      set listFlag = 1
      breaksw
    case -*:
      echo $arg is an illegal option
      goto error
      breaksw
    default:
      set fileFlag = 1
      set fileList = ($fileList $arg) # append to list.
      breaksw
  endsw
end
#
# Check for too many options.
#
@ total = $listFlag + $purgeFlag + $fileFlag
if ($total != 1) goto error
#
# If junk directory doesn't exist, create it.
#
if (!(-e $junk)) then
  'mkdir' $junk
endif
#
# Process options.
#
if ($listFlag) then
  'ls' -lgF $junk              # list junk directory.
  exit 0
endif
#
if ($purgeFlag) then
  'rm' $junk/*                 # remove contents of junk directory.
  exit 0
endif
#
if ($fileFlag) then
  'mv' $fileList $junk         # move files to junk directory.
  exit 0
endif
#
exit 0
#
# Display error message and quit.
#
error:
cat << ENDOFTEXT
Dear $USER, the usage of junk is as follows:
  junk -p means "purge all files"
  junk -l means "list junked files"
```

```
    junk <list of files> to junk them
ENDOFTEXT
exit 1
```

ENHANCEMENTS

In addition to the new facilities that have already been described, the C shell also enhances the common core-shell facilities in the following areas:

- a shortcut for command reexecution
- the "{}" metacharacters
- filename substitution
- redirection
- piping
- job control

The next set of subsections describe each enhancement.

Command Reexecution: A Shortcut

It's quite common to want to reexecute the previous command with a slight modification. For example, say that you misspelled the name of a file: Instead of typing "fil.txt", you meant to type "file.txt". There's a convenient shorthand way to correct such a mistake. If you type the command

```
^pat1^pat2
```

where *pat1* is the part of the previous command that you want to replace and *pat2* is the replacement, then the previous command is reexecuted after the first occurrence of *pat1* is replaced by *pat2*. This shortcut procedure applies only to the previous command. Here's an example of its use:

```
% cc fil.txt              ...whoops!
ld crt0.o fatal: Can't open file fil.txt for input
% ^fil^file               ...quick correction.
cc file.txt               ...OK.
% _
```

Metacharacters: {}

You may use braces around filenames in order to save time that would be used for typing common prefixes and suffixes. The notation

```
a{b,c}d
```

is textually replaced with

```
abd acd
```

In the following example, I copied the files "/usr/include/stdio.h" and "/usr/include/signal.h" (which have a common prefix and suffix) into my home directory:

```
% cp /usr/include/{stdio,signal}.h        ...copy two files.
% _
```

Filename Substitution

In addition to the common filename-substitution facilities, the C shell supports two new features: the ability to disable filename substitution and the ability to specify what action should be taken if a pattern has no matches.

Disabling Filename Substitution   To disable filename substitution, set the $noglob variable. If you set this variable, wildcards lose their special meaning. The $noglob variable is not set by default. Here's an example of the effects of setting it:

```
% echo a* p*    ...one wildcard pair matches: "p*".
prog1.c prog2.c prog3.c prog4.c
% set noglob    ...inhibit wildcard processing.
% echo a* p*
a* p*
% _
```

No-Match Situations   If several patterns are present in a command and at least one of them has a match, then no error occurs. However, if none of the patterns has a match, the shell issues an error message by default. However, if the $nonomatch variable is set and no matches occur, then the original patterns are used as is; that is, wildcard processing becomes disabled for such cases. The $nonomatch variable is not set by default. Here's an example of the effects of setting it:

```
% echo a* p*       ...one wildcard pair matches: "p*".
prog1.c prog2.c    prog3.c        prog4.c
% echo a* b*       ...no wildcards match.
echo: No match.    ...error occurs by default.
% set nonomatch    ...set special nonomatch variable.
% echo a* b*       ...wildcards lose their special meaning.
a* b*              ...no error occurs.
% _
```

Redirection

In addition to the common redirection facilities, the C shell supports a couple of enhancements: the ability to redirect the standard error channel and the ability to protect files against accidental overwrites.

Redirecting the Standard Error Channel   To redirect the standard error channel in addition to the standard output channel, simply append an "&" character to the ">" or ">>" redirection operator:

```
% cc a.c > errors        ...cc sends errors to the standard error
                         ...channel.
printf (1\n");
```

```
******** Line 8 of "a.c": Improper expression; "BAD CHAR: '\'
scanf ("%d", &i);
******** Line 9 of "a.c": Improper argument list; "scanf" found.
% cc a.c >& errors        ...redirect the standard error channel too.
% _
```

Although there's no easy way to redirect just the error channel, it can be done using the following "trick":

```
(process1 > file1) >& file2
```

This trick works by redirecting all of the standard output from *process1* to *file1* (which can be "/dev/null" if you don't want to save the output), allowing only the standard errors to leave the command group. The command group's output and error channels are then redirected to *file2*.

Protecting Files Against Accidental Overwrites You may protect existing files from accidental overwrites and nonexistent files from accidental appends by setting the $noclobber variable. If a shell command tries to perform either action, it fails and issues an error message. Note that regular system calls such as "write ()" are unaffected. $noclobber is not set by default. Here's an example of its effects:

```
% ls -l errors            ...look at existing file.
-rw-r-xr-x 1 glass        225 Feb 14 10:59 errors
% set noclobber           ...protect files.
% cc a.c >& errors        ...cannot overwrite.
errors: File exists.
% _
```

To temporarily override the effect of $noclobber, append a "!" character to the redirection operator:

```
% cc a.c >&! errors       ...existing file is overwritten.
% _
```

Piping

In addition to the common piping facilities, the C shell also allows you to pipe the standard output and standard error channel from *process1* to *process2* using the following syntax:

process1 |& process2

In the following example, I piped the standard output and error channels from the **cc** utility to **more**:

```
% cc a.c |& more            ...pipe standard output and error channels.
printf (1\n");
******** Line 8 of "a.c": Improper expression; "BAD CHAR: '\'
scanf ("%d", &i);
******** Line 9 of "a.c": Improper argument list; "scanf" found.
% _
```

Although there's no direct way to pipe just the error channel, it can be done using the following "trick":

(process1>file) |& *process2*

This trick works by redirecting all of the standard output from *process1* to *file* (which can be "/dev/null" if you don't want to save the output), allowing only the standard errors to leave the command group. The command group's output and error channels are then piped to *process2*.

Job Control

The job-control facilities of the C shell are the same as those of the Korn shell, with the following additional built-in commands:

- *stop*
- *suspend*
- *nice*
- *nohup*
- *notify*

The next set of subsections contain descriptions of these commands.

Stop   To suspend a specified job, use the *stop* command as follows:

Shell Command: stop { %job }*

stop suspends the jobs that are specified using the standard format of the job specifier described in the chapter on the Korn shell. If no arguments are supplied, the last referenced job is suspended.

Suspend

Shell Command: suspend

suspend suspends the shell that invokes it. It only makes sense to use *suspend* when the shell is a subshell of the login shell, and *suspend* is most commonly used to suspend a shell invoked by the **su** or **script** utilities.

Nice   To set the priority level of the shell or a command, use the *nice* command as follows:

Shell Command: nice [+/− number] [command]

nice runs *command* with priority level *number.* In general, the higher the priority, the slower the process will run. Only a super-user can specify a negative priority level. If the priority level is omitted, a priority level of four is assumed. If no arguments are specified, the shell's priority level is set.

For more information about process priorities, consult Chapter 12.

Nohup   To protect a command from hang-up conditions, use the built-in *nohup* command as follows:

Shell Command: nohup [command]

nohup executes *command* and protects it from hang-up signals. If no arguments are supplied, then all further commands executed from the shell are nohup'ed. Note that all background commands are automatically nohup'ed.

Notify   The shell normally notifies you of a change in a job's status just before it displays a new prompt. If you want immediate (asynchronous) notification of changes in job status, use the built-in *notify* command as follows:

Shell Command: *notify* { *%job* }*

notify instructs the shell to inform you immediately when the specified jobs change status. Jobs must be specified following the standard format of the job specifier described in the chapter on the Korn shell. If no job is specified, the last referenced job is used. To enable immediate notification of all jobs, set the $notify variable.

Terminating a Login Shell

The *logout* command terminates a login shell. Unlike *exit*, it cannot be used to terminate an interactive subshell. Therefore, you may terminate a login C shell in one of three ways:

- Press *Control*-D on a line by itself (as long as $ignoreeof is not set).
- Use the built-in *exit* command.
- Use the built-in *logout* command.

Here's an example of the use of these methods:

```
% set ignoreeof        ...set to prevent ^D exit.
% ^D                   ...won't work now.
Use "logout" to logout.
% logout               ...a better way to log out.
login: _
```

When a login C shell is terminated, it searches for "finish-up" files. The commands in each file, if found, are executed in sequence. The user's finish-up file is "$HOME/.logout", and it is executed if found. Then, any global finish-up file is executed. The name of this file might be "/etc/logout" or "/.logout", depending on your version of UNIX.

A finish-up file typically contains commands for cleaning up temporary directories, other such clean-up operations, and a goodbye message.

If a nonlogin C shell is terminated using *exit* or *Control*-D, no finish-up files are executed.

BUILT-IN COMMANDS

The C shell provides the following extra built-in commands:

- *chdir*
- *glob*
- *source*

The next few subsections contain a description of each built-in command.

chdir

Shell Command: chdir [path]

chdir works in the same way as cd does.

glob

Shell Command: glob { arg }

glob works in the same way as echo does, printing a list of arguments after they have been processed by the shell's metacharacter mechanisms. The difference is that the list of arguments for glob are delimited by nulls (ASCII 0) in the final output instead of by spaces. This feature makes the output ideally suited for use by C programs that prefer strings to be terminated by null characters.

source

When a script is executed, it is interpreted by a subshell. Any aliases and/or assignments of local variables performed by the script therefore have no effect on the original shell. If you want a script to be interpreted by the current shell and, thus, affect it, use the built-in source command as follows:

Shell Command: source [-h] fileName

source causes a shell to execute every command in the script called fileName without invoking a subshell. The commands in the script are only placed in the history list if the -h option is used. It is perfectly legal for fileName to contain further source commands. If an error occurs during the execution of fileName, control is returned to the original shell.

In the next example, I used source to reexecute an edited ".login" file. The only other way to reexecute it would have been to log out and then log back in again.

```
% vi .login                    ...edit my ".login" file.
...assume that I edited the file and have now returned to the prompt.
% source .login                ...reexecute it.
Enter your terminal type (default is vt100): vt52
% _
```

THE DIRECTORY STACK

The C shell allows you to create and manipulate a directory stack, which makes life a little easier when you're flipping back and forth between a small working set of directories. To push a directory onto the directory stack, use the *pushd* command:

Shell Command: pushd [+number | name]

pushd pushes the specified directory onto the directory stack and works like this:

- When *name* is supplied, the current working directory is pushed onto the stack and the shell moves to the named directory.
- When no arguments are supplied, the top two elements of the directory stack are swapped.
- When *number* is supplied, the *number*th element of the directory stack is rotated to the top of the stack and becomes the current working directory. The elements of the stack are numbered in ascending order, with the top as number zero.

To pop a directory from the directory stack, use the *popd* command, which works as follows:

Shell Command: popd [+number]

popd pops a directory from the directory stack and works like this:

- When no argument is supplied, the shell moves to the directory that's on the top of the directory stack and then pops it.
- When a *number* is supplied, the shell moves to the *number*th directory on the stack and discards it.

The *dirs* command is also useful for directory stacks:

Shell Command: *dirs*

dirs lists the current directory stack.

Here are some examples of directory-stack manipulation:

```
% pwd                    ...I'm in my home directory.
/home/glass
% pushd /                ...go to root directory; push home directory.
/ ~                      ...displays directory stack automatically.
% pushd /usr/include ...push another directory.
/usr/include / ~
% pushd                  ...swap two stack elements, go back to root directory.
/ /usr/include ~
% pushd                  ...swap them again; go back to "/usr/include".
/usr/include / ~
% popd                   ...pop a directory; go back to root directory.
/ ~
% popd                   ...pop a directory; go back to home directory.
~
% _
```

The Hash Table

As described in Chapter 3, the $PATH variable is used when searching for an executable file. To speed up this process, the C shell stores an internal data structure, called a *hash table*, that allows the directory hierarchy to be searched more quickly. The hash table is constructed automatically whenever the ".cshrc" file is read. In order for the hash table to work correctly, however, it must be reconstructed whenever $PATH is changed or whenever a new executable file is added to any directory in the $PATH sequence. The C shell takes care of the first case automatically, but *you* must take care of the second.

If you add or rename an executable in any of the directories in the $PATH sequence except for your current directory, you should use the *rehash* command to instruct the C shell to reconstruct the hash table. If you wish, you may use the *unhash* command to disable the hash-table facility, thereby slowing down the search process.

The *hashstat* command may be used to examine the effectiveness of the hashing system. The output of this command doesn't mean anything unless you're familiar with hashing algorithms.

In the next example, I added a new executable into the directory "~/bin", which was in my search path. The shell couldn't find it until I performed a *rehash*.

```
% pwd                                    ...I'm in my home directory.
/home/glass
% echo $PATH                             ...list my $PATH variable.
.:/home/glass/bin:/usr/bin:/usr/local/bin:/bin:
% cat > bin/script.csh                   ...create a new script.
#
echo found the script
^D                                       ...end of input.
% chmod +x bin/script.csh                ...make executable.
% script.csh                             ...try to run it.
script.csh: Command not found.
% rehash                                 ...make the shell rehash.
% script.csh                             ...try to run it again.
found the script                         ...success!
% hashstat                               ...display hash statistics.
5 hits, 6 misses, 45%
% _
```

COMMAND-LINE OPTIONS

If the first command-line argument is a "-", the C shell is started as a login shell. In addition to this option, the C shell supports the following command-line options:

Option	Meaning
-c *string*	Create a shell to execute the command *string*.
-e	Shell terminates if any command returns a nonzero exit code.
-f	Start shell, but don't search for or read commands from ".cshrc".
-i	Create an interactive shell; like the "-s" option except that the SIGTERM, SIGINT, and SIGQUIT messages are all ignored.
-n	Parse commands, but do not execute them; for debugging only.
-s	Create a shell that reads commands from standard input and sends shell messages to the standard error channel.
-t	Read and execute a single line from standard input.
-v	Causes $verbose, which was described earlier, to be set.
-V	Like "-v", except that $verbose is set before ".cshrc" is executed.
-x	Causes the $echo variable, which was described earlier, to be set.
-X	Like "-x", except that $echo is set before ".cshrc" is read.
fileName	Execute the shell commands in *fileName* if none of the "-c", "-i", "-s", or "-t" options are used. *fileName* is $0 within the *fileName* script.

CHAPTER REVIEW

Checklist

In this chapter, I described:

- the creation of a C-shell start-up file

- simple variables and lists
- expressions, including integer arithmetic
- aliases and the history mechanism
- several control structures
- enhanced job control
- several new built-in commands

Quiz

1. Why do you think integer expressions must be preceded by an "@" sign?
2. What's a good way to correct a simple typing mistake in the previous command?
3. What's the function of the "{}" metacharacters?
4. How do you protect files from accidental overwrites?
5. How do you protect scripts from *Control*-C interrupts?

Exercises

1. Write a C-shell version of the "track" script that was described in the chapter on the Bourne shell. [level: *easy*]
2. Write a utility called "hunt" that acts as a front end to **find:** It takes the name of a file as its single parameter and displays the full pathname of every filename that matches, searching downward from the current directory. **find** is described in Chapter 7. [level: *easy*]

Projects

Study the current trends in object-oriented programming and then design an object-oriented shell (perhaps a C++ shell?). [level: *hard*]

CHAPTER 7

Utilities

Motivation

In addition to the common file-oriented UNIX utilities, there are plenty of other utilities that process text, schedule commands, archive files, and sort files. This chapter contains descriptions and examples of the most useful utilities that will increase your productivity.

Prerequisites

In order to understand this chapter, you must have already read Chapters 1 and 2. It also helps if you have access to a UNIX system so that you can try out the various utilities that I discuss.

Objectives

In this chapter, I show you how to use about 30 useful utilities.

Presentation

The information in this section is presented in the form of several sample UNIX sessions.

Utilities

This chapter introduces the following utilities, listed in alphabetical order:

at	crontab	grep	tar
awk	crypt	ln	tr
biff	diff	mount	ul
cmp	dump	od	umount
compress	egrep	sed	uncompress
cpio	fgrep	sort	uniq
cron	find	su	whoami

In addition to information on these standard UNIX utilities, this chapter also provides a brief introduction to Perl because, while it does not come with most versions of UNIX, it has become an integral part of many UNIX environments.

INTRODUCTION

In this chapter, I introduce about thirty useful utilities. Rather than describe them in alphabetical order, I've grouped them into fairly logical sets, as follows:

Section	Utilties
filtering files	**egrep, fgrep, grep, uniq**
sorting files	**sort**
comparing files	**cmp, diff**
archiving files	**tar, cpio, dump**
searching for files	**find**
scheduling commands	**at, cron, crontab**
programmable text processing	**awk**
hard and soft links	**ln**
switching users	**su**
checking for mail	**biff**
transforming files	**compress, crypt, sed, tr, ul, uncompress**
looking at raw file contents	**od**
mounting file systems	**mount, umount**
identifying shells	**whoami**
document preparation	**nroff, spell, style, troff**

The remainder of this chapter goes through each group in turn, describing the utilities using worked examples. Note that while most of these utilities exist in all versions of UNIX, this case is not true for absolutely every one of them.

FILTERING FILES

There are many times when it's handy to be able to filter the contents of a file, selecting only those lines that match some kind of criteria. The utilities that do this task include the following:

- **egrep**, **fgrep**, and **grep**, which filter out all lines that do not contain a specified pattern
- **uniq**, which filters out duplicate adjacent lines

The next couple of subsections describe these utilities.

Filtering Patterns: *egrep*, *fgrep*, and *grep*

egrep, **fgrep**, and **grep** allow you to scan a file and filter out all of the lines that don't contain a specified pattern. They are very similar in nature, the main difference being the kind of text patterns that each can filter out. I'll begin by describing the common features of all three and then finish up by illustrating their differences. Here's a brief synopsis of the three utilities:

Utility: **grep** -hilnvw *pattern* { *fileName* } *
   fgrep -hilnvwx *string* { *fileName* } *
   egrep -hilnvw *pattern* { *fileName* } *

grep is a utility that allows you to search for a pattern in a list of files. If no files are specified, it searches standard input instead. *pattern* may be a regular expression. All lines that match the pattern are displayed to standard output. If more than one file is specified, each matching line is preceded by the name of the file unless the **-h** option is specified. The **-n** option precedes each matching line by its line number. The **-i** option causes the case of the patterns to be ignored. The **-l** option displays a list of the files that contain the specified pattern. The **-v** option causes **grep** to display all of the lines that *don't* match the pattern. The **-w** option restricts matching to occur on whole words only. **fgrep** is a fast version of **grep** that can only search for fixed strings. **egrep** is a version of **grep** that supports extended regular expressions. **fgrep** supports an additional option: The **-x** option outputs only lines that are exactly equal to *string*. For more information about regular expressions, consult the appendix.

To obtain a list of all of the lines in a file that contain a particular string, follow **grep** by the string and the name of the file to scan. Here's an example of this use of **grep**:

```
$ cat grepfile          ...list the file to be filtered.
Well you know it's your bedtime,
So turn off the light,
Say all your prayers and then,
Oh you sleepy young heads dream of wonderful things,
Beautiful mermaids will swim through the sea,
And you will be swimming there too.
$ grep the grepfile     ...search for the word "the".
So turn off the light,
Say all your prayers and then,
Beautiful mermaids will swim through the sea,
And you will be swimming there too.
$ _
```

Notice that words that contain the string "the" as only a part of them also satisfied the matching condition. Here's an example of the use of the "-w" and "-n" options:

```
$ grep -wn the grepfile   ...we will be more particular this time!
2:So turn off the light,
5:Beautiful mermaids will swim through the sea,
$ _
```

To display only those lines in a file that don't match the specified pattern, use the "-v" option:

```
$ grep -wnv the grepfile      ...reverse the filter.
1:Well you know it's your bedtime,
3:Say all your prayers and then,
4:Oh you sleepy young heads dream of wonderful things,
6:And you will be swimming there too.
$ _
```

If you specify more than one file to search, each selected line is preceded by the name of the file in which it appears. In the next example, I searched my C source files for the string "x". Please consult Chapter 3 for a description of the shell file-wildcard mechanism.

```
$ grep -w x *.c      ...search all files ending in ".c".
a.c:test (int x)
fact2.c:long factorial (x)
fact2.c:int x;
fact2.c:  if ((x == 1) || (x == 0))
fact2.c:    result = x * factorial (x-1);
$ grep -wl x *.c      ...list names of files that contain matches.
a.c
fact2.c
$ _
```

fgrep, **grep**, and **egrep** all support the options that I've described so far. The difference between them is that each allows a different kind of text pattern to be matched:

Utility	Kind of pattern that may be searched for
fgrep	fixed string only
grep	regular expression
egrep	extended regular expression

For information about regular expressions and extended regular expressions, consult the appendix.

To illustrate the use of **grep** and **egrep** for finding regular expressions, presented below is a piece of text followed by a table displaying the lines of text that would match various regular expressions. When using **egrep** or **grep**, you should place regular expressions inside single quotes to prevent interference from the shell. In the table below, the portion of each line of the example text that satisfies the regular expression is italicized. The example text—the poem we used earlier—is repeated here:

```
Well you know it's your bedtime,
So turn off the light,
Say all your prayers and then,
Oh you sleepy young heads dream of wonderful things,
Beautiful mermaids will swim through the sea,
And you will be swimming there too.
```

Matching Patterns

grep Pattern	Lines That Match
.nd	Say all your prayers *and* then, Oh you sleepy young heads dream of *wonderful* things, *And* you will be swimming there too.
^.nd	*And* you will be swimming there too.
sw.*ng	And you will be *swimming* there too.
[A-D]	*Beautiful* mermaids will swim through the sea, And you will be swimming there too.
\.	And you will be swimming there too.
a.	*Say* all your prayers and then, Oh you sleepy young h*eads* dream of wonderful things, Be*au*tiful mermaids will swim through the sea,
a.$	Beautiful mermaids will swim through the *sea,*
[a-m]nd	Say all your prayers *and* then,
[^a-m]nd	Oh you sleepy young heads dream of *wond*erful things, *And* you will be swimming there too.

egrep Pattern	Lines That Match
s.*w	Oh you *sleepy young heads dream of* wonderful things, Beautiful mermaids *will swim* through the sea, And you will be *sw*imming there too.
s.+w	Oh you *sleepy young heads dream of* wonderful things, Beautiful mermaids *will sw*im through the sea,
off|will	So turn *off* the light, Beautiful mermaids *will* swim through the sea, And you *will* be swimming there too.
im*ing	And you will be swimming there too.
im?ing	<no matches>

Removing Duplicate Lines: uniq

The **uniq** utility displays a file with all of its identical adjacent lines replaced by a single occurrence of the repeated line, and it works like this:

Utility: **uniq** -c -number [*inputfile* [*outputfile*]]

uniq is a utility that displays its input file with all adjacent repeated lines collapsed to a single occurrence of the repeated line. If an input file is not specified, standard input is read. The **-c** option causes each line to be preceded by the number of occurrences that were found. If *number* is specified, then *number* fields of each line are ignored.

Here's an example of the use of the **uniq** utility:

```
$ cat animals          ...look at the test file.
cat snake
monkey snake
dolphin elephant
dolphin elephant
goat elephant
pig pig
pig pig
monkey pig
$ uniq animals         ...filter out duplicate adjacent lines.
cat snake
monkey snake
dolphin elephant
goat elephant
pig pig
monkey pig
$ uniq -c animals      ...display a count with the lines.
   1 cat snake
   1 monkey snake
   2 dolphin elephant
   1 goat elephant
   2 pig pig
   1 monkey pig
$ uniq -1 animals      ...ignore the first field of each line.
cat snake
dolphin elephant
pig pig
$ _
```

SORTING FILES: SORT

The **sort** utility sorts a file in ascending or descending order based on one or more *sort fields*, and it works as follows:

Utility: **sort** -tc -r { *sortField* -bfMn }* { *fileName* }*

sort is a utility that sorts lines in one or more files based on a sorting criteria. By default, lines are sorted into ascending order. The **-r** option specifies descending order instead. Input lines are split into fields separated by spaces and/or tabs. To specify a different field separator, use the **-t** option. By default, all of a line's fields are considered when the sort is being performed. This default may be overridden by specifying one or more sort fields, the format of which is described later in this section. Individual sort fields may be customized by following them by one or more options. The **-f** option causes **sort** to ignore the case of the field. The **-M** option sorts the field in order by month. The **-n** option sorts the field in numerical order. The **-b** option ignores leading spaces.

Individual fields are ordered lexicographically, which means that corresponding characters are compared based on their respective ASCII values. (Use the command "man ascii" for a list of all characters and their corresponding values.) Two consequences of this order are that an uppercase letter is considered to be "less" than its lowercase equivalent and a space is considered to be "less" than a letter. In the following example, I sorted a text file in ascending order and then in descending order using the default ordering rule:

```
$ cat sortfile              ...list the file to be sorted.
jan  Start chapter 3   10th
Jan  Start chapter 1   30th
 Jan  Start chapter 5   23rd
 Jan  End chapter 3   23rd
Mar  Start chapter 7   27
 may  End chapter 7   17th
Apr  End Chapter 5   1
 Feb  End chapter 1   14
$ sort sortfile             ...sort it.
 Feb  End chapter 1   14
 Jan  End chapter 3   23rd
 Jan  Start chapter  5 23rd
 may  End chapter 7   17th
Apr  End Chapter 5   1
```

```
Jan   Start chapter 1   30th
Mar   Start chapter 7   27
jan   Start chapter 3   10th
$ sort -r sortfile              ...sort it in reverse order.
jan   Start chapter 3   10th
Mar   Start chapter 7   27
Jan   Start chapter 1   30th
Apr   End Chapter 5   1
 may  End chapter 7   17th
 Jan  Start chapter 5   23rd
 Jan  End chapter 3   23rd
 Feb  End chapter 1   14
$ _
```

To sort a particular field, you must specify the starting field number using a "+" prefix, followed by the noninclusive number of the stop field with a "-" prefix. Field
numbers start at index zero. If you leave off the number of the stop field, all fields
following the start field are included. In the next example, I sorted the same text file
on the first field only, which has an index of zero:

```
$ sort +0 -1 sortfile        ...sort first field only.
 Feb  End chapter 1   14
 Jan  End chapter 3   23rd
 Jan  Start chapter   5 23rd
 may  End chapter 7   17th
Apr   End Chapter 5   1
Jan   Start chapter   1 30th
Mar   Start chapter   7 27
jan   Start chapter   3 10th
$ _
```

Note that the leading spaces were counted as part of the first field, which resulted in
a strange sorting sequence. Additionally, I would have preferred the months to be
sorted in correct order, with "Jan" before "Feb", etc. The "-b" option ignores leading
blanks, and the "-M" option sorts a field by month. Here's an example that worked
better:

```
$ sort +0 -1 -bM sortfile        ...sort by month in the first field.
Jan   End chapter 3   23rd
Jan   Start chapter   5 23rd
Jan   Start chapter   1 30th
jan   Start chapter   3 10th
 Feb  End chapter 1   14
Mar   Start chapter   7 27
Apr   End Chapter 5   1
 may  End chapter 7   17th
$ _
```

The example text file was correctly sorted by month, but the dates were still out of order. You may specify multiple sort fields on the command line to deal with this problem. The **sort** utility first sorts all of the lines based on the first sort specifier and then uses the second sort specifier to order lines that compared equally by the first specifier. Therefore, to sort the example text file by month and date, it had to be sorted based on the first field and then on the fifth. In addition, the fifth field had to be sorted numerically by using the "-n" option.

```
$ sort +0 -1 -bM +4 -n sortfile      ...sort first field by month and fifth
                                     ...field numerically.
jan   Start chapter 3   10th
 Jan   End chapter 3   23rd
 Jan   Start chapter   5 23rd
 Jan   Start chapter   1 30th
 Feb   End chapter 1   14
Mar   Start chapter   7 27
Apr   End Chapter 5   1
 may   End chapter 7   17th
$ _
```

Fields are often delimited by characters other than spaces. For example, the "/etc/passwd" file contains user information stored in fields separated by colons. You may use the "-t" option to specify an alternative field separator. In the following example, I sorted a file based on fields separated by ":" characters.

```
$ cat sortfile2                      ...look at the test file.
jan:Start chapter 3:10th
Jan:Start chapter 1:30th
Jan:Start chapter 5:23rd
Jan:End chapter 3:23rd
Mar:Start chapter 7:27
may:End chapter 7:17th
Apr:End Chapter 5:1
Feb:End chapter 1:14
$ sort -t: +0 -1 -bM +2 -n sortfile2  ...colon delimiters.
jan:Start chapter 3:10th
Jan:End chapter 3:23rd
Jan:Start chapter 5:23rd
Jan:Start chapter 1:30th
Feb:End chapter 1:14
Mar:Start chapter 7:27
Apr:End Chapter 5:1
may:End chapter 7:17th
$ _
```

sort contains several other options that are too detailed to describe here; I suggest that you use the **man** utility to find out more about them.

COMPARING FILES

There are two utilities that allow you to compare the contents of two files:

- **cmp**, which finds the first byte that differs between two files
- **diff**, which displays all of the differences and similarities between two files

The next couple of subsections describe these utilities.

Testing for Sameness: cmp

The **cmp** utility determines whether two files are the same and works as follows:

Utility: **cmp** -ls *fileName1 fileName2 offset1 offset2*

cmp is a utility that tests two files for equality. If *fileName1* and *fileName2* are exactly equal, then **cmp** returns the exit code 0 and displays nothing; otherwise, it returns the exit code 1 and displays the offset and line number of the first mismatched byte. If one file is a prefix of the other, then the EOF message is displayed for the file that is shorter. The -**l** option displays the offsets and values of all mismatched bytes. The -**s** option causes all output to be inhibited. The optional values *offset1* and *offset2* specify the starting offset in *fileName1* and *fileName2*, respectively, at which the comparison should begin.

In the following example, I compared the files "lady1", "lady2", and "lady3":

```
$ cat lady1              ...look at the first test file.
Lady of the night,
I hold you close to me,
And all those loving words you say are right.
$ cat lady2              ...look at the second test file.
Lady of the night,
I hold you close to me,
And everything you say to me is right.
$ cat lady3              ...look at the third test file.
Lady of the night,
I hold you close to me,
And everything you say to me is right.
It makes me feel,
I'm so in love with you.
Even in the dark I see your light.
$ cmp lady1 lady2        ...files differ.
lady1 lady2 differ: char 48, line 3
$ cmp lady2 lady3        ...file2 is a prefix of file3.
cmp: EOF on lady2
$ cmp lady3 lady3        ...the files are exactly the same.
$ _
```

The "-l" option displays the byte offset and value of every byte that doesn't match:

```
$ cmp -l lady1 lady2      ...display bytes that don't match.
48 141 145
49 154 166
. . .
81 145 56
82 40 12
cmp: EOF on lady2         ...lady2 is smaller than lady1.
$ _
```

File Differences: diff

The **diff** utility compares two files and displays a list of editing changes that would convert the first file into the second file. It works as follows:

Utility: **diff -i** *-dflag fileName1 fileName2*

diff is a utility that compares two files and outputs a description of their differences. See the rest of this section for information on the format of this output. The **-i** flag makes **diff** ignore the case of the lines. The **-D** option causes **diff** to generate output designed for the C preprocessor.

There are three kinds of editing changes: adding lines (a), changing lines (c), and deleting lines (d). Here is the format that **diff** uses to describe each kind of edit:

Additions

---

firstStart a *secondStart, secondStop*
> lines from the second file to add to the first file

Deletions

---

firstStart, firstStop d *lineCount*
< lines from the first file to delete

Changes

---

firstStart, firstStop c *secondStart, secondStop*
< lines in the first file to be replaced
--
> lines in the second file to be used for the replacement

---

firstStart and *firstStop* denote line numbers in the first file, and *secondStart* and *secondStop* denote line numbers in the second file.

In the following example, I compared several text files to observe their differences:

```
$ cat lady1          ...look at the first test file.
Lady of the night,
I hold you close to me,
And all those loving words you say are right.
$ cat lady2          ...look at the second test file.
Lady of the night,
I hold you close to me,
And everything you say to me is right.
$ cat lady3          ...look at the third test file.
Lady of the night,
I hold you close to me,
And everything you say to me is right.
It makes me feel,
I'm so in love with you.
Even in the dark I see your light.
$ cat lady4          ...look at the fourth test file.
Lady of the night,
I'm so in love with you.
Even in the dark I see your light.
$ diff lady1 lady2     ...compare lady1 and lady2.
3c3
< And all those loving words you say are right.
---
> And everything you say to me is right.
$ diff lady2 lady3     ...compare lady2 and lady3.
3a4,6
> It makes me feel,
> I'm so in love with you.
> Even in the dark I see your light.
$ diff lady3 lady4     ...compare lady3 and lady4.
2,4d1
< I hold you close to me,
< And everything you say to me is right.
< It makes me feel,
$ _
```

The "-D" option of **diff** is useful for merging two files into a single file that contains directives for the C preprocessor. Each version of the file can be re-created by using the **cc** compiler with suitable options and macro definitions.

```
$ diff -Dflag lady3 lady4              ...look at the output.
Lady of the night,
#ifndef flag                           ...preprocessor directive.
I hold you close to me,
And everything you say to me is right.
It makes me feel,
#endif flag                            ...preprocessor directive.
I'm so in love with you.
Even in the dark I see your light.
$ diff -Dflag lady2 lady4 > lady.diff  ...store output.
$ cc -P lady.diff                      ...invoke the preprocessor.
$ cat lady.i                           ...look at the output.
Lady of the night,
I hold you close to me,
And everything you say to me is right.
$ cc -Dflag -P lady.diff               ...obtain the other version.
$ cat lady.i                           ...look at the output.
Lady of the night,
I'm so in love with you.
Even in the dark I see your light.
$ _
```

ARCHIVES

There are several occasions on which you'll want to save some files to a secondary storage medium such as a disk or tape:

- for daily, weekly, or monthly backups
- for transport between nonnetworked UNIX sites
- for posterity

There is a family of three utilities that allows you to archive files, each of which has its own strengths and weaknesses. In my opinion, it would be much better to have a single, powerful, general-purpose archive utility, but no standard utility has these qualities. Here is a list of the utilities, together with a brief description of each:

- **cpio**, which allows you to save directory structures onto a single backup volume. It's handy for saving small quantities of data, but the single-volume restriction makes it useless for large backups.
- **tar**, which allows you to save directory structures onto a single backup volume. It's specially designed to save files onto tape, so it always archives files onto

the end of the storage medium. As before, the single-volume restriction makes it unusable for large backups.

- **dump**, which allows you to save a file system onto multiple backup volumes. It's specially designed for doing total and incremental backups, but it's tricky to restore individual files. Note: In many System V–based versions of UNIX, the **ufsdump** program is equivalent to **dump**.

The next few subsections describe these utilities.

Copying Files: cpio

The **cpio** utility allows you to create and access special **cpio**-format files. These special-format files are useful for backing up small subdirectories, thereby avoiding the heavy-duty **dump** utility. Unfortunately, the **cpio** utility is unable to write special-format files to multiple volumes, so the entire backup file must be able to reside on a single storage medium. If the backup is too large for a single storage medium: use the **dump** utility instead. **cpio** works like this:

Utility: **cpio** -ov
cpio -idtu *patterns*
cpio -pl *directory*

cpio allows you to create and access special **cpio**-format files.

The **-o** option takes a list of filenames from standard input and creates a **cpio**-format file that contains a backup of the files. The **-v** option causes the name of each file to be displayed as it's copied.

The **-i** option reads a **cpio**-format file from standard input and re-creates all of the files from the input channel whose name matches a specified pattern. By default, older files are not copied over younger files. The **-u** option causes unconditional copying. The **-d** option causes directories to be created if they are needed during the copying process. The **-t** option causes a table of contents to be displayed instead of performing the copy.

The **-p** option takes a list of filenames from standard input and copies their contents to a named directory. This option is useful for copying one subdirectory to another place, although most uses of this option can be performed more easily using the **cp** utility with the **-r** (recursive) option. The **-l** option creates links instead of performing physical copies whenever possible.

To demonstrate the "-o" and "-i" options, I created a backup version of all of the C source files in my current directory, deleted the source files, and then restored them:

```
$ ls -l *.c                          ...list the files to be saved.
-rw-r--r--  1 glass     172 Jan  5 19:44 main1.c
-rw-r--r--  1 glass     198 Jan  5 19:44 main2.c
-rw-r--r--  1 glass     224 Jan  5 19:44 palindrome.c
-rw-r--r--  1 glass     266 Jan  5 23:46 reverse.c
$ ls *.c | cpio -ov > backup         ...save in "backup".
main1.c
main2.c
palindrome.c
reverse.c
3 blocks
$ ls -l backup                       ...examine "backup".
-rw-r--r--  1 glass    1536 Jan  9 18:34 backup
$ rm *.c                             ...remove the original files.
$ cpio -it < backup                  ...restore the files.
main1.c
main2.c
palindrome.c
reverse.c
3 blocks
$ ls -l *.c                          ...confirm their restoration.
-rw-r--r--  1 glass     172 Jan  5 19:44 main1.c
-rw-r--r--  1 glass     198 Jan  5 19:44 main2.c
-rw-r--r--  1 glass     224 Jan  5 19:44 palindrome.c
-rw-r--r--  1 glass     266 Jan  5 23:46 reverse.c
$ _
```

To backup all of the files that match the pattern "*.c", including subdirectories, use
the output from the **find** (described in the next section) utility as the input to **cpio**.
In the following example, note that I escaped the "*" character in the argument to
the "-name" option so that it was not expanded by the shell:

```
$ find . -name \*.c -print | cpio -ov > backup2
main1.c
main2.c
palindrome.c
reverse.c
tmp/b.c
tmp/a.c
3 blocks
$ rm -r *.c                ...remove the original files.
$ rm tmp/*.c               ...remove the lower level files.
$ cpio -it < backup2       ...restore the files.
main1.c
main2.c
palindrome.c
reverse.c
tmp/b.c
tmp/a.c
3 blocks
$ _
```

To demonstrate the "-p" option, I obtained a list of all of the files in my current directory that were modified in the last two days (using the **find** utility) and then copied them into the parent directory. Without the "-l" option, the files were physically copied, resulting in a total increase in disk usage of 153 blocks. With the "-l" option, however, the files were linked, resulting in no disk usage at all.

```
$ find . -mtime -2 -print | cpio -p ..    ...copy.
153 blocks
$ ls -l ../reverse.c                       ...look at the copied file.
-rw-r--r--  1 glass     266 Jan  9 18:42 ../reverse.c
$ find . -mtime -2 -print | cpio -pl ..    ...link
0 blocks
$ ls -l ../reverse.c                       ...look at the linked file.
-rw-r--r--  2 glass     266 Jan  7 15:26 ../reverse.c
$ _
```

Tape Archiving: tar

The **tar** utility was designed specifically for maintaining an archive of files on a magnetic tape. When you add a file to an archive file using **tar**, the file is *always* placed on the end of the archive file, since you cannot modify the middle of a file that is stored on tape. If you're not archiving files onto a tape, I suggest that you use the **cpio** utility instead. Here's how **tar** works:

Utility: **tar** -cfrtuvx [*tarFileName*] *fileList*

tar allows you to create and access special **tar**-format archive files. The **-c** option creates a **tar**-format file. The name of the **tar**-format file is "/dev/rmt0" by default (this name may vary with different versions of UNIX), although this default may be overriden by setting the $TAPE environment variable or by using the **-f** option followed by the required filename. The **-v** option encourages verbose output. The **-x** option allows you to extract named files, and the **-t** option generates a table of contents. The **-r** option unconditionally appends the listed files to the archive file. The **-u** option appends only files that are more recent than those already archived. If the file list contains directory names, the contents of the directories are appended or extracted recursively.

In the following example, I saved all of the files in the current directory to the archive file "tarfile":

```
$ ls                    ...look at the current directory.
main1*      main2       palindrome.c    reverse.h
main1.c     main2.c     palindrome.h    tarfile
main1.make  main2.make  reverse.c       tmp/
```

```
$ ls tmp                    ...look in the "tmp" directory.
a.c            b.c
$ tar -cvf tarfile .        ...archive the current directory.
a ./main1.c 1 blocks
a ./main2.c 1 blocks
...etc.; edited out for space considerations.
a ./main2 48 blocks
a ./tmp/b.c 1 blocks
a ./tmp/a.c 1 blocks
$ ls -l tarfile             ...look at the archive file "tarfile".
-rw-r--r--  1 glass     65536 Jan 10 12:44 tarfile
$ _
```

To obtain a table of contents of a **tar** archive, use the "-t" option:

```
$ tar -tvf tarfile      ...look at the table of contents.
rwxr-xr-x  496/62       0 Jan 10 12:44 1998 ./
rw-r--r--  496/62     172 Jan 10 12:41 1998 ./main1.c
rw-r--r--  496/62     198 Jan  9 18:36 1998 ./main2.c
...        edited out for space considerations.
rw-r--r--  496/62   24576 Jan  7 15:26 1998 ./main2
rwxr-xr-x  496/62       0 Jan 10 12:42 1998 ./tmp/
rw-r--r--  496/62       9 Jan 10 12:42 1998 ./tmp/b.c
rw-r--r--  496/62       9 Jan 10 12:42 1998 ./tmp/a.c
$_
```

To unconditionally append a file to the end of a tar archive, use the "-r" option followed by a list of files and/or directories to append. Notice in the following example that the **tar** archive ended up holding two copies of "reverse.c":

```
$ tar -rvf tarfile reverse.c    ...unconditionally append.
a reverse.c 1 blocks
$ tar -tvf tarfile              ...look at the table of contents.
rwxr-xr-x  496/62       0 Jan 10 12:44 1998 ./
rw-r--r--  496/62     172 Jan 10 12:41 1998 ./main1.c
...etc.
rw-r--r--  496/62     266 Jan  9 18:36 1998 ./reverse.c
...etc.
rw-r--r--  496/62     266 Jan 10 12:46 1998 reverse.c
$ _
```

To append a file only if it isn't already in the archive or if it has been modified since it was last archived, use the "-u" option instead of the "-r" option. In the following example, note that "reverse.c" was not archived because it hadn't been modified:

```
$ tar -rvf tarfile reverse.c    ...unconditionally append.
a reverse.c 1 blocks
$ tar -uvf tarfile reverse.c    ...conditionally append.
$
```

To extract a file from an archive file, use the "-x" option followed by a list of files and/or directories. If a directory name is specified, it is recursively extracted:

```
$ rm tmp/*                    ...remove all files from "tmp".
$ tar -vxf tarfile ./tmp      ...extract archived "tmp" files.
x ./tmp/b.c, 9 bytes, 1 tape blocks
x ./tmp/a.c, 9 bytes, 1 tape blocks
$ ls tmp                      ...confirm restoration.
a.c        b.c
$ _
```

Unfortunately, **tar** doesn't support pattern matching of the name list, so to extract files that match a particular pattern, be crafty and use **grep** as part of the command sequence, like this:

```
$ tar -xvf tarfile 'tar -tf tarfile | grep '.*\.c''
x ./main1.c, 172 bytes, 1 tape blocks
x ./main2.c, 198 bytes, 1 tape blocks
x ./palindrome.c, 224 bytes, 1 tape blocks
x ./reverse.c, 266 bytes, 1 tape blocks
x ./tmp/b.c, 9 bytes, 1 tape blocks
x ./tmp/a.c, 9 bytes, 1 tape blocks
$ _
```

If you change into another directory and then extract files that were stored using relative pathnames, the names are interpreted as being relative to the current directory. In the next example, I restored "reverse.c" from the previously created **tar** file to a new directory called "tmp2". Note that each copy of "reverse.c" overwrote the previous one so that the latest version was the one that was left intact:

```
$ mkdir tmp2                  ...create a new directory.
$ cd tmp2                     ...move there.
$ tar -vxf ../tarfile reverse.c   ...restore single file.
x reverse.c, 266 bytes, 1 tape blocks
x reverse.c, 266 bytes, 1 tape blocks
$ ls -l                       ...confirm restoration.
total 1
-rw-r--r-- 1 glass       266 Jan 10 12:48 reverse.c
$ _
```

Incremental Backups: dump and restore

The **dump** and **restore** utilities came from the Berkeley version of UNIX, but have been added to most other versions. (In many System V–based versions of UNIX, they are called **ufsdump** and **ufsrestore**.) Here's a system administrator's typical backup strategy:

- Perform a weekly total-file system backup.
- Perform a daily incremental backup, storing only those files that were changed since the last incremental backup.

This kind of backup strategy is supported nicely by the **dump** and **restore** utilities. **dump** works like this:

Utility: **dump** [*level*] [f *dumpFile*] [v] [w] *fileSystem*
    dump [*level*] [f *dumpFile*] [v] [w] { *fileName* }+

The **dump** utility has two forms. The first form of the **dump** utility copies files from the specified file system to *dumpFile*, which is "/dev/rmt0" by default (this name may vary in different versions of UNIX). If the dump level is specified as a number *n*, then all of the files that have been modified since the last dump at a lower level than n are copied. For example, a level-zero dump will always dump all files, whereas a level-two dump will dump all of the files modified since the last level-zero or level-one dump. If no dump level is specified, it is set to nine. The "v" option causes **dump** to verify each volume of media after it is written. The "w" option causes **dump** to display a list of all the file systems that need to be dumped instead of performing a backup.

The second form of **dump** allows you to specify the names of files to be dumped.

Both forms prompt the user to insert and/or remove dump media when necessary. For example, a large system dump to a tape drive often requires an operator to remove a full tape and replace it with an empty one. When a dump is performed, information about the dump is recorded in the "/etc/dumpdates" file for use by future invocations of **dump**.

Here's an example of **dump** that performs a level-zero dump of the filesystem on "/dev/da0" to the tape drive "/dev/rmt0" with verification:

```
$ dump 0 fv /dev/rmt0 /dev/da0
```

The **restore** utility allows you to restore files from a **dump** backup and works as follows:

Utility: **restore** -irtx [f *dumpFile*] { *fileName* }*

The **restore** utility allows you to restore a set of files from a previous dump file. If *dumpFile* is not specified, "/dev/rtm0" is used by default. (Again, this name could vary in different versions of UNIX.) The **-r** option causes every file on *dumpFile* to be restored into the current directory, so use this option with care. The **-t** option causes a table of contents of *dumpFile* to be displayed instead of restoring any files. The **-x** option causes **restore** to restore only the specified filename(s) from *dumpFile*. If a filename is the name of a directory, its contents are recursively restored.

The **-i** option causes **restore** to read the table of contents of *dumpFile* and then enter an interactive mode that allows you to choose the files that you wish to restore. For more information on this interactive mode, issue the command "man restore".

In the following example, I used **restore** to extract a couple of previously saved files from the dump device "/dev/rmt0":

```
$ restore -x f /dev/rmt0 wine.c hacking.c
```

FINDING FILES: FIND

The **find** utility can do much more than simply locate a named file; it can perform actions on a set of files that satisfy specific conditions. For example, you can use **find** to erase all of the files belonging to a particular user that haven't been modified for a particular number of days. Here's a formal description of the **find** utility:

Utility: **find** *pathList expression*

The **find** utility recursively descends through *pathList* and applies *expression* to every file. The syntax of *expression* is described below, followed by some examples of the use of **find**.

Here is a table that describes the syntax of *expression*:

Expression	Value/Action
-name *pattern*	True if the file's name matches *pattern*, which may include the shell metacharacters "*", "[", "]", and "?".
-perm *oct*	True if the octal description of the file's permission flags are exactly equal to *oct*.
-type *ch*	True if the type of the file is *ch* ("b" = block, "c" = char, etc.).
-user *userId*	True if the owner of the file is *userId*.
-group *groupId*	True if the group of the file is *groupId*.
-atime *count*	True if the file has been accessed within *count* days.
-mtime *count*	True if the contents of the file have been modified within *count* days.
-ctime *count*	True if the contents of the file have been modified within *count* days or if any of its attributes have been altered.
-exec *command*	True if the exit code from executing *command* is zero. *command* must be terminated by an escaped semicolon (\;). If you specify "{}" as a command line argument, it is replaced by the name of the current file.
-print	Prints out the name of the current file and returns true.
-ls	Displays the current file's attributes and returns true.
-cpio *device*	Writes the current file in **cpio** format to *device* and returns true.
!*expression*	Returns the logical negation of *expression*.
expr1 [-a] *expr2*	Short-circuiting "and"; if *expr1* is false, it returns false and *expr2* is not executed. If *expr1* is true, it returns the value of *expr2*.
expr1 -o *expr2*	Short-circuiting "or"; if *expr1* is true, it returns true. If *expr1* is false, it returns the value of *expr2*.

Here are some examples of **find** in action:

```
$ find . -name '*.c' -print    ...print C source files
                               ...in the current directory or any of its
                               ...subdirectories.
./proj/fall.89/play.c
./proj/fall.89/referee.c
./proj/fall.89/player.c
./rock/guess.c
./rock/play.c
./rock/player.c
./rock/referee.c
$ find . -mtime -14 -ls     ...ls-modified files during the last 14 days.
-rw-r--r--  1 glass  cs 14151 May  1 16:58 ./stty.txt
-rw-r--r--  1 glass  cs    48 May  1 14:02 ./myFile.doc
-rw-r--r--  1 glass  cs    10 May  1 14:02 ./rain.doc
-rw-r--r--  1 glass  cs 14855 May  1 16:58 ./tset.txt
-rw-r--r--  1 glass  cs 47794 May  2 10:56 ./mail.txt
$ find . -name '*.bak' -ls -exec rm {} \;
                               ...ls and then remove all files
                               ...that end with ".bak".
-rw-r--r--  1 glass  cs     9 May 16 12:01 ./a.bak
-rw-r--r--  1 glass  cs     9 May 16 12:01 ./b.bak
```

```
-rw-r--r--  1 glass  cs 15630 Jan 26 00:14 ./s6/gosh.bak
-rw-r--r--  1 glass  cs 18481 Jan 26 12:59 ./s6/gosh2.bak
$ find . \( -name '*.c' -o -name '*.txt' \) -print
                  ...print the names of all files that
                  ...end in ".c" or ".txt".
./proj/fall.89/play.c
./proj/fall.89/referee.c
./proj/fall.89/player.c
./rock/guess.c
./rock/play.c
./rock/player.c
./rock/referee.c
./stty.txt
./tset.txt
./mail.txt
$ _
```

SCHEDULING COMMANDS

There are two utilities that allow you to schedule commands to be executed at a later point in time:

- **crontab**, which allows you to create a scheduling table that describes a series of jobs to be executed on a periodic basis
- **at**, which allows you to schedule jobs to be executed on a one-time basis

The next couple of subsections describe each utility.

Periodic Execution: cron and crontab

The **crontab** utility allows you to schedule a series of jobs to be executed on a periodic basis and works as follows:

To use **crontab**, you must prepare an input file that contains lines of the format

```
minute   hour   day   month   weekday   command
```

Utility: **crontab** *crontabName*
   crontab -ler [*userName*]

crontab is the user interface to the UNIX "cron" system. When **crontab** is used without any options, the crontab file called *crontabName* is registered and its commands are executed according to the specified timing rules. The **-l** option lists the contents of a registered crontab file. The **-e** option edits and then registers a registered crontab file. The **-r** option unregisters a registered crontab file. The **-l**, **-e**, and **-r** options may be used by a super-user to access another user's crontab file by supplying the user's name as an optional argument. The anatomy of a crontab file is described shortly.

---

where the values of each field are as follows:

Field	Valid Value
minute	0–59
hour	0–23
day	1–31
month	1–12
weekday	1–7 (1 = Mon., 2 = Tue., 3 = Wed., 4 = Thu., 5 = Fri., 6 = Sat., 7 = Sun.)
command	any UNIX command

Files of this nature are called "crontab files." Whenever the current time matches a line's description, the associated command is executed by the shell specified in the $SHELL environment variable. A Bourne shell is used if this variable is not set. If any of the first five fields contain an "*" instead of a number, the field always matches. The standard output of the command is automatically sent to the user via **mail**. Any characters following a "%" are copied into a temporary file and used as the command's standard input. Here is a sample crontab file that I created in my home directory and called "crontab.cron":

```
$ cat crontab.cron       ...list the crontab file.
0    8    *    *    1     echo Happy Monday Morning
*    *    *    *    *      echo One Minute Passed > /dev/tty1
30   14   1    *    1     mail users % Jan Meeting At 3pm
$ _
```

The first line mails me "Happy Monday Morning" at 8 AM every Monday. The next line echoes "One Minute Passed" every minute to the device "/dev/tty1", which happens to be my terminal. The last line sends mail to all users on the first of January at 2:30 pm to remind them of an impending meeting.

There is a single process called "cron" that is responsible for executing the commands in registered crontab files in a timely fashion. It is started when the UNIX system is booted and does not stop until the UNIX system is shut down. Copies of all registered crontab files are stored in the directory "/var/spool/cron/crontabs".

To register a crontab file, use the **crontab** utility with the name of the crontab file as the single argument:

```
$ crontab crontab.cron   ...register the crontab file.
$ _
```

If you already have a registered crontab file, the new one is registered in place of the old one. To list the contents of your registered crontab file, use the "-l" option. To list someone else's crontab file, add their name as an argument. Only a super-user can use this option. In the example that follows, note that one of my previously registered crontab-file entries triggered coincidentally after I used the **crontab** utility:

```
$ crontab -l         ...list contents of current crontab file.
0    8    *    *    1     echo Happy Monday Morning
*    *    *    *    *      echo One Minute Passed > /dev/tty1
30   14   1    *    1     mail users % Jan Meeting At 3pm
```

```
$ One Minute Passed    ...output from one crontab command.
$ _
```

To edit your crontab file and then resave it, use the "-e" option. To unregister a crontab file, use the "-r" option:

```
$ crontab -r          ...unregister my crontab file.
$ _
```

A super-user may create files called "cron.allow" and "cron.deny" in the "/var/spool/cron" directory to enable and inhibit individual users from using the **crontab** facility. Each file consists of a list of user names on separate lines. If neither of the files exist, only a super-user may use **crontab**. If "cron.deny" is empty and "cron.allow" doesn't exist, all users may use **crontab**.

One-Time Execution: at

The **at** utility allows you to schedule one-time commands and/or scripts, and it works like this:

Utility: **at** -csm *time* [*date* [, *year*]] [+*increment*] [*script*]
    at -r { *jobId* }+
    at -l { *jobId* }*

at allows you to schedule one-time commands and/or scripts. It supports a flexible format for time specification. The **-c** and **-s** options allow you to specify that commands are run by a C shell or Bourne shell, respectively. The **-m** option instructs **at** to send you mail when the job is completed. If no script name is specified, **at** takes a list of commands from standard input. The **-r** option removes the specified jobs from the **at** queue, and the **-l** option lists the pending jobs. A job is removed from the **at** queue after it has executed.

    time is of the format HH or HHMM followed by an optional AM/PM specifier, and *date* is spelled out using the first three letters of the day and/or month. The keyword "now" may be used in place of the time sequence. The keywords "today" and "tomorrow" may be used in place of *date*. If no *date* is supplied, then **at** uses the following rules:

- If *time* is after the current time, then *date* is assumed to be "today".
- If *time* is before the current time, then *date* is assumed to be "tomorrow".

The stated time may be augmented by an *increment,* which is a number followed by one of the words "minutes", "hours", "days", "weeks", "months", or "years".

    A script is executed by the shell specified by the $SHELL environment variable or by a Bourne shell if this variable is not set. All standard output from an **at** script is mailed to the user.

In the following example, I scheduled an **at** script to send a message to my terminal "/dev/tty1":

```
$ cat at.csh                        ...look at the script to be scheduled.
#! /bin/csh
echo at done > /dev/tty1             ...echo output to terminal.
$ date                              ...look at the current time.
Sat Jan 10 17:27:42 CST 1998
$ at now + 2 minutes at.csh          ...schedule script to
                                     ...execute in two minutes.
job 2519 at Sat Jan 10 17:30:00 1998
$ at -l                              ...look at the at schedule.
      2519 a       Sat Jan 10 17:30:00 1998
$ _
at done                              ...output from scheduled script.
$ at 17:35 at.csh                    ...schedule the script again.
job 2520 at Sat Jan 10 17:35:00 1998
$ at -r 2520                         ...deschedule.
$ at -l                              ...look at the at schedule.
$ _
```

Here are some more examples of legal time formats for **at**:

```
0934am Sep 18 at.csh
9:34 Sep 18 , 1994 at.csh
11:00pm tomorrow at.csh
now + 1 day at.csh
9pm Jan 13 at.csh
10pm Wed at.csh
```

If you omit the command name, **at** displays a prompt and then waits for a list of commands to be entered from standard input. To terminate the command list, press *Control*-D. Here's an example of this method:

```
$ at 8pm                ...enter commands to be scheduled from keyboard.
at> echo at done > /dev/ttyp1
at> ^D                  ...end of input.
job 2530 at Sat Jan 10 17:35:00 1998
$ _
```

You may program a script to reschedule itself by calling **at** within the script:

```
$ cat at.csh            ...a script that reschedules itself.
#! /bin/csh
date > /dev/tty1
# Reschedule script
at now + 2 minutes at.csh
$ _
```

A super-user may create files called "at.allow" and "at.deny" in the "/var/spool/ cron" directory to enable and inhibit individual users from using the **at** facility. Each file should consist of a list of user names on separate lines. If neither of the files exist, only a super-user may use **at**. If "at.deny" is empty and "at.allow" doesn't exist, all users may use **at**.

PROGRAMMABLE TEXT PROCESSING: awk

The **awk** utility scans one or more files and performs an action on all of the lines that match a particular condition. The actions and conditions are described by an **awk** program and range from the very simple to the complex.

awk got its name from the combined first letters of its authors' surnames: Aho, Weinberger, and Kernighan. It borrows its control structures and expression syntax from the language of C. If you already know C, then learning **awk** is quite straightforward.

awk is a comprehensive utility, so comprehensive, in fact, that there's an entire book on it! Because of its comprehensiveness, I've attempted to describe only the main features and options of **awk**; however, I think that the material that I describe in this section will allow you to write a good number of useful **awk** applications. Here's a synopsis of **awk**:

Utility: **awk** -Fc [-f *fileName*] *program* { *variable=value* }* { *fileName* }*

awk is a programmable text-processing utility that scans the lines of its input and performs actions on every line that matches a particular criteria. An **awk** program may be included on the command line, in which case it should be surrounded by single quotes; alternatively, it may be stored in a file and specified using the **-f** option. The initial values of variables may be specified on the command line. The default field separators are tabs and spaces. To override this default, use the **-F** option followed by the new field separator. If no filenames are specified, **awk** reads from standard input.

The next few subsections describe the various features of **awk** and include many examples.

awk Programs

An **awk** program may be supplied on the command line, but it's much more common to place it in a text file and specify the file using the "-f" option. If you decide to place an **awk** program on the command line, surround it by single quotes.

When **awk** reads a line, it breaks it into fields that are separated by tabs and/or spaces. The field separator may be overridden by using the "-F" option, as you'll see later in this section. An **awk** program is a list of one or more commands of the form:

```
[ condition ] [ \{ action \} ]
```

condition is one of the following:

- the special token BEGIN or END
- an expression involving logical operators, relational operators, and/or regular expressions

action is a list of one or more of the following kinds of C-like statements, terminated by semicolons:

- **if** (conditional) statement [**else** statement]
- **while** (conditional) statement
- **for** (expression; conditional; expression) statement
- **break**
- **continue**
- variable = expression
- **print** [list of expressions] [> expression]
- **printf** format [, list of expressions] [> expression]
- **next** (skips the remaining patterns on the current line of input)
- **exit** (skips the rest of the current line)
- {list of statements}

action is performed on every line that matches *condition*. If *condition* is not provided, *action* is performed on every line. If *action* is not provided, then all matching lines are simply sent to standard output. The statements in an **awk** program may be indented and formatted using spaces, tabs, and new lines.

Accessing Individual Fields

The first field of the current line may be accessed by "$1", the second by "$2", and so on. "$0" stands for the entire line. The built-in variable "NF" is equal to the number of fields in the current line. In the following example, I ran a simple **awk** program on the text file "float" to insert the number of fields into each line:

```
$ cat float                    ...look at the original file.
Wish I was floating in blue across the sky,
My imagination is strong,
And I often visit the days
When everything seemed so clear.
Now I wonder what I'm doing here at all...
$ awk '{ print NF, $0 }' float    ...execute the command.
9 Wish I was floating in blue across the sky,
4 My imagination is strong,
6 And I often visit the days
5 When everything seemed so clear.
9 Now I wonder what I'm doing here at all...
$ _
```

BEGIN and END

The special condition BEGIN is triggered before the first line is read, and the special condition END is triggered after the last line has been read. When expressions are listed in a *print* statement, no space is placed between them, and a new line is printed by default. The built-in variable FILENAME is equal to the name of the input file. In the following example, I ran a program that displayed the first, third, and last fields of every line:

```
$ cat awk2                              ...look at the awk script.
BEGIN { print "Start of file:", FILENAME }
{ print $1 $3 $NF }                     ...print first, third and last fields.
END { print "End of file" }
$ awk -f awk2 float                     ...execute the script.
Start of file: float
Wishwassky,
Myisstrong,
Andoftendays
Whenseemedclear.
Nowwonderall...
End of file
$ _
```

Operators

When commas are placed between the expressions in a *print* statement, a space is printed. All of the usual C operators are available in **awk**. The built-in variable "NR" contains the line number of the current line. In the next example, I ran a program that displayed the first, third, and last fields of lines 2 and 3 of "float":

```
$ cat awk3                ...look at the awk script.
NR > 1 && NR < 4 { print NR, $1, $3, $NF }
$ awk -f awk3 float       ...execute the script.
2 My is strong,
3 And often days
$ _
```

Variables

awk supports user-defined variables. There is no need to declare variables. A variable's initial value is a null string or zero, depending on how you use it. In the next example, the program counted the number of lines and words in a file as it echoed the lines to standard output:

```
$ cat awk4                ...look at the awk script.
BEGIN { print "Scanning file" }
{
 printf "line %d: %s\n", NR, $0;
 lineCount++;
 wordCount += NF;
}
```

```
END { printf "lines = %d, words = %d\n", lineCount, wordCount }
$ awk -f awk4 float      ...execute the script.
Scanning file
line 1: Wish I was floating in blue across the sky,
line 2: My imagination is strong,
line 3: And I often visit the days
line 4: When everything seemed so clear.
line 5: Now I wonder what I'm doing here at all...
lines = 5, words = 33
$ _
```

Control Structures

awk supports most of the standard control structures of C. In the following example, I printed the fields in each line in reverse order:

```
$ cat awk5              ...look at the awk script.
{
  for (i = NF; i >= 1; i--)
    printf "%s ", $i;
    printf "\n";
}
$ awk -f awk5 float     ...execute the script.
sky, the across blue in floating was I Wish
strong, is imagination My
days the visit often I And
clear. so seemed everything When
all...at here doing I'm what wonder I Now
$ _
```

Extended Regular Expressions

The condition for line matching can be an extended regular expression, which is defined in the appendix of this book. Regular expressions must be placed between "/" characters. In the next example, I displayed all of the lines that contained a "t" followed by an "e", with any number of characters in between. For the sake of clarity, I've italicized the character sequences of the output lines that satisfied the condition.

```
$ cat awk6              ...look at the script.
/t.*e/ { print $0 }
$ awk -f awk6 float ...execute the script.
Wish I was floating in blue across the sky,
And often visit the days
When everything seemed so clear.
Now I wonder what I'm doing here at all...
$ _
```

Condition Ranges

A condition may be two expressions separated by a comma. In this case, **awk** performs *action* on every line from the first line that matches the first condition to the next line that satisfies the second condition:

```
$ cat awk7               ...look at the awk script.
/strong/ , /clear/ { print $0 }
$ awk -f awk7 float      ...execute the script.
My imagination is strong,
And I often visit the days
When everything seemed so clear.
$ _
```

Field Separators

If the field separators in a file are not spaces, use the "-F" option to specify the separator character. In the next example, I processed a file whose fields were separated by colons:

```
$ cat awk3                   ...look at the awk script.
NR > 1 && NR < 4 { print $1, $3, $NF }
$ cat float2                 ...look at the input file.
Wish:I:was:floating:in:blue:across:the:sky,
My:imagination:is:strong,
And:I:often:visit:the:days
When:everything:seemed:so:clear.
Now:I:wonder:what:I'm:doing:here:at:all...
$ awk -F: -f awk3 float2     ...execute the script.
My is strong,
And often days
$ _
```

Built-In Functions

awk supports several built-in functions, including "exp ()", "log ()", "sqrt ()", "int ()", and "substr ()". The first four functions work just like their standard counterparts in C. The "substr (str, x, y)" function returns the substring of *str* from the *x*th character to the *y*th character. Here's an example of the use of these functions:

```
$ cat test               ...look at the input file.
1.1 a
2.2 at
3.3 eat
4.4 beat
$ cat awk8               ...look at the awk script.
{
 printf "$1 = %g ", $1;
 printf "exp = %.2g ", exp ($1);
 printf "log = %.2g ", log ($1);
```

```
printf "sqrt = %.2g ", sqrt ($1);
printf "int = %d ", int ($1);
printf "substr (%s, 1, 2) = %s\n", $2, substr($2, 1, 2);
}
$ awk -f awk8 test        ...execute the script.
$1 = 1.1 exp = 3 log = 0.095 sqrt = 1 int = 1 substr (a, 1, 2) = a
$1 = 2.2 exp = 9 log = 0.79 sqrt = 1.5 int = 2 substr (at, 1, 2) = at
$1 = 3.3 exp = 27 log = 1.2 sqrt = 1.8 int = 3 substr (eat, 1, 2) = ea
$1 = 4.4 exp = 81 log = 1.5 sqrt = 2.1 int = 4 substr (beat, 1, 2) = be
$ _
```

HARD AND SOFT LINKS: ln

The **ln** utility allows you to create both hard links and symbolic (soft) links between files, and it works like this:

Utility: **ln** -sf *original* [*newLink*]
    ln -sf { *original* }+ *directory*

ln is a utility that allows you to create hard links or symbolic (soft) links to existing files.

To create a hard link between two regular files, specify the existing file label as the *original* filename and the new file label as *newLink*. Both labels will then refer to the same physical file, and this arrangement will be reflected in the hard-link count shown by the **ls** utility. The file can then be accessed via either label and is removed from the file system only when all of its associated labels are deleted. If *newLink* is omitted, the last component of *original* is assumed. If the last argument is the name of a directory, then hard links are made from that directory to all of the specified original filenames. Hard links may not span file systems.

The **-s** option causes **ln** to create symbolic links, which may span file systems. The **-f** option allows a super-user to create a hard link to a directory.

In the following example, I added a new label "hold" to the file referenced by the existing label "hold.3". Note that the hard-link count field was incremented from one to two when the hard link was added and then went back to one again when the hard link was deleted:

```
$ ls -l                 ...look at the current contents of the directory.
total 3
-rw-r--r--  1 glass          124 Jan 12 17:32 hold.1
-rw-r--r--  1 glass           89 Jan 12 17:34 hold.2
-rw-r--r--  1 glass           91 Jan 12 17:34 hold.3
```

```
$ ln hold.3 hold          ...create a new hard link.
$ ls -l                   ...look at the new contents of the directory.
total 4
-rw-r--r--  2 glass       91 Jan 12 17:34 hold
-rw-r--r--  1 glass      124 Jan 12 17:32 hold.1
-rw-r--r--  1 glass       89 Jan 12 17:34 hold.2
-rw-r--r--  2 glass       91 Jan 12 17:34 hold.3
$ rm hold                 ...remove one of the links.
$ ls -l                   ...look at the updated contents of the directory.
total 3
-rw-r--r--  1 glass      124 Jan 12 17:32 hold.1
-rw-r--r--  1 glass       89 Jan 12 17:34 hold.2
-rw-r--r--  1 glass       91 Jan 12 17:34 hold.3
$ _
```

A series of hard links may be added to an existing directory if the directory's name is specified as the second argument of **ln**. In the following example, I created links in the "tmp" directory to all of the files matched by the pattern "hold.*":

```
$ mkdir tmp               ...create a new directory.
$ ln hold.* tmp           ...create a series of links in "tmp".
$ ls -l tmp               ...look at the contents of "tmp".
total 3
-rw-r--r--  2 glass      124 Jan 12 17:32 hold.1
-rw-r--r--  2 glass       89 Jan 12 17:34 hold.2
-rw-r--r--  2 glass       91 Jan 12 17:34 hold.3
$ _
```

A hard link may not be created from a file on one file system to a file on a different file system. To get around this problem, create a *symbolic* link instead; a symbolic link may span file systems. To create a symbolic link, use the "-s" option of **ln**. In the next example, I tried to create a hard link from my home directory to the file "/usr/include/stdio.h". Unfortunately, that file was on a different file system, and so the **ln** command failed. However, the **ln** command with the "-s" option succeeded. When **ls** is used with the "-F" option, symbolic links are preceded by an "@" character. By default, **ls** displays the contents of the symbolic link; to obtain information about the file to which the link refers, use the "-L" option.

```
$ ln /usr/include/stdio.h stdio.h        ...a hard link cannot be made.
ln: stdio.h: Cross-device link
$ ln -s /usr/include/stdio.h stdio.h     ...a symbolic link can be made.
$ ls -l stdio.h                          ...examine the file.
lrwxrwxrwx  1 glass  20 Jan 12 17:58 stdio.h -> /usr/include/stdio.h
$ ls -F                                  ..."@" indicates a symbolic link.
stdio.h@
$ ls -lL stdio.h                         ...look at the link itself.
-r--r--r--  1 root   1732 Oct 13 1998 stdio.h
$ cat stdio.h                            ...look at the file.
# ifndef FILE
#define    BUFSIZ    1024
```

```
#define SBFSIZ    8
extern       struct    iobuf {
...etc. (No need to take up space by displaying the rest of the file.)
$ _
```

SUBSTITUTING A USER: su

A lot of people think that the name of the **su** utility stands for "super-user," but it doesn't. Instead, it stands for "substitute user," and this utility allows you to create a subshell owned by another user. It works like this:

Utility: **su** [-] [*userName*] [*args*]

su creates a temporary shell with *userName*'s real and effective user and group IDs. If *userName* is not specified, "root" is assumed and the new shell's prompt is set to a "#" as a reminder. While you're in the subshell, you are effectively logged on as that user; when you terminate the subshell by pressing *Control*-D, you are returned to your original shell. Of course, you must know the other user's password to use this utility. The $SHELL and $HOME environment variables are set from *userName*'s entry in the password file. If *userName* is not "root", the $USER environment variable is also set. The new shell does not go through its login sequence unless the "-" option is supplied. All other arguments are passed as command-line arguments to the new shell.

Here's an example of the use of **su**:

```
$ whoami            ...find out my current user ID.
glass
$ su                ...substitute user.
Password:           ...enter super-user password here.
$ whoami            ...confirm my current user ID has changed.
root
$ ...perform super-user tasks here (edited out for space considerations).
$ ^D                ...terminate the child shell.
$ whoami            ...confirm that current user ID is restored.
glass
$ _
```

CHECKING FOR MAIL: BIFF

The UNIX shells check for incoming mail periodically, which means that several minutes may pass between the reception of mail at your mailbox and the shell's notification to your terminal. To avoid this delay, you may enable instant mail notification by using the **biff** utility, which works as follows:

Utility: **biff** [y | n]

The **biff** utility allows you to enable and disable instant mail notification. To see your current **biff** setting, use **biff** with no parameters. Use "y" to enable instant notification and "n" to disable it. Why is this utility called **biff?** The woman at the University of California at Berkeley who wrote this utility for BSD UNIX named it after her dog Biff, who always barked when the mailman brought the mail.

Here's an example of the use of **biff**:

```
$ biff          ...display current biff setting.
biff is n
$ biff y        ...enable instant mail notification.
$ biff          ...confirm new biff setting.
biff is y
$ _
```

TRANSFORMING FILES

There are several utilities that perform a transformation on the contents of a file, including the following utilities:

- **compress** and **uncompress**, which convert a file into a space-efficient intermediate format and then back again. This utility is useful for saving disk space.
- **crypt**, which encodes a file so that other users can't understand it.
- **sed**, a general-purpose programmable stream editor that edits a file according to a preprepared set of instructions.
- **tr**, which maps characters from one set to another. This utility is useful for performing simple mappings such as converting the text of a file from uppercase to lowercase.
- **ul**, which converts embedded underline sequences in a file to a form that is suitable for a particular terminal.

The next few subsections contain a description of each utility in the previous list.

Compressing Files: compress and uncompress

The **compress** utility encodes a file into a more compact format that is to be decoded later using the **uncompress** utility. The two utilities work as follows:

Utility: **compress** -cv { *fileName* }+
             uncompress -cv { *fileName* }+

compress replaces a file by its compressed version, appending a ".Z" suffix to the file's name. The **-c** option sends the compressed version to standard output rather than overwriting the original file. The **-v** option displays the amount of compression that takes place.

    uncompress reverses the effect of **compress,** re-creating the original file from its compressed version.

---

compress is useful for reducing the amount of disk space that you take up and packing more files into an archive file. Here's an example of its use:

```
$ ls -l palindrome.c reverse.c              ...examine the original files.
-rw-r--r--  1 glass          224 Jan 10 13:05 palindrome.c
-rw-r--r--  1 glass          266 Jan 10 13:05 reverse.c
$ compress -v palindrome.c reverse.c        ...compress them.
palindrome.c: Compression: 20.08% -- replaced with palindrome.c.Z
reverse.c: Compression: 22.93%    -- replaced with reverse.c.Z
$ ls -l palindrome.c.Z reverse.c.Z
-rw-r--r--  1 glass          179 Jan 10 13:05 palindrome.c.Z
-rw-r--r--  1 glass          205 Jan 10 13:05 reverse.c.Z
$ uncompress -v *.Z                         ...restore the original files.
palindrome.c.Z:  -- replaced with palindrome.c
reverse.c.Z:     -- replaced with reverse.c
$ ls -l palindrome.c reverse.c              ...confirm the restoration.
-rw-r--r--  1 glass          224 Jan 10 13:05 palindrome.c
-rw-r--r--  1 glass          266 Jan 10 13:05 reverse.c
$ _
```

File Encryption: crypt

The **crypt** utility creates a key-encoded version of a text file. The only way to retrieve the original text from the encoded file is by executing **crypt** with the same key that was used to encode the file. Here's how it works:

Utility: **crypt** [*key*]

crypt performs one of two duties:

- If the standard input is regular text, an encoded version of the text is sent to standard output using *key* as the encoding key.

- If the standard input is encoded text, a decoded version of the text is sent to standard output using *key* as the decoding key.

If *key* is not specified, **crypt** prompts you for a key that you must enter from your terminal. The key that you enter is not echoed. If you supply *key* on the command line, beware: A **ps** listing will show the value of *key*.

    crypt uses a coding algorithm similar to the one that was used in the German "Enigma" machine.

Here's an example of the use of **crypt**:

```
$ cat sample.txt                          ...list the original file.
Here's a file that will be encrypted.
$ crypt agatha < sample.txt > sample.crypt
                                          ..."agatha" is the key.
$ rm sample.txt                           ...remove original.
$ crypt agatha < sample.crypt > sample.txt ...decode.
$ cat sample.txt                          ...list original.
Here's a file that will be encrypted.
$ _
```

Stream Editing: sed

The stream-editor utility **sed** scans one or more files and performs an editing action on all of the lines that match a particular condition. The actions and conditions may be stored in a **sed** script. **sed** is useful for performing simple repetitive editing tasks.

    sed is a fairly comprehensive utility. Because of this aspect, I've attempted to describe only the main features and options of **sed**; however, I think that the material that I describe in this section will allow you to write a good number of useful **sed** scripts.

    Here's a synopsis of **sed**:

Utility: **sed** [-e *script*] [-f *scriptfile*] { *fileName* }*

sed is a utility that edits an input stream according to a script that contains editing commands. Each editing command is separated by a new line and describes an action and a line or range of lines upon which to perform the action. A **sed** script may be stored in a file and executed by using the **-f** option. If a script is placed directly on the command line, it should be surrounded by single quotes. If no files are specified, **sed** reads from standard input. The format of **sed** scripts is described in the next set of subsections.

sed Commands   A **sed** script is a list of one or more of the following commands, separated by new lines:

Command syntax	Meaning
address a\ *text*	Append *text* after the line specified by *address*.
addressRange c\ *text*	Replace the text specified by *addressRange* with *text*.
addressRange d	Delete the text specified by *addressRange*.
address i\ *text*	Insert *text* after the line specified by *address*.
address r *name*	Append the contents of the file *name* after the line specified by *address*.
addressRange s/*expr*/*str*/	Substitute the first occurrence of the regular expression *expr* by the string *str*.
addressRange a/*expr*/*str*/g	Substitute every occurrence of the regular expression *expr* by the string *str*.

The following rules apply to the commands of **sed** scripts:

- *address* must be either a line number or a regular expression. A regular expression selects all of the lines that match the expression. You may use the "$" character to select the last line.
- *addressRange* can be a single address or a couple of addresses separated by commas. If two addresses are specified, then all of the lines between the first line that matches the first address and the first line that matches the second address are selected.
- If no address is specified, then the command is applied to all of the lines.

Substituting Text   In the next example, I supplied the **sed** script on the command line. The script inserted a couple of spaces at the start of every line.

```
$ cat arms                       ...look at the original file.
People just like me,
Are all around the world,
Waiting for the loved ones that they need.
And with my heart,
I make a simple wish,
Plain enough for anyone to see.
$ sed 's/^/  /' arms > arms.indent   ...indent the file.
$ cat arms.indent                ...look at the result.
People just like me,
Are all around the world,
Waiting for the loved ones that they need.
And with my heart,
I make a simple wish,
Plain enough for anyone to see.
$ _
```

To remove all of the leading spaces from a file, use the "substitute" operator in the reverse fashion:

```
$ sed 's/^ *//' arms.indent      ...remove leading spaces.
People just like me,
Are all around the world,
Waiting for the loved ones that they need.
And with my heart,
I make a simple wish,
Plain enough for anyone to see.
$ _
```

Deleting Text   The next example illustrates a script that deleted all of the lines that contained the regular expression "a":

```
$ sed '/a/d' arms   ...remove all lines containing an "a'.
People just like me,
$ _
```

To delete only those lines that contain the word "a", as opposed to the letter "a", I surrounded the regular expression by escaped angled brackets ("\<" and "\>"):

```
$ sed '/\<a\>/d' arms
People just like me,
Are all around the world,
Waiting for the loved ones that they need.
And with my heart,
Plain enough for anyone to see.
$ _
```

Inserting Text   In the next example, I inserted a copyright notice at the top of the file by using the "insert" command. Notice that I stored the **sed** script in a file and executed it by using the "-f" option.

```
$ cat sed5              ...look at the sed script.
1i\
Copyright 1992 & 1998 by Graham Glass\
All rights reserved\
$ sed -f sed5 arms       ...insert a copyright notice.
Copyright 1992 & 1998 by Graham Glass
All rights reserved
People just like me,
Are all around the world,
Waiting for the loved ones that they need.
And with my heart,
I make a simple wish,
Plain enough for anyone to see.
$ _
```

Replacing Text   To replace lines, use the "change" function. In the following example, I replaced the group of lines 1 through 3 with a message indicating that those lines are censored:

```
$ cat sed6              ...list the sed script.
1,3c\
Lines 1-3 are censored.
$ sed -f sed6 arms      ...execute the script.
Lines 1-3 are censored.
And with my heart,
I make a simple wish,
Plain enough for anyone to see.
$ _
```

To replace individual lines, rather than an entire group of lines, with a message, supply a separate command for each line:

```
$ cat sed7              ...list the sed script.
1c\
Line 1 is censored.
2c\
Line 2 is censored.
3c\
Line 3 is censored.
$ sed -f sed7 arms      ...execute the script.
Line 1 is censored.
Line 2 is censored.
Line 3 is censored.
And with my heart,
I make a simple wish,
Plain enough for anyone to see.
$ _
```

Inserting Files   In the following example, I inserted a file that contains a message after the last line of the file containing the poem:

```
$ cat insert           ...list the file to be inserted.
The End
$ sed '$r insert' arms  ...execute the script.
People just like me,
Are all around the world,
Waiting for the loved ones that they need.
And with my heart,
I make a simple wish,
Plain enough for anyone to see.
The End
$ _
```

Multiple sed Commands   This last example illustrates the use of multiple **sed** commands. I inserted a "<<" sequence at the start of each line and appended a ">>" sequence to the end of each line:

```
$ sed -e 's/^/<< /' -e 's/$/ >>/' arms
<< People just like me, >>
<< Are all around the world, >>
<< Waiting for the loved ones that they need. >>
<< And with my heart, >>
<< I make a simple wish, >>
<< Plain enough for anyone to see. >>
$ _
```

Translating Characters: tr

The **tr** utility maps the characters in a file from one character set to another, and it works like this:

Utility: **tr** -cds *string1 string2*

tr maps all of the characters in its standard input from the character set *string1* to the character set *string2*. If the length of *string2* is less than the length of *string1, string2* padded by repeating its last character; in other words, the string "tr abc de" is equivalent to "tr abc dee".

A character set may be specified using the "[]" notation of shell filename substitution:

- To specify a character set containing only the letters "a", "d", and "f", simply type the characters as a single string: *adf.*
- To specify the character set containing the letters "a" through "z", separate the start and end characters by a dash: *a-z.*

By default, **tr** replaces every character of standard input in *string1* by its corresponding character in *string2*.

The **-c** option causes *string1* to be *complemented* before the mapping is performed. Complementing a string means that it is replaced by a string that contains every ASCII character except those in the original string. The net effect of this action is that every character of standard input that *does not* occur in *string1* is replaced.

The **-d** option causes every character in *string1* to be deleted from standard input, and the **-s** option causes every repeated output character to be condensed into a single instance.

Here are some examples of **tr** in action:

```
$ cat go.cart                       ...list the sample input file.
go cart

racing
$ tr a-z A-Z < go.cart              ...translate lower to uppercase.
GO CART

RACING
$ tr a-c D-E < go.cart              ...replace "abc" by "DEE".
go EDrt

rDEing
$ tr -c a X < go.cart              ...replace every non-"a" with "X".
XXXXaXXXXXaXXXXX                    ...even the last new line is replaced.
$ tr -c a-z '\012' < go.cart       ...replace nonalphabetic characters
                                   ...with ASCII 12 (new line).
go
cart

racing
$ tr -cs a-z '\012' < go.cart      ...repeat, but condense
go                                 ...repeated new lines.
cart
racing
$ tr -d a-c < go.cart              ...delete all characters from "a" to "c".
go rt
ring
$ _
```

Converting Underline Sequences: ul

The **ul** utility transforms a file that contains underline characters so that it appears correctly on a particular terminal type. This utility is useful for commands like **man** that generate underlined text. **ul** works like this:

Utility: **ul** *-tterminal { filename }**

ul is a utility that transforms underline characters in its input so that they will display correctly on the specified terminal. If no terminal is specified, the one defined by the $TERM environment variable is assumed. The "/etc/termcap" file (or terminfo database) is used by **ul** to determine the correct underline sequence.

For example, let's say that you want to use the **man** utility to produce a document that you wish to print on a simple ASCII-only printer. The **man** utility generates underline characters for your current terminal, so to filter the output so that it's suitable for a "dumb" printer, pipe the output of **man** through **ul** with the "dumb" terminal setting. Here's an example of this use of **ul**:

```
$ man who | ul -tdumb > man.txt
$ head man.txt              ...look at the first 10 lines.
WHO(1)                     USER COMMANDS                    WHO(1)
NAME
    who - who is logged in on the system
SYNOPSIS
    who [ who-file ] [ am i ]
$ _
```

LOOKING AT RAW FILE CONTENTS: od

The octal-dump utility, **od**, allows you to see the contents of a nontext file in a variety of formats, and it works as follows:

Utility: **od** -acbcdfhilox *fileName* [*offset*[.][b]]

od displays the contents of *fileName* in a form specified by one of several options:

OPTION	MEANING
-a	Interpret bytes as characters and print as ASCII names (e.g., 0 = nul).
-b	Interpret bytes as unsigned octal.
-c	Interpret bytes as characters and print in C notation (e.g., 0 = \0).
-d	Interpret two-byte pairs as unsigned decimal.
-f	Interpret four-byte pairs as floating point.
-h	Interpret two-byte pairs as unsigned hex.
-i	Interpret two-byte pairs as signed decimal.
-l	Interpret four-byte pairs as signed decimal.
-o	Interpret two-byte pairs as unsigned octal.
-s[n]	Look for strings of minimum length n (default is 3) terminated by null characters.
-x	Interpret two-byte pairs as hex.

By default, the contents are displayed as a series of octal numbers. *offset* specifies where the listing should begin. If the offset ends in "b", then it is interpreted as a number of blocks; otherwise, it is interpreted as an octal number. To specify a hex number, precede it by "x". To specify a decimal number, end it with a period.

In the following example, I displayed the contents of the "/bin/od" executable as octal numbers and then as characters starting from location 1000 (octal):

```
$ od /bin/od                    ...dump the "/bin/od" file in octal.
0000000  100002 000410 000000 017250 000000 003630 000000 006320
0000020  000000 000000 000000 020000 000000 000000 000000 000000
0000040  046770 000000 022027 043757 000004 021002 162601 044763
0000060  014004 021714 000002 000410 045271 000000 020746 063400
0000100  000006 060400 000052 044124 044123 027402 047271 000000
0000120  021170 047271 000000 021200 157374 000014 027400 047271
0000140  000002 000150 054217 027400 047271 000002 000160 047126
...etc. (Edited out for space considerations.)
$ od -c /bin/od 1000             ...dump "/bin/od" as characters.
0001000 H   x  \0  001  N   @  \0  002 \0  \0   /   u   s   r   /   l
0001020 i   b   /   l   d   .   s   o  \0   /   d   e   v   /   z   e
0001040 r   o  \0  \0  \0  \0  \0 030   c   r   t   0   :       n   o
0001060     /   u   s   r   /   l   i   b   /   l   d   .   s   o  \n
0001100 \0  \0  \0   %   c   r   t   0   :       /   u   s   r   /   l
0001120 i   b   /   l   d   .   s   o       m   a   p   p   i   n   g
0001140     f   a   i   l   u   r   e  \n  \0  \0  \0  \0 023   c   r
0001160 t   0   :       n   o       /   d   e   v   /   z   e   r   o
0001200 \n  \0 200  \0  \0 002 200  \0  \0 022  \0  \0  \0 007  \0  \0
...etc. (Edited out for space considerations.)
$ _
```

You may search for strings of a minimum length by using the "-s" option, as shown in the next example. Any series of characters followed by an ASCII null is considered to be a string.

```
$ od -s7 /bin/od   ...search for strings of seven characters or more.
0000665 \fN^Nu o
0001012 /usr/lib/ld.so
0001031 /dev/zero
0001050 crt0: no /usr/lib/ld.so\n
0001103 %crt0: /usr/lib/ld.so mapping failure\n
...etc. (Edited out for space considerations.)
$ _
```

MOUNTING FILE SYSTEMS: mount and unmount

A super-user may extend the file system by using the **mount** utility and reverse the effect of the **mount** utility by using the **umount** utility. These utilities work as follows:

Utility: **mount** -o*options* [*deviceName directory*]
        umount *deviceName*

mount is a utility that allows you to "splice" a device's file system into the root hierarchy. When used without any arguments, **mount** displays a list of the currently mounted devices. To specify special options, follow **-o** by a list of valid codes. These codes include "rw", which mounts a file system for read and write, and "ro", which mounts a file system for read only. The **umount** utility unmounts a previously mounted file system.

In the next example, I spliced the file system contained on the "/dev/dsk2" device onto the "/usr" directory. Notice that before I performed the mount, the "/usr" directory was empty; after the mount, the files stored on the "/dev/dsk2" device appeared inside this directory.

```
$ mount                   ...list the currently mounted devices.
/dev/dsk1 on /  (rw)
$ ls /usr                 ..."/usr" is currently empty.
$ mount /dev/dsk2 /usr    ...mount the "/dev/dsk2" device.
$ mount                   ...list the currently mounted devices.
/dev/dsk1 on /  (rw)
/dev/dsk2 on /usr (rw)
$ ls /usr                 ...list the contents of the mounted device.
bin/     etc/    include/ lost+found/ src/     ucb/
demo/    games/  lib/     pub/        sys/     ucblib/
dict/    hosts/  local/   spool/      tmp/
$ _
```

To unmount a device, use the **umount** utility. In the next example, I unmounted the "/dev/dsk2" device and then listed the "/usr" directory. The files were no longer accessible.

```
$ umount /dev/dsk2   ...unmount the device.
$ mount              ...list the currently mounted devices.
/dev/dsk1 on /  (rw)
$ ls /usr            ...note that "/usr" is empty again.
$ _
```

IDENTIFYING SHELLS: whoami

Let's say that you come across a vacated terminal and there's a shell prompt on the screen. Obviously, someone was working on the UNIX system and forgot to log off. You wonder curiously who that person is. To solve the mystery, you can use the **whoami** utility, which displays the owner of a shell:

Utility: **whoami**

Displays the owner of a shell.

For example, when I executed **whoami** at my terminal, I saw this:

```
$ whoami
glass
$ _
```

IDENTIFYING TERMINALS: tty

The **tty** utility identifies the name of your terminal and works as follows:

Utility: **tty**

tty displays the pathname of your terminal. It returns zero if its standard input is a terminal; otherwise, it returns 1.

In the following example, my login terminal was the special file "/dev/ttyp0":

```
$ tty          ...display the pathname of my terminal.
/dev/ttyp0
$ _
```

TEXT FORMATTING: nroff, troff, style, AND spell

One of the first uses of UNIX was to support the text-processing facilities at Bell Laboratories. Several utilities, including **nroff, troff, style,** and **spell** were created for text formatting. Although these utilities were reasonable in their time, they have been made virtually obsolete by far more sophisticated WYSIWYG (what you see is what you get) tools. For example, **nroff** requires you to manually place special commands such as ".pa" inside a text document in order for it to format correctly, whereas modern tools allow you to do this formatting graphically.

For more information about these old-style text-processing utilities, see [1,159].

ROLLING YOUR OWN PROGRAMS: Perl

In earlier times, when what you needed to do required combining two or more of the UNIX utilities we've seen, you had to write a shell script in one of the shell languages that we examined in earlier chapters. Shell scripts are slower than C programs because they are interpreted instead of compiled, but they are also much easier to write and debug. C programs allow you to take advantage of many more UNIX features, but generally require more time both to write and to modify.

In 1986, Larry Wall found that shell scripts weren't enough and C programs were overkill for many purposes. He set out to write a scripting language that would be the best of both worlds. The result was Perl. The Practical Extraction Report Language addressed many of Larry's problems with generating reports and other text-oriented functions, and it also provides easy access to many other UNIX facilities that shell scripts do not.

Perl will look familiar to shell and C programmers, since much of its syntax was taken from elements of both. I can only hope to give you a basic view of Perl here. Like with **awk**, there are entire books that describe Perl in detail (e.g. [23], [28]). That level of detail is beyond the scope of this book, but by whetting your appetite with an introduction, I'm sure you'll want to find out more about Perl.

Printing Text

Without the ability to print output, most programs wouldn't accomplish much. So, in the tradition of UNIX, I'll start our examples of Perl scripts with one that prints a single line:

```
print "hello world.\n";
```

Just from this simple example, you can infer that each line in Perl must end with a semicolon (;). Also, note the "\n" is used, like in the programming language of C, to print a new-line character at the end of the line.

Variables, Strings, and Integers

To write useful programs, of course, requires the ability to assign and modify values like strings and integers. Perl provides variables much like those of shells. These variables can be assigned any type of value, and Perl keeps track of the variable type for you. The major difference between Perl variables and shell variables is that the dollar sign ($) is not used simply to expand the value of the variable, but is *always* used to denote the variable. Even when assigning a value to a variable, such as in the statement

```
$i = 3;
```

you must put the "$" in front of the variable. This aspect is probably the most difficult adjustment for seasoned shell programmers to make.

In addition to all of the "typical" mathematical operators (add, subtract, etc.), integers also support a *range operator*, "..", which is used to specify a range of integers. This operator is useful when building a loop around a range of values, as we will see later.

Strings, as in most languages, are specified by text in quotation marks. Strings also support a concatenation operator, ".", which puts strings together. The use of the range operator, the specification of strings, and the use of the concatenation operator are demonstrated as follows:

```
print 1, 2, 3..15, "\n";      # range operator
print "A", "B", "C", "\n";    # strings
$i = "A"."B" ;                # concatenation operator
print "$i", "\n" ;
```

The previous example of lines of Perl generates the following output:

```
123456789101112131415
ABC
AB
```

You can see that each value, and only each value, is printed, giving you control over all spacing.

Arrays

Most programming languages provide *arrays*, which are lists of data values. Perl's arrays are quite simple to use, as they are dynamically allocated, which means that you don't have to define how large they will be, and if you use more than the space that is currently allocated, Perl will allocate more space and enlarge the array. The syntax for arrays is probably new, however. Rather than using a dollar sign, as you do with Perl variables, an array is denoted by an "at" sign (@):

```
@arr = (1,2,3,4,5);
```

The previous line defines the array "arr" and puts five values in it. You could also define the same array with the line

```
@arr = (1..5);
```

using the range operator with integers.

You can access a single element with an index number in brackets, such as follows:

```
print @arr[0],"\n";
```

As with most array implementations, the first element is numbered as zero. Using the definition of the "print" command from before, the previous line would print "1", since it's the first value in the array.

If you print an array without providing any index numbers, all defined values in the array are printed. If you use the name of the array without any index numbers in a place where a scalar value is expected, the number of elements in the array is used. These features are demonstrated in the following example:

```
@a1 = (1);              # array of 1 element
@a2 = (1,2,3,4,5);      # array of 5 elements
@a3 = (1..10);          # array of 10 elements

print @a1, " ", @a2, " ", @a3, "\n";

print @a1[0], " ", @a2[1], " ", @a3[2], "\n";

# using the array as a scalar will yield the number of items in it.
print @a2 + @a3, "\n";
```

This code will result in the following output:

```
1 12345 12345678910
1 2 3
15
```

Mathematical and Logical Operators

Once you have assigned your variables, the next thing you usually want to do with them is to change their values. Most operations on values are familiar from C programming. The typical operators for adding, subtracting, multiplying, and dividing are "+", "−", "*", and "/", respectively, for both integers and real numbers. Integers also support the C constructs to increment and decrement before and after the value is used and logical "and"s and "or"s. Notice that in the following example, I have to add a backslash before the "$" used in the text of "print" statement since I actually want the name of the variable with the "$" preceding it to be printed instead of the value of the variable in those places:

```
$n = 2;
print ("\$n=", $n, "\n");

$n = 2 ; print ("increment after \$n=", $n++, "\n");
$n = 2 ; print ("increment before \$n=", ++$n, "\n");
$n = 2 ; print ("decrement after \$n=", $n--, "\n");
$n = 2 ; print ("decrement before \$n=", --$n, "\n");

$n = 2;                          # reset
print ("\$n+2=", $n + 2, "\n");
print ("\$n-2=", $n - 2, "\n");
print ("\$n*2=", $n * 2, "\n");
print ("\$n/2=", $n / 2, "\n");
```

```
$r = 3.14;                # real number
print ("\$r=", $r, "\n");

print ("\$r*2=", $r * 2, "\n"); # double
print ("\$r/2=", $r / 2, "\n"); # cut in half

print ("1 && 1 -> ", 1 && 1, "\n");

print ("1 && 0 -> ", 1 && 0, "\n");
print ("1 || 1 -> ", 1 || 1, "\n");
print ("1 || 0 -> ", 1 || 0, "\n");
```

This script generates the following output:

```
$n=2
increment after $n=2
increment before $n=3
decrement after $n=2
decrement before $n=1
$n+2=4
$n-2=0
$n*2=4
$n/2=1
$r=3.14
$r*2=6.28
$r/2=1.57
1 && 1 -> 1
1 && 0 -> 0
1 || 1 -> 1
1 || 0 -> 1
```

"if", "while", "for" and "foreach" Loop Constructs

An essential part of any programming language is the ability to execute different statements, depending on the value of a variable, and create loops for repetitive tasks or for indexing through array values. "if" statements and "while" loops in Perl are similar to those in the language of C.

In an "if" statement, a "comparison" operator is used to compare two values, and different sets of statements are executed, depending on the result of the comparison (true or false):

```
$i = 0;
if ( $i == 0 ) {
    print "it's true\n";
} else {
    print "it's false\n";
}
```

The previous code results in "it's true" being printed. As in C, other comparison operators are "!=" (not equal), "<" (less than), and ">" (greater than), among others.

In the previous example, you could also loop in a "while" statement to print the text until the comparison is no longer true:

```
while ( $i == 0 ) {
    print "it's true\n";
    $i++;
}
```

Of course, the comparison will be true the next time through the loop, since "$i" was incremented.

Perl also handles "for" loops from C and "foreach" loops from the C shell. An example of a "for" loop in Perl is the following:

```
for ($i = 0 ; $i < 10 ; $i++ ) {
    print $i, " ";
}
print "\n";
```

This code counts from zero to nine and prints the value (without a new line until the end), generating the following output:

```
0 1 2 3 4 5 6 7 8 9
```

A foreach loop in Perl looks like this:

```
foreach $n (1..15) {
    print $n, " ";
}
print "\n";
```

This code generates about what you would expect:

```
1 2 3 4 5 6 7 8 9 10 11 12 13 14 15
```

File I/O

One big improvement that Perl made over shell scripts is that it has the ability to take input from and send output to specific files rather than just the standard input, output, or error channels. You still can access standard input and output, however:

```
@line=<stdin>;
foreach $i (@line) {
    print "->", $i;    # also reads in EOL
}
```

The previous script reads each line from the standard input and prints it. However, if you have a specific data file from which you wish to read, then code like the following is more appropriate:

```
-$FILE="info.dat";
open (FILE);                # name of var, not eval
@array = <FILE>;
close (FILE);
foreach $line (@array) {
    print "$line";
}
```

This Perl script opens a file called "info.dat" and reads all of its lines into the array called "array" (clever name, wouldn't you say?). It then does the same as the previous script does and prints out each line.

Functions

To be able to effectively separate various tasks that a program performs, especially if the same task is needed in several places, a programming language needs to provide a *subroutine*, or *function*, capability. The Korn shell provides a weak type of function implemented through the command interface, and it is the only major shell that provides functions at all. Of course, the language of C does, but script writers had a harder time of it before Perl came along.

Perl functions are simple to use, although their syntax can get complicated. A simple example of a Perl function will give you the idea:

```
sub pounds2dollars {
    $EXCHANGE_RATE = 1.54;     # modify when necessary
    $pounds = $_[0];
    return ($EXCHANGE_RATE * $pounds);
}
```

This function changes a value specified in pounds sterling (British money) into U. S. dollars (given an exchange rate of $1.54 to the pound, which can be modified as necessary). The special variable "$_[0]" references the first argument to the function. To call the function, our Perl script would look like this:

```
$book = 3.0;        # price in British pounds
$value = pounds2dollars($book);
print "Value in dollars = $value\n";
```

When we run this script (which includes the function at the end), we get:

```
Value in dollars = 4.62
```

In the next section, we'll see an example of a function that returns more than one value.

System Calls

One capability that is conspicuously absent from shell scripting is that of making UNIX system calls. Perl provides an interface to many UNIX system calls. The interface is via Perl functions, not directly through the system-call library; therefore, its use is dependent on the implementation and version of Perl, and you should consult the documentation for your version for specific information. When an interface is available, it is usually very much like its counterpart in the C library.

A simple example of a system call gives us the time and date:

```
($s,$m,$h,$dy,$mo,$yr,$wd,$yd,$dst) = gmtime();
$mo++;      # month begins counting at zero
print "The date is $mo/$dy/$yr.\n";
print "The time is $h:$m:$s.\n";
```

The previous code results in:

```
The date is 4/25/98.
The time is 13:40:27.
```

Note that "gmtime()" returns nine values. The Perl syntax is to specify these values in parentheses (as you would if you were assigning multiple values to an array).

Command-Line Arguments

Another useful capability is to be able to pass command-line arguments to a Perl script. Shell scripts provide a very simple interface to command-line arguments, while C programs provide a slightly more complex, but more flexible, interface. The Perl interface is somewhere in between, and an example of its use is as follows:

```
$n = $#ARGV+1;  # number of arguments (beginning at zero)
print $n, " args: \n";
for ( $i = 0 ; $i < $n ; $i++ ) {
   print " @ARGV[$i]\n";
}
```

This Perl script prints the number of arguments that were supplied on the Perl command (after the name of the Perl script itself) and then prints out each argument on a separate line.

We can modify our pounds-to-dollars script from before to allow a value in British pounds to be specified on the command line:

```
if ( $#ARGV < 0 ) { # if no argument given
   print "Specify value in pounds to convert to dollars\n";
   exit
}
```

```
$poundvalue = @ARGV[0];   # get value from command line
$dollarvalue = pounds2dollars($poundvalue);
print "Value in dollars = $dollarvalue\n";

sub pounds2dollars {
   $EXCHANGE_RATE = 1.54; # modify when necessary

   $pounds = $_[0];
   return ($EXCHANGE_RATE * $pounds);
}
```

A Real-World Example

All of these short examples of Perl code should have given you the flavor for how Perl works, but so far, we haven't done anything that's really very useful. So let's take what we've learned and write a Perl script to print out a table of information about a loan. We define the command that runs our script as having the following syntax:

Utility: **loan** -a *amount* -p *payment* -r *rate*

loan prints out a table, given a loan amount, interest rate, and payment to be made each month. The table shows how many months are required to pay off the loan, as well as how much interest and principal will be paid each month. All arguments are required.

The Perl script looks like this:

```
# show loan interest

$i=0;
while ( $i < $#ARGV) {              # process arguments
   if ( @ARGV[$i] eq "-r" ) {
      $RATE=@ARGV[++$i];            # interest rate
   } else {

      if ( @ARGV[$i] eq "-a" ) {
         $AMOUNT=@ARGV[++$i];# loan amount
      } else {
         if ( @ARGV[$i] eq "-p" ) {
            $PAYMENT=@ARGV[++$i];# payment amount
         } else {
            print "Unknown argument (@ARGV[$i])\n";
            exit
```

```
      }
    }
  }
  $i++;
}

if ($AMOUNT == 0 || $RATE == 0 || $PAYMENT == 0) {
  print "Specify -r rate -a amount -p payment\n";
  exit
}

print "Original balance: \$$AMOUNT\n";
print "Interest rate:     ${RATE}%\n";
print "Monthly payment:   \$$PAYMENT\n";
print "\n";
print "Month\tPayment\tInterest\tPrincipal\tBalance\n\n";

$month=1;
$rate=$RATE/12/100; #   get actual monthly percentage rate
$balance=$AMOUNT;
$payment=$PAYMENT;

while ($balance > 0) {
# round up interest amount
    $interest=roundUpAmount($rate * $balance);
    $principal=roundUpAmount($payment - $interest);
    if ( $balance < $principal ) {      # last payment
        $principal=$balance;                 # don't pay too much!
        $payment=$principal + $interest;
    }
    $balance = roundUpAmount($balance - $principal);
    print
"$month\t\$$payment\t\$$interest\t\t\$$principal\t\t\$$balance\n";
    $month++;
}

sub roundUpAmount {
#
# in: floating-point monetary value
# out: value rounded (and truncated) to the nearest cent
#
    $value=$_[0];

    $newvalue = ( int ( ( $value * 100 ) +.5 ) ) / 100;

    return ($newvalue);
}
```

If I want to pay $30 a month on my $300 credit-card balance and the interest rate is 12.9% APR, my payment schedule—the output of the **loan** utility—looks like the following:

```
Original balance: $300
Interest rate:     12.5%
Monthly payment:   $30
```

Month	Payment	Interest	Principal	Balance
1	$30	$3.13	$26.87	$273.13
2	$30	$2.85	$27.15	$245.98
3	$30	$2.56	$27.44	$218.54
4	$30	$2.28	$27.72	$190.82
5	$30	$1.99	$28.01	$162.81
6	$30	$1.7	$28.3	$134.51
7	$30	$1.4	$28.6	$105.91
8	$30	$1.1	$28.9	$77.01
9	$30	$0.8	$29.2	$47.81
10	$30	$0.5	$29.5	$18.31
11	$18.5	$0.19	$18.31	$0

So, I find that it will take 11 months to pay off the balance at $30 per month, but the last payment will only be $18.31. If I want to pay it off faster than that, I know that I need to raise my monthly payment!

CHAPTER REVIEW

Checklist

In this chapter, I described utilities that:

- filter files
- sort files
- compare files
- archive files
- find files
- schedule commands
- support programmable text processing
- create hard and soft links
- substitute users
- check for mail
- transform files
- look at raw file contents
- mount file systems
- prepare documents
- writing scripts using Perl

Quiz

1. Under what circumstances would you archive files using **tar?**
2. How would you convert the text of a file to uppercase?
3. Describe what it means to "mount" a file system.

4. Which process serves the **crontab** system?
5. What additional functionality does an extended regular expression have?
6. What are the main differences between **sed** and **awk?**
7. How did **awk** get its name?
8. Under what circumstances would you use a symbolic link instead of a hard link?
9. What are the drawbacks of using a symbolic link?
10. What is meant by an incremental backup, and how would you perform one?
11. What are some ways that Perl makes script programming easier than do conventional shell scripts?

Exercises

1. Perform some timing tests on **grep** and **fgrep** to determine the advantages of using **fgrep**'s speed. [level: *easy*]
2. Ask the system administrator to demonstrate the use of **tar** to produce a backup tape of your files. [level: *easy*]
3. Use **crontab** to schedule a script that removes your old core files at the start of each day. [level: *medium*]
4. Write a script called **squirrel** that takes two arguments: a filename and a key string. **squirrel** should compress the specified file and then encrypt the compressed version using the key. Write a companion script called **dig** that also takes two arguments: a filename and a key string. **dig** should decrypt the file using the key and then uncompress it. [level: *easy*]

Project

1. After you've read Chapter 4, design a script that periodically finds all of your files in the file system that haven't been accessed for a specified time and archives them in a compressed format. The archived files should be stored in a subdirectory for easy retrieval. [level: *medium*]
2. Modify the **loan** Perl script so that you can pass a list of payments to it rather than using the same payment value for every month. [level: *medium*]

CHAPTER 8

Networking

Motivation

One of the most significant advantages of UNIX over other competing operating systems during its origin was that it was one of the first operating systems to provide access to widely distributed local networks as well as the large Internet network that spans the globe. Today, millions of users and programs share information on these networks for a myriad of reasons, from distributing large computational tasks to exchanging a good recipe for lasagna. To make the best use of these network resources, you should understand the utilities that manage the exchange of information. This chapter describes the most useful network utilities of UNIX. While these utilities are applicable to both local networks and the Internet, I will defer most specific Internet-related topics until Chapter 9.

Prerequisites

In order to understand this chapter, you should have already read Chapters 1 and 2. It also helps if you have access to a UNIX system so that you can try out the various utilities that I discuss.

Objectives

In this chapter, I'll show you how to find out what's on the network, how to talk to other users, how to copy files across a network, and how to execute processes on other computers on the network.

Presentation

This chapter begins with an overview of network concepts and terminology and then describes the UNIX network utilities.

Commands

This section introduces the following utilities, listed in alphabetical order:

finger	rsh	w
ftp	rusers	wall
hostname	rwho	who

Commands (continued)

mesg	talk	whois
rcp	telnet	write
rlogin	users	

INTRODUCTION

A network is an interconnected system of cooperating computers. Through a network, you can share resources with other users via an ever-increasing number of network applications, such as Web browsers and electronic-mail messaging systems.

There has been a huge explosion in the use of UNIX networks in the 1990s. For example, the client–server paradigm described in Chapter 1 has been adopted by many of the major computer corporations, and relies heavily on the operating system's network capabilities to distribute the workload between the server and its clients.

In order to prepare yourself for the advent of widespread networking, it's important to know the following items:

- common network terminology
- how networks are built
- how to talk to other people on the network
- how to use other computers on the network

This chapter covers all of these issues and more.

BUILDING A NETWORK

One of the best ways to understand how modern networks work is to look at how they evolved. Imagine that two people in an office want to hook their computers together so that they can share data. The easiest way to do so is to connect a cable between their serial ports. This connection is the simplest form of *local-area network* (LAN) and requires virtually no special software or hardware. When one computer wants to send information to the other, it simply sends it out of its serial port:

FIGURE 8.1   The simplest LAN

Ethernets

To make things a little more interesting, let's assume that another person wants to tie into the other two peoples' existing network. With three computers in the network, we need an addressing scheme so that the computers can be differentiated. We would also like to keep the number of connections down to a minimum. The most common implementation of this kind of LAN is called an *Ethernet*®. Ethernet is a hardware standard defining cabling, signaling, and behaviors that allow data to pass across a length of wire. The format of this data is defined by *network protocols*, which we'll look at a bit later. The Ethernet standard was originally developed by Xerox Corporation and works like this:

- Each computer contains an Ethernet card, which is a special piece of hardware that has a unique Ethernet address.
- Every computer's Ethernet card is connected to the same single piece of wire.
- When a computer wishes to send a message to another computer with a particular Ethernet address, it broadcasts the message onto the Ethernet together with Ethernet header and trailer information that contain the Ethernet destination address. Only the Ethernet card whose address matches the destination address accepts the message.
- The situation in which two computers try to broadcast to the Ethernet at the same time is known as a *collision*. When a collision occurs, both computers wait a random period of time and then try again.

Here's a diagram:

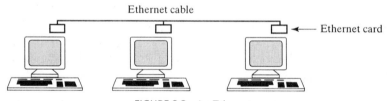

FIGURE 8.2   An Ethernet

Ethernet networks can transmit data on the order of tens or hundreds of megabytes per second.

Bridges

Let's assume that the Ethernet in the office works so well that the people in the office next door build themselves an Ethernet too. How does one computer on one Ethernet talk to another computer on another Ethernet? One solution might be to connect a special bit of hardware called a *bridge* between the networks. A bridge passes an Ethernet message between the different *segments* (wires) of the network as if both segments were a single Ethernet network cable. A bridge is used when you need to extend a network past the allowed length of a single section of wire. (The length of these wires is limited by signal degradation over a distance.)

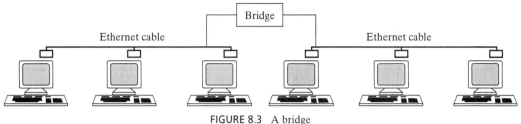

FIGURE 8.3   A bridge

Routers

The use of bridges facilitates the construction of small serially linked sections of Ethernet, but it's a pretty inefficient way to link together large numbers of networks. For example, assume that a corporation has four LANs that it wishes to interconnect in an efficient way. Stringing them all together with bridges would cause data to pass across the "middle" sections to get to the ends when hosts on those middle sections have no interest in the data. To pass data directly from the originating network to the destination network, a *router* can be used. A router is a device that hooks together two or more networks and automatically routes incoming messages to the correct network.

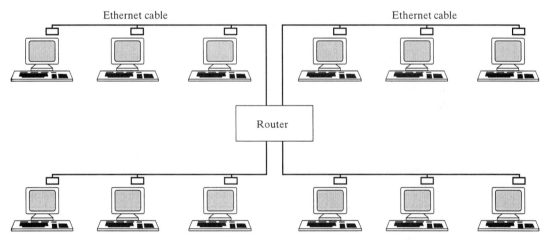

FIGURE 8.4   A router

Gateways

The final stage in network evolution occurs when many corporations wish to connect their local area networks together into a single, large wide-area network (WAN). To do so, several high-capacity routers called *gateways* are placed throughout the country, and each corporation ties its LAN into the nearest gateway.

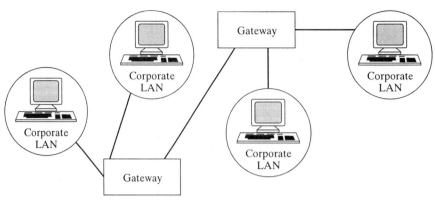

FIGURE 8.5 Gateways

INTERNET WORKING

In order for a collection of LANs and WANs to be able route information amongst themselves, they must agree upon a network-wide addressing and routing scheme. This large-scale interconnection of different networks is known as *internetworking*. Any group of two or more networks connected together may properly be call "an internet." However, the largest and best known such network has become known as "the Internet."

Universities, large corporations, government offices, and military sites all have computers that are part of the Internet; these computers are generally linked together by high-speed data links. The largest of these computer systems are joined together to form what is known as the *backbone* of the Internet. Other smaller establishments link their LANs to the backbone via gateways.

Packet Switching

Today's digital computer networks are *packet-switched* networks. When one node on the network sends a message to another node, the message is split up into small packets, each of which can be routed independently, or switched, through the network.

These packets contain special information that allows them to be recombined at the destination. They also contain information for routing purposes, including the addresses of the source and destination nodes. The combined set of protocols is called the TCP/IP (Transmission Control Protocol and Internet Protocol) protocol suite. UNIX interprocess communication (IPC) uses TCP/IP to allow UNIX processes on different machines to talk to each other.

Internet Addresses

Hosts on the Internet, as well as many on private internets, also use TCP/IP to send data. While it is most popularly implemented on Ethernet networks, TCP/IP can also be used on other types of networks. This flexible usage makes it useful for connecting different types of networks, for not all computers are connected by

Ethernet. For example, some LANs may use the IBM Token Ring system. Therefore, the IP-addressing system uses a hardware-independent labeling scheme; the bridges, routers, and gateways transmit messages based purely on their destination IP address. The IP address is mapped to a physical-hardware address only when the message reaches the destination host's LAN. Thus, the computer sending the message does not need to understand hardware-specific information of the computer to which the message is to be sent.

The IP-addressing mechanism works the same whether or not you actually connect your computers to the Internet. When an organization sets up a LAN that is to be part of the Internet, they must get a unique address range assigned to their computers, a process that we will examine in Chapter 9. For now, let's assume that we're using a local IP network.

An IP address is a 32-bit value that is written as four dot-separated numbers, each number representing eight of the 32 bits of the address. Because each part represents an eight-bit value, the maximum value that the part may have is 255.

Due to the explosive growth of the Internet, the seemingly endless supply of 32-bit addresses is quickly being used up. The current IP-protocol standard (IP version 4) is being modified to allow larger addresses; IPv6 will define 128-bit IP addresses so that many more addresses can be assigned. See Chapter 15 for more information on IPv6.

Naming

These numerical addresses are not very convenient for humans to use to access remote computers. Humans are much more used to naming things. (Think about how we refer to people, pets, and cars.) So, we have taken to naming our computers as well.

When a *hostname* is assigned to a particular computer, a correlation can be established between its name and its numerical IP address. This way, a user can type the computer's name to reference it, and the software can translate this name to an IP address automatically.

The mapping of IP addresses to local host names is kept by each LAN's system administrator in a file called "/etc/hosts". To show you what this file looks like, here's a small section of the file from the University of Texas at Dallas:

```
129.110.41.1     manmax03
129.110.42.1     csservr2
129.110.43.2     ncube01
129.110.43.128   vanguard
129.110.43.129   jupiter
129.110.66.8     neocortex
129.110.102.10   corvette
```

Routing

The Internet Protocol performs two kinds of routing: static and dynamic. Static routing information is kept in the file "/etc/route" and is of the form: "You may get to the destination *DEST* via the gateway *GATE* with *X* hops." When a router has to forward a message, it can use the information in this file to determine the best route. Dynamic routing information is shared between hosts via the "/etc/routed" or "/etc/gated" daemons.[1] These programs constantly update their local routing tables based on information gleaned from network traffic and periodically share their information with other neighboring daemons.

Security

Several of the UNIX networking utilities that I discuss later in this chapter allow a user with accounts on several machines to execute a command on one of these machines from another. For example, I have an account on both the "csservr2" and "vanguard" machines at the University of Texas at Dallas. To execute the **date** command on the "vanguard" machine from the "csservr2" machine, I can use the **rsh** utility as follows:

```
$ rsh vanguard date    ...execute date on vanguard.
```

The interesting thing about **rsh** and a few other utilities is that they are able to obtain a shell on the remote host *without requiring a password*. They can do so because of a UNIX facility called *machine equivalence*. If you create a file called ".rhosts" in your home directory that contains a list of host names, then any user with the same user ID as your own may log into your account from these hosts without supplying a password. Both my "csservr2" and "vanguard" home directories contain a file ".rhosts" that contains the following lines:

```
csservr2.utdallas.edu
vanguard.utdallas.edu
```

We must use the "official" hostname, which includes the Internet domain, in the ".rhosts" file. I will discuss Internet domains in Chapter 9.

Machine equivalence allows me to execute remote commands from either computer without any hassle. UNIX also allows a system administrator to list globally equivalent machines in the file "/etc/hosts.equiv". Global equivalence means that *any* user on the listed machines can log into the local host without a password. For example, if the "vanguard" "/etc/hosts.equiv" file contained the lines

```
csservr2.utdallas.edu
vanguard.utdallas.edu
```

then any user on "csservr2" could log into "vanguard" or execute a remote command on it without a password. Global equivalence should be used, if ever, with great care.

---

[1] A daemon is a fancy term for a constantly running background process that is normally started when the system is booted.

Ports and Common Services

When one network host talks to another, it does so via a set of numbered ports. Every host supports some standard ports for common uses and allows application programs to create other ports for transient communication. The file "/etc/services" contains a list of the standard ports. Here's a snippet from the file at the University of Texas at Dallas file:

```
echo         7/tcp
discard      9/tcp             sink null
systat      11/tcp             users
daytime     13/tcp
ftp-data    20/tcp
ftp         21/tcp
telnet      23/tcp
smtp        25/tcp             mail
time        37/tcp             timserver
rlp         39/udp             resource
whois       43/tcp
finger      79/tcp
sunrpc     111/tcp
exec       512/tcp
login      513/tcp
```

The description of the **telnet** utility later in this chapter contains some examples in which I connected to some of these standard ports.

Network Programming

The UNIX interprocess communication allows you to communicate with other programs at a known IP address and port. This facility is described near the end of Chapter 12, together with the full source code for an "Internet shell" that can pipe and redirect to other Internet shells on different hosts.

USERS

UNIX networking is all about moving around the network and talking to other people. Therefore, one of the most basic things to learn is how to find out who's on a particular host. There are several utilities that accomplish this task, each with its own strengths:

- **users**, which lists all of the users on your local host
- **rusers**, which lists all of the users on your local network
- **who**, which is like **users**, except that it gives you more information
- **rwho**, which is like **rusers**, except that it gives you more information
- **w**, which is like **who**, except that it gives you *even more* information
- **whois**, which allows you to obtain information about major Internet sites
- **hostname**, which displays your local host's name.

The next few subsections describe each of these utilities in turn.

Listing Users: users and rusers

The **users** and **rusers** utilities simply list the current users of your local host and local network, respectively:

Utility: **users**

users displays a simple, terse list of the users on your local host.

Utility: **rusers** -a { *host* }*

rusers displays a list of the users on your local network. By default, all of the machines on the local network are interrogated, although you may override this default by supplying a list of host names. **rusers** works by broadcasting a request for information to all of the hosts and then displays the responses as they arrive. In order for a host to respond, it must be running the **rusersd** daemon (see Chapter 14 for more information about daemons). The **-a** argument causes **rusers** to print information for all responding machines, not just those with users logged in. The **-l** argument prints a long (more detailed) listing.

Here's an example of **users** and **rusers** in action:

```
$ users              ...display users on the local host.
glass posey
$ rusers -al         ...display users on the local network.
csservr4.utd posey
vanguard.utd huynh posey datta venky
csservr2.utd posey glass
$ _
```

More User Listings: who, rwho, and w

The **who** and **rwho** utilities supply a little more information than do the **users** and **rusers** utilities:

Utility: **who** [*whoFile*] [am i]

By default, **who** displays a list of every user on your local host. If you supply the arguments "am i", **who** only describes yourself.

Whenever a user logs in or out, the file "/var/adm/wtmp" is updated with information about their login session. You may give the name of this file (or a file in the same format) as the *whoFile* argument, in which case **who** decodes this information and presents it in the typical **who** format.

Here's an example of the use of **who**:

Utility: **rwho**

rwho is just like **who**, except that it displays a list of the users logged onto all of the remote hosts on your local network.

```
$ who                       ...list all users currently on local host.
posey       ttyp0    May 15 16:31 (blackfoot.utdall)
glass       ttyp2    May 17 17:00 (bridge05.utdalla)
$ who am i                  ...list myself.
csservr2!glass     ttyp2       May 17 17:00 (bridge05.utdalla)
$ who /var/adm/wtmp         ...examine the "who" file.
lcui        ttyp2    May 17 12:48 (bridge05.utdalla)
juang       ttyp3    May 17 12:49 (annex.utdallas.e)
            ttyp3    May 17 12:52
            ttyp2    May 17 12:57
weidman     ttyp2    May 17 16:25 (annex.utdallas.e)
            ttyp2    May 17 16:33
glass       ttyp2    May 17 17:00 (bridge05.utdalla)
$ _
```

The **w** utility is just as easy to use:

Utility: **w** { *userId* }*

w displays a list that describes what each specified user is doing.

Here's an example of the use of **w**:

```
$ w             ...obtain more detailed information than that given by "who".
5:27pm  up 11 days, 11 mins, 3 users, load average: 0.08, 0.03, 0.01
User      tty        login@ idle  JCPU  PCPU  what
posey     ttyp0    Fri 4pm 2days     1          -csh
glass     ttyp2      5:00pm     1     13     1  w
$ w glass  ...examine just myself.
5:27pm  up 11 days, 11 mins, 3 users, load average: 0.08, 0.03, 0.01
User      tty        login@ idle  JCPU  PCPU  what
glass     ttyp2      5:00pm           13     1  w glass
$ _
```

Your Own Host's Name: hostname

To find out the name of your local host, use **hostname**:

Utility: **hostname** [*hostName*]

When used with no parameters, **hostname** displays the name of your local host. A super-user may change this name by supplying the new hostname as an argument, which is usually done automatically in the "/etc/rc.local" file. For more information about this file, see Chapter 14.

Here's an example of the use of **hostname**:

```
$ hostname      ...display my host's name.
csservr2
$ _
```

Personal Data: finger

Once you've obtained a list of the people on your system, it's handy to be able to learn a little bit more about them. The **finger** utility allows you to do so:

Utility: **finger** {*userId* }*

finger displays information about a list of users that is gleaned from several sources:

- The user's home directory, startup shell, and full name are read from the password file "/etc/passwd".

- If the user supplies a file called ".plan" in his/her home directory, its contents are displayed as the user's "plan".
- If the user supplies a file called ".project" in his/her home directory, its contents are displayed as the user's "project".

If no user IDs are listed, **finger** displays information about every user that is currently logged on. You may finger a user on a remote host by using the "@" syntax, in which case the remote host's **finger** daemon is used to reply to the local **finger's** request.

I recommend that you create your own ".plan" and ".project" files in your home directory so that people can "finger" *you* back. Have fun!

In the following example, I fingered everyone on the system and then fingered myself:

```
$ finger              ...finger everyone on the system.
Login       Name      TTY Idle   When    Where
posey    John Posey   p0   2d Fri 16:31  blackfoot.utdall
glass    Graham Glass p2      Sun 17:00  bridge05.utdalla
$ finger glass        ...finger myself.
Login name: glass              In real life: Graham Glass
Directory: /home/glass         Shell: /bin/ksh
On since May 17 17:00:47 on ttyp2 from bridge05.utdalla
No unread mail
Project: To earn an enjoyable, honest living.
Plan: To work hard and have fun and not notice the difference.
$ _
```

In the next example, I listed the three sources of **finger**'s information about me:

```
$ cat .plan               ...list the ".plan" file.
To work hard and have fun and not notice any difference.
$ cat .project            ...list the ".project" file.
To earn an enjoyable, honest living.
$ grep glass /etc/passwd  ...look at the password file.
glass:##glass:496:62:Graham Glass:/home/glass:/bin/ksh
$ _
```

In this final example, I used **rusers** to get a listing of the remote users and then performed a remote **finger** to learn all about "susan":

```
$ rusers                    ...look at remote users.
csservr4.utd posey
vanguard.utd huynh posey datta venky
centaur.utda susan
```

```
csservr2.utd posey posey lcui glass
$ finger susan@centaur          ...do a remote finger.
[centaur.utdallas.edu]
Login name: susan               In real life: Susan Marsh
Directory: /home/susan          Shell: /bin/csh
On since May 11 11:00:55 on console 1 day Idle Time
New mail received Fri May 15 19:24:01 1998;
 unread since Fri May 15 16:40:28 1998
No Plan.
$ _
```

COMMUNICATING WITH USERS

There are several utilities that allow you to communicate with a user:

- **write**, which allows you to send individual lines to a user, one at a time
- **talk**, which allows you to have an interactive split-screen two-way conversation
- **wall**, which allows you to send a message to everyone on the local host
- **mail**, which allows you to send mail messages

The **mail** utility was described in Chapter 2, and it supports the full standard Internet-addressing scheme. The rest of these utilities are described in this section, together with a simple utility called **mesg** that allows you to shield yourself from receiving other people's messages.

Shielding Yourself from Communication: mesg

The **write**, **talk**, and **wall** utilities communicate with other users by writing directly to their terminals. You may disable the ability of other users to write to your terminal by using the **mesg** utility:

Utility: **mesg** [n|y]

mesg allows you to prevent other users from writing to your terminal. It works by modifying the write permission of your tty device. The "n" and "y" arguments disable and enable writes, respectively. If no arguments are supplied, your current status is displayed.

In the following example, **mesg** prevented me from receiving a **write** message:

```
$ mesg n            ...protect terminal.
$ write glass       ...try to write to myself.
write: You have write permission turned off
$ _
```

Sending One Line at a Time: write

The **write** command is a simple utility that allows you to send one line at a time to a named user:

Utility: **write** *userId* [*tty*]

write copies its standard input, one line at a time, to the terminal associated with *userId*. If the user is logged onto more than one terminal, you may specify the particular tty as an optional argument.
    The first line of input that you send to a user via **write** is preceded by the message

```
Message from yourHost!yourId on yourTty
```

so that the receiver may initiate a **write** command to talk back to you. To exit **write**, press *Control*-D on a line of its own. You may disable writes to your terminal by using **mesg**.

In the following example, I received a **write** message from my friend Tim and then initiated my own **write** command to respond. We used the "-o-" (over) and "-oo-" (over and out) conventions for synchronization:

```
$
Message from tim@csservr2 on ttyp2 at 18:04
hi Graham -o-                        ...from tim.
$ write tim                          ...initiate a reply.
hi Tim -o-                           ...from me.
don't forget the movie later -oo- ...from tim.
OK -oo-                              ...from me.
^D                                   ...end of my input.
$ _
```

Although you can have a two-way conversation using **write**, it's awfully clumsy. A better way is to use the **talk** utility, which is described next.

Interactive Conversations: talk

The **talk** utility allows you to have a two-way conversation across a network:

Utility: **talk** *userId* [*tty*]

The **talk** command allows you to talk to another user on the network via a split-screen interface. If the user is logged onto more than one terminal, you may choose a particular terminal by supplying a specific tty name.

To talk to someone, type the following at your terminal, filling in their specific information for "theirUserId" and "theirHost":

```
$ talk theirUserId@theirHost
```

This command causes the following message to appear on their screen (with your specific information supplied in place of "yourUserId" and "yourHost" and their hostname in place of "theirHost"):

```
Message from TalkDaemon@theirHost...
talk: connection requested by yourUserId@yourHost
talk: respond with: talk yourUserId@yourHost
```

If they agree to your invitation, they'll type the following at their shell prompt, filling in your specific information for "yourUserId" and "yourHost":

```
$ talk yourUserId@yourHost
```

At this point, your screen divides into two portions, one containing your keyboard input, and the other containing the other person's. Everything that you type is echoed at the other person's terminal, and vice versa. To redraw the screen if it ever gets messed up, press *Control-L*. To quit from **talk**, press *Control-C*.

To prevent other people from talking to you, use the **mesg** utility.

talk is a fun utility that is worth exploring with a friend.

Messages to Everyone: wall

If you ever have something important to say to the world (or at least to everyone on your local host), **wall** is the way to say it. **wall** stands for "write all", and it allows you to broadcast a message as follows:

Utility: **wall** [*fileName*]

wall copies its standard input (or the contents of *fileName*, if supplied) to the terminal of every user on the local host, preceding it with the message "Broadcast Message ...". If a user has disabled terminal communication by using **mesg**, the message will not be received unless the user of **wall** is a super-user.

In the following example, I sent a one-line message to everyone on the local host, including myself:

```
$ wall                                   ...write to everyone.
this is a test of the broadcast system
^D                                       ...end of input.
Broadcast Message from glass@csservr2 (ttyp2) at 18:04...
this is a test of the broadcast system
$ _
```

The **wall** command is most often used by system administrators to send users important, timely information (like "system going down in five minutes!").

DISTRIBUTING DATA

A very basic kind of remote operation is the transmission of files, and once again, UNIX has several utilities for performing this operation:

- **rcp** (remote copy) allows you to copy files between your local UNIX host and another remote UNIX host.
- **ftp** (file transfer protocol) allows you to copy files between your local UNIX host and any other host (possibly non-UNIX) that supports the **ftp** protocol. **ftp** is thus more powerful than rcp.
- **uucp** (UNIX-to-UNIX copy) is similar to **rcp**, and it allows you to copy files between any two UNIX hosts.

The next couple of sections describe **rcp** and **ftp**. **uucp** is not suited to use by regular users (but more for e-mail and news transmission over dial-up lines) so is not covered here.

Copying Files Between Two UNIX Hosts: rcp

rcp allows you to copy files between UNIX hosts:

Utility: **rcp** -p *originalFile newFile*
       rcp -pr { *fileName* } + *directory*

rcp allows you to copy files between UNIX hosts. Both your local host
and the remote host must be registered as equivalent machines. (See the
discussion of security earlier in this chapter for more information.) To
specify a remote file on *host*, use the following syntax:

```
host:pathName
```

If *pathName* is relative, it's interpreted as being relative to your home
directory on *host*. The **-p** option tries to preserve the last modification
time, last access time, and permission flags during the copy. The **-r** option
causes any file that is a directory to be recursively copied.

In the following example, I copied the file "original.txt" from the remote "vanguard" host to a file called "new.txt" on my local "csservr2" host. I then copied the
file "original2.txt" from my local host to the file "new2.txt" on the remote host.

```
$ rcp vanguard:original.txt new.txt        ...copying from remote to local.
$ rcp original2.txt vanguard:new2.txt      ...copying from local to remote.
$ _
```

Copying Files Using the File Transfer Protocol: ftp

The file transfer protocol is a generic protocol for the transmission of files and is supported by many machines. Therefore, you can use it to transfer files from your local
UNIX host to any other kind of remote host as long as you know the Internet address
of the remote host's ftp server. Users of non-UNIX computers often use **ftp** for transferring files between UNIX and their own system. Here's a brief description of **ftp**:

Utility: **ftp** -n [*hostName*]

ftp allows you to manipulate files and directories on both your local host
and a remote host. If you supply a remote hostname, **ftp** searches the
".netrc" file to see if the remote host has a passwordless anonymous **ftp**
account. If it does, it uses that account to log you into the remote host.
If it doesn't have an anonymous account, it assumes that you have an

account on the remote host and prompts you for its user ID and password. If the login is successful, **ftp** enters its command mode and displays the prompt "ftp>". If you don't supply a remote hostname, **ftp** enters its command mode immediately and you must use the "open" command to connect to a remote host.

The **-n** option prevents **ftp** from attempting the initial automatic login sequence.

ftp's command mode supports many commands for file manipulation. The most common of these commands are described in the next table. You may abort file transfers without quitting **ftp** by pressing *Control*-C.

Here's a list of the most useful **ftp** commands that are available from **ftp**'s command mode:

Command	Meaning
!*command*	Executes *command* on local host.
append *localFile remoteFile*	Appends the local file *localFile* to the remote file *remoteFile*.
bell	Causes a beep to be sounded after every file transfer.
bye	Shuts down the current connection to the remote host and then quits **ftp**.
cd *remoteDirectory*	Changes your current remote working directory to *remoteDirectory*.
close	Shuts down the current connection to the remote host.
delete *remoteFile*	Deletes *remoteFile* from the remote host.
get *remoteFile* [*localFile*]	Copies the remote file *remoteFile* to the local file *localFile*. If *localFile* is omitted, the local file is given the same name as that of the remote file.
help [*command*]	Displays help about *command*. If *command* is omitted, a list of all **ftp** commands is displayed.
lcd *localDirectory*	Changes your current local working directory to *localDirectory*.
ls *remoteDirectory*	Lists the contents of your current remote working directory.
mkdir *remoteDirectory*	Creates *remoteDirectory* on the remote host.
open *hostName* [*port*]	Attempts a connection to the host with name *hostName*. If you specify a port number, **ftp** assumes that this port is an **ftp** server.
put *localFile* [*remoteFile*]	Copies the local file *localFile* to the remote file *remoteFile*. If *remoteFile* is omitted, the remote file is given the same name as that of the local file.
pwd	Displays your current remote working directory.
quit	Same as "bye".
rename *remoteFrom remoteTo*	Renames the remote file *remoteFrom* as *remoteTo*.
rmdir *remoteDirectory*	Deletes the remote directory *remoteDirectory*.

In the following example, I copied "writer.c" from the remote host "vanguard" to my local host and then copied "who.c" from my local host to the remote host:

```
$ ftp vanguard              ...open ftp connection to "vanguard".
Connected to vanguard.utdallas.edu.
vanguard FTP server (SunOS 5.4) ready.
Name (vanguard:glass): glass...login
Password required for glass.
Password:                   ...secret!
User glass logged in.
ftp> ls                     ...obtain directory listing of remote host.
PORT command successful.
ASCII data connection for /bin/ls (129.110.42.1,4919) (0 bytes).
...                         ...lots of files were listed here, but are not
                            ...printed for space considerations.
uniq
upgrade
who.c
writer.c
ASCII Transfer complete.
1469 bytes received in 0.53 seconds (2.7 Kbytes/s)
ftp> get writer.c          ...copy from remote host.
PORT command successful.
ASCII data connection for writer.c (129.110.42.1,4920) (1276 bytes).
ASCII Transfer complete.
local: writer.c remote: writer.c
1300 bytes received in 0.012 seconds (1e+02 Kbytes/s)
ftp> !ls                    ...obtain directory listing of local host.
reader.c who.c writer.c
ftp> put who.c              ...copy file to remote host.
PORT command successful.
ASCII data connection for who.c (129.110.42.1,4922).
ASCII Transfer complete.
ftp> quit                   ...disconnect.
Goodbye.
$ _
```

DISTRIBUTING PROCESSING

The power of distributed systems becomes clearer when you start moving around the network and logging into different hosts. Some hosts supply limited password-less accounts with user IDs like "guest" so that explorers can roam the network without causing any harm, although this practice is fading away as more people abuse the privilege. These days, you almost always have to have an account on a remote computer in order to log into it. Three utilities for distributed access are:

- **rlogin**, which allows you to log into a remote UNIX host
- **rsh**, which allows you to execute a command on a remote UNIX host
- **telnet**, which allows you to execute commands on any remote host that has a telnet server

Of these utilities, **telnet** is the most flexible, as there are other systems in addition to UNIX that support telnet servers. These three utilities are described in the next set of subsections.

Remote Logins: rlogin

To log into a remote host, use **rlogin**:

Utility: **rlogin** -e*char* [-l *userId*] *hostName*

rlogin attempts to log you into the remote host *hostName*. If you don't supply a user ID by using the **-l** option, your local user ID is used during the login process.

If the remote host isn't set as an equivalent of your local host in your "$HOME/.rhost" file, you are asked for your password on the remote host.

Once you have connected, your local shell goes to sleep and the remote shell starts to execute. When you're finished with the remote login shell, terminate it in the normal fashion (usually with a *Control*-D) and your local shell will then awaken.

There are a few special "escape commands" that you may type that have a special meaning; each is preceded by the escape character, which is a tilde (~) by default. You may change this escape character by following the **-e** option with the preferred escape character. Here is a list of the escape commands:

SEQUENCE	MEANING
~.	Disconnect immediately from remote host.
~susp	Suspend remote login session. Restart remote login session using the command "*fg*".
~dsusp	Suspend input half of remote login session, but still echo output from login session to your local terminal. Restart remote login session using the command "*fg*".

In the following example, I logged into the remote host "vanguard" from my local host "csservr2", executed the **date** utility, and then disconnected:

```
$ rlogin vanguard                    ...remote login.
Last login: Tue May 19 17:23:51 from csservr2.utdallas
vanguard% date                       ...execute a command on "vanguard".
Wed May 20 18:50:47 CDT 1998
vanguard% ^D                         ...terminate the remote login shell.
Connection closed.
$                                    ...back home again at csservr2!
```

Executing Remote Commands: rsh

If you want to execute just a single command on a remote host, **rsh** is much handier than **rlogin**. Here's how it works:

Utility: **rsh** [-l *userId*] *hostName* [*command*]

rsh attempts to create a remote shell on the host *hostName* to execute *command.* **rsh** copies its standard input to *command* and copies the standard output and errors from *command* to its own standard output and error channels. Interrupt, quit, and terminate signals are forwarded to *command* so you may stop a remote command by pressing *Control-C.* **rsh** terminates immediately after *command* terminates.

If you do not supply a user ID by using the **-l** option, your local user ID is used during the connection. If no command is specified, **rsh** gives you a remote shell by invoking **rlogin.**

Quoted metacharacters are processed by the remote host; unquoted metacharacters are processed by the local shell.

In the following example, I executed the **hostname** utility on both my local "csservr2" host and the remote "vanguard" host:

```
$ hostname                    ...execute on my local host.
csservr2
$ rsh vanguard hostname       ...execute on a remote host.
vanguard
$ _
```

Remote Connections: telnet

telnet allows you to communicate with any remote host on the Internet that has a **telnet** server. Here's how it works:

Utility: **telnet** [*host* [*port*]]

telnet establishes a two-way connection with a remote port. If you supply a hostname but not a port specifier, you are automatically connected to a **telnet** server on the specified host, which typically allows you to log into the remote machine. If you don't even supply a host name, **telnet** goes directly into command mode (in the same fashion as does **ftp**).

What happens after the connection is complete depends on the functionality of the port to which you're connected. For example, port 13 of any Internet machine will send you the date and time and then disconnect, whereas port 7 will echo ("ping") back to you anything that you enter from the keyboard.

To enter **telnet** command mode after you've established a connection, press the sequence *Control*-], which is the **telnet** escape sequence. This sequence causes the command-mode prompt to be displayed; this prompt accepts commands that include the following:

COMMAND	MEANING
close	Close current connection.
open *host* [*port*]	Connect to *host* with optional *port* specifier.
quit	Exit **telnet**.
z	Suspend **telnet**.
?	Print summary of **telnet** commands.

Therefore, to terminate a **telnet** connection, press *Control*-] and then type the command "quit".

In the following example, I used **telnet** to emulate the **rlogin** functionality by omitting an explicit port number with the "open" command:

```
$ telnet                        ...start telnet.
telnet> ?                       ...get help.
Commands may be abbreviated.  Commands are:
close      close current connection
display    display operating parameters
mode       try to enter line-by-line or character-at-a-time mode
open       connect to a site
quit       exit telnet
send       transmit special characters ("send ?' for more)
set        set operating parameters ("set ?' for more)
status     print status information
toggle     toggle operating parameters ("toggle ?' for more)
z          suspend telnet
?          print help information
telnet> open vanguard          ...get a login shell from vanguard.
Trying 129.110.43.128...
Connected to vanguard.utdallas.edu.
Escape character is "^]'.
SunOS 5.4 (vanguard)
login: glass                    ...enter my user ID.
Password:                       ...secret!
Last login: Tue May 19 17:22:45 from csservr2.utdalla
***  For assistance, send mail to UNIXINFO.
```

```
Tue May 19 17:23:21 CDT 1998
Erase is Backspace
vanguard% date                    ...execute a command.
Tue May 19 17:23:24 CDT 1998
vanguard% ^D                      ...disconnect from remote host.
Connection closed by foreign host.
$ _                               ...telnet terminates.
```

You may specify the hostname directly on the command line, if you like:

```
$ telnet vanguard               ...specify hostname on command line.
Trying 129.110.43.128...
Connected to vanguard.utdallas.edu.
Escape character is "^]".
SunOS 5.4 (vanguard)
login: glass                      ...enter user ID, etc....
```

You may use **telnet** to try out some of the standard port services that I described earlier in this chapter. For example, port 13 prints the date and time on the remote host and then immediately disconnects:

```
$ telnet vanguard 13              ...what's the remote time and date?
Trying 129.110.43.128...
Connected to vanguard.utdallas.edu.
Escape character is "^]".
Tue May 19 17:26:32 1998
Connection closed by foreign host   ...telnet terminates.
$ _
```

Similarly, port 79 allows you to enter the name of a remote user and obtain finger information on that user:

```
$ telnet vanguard 79              ...manually perform a remote finger.
Trying 129.110.43.128 ...
Connected to vanguard.utdallas.edu.
Escape character is "^]".
glass                             ...enter the user ID.
Login name: glass          In real life: Graham Glass
Directory: /home/glass         Shell: /bin/csh
Last login Tue May 19 17:23 on from csservr2.utdalla
No unread mail
No Plan.
Connection closed by foreign host.   ...telnet terminates.
$ _
```

When system administrators are testing a network, they often use port 7 to check host connections. Port 7 echoes everything that you type back to your terminal and is sometimes known as a "ping port":

```
$ telnet vanguard 7                    ...try a ping.
Trying 129.110.43.128...
Connected to vanguard.utdallas.edu.
Escape character is "^]'.
hi                                     ...my line.
hi                                     ...the echo.
there
there
^]                                     ...escape to command mode.
telnet> quit                           ...terminate connection.
Connection closed.
$ _
```

telnet accepts numerical Internet addresses as well as symbolic names:

```
$ telnet 129.110.43.128 7              ..."vanguard"'s numerical address.
Trying 129.110.43.128...
Connected to 129.110.43.128.
Escape character is "^]'.
hi                                     ...my line.
hi...the echo.
^]                                     ...escape to command mode.
telnet> quit                           ...disconnect.
Connection closed.
$ _
```

NETWORK FILE SYSTEM: NFS

In order to make good use of UNIX's network capabilities, Sun Microsystems introduced a public-domain specification for a network file system (NFS). NFS supports
the following useful features:

- It allows several local file systems to be mounted into a single-network file
  hierarchy that may be transparently accessed from any host. To support this
  feature, NFS includes a remote mounting facility.
- RPC (remote procedure call) is used by NFS to allow one machine to make a
  procedure call to another machine, thereby encouraging distributed computation.
- XDR (external data representation) is the host-neutral data-representation
  scheme supported by NFS that allows programmers to create data structures
  that may be shared by hosts that have different byte ordering and word lengths.

NFS is very popular and is used on most machines that run UNIX. See [16, 280] for
more details on NFS.

FOR MORE INFORMATION

If you've enjoyed this overview of UNIX networking and you wish to find out more,
then I recommend that you read *UNIX Network Programming* [13], *UNIX Communications* [12], and the network section of *UNIX System Administration Handbook*
[16, 218].

CHAPTER REVIEW

Checklist

In this chapter, I described:

- the main UNIX network concepts and terminology
- utilities for listing users and communicating with them
- utilities for manipulating remote files
- utilities for obtaining remote login shells and executing remote commands

Quiz

1. What's the difference between a bridge, a router, and a gateway?
2. What's a good way for a system administrator to tell people about important events?
3. Why is **ftp** more powerful than **rcp?**
4. Describe some uses of common ports.
5. What does "machine equivalence" mean and how can you make use of it?

Exercises

1. Write a shell script that operates in the background on two machines and that ensures that the contents of a named directory on one machine are always a mirror image of those of another named directory on the other machine. [level: *hard*]
2. If you have accounts on different machines, write a "worm" program that moves between these accounts and performs some kind of benign operation. If you're the owner of the system, you can make the worm do some fun stuff, such as replicating and mutating now and again. [level: *hard*]
3. Try out **rcp** and **rsh** as follows:
   - Copy a single file from your local host to a remote host by using **rcp**.
   - Obtain a shell on the remote host using **rsh** and edit the file that you just copied.
   - Exit the remote shell using *exit.*
   - Copy the file from the remote host back to the local host using **rcp**.
     [level: *easy*]
4. Use **telnet** to obtain the time of day at several remote host sites. Are the times accurate relative to each other? [level: *medium*]

# CHAPTER 9

The Internet

Motivation

The Internet is probably the most visible aspect of computing in the history of the industry. What started out as a network tool to connect university and government users has grown into a huge entity used by millions worldwide. Even the most computer-illiterate people in the United States have at least heard of the Internet. Much of the appeal of having a home computer nowadays is to be able to access information on the Internet. This chapter will provide you with a solid understanding of what the Internet is and what you can do with it.

Prerequisites

While you don't really have to understand the nuts and bolts of the Internet Protocols (discussed in Chapter 8) to benefit from this chapter, the more familiar you are with generic UNIX networking issues, the more of this chapter you will find to be helpful.

Objectives

After reading this chapter, you will have a solid understanding of what the Internet is, how it came about, how it works, and what you can use it for.

Presentation

To really understand any topic, an understanding of its history is critical. I will first describe how the Internet came to be what it is today given its inauspicious start. After a survey of the tools that are used to access information on the Internet, I will also discuss where the future may take Internet users.

THE EVOLUTION OF THE INTERNET

As the local networks we looked at in Chapter 8 began to grow larger and to be connected together, an evolution began. First, some companies connected their own LANs together via private connections. Others transferred data across a network implemented on the public telephone network. Ultimately, the network research being funded by the U. S. Government brought it all together.

It may sound hard to believe, but what we know today as "the Internet" was almost inevitable. Although it began in a computer lab and, at the time, most people thought only high-powered computer scientists would ever use it, the way we stored and used information almost dictated that we find a better way to move information from one place to another.

Now when I watch television and see web page addresses at the end of commercials for mainstream products, I know that the Internet has truly reached common usage. Not only do high-tech companies maintain web pages, but even cereal companies have web sites. One may argue about the usefulness of some of these sites, but the fact that they exist tells us a great deal about how society has embraced the new technology.

It makes you wonder how we got here and where we might go with it all.

In the Beginning: The 1960s

In the 1960s, man was about to reach the moon, society was going through upheavals on several fronts, and technology was changing more rapidly than ever before. The Advanced Research Projects Agency (ARPA) of the Department of Defense (*DOD*) was attempting to develop a computer network to connect government computers (and the computers of some government contractors) together. As with so many advances in our society, some of the motivation (and funding) came from a government that hoped to leverage an advance in military and/or defensive capability. High-speed data communication might be required to help win a war at some point. Our interstate-highway system (network) has its roots in much the same type of motivation.

In the 1960s, mainframe computers still dominated computing and would continue to do so for some time. Removable disk packs, small cartridge tapes, and compact-disc technology were still in the future. Moving data from one of these mainframe computers to another usually required writing the data on a bulky tape device or some large disk device, physically carrying that media to the other mainframe computer, and then loading the data onto that computer. While this process was used, it was extremely inconvenient.

A Network Connection   Though computer networking was still in its infancy, local networks did exist and were the inspiration for what would ultimately become the Internet. During 1968 and 1969, ARPA experimented with connections between a few government computers. The basic architecture was a 50KB-dedicated telephone circuit connected to a machine at each site called an Interface Message Processor (IMP). Conceptually, this system is not unlike your personal Internet connection today if you consider that your modem does the job of the IMP. (Of course, the IMP was a much more complex device.) At each site, the IMP connected to the computer or computers that were to access the network.

The ARPANET   The ARPANET was born in September of 1969 when the first four IMPs were installed at the University of Southern California, Stanford Research Institute, the University of California at Santa Barbara, and the University of Utah. All of these sites had significant numbers of ARPA contractors. The success of the initial experiments between these four sites generated a great deal of interest on the part of ARPA as well as the academic community. Computing would never be the same.

Standardizing the Internet: The 1970s

The problem with the first connections to the ARPANET was that each IMP was, to some degree, custom designed for each site, depending on the operating systems and network configurations of their other computers. Much time and effort had been expended to get this network up to four sites. Hundreds of sites would require hundreds of times this much custom work if it were done in the same fashion.

It became clear that if all of the computers connected to the network in the same way and used the same software protocols, they could all connect to each other more efficiently and with much less effort at each site. But at this time, different computer vendors supplied their own operating systems with their hardware, and there was very little in the way of standards to help them interact or cooperate. What was required was a set of standards that could be implemented in software on different systems that could share data in a form that different computers could still understand.

Although the genesis of standard networking protocols began in the 1970s, it would be 1983 before all members of the ARPANET used them exclusively.

The Internet Protocol Family   In the early 1970s, researchers began to design the Internet Protocol. The word "internet" was used because it was more generic (at the time) than ARPANET, which referred to a specific network. The word "internet" referred to the generic internetworking of computers to allow them to communicate.

The Internet Protocol is the fundamental software mechanism that moves data from one place to another across a network. Data to be sent is divided into *packets*, which are the basic data units used on a digital computer network. IP does not guarantee that any single packet will arrive at the other end or in what order the packets will arrive, but it does guarantee that if the packet arrives, it will arrive unchanged from the original. This guarantee may not seem very useful at first, but stay with me for a moment.

TCP/IP   Once you can transmit a packet to another computer and know that if it arrives at all, it will be correct, other protocols can be added "on top" of the basic IP to provide other functionality. The Transmission Control Protocol (TCP) is the most often-used protocol along with IP (used together they are referred to as TCP/IP). As the name might imply to you, TCP controls the actual transmission of the stream of data packets. TCP adds sequencing and acknowledgement information to each packet, and each end of a TCP "conversation" cooperates to make sure that the original data stream is reconstructed in the same order as that of the original. When a single packet fails to arrive at the other end due to some failure in the network, the receiving TCP software figures this problem out because the packet's sequence number is missing. It can contact the sender and have it send the packet again. Alternatively, the sender, having likely not received an acknowledgment for the packet in question, will eventually retransmit the packet on its own, assuming that it was not received. If it was received and only the acknowledgement was lost, the receiving TCP software, upon receiving a second copy, will drop it, since it has already received the first one. The receiver will still send the acknowledgement for which the sending TCP software was waiting.

TCP is a connection-oriented protocol. An application program opens a TCP connection to another program on another computer, and they send data back and forth to each other. When they have completed their work, they close down the connection. If one end (or a network break) closes the connection unexpectedly, this interruption is considered an error by the other end.

UDP/IP   Another useful protocol that cooperates with IP is the Unreliable Datagram Protocol (UDP). Based on the name, you may wonder how useful an unreliable protocol can be, but there are occasions for which an application needs to send status information to another application (such as a management agent sending status information to a network or systems-management application). The information is not of critical importance, and if it does not arrive, either it will be sent again later or it may not be necessary for each and every instance of the data to be received by the application. Of course, this scenario assumes that any failure would be due to some transient failure and that the next time, the transmission it would work. If it fails all of the time, it would imply the existence of a network problem that might not become apparent.

In such a case, the overhead required to open and maintain a TCP connection is more work than is really necessary; you just want to send a short status message. You don't really care if the other end gets it (since if they don't, they probably will get the next one), and you certainly don't want to wait around for it to be acknowledged. So, an unreliable protocol fits the bill nicely.

Internet Addressing   When an organization is setting up a LAN that it wishes to be part of the Internet, it requests a unique Internet IP address from the NIC (the Network Information Center). The number that is allocated depends on the size of the organization:

- A huge organization, such as a country or a massive corporation, is allocated a Class A address. A Class A address is a number that is the first eight bits of a 32-bit IP address. The organization is then free to use the remaining 24 bits for labeling its local hosts. The NIC rarely allocates these Class A addresses, as each one uses up a lot of the total 32-bit number space.
- A medium-sized organization, such as a mid-size corporation, is allocated a Class B address. A Class B address is a number that is the first 16 bits of a 32-bit IP address. The organization can then use the remaining 16 bits to label its local hosts.
- A small organization is allocated a Class C address, which is the first 24 bits of a 32-bit IP address.

For example, the University of Texas at Dallas is classified as a medium-sized organization, and its LAN was allocated the 16-bit number 33134. IP addresses are written as a series of four eight-bit numbers, with the most significant byte written first. All computers on the LAN of the University of Texas at Dallas therefore have an IP address of the form 129.110.XXX.YYY,[1] where XXX and YYY are numbers between zero. and 255.

Internet Applications   Once there existed a family of protocols that allowed easy transmission of data to a remote network host, the next step was to provide application programs that took advantage of these protocols. The first applications to be used with TCP/IP were two programs in wide use even before TCP/IP was used on the ARPANET. I described the use of these programs in the previous chapter.

The telnet program was (and still is) used to connect one computer to another computer on the network in order for the user of the first computer to log in and use that computer from his or her local computer or terminal. This program is quite useful in these days of high-priced computing resources. Your organization might not have its own supercomputer, but you might have access to one at another site. Telnet allows you to log in remotely without having to travel to the other site.

The ftp program was used to transfer files back and forth. While ftp is still available today, most people use web browsers or network file systems to move data files from one computer to another.

Redesigning and Renaming the Internet: The 1980s

As more universities and government agencies began using the ARPANET, word of its usefulness spread. Soon, corporations were getting connected. At first, because of the funding involved, a corporation had to have some kind of government contract in order to qualify. Over time, this requirement was enforced less and less.

With this growth came headaches. As with a local network, the smaller it is, the fewer nodes that are connected and the easier it is to administer. As the network grows, the complexity of managing the whole thing grows as well. It became clear that the growth rate that the ARPANET was experiencing would soon outgrow the Defense Department's ability to manage the network.

The rate of new hosts being added was now requiring modifications to the network host table on a daily basis. This growth rate also required each ARPANET site to download new host tables every day if they wished to have up-to-date tables. In addition, the number of available hostnames was dwindling, since each hostname had to be unique across the entire network.

Domain Name Service   Enter DNS, the Domain Name Service. DNS and BIND, the Berkeley Internet Name Daemon, proposed the hierarchy of domain naming of network hosts and the method for providing address information to anyone on the network as they request it.

In the new system, top-level domain names were established, under which each network site could establish a subdomain. The DOD would managed the top-level domains and delegated the management of each subdomain to the entity or organization that registered the domain. The DNS/BIND software provided the method for any network site to do a search for network-address information for a particular host.

---

[1]$129 * 256 + 110 = 33134.$

Let's look at a real-world example of how a hostname is resolved to an address. One of the most popular top-level domains is "com", so we'll use that domain in our example, as most people are familiar with the naming convention. The DOD maintains the server for the "com" domain. All subdomains registered in the "com" domain are known to this server. When another network host needs an address for a hostname under the "com" domain, it queries the "com" name server.

For example, if you attempt to make a connection to "snoopy.hp.com", your machine would not know the IP address because there is no information in your local host table for "snoopy.hp.com". Your machine would then contact the domain-name server for the "com" domain to ask it for the address. However, that server only knows the address for the "hp.com" name server; it does not need to know about everything under that particular domain. But since "hp.com" is registered with the "com" name server, it can query the "hp.com" name server for the address.[2] Once a name server that has authority for the "hp.com" domain is contacted, an address for "snoopy.hp.com" (or a message that the host does not exist) is returned to the requestor.

Up to this point, every hostname on the ARPANET was just a name, like "utexas" for the ARPANET host at the University of Texas. Under the new system, this machine was renamed to be a member of the "utexas.edu" domain. However, this change could not be made everywhere overnight. So for a time, a default domain ".arpa" was established. By default, all hosts began to be known under this domain (i.e., "utexas" changed its name to "utexas.arpa"). Once a site had taken that single step, it was easier for it to become a member of its new domain, since most of the remaining pain only involved implementing software that understands the domain-name system.

Once the ARPANET community adopted this system, all kinds of problems were solved. Suddenly, a hostname only had to be unique within a subdomain. Just because HP had a machine called "snoopy" didn't mean that someone at the University of Texas couldn't also use that name, since "snoopy.hp.com" and "snoopy.utexas.edu" are different names. This issue had not been such a big problem when only mainframe computers were connected to the network, but we were quickly approaching the explosion of workstations, and it would have been a huge problem after that. The other big advantage of this system was that a single network-wide host table no longer had to be maintained and updated on a daily basis. Each site kept its own local host tables up to date, and would simply query the name server when an address for a host at another site was needed. By querying other name servers, you were always guaranteed to receive the most up-to-date information.

The top-level domains that are most often encountered are shown in the following table:

---

[2]Two options are available in the protocols. The first is that the requesting machine may be redirected to a "more knowledgeable" host and may then make follow-up requests until it obtains the information it needs. The other possibility is that the original machine may make a single request, and each subsequent machine that doesn't have the address can make the follow-up request of the more knowledgeable host on behalf of the original host. This choice is a configuration option in the domain-resolution software and has no effect on how many requests are made or on the efficiency of the requests.

Name	Category
com	commercial
edu	educational
gov	governmental
org	nonprofit organization
mil	military
XX	two-letter country code

For example, the LAN of the University of Texas at Dallas was allocated the name "utdallas.edu". Once an organization has obtained its unique IP address and domain name, it may use the rest of the IP number to assign addresses to the other hosts on the LAN.

DOD Lets Go   Like a parent whose child has grown up and needs its independence, the Department of Defense was coming to a point where its child, the ARPANET, needed to move out of the house and be on its own. The DOD originally started the network as a research project, a proof of concept. The network became valuable, so the DOD continued to run and manage it. But as membership in the ARPANET grew, the management of this network took more and more resources and provided the DOD with fewer and fewer payoffs as non-DOD-related entities got connected. It was time for the Department of Defense to get out of the network-management business.

In the late 1980s, the National Science Foundation (NSF) began to build NSFNET. NSFNET took a unique approach to large-scale networking at the time in that it was constructed as a "backbone" network to which other regional networks could connect. NSFNET was originally intended to link supercomputer centers.

Using the same types of equipment and protocols as those making up the ARPANET, NSFNET provided an alternative medium with much freer and easier access than the government-run ARPANET. To most people, except the programmers and managers involved, the ARPANET appears to have mutated into the Internet of today. In reality, connections to NSFNET (and their regional networks) were created and ARPANET connections were severed, but because of the sharing of naming conventions and appearances, the change was much less obvious to the casual user.

The end result was a network that, to the user, worked in the same way as the ARPANET had, but that as it grew, was made up of many more corporations and nongovernment agencies. More importantly, this new network was not funded by government money; it was surviving through private funding from those using it.

The Web: The 1990s

The 1990s saw the Internet come into popular use. Although it had grown consistently since its inception, it was still predominately a world belonging to computer users and programmers. Two things happened to spring the Internet on an unsuspecting public: the continued growth of personal computers in the home and one amazingly good idea.

The "Killer App"   Again, timing played a role in the history of the Internet. The network itself was growing and being used by millions of people, but still was not considered mainstream. The more sophisticated home users were getting connected to the Internet via a connection to their employer's network or by subscribing with a company that provided access to the Internet. These companies came to be known as *ISP*s, Internet Service Providers. In the early 1990s, only a handful of these companies existed, as only a few people recognized that there was a business in providing Internet access to anyone who wanted it. However, at the time, the demand was small.

Then came "mosaic". Mosaic was the first "browser" and was conceived by software designers at the National Center for Supercomputing Applications (NCSA) at the University of Illinois at Urbana-Champaign. With Mosaic, a computer user could access information from other sites on the Internet without having to use the complicated and nonintuitive tools that were popular at the time (e.g., telnet, ftp, gopher).

Mosaic was—and browsers in general, are—an application that displayed a page of information both textually and graphically. It displayed information described by a page-description language called HTML, HyperText Markup Language. HTML was developed as a documentation and information technology. Its most revolutionary aspect was that of a hyperlink, a way to link information in one place in a document to other information in another part of the document or, more generically, in another document.

By designing a page with HTML, you could display information and include links to other parts of the page or to other pages at other sites that contained related information. This ability created a document that could be "navigated" to allow the user to obtain the specific information in which they were interested rather than having to read or search the document in a sequential fashion, as was typical before the advent of HTML.

Almost overnight, servers that provided information that could be viewed by Mosaic sprang up across the Internet. Now, rather than maintaining an anonymous FTP site, a site could maintain its publicly accessible information in a much more presentable format. Anonymous FTP sites usually required that the users accessing them know what they are trying to find, or, at best, that the users get the README file that would help them find what they want. On the other hand, with a server that provided HTML, the user could simply point and click and be taken to the page containing the information that they sought.

Of course, not all of this magic happened automatically, for each site that maintained any information for external users had to set up a server and format the information. But this task was not significantly more work than the task of providing the information via anonymous FTP. As sites became more sophisticated and involved, the work required increased, but the payoff in presentation also increased. Early on, as people switched from providing information via FTP-based tools to using Web-based tools, the two alternatives became comparable.

Some of the people involved in the early releases of Mosaic later formed Netscape Communications Corporation, where they applied the lessons that they had learned from early browser development and produced Netscape, the next generation in browsers. Since then, browsers, lead by Netscape and Microsoft Internet Explorer, have evolved to become very sophisticated applications and introduce significant advances in both browsing and publishing every year.

The Web vs. the Internet   Alert readers will notice that I avoided using the word "web" in the previous section. The word means many different things in different contexts to different people and causes as much confusion as it conveys information. All of the words before which I didn't use the term in the previous section (e.g., "web browsers," "web publishing," "web pages") have the same basic meaning with or without the word "web" to modify them. So where does this word really come from?

Before Mosaic and other browsers, there was just the Internet. As we have already seen, the Internet is simply a worldwide network of computers.[3] This definition in itself can be diagrammed as a web of network connections, but this definition is not the meaning of the word "web" as used in its present context.

When Mosaic, using HTML, provided the capability to jump around from one place to another on the Internet, yet another conceptual "web" emerged. Not only is my computer connected to several others, forming a web, but now my HTML document is also connected to several others by hyperlinks, creating a virtual spider web of information. This web is the "web" that gave rise to the terms "web pages" and "web browsing."

When someone talks about the Web today, they may mean the Internet itself or they may mean the web of information available on the Internet. Although not originally intended to be, the nomenclature the Web and "the Internet" are often used interchangeably today. However, in proper usage, the Web refers to the information that is available from the infrastructure of "the Internet."

Web Addressing   Web page addresses require three pieces of information: the protocol to use to obtain the page, the address from which to obtain the page, and the file representing the page itself.[4]

The protocol used to serve HTML is http (HyperText Transport Protocol). Many web browsers also support other protocols, like ftp, which gives you window-based interface to an FTP daemon. Hostnames of web servers often begin with "www" (standing for World Wide Web—for example, "www.hp.com" or w3 (meaning "w" used three times). The specification for the file may be missing, in which case "/" is assumed. (This character refers to the root node of the public area of the web server, not the root directory of the system.)

Accessibility   A few ISPs had sprung up even as the Web was coming into existence. Once the concept of the Web gained visibility, it seemed like everyone suddenly wanted to get on the Internet. While electronic mail was always usable and remains one of the most talked-about services provided by access to the Internet, web browsing had the visibility and the public-relations appeal to win over the general public.

All of a sudden, the average person saw useful (or at least fun) things they could get from being connected to the Internet, which was no longer the sole domain of computer geeks. For better or worse, the Internet would change rapidly.

---

[3]Of course, this definition is an *extreme* oversimplification.

[4]A fourth piece of information, usually not specified, is the port number to contact to obtain the information. The default port number for a web page server daemon is 80, but this number can be changed or multiple web servers can be run on different ports to serve different information.

More people, more information, and more demand caused great growth in its usage and availability. Of course, with more people comes more inexperienced people and more congestion. Popularity is always a double-edged sword.

Another factor enabling the general public to access the Internet was the geometric increase in modem speeds. While large companies have direct connections to the Internet, most private connections are dial-up connections over home phone lines, requiring the use of modems. When the top modem speed was 2400 bps (bytes per second), which wasn't all that long ago, downloading a web page would have been intolerably slow. As modem speeds have increased to 56 Kbps (56,000 bps) and are still increasing, it has become much more reasonable to have more than just a terminal connection on a dial-up connection.

Price has also played a part in the interest of the general public; most of these private connections can be had for between $10–$30 per month, depending on the usage. An Internet bill that is comparable with a cable bill or a phone bill is tolerable. The general public was not likely to have embraced an Internet bill that was an order of magnitude higher than other utility bills.

Changes in the Internet   As the public has played a larger and larger part in the direction of the evolution of the Internet, some of the original spirit of what the Internet was has changed.

The Internet was originally developed "just to prove it could be done," but not as a profit-making enterprise. The original spirit of the Internet, especially in its ARPANET days, was that information and software should be free to others with similar interests and objectives. Much of the original code that ran the Internet (the Internet Protocol protocol suite, tools such as ftp and Telnet, etc.) was given away by the original authors and modified by others who contributed their changes back to the original authors for "the greater good."

This spirit was probably what allowed the Internet to grow and thrive in its youth. However, today, business takes place over the Internet, and a smaller proportion of information is freely available. This is not to say that everybody is out to do nothing but make money, or even that making money is bad. But it is a change in the culture of the Internet, and there are those who would argue that it is a battle between good and evil.

Of course, it would be wonderful to live in a world where you could have anything you want and you could do anything you want to contribute to society. In reality, this system rarely works very well; everyone wants to do the fun things, but no one wants to do the things that aren't so fun! In a capitalist society, money provides the motivation for many things that need to be done, including software development.

The Internet needed the "free spirit" origins that it had, but now that mainstream society is using the Internet, it is only natural that it has changed to a more capitalist medium. Advertising on Web sites is common, and some web sites require each user to pay a subscription fee in order to be able to log in to gain access to information on their web pages. Commerce over the Internet (such as on-line ordering of goods and services, including on-line information) is expected to experience explosive growth over the next few years and into the next century.

Security   Entire books concerning Internet security exist [30]. In the future, as more commercial activity takes place across the Internet, the needs for and concerns about the security of operations that take place across the Internet will only increase.

In general, a single transfer of data is responsible for its own security. In other words, if you are making a purchase, the vendor will probably use secure protocols to acquire purchase information from you, like credit-card information.

Four major risks confront an Internet web server or surfer: information copying, information modification, impersonation, and denial of service. Encryption services can prevent the copying or modifying of information. User education can help minimize impersonation.

The most feared—and ironically, the least often-occurring—hazard is the copying of information that travels across the network. The Internet is a public network, and therefore, any information sent "in the clear" (unencrypted) could be copied by someone between the sender and the recipient. In reality, since information is divided into packets that may or may not travel via the same route to their destination, it is often impractical to try to eavesdrop in order to obtain useful information.

Modification of information that is in transit has the same difficulties as those of eavesdropping, with the additional problem of making the modification. While not impossible, it is a very difficult process and usually not worth the effort.

Impersonation of a user, either through a login interface or an e-mail message, is probably the most common type of security breach. Users often do not safeguard their passwords. Once another person knows a user's username and password, the person can log in and have all of the same rights and privileges as the legitimate user. Unfortunately, it is also trivial to send an e-mail message with forged headers to make it appear that the message came from another user. Close examination of the headers can usually authenticate them or prove them to be forged, but this falsification can still lead to confusion, especially if an inexperienced user receives the message. One might also impersonate another network host by claiming to use its network address. This act is known as *spoofing*. Spoofing is not a trivial exercise, but an experienced network programmer or administrator can pull it off.

A denial-of-service attack occurs when an outside attacker sends a huge amount of information to a server to overload its capability to do its job. The server gets so bogged down that it either becomes unusable or it completely crashes so that no one can use it.

Copyright   One of the biggest challenges in the development of information exchange on the Internet is that of copyright. In traditional print media, time is required to reproduce information, and proof of that reproduction will exist. In other words, if I reprint someone else's text without their permission, the copy that I create would prove the action. On the Internet, however, information can be reproduced literally at the speed of light. In the amount of time that it takes to copy a file, a copyright can be violated with very little evidence of the action left behind.

Censorship   In any environment where information can be distributed, there will be those who want to be able to limit who can gain access to what information. If the information is mine and I want to limit your access to it, this desire is called my right to privacy. If the information is someone else's and I want to limit your access to it, this desire is called censorship.

This is not to say that censorship is bad. As with so much in our society, the idea alone is not the problem, but rather the interpretation of the idea. Censorship on the Internet is, to put it mildly, a complex issue. Governments and organizations may try to limit certain kinds of access to certain kinds of materials, often with the best of intentions. The problem is that since the Internet is a worldwide resource, local laws have very little jurisdiction over the whole of the Internet. How can a law in Nashville be applied to a web server in Sydney? If someone in Nashville decides that the web server in Sydney *is* doing something illegal, who will prosecute?

Misinformation   As much of a problem as copyrighted or offensive material may be, much more trouble is caused by information that is simply incorrect. Since there is no information authority that approves and validates information put on the 'Net, anyone can publish anything. This ability is a great thing for free speech, but humans tend to believe almost any information that they see in print. I can't tell you how many stories I've heard about people acting on information they found on the Web that turned out to be misleading or wrong. How much credence would you give to a rumor you were told by someone you didn't know? That's how much credence you should give to information you pick up off of the Web, at least when you aren't sure of the source.

Acceptable Use   Many ISPs have an Acceptable-Use policy that you must adhere to in order to use their services. Over time, this policy may well solve many of the problems that the Internet has had in its formative years. Most of these policies basically ask users to behave themselves and not to do anything illegal or abusive to other users, which includes sending harassing e-mail, copying files that don't belong to you, and so on.

There is a perceived anonymity of users of the Internet.[5] If you send me an e-mail message with which I disagree, it may be difficult for me to walk over to you and yell at you personally. I might have to settle for YELLING AT YOU OVER E-MAIL.[6] Because of this capability of avoiding in-person confrontation, people tend to behave in ways that they would not in person. As the Internet and its users grow up, this problem should lessen.

USING TODAY'S INTERNET

In the past, using the Internet meant keeping track of a collection of commands and ftp sites. You had to keep track of the resources as well as of the methods of accessing them.

Today, almost everything that you access on the Internet is web based—that is, accessible via a web browser. Many web browsers have been written, but by far, the most popular browser for UNIX computers is Netscape written by Netscape Communications.

---

[5]I say "perceived" here because it is actually possible to find the identities of most people if you're willing to do enough work. Even people who have filtered threatening e-mail through "anonymous" e-mail services have been found by law-enforcement officials. ISPs will cooperate with the authorities when arrest warrants are involved!

[6]Text in all caps is typically interpreted as the written equivalent to speaking the words in a loud voice. This rule does not include those few users who still use computers or terminals that can only generate uppercase characters.

Web Browsing

A web browser is a program, much like any other window-based program, with menu buttons, a control area, and a display area. You type in or select a web address (also known as a *URL*, a Uniform Resource Locator), and the browser makes the request from the specified host on the network (either the local network or the Internet) and displays the information that is returned in the window. A Netscape browser "pointing to" Prentice Hall's web site looks like this:

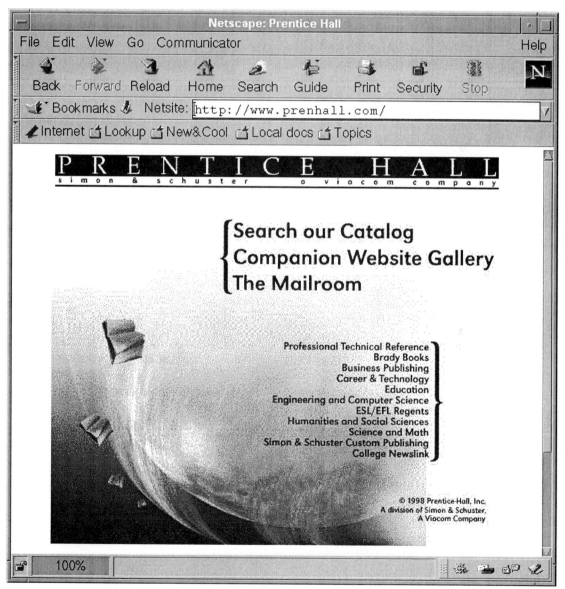

FIGURE 9.1 A Netscape window. Copyright 1998 Netscape Communications Corp. Used with permission. All rights reserved. This page may not be reprinted or copied without the express written permission of Netscape.

I won't spend much time describing how to use Netscape, since playing with it is the best way to learn how to use it. Each page that you access has text and may have hypertext links, which provide you with a way to access other related pages. You can type a new address in the address window. You can click on the "Back" button to return to a previous page. Netscape provides a history of the pages that you have visited so that you can easily find them again.

URLs

The Uniform Resource Locator (URL) is the name for a Web address used by a web browser. The URL of the page in Figure 9.1 is "http://www.prenhall.com" and can be found in the URL window. You can select the text in that window and type a new URL or access another web page by clicking on a link contained in the text of that page.

The components of a URL are the protocol, the Internet address, an optional port number, and an optional filename. In the case of the URL in Figure 9.1, the port number and filename are left off, so the default port of the web server (port 80) is used and the default file (/) is requested. The most common protocol is http (HyperText Transport Protocol), which is the common protocol for accessing HTML. An encrypted channel can be accessed using Secure HTTP (https). Most web browsers also support the ftp protocol, which gives you a GUI-based way of accessing anonymous ftp sites through your browser. If no protocol is specified, most browsers will assume that "http://" goes on the front of the address, so you can usually leave that text off when manually typing in a URL.

Web Searches

So now that you have a browser window and can access web sites, how do you find whatever you want? Many people discussed with me what I should put in this section to help you navigate the Web. However, by the time that this book is published, many of the sites that I might have listed may no longer work. Rather than just giving you a fish, I'd rather show you how to fish so that you can find anything that you might need on your own.

There are more than a few web search "engines" on the Internet. These search engines are sites that continuously build a database of web pages and keyword indices relating to the web pages. Normally, these sites provide free services; the pages that show you the results of the search usually have advertisements on them that sponsors pay for to support the cost of running the site.

At the time of this writing, the most popular search engines, in alphabetical order in order not to show any preferences, are:

- www.altavista.com
- www.excite.com
- www.infoseek.com
- www.lycos.com
- www.webcrawler.com
- www.yahoo.com

I have my own preferences, and so will you. Your favorite site may depend on the speed of the response, the layout of the information, the quality of what it finds, the ease with which you can build a query, or some of the other services the site may provide.

Today, there are so many sites on the Internet that the biggest problem with search engines is being able to build a query specific enough so that you don't get hundreds of links back, most of which aren't what you really want.

If you are trying to find a mainstream company, you can often get lucky by guessing. A URL of the format "www.companyname.com" probably works as often as it doesn't.

Finding Users and Domains

The NIC provides web page access to the database of registered Internet users and Internet domains. The user database does not contain every Internet user; it contains only users who have registered with the NIC. This group of people usually includes system and network administrators who manage domain information for a site.

The NIC's hostname is "rs.internic.net" and its web page can point you to the resources with which you can perform all sorts of searches for domain and Internet information.

Factors Affecting Future Use

Will the Internet continue to grow as it has over the past 10 years? The only factor limiting its use before now has been accessibility. With ISPs continuing to pop up and expand, my guess would be that the accessibility problem has been solved.

Today, millions of people access the Internet each day. Some use it to send and receive e-mail and read discussion bulletin boards. Some use it to look up information of all kinds on the Web servers of corporate and educational institutions. Many use it to order products. As convenience becomes a priority in people's busy lives, net access may prove to be the most efficient way of finding information, even on a the local level.

With millions of people using the Internet now and even more expected to use it in the future, advertisers are eager to get their messages to this new market. As Web servers and applications become more sophisticated, advertisers will be able to target their message to only those users who are interested. This ability is an advantage to both the merchant and the customer, since it helps reduce the information overload we are already suffering from these days.

CHAPTER REVIEW

Checklist

In this chapter, I described:

- the history of the Internet
- protocols used on the Internet
- applications that access the Internet

- the Domain Name Service used on the Internet
- the World Wide Web, web browsing, and web searching

Quiz

1. Why does the NIC allocate very few Class A addresses?
2. What is the difference between the http and https protocols?
3. If you were looking for Sun Microsystems' web page, what address would you try first?
4. What are the two most significant differences between the TCP and UDP protocols?

Exercises

1. Use your web browser to go to NIC's web site (rs.internic.net) and look up information about your domain name (or your ISP's domain name). [level: *medium*]
2. Pick some companies you know and try to access their web pages with URLs that you make up in the form of www.companyname.com. [level: *easy*]

Projects

1. Connect to the "rs.internic.net" web site and explore it to find out what kinds of services the NIC provides. [level: *medium*]
2. Pretend that you want to buy the latest CD of your favorite group, but you don't know of an Internet site that sells CDs (there are several). Do a web search with several keywords (like "music", "CD", "purchase", and the name of the group). See if you find a way to buy the CD, and explore some of the other sites that come up to find out why they satisfied your search so that you know how to make a better search next time. [level: *medium*]

C H A P T E R   1 0

Windowing Systems

Motivation

Virtually all UNIX computers now employ some form of windowing system. The vast majority of these are based on MIT's X Window System™. A familiarity with the X Window System should allow you to function on virtually any UNIX-based window system in use today.

Prerequisites

Since the X Window System takes advantage of several UNIX networking facilities, you should have read or be familiar with the issues discussed in Chapter 8 prior to reading this chapter.

Objectives

In this chapter I will provide you with a general overview of the X Window System, show how to use some of its most common features, and show you how it can improve your productivity. Many other books (e.g., [24], [25], and [26]) go into much greater detail about this complicated subject. The goal here is to give you enough information to get you started using the X Window System and to give you an understanding upon which to build.

Presentation

First, I will give you a brief history of window systems in general, followed by an examination of the X Window System, what it looks like, how it works, and the UNIX commands involved in using it.

INTRODUCTION

In the early days of UNIX systems, a character terminal was the only interface to the system. You logged in and did all your work in a single, character-based terminal session. If you were lucky, it was a terminal with "smart" cursor capabilities for which full-screen manipulations were possible by moving the cursor around on the screen, which allowed screen-oriented text editing or debugging. Usually, however, you simply had a line-oriented terminal where you typed in a line of text (a command) and

315

got back one or more lines of text in response. And you were happy to have it instead of the punch cards you used before that!

Graphical User Interfaces

As computer systems became more sophisticated, bitmapped displays (where each bit on the screen can be tuned on or off rather than simply displaying a character in a certain space) allowed user interfaces to become more sophisticated. The *Graphical User Interface* (GUI, often pronounced "gooey") was born. The first semi-well-known GUI was that of the Xerox STAR. This computer was purely a text-processing system and was the first to use the icon representing a document that looked like a page with one corner folded over. The Xerox STAR had icons for folders, documents, and printers on a *desktop* (the screen) rather than a command-line-driven interface, as had been the norm to that time.

The ability to click on a picture of a document to edit it and to drag it on the top of a printer icon to print it, rather than having to remember what the commands to perform these functions were, was, at the time, revolutionary. Some of the engineers from Xerox moved on to Apple Computer and the Apple Lisa was introduced, followed later by the Apple Macintosh.

UNIX also got into the GUI act. Sun Microsystems introduced "suntools" early in the history of SunOS (the predecessor of Solaris, Sun's current version of UNIX). Suntools allowed multiple terminal windows on the same screen with a cut-and-paste ability between them. At first, there were only a few applications that provided real GUI functionality. A performance meter could display system-performance statistics in a meter display rather than by numbers on a chart. The "mailtool" program allowed you to read e-mail with something other than the traditional "/bin/mail" program. But under conventional windowing systems, an application could only display information on the screen of the computer on which the application was running. The next step in the evolution was still to come.

MIT

In 1984, the Massachusetts Institute of Technology released the X Window System. Recognizing the usefulness of window systems, but unimpressed at what UNIX vendors were providing, students at MIT, in a move comparable to the BSD movement at Berkeley and to the origin of UNIX itself, set out to write a window system of their own. Digital Equipment Corporation initially helped fund Project Athena, where X had its origins.

The revolutionary idea behind the X Window System, which has yet to be rivaled in any modern computer system, is the distinction between the functions of client and server in the process of drawing an image on a computer screen. Unlike most windowing systems, X is defined by a network protocol, replacing the traditional procedure call interface. Rather than simply having an application draw its image directly to the screen, as previous window systems had done, the X Window System split the two functions apart. The X server takes care of drawing on and managing the contents of the computer's bitmapped display and communicating with all clients who wish to draw on the screen. An X client doesn't draw directly on a screen, but instead communicates with an X server running on the computer where the screen on which it wishes to draw is located. By allowing this communication to be between two processes on the same machine or via a network connection between two processes on different machines, suddenly you have the capability to draw graphics on a screen on a different computer. This capability opens the door to all sorts of new possibilities, as well as security problems.

The X Window System is often referred to simply as "X" or "X11," referring to its most recent version. The current release of X11 is the sixth release; hence, the complete reference is sometimes called "X11R6".

X SERVERS

An *X server* starts up and "takes over" the bitmapped display on a computer system. This action may happen automatically when a user logs in, or it may happen when the user executes a command to start the X server, depending on the implementation.

Usually, at the time that the X server starts, one or two *X clients* are also started. X clients are programs that communicate with one or more X servers in order to communicate with a user. Some other program must be started that will allow the user access to the system. (A screen being driven by an X server, but not running any application, would not allow you to do anything on it.) A terminal window and a window manager are usually the types of programs that you start at this point, as we will see later.

On systems that don't start an X server for you at login time, there is usually a command such as "xinit" or "xstart" that you can either type manually or add to your login or profile script so that the server will be started automatically when you login.

Screen Geometry

The layout of the screen is called *geometry*. A bitmapped display has a certain size, measured in pixels. Pixels are the dots on a display that can be set to on or off (white or black) or to some color value. A small screen might be 600×480 pixels (a typical low-resolution PC monitor). A larger screen might be 1280×1000 pixels or even larger for very high-resolution graphics.

Screen geometry is specified either by referencing a specific position on the screen (e. g., 500×200) or by referencing positions relative to a corner of the screen. For example, position $+0+0$ is the upper left corner of the screen, $-0-0$ is the lower right corner, $-0+0$ is the upper right corner, and $+0-0$ is the lower left corner. Therefore, $+500+500$ would be 500 pixels away from the upper left corner of the screen in both the x and y directions. We will see examples of such referencing when we discuss X clients.

Security and Authorization

As you may have guessed by now, the ability to scribble on any computer screen in your network could lead to security problems. These security problems would exist not so much because the act of writing on someone else's screen is anything more than annoying if the operation is not wanted by the recipient, but because I/O to an

X server is just that, input and output. Write access to an X server also gives you the ability to query that system for a current copy of the display or even keyboard input that is being typed (e. g. a password).

Because of this issue, the X Window System has a certain amount of security built into the X server. It isn't highly rated security, but it is enough to keep the casual snoop from having unauthorized access. By default, the X server running on any computer system only allows X clients on that same system to talk to it. The X server does not accept connections from "foreign" X clients without knowing who they are. This rule causes the default configuration of an X server to be very much like a conventional window system, for which only applications running on that computer can write to that computer's display. In order to take advantage of the network capabilities of the X Window System, however, you have to allow outside access.

The **xhost** command is used to allow X clients on other systems to display to your system and works as follows:

Utility: **xhost** [+|−][*hostname*]

The **xhost** command allows or denies access to the X server on a system. With no arguments, **xhost** prints its current settings and which hosts (if any) have access. By specifying only "+", you can give access to all hosts, or by specifying only "−", you can deny access to all hosts. When a hostname is specified after a "+" or "−", access is granted or denied, respectively, to that host. In the case of allowing access, the "+" is optional.

```
xhost +bluenote
```

allows X clients running on the computer called "bluenote" to write to the display on the system on which the **xhost** command was run. Later, when whatever you needed to run is finished, you can remove access to "bluenote" with the command

```
xhost -bluenote
```

In a secure environment where you aren't afraid of other systems writing to your display, you can allow any X client on the network to write to your display with the command

```
xhost +
```

You can also take away access from all X clients with the command

```
xhost -
```

X WINDOW MANAGERS

All of this ability to write to a display isn't really very useful if you just sit there and watch windows pop up and go away, but you can't do anything with them. This point is where window managers come in. A window manager is a program (an X client) that communicates with the X server and with the keyboard and mouse on the system. It provides the interface for the user to give instructions to the X server about what to do with the windows.

Although window managers are usually run on the same computer as the display that they manage, this situation is not a requirement. If you have a special X window manager that only runs on one specific type of computer, it is possible to set it up to manage your workstation from a remote computer. Of course, there are inherent problems involved in doing so. What if the remote machine running the window manager or the network were to go down? Your X server would no longer be managed because it could not communicate with the window manager, and your keyboard and mouse likely would not respond—at least, not properly—to your input. But the fact that it could be done this way is a testament to how flexible the X window system architecture is.

One of the important features provided by a window manager is the "look and feel" of the desktop. The look and feel of the interior of a window depend on the application creating the window. While all window managers provide similar basic functionality, the appearance of each can vary widely.

Focus

The most important job of a window manager is to maintain the window *focus.* "Focus" is the term used to describe which window is currently selected or active. If you type on the keyboard, the window with focus is where the data will be sent. Focus is what allows you to move from one window to another and do multiple things in different windows. Generally, a window with focus has a different border than the other windows, although this aspect is configurable.

Window focus can be configured so that it is set when a window border or title bar is selected or simply when the mouse pointer is moved onto the window, depending on user preference.

Program Start-up

Most window managers also provide a *menu-pulldown capability* that can be customized to allow you to start different often-used applications. For example, if your pointer is on the root window (the desktop itself, not an application window) and you click and hold down a mouse button, most window managers will bring up a menu with a list of things that you can select to perform a function. This list usually includes functions like starting a new terminal window or exiting the window manager. The specific functions vary from one window manager to another and can be heavily customized by each user. Also, different mouse buttons can be customized to bring up different lists of functions.

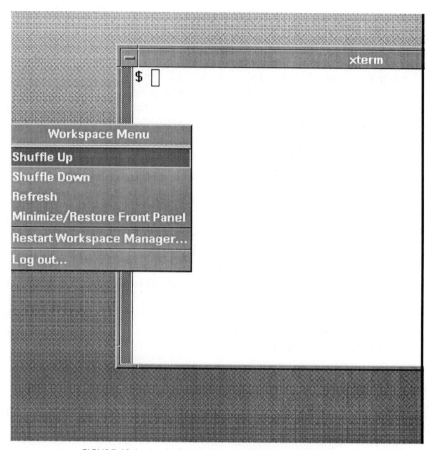

FIGURE 10.1   A window and a root window pulldown menu

Opened and Closed Windows

The window manager also takes care of displaying active windows and positioning icons that represent windows that are not open. If you start up a new terminal window and are finished with it, but don't want to terminate it, as you may need it later, you can close the terminal window. The window manager will create an icon on the desktop that represents the terminal-window program, but it won't take up much space. You will still be able to see it, and you can click (or perhaps double click, depending on the window manager you use) on it later to have it restored. The program itself is still running while it is *iconified,* but the terminal window is conve-

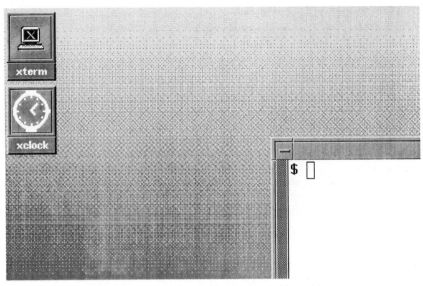

FIGURE 10.2   A desktop with an open window and icons

niently out of your way. The X server itself knows nothing of this function, as you will see if you ever kill your window manager. (All of your iconified processes will pop open all over your screen!)

Choices of Window Managers

Many different window managers are available for X servers. Most are based on the Motif standard, developed by the Open Software Foundation. Several window managers have a common lineage from the original Motif window manager:

- mwm (Motif Window Manager) is the original and probably still the most common window manager.
- twm/tvtwm (Tom's Window Manager and Tom's Virtual Window Manager) was written by Tom LaStrange to correct some of the things that he didn't like about Motif. tvtwm is interesting in that it manages a larger screen area than can be displayed and lets you virtually move around in its different sections, effectively giving you a new screen area in which to work.
- vuewm is Hewlett-Packard's VUE Window Manager.
- olwm is Sun Microsystems' OpenLook Window Manager.

For the sake of simplicity, I will talk about Motif window managers in a generic sense, as the aspects of interest are common to all of these specific window managers.

The Motif window manager provides additional components of a window that the application does not have to worry about. Motif draws a border around a window that can be selected with the mouse in order to change focus onto the window, move (drag) the window, or change its size. The window border contains a title and buttons that allow it to be moved, resized, minimized (closed to an icon), made to fill the entire screen, or terminated.

WIDGETS

A *widget* is the term used to describe each individual component of an X window. Buttons, borders, and scrolling boxes are all widgets. Each X toolkit can define its own set of widgets. Since we are focusing on Motif environments, we will concern ourselves only with the Motif widget set, which is provided to the application program via the Motif *Application Programming Interface* (API).

Menus

Menu buttons provide GUI access to functions provided by the application. These functions are often those not directly related to the contents of any particular window. For example, they do things like opening files, setting options, and exiting. Menu buttons are found along the top of a window.

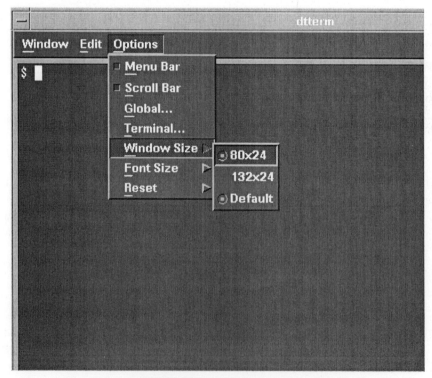

FIGURE 10.3   A pull down menu

Pushbuttons

Pushbuttons can be laid out in any fashion required by an application. The typical pushbutton example is the OK/Cancel *dialog box* (an additional window that pops up with new information or one that queries the user for more information).

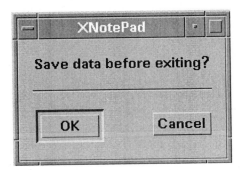

FIGURE 10.4   A dialog box with pushbuttons

Check Boxes and Radio Buttons

Check boxes and *radio buttons* are both input-gathering widgets. Check boxes are a yes/no type of button. If checked, the item to which the box refers is true, yes, or present, depending on the context of the statement. Radio buttons are a collection of mutually exclusive selections; when one is selected, any other that was selected before is deselected.

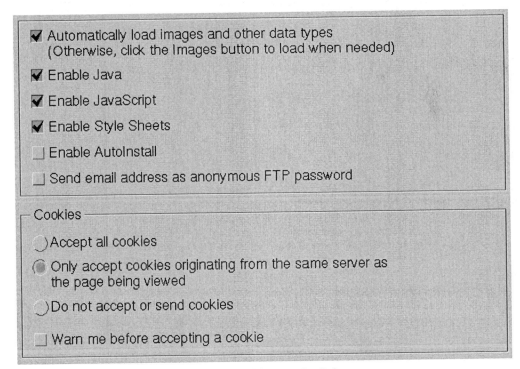

FIGURE 10.5   Check boxes and radio buttons

Scroll Bars

Scroll bars allow you to scroll back and forth in a window or a part of a window. This capability is often useful when a lot of text is involved, but only a short display area is available such that not all of the text fits. Scroll bars may be either horizontal or vertical.

FIGURE 10.6 Two views of the same window with the scroll bar moved. Copyright 1998 Netscape Communications Corp. Used with permission. All rights reserved. This page may not be reprinted or copied without the express written permission of Netscape.

FUNCTIONS OF MOTIF WINDOW MANAGERS

Functions performed on windows and icons on the desktop under the Motif Window Manager are similar to those of other X Window System window managers, although some details might vary slightly.

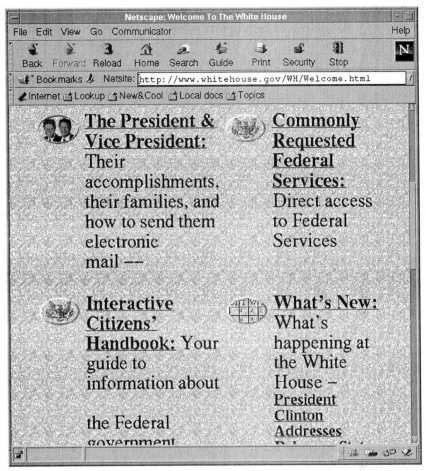

FIGURE 10.6 (*continued*)

Bringing Up the Root Menu

The root menu contains the basic functions needed to control your X session. The default list includes starting a terminal window, moving focus to another window, and exiting the window manager. The root menu is customizable and is often heavily customized to add commonly used X applications to make them easy to start. It is possible to have a different menu brought up for each of the different mouse buttons.

Opening a Window

Opening, or deiconifying, a window is done by double clicking on the icon representing the closed window.

Closing a Window

Closing, or iconifying, a window is done by clicking on the "close" tab in the window border. Pulling down the window's menu by selecting the border of the window and selecting "Close" can also close the window. Most window managers also provide a way to define a keyboard shortcut that can be used to close the window when the focus is on the window.

Moving a Window

You can move a window by selecting the border of the window, holding down the middle mouse button, and then dragging the window to the new location. A window-border pulldown menu also usually has a "Move" selection that accomplishes the same task.

Resizing a Window

Most windows can be resized by selecting the resize border area of any corner of the window with the left mouse button and dragging the corner to reach the new size. By dragging a corner, sizes in both the x and y directions may be modified. Selecting a top, bottom, or side border and dragging will only change the window's size in the one direction.

Raising or Lowering a Window

A window can be virtually raised to the top (to appear over other windows) simply by selecting its border. This action also sets focus on the window.

Bringing Up a Window Menu

The window manager can supply a menu for each window. These menus generally provide one or more of the functions listed previously, but can also be customized to include functions commonly used by particular users. To bring up the window menu, you can either click on the menu button in the upper left corner of the window or hold down the right mouse button anywhere in the window border or title bar.

CLIENT APPLICATIONS

Every program that writes to the screen of an X server is known as an X client. Many useful X clients are included with the X Window System.

Some X Clients

Here are a few of the simplest X clients, which also turn out to be the ones beginners tend to use first to get used to the X Window System. You should consult the "man" page for each program to find out about the optional arguments that can be used to customize the client program.

xclock

Utility: **xclock** [-digital]

The **xclock** command provides a simple clock on your desktop. The default clock is an analog clock (with sweeping hands). If the **-digital** argument is specified, a digital clock is displayed instead.

The **xclock** command can be started by hand or in your initialization file.

FIGURE 10.7   An **xclock** client

xbiff   The **xbiff** program is basically an X Window System version of the Berkeley UNIX **biff** program that tells you when you have new mail. As the legend goes, one of the developers at the University of California at Berkeley had a dog named Biff who always barked when the postman came by. Many other such X client programs have been written to do more sophisticated types of notifications, but **xbiff** is the original.

Utility: **xbiff**

The **xbiff** client displays a mailbox or an inbox icon on the desktop (depending on the version). If the user running **xbiff** has no new mail, the flag on the mailbox is down (or the inbox is empty). When mail is delivered, the flag goes up (or the inbox has something in it) and the icon may change color.

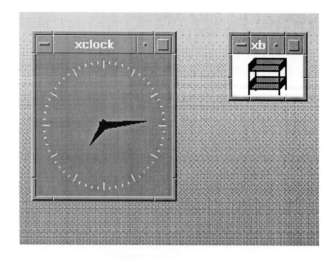

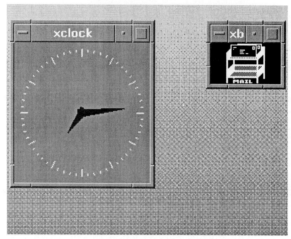

FIGURE 10.8   Two views of the **xbiff** client

xterm   **xterm** is probably the most commonly used X client among UNIX users. It provides a terminal interface window to the system. Early window-system users used their X terminals to provide multiple terminal interfaces in the system to consolidated monitors on their desktop. As X clients become more sophisticated, **xterm** is used less and less, but it is still quite useful if you use the UNIX shell interface. We saw an example of an **xterm** earlier in this chapter. The **xterm** has a myriad of arguments that allow the window's size, color, and font to be defined at the command line. See the "man" page for **xterm** for details.

Utility: **xterm** [-C]

The **xterm** command starts a terminal window on the desktop. If the **-C** argument is included, this terminal window will receive console messages. This feature is useful to keep console messages from being written across the screen on a system for which the bitmapped display is also the console device.

Standard Arguments for X Clients

Most X clients accept standard arguments that allow their size and position to be customized when started.

-geometry   X client geometry is specified by the "-geometry" argument. You can specify not only the size of the client, but also the offset position where it will appear on the screen. The general format is "$X \times Y$" for the position, followed by "$+X+Y$" for the offset position. For example, to start an **xclock** positioned 10 pixels in each direction from the upper right-hand corner of the screen and 100 pixels in both width and height, you would use the command

```
xclock -geometry 100x100-10+10
```

Note that the value of the "-geometry" argument is a single shell token; in other words, there are no spaces imbedded in it.

-foreground and -background   Foreground and background colors can be set with the "-foreground" and "-background" arguments. The following **xterm** command creates a terminal window with cyan (a light shade of blue) letters on a black background:

```
xterm -foreground cyan -background black
```

I find this combination of colors very easy to work with, but everyone has their own favorites.

-title   The "-title" argument sets the title in the title bar of a window. This feature is often useful for labeling one of many terminal windows used for a remote login session to another machine to help keep windows straight. An example of a command that sets such a title is

```
xterm -title "Remote access to mail server"
```

-iconic   The "-iconic" argument is used to start an X client, but to have the window closed (minimized) so that only the icon representing it shows up on the desktop. This feature is useful for an application that you will be using, but not necessarily at the moment that it starts up, like a mail reader or Web browser.

ADVANCED TOPICS

Some of the topics that we want to examine here fall into one or more of the previous sections, but you needed to have a good basic understanding of the X Window System before we launched into these topics. Here are some capabilities of the X Window System that make it unusually useful as compared to other windowing systems.

Copy and Paste

The *copy-and-paste function* is one of the more useful features of the X Window System. The ability to select text in one window and copy it to another window without having to retype it is a great timesaver. I am discussing this feature outside the range of the window manager because, even though it feels like the window manager provides the capability, it is actually provided by the X server itself. You can prove this situation by using it even when no window manager is running.

To copy text into the copy-and-paste text buffer, you simply click and hold down the left mouse button with the pointer set at one end of the text that you wish to select and drag the pointer to the other end of the text. (You can do this task either forward or backward.) When you release the mouse button, the highlighted text has been copied to the buffer, unlike on a PC, where you then have to tell the application to copy the highlighted text to the buffer.) You then go to the window where you wish to paste the text and click the middle mouse button (or both mouse buttons at once on a system that has only two mouse buttons), and the text is inserted. Some applications will insert the text at the current cursor position, and others will insert it at the point where you click the middle mouse button. This detail is application specific.

In the example in Figure 10.9, I executed a **who** command to find out who was logged into the system. To copy and paste the line showing Graham's login, I moved the mouse pointer to the beginning of the line and dragged the pointer to the end of the line before letting go. This action highlighted the text and put it in the copy-and-paste buffer. Then, when I sent an e-mail message to Graham, I clicked on the middle mouse button (the equivalent procedure on a two-button mouse is to click both the left and right buttons at the same time) to paste the text into the mail message at the current point.

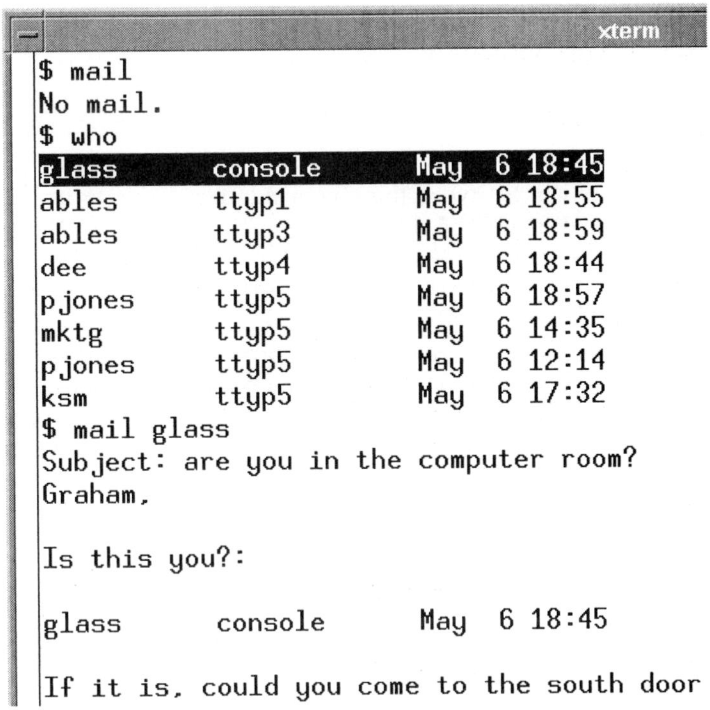

```
─                                                          xterm
$ mail
No mail.
$ who
glass          console          May   6 18:45
ables          ttyp1            May   6 18:55
ables          ttyp3            May   6 18:59
dee            ttyp4            May   6 18:44
pjones         ttyp5            May   6 18:57
mktg           ttyp5            May   6 14:35
pjones         ttyp5            May   6 12:14
ksm            ttyp5            May   6 17:32
$ mail glass
Subject: are you in the computer room?
Graham,

Is this you?:

glass          console          May   6 18:45

If it is, could you come to the south door
```

FIGURE 10.9   An example of copy and paste

Networking Capabilities

I mentioned earlier that the X Window System was a networked windowing system and that it was possible to display information from an X client running on one computer on an X server running on another.

The nuts and bolts of this procedure are quite simple. Another of the standard arguments of X clients that we did not discuss previously is the "-display" argument. This command is used to tell the X client which X server to contact to display its widgets. By default, the display is the local machine upon which the client is running. To start an **xterm** on the host "savoy", we would issue the command

```
xterm -display savoy:0.0
```

The specification of ":0.0" is a method of uniquely identifying a display and X server running on the computer. While it is possible to run multiple X servers as well as to have multiple monitors connected to a single computer, in general usage, each computer will only have one monitor and be running only one X server, so this value will almost always be ":0.0" to denote this arrangement. The default display name for the local system would be "unix:0.0", or perhaps ":0.0" without a hostname. The "unix" name has the special meaning of "the local computer," and therefore, it will not work remotely if you actually have a local host called "unix".

If I type the command

```
xterm -display bluenote.utexas.edu:0.0
```

and if the user on "bluenote" has used the **xhost** command to allow access to the machine on which I typed this command, then the X terminal window that is created will be displayed on "bluenote".

Application Resources

Application *resources* are both a Pandora's box of detail as well as one of the most revolutionary aspects of the X Window System. X resources allow a user to customize the look and feel of their desktop and the applications that they run to a degree that no other window system provides. Here, we will take a quick look at the most basic parts of using X resources. I strongly urge you to read the chapter "Setting Resources" in [24] for exhaustive details.

How Resources Work Every application, including the window manager itself, can take advantage of X Resources. An X resource is a text string, like a variable name, and a value, which is set as part of the X server. The value of a resource is tied to a specific widget. When the X server draws a specific widget, it looks up the value(s) associated with the widget in its list of resources and sets the described attribute appropriately.

For example, consider the hypothetical application called "xask". This application is simply a dialog box containing a text message (a question) and two buttons: "yes" and "no". It might be defined with (at least) the following resources:

```
xask.Button.yes.text
xask.Button.no.text
```

The application may have default values in case these resources are not set. With no resources set, when you run "xask", you might see a window like the one in Figure 10.10.

FIGURE 10.10 The mythical "xask" application

But what if you would rather have something more interesting than "yes" and "no" for choices? Maybe you need to change the language used by the application, but you do not wish to have a separate version for each language you need to use.

The answer is to customize the values with X resources. In our example, we'll set the following resources for "xask":

```
xask.Button.yes.text:  Sure
xask.Button.no.text:   No way
```

Of course, this example is trivial, but you see the power of X resources. By setting the previous values to those resources in the X server, the next time you run "xask", you see the display shown in Figure 10.11.

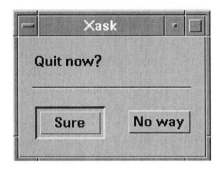

FIGURE 10.11   The "xask" application with customized X resources

If I set these X resources on my X server and run "xask", and you do not set any resources on your X server and run the exact same copy of "xask", we both will see a different window!

X resources are used to set attributes like sizes, colors, fonts, and values of text strings. While these attributes are typical, there is really no limit to what you could allow to be customized in an application.

Every X application uses some number of X resources, and they should be defined in the documentation for the application. The larger, and thus more complex, the application, the more resources it will use. For instance, the Motif window manager has what seems like an endless number of resources that allow you to customize nearly everything about it.

Defining Resources   Once you know which resources you want to set, how do you set them? X resources are resources of the X server; therefore, they set on the machine on which the X server runs. There are many ways to load resources onto an X server.

The most manual method of accessing the X resource database in the X server is with the **xrdb** command:

Utility: **xrdb** [*-query*|*-load*|*-merge*|*-remove*] [*filename*]

The **xrdb** command provides access to the X Resource database for the X server. Used with the **-query** argument, **xrdb** prints the resources defined to the X server. The **-load** argument causes new resource information to be loaded into the resource database, replacing the previous information. If a filename is specified, the resource information is loaded from that file; otherwise the standard input channel is read to find the resource information. The **-merge** argument loads new resource information in a manner similar to that of the **-load** argument, except that existing information is not removed. (Information about duplicate resources is overwritten.) Finally, the **-remove** argument clears out the X resource database.

You can add or remove individual resources or groups of resources anytime you wish.

Manually adding and removing X resources gets tedious very quickly. What we really want is a way to specify a resource that will apply every time that we run a given application. We accomplish this goal by setting up a default resource file called ".Xdefaults". This file is an initialization file recognized by the X server program when run by the user. Upon start-up, the X server loads all resources listed in this file. For example, if we always wanted our "xask" program to use the more casual text in the response buttons, as in our earlier example, we could enter those resources into our ".Xdefaults" file, and the next time we start the X server, these resources will be set. Note that we could also run **xrdb** on our ".Xdefaults" file itself to load or reload these resources at any time.

If you customize a great number of resources in many applications, putting all of these lines for customized resources in your .Xdefaults file, over time you will find that this file gets extremely large. While this aspect isn't a real problem, it makes the contents of the file harder to manage. Also, some applications come with a default set of resources that specify the default attributes of widgets used by the application rather than setting these default values in the code itself. In such a case, we need a way to load these resources into the X server when we run the application.

This goal is accomplished by specifying a directory where X resources are kept. Lists of resources for an application are stored in a file named such that the application will find it. (This name is usually the same as that of the application, but is defined by the application itself.) In this way, resources can be managed more easily, since each file contains only the resources for that application. You may find tens, or even hundreds, of files in this directory, but each file will be of a manageable size.

With regard to our previous example of "xask", we might put our resources in a file called "Xask" that we know is used by the application. Then, all we need is a way to tell applications where to look for these files. We do so by defining a shell variable called $XAPPLRESDIR (X application resource directory). In the C shell, this variable should be an environment variable so that child shells inherit the value; in Bourne-based shells, this variable should be exported when it is set.

Configuration and Start-up

It may seem strange that I left this section until the end of the chapter, but trying to run the X Window System without any idea about how it works sometimes proves to be quite an impediment. Knowing the relationship between the X server and client and where the window manager fits into the picture should help this section seem simple. The details of how you start X also varies from platform to platform and implementation to implementation.

xinit and .xinitrc   When running the "generic" X Window System distribution from MIT, you log into the UNIX computer the way you normally do. You can then type the "xinit" command to start the X server, or you might have this command in your shell-initialization file. For example, it may be in ".cshrc" if your login shell is the C shell or in ".profile" if your login shell is the Bourne or Korn shell.

The **xinit** command starts the X server and runs commands found in a shell-script file called ".xinitrc". In this file, you can specify any application that you wish to be started when the X server starts. (Remember how we said earlier that simply starting an X server with no application is not really very useful.) Typical commands found in the ".xinitrc" file would be xterms and mail programs, or perhaps the command to start up your favorite Web browser. You will also start up your window manager of choice in this file.

The real trick to setting up a proper ".xinitrc" file is to understand that your X server runs the commands in this file and when the file exists (i.e., all of the commands have completed), the X server terminates. This point is key. Often, people put commands into their ".xinitrc" file and use the "&" sign after them to fork off the processes. But they also do so the last command in the list. In this case, the ".xinitrc" script exists and the X server terminates. The appearance is that the X server starts, begins to fire up applications, and then abruptly exists. The reason is that the last application started in the ".xinitrc" file should *not* be started in the background (which is the effect of the "&" on the end of the command)! Then, when this particular application exits, the X server itself exists.

Some people choose to make this last application the window manager (e.g. mwm). Advanced users sometimes make this last command the special "console" terminal window because they want to be able to stop and start their window manager without the X server terminating. In this case, to cause the X server to exit, you would simply terminate your console window.

This whole discussion may sound simple, but this simple idea has caused more than its share of grief for the novice X Window System user!

mwm and .mwmrc   Just as ".xinitrc" is the start-up file for "xinit", ".mwmrc" is the initialization file for mwm. When you start the Motif Window Manager, it must be instructed how to map mouse buttons, what to do when you click on various widgets, and how to behave in general. Usually, your account will be provided with a default copy of the ".mwmrc" file, which you may edit to customize your window manager.

Within the ".mwmrc" file, all of the pulldown menus that will be available to you are defined. This method provides the one way that you can do anything useful when the X server is running without starting other applications (in your ".xinitrc" file). Over time, you may find certain applications to be so useful that you add a command to add them to your pulldown menus so that you can start them with a mouse click. You should consult [25] for all of the details about customizing your ".mwmrc" file.

A (LIMITED) SURVEY OF OTHER X-COMPATIBLE DESKTOPS

Open Windows

Sun Microsystems found themselves in the precarious position of having provided Suntools for their platform, but having had the world move in the direction of X. MIT wrote X so that it could be run on several UNIX platforms. Therefore, people were running X instead of Suntools.

Acknowledging that Suntools was not the answer, Sun abandoned it and developed their own X-based window system called "OpenWindows." While based on X and capable of running X clients, OpenWindows provided a new look and feel and a new widget set (and, of course, a new set of applications). This new style was called "Open Look."

While the Open Look style and OpenWindows were embraced by Sun users, they never really took off in the rest of the X community to become the standard that Sun had hoped they would be.

VUE

Hewlett-Packard also wanted to improve on the original X concept while staying compatible with generic X clients. The HP Visual User Environment (VUE) implemented an X server and a Motif-based window manager called "vuewm." The major difference between X and VUE was a new desktop design and a new start-up paradigm.

The desktop contained a front panel with icons that provided access to many client programs, like a filemanager, a printer manager, and a help interface. It also provided use of the concept of different virtual screens (much as those of "tvtwm," which we mentioned earlier) between which the user could switch back and forth.

VUE provided a login screen so that the user never saw a generic UNIX login or shell prompt on the terminal. VUE ran when the computer started and turned control over to the user's initialization files when he or she logged in. VUE also provided a useful set of default files so that the environment worked well initially, but it could still be customized by the experienced X user.

While with X, the user had to edit initialization files to modify the behavior of the window system, VUE provided many methods for modifying behavior via the GUI, which was easier for the average user to work with.

CDE

With these (and other) companies developing their own implementations of X servers and adding their own bells and whistles to them, it became clear that X environments were getting very complicated and diverse.

Hewlett-Packard, IBM, SunSoft, and Novell got together to define a new X implementation that could be shared and used by all UNIX platforms. The Common Desktop Environment (CDE) was the result.

CDE's outward appearance is very much like that of VUE, although there are also influences by OpenWindows apparent throughout. It is also Motif based, like VUE, and has a login and session manager.

CDE does not provide any great technological leap over OpenWindows, VUE, or even X itself. What it provides is, as its name implies, a common environment shared by major UNIX vendors and available to UNIX users who use different UNIX platforms. Just as OpenWindows and VUE were not the ultimate solution to the UNIX window-system challenge, it remains to be seen if CDE is the great panacea. It certainly solves some of the major problems that the UNIX world has faced with windowing systems.

CHAPTER REVIEW

Checklist

In this chapter, I described:

- What a Graphical User Interface does
- MIT's X Window System
- X servers, X clients, and X widgets
- The Motif window manager
- X application resources

Quiz

1. Which command is used to change access permissions on an X server?
2. Which Motif widget would you use in a window for which you want to give the user a choice between several options out of which they can only choose one?
3. What is the X application argument used to cause the application's window to show up on a different computer's screen?
4. What attribute of an X server allows you to change the appearance of an X application without having to modify the program?

Exercises

1. Explain why a window manager is an X client. [level: *easy*]
2. Assume that your window manager has exited and you cannot get focus in a window to type in a command to bring up a new one (and that you have no root-menu button that starts a new one). Explain how you might still be able to use copy and paste with your existing windows to execute a command (e.g., the command to start a new window manager). [level: *hard*]

Project

Use the **xrdb** command to print the resource database of a running X server. Study the output to learn what types of applications use what types of resources. [level: *medium*]

CHAPTER 11

C Programming Tools

Motivation

The most commonly used programming languages on UNIX systems are C and C++. This fact isn't surprising, since UNIX was written in C and, up until recently, has always come with a standard C compiler.[1] Most UNIX utilities and many commercial products are written in C or C++. Therefore, it's likely that you will find knowledge about writing, compiling, and running C programs very useful. Of course, UNIX supports many other popular programming languages, but this chapter applies primarily to the language of C and its supporting tools, since a C compiler comes with most (but no longer all) versions of UNIX.

Prerequisites

This chapter assumes that you already know the language of C and have compiled programs on at least one platform. For example, many readers may have used the Borland or Microsoft C compilers.

Objectives

In this chapter, I describe the tools that support the various stages of program development: compilation, debugging, maintaining libraries, profiling, and source-code control.

Presentation

The C programming environment is introduced in a natural fashion, with plenty of examples and small programs.

Utilities

This section introduces the following utilities, listed in alphabetical order:

---

[1] Unfortunately, some vendors have now chosen to "unroll" the C compiler from their Unix distributions and sell them separately. Depending on your needs, you should check on this issue for any version of UNIX that you are considering using.

338

admin	ld	sact
ar	lint	strip
cc	lorder	touch
comb	make	tsort
dbx	prof	unget
get	prs	
help	ranlib	

THE C LANGUAGE

Before we get into any source code, I'd like to make an important point: *The source code in this book does not use all of features of ANSI C.* This situation is unfortunate because ANSI C contains several nice syntactical and type-checking facilities that encourage maintainable and readable programs. The only reason that I did not use these features is because several major corporations and universities that I know of firsthand only support K&R C (an older standard). In order to make my source code as portable and useful as possible, I tailored the code to the most reasonable lowest common denominator. However, I didn't enjoy doing this, as I'm a professional software developer as well as an author, and it really goes against my grain. In fact, I'd rather have written all of the code in C++, but that's another story.

SINGLE-MODULE PROGRAMS

Let's examine a C program that performs a simple task: reversing a string. To begin with, I'll show you how to write, compile, link, and execute a program that solves the problem using a single source file. Then, I'll explain why it's better to split the program up into several independent modules, and I'll show you how to do so. Here's a source-code listing of the first version of the "reverse" program:

```
 1   /* REVERSE.C */
 2
 3   #include <stdio.h>
 4
 5   /* Function Prototype */
 6   reverse ();
 7
 8   /*****************************************************************/
 9
10   main ()
11
12   {
13       char str [100]; /* Buffer to hold reversed string */
14
15       reverse ("cat", str); /* Reverse the string "cat" */
16       printf ("reverse ("cat") = %s\n", str); /* Display result */
17       reverse ("noon", str); /* Reverse the string "noon" */
```

```
18       printf ("reverse ("noon") = %s\n", str); /* Display Result */
19  }
20
21  /********************************************************************/
22
23  reverse (before, after)
24
25  char *before; /* A pointer to the source string */
26  char *after; /* A pointer to the reversed string */
27
28  {
29      int i;
30      int j;
31      int len;
32
33      len = strlen (before);
34
35      for (j = len - 1; i = 0; j >= 0; j-; i++) /* Reverse loop */
36        after[i] = before[j];
37
38      after[len] = NULL; /* NULL terminate reversed string */
39  }
```

Compiling a C Program

To create and run the "reverse" program, I first created a subdirectory called "reverse" inside my home directory and then created the file "reverse.c" using the UNIX **emacs** editor. I then compiled the C program using the **cc** utility.

To prepare an executable version of a single, self-contained program, follow **cc** by the name of the source-code file, which must end in a ".c" suffix. **cc** doesn't produce any output when the compilation is successful. By default, **cc** creates an executable file called "a.out" in the current directory. To run the program, type "a.out". Any errors that are encountered are sent to the standard error channel, which is connected by default to your terminal's screen.

Here's what happened when I compiled the "reverse.c" file:

```
$ mkdir reverse            ...create a subdirectory for the source code.
$ cd reverse
$ ... I created the file "reverse.c" using emacs.
$ cc reverse.c             ...compile source.
"reverse.c", line 16: syntax error at or near variable name "cat"
"reverse.c", line 18: syntax error at or near variable name "noon"
"reverse.c", line 35: syntax error at or near symbol ;
"reverse.c", line 35: syntax error at or near symbol )
$ _
```

As you can see, **cc** found a number of compile-time errors:

- The errors on lines 16 and 18 were due to the inappropriate use of double quotes within double quotes.
- The errors on line 35 were due to an illegal use of a semicolon (;).

Since these errors were easy to correct, I copied the error-laden "reverse.c" file to a file called "reverse.old1.c" and then removed the compile-time errors using **emacs**. I left the original file in the directory so that I could see the evolution of my programming attempts.

A Listing of the Corrected "Reverse" Program

Here is the second, corrected version of the "reverse" program. The lines containing the errors that I corrected are in italics:

```
 1  /* REVERSE.C */
 2
 3  #include <stdio.h>
 4
 5  /* Function Prototype */
 6  reverse ();
 7
 8  /*************************************************************/
 9
10   main ()
11
12   {
13      char str [100]; /* Buffer to hold reversed string */
14
15      reverse ("cat", str); /* Reverse the string "cat" */
16      printf ("reverse (\"cat\") = %s\n", str); /* Display */
17      reverse ("noon", str); /* Reverse the string "noon" */
18      printf ("reverse (\"noon\") = %s\n", str); /* Display */
19   }
20
21   /*************************************************************/
22
23   reverse (before, after)
24
25   char *before; /* A pointer to the source string */
26   char *after; /* A pointer to the reversed string */
27
28   {
29      int i;
30      int j;
31      int len;
32
33      len = strlen (before);
34
```

```
35     for (j = len - 1, i = 0; j >= 0; j--, i++) /* Reverse loop */
36        after[i] = before[j];
37
38     after[len] = NULL; /* NULL terminate reversed string */
39   }
```

Running a C Program

After compiling the second version of "reverse.c", I ran it by typing the name of the executable file, "a.out". As you can see, the answers were correct:

```
$ cc reverse.c                      ...compile source.
$ ls -l reverse.c a.out             ...list file information.
-rwxr-xr-x  1 glass       24576 Jan5 16:16 a.out*
-rw-r--r--  1 glass         439 Jan5 16:15 reverse.c
$ a.out                             ...run program.
reverse ("cat") = tac
reverse ("noon") = noon
$ _
```

Overriding the Default Executable Name

The name of the default executable, "a.out", is rather cryptic, and an "a.out" file produced by a subsequent compilation would overwrite the one that I just produced. To avoid both problems, it's best to use the "-o" option with **cc**, which allows you to specify the name of the executable file that you wish to create:

```
$ cc reverse.c -o reverse       ...call the executable file "reverse".
$ ls -l reverse
-rwxr-xr-x 1 glass       24576 Jan  5 16:19 reverse*
$ reverse                       ...run the executable file "reverse".
reverse ("cat") = tac
reverse ("noon") = noon
$ _
```

MULTIMODULE PROGRAMS

The trouble with the way that I built the "reverse" program is that the "reverse" function cannot easily be used in other programs. For example, let's say that I wanted to write a function that returns a value of 1 if a string is a palindrome and a value of 0 otherwise. A palindrome is a string that reads the same forward and backward; for example, "noon" is a palindrome, but "nono" is not. I could use the "reverse" function to implement my "palindrome" function. One way to do so is to cut and paste "reverse ()" into the "palindrome" program, but this technique is poor for at least three reasons:

- Performing a cut-and-paste operation is slow.
- If we came up with a better piece of code for performing a "reverse" operation, we'd have to replace every copy of the old version with the new version, which is a maintenance nightmare.

- Each copy of "reverse ()" soaks up disk space.

As I'm sure you realize, there's a better way to share functions.

Reusable Functions

A better strategy for sharing "reverse ()" is to remove "reverse ()" from the "reverse" program, compile it separately, and then link the resultant object module into whichever programs wish to use it. This technique therefore avoids all three of the problems listed in the previous section and allows the function to be used in many different programs. Functions with this property are termed *reusable functions*.

Preparing a Reusable Function

To prepare a reusable function, create a source-code module that contains the source code of the function, together with a header file that contains the function's prototype. The header file should be named with a suffix of "oh". Then compile the source-code module into an object module by using the "-c" option of **cc**. An object module contains machine code, together with symbol-table information, that allows it to be combined with other object modules when an executable file is being created. Here are the listings of the new "reverse.c" and "reverse.h" files:

reverse.h

```
1   /* REVERSE.H */
2
3   reverse (); /* Declare but do not define this function */
```

reverse.c

```
1   /* REVERSE.C */
2
3   #include <stdio.h>
4   #include "reverse.h"
5
6   /********************************************************************/
7
8   reverse (before, after)
9
10  char *before; /* A pointer to the original string */
11  char *after; /* A pointer to the reversed string */
12
13  {
14     int i;
15     int j;
16     int len;
17
18     len = strlen (before);
19
20     for (j = len - 1, i = 0; j >= 0; j--, i++) /* Reverse loop */
```

```
21     after[i] = before[j];
22
23   after[len] = NULL; /* NULL terminate reversed string */
24 }
```

Here's a listing of a main program that uses "reverse ()":

main1.c

```
1  /* MAIN1.C */
2
3  #include <stdio.h>
4  #include "reverse.h" /* Contains the prototype of reverse () */
5
6  /*******************************************************************/
7
8  main ()
9
10 {
11    char str [100];
12
13    reverse ("cat", str); /* Invoke external function */
14    printf ("reverse (\"cat\") = %s\n", str);
15    reverse ("noon", str); /* Invoke external function */
16    printf ("reverse (\"noon\") = %s\n", str);
17 }
```

Separately Compiling and Linking Modules

To compile each source-code file separately, use the "-c" option of **cc**. This action creates a separate object module for each source-code file, each with a ".o" suffix:

```
$ cc -c reverse.c      ...compile "reverse.c" to "reverse.o".
$ cc -c main1.c        ...compile "main1.c" to "main1.o".
$ ls -l reverse.o main1.o
-rw-r--r-- 1 glass              311 Jan 5 18:24 main1.o
-rw-r--r-- 1 glass              181 Jan 5 18:08 reverse.o
$ _
```

Alternatively, you can place all of the source-code files on one line instead of issuing multiple commands:

```
$ cc -c reverse.c main1.c     ...compile each ".c" file to a ".o" file.
$ _
```

To link them all together into an executable called "main1", list the names of all of the object modules after the **cc** command:

```
$ cc reverse.o main1.o -o main1        ...link object modules.
$ ls -l main1                          ...examine the executable.
-rwxr-xr-x 1 glass       24576 Jan 5 18:25 main1*
$ main1                                 ...run the executable.
reverse ("cat") = tac
reverse ("noon") = noon
$ _
```

The Stand-alone Loader: ld

When **cc** is used to link several object modules, it transparently invokes the UNIX stand-alone loader, **ld**, to do the job. The loader is better known as the *linker*. Although most C programmers don't ever need to invoke **ld** directly, it's wise to know a little bit about it:

Utility: **ld** -n {-L*path* }* { *objModule* }* { *library* }* {-l*x*}* [-o *outputFile*]

ld links together the specified object and library modules to produce an executable file. You may override the default name of the executable, "a.out", by using the **-o** option. If you wish to create a stand-alone executable (as opposed to a dynamic-link module, which is beyond the scope of this book), then you should specify the **-n** option.

When **ld** encounters an option of the form **-l*x***, it searches the standard directories "/lib", "/usr/lib", and "/usr/local/lib" for a library with the name "lib*x*.a". To insert the directory *path* into this search path, use the **-L*path*** option.

The **ld** command varies wildly from version to version, even more than do most other UNIX commands. I strongly suggest that you consult the documentation for your version of UNIX when using it.

If you link a C program manually, it's important to specify the C runtime object module, "/lib/crt0.o", as the first object module and to specify the standard C library, "/lib/libc.a", as a library module. Here's an example of those specifications in a manual link:

```
$ ld -n /lib/crt0.o main1.o reverse.o -lc -o main1     ...manual link.
$ main1                                                  ...run program.
reverse ("cat") = tac
reverse ("noon") = noon
$ _
```

Reusing the Reverse Function

Now that you've seen how the original "reverse" program may be built out of a couple of modules, let's use the "reverse" module to build the "palindrome" program. Here's the header and source-code listing of the "palindrome" function:

palindrome.h

```
1  /* PALINDROME.H */
2
3  int palindrome (); /* Declare but do not define */
```

palindrome.c

```
1  /* PALINDROME.C */
2
3  #include "palindrome.h"
4  #include "reverse.h"
5  #include <string.h>
6
7  /***************************************************************/
8
9  int palindrome (str)
10
11   char *str;
12
13   {
14     char reversedStr [100];
15     reverse (str, reversedStr); /* Reverse original */
16     return (strcmp (str, reversedStr) == 0); /* Compare the two */
17   }
```

Here's the source code of the program "main2.c" that tests "palindrome ()":

```
1  /* MAIN2.C */
2
3  #include <stdio.h>
4  #include "palindrome.h"
5
6  /***************************************************************/
7
8  main ()
9
10  {
11    printf ("palindrome (\"cat\") = %d\n", palindrome ("cat"));
12    printf ("palindrome (\"noon\") = %d\n", palindrome ("noon"));
13  }
```

The way to combine the "reverse", "palindrome", and "main2" modules is as before: Compile the object modules and then link them. We don't have to recompile "reverse.c", as it hasn't changed since the "reverse.o" object file was created.

```
$ cc -c palindrome.c          ...compile "palindrome.c" to "palindrome.o".
$ cc -c main2.c               ...compile "main2.c" to "main2.o".
$ cc reverse.o palindrome.o main2.o -o main2 ...link them all.
$ ls -l reverse.o palindrome.o main2.o main2
-rwxr-xr-x 1 glass         24576 Jan 5 19:09 main2*
-rw-r--r-- 1 glass           306 Jan 5 19:00 main2.o
-rw-r--r-- 1 glass           189 Jan 5 18:59 palindrome.o
-rw-r--r-- 1 glass           181 Jan 5 18:08 reverse.o
$ main2                        ...run the program.
palindrome ("cat") = 0
palindrome ("noon") = 1
$ _
```

Maintaining Multimodule Programs

Several different issues must be considered when maintaining multimodule systems:

Q1. What ensures that object modules and executables are kept up to date?

Q2. What stores the object modules?

Q3. What tracks each version of source and header files?

Fortunately, there are UNIX utilities that address each problem. Here are solutions to each question:

A1. **make**, the UNIX file-dependency system

A2. **ar**, the UNIX archive system

A3. **sccs**, the UNIX source-code-control system

The next few subsections discuss each utility in turn.

THE UNIX FILE-DEPENDENCY SYSTEM: MAKE

You've now seen how several independent object modules may be linked into a single executable. You've also seen that the same object module may be linked into several different executables. Although multimodule programs are efficient in terms of reusability and disk space, they must also be carefully maintained. For example, let's assume that we change the source code of "reverse.c" to use pointers instead of array subscripts. This change would result in a faster "reverse" function. In order to update the two main program executables "main1" and "main2" manually, we'd have to perform the following steps, in order:

1. Recompile "reverse.c".
2. Link "reverse.o" and "main1.o" to produce a new version of "main1".
3. Link "reverse.o" and "main2.o" to produce a new version of "main2".

Similarly, imagine a situation in which a "#define" statement in a header file is changed. All of the source-code files that directly or indirectly include the file must be recompiled, and then all of the executable modules that refer to the changed object modules must be relinked.

Although these tasks might not seem like a big deal, imagine a system with 1000 object modules and 50 executable programs. Remembering all of the relationships between the headers, source-code files, object modules, and executable files would be a nightmare. One way to avoid these problems is to use the UNIX **make** utility, which allows you to create a *makefile* that contains a list of all file interdependencies for each executable. Once such a file is created, to re-create the executable is easy; you just use the **make** command as follows:

```
$ make -f makefile
```

Here's a synopsis of **make**:

Utility: **make** [-f *makefile*]

make is a utility that updates a file based on a series of dependency rules stored in a special-format "make file". The **-f** option allows you to specify your own make-filename; if none is specified, the name "makefile" is assumed. For details on make-file formats and rules, consult the rest of this section.

Make Files

To use the **make** utility to maintain an executable file, you must first create a make file. This file contains a list of all of the interdependencies that exist between the files that are used to create the executable. A make file may have any name; I recommend that you name a make file by taking the name of the executable and adding a ".make" suffix. Thus, the name of the make file for "main1" would be called "main1.make". In its simplest form, a make file contains make rules of the form

---

targetList:*dependencyList*
        commandList

---

where *targetList* is a list of target files and *dependencyList* is a list of files on which the files in *targetList* depend. *commandList* is a list of zero or more commands, separated by new lines, that reconstructs the target files from the dependency files. Each line in *commandList* must start with a "tab" character. Rules must be separated by at least one blank line.

For example, let's think about the file interdependencies related to the executable file "main1". This file is built out of two object modules: "main1.o" and "reverse.o". If either file is changed, then "main1" may be reconstructed by linking the files using the **cc** utility. Therefore, one rule in "main1.make" would be:

```
main1: main1.o reverse.o
       cc main1.o reverse.o -o main1
```

This line of reasoning must now be carried forward to the two object files. The file "main1.o" is built from two files: "main1.c" and "reverse.h". (Remember that any file that is either directly or indirectly "#include"d in a source file is effectively part of that file.) If either file is changed, then "main1.o" may be reconstructed by compiling "main1.c". Here, therefore, are the remaining rules in "main1.make":

```
main1.o: main1.c reverse.h
         cc -c main1.c
reverse.o: reverse.c reverse.h
           cc -c reverse.c
```

The Order of Make Rules

The order of make rules is important. The **make** utility creates a "tree" of interdependencies by initially examining the first rule. Each target file in the first rule is a root node of a dependency tree, and each file in its dependency list is added as a leaf of each root node. In our example, the initial tree would look like this:

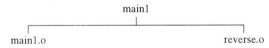

FIGURE 11.1   Initial **make** dependency tree

The **make** utility then visits each rule associated with each file in the dependency list and performs the same actions. In our example, the final tree would therefore look like this:

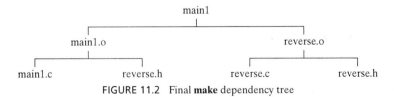

FIGURE 11.2   Final **make** dependency tree

Finally, the make utility works up the tree from the bottom leaf nodes to the root node, looking to see if the last modification time of each child node is more recent than the last modification time of its immediate parent node. For every case in which this situation is so, the associated parent's rule is executed. If a file is not present, its rule is executed regardless of the last modification times of its children. To illustrate this process, I've numbered the following diagram to illustrate the order in which the nodes would be examined:

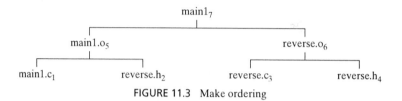

FIGURE 11.3   Make ordering

Executing a Make

Once a make file has been created, the make process is set into action by using the **make** utility as follows:

make [-f *makeFileName*]

This command causes the **make** utility to re-create the executable file whose dependency information is stored in the file *makeFileName*. If the "-f" option is omitted, the default make-file name "makefile" is used.

To show you how this process works, I deleted all of the object modules and the executable to force every command list to execute. When I performed the make, here's what I saw:

```
$ make -f main1.make      ...make the executable up to date.
cc -c main1.c
cc -c reverse.c
cc main1.o reverse.o -o main1
$ _
```

Notice that every make rule was executed in the exact order shown in the previous diagram.

Since I created a second executable when I made the "palindrome" program, I also fashioned a second make file, called "main2.make". Here it is:

```
main2:        main2.o reverse.o palindrome.o
              cc main2.o reverse.o palindrome.o -o main2
main2.o:      main2.c palindrome.h
              cc -c main2.c
```

```
reverse.o:      reverse.c reverse.h
                cc -c reverse.c
palindrome.o:   palindrome.c palindrome.h reverse.h
                cc -c palindrome.c
```

When I performed a make using this file, I saw the following output:

```
$ make -f main2.make   ...make the executable up to date.
cc -c main2.c
cc -c palindrome.c
cc main2.o reverse.o palindrome.o -o main2
$ _
```

Notice that "reverse.c" was not recompiled. It was not recompiled because the previous make had already created an up to date object module, and **make** only recompiles files when necessary.

Make Rules

The make files that I've shown you so far are larger than they need to be because some of the make rules that I supplied are already known by the **make** utility in a more general way. For example, note that several of the rules are of the form

```
xxx.o:      reverse.c reverse.h
            cc -c xxx.c
```

where xxx varies between rules. The **make** utility contains a predefined rule similar to the following:

```
.c.o:
            /bin/cc -c -O $<
```

This cryptic-looking rule tells the **make** utility how to create an object module from a C source-code file. The existence of this general rule allows me to leave off the C recompilation rule. Here, therefore, is a sleeker version of "main2.make":

```
main2:          main2.o reverse.o palindrome.o
                cc main2.o reverse.o palindrome.o -o main2
main2.o:        main2.c palindrome.h
reverse.o:      reverse.c reverse.h
palindrome.o:   palindrome.c palindrome.h reverse.h
```

The **make** utility also includes other inference rules. For example, **make** knows that the name of an object module and its corresponding source-code file are usually related. It uses this information to infer standard dependencies. For example, it deduces that "main2.o" is dependent on "main2.c", and thus you may leave this information off the dependency list. Here, then, is an even sleeker version of "main2.make":

```
main2:            main2.o reverse.o palindrome.o
                  cc main2.o reverse.o palindrome.o -o main2
main2.o:          palindrome.h
reverse.o:        reverse.h
palindrome.o:     palindrome.h reverse.h
```

Writing Your Own Rules

Unfortunately, the method for writing your own rules, or even understanding the ones that already exist, is beyond the scope of this book. For more information, I suggest that you consult one of the sources listed in the section "Other Make Facilities" later in this chapter.

Touch

To confirm that the new version of the make file worked, I requested a make and obtained the following output:

```
$ make -f main2.make
'main2' is up to date.
$ _
```

Obviously, since I'd already performed a successful make, another one wasn't going to trigger any rules! To force a make to be able to occur for testing purposes, I used a handy utility called **touch**, which makes the last modification time of all of the named files equal to the current system time. Here's a brief synopsis of **touch**:

Utility: **touch** -c { *fileName* }+

touch updates the last modification and access times of the named files to the current time. By default, if a specified file doesn't exist, it is created with zero size. To prevent this default from occurring, use the "-c" option.

So, I "touched" the file "reverse.h", which subsequently caused the recompilation of several source files:

```
$ touch reverse.h        ...fool the make utility.
$ make -f main2.make
/bin/cc -c -O reverse.c
/bin/cc -c -O palindrome.c
cc main2.o reverse.o palindrome.o -o main2
$ _
```

Macros

The **make** utility supports primitive macros. If you contain a line of the form

token = replacementText

at the top of a make file, every occurrence of $(*token*) in the make file is replaced by *replacementText*. In addition to containing rules, the standard-rules file contains default definitions of macros, such as "CFLAGS", that are used by some of the built-in rules. For example, the rule that tells the **make** utility how to update an object file from a C source file looks like this:

```
.c.o:
        /bin/cc -c $(CFLAGS) $<
```

The standard-rules file contains a line of the form:

CFLAGS =   -O

If you wanted to recompile a suite of programs using the "-p" option of **cc**, you would override the default value of CFLAGS at the top of the make file and use the "-p" option in the final call to **cc** in the "main2" rule, like this:

```
CFLAGS =        -p
main2:          main2.o reverse.o palindrome.o
                cc -p main2.o reverse.o palindrome.o -o main2
main2.o:        palindrome.h
reverse.o:      reverse.h
palindrome.o:   palindrome.h reverse.h
```

To recompile the suite of programs, I used the **touch** utility to force recompilation of all of the source files:

```
$ touch *.c   ...force make to recompile everything.
$ make -f main2.make
/bin/cc -c -p main2.c
/bin/cc -c -p palindrome.c
/bin/cc -c -p reverse.c
cc -p main2.o reverse.o palindrome.o -o main2
$ _
```

Other Make Facilities

make is a rather complicated utility, and it includes provisions for handling libraries and inference rules. Information on all parts of **make** except the library facilities is included in this book, and many other books contain less information about **make** than this one, so I suggest that you consult the UNIX "man" pages for more details.

THE UNIX ARCHIVE SYSTEM: AR

A medium-sized C project typically uses several hundred object modules. Specifying this many object modules in a make-file rule can get rather tedious, so I recommend that you learn how to use the UNIX archive utility, **ar**, to organize and group your object modules. An archive utility is sometimes known as a *librarian*. It allows you to perform the following tasks:

- creating a special archive-format file, which ends in a ".a" suffix
- adding, removing, replacing, and appending any kind of file to an archive
- obtaining an archive's table of contents

Here's a synopsis of **ar**:

Utility: **ar** *key archiveName* { *fileName* }*

ar allows you to create and manipulate archives. *archiveName* is the name of the archive file that you wish to access, and it should end with a ".a" suffix. *key* may be one of the following letters:

- "d", deletes a file from an archive
- "q", which appends a file onto the end of an archive, even if it's already present
- "r", which adds a file to an archive if it isn't already there, or replaces the current version if it is
- "t", which displays an archive's table of contents to standard output
- "x", which copies a list of files from an archive into the current directory
- "v", which generates verbose output

When a set of object modules is stored in an archive file, it may be accessed from the **cc** compiler and the **ld** loader by simply supplying the name of the archive file as an argument. Any object modules that are needed from the archive file are automatically linked as necessary. This feature greatly reduces the number of parameters for these utilities when linking large numbers of object modules. An example of this advantage is given later in this section.

The rest of this section contains examples of the use of each **ar** option.

Creating an Archive

An archive is automatically created when the first file is added. Therefore, to see how an archive is created, please read the next subsection: "Adding A File".

Adding a File

To add a file to a named archive, use the **ar** utility with the "r" option as follows:

ar r *archiveName* { *fileName* }+

This option adds all of the specified files to the archive file *archiveName*, replacing files if they already exist. If the archive file doesn't exist, it is automatically created. The name of the archive should have a ".a" suffix.

Appending a File

To append a file to a named archive, use the **ar** utility with the "q" option as follows:

ar q *archiveName* { *fileName* }+

This option appends all of the specified files to the archive file *archiveName*, regardless of whether they already exist. If the archive file doesn't exist, it is automatically created. This option is handy if you know that a particular file isn't already present, as it allows **ar** to avoid searching through the archive.

Obtaining a Table of Contents

To obtain a table of contents of an archive, use the **ar** utility with the "t" option as follows:

ar t *archiveName*

Deleting a File

To delete a list of files from an archive, use the **ar** utility with the "d" option as follows:

---

ar d *archiveName* {*fileName* }+

Extracting a File

To copy a list of files from an archive to the current directory, use the **ar** utility with the "x" option. If you don't specify a list of files, then all of the files in the archive are copied. The "x" option is used with the **ar** utility as follows:

---

ar x *archiveName* { *fileName* }+

Maintaining an Archive from the Command Line

Here is an example that illustrates how an archive may be built and manipulated from the command line, using the object modules built earlier in this chapter. Later in this section, I'll show how a library can be maintained automatically from a make file.

First, I built an archive file called "string.a" to hold all of my string-related object modules. Next, I added each module in turn by using the "r" option. Finally, I demonstrated the various **ar** options:

```
$ cc -c reverse.c palindrome.c main2.c      ...create object modules.
$ ls *.o                                     ...confirm.
main2.o      palindrome.o        reverse.o
$ ar r string.a reverse.o palindrome.o       ...add them to an archive.
ar: creating string.a
$ ar t string.a                              ...obtain a table of contents.
reverse.o
palindrome.o
$ cc main2.o string.a -o main2               ...link the object modules.
$ main2                                       ...execute the program.
palindrome ("cat") = 0
palindrome ("noon") = 1
$ ar d string.a reverse.o                     ...delete a module.
$ ar t string.a                              ...confirm deletion.
palindrome.o
$ ar r string.a reverse.o                     ...put it back again.
```

```
$ ar t string.a                    ...confirm addition.
palindrome.o
reverse.o
$ rm palindrome.o reverse.o        ...delete originals.
$ ls *.o                           ...confirm.
main2.o
$ ar x string.a reverse.o          ...copy them back again.
$ ls *.o                           ...confirm.
main2.oreverse.o
$ _
```

Maintaining an Archive Using make

Although an archive can be built and maintained from the command line, it's much better to use **make**. To refer to an object file inside an archive, place the name of the object file inside parentheses, preceded by the name of the archive. The **make** utility has built-in rules that take care of the archive operations automatically. Here is the updated "main2.make" file that uses archives instead of plain object files:

```
main2:              main2.o string.a(reverse.o) string.a(palindrome.o)
                    cc main2.o string.a -o main2
main2.o:            palindrome.h
string.a(reverse.o):    reverse.h
string.a(palindrome.o): palindrome.h reverse.h
```

Here is the output from a **make** performed using this file:

```
$ rm *.o                        ...remove all object modules.
$ make -f main2.make            ...perform a make.
cc -c main2.c
cc -c reverse.c
ar rv string.a reverse.o        ...object module is automatically saved.
a - reverse.o
ar: creating string.a
rm -f reverse.o                 ...original is removed automatically.
cc -c palindrome.c
ar rv string.a palindrome.o
a - palindrome.o
rm -f palindrome.o
cc main2.o string.a -o main2    ...archived object modules are accessed.
$ _
```

Notice that the built-in make rules automatically removed the original object file once it had been copied into the archive.

Ordering Archives

The built-in make rules do not maintain any particular order in an archive file. On most systems, this situation is fine, as the **cc** and **ld** utilities are able to extract object modules and resolve external references regardless of order. However, on some older systems, this ability is unfortunately not the case. Instead, if an object module *A* contains a function that calls a function in an object module *B*, then *B* must come before *A* in the link sequence. If *A* and *B* are in the same library, then *B* must appear before *A* in the library. If your system is one of these older types, then you'll probably get the following error at the end of the make shown in the last example:

```
ld: Undefined symbol
   _reverse
*** Error code 2
make: Fatal error: Command failed for target 'main2'
```

This cryptic error occurs because "reverse.o" contains a call to "palindrome ()" in "palindrome.o", which means that "reverse.o" should be *after* "palindrome.o" in the archive, but isn't. To resolve this error, you must either reorder the modules in the archive using the **lorder** and **tsort** utilities or use **ranlib**, as described in the next subsection. In the next example, I created a new ordered version of the old archive and then renamed it to replace the original. The make file then worked correctly.

```
$ ar cr string2.a `lorder string.a | tsort`   ...order archive.
$ ar t string.a                                ...old order.
reverse.o
palindrome.o
$ ar t string2.a                               ...new order.
palindrome.o
reverse.o
$ mv string2.a string.a                        ...replace old archive.
$ make -f main2d.make                          ...try make again.
cc main2.o string.a -o main2
$ _
```

For more information on **lorder** and **tsort**, please use the **man** facility.

Creating a Table of Contents: ranlib

On older systems where this ordering is a problem, you can help the linker to resolve out-of-order object modules by adding a table of contents to each archive by using the **ranlib** utility (if **ranlib** does not exist on your system, then you don't need to worry about ordering):

Utility: **ranlib** { *archive* }+

ranlib adds a table of contents to each specified archive. It does so by inserting an entry called "__.SYMDEF" into the archive.

In the next example, the unresolved reference error was due to an out-of-order sequence of object modules in the "string.a" archive. **cc** reminded me that I should add a table of contents, so I followed its recommendation. As you can see, the next link was successful.

```
$ ar r string.a reverse.o palindrome.o        ...this order causes problems.
ar: creating string.a
$ cc main2.o string.a -o main2                 ...compile fails.
ld: string.a: warning: archive has no table of contents; add one using
ranlib(1)
ld: Undefined symbol
 _reverse
$ ranlib string.a                              ...add a table of contents.
$ cc main2.o string.a -o main2                 ...no problem.
$ main2                                         ...program runs fine.
palindrome ("cat") = 0
palindrome ("noon") = 1
$ _
```

Shared Libraries

Static libraries work just fine for many applications. However, as processor speed increases and the prices of disks and memory come down, code has been allowed to become more complex. Therefore, programs linked with large archive libraries will result in very large executable files; a small program that creates a single X window can be as large as one megabyte when linked with the required X libraries.

To reduce the size of your generated object code, you can link your program to a *shared library* instead. A shared, or dynamic, library is associated with a compiled program, but its functions are loaded in dynamically as they are needed, rather than all at once at load time. The resulting object code is smaller because it does not include the text of the library, as it does when it is linked with a static library.

The one disadvantage of using a shared library is that your object code will have been written for a specific version of the library. If bug fixes, but no interface changes, are made, then your program will benefit from the newer library that works better. However, if calling interface changes are made, then when your program links with the newer version of the library at run time, problems may, and probably will, result. It is therefore important to be aware of changes in supporting libraries when writing an application.

The **ld** command includes arguments to allow you to specify for it to build a shared library (on systems that support shared libraries) rather than a static library when it runs. These arguments vary in different versions of UNIX, and you should check the documentation for your version of UNIX. The most common version of this argument is "-shared". You can also instruct **ld** to link against either static or dynamic libraries with the "-B" argument ("-Bstatic" or "-Bdynamic"). Depending on your C compiler, the **cc** command may also have one of these arguments or a different one to allow you to create a shared library at compile time.

THE UNIX SOURCE CODE CONTROL SYSTEM: SCCS

To maintain a large project properly, it's important to be able to store, access, and protect all of the versions of source code files. For example, if I decided to change "reverse ()" to use pointers for efficiency reasons, it would be nice if I could easily go back and see how the source file looked *before* the changes were made. Similarly, it's important to be able to "lock out" other users from altering a file while you're actively modifying it. Here is an outline of how the UNIX source code control system (SCCS) works:

- When you create the original version of a function, you convert it into a special "sccs-format" file using the **admin** utility. An sccs-format file is stored specially, and it may not be edited or compiled in the usual manner. This file contains information about the time of creation and user creating it. Future modifications will contain information about what changes have been made from the previous version.
- Whenever you wish to edit an sccs-format file, you must first "check out" the latest version of the file using the **get** utility. This utility creates a standard-format text file that you may edit and compile. The **get** utility also allows you to obtain a previous version of a file.
- When the new version of the file is complete, you must return it to the sccs file using the **delta** utility. This command optimizes the storage of the sccs file by only saving the differences between the old version and the new version. The **get** utility does not allow anyone else to check out the file until you return it.
- The **sact** utility allows you to see the current editing activity on a particular sccs file.

The source code control system also contains several other utilities, namely **help**, **prs**, **comb**, **what**, and **unget**. Before we investigate the more advanced sccs options, let's look at a sample sccs session.

Warning: Some systems vary in the way that sccs works; I suggest that you consult **man** to see if the sccs examples in this book tally with your own system's version of sccs. I discuss sccs since it comes with most versions of UNIX. Other source code control software is available, both free from the Internet (such as RCS), and commercially, which may better suit your needs.

Creating an sccs File

To create an sccs file, use the **admin** utility, which works as follows:

Utility: **admin** -i*name* -fl*list* -dl*list* -e*name* -a*name* sccsfile

admin is an sccs utility that allows you to create and manipulate an sccs-format file. The **-i** option creates an sccs format file called *sccsfile* from the file *name*. *sccsfile* should have a ".s" prefix. The **-fl** and **-dl** options allow you to lock and unlock a set of listed releases, respectively. The **-a** and **-e** options allow you to add and subtract named users from the list of users that are able to obtain an editable version of the sccs file. Once the sccs file has been created, you may delete the original. If you get an error from any sccs-related utility, invoke the sccs **help** utility with the code of the message as its argument.

In the following example, I created an sccs version of the "reverse.c" source file:

```
$ ls -l reverse.c                    ...look at the original.
-rw-r--r--   1 gglass         266 Jan  7 16:37 reverse.c
$ admin -ireverse.c s.reverse.c      ...create an sccs file.
No id keywords (cm7)
$ help cm7                           ...get help on "cm7".
cm7: "No id keywords"
No SCCS identification keywords were substituted for. You may not have
any keywords in the file, in which case you can ignore this warning. If
this message came from delta then you just made a delta without any
keywords. If this message came from get then the last time you made a
delta you changed the lines on which they appeared. It's a little late to
be telling you that you messed up the last time you made a delta, but
this is the best we can do for now, and it's better than nothing.
This isn't an error, only a warning.
$ ls -l s.reverse.c                  ...look at the sccs file.
-r--r--r--   1 gglass         411 Jan  7 17:39 s.reverse.c
$ rm reverse.c                       ...remove the original.
$ _
```

Here's a synopsis of the **help** utility:

Utility: **help** { *message* }+

help is an sccs utility that displays an explanation of the named key messages. Key messages are generated by other sccs utilities in the case of warning or fatal-error situations.

Checking out a File

To make a read-only copy of an sccs file, use the **get** utility:

Utility: **get** -e -p -r*revision sccsfile*

get is an sccs utility that checks out a revision of a file from its sccs counterpart. If no version number is supplied, the latest version is checked
out. If the -e option is used, the file is modifiable and should be returned
to the sccs file using delta; otherwise, it is read-only and should not be
returned. The -p option causes a read-only copy of the file to be displayed to standard output; no file is created.

In the following example, I checked out a read-only copy of the latest version of the
"reverse.c" file:

```
$ get s.reverse.c              ...check out a read-only copy.
1.1                            ...version number.
29 lines                       ...number of lines in file.
No id keywords (cm7)
$ ls -l reverse.c              ...look at the copy.
-r--r--r--   1 gglass       266 Jan  7 18:04 reverse.c
$ _
```

The get command displays the version number of the file that is being copied out; in
this case, it's the default, version 1.1. A version number is of the form:

release.delta

Every time a change is saved to an sccs file, the delta number is incremented automatically. The release number is changed only when explicitly done so using the get
utility. I'll show you how to create a new release later in this section.

When you obtain a read-only version of a file, it may not be edited, and its
read-only status does not prevent anyone else from accessing the sccs file at the
same time. To check out an editable version of an sccs file, use the "-e" option of **get**.
This option creates a writeable file and prevents multiple "gets":

```
$ get -e s.reverse.c           ...check out a writeable version.
1.1
new delta 1.2                  ...editable version is 1.2.
29 lines
```

```
$ ls -l reverse.c            ...look at it.
-rw-r-xr-x 1 gglass          266 Jan 7 18:05 reverse.c
$ get -e s.reverse.c         ...version is locked.
ERROR [s.reverse.c]: writable ereverse.c' exists (ge4)
$ _
```

Monitoring sccs Activity

The **sact** utility displays a list of the current activity related to a named file, and it works like this:

Utility: **sact** {*sccsfile* }+

sact is an sccs utility that displays the current editing activity on the named sccs files (). The output contains the version of the existing delta, the version of the new delta, the user that checked out the file using the command "get -e", and the date and time that the "get -e" command was executed.

Here's the output of **sact** after the previous example:

```
$ sact s.reverse.c      ...monitor activity on "reverse.c".
1.1 1.2 gglass 98/01/07 18:05:11
$ _
```

Undoing a Check-Out/Returning a File

If you perform a **get** and then wish that you hadn't, you may undo the **get** by using the **unget** utility, which works like this:

Utility: **unget** -r*revision* -n { *sccsfile* }+

unget is an sccs utility that reverses the effect of a previous **get**. It restores the sccs file to its previous state, deletes the non-sccs version of the file, and unlocks the file for other people to use. If there are several revisions that are currently being edited, use the **-r** option to specify which revision you which to **unget**. By default, **unget** moves the file back into the sccs file. The **-n** option causes unget to *copy* the file instead, leaving the checked-out version in place.

In the following example, assume that I had just performed a **get** on "reverse.c" and then changed my mind:

```
$ ls -l reverse.c              ...look at the checked-out file.
-rw-r-xr-x 1 gglass            266 Jan 7 18:05 reverse.c
$ unget s.reverse.c            ...return it.
1.2                            ...version of returned file.
$ ls -l reverse.c              ...original is gone.
reverse.c not found
$ sacts.reverse.c              ...original activity is gone.
No outstanding deltas for: s.reverse.c
$ _
```

Creating a New Delta

Let's say that you check out an editable version of "reverse.c" and change it so that it uses pointers instead of array subscripts. Here is a listing of the new version:

```
1   /* REVERSE.C */
2
3   #include <stdio.h>
4   #include "reverse.h"
5
6
7   reverse (before, after)
8
9   char *before;
10  char *after;
11
12  {
13     char* p;
14
15     p = before + strlen (before);
16
17     while (p-- != before)
18        *after++ = *p;
19
20     *after = NULL;
21  }
```

When the new version of the file is saved, you must return it to the sccs file using the **delta** command, which works like this:

Utility: **delta** -r*revision* -n { *sccsfile* }+

delta is an sccs utility that returns a checked-out file back to the specified sccs file. The new version's delta number is equal to the old delta number plus one. As a bonus, **delta** describes the changes that you made to the file, and **delta** prompts you for a comment before returning the file. If the same user has two outstanding versions and wishes to return one of them, the **-r** option must be used to specify the revision number. By default, a file is removed from the user's directory after it is returned. The **-n** option prevents this removal from occurring.

Here's an example of the use of **delta**:

```
$ delta s.reverse.c        ...return the modified checked-out version.
comments? converted the function to use pointers    ...comment.
No id keywords (cm7)
1.2                        ...new version number.
5 inserted                 ...description of modifications.
7 deleted
16 unchanged
$ ls -l reverse.c          ...the original was removed.
reverse.c not found
$ _
```

Obtaining a File's History

To get a listing of an sccs file's modification history, use the **prs** utility, which works like this:

Utility: **prs** -r*revision* { *sccsfile* }+

prs is an sccs utility that displays the history associated with the named sccs files (). By default, all of a file's history is displayed. You may limit the output to a particular version by using the **-r** option. The numbers in the right-hand column of the output refer to the number of lines inserted, deleted, and unchanged, respectively.

Here's an example of the use of the **prs** utility:

```
$ prs s.reverse.c        ...display the history.
s.reverse.c:
D 1.2 98/01/07 18:45:47 gglass 2 1        00005/00007/00016
MRs:
COMMENTS:
converted the function to use pointers
D 1.1 98/01/07 18:28:53 gglass 1 0        00023/00000/00000
MRs:
COMMENTS:
date and time created 98/01/07 18:28:53 by gglass
$ _
```

sccs Identification Keywords

Several special character sequences can be placed in a source file and processed specially by **get** when read-only copies of a version are obtained. Here are a few of the most common sequences:

Sequence	Replaced with
%M%	the name of the source-code file
%I%	the *release.delta.branch.sequence* number
%D%	the current date
%H%	the current hour
%T%	the current time

It's handy to place these sequences in a comment at the top of a source file. The comment won't affect your source-code program, and it will easily be visible when the file is read. The next subsection contains an example of how these sequences are used.

Creating a New Release

To create a new release of an sccs file, specify the new release number by using the "-r" option of **get**. The new release number is based on the most recent version of the previous release. In the next example, I created release 2 of the "reverse.c" file and inserted the identification keywords described in the previous subsection. Note that they were replaced when I obtained a read-only copy of version 2 later in the example.

```
$ get -e -r2 s.reverse.c        ...check out version 2.
1.2                             ...previous version number.
new delta 2.1                   ...new version number.
21 lines
$ vi reverse.c                  ...edit the writeable copy.
... I added the following lines at the top of the program:
/*
   Module: %M%
  SCCS Id: %I%
     Time: %D% %T%
*/
... and then saved the file.
$ delta s.reverse.c             ...return the new version.
comments? added SCCS identification keywords
2.1
6 inserted
0 deleted
21 unchanged
```

```
$ get -p s.reverse.c              ...display the file to standard output.
2.1
/* REVERSE.H */
/*
  Module: reverse.c
  SCCS Id: 2.1
     Time: 98/01/07 22:32:38
*/
...rest of file (edited out to eliminate redundancy).
$ _
```

Checking Out Read-Only Copies of Previous Versions

To check out a version other than the latest, use the "-r" option of **get** to specify the version number. For example, let's say that I wanted to obtain a read-only copy of version 1.1 of "reverse.c". Here's how it's done:

```
$ get -r1.1 s.reverse.c        ...check out version 1.1.
1.1
23 lines
$ _
```

Checking Out Editable Copies of Previous Versions

If you want to obtain an editable copy of a previous version, use the "-e" or "-r" option of **get**. Let's say that I wanted to obtain an editable copy of version 1.1 of "reverse.c". The version of the editable copy cannot be called version 1.2, since that version already exists. Instead, **get** creates a new "branch" off of the 1.1 version numbered 1.1.1.1. Deltas added to this branch are numbered 1.1.1.2, 1.1.1.3, etc.

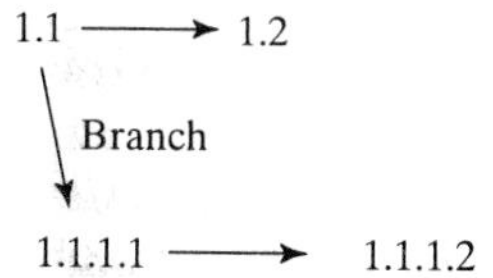

FIGURE 11.4   Delta branching

Here's an example of this action:

```
$ get -e -r1.1 s.reverse.c      ...get a branch off of version 1.1.
1.1
new delta 1.1.1.1
23 lines
$ _
```

Editing Multiple Versions

You may edit multiple revisions of a file at one time. If you do so, you must specify the revision number of the file that you're returning when you perform the **delta**.

You must also rename the name of the copy when obtaining another copy, since all copies are given the same name. In the following example, I obtained a copy of version 1.1 and version 2.1 of "reverse.c" for editing, and then saved them both:

```
$ get -e -r1.1 s.reverse.c    ...edit a new version based on version 1.1.
1.1
new delta 1.1.1.1
23 lines
$ mv reverse.c reverse2.c      ...rename version 1.1.1.1.
$ get -e -r2.1 s.reverse.c     ...edit a new version based on version 2.1.
2.1
new delta 2.2
27 lines
$ sact s.reverse.c             ...view sccs activity.
1.1 1.1.1.1 gglass 98/01/07 22:42:26
2.1 2.2 gglass 98/01/07 22:42:49
$ delta s.reverse.c            ...ambiguous return.
comments? try it
ERROR [s.reverse.c]: missing -r argument (de1)
$ delta -r2.1 s.reverse.c      ...return modified version 2.1.
comments? try again
2.2
0 inserted
0 deleted
27 unchanged
$ mv reverse2.c reverse.c      ...rename the other version.
$ delta s.reverse.c            ...unambiguous return.
comments? save it
No id keywords (cm7)
1.1.1.1
0 inserted
0 deleted
23 unchanged
$ sact s.reverse.c
No outstanding deltas for: s.reverse.c
$ _
```

Deleting Versions

You may remove a delta from an sccs file as long as it's a leaf node on the sccs version tree. To do so, use the **rmdel** utility, which works as follows:

Utility: **rmdel** -r*revision sccsfile*

rmdel removes the specified version from an sccs file as long as it's a leaf node.

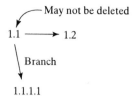

FIGURE 11.5   Only leaf nodes may be deleted

In the following example, I wasn't allowed to delete version 1.1, as it's not a leaf node, but I was allowed to delete version 1.1.1.1:

```
$ rmdel -r1.1 s.reverse.c          ...try removing non-leaf node 1.1.
ERROR [s.reverse.c]: not a 'leaf' delta (rc5)
$ rmdel -r1.1.1.1 s.reverse.c      ...remove leaf node 1.1.1.1.
$ _
```

Compressing sccs Files

You may compress an sccs file and remove any unnecessary deltas by using the **comb** utility, which works like this:

Utility: **comb** { *sccsfile* }+

comb compresses an sccs file so that it contains only the latest version of the source. Only the latest delta and the deltas that have branches remain. It works by generating a Bourne-shell script that must then be run to perform the actual compression. The script is sent to standard output, so it must be saved and then executed.

In the next example, assume that "s.reverse.c" contained several different versions. I compressed it into a smaller file containing just the latest version.

```
$ comb s.reverse.c > comb.out     ...generate script.
$ cat comb.out                    ...look at the script.
trap "rm -f COMB$$ comb$$ s.COMB$$; exit 2" 1 2 3 15
get -s -k -r2.3 -p s.reverse.c > COMB$$
...other lines go here; they have been omitted for space considerations.
rm comb$$
rm -f s.reverse.c
mv s.COMB$$ s.reverse.c
admin -dv s.reverse.c
$ chmod +x comb.out               ...make the script executable.
$ comb.out                        ...execute the script.
$ prs s.reverse.c                 ...look at the history.
```

```
s.reverse.c:
D 2.3 98/01/08 15:35:53 gglass 1 0   00028/00000/00000
MRs:
COMMENTS:
This was COMBined
$ _
```

Restricting Access to sccs Files

By default, a file may be checked out of an sccs file by anyone. However, you may restrict access to one or more users and/or groups by using the "-a" and "-e" options of **admin**. The "-a" option may be followed by a couple of values:

- a username, in which case the user is added to the list of users that may check out the file
- a group number, in which case any user in the group may check out the file

If the value is preceded by an exclamation point (!), then the specified user or group is *denied* check-out rights. If you're using the C shell, be sure to escape the "!" to prevent accidental reference to the history list. To remove a user from the list, use the "-e" option instead. Multiple "-a" and "-e" options may occur on a single command line. In the following example, I denied my own access rights and then restored them:

```
$ admin -a\!glass s.reverse.c     ...remove rights of user "glass".
$ get -e s.reverse.c              ...try to access.
2.3
ERROR [s.reverse.c]: not authorized to make deltas (co14)
$ admin -aglass s.reverse.c       ...restore access.
$ get -e s.reverse.c              ...no problem.
2.3
new delta 2.4
28 lines
$ unget s.reverse.c               ...return file.
2.4
$ admin -atim s.reverse.c         ...add "tim" to user list.
$ admin -eglass s.reverse.c       ...deny "glass" access rights.
$ get -e s.reverse.c              ...try to access.
2.3
ERROR [s.reverse.c]: not authorized to make deltas (co14)
$ admin -aglass s.reverse.c       ...restore rights to "glass".
$ admin -a182 s.reverse.c         ...give access to group 182.
$ _
```

Locking Releases

You may prevent either a single release or all releases from being edited by using **admin** with the "-fl" and "-dl" options. To lock a particular release, follow "-fl" with the number of the release. To lock all releases, follow "-fl" with the letter "a". To release a lock, use the same rules, but with the "-dl" option instead. Here's an example of the use of these options:

```
$ admin -fla s.reverse.c              ...lock all releases.
$ get -e -r2.1 s.reverse.c            ...try to access.
2.1
ERROR [s.reverse.c]: SCCS file locked against editing (co23)
$ admin -dla s.reverse.c              ...release all locks.
$ get -e -r1.1 s.reverse.c            ...no problem.
1.1
new delta 1.1.1.1
21 lines
$ _
```

THE UNIX PROFILER: PROF

It's often handy to be able to see where a program is spending its time. For example, if an amount of time that is greater than expected is being spent in a particular function, it might be worth optimizing the function by hand for better performance. The **prof** utility allows you to obtain a program's profile, and it works like this:

Utility: **prof** -ln [*executableFile* [*profileFile*]]

prof is the standard UNIX profiler. It generates a table of time and repetitions of each function in the executable *executableFile* based on the performance trace stored in the file *profileFile*. If *profileFile* is omitted, the filename "mon.out" is assumed. If *executableFile* is omitted, the filename "a.out" is assumed. The executable file must have been compiled using the **-p** option of **cc**, which instructs the compiler to generate special code that writes a "mon.out" file when the program runs. The **prof** utility then looks at this output file after the program has terminated and displays the information contained therein. For information on how to make a file using the **-p** option, refer to the section of this chapter on the **make** utility. By default, the profile information is listed in descending order of time. The **-l** option orders the information by name, and the **-n** option orders the information by cumulative time.

Here's an example of **prof** in action:

```
$ main2                    ...execute the program.
palindrome ("cat") = 0     ...program output.
palindrome ("noon") = 1
$ ls -l mon.out            ...list the file for monitor output.
-rw-r-xr-x    1 gglass       1472 Jan  8 17:19 mon.out
$ prof main2 mon.out       ...profile the program.
%Time Seconds Cumsecs  #Calls   msec/call  Name
 42.9    0.05    0.05                        rdpcs
 42.9    0.05    0.10    2002     0.025      reverse
```

```
14.3     0.02    0.12    2002        0.008   palindrome
 0.0     0.00    0.12       1        0.      main
$ prof -l main2                    ...order the profile by name.
%Time Seconds Cumsecs   #Calls   msec/call   Name
 0.0     0.00    0.05       1        0.      main
14.3     0.02    0.07    2002        0.008   palindrome
42.9     0.05    0.05                        rdpcs
42.9     0.05    0.12    2002        0.025   reverse
$ _
```

After you view a profile, you may decide to do some handtuning of the program and then obtain another profile.

DOUBLE-CHECKING PROGRAMS: LINT

There's a handy utility called **lint** that checks your program more thoroughly than **cc** does:

Utility: **lint** { *fileName* }*

lint scans the specified source files and displays any potential errors that it finds.

If you're building a program out of several source modules, it's a good idea to specify them all on the same command line so that **lint** can check module interactions. Here's an example that demonstrates the difference between single-module checking and multimodule checking:

```
$ lint reverse.c                                ...check "reverse.c".
reverse defined( reverse.c(12) ), but never used
$ lint palindrome.c                             ...check "palindrome.c".
palindrome defined( palindrome.c(12) ), but never used
reverse used( palindrome.c(14) ), but not defined
$ lint main2.c                                  ...check "main2.c".
main2.c(11): warning: main() returns random value to invocation environment
printf returns value which is always ignored
palindrome used( main2.c(9) ), but not defined
$ lint main2.c reverse.c palindrome.c           ...check all modules together.
main2.c:
main2.c(11): warning: main() returns random value to invocation environment
reverse.c:
palindrome.c:
Lint pass2:
printf returns value which is always ignored
$ _
```

THE UNIX DEBUGGER: DBX

The UNIX debugger **dbx** allows you to symbolically debug a program. Although it's not as good as most professional debuggers on the market, it comes as a handy standard utility in most versions of UNIX. **dbx** includes the following facilities:

- single stepping
- breakpoints
- editing from within the debugger
- accessing and modifying variables
- searching for functions
- tracing

Here's a synopsis of **dbx**:

Utility: **dbx** *executableFilename*

dbx is a standard UNIX debugger. The named executable file is loaded into the debugger, and a user prompt is displayed. To obtain information on the various **dbx** commands, enter **help** at the prompt.

To demonstrate **dbx**, let's debug the following recursive version of "palindrome ()":

```
1   /* PALINDROME.C */
2
3   #include "palindrome.h"
4   #include <string.h>
5
6
7   enum { FALSE, TRUE };
8
9
10   int palindrome (str)
11
12   char *str;
13
14   {
15      return (palinAux (str, 1, strlen (str)));
16   }
17
18   /********************************************************************/
19
20   int palinAux (str, start, stop)
```

```
21
22   char *str;
23   int start;
24   int stop;
25
26  }
27     if (start >= stop)
28        return (TRUE);
29     else if (str[start] != str[stop])
30        return (FALSE);
31     else
32        return (palinAux (str, start + 1, stop - 1));
33  }
```

Preparing a Program for Debugging

To debug a program, it must have been compiled using the "-g" option to "-cc", which places debugging information into the object module.

Entering the Debugger

Once a program has been compiled correctly, invoke **dbx** with the name of the executable as the first argument. **dbx** then presents you with a prompt. I recommend that you enter **help** at the prompt to see a list of all of the **dbx** commands:

```
$ dbx main2        ...enter the debugger.
dbx version sr10.3(4) of 7/6/90 17:52
reading symbolic information ...
Type 'help' for help.
(dbx) help           ...obtain help.
run [args]                  - begin execution of the program
stop at <line>             - suspend execution at the line
stop in <func>             - suspend execution when <func> is called
stop if <cond>             - suspend execution when <cond> is true
trace <line#>              - trace execution of the line
trace <func>               - trace calls to the function
trace <var>                - trace changes to the variable
trace <exp> at <line#>     - print <exp> when <line> is reached
status                - print numbered list of traces and stops in effect
delete <#> [<#> ...]       - cancel trace or stop of each number given
cont                       - continue execution from where it stopped
step                  - execute one source line, stepping into functions
next                  - execute one source line, skipping over calls
return                     - continue until the current function returns
call <func>(<params>)      - execute the given function call
print <exp> [, <exp> ...]  - print the values of the expressions
where                      - print currently active procedures
whatis <name>              - print the declaration of the name
assign <var> = <exp> - assign the program variable the value of <exp>
```

```
dump <func>                    - print all variables in the active function
list [<line#> ], <line#>>  - list source lines
use <directory-list>           - set the search path for source files
sh <command-line>              - pass the command line to the shell
quit                           - exit dbx
(dbx) _
```

Running A Program

To run your program through the debugger, enter the "run" command. This command runs the program to completion:

```
(dbx) run                    ...run the program.
palindrome ("cat") = 0
palindrome ("noon") = 0
program exited
(dbx) _
```

Oops! The string "noon" is a palindrome, but my function thinks that it isn't. Time to delve into **dbx** . . .

Tracing a Program

To obtain a line-by-line trace, use the "trace" command. When any kind of trace is requested, **dbx** returns you an index number that can be used by the "delete" command to turn off the trace. In the continuation of our previous example, I restarted the program from the beginning by using the "rerun" command:

```
(dbx) trace...request a trace.
[1] trace  ...request is #1.
(dbx) rerun...run the program from the start.
trace:      9  printf ("palindrome (\"cat\") = %d\n", palindrome ("cat"));
trace:     10  int palindrome (str)
trace:     15    return (palinAux (str, 1, strlen (str)));
trace:     20  int palinAux (str, start, stop)
trace:     27  if (start >= stop)
trace:     29    else if (str[start] != str[stop])
trace:     30      return (FALSE);
trace:     33  }
trace:     33  }
trace:     16  }
palindrome ("cat") = 0
trace: 10          printf ("palindrome (\"noon\") = %d\n", palindrome ("noon"));
trace:     10  int palindrome (str)
trace:     15    return (palinAux (str, 1, strlen (str)));
trace:     20  int palinAux (str, start, stop)
trace:     27   if (start >= stop)
trace:     29    else if (str[start] != str[stop])
```

```
trace:      30        return (FALSE);
trace:      33   }
trace:      33   }
trace:      16   }
palindrome ("noon") = 0
trace:      11   }
trace:      11   }
program exited
(dbx) _
```

Tracing Variables and Function Calls

A trace may be placed on a variable's value or on a call to a particular function by adding parameters to the "trace" command. To trace a variable, the syntax is

```
trace variable in function
```

and to trace a call to a named function, use the syntax

```
trace function
```

Here's the output from **dbx** when three new traces were added and then the program was restarted:

```
(dbx) trace start in palinAux ...trace the variable called "start".
[2] trace start in palinAux
(dbx) trace stop in palinAux   ...trace the variable called "stop".
[3] trace stop in palinAux
(dbx) trace palinAux           ...trace the function "palinAux".
[4] trace palinAux
(dbx) rerun                    ...run the program from the start.
trace:      9    printf ("palindrome (\"cat\") = %d\n", palindrome ("cat"));
trace:     10    int palindrome (str)
trace:     15      return (palinAux (str, 1, strlen (str)));
trace:     20    int palinAux (str, start, stop)
calling palinAux(str = "cat", start = 1, stop = 3) from function
palindrome.palindrome
trace:     27      if (start >= stop)
initially (at line 27 in "/home/glass/reverse/palindrome.c"): start = 1
```

```
initially (at line 27 in "/home/glass/reverse/palindrome.c"): stop = 3
trace:      29      else if (str[start] != str[stop])
trace:      30          return (FALSE);
trace:      33   }
trace:      33   }
trace:      16   }
palindrome ("cat") = 0
trace:      10   printf ("palindrome (\"noon\") = %d\n", palindrome ("noon"));
trace:      10   int palindrome (str)
trace:      15      return (palinAux (str, 1, strlen (str)));
trace:      20   int palinAux (str, start, stop)
after line 20 in "/home/glass/reverse/palindrome.c": stop = 4
calling palinAux(str = "noon", start = 1, stop = 4) from function palindrome.palindrome
trace:      27      if (start ,= stop)
trace:      29      else if (str[start] != str[stop])
trace:      30          return (FALSE);
trace:      33   }
trace:      33   }
trace:      16   }
palindrome ("noon") = 0
trace:      11   }
trace:      11   }
program exited
(dbx) _
```

The Bug

By now, the bug is fairly clear; the values of *start* and *stop* are incorrect, each being one value greater than they should be. It's a very common error to forget that array indices in C begin at 0 rather than at 1. To fix this bug, you may call up the editor specified by the $EDITOR environment variable by using the "edit" command. This editor is handy for correcting errors on the fly, although you must remember to recompile the program before debugging it again.

Here is the correct version of the "palindrome ()" function:

```
int palindrome (str)
char *str;
{
 return (palinAux (str, 0, strlen (str) - 1));
}
```

I'll end this section with a brief discussion of some useful miscellaneous **dbx** commands for setting breakpoints, single stepping, accessing variables, and listing portions of the program.

Breakpoints

To make **dbx** stop when it encounters a particular function, use the "stop" command. This command allows you to run a program at full speed until the function that you wish to examine more closely is executed:

```
(dbx) stop in palinAux          ...set breakpoint.
[7] stop in palinAux
(dbx) rerun                     ...run the program from the start.
trace:      9      printf ("palindrome (\"cat\") = %d\n", palindrome ("cat"));
trace:     10      int palindrome (str)
trace:     15         return (palinAux (str, 1, strlen (str)));
trace:     20      int palinAux (str, start, stop)
calling palinAux(str = "cat", start = 1, stop = 3) from function palindrome.palindrome
[7] stopped in palinAux at line 27 in file "/home/glass/reverse/palindrome.c"
   27      if (start >= stop)
(dbx) _
```

Single Stepping

To step through a program one line at a time, use the "step" command. This command causes **dbx** to redisplay its prompt immediately after the next line of program has been executed, and it is useful for high-resolution interrogation of a function. In the following example, I entered "step" after my program stopped at line 27:

```
(dbx) step          ...execute line after #27 and then stop.
trace:     29      else if (str[start] != str[stop])
initially (at line 29 in "/home/glass/reverse/palindrome.c"):
start = 1
initially (at line 29 in "/home/glass/reverse/palindrome.c"):
stop = 3
stopped in palinAux at line 29 in file "/home/glass/reverse/palindrome.c"
   29      else if (str[start] != str[stop])
(dbx) _
```

Accessing Variables

To print the value of a particular variable at any time, use the "print" command. The "whatis" command displays a variable's declaration, and the "which" command tells you where the variable is declared. The "where" command displays a complete stack trace, and the "whereis" command tells you where a particular function is located. These commands are demonstrated as follows:

```
(dbx) print start           ...display current value of start.
1
(dbx) whatis start          ...get type information.
int start;
(dbx) which start           ...find its location.
palindrome.palinAux.start
(dbx) where                 ...obtain stack trace.
palinAux(str = "cat", start = 1, stop = 3), line 29 in "/home/glass/reverse/palindrome.c"
palindrome.palindrome(str = "cat"), line 15 in "/home/glass/reverse/palindrome.c"
main(), line 9 in "/home/glass/reverse/main2.c"
unix_$main() at 0x3b4e7a14
_start(), line 137 in "//garcon/unix_src/lang/sgs/src/crt0/crt0.c"
```

```
(dbx) whereis palinAux   ...locate a function.
palindrome.palinAux
(dbx) whereis start           ...locate a variable.
palindrome.palinAux.start
(dbx) _
```

Listing a Program

The "list" command allows you to list 10 lines of a function at a time, and the "/" and "?" commands allow you to search forward and backward through text, respectively:

```
(dbx) list palindrome ...list 10 lines.
    5
    6
    7    enum { FALSE, TRUE };
    8
    9
   10    int palindrome (str)
   11
   12    char* str;
   13
   14    {
   15      return (palinAux (str, 1, strlen (str)));
(dbx) list 10,20         ...list lines 10 thru 20.
   10    int palindrome (str)
   11
   12    char* str;
   13
   14    }
   15      return (palinAux (str, 1, strlen (str)));
   16    {
   17
   18    /************************************************************/
   19
   20    int palinAux (str, start, stop)
   21
(dbx) ?palinAux          ...search backward for string "palinAux".
   20    int palinAux (str, start, stop)
(dbx) /palinAux          ...search forward for string "palinAux".
   32        return (palinAux (str, start + 1, stop - 1));
(dbx) _
```

Leaving the Debugger

To quit out of **dbx**, use the "quit" command. This command exits you back to your shell:

```
(dbx) quit             ...leave the debugger.
$ _
```

Summary

I've presented a smattering of the commonly used **dbx** commands. Used wisely, they can provide useful hints about the errors in your program. In my own opinion, **dbx** is actually a pretty poor debugger compared to some of the popular PC debuggers, such as Borland's Turbo Debugger, and advanced UNIX systems, like ObjectWorks\C++. On the positive side, at least it's available on most UNIX machines, which makes a rudimentary understanding of its operation handy.

WHEN YOU'RE DONE: STRIP

The debugger and profiler, utilities both require that you compile a program using special options, each of which adds code to the executable file. To remove this extra code after debugging and profiling are done with, use the **strip** utility, which works as follows:

Utility: **strip** { *fileName* }+

strip removes all of the symbol table, relocation, debugging, and profiling information from the named file(s).

Here's an example of how much space you can save by using **strip**:

```
$ ls -l main2        ...look at original file.
-rwxr-xr-x 1 gglass    5904 Jan 8 22:18 main2*
$ strip main2        ...strip out spurious information.
$ ls -l main2        ...look at stripped version.
-rwxr-xr-x 1 gglass    3373 Jan 8 23:17 main2*
$ _
```

CHAPTER REVIEW

Checklist

In this chapter, I described utilities that:

- compile C programs
- manage the compilation of multimodule programs
- maintain archives
- maintain multiple versions of source code
- profile executable files
- debug executable files

Quiz

1. What's the definition of a leaf node on an sccs delta tree?
2. What's the benefit of the "-q" option of **ar**?
3. Can the **make** utility use object modules stored in an archive file?
4. What does the term "reusable function" mean?
5. Why would you profile an executable file?
6. Describe briefly what the **strip** utility does.

Exercises

1. Compile "reverse.c" and "palindrome.c" and place them into an archive called "string.a". Write a main program called "prompt.c" that prompts the user for a string and then outputs a value of 1 if the string is a palindrome and a value of 0 otherwise. Create a make file for the program that links "prompt.o" with the "reverse ()" and "palindrome ()" functions stored in "string.a". Use **dbx** to debug your code if any bugs exist. [level: *medium*]
2. Replace the original version of "palindrome ()" stored in "palindrome.c" with a pointer-based version. Use sccs to manage the source-code changes and **ar** to replace the old version in "string.a". [level: *medium*].
3. Try a modern debugger such as the Borland C++ source-level debugger. How does it compare **dbx**? [level: *medium*].

Project

Write a paper that describes how you would use the utilities in this section to help manage a 10-person computing team. [level: *medium*]

CHAPTER 12

Systems Programming

Motivation

If you're a C programmer and you wish to take advantage of the UNIX multi-tasking and interprocess-communication facilities, it's essential that you have a good knowledge of the UNIX system calls.

Prerequisites

In order to understand this chapter, you should have a good working knowledge of C. For the section of this chapter on the Internet, it helps if you have read Chapters 8 and 9.

Objectives

In this chapter, I'll explain and demonstrate a majority of the UNIX system calls, including those that support I/O, process management, and interprocess communication.

Presentation

The information in this section is presented in the form of several sample programs, including a shell designed for the Internet.

System and Library Calls

This section contains information on the following system calls and library calls, listed in alphabetical order:

accept	getdents	nice
alarm	getegid	open
bind	geteuid	pause
chdir	getgid	perror
chmod	gethostname	pipe
chown	getpgid	read
close	getpid	setegid
connect	getppid	seteuid
dup	getuid	setgid
dup2	htonl	setpgid

execl	htons	setuid
execlp	inet_addr	signal
execv	inet_ntoa	socket
execvp	ioctl	stat
exit	kill	sync
fchmod	lchown	truncate
fchown	link	unlink
fcntl	listen	wait
fork	lseek	write
fstat	lstat	
ftruncate	mknod	

INTRODUCTION

In order to make use of services such as file creation, process duplication, and inter-process communication, application programs must talk to the operating system. They can do so via a collection of routines called *system calls*, which are the programmer's functional interface to the UNIX kernel. System calls are just like library routines, except that they perform a subroutine call directly into the heart of UNIX.

The UNIX system calls can be loosely grouped into three main categories:

- file management
- process management
- error handling

Interprocess communication (IPC) is, in fact, a subset of file management, since UNIX treats IPC mechanisms as special files. Here's a diagram that illustrates the file-management system call hierarchy:

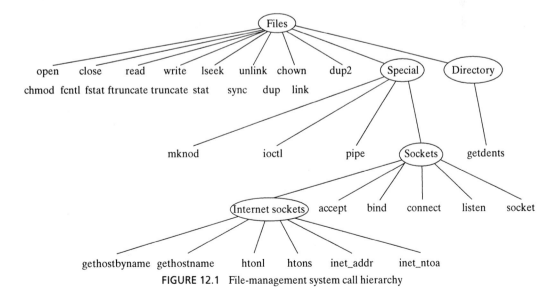

FIGURE 12.1   File-management system call hierarchy

The process management system call hierarchy includes routines for duplicating, differentiating, and terminating processes, and it looks like this:

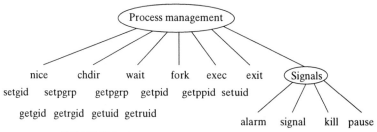

FIGURE 12.2 Process management system call hierarchy

The only system call that supports error handling is "perror ( )", which I'll also put it in a hierarchy just to be consistent:

FIGURE 12.3 Error-handling hierarchy

This chapter covers the system calls shown in these hierarchy diagrams in the following order:

- Error handling: I start the chapter with a description of "perror ( )".
- Regular file management: The section on this topic includes information on how to create, open, close, read, and write regular files. We'll also see a short overview of STREAMS.
- Process management: The section on this topic explains how to duplicate, differentiate, suspend, and terminate processes and briefly discusses multithreaded processes.
- Signals: Although the signal facility could come under the heading of either process management or interprocess communication, it's a significant-enough topic to warrant a section of its own.
- IPC: The section on this topic describes interprocess communication via pipes (both unnamed pipes and named pipes) and sockets (including information about Internet sockets) and provides short overviews of newer IPC mechanisms—shared memory and semaphores—found in some versions of UNIX.

This chapter ends with a source-code listing and discussion of a complete Internet shell, which is a shell that supports piping and redirection to other Internet shells on remote hosts. The Internet shell program uses most of the facilities that are described in this chapter.

ERROR HANDLING: PERROR ( )

Most system calls are capable of failing in some way. For example, the "open ( )" system call will fail if you try to open a nonexistent file for reading. By convention, all system calls return a value of −1 if an error occurs. However, this value doesn't tell you much about *why* the error occurred; the "open ( )" system call can fail for one of several different reasons. If you want to deal with system-call errors in a systematic way, you must know about two things:

- "errno", a global variable that holds the numerical code of the last system-call error
- "perror ( )", a subroutine that describes system-call errors

Every process contains a global variable called "errno", that is originally set to zero when the process is created. When a system call error occurs, "errno" is set to the numerical code associated with the cause of the error. For example, if you try to open a file that doesn't exist for reading, "errno" is set to 2. The file "/usr/include/sys/errno.h" contains a list of the predefined error codes. Here's a snippet of that file:

```
#define      EPERM        1    /* Not owner */
#define      ENOENT       2    /* No such file or directory */
#define      ESRCH        3    /* No such process */
#define      EINTR        4    /* Interrupted system call */
#define      EIO          5    /* I/O error */
```

A successful system call never affects the current value of "errno", and an unsuccessful system call always overwrites the current value of "errno". To access "errno" from your program, include "errno.h". The "perror ( )" subroutine converts the current value of "errno" into a description in English and works like this:

Library Routine: void perror (char* *str*)

"perror ( )" displays the string *str*, followed by a colon, followed by a description of the last system call error. If there is no error to report, it displays the string "Error 0". Actually, "perror ( )" isn't a system call— it's a standard C library routine.

Your programs should check system calls for a return value of −1 and then deal with the problems immediately if this value is returned. One of the first things to do in such situations, especially during debugging, is to call "perror ( )" for a description of the error.

In the next example, I forced a couple of system call errors to demonstrate "perror ( )", and then demonstrated that "errno" retained the last system call error code even after a successful call was made. The only way to reset "errno" is to assign it manually to zero. When you read the example, don't worry about how "open ( )" works; I'll describe it later in this chapter.

```
$ cat showErrno.c
#include <stdio.h>
#include <sys/file.h>
#include <errno.h>
main ( )
{
  int fd;
  /* Open a nonexistent file to cause an error "/
fd = open ("nonexist.txt", O_RDONLY);
if (fd == -1) /* fd == -1 =, an error occurred */
    {
    printf ("errno = %d\n", errno);
    perror ("main");
    }
fd = open ("/", O_WRONLY); /* Force a different error */
if (fd == -1)
    {
    printf ("errno = %d\n", errno);
    perror ("main");
    }
/* Execute a successful system call */
fd = open ("nonexist.txt", O_RDONLY | O_CREAT, 0644);
printf ("errno = %d\n", errno); /* Display after successful call */
perror ("main");
errno = 0; /* Manually reset error variable */
perror ("main");
}
```

Here's the output from this program:

```
$ showErrno                ...run the program.
errno = 2
main: No such file or directory
errno = 21                 ...even after a successful call.0
main: Is a directory
errno = 21
main: Is a directory
main: Error 0
$ _
```

REGULAR FILE MANAGEMENT

My description of file-management system calls is split up into four main subsections:

- a primer that describes the main concepts behind UNIX files and file descriptors
- a description of the basic file-management system calls, which are demonstrated by a sample program called "reverse" that reverses the lines of a file

- an explanation of a few advanced system calls, which are demonstrated by a sample program called "monitor" that periodically scans directories and displays the names of files within them that have changed since the last scan
- a description of the remaining file-management system calls, which are demonstrated by some miscellaneous snippets of source code.

A File-Management Primer

The file-management system calls allow you to manipulate the full collection of regular, directory, and special files, including:

- disk-based files
- terminals
- printers
- interprocess communication facilities, such as pipes and sockets

In most cases, "open ( )" is initially used to access or create a file. If the system call succeeds, it returns a small integer called a *file descriptor* that is used in subsequent I/O operations on that file. If "open ( )" fails, it returns a value of −1. Here's a snippet of code that illustrates a typical sequence of events:

```
int fd; /* File descriptor */
...
fd = open (fileName, ...); /* Open file, return file descriptor */
if (fd == -1) { /* deal with error condition */ }
...
fcntl (fd, ...); /* Set some I/O flags if necessary */
...
read (fd, ...); /* Read from file */
...
write (fd, ...); /* Write to file */
...
lseek (fd, ...); /* Seek within file*/
...
close (fd); /* Close the file, freeing file descriptor */
```

When a process no longer needs to access an open file, it should close it using the "close ( )" system call. All of a process' open files are automatically closed when the process terminates. Although this automatic closure means that you may omit an explicit call to "close ( )", it's better programming practice to explicitly close your files.

File descriptors are numbered sequentially, starting from zero. By convention, the first three file descriptor values have a special meaning:

Value	Meaning
0	standard input
1	standard output
2	standard error

For example, the "printf ( )" library function always sends its output using file descriptor 1, and "scanf ( )" always reads its input using file descriptor 0. When a reference to a file is closed, the file descriptor is freed and may be reassigned by a subsequent "open ( )". Most I/O system calls require a file descriptor as their first argument so that they know which file to operate on.

A single file may be opened several times and, thus, may have several file descriptors associated with it:

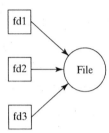

FIGURE 12.4   Many file descriptors, one file

Each file descriptor has its own private set of properties that have nothing to do with the file that it is associated with, including:

- A file pointer that records the offset in the file where it is reading and/or writing. When a file descriptor is created, its file pointer is positioned at offset 0 in the file (the first character) by default. As the process reads and/or writes, the file pointer is updated accordingly. For example, if a process opened a file and then read 10 bytes from the file, the file pointer would end up being positioned at offset 10. If the process then wrote 20 bytes, the bytes at offsets 10 to 29 in the file would be overwritten and the file pointer would end up being positioned at offset 30.
- A flag that indicates whether the descriptor should be automatically closed if the process execs. "exec ( )" is described in the "Process Management" section of this chapter.
- A flag that indicates whether all of the output to the file should be appended to the end of the file.

In addition to these values, some other values are meaningful only if the file is a special file, such as a pipe or a socket:

- A flag that indicates whether a process should block (wait) on input from the file if the file doesn't currently contain any input.
- A number that indicates a process ID or process group that should be sent a SIGIO signal if input becomes available on the file. Signals and process groups are discussed later in this chapter.

The system calls "open ( )" and "fcntl ( )" allow you to manipulate these flags and are described later in this section.

First Example: reverse

In this first section, I'll describe the most basic I/O system calls. Here's a list of them, together with a brief description of their respective functions:

Name	Function
open	opens/creates a file
read	reads bytes from a file into a buffer
write	writes bytes from a buffer to a file
lseek	moves to a particular offset in a file
close	closes a file
unlink	removes a file

To illustrate the use of these system calls, I'll use a small utility program called "reverse.c". As well as being a good vehicle for my presentation, it also doubles as a nice example of how to write a UNIX utility. Here's a description of **reverse**:

Utility: **reverse** -c [*fileName*]

reverse reverses the lines of its input read from *fileName* and displays them to standard output. If no filename is specified, **reverse** reverses its standard input. When the **-c** option is used, **reverse** also reverses the characters in each line.

Here's an example of **reverse** in action:

```
$ cc reverse.c -o reverse            ...compile the program.
$ cat test                           ...list the test file.
Christmas is coming,
The days that grow shorter,
Remind me of seasons I knew in the past.
$ reverse test                       ...reverse the file.
Remind me of seasons I knew in the past.
The days that grow shorter,
Christmas is coming,
$ reverse -c test                    ...reverse the lines too.
.tsap eht ni wenk I snosaes fo em dnimeR
,retrohs worg taht syad ehT
,gnimoc si samtsirhC
```

```
$ cat test | reverse                    ...pipe output to "reverse".
Remind me of seasons I knew in the past.
The days that grow shorter,
Christmas is coming,
$ _
```

How reverse Works

The **reverse** utility works by performing two passes over its input. During the first pass, it notes the starting offset of each line in the file and stores this information in an array. During the second pass, it jumps to the start of each line in reverse order, copying it from the original input file to its standard output.

If no file name is specified on the command line, **reverse** reads from its standard input during the first pass and copies it into a temporary file for the second pass. When the program is finished, the temporary file is removed.

Here's an overview of the program flow, together with a list of the functions that are associated with each action, and a list of the system calls used by each step:

Step	Action	Functions	System calls
1	Parse command line.	parseCommandLine, processOptions	open
2	If reading from standard input, create a temporary file to store input; otherwise, open the input file for reading.	pass1	open
3	Read from the file in chunks, storing the starting offset of each line in an array. If reading from standard input, copy each chunk to the temporary file.	pass1, trackLines	read, write
4	Read the input file again, but backward this time, copying each line to standard output. Reverse the line if the "-c" option was chosen.	pass2, processLine, reverseLine	lseek
5	Close the file, removing it if it was a temporary file.	pass2	close

The next few pages contain a complete listing of "reverse.c", the source code of **reverse.** I suggest that you skim through it and then read the descriptions of the system calls that follow.

"reverse.c": Listing

```
1  #include <fcntl.h> /* For file-mode definitions */
2  #include <stdio.h>
3  #include <stdlib.h>
```

```
 4
 5
 6   /* Enumerator */
 7   enum { FALSE, TRUE }; /* Standard false and true values */
 8   enum { STDIN, STDOUT, STDERR }; /* Standard I/O-channel indices */
 9
10
11   /* #define Statements */
12   #define BUFFER_SIZE    4096    /* Copy buffer size */
13   #define NAME_SIZE      12
14   #define MAX_LINES      100000  /* Max lines in file */
15
16
17   /* Globals */
18   char *fileName = NULL; /* Points to file name */
19   char tmpName [NAME_SIZE];
20   int charOption = FALSE; /* Set to true if "-c" option is used */
21   int standardInput = FALSE; /* Set to true if reading stdin */
22   int lineCount = 0; /* Total number of lines in input */
23   int lineStart [MAX_LINES]; /* Store offsets of each line */
24   int fileOffset = 0; /* Current position in input */
25   int fd; /* File descriptor of input */
26
27   /*******************************************************************/
28
29   main (argc, argv)
30
31   int argc;
32   char* argv [];
33
34   {
35     parseCommandLine (argc,argv); /* Parse command line */
36     pass1 ( ); /* Perform first pass through input */
37     pass2 ( ); /* Perform second pass through input */
38     return (/* EXITSUCCESS */ 0); /* Done */
39   }
40
41   /*******************************************************************/
42
43   parseCommandLine (argc, argv)
44
45   int argc;
46   char* argv [];
47
48   /* Parse command-line arguments */
49
50   {
51     int i;
52
53     for (i= 1; i < argc; i++)
54       {
```

```
55        if(argv[i][0] == '-')
56           processOptions (argv[i]);
57        else if (fileName == NULL)
58           fileName= argv[i];
59        else
60           usageError (); /* An error occurred */
61     }
62
63    standardInput = (fileName == NULL);
64 }
65
66 /*******************************************************************/
67
68 processOptions (str)
69
70 char* str;
71
72 /* Parse options */
73
74 {
75    int j;
76
77    for (j= 1; str[j] != NULL; j++)
78      {
79        switch(str[j]) /* Switch on command-line flag */
80          {
81            case'c':
82               charOption = TRUE;
83               break;
84
85            default:
86               usageError ( );
87               break;
88          }
89      }
90 }
91
92 /*******************************************************************/
93
94 usageError ( )
95
96 {
97    fprintf (stderr, "Usage: reverse -c [filename]\n");
98    exit (/* EXITFAILURE */ 1);
99 }
100
101 /*******************************************************************/
102
103 pass1 ( )
104
105 /* Perform first scan through file */
```

```
106
107   {
108     int tmpfd, charsRead, charsWritten;
109     char buffer [BUFFER_SIZE];
110
111     if (standardInput) /* Read from standard input */
112       {
113         fd = STDIN;
114         sprintf (tmpName, ".rev.%d",getpid ( )); /* Random name */
115         /* Create temporary file to store copy of input */
116         tmpfd = open (tmpName, O_CREAT | O_RDWR, 0600);
117         if (tmpfd == -1) fatalError ( );
118       }
119     else /* Open named file for reading */
120       {
121         fd = open (fileName, O_RDONLY);
122         if (fd == -1) fatalError ( );
123       }
124
125     lineStart[0] = 0; /* Offset of first line */
126
127     while (TRUE) /* Read all input */
128       {
129         /* Fill buffer */
130         charsRead = read (fd, buffer, BUFFER_SIZE);
131         if (charsRead == 0) break; /* EOF */
132         if (charsRead == -1) fatalError ( ); /* Error */
133         trackLines (buffer, charsRead); /* Process line */
134         /* Copy line to temporary file if reading from stdin */
135         if (standardInput)
136           {
137             charsWritten = write (tmpfd, buffer, charsRead);
138             if(charsWritten != charsRead) fatalError ( );
139           }
140       }
141
142     /* Store offset of trailing line, if present */
143     lineStart[lineCount + 1] = fileOffset;
144
145     /* If reading from standard input, prepare fd for pass2 */
146     if (standardInput) fd = tmpfd;
147   }
148
149   /*****************************************************************/
150
151   trackLines (buffer, charsRead)
152
153   char* buffer;
154   int charsRead;
155
156   /* Store offsets of each line start in buffer */
```

```
157
158  {
159    int i;
160
161    for (i = 0; i < charsRead; i++)
162      {
163        ++fileOffset; /* Update current file position */
164        if (buffer[i] == '\n') lineStart[++lineCount] = fileOffset;
165      }
166  }
167
168  /*******************************************************************/
169
170  int pass2 ( )
171
172  /* Scan input file again, displaying lines in reverse order */
173
174  {
175    int i;
176
177    for (i = lineCount - 1; i >= 0; i--)
178      processLine (i);
179
180    close (fd); /* Close input file */
181    if (standardInput) unlink (tmpName); /* Remove temp file */
182  }
183
184  /*******************************************************************/
185
186  processLine (i)
187
188  int i;
189
190  /* Read a line and display it */
191
192  {
193    int charsRead;
194    char buffer [BUFFER_SIZE];
195
196    lseek (fd, lineStart[i], SEEK_SET); /* Find and read the line */
197    charsRead = read (fd, buffer, lineStart[i+1] - lineStart[i]);
198    /* Reverse line if "-c" option was selected */
199    if (charOption) reverseLine (buffer, charsRead);
200    write (1, buffer, charsRead); /* Write it to standard output */
201  }
202
203  /*******************************************************************/
204
205  reverseLine (buffer, size)
206
207  char* buffer;
208  int size;
```

```
209
210    /* Reverse all the characters in the buffer */
211
212    {
213      int start = 0, end = size - 1;
214      char tmp;
215
216      if (buffer[end] == '\n') --end; /* Leave trailing new line */
217
218      /* Swap characters in a pairwise fashion */
219      while (start < end)
220        {
221          tmp = buffer[start];
222          buffer[start] = buffer[end];
223          buffer[end] = tmp;
224          ++start; /* Increment start index */
225          --end; /* Decrement end index */
226        }
227    }
228
229    /*****************************************************************/
230
231    fatalError ( )
232
233    {
234      perror ("reverse:"); /* Describe error */
235      exit (1);
236    }
```

Opening a File: open ( )

The **reverse** utility begins by executing "parseCommandLine ( )" [line 43], which sets various flags, depending on which options are chosen. If a filename is specified, the variable "fileName" is set to point to the filename and "standardInput" is set to FALSE; otherwise, "fileName" is set to NULL and "standardInput" is set to TRUE. Next, "pass1 ( )" [line 103], which performs one of the following actions, is executed:

- If **reverse** is reading from standard input, a temporary file is created. The file is created with read and write permissions for the owner and no permissions for anyone else (octal mode 600). It is opened in read/write mode and is used to store a copy of the standard input for use during "pass 2 ( )". During "pass 1 ( )", the input is taken from standard input, and so the file descriptor "fd" is set to "STDIN", which was defined to be zero at the top of the program. Recall that standard input is always indicated by a file descriptor of zero.

- If **reverse** is reading from a named file, the file is opened in read-only mode so that its contents may be read during pass 1 using the file descriptor "fd".

Each action uses the "open ( )" system call; the first action uses it to create a file, and the second action uses it to access an existing file. The "open ( )" system call is defined as follows:

System Call: int open (char* *fileName,* int *mode* [, int *permissions*])

"open ( )" allows you to open or create a file for reading and/or writing. *fileName* is an absolute or relative pathname, and *mode* is a bitwise or'ing of a read/write flag together with zero or more miscellaneous flags. *permissions* is a number that encodes the value of the file's permission flags and should only be supplied when a file is being created. It is usually written using the octal encoding scheme described in Chapter 2. The *permissions* value is affected by the process' **umask** value, described in Chapter 3. The values of the predefined read/write and miscellaneous flags are defined in "/usr/include/fcntl.h". The read/write flags are as follows:

FLAG	MEANING
O_RDONLY	Open for read only.
O_WRONLY	Open for write only.
O_RDWR	Open for both read and write.

The miscellaneous flags are as follows:

FLAG	MEANING
O_APPEND	Position the file pointer at the end of the file before each "write ( )".
O_CREAT	If the file doesn't exist, create the file and set the owner ID to the process' effective UID. The **umask** value is used when determining the initial permission-flag settings.
O_EXCL	If O_CREAT is set and the file exists, then "open ( )" fails.
O_NONBLOCK (Called O_NDELAY on some systems.)	This setting works only for named pipes. If set, an "open" for a read-only file will return immediately, regardless of whether the write end is open, and an "open" for a write-only file will fail if the read end isn't open. If clear, an "open" for a read, only or write-only file will block until the other end is also open.
O_TRUNC	If the file exists, it is truncated to length zero.

"open ( )" returns a nonnegative file descriptor if successful; otherwise, it returns a value of −1.

Creating a File   To create a file, use the O_CREAT flag as part of the mode flags and supply the initial file-permission flag settings as an octal value. For example, lines 114 to 117 create a temporary file with read and write permissions for the owner and then open it for reading and writing:

```
114        sprintf (tmpName, ".rev.%d", getpid ()); /* Random name */
115        /* Create temporary file to store copy of input */
116        tmpfd = open (tmpName, O_CREAT | O_RDWR, 0600);
117        if (tmpfd == -1) fatalError ();
```

The "getpid ( )" function is a system call that returns the process' ID number (PID), which is guaranteed to be unique. This function is a handy way to generate unique names for temporary files. For more details on this system call, see the "Process Management" section of this chapter. Note that I chose the name of the temporary file to begin with a period so that it doesn't show up in an **ls** listing. Files that begin with a period are sometimes known as *hidden files*.

Opening an Existing File   To open an existing file, specify the mode flags only. Lines 121 and 122 open a named file for read-only access:

```
121        fd = open (fileName, O_RDONLY);
122        if (fd == -1) fatalError ();
```

Other Flags for "Open ( )"   The other more complicated flag settings for "open ( )", such as O_NONBLOCK, are intended for use with the pipes, sockets, and STREAMS that are described later in this chapter. Right now, the O_CREAT flag is probably the only miscellaneous flag that you'll need.

Reading From a File: read ( )

Once **reverse** has initialized the file descriptor "fd" for input, it reads chunks of input and processes them until the end of the file is reached. To read bytes from a file, it uses the "read ( )" system call, which works as follows:

System Call: ssize_t read (int *fd*, void* *buf*, size_t *count*)

Note: *This synopsis describes how "read ( )" operates when reading a regular file. For information on reading from special files, please refer to later sections of this chapter.*
       "read ( )" copies *count* bytes from the file referenced by the file descriptor *fd* into the buffer *buf*. The bytes are read from the current file position, which is then updated accordingly. "read ( )" copies as many bytes from the file as it can, up to the number specified by *count*, and returns the number of bytes actually copied. If "read ( )" is attempted after the last byte has already been read, it returns a value of zero, which indicates the end of the file.
       If successful, "read ( )" returns the number of bytes that it read; otherwise, it returns a value of −1.

The "read ( )" system call performs low-level input and has none of the formatting capabilities of "scanf ( )". The benefit of "read ( )" is that it bypasses the additional layer of buffering supplied by the C library functions and is therefore very fast. Although I could have read one character of input at a time, doing so would have resulted in a large number of system calls, thus slowing down the execution of my program considerably. Instead, I used "read ( )" to read up to "BUFFER_SIZE" characters at a time. For efficient copying, "BUFFER_SIZE" was chosen to be a multiple of the disk's block size. Lines 130 to 132 perform the "read" and test the return result:

```
130         charsRead = read (fd, buffer, BUFFER_SIZE);
131         if (charsRead == 0) break; /* EOF */
132         if (charsRead == -1) fatalError (); /* Error */
```

As each chunk of input is read, it is passed to the "trackLines ( )" function. This function scans the input buffer for new lines and stores the offset of the first character in each line in the "lineStart" array. The variable "fileOffset" is used to maintain the current file offset. The contents of "lineStart" are used during the second pass.

Writing to a File: write ( )

When **reverse** is reading from standard input, it creates a copy of the input for use during the second pass. To make this copy, it sets the file descriptor "tmpfd" to refer to a temporary file and then writes each chunk of input to the file during the "read" loop. To write bytes to a file, it uses the "write ( )" system call, which works as follows:

System Call: ssize_t write (int *fd*, void* *buf*, size_t *count*)

Note: This synopsis describes how "write ( )" operates when writing to a regular file. For information on writing to special files, please refer to later sections of this chapter.

"write ( )" copies *count* bytes from a buffer *buf* to the file referenced by the file descriptor *fd*. The bytes are written at the current file position, which is then updated accordingly. If the O_APPEND flag was set for *fd*, the file position is set to the end of the file before each "write".

"write ( )" copies as many bytes from the buffer as it can, up to the number specified by *count*, and returns the number of bytes actually copied. Your process should always check the return value. If the return value isn't *count*, then the disk probably filled up and no space was left.

If successful, "write ( )" returns the number of bytes that were written; otherwise, it returns a value of −1.

The "write ( )" system call performs low-level output and has none of the formatting capabilities of "printf ( )". The benefit of "write ( )" is that it bypasses the additional layer of buffering supplied by the functions of the C library and is therefore very fast. Lines 134 to 139 perform the "write" operation:

```
134     /* Copy line to temporary file if reading standard input */
135     if (standardInput)
136         {
137         charsWritten = write (tmpfd, buffer, charsRead);
138         if (charsWritten != charsRead) fatalError ();
139         }
```

Moving in a File: lseek ( )

Once the first pass has completed, the array "lineStart" contains the respective offsets of the first character of each line of the input file. During the second pass, the lines are read in reverse order and displayed to standard output. In order to read the lines out of sequence, the program makes use of "lseek ( )", which is a system call that allows a descriptor's file pointer to be changed. Here's a descripton of "lseek ( )":

System Call: off_t lseek (int *fd*, off_t *offset*, int *mode*)

"lseek ( )" allows you to change a descriptor's current file position. *fd* is the file descriptor, *offset* is a long integer, and *mode* describes how *offset* should be interpreted. The three possible values of *mode* are defined in "/usr/include/stdio.h" and have the following meanings:

VALUE	MEANING
SEEK_SET	*offset* is relative to the start of the file.
SEEK_CUR	*offset* is relative to the current file position.
SEEK_END	*offset* is relative to the end of the file.

"lseek ( )" fails if you try to move to a point that comes before the start of the file.

   If successful, "lseek ( )" returns the current file position; otherwise, it returns a value of −1. On some systems, these values are defined in "/usr/include/unistd.h".

Lines 196 and 197 "seek" to the start of a line and then read in all of its characters. Note that the number of characters to read is calculated by subtracting the offset value of the start of the next line from the offset value of the start of the current line:

```
196     lseek (fd, lineStart[i], SEEK_SET); /* Find line and read it */
197     charsRead = read (fd, buffer, lineStart[i+1] - lineStart[i]);
```

If you want to find out your current location without moving, use an offset value of zero relative to the current position:

```
currentOffset = lseek (fd, 0, SEEK_CUR);
```

If you move past the end of the file and then perform a "write ( )", the kernel automatically extends the size of the file and treats the intermediate area of the file as if it were filled with NULL (ASCII 0) characters. Interestingly enough, it doesn't allocate disk space for the intermediate area, a situation that is confirmed by the following example:

```
$ cat sparse.c                       ...list the test file.
#include <fcntl.h>
#include <stdio.h>
#include <stdlib.h>
/*******************************************************************/
main ()
{
  int i, fd;
  /* Create a sparse file */
  fd = open ("sparse.txt", O_CREAT | O_RDWR, 0600);
  write (fd, "sparse", 6);
  lseek (fd, 60006, SEEK_SET);
  write (fd, "file", 4);
  close (fd);
  /* Create a normal file */
  fd = open ("normal.txt", O_CREAT | O_RDWR, 0600);
  write (fd, "normal", 6);
  for (i = 1; i <= 60000; i++)
    write (fd, "/0", 1);
  write (fd, "file", 4);
  close (fd);
}
$ sparse                        ...execute the file.
$ ls -l *.txt                   ...look at the files.
-rw-r--r-- 1 glass           60010 Feb 14 15:06 normal.txt
-rw-r--r-- 1 glass           60010 Feb 14 15:06 sparse.txt
$ ls -s *.txt                   ...list their block usage.
  60 normal.txt*               ...uses a full 60 blocks.
   8 sparse.txt*               ...only uses eight blocks.
$ _
```

Files that contain "gaps" like this are termed "sparse" files. For details on how they are actually stored, consult Chapter 13.

Closing a File: "close ( )"

When the second pass is over, **reverse** uses the "close ( )" system call to free the file descriptor of the input. Here's a description of "close ( )":

System Call: int close (int *fd*)

"close ( )" frees the file descriptor *fd*. If *fd* is the last file descriptor associated with a particular open file, the kernel resources associated with the file are deallocated. When a process terminates, all of its file descriptors are automatically closed, but it's better programming practice to close a file when you're done with it. If you close a file descriptor that's already closed, an error occurs.

　　If successful, "close ( )" returns a value of 0; otherwise, it returns a value of −1.

Line 180 contains the call to "close ( )":

```
180     close (fd); /* Close input file */
```

When a file is closed, it does not guarantee that the file's buffers are immediately flushed to disk. For more information on file buffering, consult Chapter 13.

Deleting a File: unlink ( )

If **reverse** reads from standard input, it stores a copy of the input in a temporary file. At the end of the second pass, it removes this file using the "unlink ( )" system call, which works like this:

System Call: int unlink (const char* *fileName*)

"unlink ( )" removes the hard link from the name *fileName* to its file. If *fileName* is the last link to the file, the file's resources are deallocated. In this case, if any process' file descriptors are currently associated with the file, the directory entry is removed immediately, but the file is only deallocated after all of the file descriptors are closed. This condition means that an executable file can "unlink" itself during execution and still continue to completion.

　　If successful, "unlink ( )" returns a value of 0; otherwise, it returns a value of −1.

Line 181 contains the call to "unlink ( )":

```
181     if (standardInput) unlink (tmpName); /* Remove temp file */
```

For more information about hard links, consult Chapter 13.

Second Example: monitor

This section contains a description of some more advanced system calls:

Name	Function
stat	obtains status information about a file
fstat	works just like stat
getdents	obtains directory entries

These calls are demonstrated in the context of a program called "monitor", which allows a user to monitor a series of named files and obtain information whenever any of them are modified. Here's a description of **monitor**:

Utility: **monitor** [-t *delay*] [-l *count*]{ *fileName* }+

monitor scans all of the specified files every *delay* seconds and displays information about any of the specified files that were modified since the last scan. If *fileName* is a directory, all of the files inside that directory are scanned. File modification is indicated in one of three ways:

LABEL	MEANING
ADDED	Indicates that the file was created since the last scan. Every file in the file list is given this label during the first scan.
CHANGED	Indicates that the file was modified since the last scan.
DELETED	Indicates that the file was deleted since the last scan.

By default, **monitor** will scan forever, although you can specify the total number of scans by using the **-l** option. The default delay time is 10 seconds between scans, although this default may be overridden by using the **-t** option.

In the next example, I monitored an individual file and a directory, storing the output of **monitor** into a temporary file. Notice how the contents of the "monitor.out" file reflected the additions, modifications, and deletions of the monitored file and directory:

```
% ls                            ...look at home directory.
monitor.c    monitor    tmp/
% ls tmp                        ...look at "tmp" directory.
b
% monitor tmp myFile.txt >& monitor.out &  ...start monitoring.
[1] 12841
% cat > tmp/a                   ...create a file in "y/tmp".
hi there
^D
% cat > myFile.txt              ...create "myFile.txt".
hi there
^D
% cat >> myFile.txt             ...change "myFile.txt".
hi again
^D
% rm tmp/a                      ...delete "tmp/a".
% jobs                          ...look at jobs.
[1] + Running               monitor tmp myFile.txt >& monitor.out
% kill %1                       ...kill "monitor" job.
[1] Terminated              monitor tmp myFile.txt >& monitor.out
% cat monitor.out               ...look at output.
ADDED tmp/b size 9 bytes, mod. time = Sun Jan 18 00:38:55 1998
ADDED tmp/a size 9 bytes, mod. time = Fri Feb 13 18:51:09 1998
ADDED myFile.txt size 9 bytes, mod. time = Fri Feb 13 18:51:21 1998
CHANGED myFile.txt size 18 bytes, mod. time = Fri Feb 13 18:51:49 1998
DELETED tmp/a
% _
```

How monitor Works

The **monitor** utility continually scans the specified files and directories for modifications. It uses the "stat ( )" system call to obtain status information about named files, including their type and last modification time, and the "getdents ( )" system call to scan directories. It maintains a status table called "stats", that holds the following information about each file that it finds:

- the name of the file
- the status information obtained by the "stat ( )" system call
- a record of whether the file was present during the present scan and the previous scan

During a scan, **monitor** processes each file as follows:

- If the file isn't currently in the scan table, it's added and the message "ADDED" is displayed.
- If the file is already in the scan table and has been modified since the last scan, the message "CHANGED" is displayed.

At the end of a scan, all entries that were present during the previous scan, but not during the current scan, are removed from the table and the message "DELETED" is displayed.

Below is a complete listing of "monitor.c", the source code of **monitor.** I suggest that you skim through it and then read the description of the system calls that follow.

monitor.c: Listing

```
1   #include <stdio.h>              /* For printf, fprintf */
2   #include <string.h>            /* For strcmp */
3   #include <ctype.h>             /* For isdigit */
4   #include <fcntl.h>             /* For O_RDONLY */
5   #include <sys/dirent.h>        /* For getdents */
6   #include <sys/stat.h>          /* For IS macros */
7   #include <sys/types.h>         /* For modet */
8   #include <time.h>              /* For localtime, asctime */
9
10
11  /* #define Statements */
12  #define MAX_FILES              100
13  #define MAX_FILENAME           50
14  #define NOT_FOUND              -1
15  #define FOREVER                -1
16  #define DEFAULT_DELAY_TIME     10
17  #define DEFAULT_LOOP_COUNT     FOREVER
18
19
20  /* Booleans */
21  enum { FALSE, TRUE };
22
23
24  /* Status structure, one per file. */
25  struct statStruct
26    {
27      char fileName [MAX_FILENAME]; /* File name */
28      int lastCycle, thisCycle; /* To detect changes */
29      struct stat status; /* Information from stat () */
30    };
31
32
33  /* Globals */
34  char* fileNames [MAX_FILES]; /* One per file on command line */
35  int fileCount; /* Count of files on command line */
36  struct statStruct stats [MAX_FILES]; /* One per matching file */
37  int loopCount = DEFAULT_LOOP_COUNT; /* Number of times to loop */
38  int delayTime = DEFAULT_DELAY_TIME; /* Seconds between loops */
39
40  /**********************************************************************/
41
```

```
42  main (argc, argv)
43
44  int argc;
45  char* argv [];
46
47  {
48    parseCommandLine (argc, argv); /* Parse command line */
49    monitorLoop (); /* Execute main monitor loop */
50    return (/* EXIT_SUCCESS */ 0);
51  }
52
53  /*******************************************************************/
54
55  parseCommandLine (argc, argv)
56
57  int argc;
58  char* argv [];
59
60  /* Parse command-line arguments */
61
62  {
63    int i;
64
65    for (i = 1; ( (i < argc) && (i < MAX_FILES) ); i++)
66      {
67        if (argv[i][0] == '-')
68          processOptions (argv[i]);
69        else
70          fileNames[fileCount++] = argv[i];
71      }
72
73    if (fileCount == 0) usageError ();
74  }
75
76  /*******************************************************************/
77
78  processOptions (str)
79
80  char* str;
81
82  /* Parse options */
83
84  {
85    int j;
86
87    for (j = 1; str[j] != NULL; j++)
88      {
89        switch(str[j]) /* Switch on option letter */
90          {
91            case 't':
92              delayTime = getNumber (str, &j);
```

```
 93                break;
 94
 95            case 'l':
 96                loopCount = getNumber (str, &j);
 97                break;
 98          }
 99        }
100  }
101
102  /****************************************************************/
103
104  getNumber (str, i)
105
106  char* str;
107  int* i;
108
109  /* Convert a numeric ASCII option to a number */
110
111  {
112    int number = 0;
113    int digits = 0; /* Count the digits in the number */
114
115    while (isdigit (str[(*i) + 1])) /* Convert chars to ints */
116      {
117        number = number * 10 + str[++(*i)] - '0';
118        ++digits;
119      }
120
121    if (digits == 0) usageError (); /* There must be a number */
122    return (number);
123  }
124
125  /****************************************************************/
126
127  usageError ()
128
129  {
130    fprintf (stderr, "Usage: monitor -t<seconds> -l<loops> {filename}+\n");
131    exit (/* EXIT_FAILURE */ 1);
132  }
133
134  /****************************************************************/
135
136  monitorLoop ()
137
138  /* The main monitor loop */
139
140  {
141    do
142      {
143        monitorFiles (); /* Scan all files */
```

```
144         fflush (stdout); /* Flush standard output */
145         fflush (stderr); /* Flush standard error */
146         sleep (delayTime); /* Wait until next loop */
147       }
148     while (loopCount == FOREVER || --loopCount > 0);
149   }
150
151   /****************************************************************/
152
153   monitorFiles ()
154
155   /* Process all files */
156
157   {
158     int i;
159
160     for (i = 0; i < fileCount; i++)
161       monitorFile (fileNames[i]);
162
163     for (i = 0; i< MAX_FILES; i++) /* Update stat array */
164       {
165         if (stats[i].lastCycle && !stats[i].thisCycle)
166           printf ("DELETED %s\n", stats[i].fileName);
167
168         stats[i].lastCycle = stats[i].thisCycle;
169         stats[i].thisCycle = FALSE;
170       }
171   }
172
173   /****************************************************************/
174
175   monitorFile (fileName)
176
177   char* fileName;
178
179   /* Process a single file/directory*/
180
181   {
182     struct stat statBuf;
183     mode_t mode;
184     int result;
185
186     result = stat (fileName, &statBuf); /* Obtain file status */
187
188     if (result == -1) /* Status was not available */
189       {
190         fprintf (stderr, "Cannot stat %s\n", fileName);
191         return;
192       }
193
194     mode = statBuf.st_mode; /* Mode of file */
```

```
195
196   if(S_ISDIR (mode)) /* Directory */
197     processDirectory (fileName);
198   else if (S_ISREG (mode) || S_ISCHR (mode) || S_ISBLK (mode))
199     updateStat (fileName, &statBuf); /* Regular file */
200 }
201
202 /*******************************************************************/
203
204 processDirectory (dirName)
205
206 char* dirName;
207
208 /* Process all files in the named directory */
209
210 {
211   int fd, charsRead;
212   struct dirent dirEntry;
213   char fileName [MAX_FILENAME];
214
215   fd = open (dirName, O_RDONLY); /* Open for reading */
216   if (fd == -1) fatalError ();
217
218   while (TRUE) /* Read all directory entries */
219     {
220       charsRead = getdents(fd, &dirEntry, sizeof (struct dirent));
221       if (charsRead == -1) fatalError ();
222       if (charsRead == 0) break; /* EOF */
223       if (strcmp (dirEntry.d_name, ".") != 0&&
224           strcmp (dirEntry.d_name, "..") != 0) /* Skip . and .. */
225         {
226           sprintf (fileName, "%s/%s", dirName, dirEntry.d_name);
227           monitorFile (fileName); /* Call recursively */
228         }
229
230       lseek (fd, dirEntry.d_off, SEEK_SET); /* Find next entry */
231     }
232
233   close (fd); /* Close directory */
234 }
235
236 /*******************************************************************/
237
238 updateStat (fileName, statBuf)
239
240 char* fileName;
241 struct stat* statBuf;
242
243 /* Add a status entry if necessary */
244
245 {
```

```
246    int entryIndex;
247
248    entryIndex = findEntry (fileName); /* Find existing entry */
249
250    if (entryIndex == NOT_FOUND)
251      entryIndex = addEntry (fileName, statBuf); /* Add new entry */
252    else
253      updateEntry (entryIndex, statBuf); /* Update existing entry */
254
255    if (entryIndex != NOT_FOUND)
256    stats[entryIndex].thisCycle = TRUE; /* Update status array */
257  }
258
259  /*******************************************************************/
260
261  findEntry (fileName)
262
263  char* fileName;
264
265  /* Locate the index of a named file in the status array */
266
267  {
268    int i;
269
270    for (i = 0; i < MAX_FILES; i++)
271      if (stats[i].lastCycle &&
272          strcmp (stats[i].fileName, fileName) == 0) return (i);
273
274    return (NOT_FOUND);
275  }
276
277  /*******************************************************************/
278
279  addEntry (fileName, statBuf)
280
281  char* fileName;
282  struct stat* statBuf;
283
284  /* Add a new entry into the status array */
285
286  {
287    int index;
288
289    index = nextFree (); /* Find the next free entry */
290    if (index == NOT_FOUND) return (NOT_FOUND); /* None left */
291    strcpy (stats[index].fileName, fileName); /* Add filename */
292    stats[index].status = *statBuf; /* Add status information */
293    printf ("ADDED"); /* Notify standard output */
294    printEntry (index); /* Display status information */
295    return (index);
296  }
```

```
297
298   /*******************************************************************/
299
300   nextFree ()
301
302   /* Return the next free index in the status array */
303
304   {
305     int i;
306
307     for (i = 0; i < MAX_FILES; i++)
308       if (!stats[i].lastCycle && !stats[i].thisCycle) return (i);
309
310     return (NOT_FOUND);
311   }
312
313   /*******************************************************************/
314
315   updateEntry (index, statBuf)
316
317   int index;
318   struct stat* statBuf;
319
320   /*Display information if the file has been modified */
321
322   {
323     if (stats[index].status.st_mtime != statBuf->st_mtime)
324       {
325         stats[index].status = *statBuf; /* Store stat information */
326         printf ("CHANGED "); /* Notify standard output */
327         printEntry (index);
328       }
329   }
330
331   /*******************************************************************/
332
333   printEntry (index)
334
335   int index;
336
337   /* Display an entry of the status array */
338
339   {
340     printf ("%s ", stats[index].fileName);
341     printStat (&stats[index].status);
342   }
343
344   /*******************************************************************/
345
346   printStat (statBuf)
347
```

```
348   struct stat* statBuf;
349
350   /* Display a status buffer */
351
352   {
353      printf ("size %lu bytes, mod. time = %s", statBuf->st_size,
354               asctime (localtime (&statBuf->st_mtime)));
355   }
356
357   /***************************************************************/
358
359   fatalError ()
360
361   {
362     perror ("monitor: ");
363     exit (/* EXIT_FAILURE */ 1);
364   }
```

Obtaining File Information: stat ( ), lstat ( ), and fstat ( )

monitor obtains its file information by calling "stat ( )", which works as follows:

System Call: int stat (const char* *name*, struct stat* *buf*)
                int lstat (const char* *name*, struct stat* *buf*)
                int fstat (int *fd*, struct stat* *buf*)

"stat ( )" fills the buffer *buf* with information about the file *name*. The "stat" structure is defined in "/usr/include/sys/stat.h". "lstat( )" returns information about a symbolic link itself rather than the file that it references. "fstat ( )" performs the same function as "stat ( )", except that it takes the file descriptor of the file to be "stat"'ed as its first parameter. The "stat" structure contains the following members:

NAME	MEANING
st_dev	the device number
st_ino	the inode number
st_mode	the permission flags
st_nlink	the hard-link count
st_uid	the user ID
st_gid	the group ID
st_size	the file size
st_atime	the last access time
st_mtime	the last modification time
st_ctime	the last status-change time

There are some predefined macros defined in "/usr/include/sys/stat.h" that take "st_mode" as their argument and return true (a value of 1) for the following file types:

MACRO	RETURNS TRUE FOR FILE TYPE
S_IFDIR	directory
S_IFCHR	character special device
S_IFBLK	block special device
S_IFREG	regular file
S_IFFIFO	pipe

The time fields may be decoded using the standard C library "asctime ( )" and "localtime ( )" subroutines.

"stat ( )" and "fstat ( )" return a value of 0 if successful and a value of −1 otherwise.

The **monitor** utility invokes "stat ( )" from "monitorFile ( )" [line 175] on line 186:

```
186     result = stat (fileName, &statBuf); /* Obtain file status */
```

It examines the mode of the file using the S_ISDIR, S_ISREG, S_ISCHR, and S_ISBLK macros, processing directory files and other files as follows:

- If the file is a directory file, it calls "processDirectory ( )" [line 204], which applies "monitorFile ( )" recursively to each of its directory entries.
- If the file is a regular file, character special file, or block special file, it calls "updateStat ( )" [line 238], which either adds or updates the file's status entry. If the status changes in any way, "updateEntry ( )" [line 315] is called to display the file's new status. The decoding of the time fields is performed by the "localtime ( )" and "asctime ( )" routines in "printStat ( )" [line 346].

Reading Directory Information: getdents ( )

"processDirectory ( )" [204] opens a directory file for reading and then uses "getdents ( )" to obtain every entry in the directory. "getdents" works as follows:

System Call: int getdents (int *fd*, struct dirent* *buf*, int *structSize*)

"getdents ( )" reads the directory file with descriptor *fd* from its current position and fills the structure pointed to by *buf* with the next entry. The

structure "dirent" is defined in "/usr/include/sys/dirent.h" and contains
the following fields:

NAME	MEANING
d_ino	the inode number
d_off	the offset of the next directory entry
d_reclen	the length of the directory entry structure
d_nam	the length of the filename

getdents ( ) returns the length of the directory entry when successful, 0
when the last directory entry has already been read, and −1 in the case
of an error.

processDirectory ( ) is careful not to trace into the "." and ".." directories, and uses
"lseek ( )" to jump from one directory entry to the next. When the directory has
been completely searched, it is closed.

Some older systems use the getdirentries ( ) system call instead of getdents ( ).
The usage of getdirentries ( ) differs somewhat from getdents ( ), you should consult
your system's man page for details.

Miscellaneous File Management System Calls

There now follows a brief description of the following miscellaneous file management system calls:

Name	Function
chown	changes a file's owner and/or group
chmod	changes a file's permission settings
dup	duplicates a file descriptor
dup2	similar to dup
fchown	works just like chown
fchmod	works just like chmod
fcntl	gives access to miscellaneous file characteristics
ftruncate	works just like truncate
ioctl	controls a device
link	creates a hard link
mknod	creates a special file
sync	schedules all file buffers to be flushed to disk
truncate	truncates a file

Changing a File's Owner and/or Group: chown ( ), lchown ( ), and fchown ( )

"chown ( )" and "fchown ( )" change the owner and/or group of a file and work like this:

System Call: int chown (const char* *fileName*, uid_t *ownerId*,
       gid_t *groupId*)
   int lchown (const char* *fileName*, uid_t *ownerId*,
       gid_t *groupId*)
   int fchown (int *fd*, uid_t *ownerId*, gid_t *groupId*)

"chown ( )" causes the owner and group IDs of *fileName* to be changed to *ownerId* and *groupId*, respectively. A value of −1 in a particular field means that its associated value should remain unchanged. "lchown( )" changes the ownership of a symbolic link itself rather than the file that the link references.

Only a super-user can change the ownership of a file, and a user may change the group only to another group of which he/she is a member. If *fileName* is a symbolic link, the owner and group of the link are changed instead of the file that the link is referencing.

"fchown ( )" is just like "chown ( )" except that it takes an open descriptor as an argument instead of a filename.

They both return a value of −1 if unsuccessful, and a value of 0 otherwise.

In the next example, I changed the group of the file "test.txt" from "music" to "cs", which has a group ID number of 62. For more information about group IDs and how to locate them, consult Chapter 14.

```
$ cat mychown.c              ...list the program.
main ()
{
int flag;
flag = chown ("test.txt", -1, 62); /* Leave user ID unchanged */
if (flag == -1) perror("mychown.c");
}
$ ls -lg test.txt              ...examine file before the change.
-rw-r--r-- 1 glass      music       3 May 25 11:42 test.txt
$ mychown                      ...run program.
$ ls -lg test.txt              ...examine file after the change.
-rw-r--r-- 1 glass      cs          3 May 25 11:42 test.txt
$ _
```

Changing a File's Permissions: chmod ( ) and fchmod ( )

"chmod ( )" and "fchmod ( )" change a file's permission flags and work like this:

System Call: int chmod (const char* *fileName*, int *mode*)
        int fchmod (int *fd*, mode_t *mode*);

"chmod ( )" changes the mode of *fileName* to *mode*, where *mode* is usually supplied as an octal number, as described in Chapter 2. The "set user ID" and "set group ID" flags have the octal values 4000 and 2000, respectively. To change a file's mode, you must either own it or be a super-user.

"fchmod ( )" works just like "chmod ( )" except that it takes an open file descriptor as an argument instead of a filename.

They both return a value of −1 if unsuccessful, and a value of 0 otherwise.

In the following example, I changed the permission flags of the file "test.txt" to 600 octal, which corresponds to read and write permission for the owner only:

```
$ cat mychmod.c                  ...list the program.
main ()
{
  int flag;
  flag = chmod ("test.txt", 0600); /* Use an octal encoding */
  if (flag == -1) perror ("mychmod.c");
}
$ ls -l test.txt                 ...examine file before the change.
-rw-r--r-- 1 glass              3 May 25 11:42 test.txt
$ mychmod                        ...run the program.
$ ls -l test.txt                 ...examine file after the change.
-rw------- 1 glass              3 May 25 11:42 test.txt
$ _
```

Duplicating a File Descriptor: dup ( ) and dup2 ( )

"dup ( )" and "dup2 ( )" allow you to duplicate file descriptors, and they work like this:

System Call: int dup (int *oldFd*)
        int dup2 (int *oldFd*, int *newFd*)

"dup ( )" finds the smallest free file-descriptor entry and points it to the same file to which *oldFd* points. "dup2 ( )" closes *newFd* if it's currently active and then points it to the same file to which *oldFd* points. In both cases, the original and copied file descriptors share the same file pointer and access mode.

They both return the index of the new file descriptor if successful and a value of −1 otherwise.

The shells use "dup2 ( )" to perform redirection and piping. For examples that show how this task is done, read the "Process Management" section of this chapter and study the Internet shell at the end of this chapter.

In the following example, I created a file called "test.txt" and wrote to it via four different file descriptors:

- The first file descriptor was the original descriptor.
- The second descriptor was a copy of the first, allocated in slot 4.
- The third descriptor was a copy of the first, allocated in slot 0 (the standard input channel), which was freed by the "close (0)" statement.
- The fourth descriptor was a copy of the third descriptor, copied over the existing descriptor in slot 2 (the standard error channel).

```
$ cat mydup.c                    ...list the file.
#include <stdio.h>
#include <fcntl.h>
main ()
{
  int fd1, fd2, fd3;
   fd1 = open ("test.txt", O_RDWR | O_TRUNC);
  printf ("fd1 = %d\n", fd1);
  write (fd1, "what's", 6);
   fd2 = dup (fd1); /* Make a copy of fd1 */
  printf ("fd2 = %d\n", fd2);
  write (fd2, "up", 3);
   close (0); /* Close standard input */
  fd3 = dup (fd1); /* Make another copy of fd1 */
  printf ("fd3 = %d\n", fd3);
  write (0, " doc", 4);
   dup2 (3, 2); /* Duplicate channel 3 to channel 2 */
  write (2, "?\n", 2);
}
$ mydup                          ...run the program.
fd1 = 3
fd2 = 4
fd3 = 0
$ cat test.txt                   ...list the output file.
what's up doc?
$ _
```

File Descriptor Operations: fcntl ( )

"fcntl ( )" directly controls the settings of the flags associated with a file descriptor, and it works as follows:

System Call: int fcntl (int *fd*, int *cmd*, int *arg*)

"fcntl ( )" performs the operation encoded by *cmd* on the file associated with the file descriptor *fd*. *arg* is an optional argument for *cmd*. Here are the most common values of *cmd*:

VALUE	OPERATION
F_SETFD	Set the close-on-exec flag to the lowest bit of *arg* (0 or 1).
F_GETFD	Return a number whose lowest bit is 1 if the close-on-exec flag is set and 0 otherwise.
F_GETFL	Return a number corresponding to the current file-status flags and access modes.
F_SETFL	Set the current file-status flags to *arg*.
F_GETOWN	Return the process ID or process group that is currently set to receive SIGIO/SIGURG signals. If the returned value is positive, it refers to a process ID. If it's negative, its absolute value refers to a process group.
F_SETOWN	Set the process ID or process group that should receive SIGIO/SIGURG signals to *arg*. The encoding scheme is as described for F_GETOWN.

fcntl ( ) returns −1 if unsuccessful.

In the following example, I opened an existing file for writing and overwrote the initial few letters with the phrase "hi there." I then used "fcntl ( )" to set the file descriptor's APPEND flag, which instructed it to append all further writes. This caused "guys" to be placed at the end of the file, even though I moved the file position pointer back to the start with lseek ( ):

```
$ cat myfcntl.c                    ...list the program.
#include <stdio.h>
#include <fcntl.h>
main ()
{
  int fd;
  fd = open ("test.txt", O_WRONLY); /* Open file for writing */
  write (fd, "hi there\n", 9);
  lseek (fd, 0, SEEK_SET); /* Seek to beginning of file */
```

```
  fcntl (fd, F_SETFL, O_WRONLY | O_APPEND); /* Set APPEND flag */
  write (fd, " guys\n", 6);
  close (fd);
}
```

```
$ cat test.txt                  ...list the original file.
here are the contents of
the original file.
$ myfcntl                       ...run the program.
$ cat test.txt                  ...list the new contents.
hi there
the contents of
the original file.
guys                            ...note that "guys" is at the end.
$ _
```

Controlling Devices: ioctl ( )

"ioctl ( )" performs many controlling functions on an input/output channel and works as follows:

System Call: int ioctl (int *fd*, int *cmd*, int *arg*)

"ioctl ( )" performs the operation encoded by *cmd* on the file associated with the file descriptor *fd*. *arg* is an optional argument for *cmd*. The valid values of *cmd* depend on the device to which *fd* refers and are typically documented in the manufacturer's operating instructions. Therefore, I supply no examples for this system call.

  "ioctl ( )" returns a value of −1 if unsuccessful.

Creating Hard Links: link ( )

"link ( )" creates a hard link to an existing file and works as follows:

System Call: int link (const char* *oldPath*, const char* *newPath*)

"link ( )" creates a new label *newPath* and links it to the same file to which the label *oldPath* is linked. The hard-link count of the associated file is incremented by one. If *oldPath* and *newPath* reside on different physical devices, a hard link cannot be made and "link ( )" fails. For more information about hard links, consult the description of **ln** in Chapter 7.

  "link ( )" returns a value of −1 if unsuccessful and a value of 0 otherwise.

In the next example, I created the filename "another.txt" and linked it to the file referenced by the existing name "original.txt". I then demonstrated that both labels were linked to the same file.

```
$ cat mylink.c                     ...list the program.
main ()
{
  link ("original.txt", "another.txt");
}
$ cat original.txt                 ...list original file.
this is a file.
$ ls -l original.txt another.txt  ...examine the files before.
another.txt not found
-rw-r--r-- 1 glass          16 May 25 12:18 original.txt
$ mylink                           ...run the program.
$ ls -l original.txt another.txt  ...examine files after.
-rw-r--r-- 2 glass          16 May 25 12:18 another.txt
-rw-r--r-- 2 glass          16 May 25 12:18 original.txt
$ cat >> another.txt               ...alter "another.txt".
hi
^D
$ ls -l original.txt another.txt  ...both labels reflect the change.
-rw-r--r-- 2 glass          20 May 25 12:19 another.txt
-rw-r--r-- 2 glass          20 May 25 12:19 original.txt
$ rm original.txt                  ...remove original label.
$ ls -l original.txt another.txt  ...examine labels.
original.txt not found
-rw-r--r-- 1 glass          20 May 25 12:19 another.txt
$ cat another.txt                  ...list contents via other label.
this is a file.
hi
$ _
```

Creating Special Files: mknod ( )

"mknod ( )" allows you to create a special file, and it works like this:

System Call: int mknod (const char* *fileName*, mode_t *type*, dev_t *device*)

"mknod ( )" creates a new regular, directory, or special file called *fileName* whose type can be one of the following:

VALUE	MEANING
S_IFDIR	directory
S_IFCHR	character-oriented file
S_IFBLK	block-oriented file
S_IFREG	regular file
S_IFIFO	named pipe

If the file is a character- or block-oriented file, then the low-order byte of *device* should specify the minor device number and the high-order byte should specify the major device number. (This specification can vary in different versions of UNIX). In other cases, the value of *device* is ignored. For more information on special files, consult Chapter 13.

Only a super-user can use "mknod ( )" to create directories, character-oriented files, or block-oriented special files. It is typical now to use the "mkdir ( )" system call to create directories.

"mknod ( )" returns a value of −1 if unsuccessful and a value of 0 otherwise.

For an example of the use of "mknod ( )", consult the section on named pipes later in this chapter.

Flushing the File-System Buffer: sync ( )

"sync ( )" flushes the file-system buffers and works as follows:

System Call: void sync ( )

"sync ( )" schedules all of the file system buffers to be written to disk. For more information on the buffer system, consult Chapter 13. "sync ( )" should be performed by any programs that bypass the file system buffers and examine the raw file system.

"sync ( )" always succeeds.

Truncating a File: truncate ( ) and ftruncate ( )

"truncate ( )" and "ftruncate ( )" set the length of a file, and they work like this:

System Call: int truncate (const char* *fileName*, off_t *length*)
              int ftruncate (int *fd*, off_t *length*)

"truncate ( )" sets the length of the file *fileName* to be *length* bytes. If the file is longer than *length,* it is truncated. If it is shorter than *length,* it is padded with ASCII NULLS.

"ftruncate ( )" works just like "truncate ( )" does, except that it takes an open file descriptor as an argument instead of a filename.

They both return a value of −1 if unsuccessful and a value of 0 otherwise.

In the next example, I set the lengths of two files to 10 bytes; one of the files was originally shorter than that length, and the other was longer.

```
$ cat truncate.c              ...list the program.
main ()
{
  truncate ("file1.txt", 10);
  truncate ("file2.txt", 10);
}
$ cat file1.txt               ...list "file1.txt".
short
$ cat file2.txt               ...list "file2.txt".
long file with lots of letters
$ ls -l file*.txt             ...examine both files.
-rw-r--r-- 1 glass         6 May 25 12:16 file1.txt
-rw-r--r-- 1 glass        32 May 25 12:17 file2.txt
$ truncate                    ...run the program.
$ ls -l file*.txt             ...examine both files again.
-rw-r--r-- 1 glass        10 May 25 12:16 file1.txt
-rw-r--r-- 1 glass        10 May 25 12:17 file2.txt
$ cat file1.txt               ..."file1.txt" is longer.
short
$ cat file2.txt               ..."file2.txt" is shorter.
long file
$ _
```

STREAMS

STREAMS is a newer and more generalized I/O facility that was introduced in System V UNIX. STREAMS is most often used to add device drivers to the kernel and to provide an interface to the network drivers, among other uses.

STREAMS was originally developed by Dennis Ritchie, one of the original developers of UNIX, and the implementation of STREAMS provides a full-duplex (two-way) path between kernel space and user-process space. The implementation is more generalized than that of previous I/O mechanisms, making it easier to implement new device drivers. One of the original motivations for the creation and implementation of STREAMS was to clean up and improve traditional UNIX character I/O to terminal devices.

System V–based versions of UNIX also include the Transport Layer Interface (TLI) networking interface to STREAMS drivers, which provides a socket-like interface to the STREAMS-based network drivers in order to communicate with other socket-based programs.

Improvements Over Traditional UNIX I/O   Traditional UNIX character-based I/O had evolved from the early days of UNIX. As with any complex software subsystem, over time, unplanned and unarchitected changes added more complexity. Some of the advantages of STREAMS come simply from the fact that it is newer and can take advantage of some of the lessons learned over the years. This newness yields a cleaner interface than was available before.

STREAMS also makes adding network protocols easier than having to write the whole driver and all of its required parts from scratch. The device-dependent code has been separated out into *modules* so that only this part must be rewritten for each new device. Common I/O housekeeping code (e.g., buffer allocation and management) has been standardized so that each module can leverage services provided by the stream.

The processingof STREAMS involves sending and receiving *streams messages* rather than just doing raw, character-by-character I/O. STREAMS also added flow control and priority processing.

Anatomy of a STREAM   Each STREAM has three parts:

- **stream head**: the access point for a user application, functions, and data structures representing the STREAM
- **module(s)**: code to process data being read or written
- **stream driver**: the back-end code that communicates with the specific device

These parts run in kernel space, although modules can be added from user space. The stream head provides the system-call interface for a user application. A stream head is created by using the "open ( )" system call. The kernel manages any memory allocation required, the *upstream* and *downstream* flow of data, queue scheduling, flow control, and error logging.

Data written to the stream head from an application program is in the form of a message that is passed to the first module for processing. This module does its specific processing on the message and passes the result to the second module. This process continues until the last module passes the message to the stream driver, where the data is written to the appropriate device. Data coming from the device takes the same path, but in the reverse direction.

STREAM System Calls   In addition to the I/O system calls we've already seen—"ioctl ( )", "open ( )", "close ( )", "read ( )", and "write ( )", the following additional system calls are useful with a stream:

- "getmsg ( )": get a message from a stream
- "putmsg ( )": put a message on a stream
- "poll ( )": poll one or more streams for activity
- "isastream ( )": find out if a given file descriptor is a stream

PROCESS MANAGEMENT

Every process in a UNIX system has the following attributes:

- some code (a.k.a. text)
- some data
- a stack
- a unique process ID number (PID)

When UNIX is first started, there's only one visible process in the system. This process is called "init," and it has a process ID of 1. The only way to create a new process in UNIX is to duplicate an existing process, so "init" is the ancestor of all subsequent processes. When a process duplicates, the parent and child processes are virtually identical (except for aspects like PIDs, PPIDs, and runtimes); the child's code, data, and stack are a copy of the parent's, and the processes even continue to execute the same code. A child process may, however, replace its code with that of another executable file, thereby differentiating itself from its parent. For example, when "init" starts executing, it quickly duplicates several times. Each of the duplicate child processes then replaces its code from the executable file called "getty", which is responsible for handling user logins. The process hierarchy therefore looks like this:

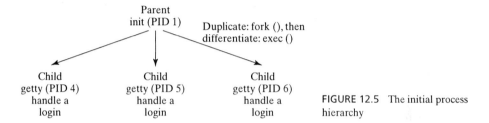

FIGURE 12.5   The initial process hierarchy

When a child process terminates, its death is communicated to its parent so that the parent may take some appropriate action.

It's very common for a parent process to suspend until one of its children terminates. For example, when a shell executes a utility in the foreground, it duplicates into two shell processes; the child-shell process replaces its code with that of the utility, whereas the parent shell waits for the child process to terminate. When the child process terminates, the original parent process awakens and presents the user with the next shell prompt.

Here's an illustration of the way that a shell executes a utility; I've indicated the system calls that are responsible for each phase of the execution:

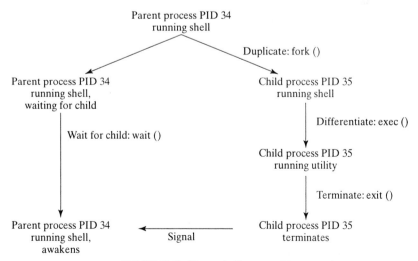

FIGURE 12.6   How a shell runs a utility

The Internet shell that I present later in this chapter has the basic process-management facilities of the classic UNIX shells and is a good place to look for some in-depth coding examples that utilize process-oriented system calls. In the meantime, let's look at some simple programs that introduce the system calls one by one. The next few subsections describe the following system calls:

Name	Function
fork	duplicates a process
getpid	obtains a process' ID number
getppid	obtains a parent process' ID number
exit	terminates a process
wait	waits for a child process
exec..	replaces the code, data, and stack of a process

Creating a New Process: fork ( )

A process may duplicate itself by using "fork ( )", which works like this:

System Call: pid_t fork (void)

"fork ( )" causes a process to duplicate. The child process is an almost-exact duplicate of the original parent process; it inherits a copy of its parent's code, data, stack, open file descriptors, and signal table. However, the parent and child processes have different process ID numbers and parent process ID numbers.

If "fork ( )" succeeds, it returns the PID of the child to the parent process and returns a value of 0 to the child process. If it fails, it returns a value of −1 to the parent process and no child process is created.

"fork ( )" is a strange system call because one process (the original) calls it, but two processes (the original and its child) return from it. Both processes continue to run the same code concurrently, but have completely separate stack and data spaces.

This system call reminds me of a great sci-fi story I read once about a man who comes across a fascinating booth at a circus. The vendor at the booth tells the man that the booth is a matter replicator; anyone who walks through the booth is duplicated. The original person walks out of the booth unharmed, but the duplicate person walks out onto the surface of Mars as a slave of the Martian construction crews. The vendor then tells the man that he'll be given a million dollars if he allows himself to be replicated, and the man agrees. He happily walks through the machine, looking forward to collecting the million dollars . . . and walks out onto the surface of Mars. Meanwhile, back on Earth, his duplicate is walking off with a stash of cash. The question is this: If you came across the booth, what would you do?

A process may obtain its own process ID and parent process ID numbers by using the "getpid ( )" and "getppid ( )" system calls, respectively. Here's a synopsis of these system calls:

System Call: pid_t getpid (void)
　　　　　　　pid_t getppid (void)

"getpid ( )" and "getppid ( )" return a process' ID number and parent process' ID number, respectively. They always succeed. The parent-process ID number of PID 1 is 1.

To illustrate the operation of "fork ( )", as well as of "getpid ( )" and "getppid ()", here's a small program that duplicates and then branches, based on the return value of "fork ( )":

```
$ cat myfork.c                  ...list the program.
#include <stdio.h>
main ()
{
int pid;
 printf ("I'm the original process with PID %d and PPID %d.\n",
         getpid (), getppid ());
pid = fork (); /* Duplicate. Child and parent continue from here */
if (pid != 0) /* pid is non-zero, so I must be the parent */
  {
    printf ("I'm the parent process with PID %d and PPID %d.\n",
            getpid (), getppid ());
    printf ("My child's PID is %d\n", pid);
  }
else /* pid is zero, so I must be the child */
  {
    printf ("I'm the child process with PID %d and PPID %d.\n",
            getpid (), getppid ());
  }
 printf ("PID %d terminates.\n", getpid () ); /* Both processes */
                                             /* execute this */
}
$ myfork                        ...run the program.
I'm the original process with PID 13292 and PPID 13273.
I'm the parent process with PID 13292 and PPID 13273.
My child's PID is 13293.
I'm the child process with PID 13293 and PPID 13292.
```

```
PID 13293 terminates.          ...child terminates.
PID 13292 terminates.          ...parent terminates.
$ _
```

The PPID of the parent process refers to the PID of the shell that executed the "myfork" program.

WARNING: As you will soon see, it is dangerous for a parent process to terminate without waiting for the death of its child. The only reason that the parent doesn't wait for its child to terminate in this example is because I haven't yet described the "wait ()" system call!

Orphan Processes

If a parent dies before its child terminates, the child is automatically adopted by the original "init" process, PID 1. To illustrate this feature, I modified the previous program by inserting a "sleep" statement into the child's code. This statement ensured that the parent process terminated before the child did.

Here's the program and its resultant output:

```
$ cat orphan.c                ...list the program.
#include <stdio.h>
main ()
{
  int pid;
  printf ("I'm the original process with PID %d and PPID %d.\n",
          getpid (), getppid ());
  pid = fork (); /* Duplicate. Child and parent continue from here */
  if (pid != 0) /* Branch based on return value from fork () */
    {
      /* pid is non-zero, so I must be the parent */
      printf ("I'm the parent process with PID %d and PPID %d.\n",
              getpid (), getppid ());
      printf ("My child's PID is %d\n", pid);
    }
  else
    {
      /* pid is zero, so I must be the child */
      sleep (5); /* Make sure that the parent terminates first */
      printf ("I'm the child process with PID %d and PPID %d.\n",
              getpid (), getppid ());
    }
  printf ("PID %d terminates.\n", getpid () ); /* Both processes */
                                              /* execute this */
}
$ orphan                  ...run the program.
I'm the original process with PID 13364 and PPID 13346.
I'm the parent process with PID 13364 and PPID 13346.
PID 13364 terminates.
   I'm the child process with PID 13365 and PPID 1. ...orphaned!
PID 13365 terminates.
$ _
```

Here's an illustration of the orphaning effect:

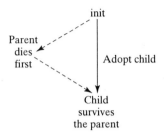

FIGURE 12.7   Adoption

Terminating a Process: exit ()

A process may terminate at any time by executing "exit ( )", which works as follows:

System Call: void exit (int *status*)

"exit ( )" closes all of a process' file descriptors; deallocates its code, data, and stack; and then terminates the process. When a child process terminates, it sends its parent a SIGCHLD signal and waits for its termination code *status* to be accepted. Only the lower eight bits of *status* are used, so values are limited to the range of 0–255. A process that is waiting for its parent to accept its return code is called a *zombie* process. A parent accepts a child's termination code by executing "wait ( )", which is described shortly.

The kernel ensures that all of a terminating process' children are orphaned and adopted by "init" by setting their PPIDs to 1. The "init" process always accepts its childrens' termination codes.

"exit ( )" never returns.

The termination code of a child process may be used for a variety of purposes by the parent process. Shells may access the termination code of their last child process via one of their special variables. For example, the C shell stores the termination code of the last command in the variable $status:

```
% cat myexit.c                    ...list the program.
#include <stdio.h>
main ()
{
 printf ("I'm going to exit with return code 42\n");
 exit (42);
```

```
}
% myexit                        ...run the program.
I'm going to exit with return code 42
% echo $status                  ...display the termination code.
42
% _
```

Zombie Processes

A process that terminates cannot leave the system until its parent accepts its return code. If its parent process is already dead, it'll already have been adopted by the "init" process, which always accepts its childrens' return codes. However, if a process' parent is alive, but the parent never executes a "wait ( )" system call, the process' return code will never be accepted and the process will remain a zombie. A zombie process doesn't have any code, data, or stack, so it doesn't use up many system resources, but it does continue to inhabit the system's fixed-size process table. Too many zombie processes can require the system administrator to intervene; see Chapter 14 for more details.

The next program created a zombie process, which was indicated in the output from the **ps** utility. When I killed the parent process, the child was adopted by "init" and allowed to rest in peace.

```
$ cat zombie.c                  ...list the program.
#include <stdio.h>
main ()
{
 int pid;
 pid = fork (); /* Duplicate */
 if (pid != 0) /* Branch based on return value from fork () */
   {
     while (1) /* Never terminate, and never execute a wait () */
       sleep (1000);
   }
 else
   {
     exit (42); /* Exit with a silly number */
   }
}
$ zombie &                      ...execute the program in the background.
[1] 13545
$ ps                            ...obtain process status.
 PID TT STAT   TIME COMMAND
13535 p2 S      0:00 -ksh (ksh) ...the shell.
13545 p2 S      0:00 zombie      ...the parent process.
13546 p2 Z      0:00 <defunct>   ...the zombie child.
13547 p2 R      0:00 ps
$ kill 13545                    ...kill the parent process.
[1]    Terminated              zombie
$ ps                            ...notice that the zombie is gone now.
 PID TT STAT   TIME COMMAND
```

```
13535 p2 S      0:00 -ksh (ksh)
13548 p2 R      0:00 ps
$ _
```

Waiting for a Child: wait ( )

A parent process may wait for one of its children to terminate and then accept its child's termination code by executing "wait ( )":

System Call: pid_t wait (int* *status*)

"wait ( )" causes a process to suspend until one of its children terminates. A successful call to "wait ( )" returns the PID of the child that terminated and places a status code into *status* that is encoded as follows:

- If the rightmost byte of *status* is zero, the leftmost byte contains the low eight bits of the value returned by the child's "exit ( )" or "return ( )" system call.
- If the rightmost byte is nonzero, the rightmost seven bits are equal to the number of the signal that caused the child to terminate, and the remaining bit of the rightmost byte is set to 1 if the child produced a core dump.

If a process executes a "wait ( )" system call and has no children, "wait ( )" returns immediately with a value of −1. If a process executes a "wait ( )" system call and one or more of its children are already zombies, "wait ( )" returns immediately with the status of one of the zombies.

In the next example, the child process terminated before the end of the program by executing an "exit ( )" system call with return code 42. Meanwhile, the parent process executed a "wait ( )" system call and suspended until it received its child's termination code. At this point, the parent displayed information about its child's demise and executed the rest of the program.

```
$ cat mywait.c                    ...list the program.
#include <stdio.h>
main ()
{
  int pid, status, childPid;
  printf ("I'm the parent process and my PID is %d\n", getpid ());
  pid = fork (); /* Duplicate */
  if (pid != 0) /* Branch based on return value from fork () */
    {
```

```
      printf ("I'm the parent process with PID %d and PPID %d\n",
             getpid (), getppid ());
      childPid = wait (&status); /* Wait for a child to terminate. */
      printf ("A child with PID %d terminated with exit code %d\n",
             childPid, status >> 8);
   }
 else
   {
      printf ("I'm the child process with PID %d and PPID %d\n",
             getpid (), getppid ());
      exit (42); /* Exit with a silly number */
   }
  printf ("PID %d terminates\n", getpid () );
}
$ mywait                          ...run the program.
I'm the parent process and my PID is 13464
I'm the child process with PID 13465 and PPID 13464
I'm the parent process with PID 13464 and PPID 13409
A child with PID 13465 terminated with exit code 42
PID 13465 terminates
$ _
```

Differentiating a Process: exec ( )

A process may replace its current code, data, and stack with those of another executable by using one of the "exec ( )" family of system calls. When a process executes an "exec ( )" system call, its PID and PPID numbers stay the same—only the code that the process is executing changes. The "exec ( )" family works like this:

System Call: int execl (const char* *path*, const char* *arg0*, const char* *arg1*, ..., const char* *argn*, NULL)
int execv (const char* *path*, const char* *argv*[])
int execlp (const char* *path*, const char* *arg0*, const char* *arg1*,..., const char* *argn*, NULL)
int execvp (const char* *path*, const char* *argv*[])

The "exec ( )" family of system calls replaces the calling process' code, data, and stack with those of the executable whose pathname is stored in *path*.

"execl ( )" is identical to "execlp ( )", and "execv ( )" is identical to "execvp ( )", except that "execl ( )" and "execv ( )" require the absolute or relative pathname of the executable file to be supplied, whereas "execlp ( )" and "execvp ( )" use the $PATH environment variable to find *path*.

If the executable is not found, the system call returns a value of −1; otherwise, the calling process replaces its code, data, and stack with those of the executable and starts to execute the new code. A successful "exec ( )" never returns.

"execl ( )" and "execlp ( )" invoke the executable with the string arguments pointed to by *arg1* through *argn*. *arg0* must be the name of the executable file itself, and the list of arguments must be null terminated.

"execv ( )" and "execvp ( )" invoke the executable with the string arguments pointed to by *argv*[1] to *argv*[n], where *argv*[n + 1] is NULL. *argv*[0] must be the name of the executable file itself.

The "exec ( )" family in the previous box isn't really made up of system calls—the C commands are library functions that invoke the "execve ( )" system call. "execve ( )" is hardly ever used directly, as it contains some rarely used options.

In the next example, the program displayed a small message and then replaced its code with that of the "ls" executable. Note that the "execl ( )" call was successful and therefore never returned.

```
$ cat myexec.c                    ...list the program.
#include <stdio.h>
main ()
{
  printf ("I'm process %d and I'm about to exec an ls -l\n", getpid ());
  execl ("/bin/ls", "ls", "-l", NULL); /* Execute ls */
  printf ("This line should never be executed\n");
}
$ myexec                          ...run the program.
I'm process 13623 and I'm about to exec an ls -l
total 125
-rw-r--r-- 1 glass              277 Feb 15 00:47 myexec.c
-rwxr-xr-x 1 glass            24576 Feb 15 00:48 myexec
$ _
```

Changing Directories: chdir ( )

Every process has a *current working directory* that is used when processing a relative pathname. A child process inherits its current working directory from its parent. For example, when a utility is executed from a shell, its process inherits the shell's current working directory. To change a process' current working directory, use "chdir ( )", which works as follows:

System Call: int chdir (const char* *pathname*)

"chdir ( )" sets a process' current working directory to the directory *pathname*. The process must have execute permission from the directory to succeed.

> "chdir ( )" returns a value of 0 if successful; otherwise, it returns a value of −1.

In the following example, the process printed its current working directory before and after executing "chdir ( )" by executing **pwd** using the "system ( )" library routine:

```
$ cat mychdir.c              ...list the source code.
#include <stdio.h>
main ()
{
 system ("pwd"); /* Display current working directory */
 chdir ("/"); /* Change working directory to root directory */
 system ("pwd"); /* Display new working directory */
 chdir ("/home/glass"); /* Change again */
 system ("pwd"); /* Display again */
}
$ mychdir                    ...execute the program.
/home/glass
/
/home/glass
$ _
```

Changing Priorities: nice ( )

Every process has a priority value between −20 and +19 that affects the amount of CPU time that it's allocated. In general, the smaller the priority value, the faster the process will run. Only super-user and kernel processes (described in Chapter 13) can have a negative priority value, and login shells start with a priority value of zero.

A child process inherits its priority value from its parent and may change it by using "nice ( )":

System Call: int nice (int *delta*)

"nice ( )" adds *delta* to a process' current priority value. Only a super-user may specify a *delta* that leads to a negative priority value. Legal priority values lie between −20 and +19. If a *delta* beyond one of these limits is specified, the priority value is truncated to the limit.

If "nice ( )" succeeds, it returns the new priority value; otherwise it returns a value of −1. Note that this return value causes an ambiguity, since a value of −1 is a legal priority value.

In the next example, the process executed **ps** commands before and after a couple of "nice ( )" calls. Note that when the process' priority value became nonzero, it was flagged with an "N" by **ps**, together with the **sh** and **ps** commands that it created due to the "system ( )" library call.

```
$ cat mynice.c              ...list the source code.
#include <stdio.h>
main ()
{
 printf ("original priority\n");
 system ("ps"); /* Execute a ps */
 nice (0); /* Add 0 to my priority */
 printf ("running at priority 0\n");
 system ("ps"); /* Execute another ps */
 nice (10); /* Add 10 to my priority */
 printf ("running at priority 10\n");
 system ("ps"); /* Execute the last ps */
}
$ mynice                    ...execute the program.
original priority
 PID TT STAT TIME COMMAND
15099 p2 S                  0:00 -sh (sh)
15206 p2 S                  0:00 a.out
15207 p2 S                  0:00 sh -c ps
15208 p2 R                  0:00 ps
running at priority 0       ...adding a priority value of zero doesn't
                            ...change the priority.

 PID TT STAT TIME COMMAND
15099 p2 S                  0:00 -sh (sh)
15206 p2 S                  0:00 a.out
15209 p2 S                  0:00 sh -c ps
15210 p2 R                  0:00 ps
running at priority 10      ...adding a priority value of 10 makes them
                            ...run slower.

 PID TT STAT TIME COMMAND
15099 p2 S                  0:00 -sh (sh)
15206 p2 S N                0:00 a.out
15211 p2 S N                0:00 sh -c ps
15212 p2 R N                0:00 ps
$ _
```

Accessing User and Group IDs

Here are the system calls that allow you to read a process' real and effective IDs:

System Call: uid_t getuid ( )
      uid_t geteuid ( )
      gid_t getgid ( )
      gid_t getegid ( )

"getuid ( )" and "geteuid ( )" return the calling process' real and effective user IDs, respectively. "getgid ( )" and "getegid ( )" return the calling process' real and effective group IDs, respectively. The ID numbers correspond to the user and group IDs listed in the "/etc/passwd" and "/etc/group" files.

These calls always succeed.

Here are the system calls that allow you to set a process' real and effective IDs:

System Call: int setuid (uid_t *id*)
int seteuid (uid_t *id*)
int setgid (gid_t *id*)
int setegid (gid_t *id*)

"seteuid ( )" and "setegid ( )" set the calling process' effective user ID and group ID, respectively. "setuid ( )" and "setgid ( )" set the calling process' effective and real user IDs and group IDs, respectively, to the specified value.

These calls succeed only if executed by a super-user, or if *id* is the real or effective user or group ID of the calling process. They return a value of 0 if successful; otherwise, they return a value of −1.

Sample Program: Background Processing

Here's a sample program that makes use of "fork ( )" and "exec ( )" to execute a program in the background. The original process creates a child to "exec" the specified executable and then terminates. The orphaned child is automatically adopted by "init." Notice how I craftily passed the argument list from "main ( )" to "execvp ( )" by passing "&argv[1]" as the second argument to "execvp ( )". Also, note that I used "execvp ( )" instead of "execv ( )" so that the program could use $PATH to find the executable file.

```
$ cat background.c      ...list the program.
#include <stdio.h>
main (argc, argv)
int argc;
char* argv [];

{
    if (fork () == 0) /* Child */
```

```
        {
          execvp (argv[1], &argv[1]); /* Execute other program */
          fprintf (stderr, "Could not execute %s\n", argv [1];
        }
    }
$ background.exe cc wait.c      ...run the program.
$ ps                            ...confirm that "cc" is in.
background.
  PID TT STAT   TIME COMMAND
13664 p0 S     0:00 -csh (csh)
13716 p0 R     0:00 ps
13717 p0 D     0:00 cc wait.c
```

Sample Program: Disk Usage

The next programming example uses a novel technique for counting the number of non-directory files in a hierarchy. When the program is started, its first argument must be the name of the directory to search. It searches through each entry in the directory, spawning off a new process for each entry. Each child process either exits with 1 if its associated file is a non-directory file, or repeats the process, summing up the exit codes of its children and exiting with the total count. This technique is interesting but silly. Not only does it create a large number of processes, which is not particularly efficient, but since it uses the termination code to return the file count, it's limited to an 8-bit total count.

```
$ cat count.c                   ...list the program
#include <stdio.h>
#include <sys/file.h>
#include <sys/dir.h>
#include <sys/stat.h>
long processFile ();
long processDirectory ();
main (argc, argv)
int argc;
char* argv [];
{
  long count;
  count = processFile (argv[1]);
  printf ("Total number of non-directory files is %ld\n", count);
  return (/* EXIT_SUCCESS */ 0);
}
long processFile (name)
char* name;
{
  struct stat statBuf; /* To hold the return data from stat () */
  mode_t mode;
  int result;
  result = stat (name, &statBuf); /* Stat the specified file */
  if (result == -1) return (0); /* Error */
  mode = statBuf.st_mode; /* Look at the file's mode */
  if (S_ISDIR (mode)) /* Directory */
    return (processDirectory (name));
```

```
      else
         return (1); /* A nondirectory file was processed */
      }
long processDirectory (dirName)
char* dirName;
{
int fd, children, i, charsRead, childPid, status;
long count, totalCount;
char fileName [100];
struct dirent dirEntry;
fd = open (dirName, O_RDONLY); /* Open directory for reading */
children = 0; /* Initialize child process count */
 while (1) /* Scan directory */
   {
     charsRead = getdents (fd, &dirEntry, sizeof (struct dirent));
     if (charsRead == 0) break; /* End of directory */
     if (strcmp (dirEntry.d_name, ".") != 0 &&
         strcmp (dirEntry.d_name, "..") != 0)
       {
         if (fork () == 0) /* Create a child to process dir. entry */
           {
             sprintf (fileName, "%s/%s", dirName, dirEntry.d_name);
             count = processFile (fileName);
             exit (count);
           }
         else
           ++children; /* Increment count of child processes */
       }
     lseek (fd, dirEntry.d_off, SEEK_SET); /* Jump to next dir. entry */
   }
close (fd); /* Close directory */
totalCount = 0; /* Initialize file count */
for (i = 1; i <= children; i++) /* Wait for children to terminate */
  {
    childPid = wait (&status); /* Accept child's termination code */
    totalCount += (status >> 8); /* Update file count */
  }
 return (totalCount); /* Return number of files in directory */
}
```

```
$ ls -F                  ...list current directory.
a.out*         disk.c          fork          tmp/        zombie*
background     myexec.c        myfork.c      mywait.c
background.c   myexit.c        orphan.c      mywait*
count*         myexit*         orphan*       zombie.c
$ ls tmp                 ...list only subdirectory.
a.out*         disk.c          myexit.c      orphan.c
background.c   myexec.c        myfork.c      mywait.c
zombie.c
$ count .                ...count regular files from ".".
Total number of non-directory files is 25
$ _
```

Threads

Multiple processes are expensive to create, either anew or by copying an existing process with the "fork ()" system call. Often, a completely new process space is not necessary for a small, yet independent, task in a program. In fact, you may want separate tasks to be able to share some resources in a process, such as memory space or an open device.

When multiprocessor systems became available, it was clear that UNIX needed a better way to take advantage of multiple processors without requiring a new process to be started in order to take advantage of the additional processor.

A *thread* is an abstraction that allows multiple "threads of control" in a single process space. It can almost be thought of as a process within a process (almost). The thread model is similar to the UNIX process model in many ways.

The terminology of some thread implementations can be confusing. You may find the term "light-weight processes" used interchangeably with "thread," or you may find places where they are used differently to distinguish subtle differences. In most cases, the idea of a process of lighter weight (a process that is less expensive) is what is intended. For the purposes of our high-level examination, we will merely refer to *threads*.

Since implementation of thread functionality varies widely in different versions of UNIX, to examine any one particular implementation would unfairly ignore others, and a complete examination of all current implementations is beyond the scope of this introductory text. We therefore will examine UNIX thread functionality at a high level that is common to all implementations. I recommend that you consult the documentation for your version of UNIX for specific system-call information.

Thread Management   Four major functions make up the common thread-management capabilities in most implementations:

- Create: Create a thread.
- Join: Suspend and wait for a created thread to terminate (similar to the "wait ( )" system call between parent and child processes).
- Detach: Allow the thread to release its resources to the system when it finishes and not to require a join. (In this case, an exit value is not available.)
- Terminate: Return resources to the process.

Thread Synchronization   In a multithreaded environment, one or more threads can be created to handle specific tasks. If the tasks are unrelated, the threads can be initiated and run to completion. If any part of the task requires information from another task, processing between threads must be synchronized.

Synchronization can often be accomplished via standard UNIX IPC mechanisms but, most thread libraries also provide synchronization primitives that are most specific to the use of threads.

A *mutex* object can be used to manage mutual exclusion between threads. Mutex objects can be created, destroyed, locked, and unlocked. The attributes of a mutex object are shared between threads and are used to let other threads know the state of the thread that the mutex object describes.

Mutex objects can also be used in conjunction with *conditional variables*, which maintain a value (such as a threshold) to allow more precise management of thread synchronization.

Thread safety   So now you've synchronized the various threads of control in your own program, but what about library functions that they call? Does your code need to synchronize its use, for example, of a graphics library to make sure that two separate threads don't try to write to the same part of the screen at the same time? What about two threads that are using a math library to update shared data? You've synchronized your use of your variables, but do the math functions use any shared variables? Is the function reentrant? That is, can more than one control point be used in the memory space of the function at the same time?

By asking these questions, you are asking if the library is *thread safe*; in other words, is it safe to call the functions in these libraries from a multithreaded program? It probably isn't hard to imagine the kinds of unforeseen problems that can crop up under these circumstances. Unless the vendor or author of the library claims that it is thread safe, you should assume that it is not and write your code accordingly (by managing mutually exclusive access to the library between the various threads in your program).

Other process-related system calls that we've already examined may be affected by the implementation of threads. For example, each thread maintains its own stack, signal mask, and local storage area. Therefore, it may not always be obvious when a system call applies only to the thread or to the entire process running the thread. It will be important for you to find out what effects your threads' implementation may have on other UNIX system calls.

Redirection

When a process forks, the child inherits a copy of its parent's file descriptors. When a process execs, all nonclose-on-exec file descriptors remain unaffected, including the standard input, output, and error channels. The UNIX shells use these two sets of file descriptors to implement redirection. For example, say that you type the following command at a terminal:

```
ls > ls.out
```

To perform the redirection, the shell performs the following series of actions:

- The parent shell forks and then waits for the child shell to terminate.
- The child shell opens the file "ls.out", creating it or truncating it as necessary.
- The child shell then duplicates the file descriptor of "ls.out" to the standard-output file descriptor, number 1, and then closes the original descriptor of "ls.out". All standard output is therefore redirected to "ls.out".
- The child shell then exec's the **ls** utility. Since the file descriptors are inherited during an "exec ( )", all of the standard output of **ls** goes to "ls.out".
- When the child shell terminates, the parent resumes. The parent's file descriptors are unaffected by the child's actions, as each process maintains its own private descriptor table.

To redirect the standard error channel in addition to standard output, the shell simply would have to duplicate the "ls.out" descriptor twice—once to descriptor 1 and once to descriptor 2.

Here's a small program that does approximately the same kind of redirection as a UNIX shell does. When invoked with the name of a file as the first parameter and a command sequence as the remaining parameters, the program "redirect" redirects the standard output of the command to the named file:

```
$ cat redirect.c            ...list the program.
#include <stdio.h>
#include <fcntl.h>
main (argc, argv)
int argc;
char* argv [];
{
    int fd;
     /* Open file for redirection */
    fd = open (argv[1], O_CREAT | O_TRUNC | O_WRONLY, 0600);
    dup2 (fd, 1); /* Duplicate descriptor to standard output */
    close (fd); /* Close original descriptor to save descriptor space */
    execvp (argv[2], &argv[2]); /* Invoke program; will inherit stdout */
    perror ("main"); /* Should never execute */
}
$ redirect ls.out ls -l  ...redirect "ls -l" to "ls.out".
$ cat ls.out             ...list the output file.
total 5
-rw-r-xr-x 1  gglass          0 Feb 15 10:35 ls.out
-rw-r-xr-x 1  gglass        449 Feb 15 10:35 redirect.c
-rwxr-xr-x 1  gglass       3697 Feb 15 10:33 redirect
$ _
```

The Internet shell described at the end of this chapter has better redirection facilities than the standard UNIX shells; it can redirect output to another Internet shell on a remote host.

SIGNALS

Programs must sometimes deal with unexpected or unpredictable events, such as:

- a floating point error
- a power failure
- an alarm clock "ring" (discussed soon)
- the death of a child process
- a termination request from a user (i.e., *Control*-C)
- a suspend request from a user (i.e., *Control*-Z)

These kind of events are sometimes called *interrupts*, as they must interrupt the regular flow of a program in order to be processed. When UNIX recognizes that such an event has occurred, it sends the corresponding process a signal.

There is a unique, numbered signal for each possible event. For example, if a process causes a floating point error, the kernel sends the offending process signal number 8:

FIGURE 12.8   Floating point error signal

The kernel isn't the only entity that can send a signal; any process can send any other process a signal, as long as it has permission to do so. The rules regarding permissions are discussed shortly.

A programmer may arrange for a particular signal to be ignored or to be processed by a special piece of code called a *signal handler*. In the latter case, the process that receives the signal suspends its current flow of control, executes the signal handler, and then resumes the original flow of control when the signal handler finishes.

By learning about signals, you can "protect" your programs from *Control*-C, arrange for an alarm clock signal to terminate your program if it takes too long to perform a task, and learn how UNIX uses signals during everyday operations.

The Defined Signals

Signals are defined in "/usr/include/sys/signal.h". A programmer may choose for a particular signal to trigger a user-supplied signal handler, trigger the default kernel-supplied handler, or be ignored. The default handler usually performs one of the following actions:

- terminate the process and generate a core file (*dump*)
- terminate the process without generating a core image file (*quit*)
- ignore and discard the signal (*ignore*)
- suspend the process (*suspend*)
- resume the process

A List of Signals

Here's a list of the System V prefined signals, along with their respective macro definitions, numerical values, and default actions, as well as a brief description of each:

Macro	#	Default	Description
SIGHUP	1	quit	hang up
SIGINT	2	quit	interrupt
SIGQUIT	3	dump	quit
SIGILL	4	dump	illegal instruction
SIGTRAP	5	dump	trace trap (used by debuggers)
SIGABRT	6	dump	abort
SIGEMT	7	dump	emulator trap instruction
SIGFPE	8	dump	arithmetic exception
SIGKILL	9	quit	kill (cannot be caught, blocked, or ignored)
SIGBUS	10	dump	bus error (bad format address)
SIGSEGV	11	dump	segmentation violation (out-of-range address)
SIGSYS	12	dump	bad argument to system call
SIGPIPE	13	quit	write on a pipe or other socket with no one to read it
SIGALRM	14	quit	alarm clock
SIGTERM	15	quit	software termination signal (default signal sent by kill)
SIGUSR1	16	quit	user signal 1
SIGUSR2	17	quit	user signal 2
SIGCHLD	18	ignore	child status changed
SIGPWR	19	ignore	power fail or restart
SIGWINCH	20	ignore	window size change
SIGURG	21	ignore	urgent socket condition
SIGPOLL	22	exit	pollable event
SIGSTOP	23	quit	stopped (signal)
SIGSTP	24	quit	stopped (user)
SIGCONT	25	ignore	continued
SIGTTIN	26	quit	stopped (tty input)
SIGTTOU	27	quit	stopped (tty output)
SIGVTALRM	28	quit	virtual timer expired
SIGPROF	29	quit	profiling timer expired
SIGXCPU	30	dump	CPU time limit exceeded
SIGXFSZ	31	dump	file size limit exceeded

Terminal Signals

The easiest way to send a signal to a foreground process is by pressing *Control*-C or *Control*-Z from the keyboard. When the terminal driver (the piece of software that supports the terminal) recognizes that *Control*-C was pressed, it sends a SIGINT signal to all of the processes in the current foreground job. Similarly,

Control-Z causes it to send a SIGTSTP signal to all of the processes in the current foreground job. By default, SIGINT terminates a process and SIGTSTP suspends a process. Later in this section, I'll show you how to perform similar actions from a C program.

Requesting an Alarm Signal: alarm ( )

One of the simplest ways to see a signal in action is to arrange for a process to receive an alarm clock signal, SIGALRM, by using "alarm ( )". The default handler for this signal displays the message "Alarm clock" and terminates the process. Here's how "alarm ( )" works:

System Call: unsigned int alarm (unsigned int *count*)

"alarm ( )" instructs the kernel to send the SIGALRM signal to the calling process after *count* seconds. If an alarm had already been scheduled, that alarm is overwritten. If *count* is 0, any pending alarm requests are cancelled.

　　"alarm ( )" returns the number of seconds that remain until the alarm signal is sent.

Here's a small program that uses "alarm ( )", together with its output:

```
$ cat alarm.c              ...list the program.
#include <stdio.h>
main ()
{
 alarm (3); /* Schedule an alarm signal in three seconds */
 printf ("Looping forever...\n");
 while (1);
 printf ("This line should never be executed\n");
}
$ alarm                    ...run the program.
Looping forever...
Alarm clock                ...occurs three seconds later.
$ _
```

The next section shows you how you override a default signal handler and make your program respond specially to a particular signal.

Handling Signals: signal ( )

The previous example program reacted to the alarm signal SIGALRM in the default manner. The "signal ( )" system call may be used to override the default action, and it works as follows:

System Call: void (*signal (int *sigCode*, void (*func*)(int))) (int)

"signal ( )" allows a process to specify the action that it will take when a particular signal is received. The parameter *sigCode* specifies the number of the signal that is to be reprogrammed, and *func* may be one of several values:

- SIG_IGN, which indicates that the specified signal should be ignored and discarded.
- SIG_DFL, which indicates that the kernel's default handler should be used.
- an address of a user-defined function, which indicates that the function should be executed when the specified signal arrives.

The valid signal numbers are stored in "/usr/include/signal.h". The signals SIGKILL and SIGSTP may not be reprogrammed. A child process inherits the signal settings from its parent during a "fork ( )". When a process performs an "exec ( )", previously ignored signals remain ignored, but installed handlers are set back to the default handler.

With the exception of SIGCHLD, signals are not stacked, which means that if a process is sleeping and three identical signals are sent to it, only one of the signals is actually processed.

"signal ( )" returns the previous *func* value associated with *sigCode* if successful; otherwise, it returns a value of −1.

I made a couple of changes to the previous program so that it caught and processed the SIGALRM signal efficiently:

- I installed my own signal handler, "alarmHandler ( )", by using "signal ( )".
- I made the "while" loop less draining on the timesharing system by making use of a system call called "pause ( )". The old version of the "while" loop had an empty code body that caused it to loop very quickly and soak up CPU resources. The new version of the "while" loop suspends each time through the loop until a signal is received.

Before I show you the updated program, here's a description of "pause ( )":

System Call: int pause (void)

"pause ( )" suspends the calling process and returns when the calling process receives a signal. It is most often used to wait efficiently for an alarm signal. "pause ( )" doesn't return anything useful.

Here's the updated version of the previous program:

```
$ cat handler.c                          ...list the program.
#include <stdio.h>
#include <signal.h>
int alarmFlag = 0; /* Global alarm flag */
void alarmHandler (); /* Forward declaration of alarm handler */
/******************************************************************/
main ()
{
  signal (SIGALRM, alarmHandler); /* Install signal handler */
  alarm (3); /* Schedule an alarm signal in three seconds */
  printf ("Looping...\n");
  while (!alarmFlag) /* Loop until flag set */
    {
      pause (); /* Wait for a signal */
    }
  printf ("Loop ends due to alarm signal\n");
    }
/******************************************************************/
void alarmHandler ()
{
  printf ("An alarm clock signal was received\n");
  alarmFlag = 1;
}
$ handler                                ...run the program.
Looping...
An alarm clock signal was received   ...occurs three seconds later.
Loop ends due to alarm signal
$ _
```

Protecting Critical Code and Chaining Interrupt Handlers

The same techniques that I just described may be used to protect critical pieces of code against *Control-C* attacks and other such signals. In these cases, it's common to save the previous value of the handler so that it can be restored after the critical code has executed. Here's the source code of a program that protects itself against SIGINT signals:

```
$ cat critical.c                    ...list the program.
#include <stdio.h>
#include <signal.h>
main ()
{
  void (*oldHandler) (); /* To hold old handler value */
   printf ("I can be Control-C'ed\n");
  sleep (3);
  oldHandler = signal (SIGINT, SIG_IGN); /* Ignore Control-C */
  printf ("I'm protected from Control-C now\n");
  sleep (3);
  signal (SIGINT, oldHandler); /* Restore old handler */
  printf ("I can be Control-C'ed again\n");
```

```
 sleep (3);
 printf ("Bye!\n");
}
$ critical                      ...run the program.
I can be Control-C'ed
^C                              ...Control-C works here.
$ critical                      ...run the program again.
I can be Control-C'ed
I'm protected from Control-C now
^C                              ...Control-C is ignored.
I can be Control-C'ed again
Bye!
$ _
```

Sending Signals: kill ( )

A process may send a signal to another process by using the "kill ( )" system call. "kill ( )" is a misnomer, since many of the signals that it can send do not terminate a process. It's called "kill ( )" because of historical reasons; the main use of signals when UNIX was first designed was to terminate processes. "kill ( )" works like this:

System Call: int kill (pid_t *pid*, int *sigCode*)

"kill ( )" sends the signal with value *sigCode* to the process with PID *pid*. "kill ( )" succeeds and the signal is sent as long as at least one of the following conditions is satisfied:

- The sending process and the receiving process have the same owner.
- The sending process is owned by a super-user.

There are a few variations on the way that "kill ( )" works:

- If *pid* is zero, the signal is sent to all of the processes in the sender's process group.
- If *pid* is −1 and the sender is owned by a super-user, the signal is sent to all processes, including the sender.
- If *pid* is −1 and the sender is not owned by a super-user, the signal is sent to all of the processes owned by the same owner as that of the sender, excluding the sending process.
- If the *pid* is negative, but not −1, the signal is sent to all of the processes in the process group.

Process groups are discussed later in this chapter. If "kill ( )" manages to send at least one signal successfully, it returns a value of 0; otherwise, it returns a value of −1.

Death of Children

When a parent's child terminates, the child process sends its parent a SIGCHLD signal. A parent process often installs a handler to deal with this signal; this handler typically executes a "wait ( )" system call to accept the child's termination code and let the child dezombify.[1]

Alternatively, the parent can choose to ignore SIGCHLD signals, in which case the child dezombifies automatically. One of the socket programs that appears later in this chapter makes use of this feature.

The next example illustrates a SIGCHLD handler and allows a user to limit the amount of time that a command takes to execute. The first parameter of "limit" is the maximum number of seconds that is allowed for execution, and the remaining parameters are the command itself. The program works by performing the following steps:

1. The parent process installs a SIGCHLD handler that is executed when its child process terminates.
2. The parent process forks a child process to execute the command.
3. The parent process sleeps for the specified number of seconds. When it wakes up, it sends its child process a SIGINT signal to kill it.
4. If the child terminates before its parent finishes sleeping, the parent's SIGCHLD handler is executed, causing the parent to terminate immediately.

Here's the source code for and sample output from the program:

```
$ cat limit.c                    ...list the program.
#include <stdio.h>
#include <signal.h>
int delay;
void childHandler ();
/****************************************************************/
main (argc, argv)
int argc;
char* argv[];
{
 int pid;
 signal (SIGCHLD, childHandler); /* Install death-of-child handler */
 pid = fork (); /* Duplicate */
 if (pid == 0) /* Child */
   {
     execvp (argv[2], &argv[2]); /* Execute command */
     perror ("limit"); /* Should never execute */
   }
 else /* Parent */
   {
```

---

[1]Dezombifying means that the child is completely laid to rest and is no longer a zombie.

```
    sscanf (argv[l], "%d", &delay); /* Read delay from command-line */
    sleep (delay); /* Sleep for the specified number of seconds */
    printf ("Child %d exceeded limit and is being killed\n", pid);
    kill (pid, SIGINT); /* Kill the child */
  }
}
/******************************************************************/
void childHandler () /* Executed if the child dies before the parent */
{
  int childPid, childStatus;
  childPid = wait (&childStatus); /* Accept child's termination code */
  printf ("Child %d terminated within %d seconds\n", childPid, delay);
  exit (/* EXITSUCCESS */ 0);
}
$ limit 5 ls               ...run the program; command finishes OK.
a.out          alarm          critical       handler    limit
alarm.c        critical.c     handler.c      limit.c
Child 4030 terminated within 5 seconds
$ limit 4 sleep 100        ...run it again; command takes too long.
Child 4032 exceeded limit and is being killed
$ _
```

Suspending and Resuming Processes

The SIGSTOP and SIGCONT signals suspend and resume a process, respectively. They are used by the UNIX shells that support job control (most besides the Bourne shell) to implement built-in commands like *stop*, *fg*, and *bg*.

In the following example, the main program created two children that both entered an infinite loop and displayed a message every second. The main program waited for three seconds and then suspended the first child. The second child continued to execute as usual. After another three seconds, the parent restarted the first child, waited a little while longer, and then terminated both children.

```
$ cat pulse.c              ...list the program.
#include <signal.h>
#include <stdio.h>
main ()
{
  int pid1;
  int pid2;
  pid1 = fork ();
  if (pid1 == 0) /* First child */
    {
      while (1) /* Infinite loop */
        {
          printf ("pid1 is alive\n");
          sleep (1);
        }
    }
  pid2 = fork (); /* Second child */
```

```
if (pid2 == 0)
  {
    while (1) /* Infinite loop */
      {
        printf ("pid2 is alive\n");
        sleep (1);
      }
  }
sleep (3);
kill (pid1, SIGSTOP); /* Suspend first child */
sleep (3);
kill (pid1, SIGCONT); /* Resume first child */
sleep (3);
kill (pid1, SIGINT); /* Kill first child */
kill (pid2, SIGINT); /* Kill second child */
}
$ pulse                        ...run the program.
pid1 is alive                  ...both run in first three seconds.
pid2 is alive
pid1 is alive
pid2 is alive
pid1 is alive
pid2 is alive
pid2 is alive                  ...just the second child runs now.
pid2 is alive
pid2 is alive
pid1 is alive                  ...the first child is resumed.
pid2 is alive
pid1 is alive
pid2 is alive
pid1 is alive
pid2 is alive
$ _
```

Process Groups and Control Terminals

When you're in a shell and you execute a program that creates several children, a single *Control*-C from the keyboard will normally terminate the program and its children and then return you to the shell. In order to support this kind of behavior, UNIX introduced a few new concepts:

- In addition to having a unique process ID number, every process is also a member of a *process group*. Several processes can be members of the same process group. When a process forks, the child inherits its process group from its parent. A process may change its process group to a new value by using "setpgid ()". When a process execs, its process group remains the same.

- Every process can have an associated *control terminal*, which is typically the terminal where the process was started. When a process forks, the child inherits its control terminal from its parent. When a process execs, its control terminal stays the same.

- Every terminal can be associated with a single *control* process. When a metacharacter such as a *Control*-C is detected, the terminal sends the appropriate signal to all of the processes in the process group of its control process.
- If a process attempts to read from its control terminal and is not a member of the same process group as the terminal's control process, the process is sent a SIGTTIN signal, which normally suspends the process.

Here's how a shell uses these features:

- When an interactive shell begins, it is the control process of a terminal and has that terminal as its control terminal. How this set-up occurs is beyond the scope of this book.
- When a shell executes a foreground process, the child shell places itself in a different process group before exec'ing the command and takes control of the terminal. Any signals generated from the terminal thus go to the foreground command rather than to the original parent shell. When the foreground command terminates, the original parent shell takes back control of the terminal.
- When a shell executes a background process, the child shell places itself in a different process group before exec'ing, but does not take control of the terminal. Any signals generated from the terminal continue to go to the shell. If the background process tries to read from its control terminal, it is suspended by a SIGTTIN signal.

The diagram in Figure 12.9 illustrates a typical setup. Assume that process 145 and process 230 are the process leaders of background jobs and that process 171 is the process leader of the foreground job.

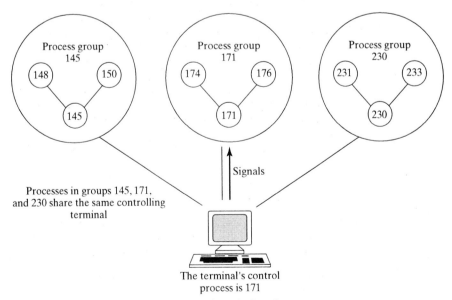

FIGURE 12.9   Control terminals and process groups

"setpgid ( )" changes a process' group, and it works as follows:

System Call: pid_t setpgid (pid_t *pid*, pid_t *pgrpId*)

"setpgid ( )" sets the process-group ID of the process with PID *pid* to *pgrpId*. If *pid* is zero, the caller's process group ID is set to *pgrpId*. In order for "setpgid ( )" to succeed and set the process group ID, at least one of the following conditions must be met:

- The caller and the specified process must have the same owner.
- The caller must be owned by a super-user.

When a process wants to start its own unique process group, it typically passes its own process ID number as the second parameter of "setpgid ( )".
   If "setpgid ( )" fails, it returns a value of −1.

A process may find out its current process-group ID by using "getpgid ( )", which works like this:

System Call: pid_t getpgid (pid_t *pid*)

"getpgid ( )" returns the process group ID of the process with PID *pid*. If *pid* is zero, the process group ID of the caller is returned.

The next example illustrates the fact that a terminal distributes signals to all of the processes in its control process' process group. Since the child inherited its process group from its parent, both the parent and child caught the SIGINT signal.

```
$ cat pgrp1.c                              ...list program.
#include <signal.h>
#include <stdio.h>
void sigintHandler ();
main ()
{
signal (SIGINT, sigintHandler); /* Handle Control-C */
if (fork () == 0)
 printf ("Child PID %d PGRP %d waits\n", getpid (),getpgid (0));
else
 printf ("Parent PID %d PGRP %d waits\n", getpid (), getpgid (0));
```

```
pause (); /* Wait for a signal */
}
void sigintHandler ()
{
printf ("Process %d got a SIGINT\n",getpid ());
}
$ pgrp1                                    ...run the program.
Parent PID 24583 PGRP 24583 waits
Child PID 24584 PGRP 24583 waits
^C                                         ...press Control-C.
Process 24584 got a SIGINT
Process 24583 got a SIGINT
$ _
```

If a process places itself into a different process group, then it is no longer associated with the terminal's control process and does not receive signals from the terminal. In the following example, the child process was not affected by *Control*-C:

```
$ cat pgrp2.c                          ...list the program.
#include <signal.h>
#include <stdio.h>
void sigintHandler ();
main()
{
 int i;
  signal (SIGINT, sigintHandler); /* Install signal handler */
 if (fork () == 0)
  setpgid (0, getpid ()); /* Place child in its own process group */
 printf ("Process PID %d PGRP %d waits\n", getpid (), getpgid (0));
 for (i = 1; i <= 3; i++) /* Loop three times */
   {
     printf ("Process %d is alive\n", getpid ());
     sleep(1);
   }
}
void sigintHandler ()
{
 printf ("Process %d got a SIGINT\n", getpid ());
 exit (1);
}
$ pgrp2                                ...run the program.
Process PID 24591 PGRP 24591 waits
Process PID 24592 PGRP 24592 waits
^C                                     ...type Control-C
Process 24591 got a SIGINT            ...parent receives signal.
Process 24592 is alive                ...child carries on.
Process 24592 is alive
Process 24592 is alive
$ _
```

If a process attempts to read from its control terminal after it disassociates itself with the terminal's control process, it is sent a SIGTTIN signal, which suspends the receiver by default. In the following example, I trapped SIGTTIN with my own handler to make the effect a little clearer:

```
$ cat pgrp3.c                  ...list the program.
#include <signal.h>
#include <stdio.h>
#include <sys/termio.h>
#include <fcntl.h>
void sigttinHandler ();
main ()
{
  int status;
  char str [100];
    if (fork () == 0) /* Child */
    {
        signal (SIGTTIN, sigttinHandler); /* Install handler */
        setpgid (0, getpid ()); /* Place myself in a new process group */
        printf ("Enter a string: ");
        scanf ("%s", str); /* Try to read from control terminal */
        printf ("You entered %s\n", str);
    }
else /* Parent */
    {
        wait (&status); /* Wait for child to terminate */
    }
}
void sigttinHandler ()
{
printf ("Attempted inappropriate read from control terminal\n");
exit (1);
}
$ pgrp3                  ...run the program.
Enter a string: Attempted inappropriate read from control terminal
$ _
```

IPC

Interprocess communication (IPC) is the generic term describing how two processes may exchange information with each other. In general, the two processes may be running on the same machine or on different machines, although some IPC mechanisms may only support local usage (e.g., signals and pipes). This communication may be an exchange of data for which two or more processes are cooperatively processing the data or synchronization information to help two independent, but related, processes schedule work so that they do not destructively overlap.

Pipes

Pipes are an interprocess communication mechanism that allow two or more processes to send information to each other. They are commonly used from within shells to connect the standard output of one utility to the standard input of another. For example, here's a simple shell command that determines how many users there are on the system:

```
$ who | wc -1
```

The **who** utility generates one line of output per user. This output is then "piped" into the **wc** utility, which, when invoked with the "-l" option, outputs the total number of lines in its input. Thus, the pipelined command craftily calculates the total number of users by counting the number of lines that **who** generates. Here's a diagram of the pipeline:

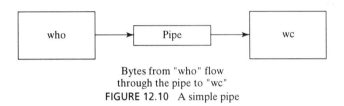

Bytes from "who" flow
through the pipe to "wc"
FIGURE 12.10   A simple pipe

It's important to realize that both the writer process and the reader process of a pipeline execute concurrently; a pipe automatically buffers the output of the writer and suspends the writer if the pipe gets too full. Similarly, if a pipe empties, the reader is suspended until some more output becomes available.

All versions of UNIX support *unnamed* pipes, which are the kind of pipes that shells use. System V also supports a more powerful kind of pipe called a *named pipe*. In this section, I'll show you how to construct both kinds of pipe, starting with unnamed pipes.

Unnamed Pipes: "pipe ( )"   An unnamed pipe is a unidirectional communications link that automatically buffers its input (the maximum size of the input varies with different versions of UNIX, but is approximately 5K) and may be created using the "pipe ( )" system call. Each end of a pipe has an associated file descriptor. The "write" end of the pipe may be written to using "write ( )", and the "read" end may be read from using "read ( )". When a process has finished with a pipe's file descriptor, it should close it using "close ( )". Here's how "pipe ( )" works:

System Call: int pipe (int *fd* [2])

"pipe ( )" creates an unnamed pipe and returns two file descriptors: The descriptor associated with the "read" end of the pipe is stored in *fd*[0], and the descriptor associated with the "write" end of the pipe is stored in *fd*[1].

The following rules apply to processes that read from a pipe:

- If a process reads from a pipe whose "write" end has been closed, the "read ( )" call returns a value of zero, indicating the end of input.
- If a process reads from an empty pipe whose "write" end is still open, it sleeps until some input becomes available.
- If a process tries to read more bytes from a pipe than are present, all of the current contents are returned and "read ( )" returns the number of bytes actually read.

The following rules apply to processes that write to a pipe:

- If a process writes to a pipe whose "read" end has been closed, the write fails and the writer is sent a SIGPIPE signal. The default action of this signal is to terminate the receiver.
- If a process writes fewer bytes to a pipe than the pipe can hold, the "write ( )" is guaranteed to be atomic; that is, the writer process will complete its system call without being preempted by another process. If a process writes more bytes to a pipe than the pipe can hold, no similar guarantees of atomicity apply.

Since access to an unnamed pipe is via the file descriptor mechanism, typically only the process that creates a pipe and its descendants may use the pipe.[2] "lseek ( )" has no meaning when applied to a pipe.

If the kernel cannot allocate enough space for a new pipe, "pipe ( )" returns a value of −1; otherwise, it returns a value of 0.

Assume that the following code was executed:

```
int fd [2];
pipe (fd);
```

In such a case, the data structures shown in Figure 12.11 would be created.

---

[2]In advanced situations, it is actually possible to pass file descriptors to unrelated processes via a pipe.

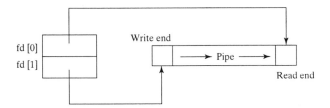

fd [0]

fd [1]

Write end

Pipe

Read end

FIGURE 12.11 An unnamed pipe

Unnamed pipes are usually used for communication between a parent process and its child, with one process writing and the other process reading. The typical sequence of events for such a communication is as follows:

1. The parent process creates an unnamed pipe using "pipe ( )".
2. The parent process forks.
3. The writer closes its "read" end of the pipe, and the designated reader closes its "write" end of the pipe.
4. The processes communicate by using "write ( )" and "read ( )" calls.
5. Each process closes its active pipe descriptor when it's finished with it.

Bidirectional communication is only possible by using two pipes.

Here's a small program that uses a pipe to allow the parent to read a message from its child:

```
$ cat talk.c                     ...list the program.
#include <stdio.h>
#define READ 0          /* The index of the "read" end of the pipe */
#define WRITE 1         /* The index of the "write" end of the pipe */
char* phrase = "Stuff this in your pipe and smoke it";
main ()
{
int fd [2], bytesRead;
char message [100]; /* Parent process' message buffer */
 pipe (fd); /*Create an unnamed pipe */
if (fork () == 0) /* Child, writer */
 {
   close(fd[READ]); /* Close unused end */
   write (fd[WRITE],phrase, strlen (phrase) + 1); /* include NULL*/
   close (fd[WRITE]); /* Close used end*/
 }
else /* Parent, reader*/
 {
   close (fd[WRITE]); /* Close unused end */
   bytesRead = read (fd[READ], message, 100);
   printf ("Read %d bytes: %s\n", bytesRead, message); /* Send */
   close (fd[READ]); /* Close usedend */
 }
}
$ talk                           ...run the program.
Read 37 bytes: Stuff this in your pipe and smoke it
$ _
```

Notice that the child included the phrase's NULL terminator as part of the message so that the parent could easily display it. When a writer process sends more than one variable-length message into a pipe, it must use a protocol to indicate to the reader the location for the end of the message. Methods for such indication include:

- sending the length of a message (in bytes) before sending the message itself
- ending a message with a special character such as a new line or a NULL

The UNIX shells use unnamed pipes to build pipelines. They use a trick similar to the redirection mechanism described in the "Process Management" section to connect the standard output of one process to the standard input of another. To illustrate this approach, here's the source code of a program that executes two named programs, connecting the standard output of the first to the standard input of the second. It assumes that neither program is invoked with options and that the names of the programs are listed on the command-line.

```
$ cat connect.c                       ...list the program.
#include <stdio.h>
#define READ    0
#define WRITE   1
main (argc, argv)
int argc;
char* argv [];
{
  int fd [2];
    pipe (fd); /* Create an unamed pipe */
    if (fork () != 0) /* Parent, writer */
      {
        close (fd[READ]); /* Close unused end */
        dup2 (fd[WRITE], 1); /* Duplicate used end to stdout */
        close (fd[WRITE]); /* Close original used end */
        execlp (argv[1], argv[1], NULL); /* Execute writer program */
        perror ("connect"); /* Should never execute */
      }
  else /* Child, reader */
      {
        close (fd[WRITE]);      /* Close unused end */
        dup2 (fd[READ], 0);     /* Duplicate used end to stdin */
        close (fd[READ]);       /* Close original used end */
        execlp (argv[2], argv[2], NULL);    /* Execute reader program */
        perror ("connect");     /* Should never execute */
    }
}
}
$ who                                 ...execute "who" by itself.
gglass                    ttyp0            Feb 15 18:45 (xyplex_3)
$ connect who wc                      ...pipe "who" through "wc".
        1         6         57    ...1 line, 6 words, 57 chars.
$ _
```

For a more sophisticated example of the use of unnamed pipes, refer to the Internet shell that is described later in this chapter. Also, note that the chapter review contains an interesting exercise that involves building a ring of pipes.

Named Pipes   Named pipes, often referred to as FIFOs (first in, first out), are less restricted than unnamed pipes and offer the following advantages:

- They have a name that exists in the file system.
- They may be used by unrelated processes.
- They exist until explicitly deleted.

Unfortunately, they are only supported by System V. All of the pipe rules that I mentioned in the "Unnamed Pipes" section apply to named pipes as well, except that named pipes have a larger buffer capacity, typically about 40K.

Named pipes exist as special files in the file system and may be created in one of two ways:

- by using the UNIX **mknod** utility
- by using the "mknod ( )" system call

To create a named pipe using **mknod**, use the "p" option. For more information about **mknod**, see Chapter 14. The mode of the named pipe may be set using **chmod**, allowing others to access the pipe that you create. Here's an example of this procedure, executed from a Korn shell:

```
$ mknod myPipe p                       ...create pipe.
$ chmod ug+rw myPipe                   ...update permissions.
$ ls -lg myPipe                        ...examine attributes.
prw-rw----  1 glass         cs         0 Feb 27 12:38 myPipe
$ _
```

Note that the type of the named pipe is "p" in the **ls** listing.

To create a named pipe using "mknod ( )", specify "S_IFIFO" as the file mode. The mode of the pipe can then be changed using "chmod ( )". Here's a snippet of C code that creates a named pipe with read and write permissions for the owner and group:

```
mknod ("myPipe", SIFIFO, 0); /* Create a named pipe */
chmod ("myPipe", 0660); /* Modify its permission flags */
```

Regardless of how you go about creating a named pipe, the end result is the same: A special file is added into the file system. Once a named pipe is opened using "open ( )", "write ( )" adds data at the start of the FIFO queue, and "read ( )" removes data from the end of the FIFO queue. When a process has finished using a named pipe, it should close it using "close ( )", and when a named pipe is no longer needed, it should be removed from the file system using "unlink ( )".

Like an unnamed pipe, a named pipe is intended only for use as a unidirectional link. Writer processes should open a named pipe for writing only, and reader processes should open a pipe for reading only. Although a process can open a named pipe for both reading and writing, this usage doesn't have much practical application. Before I show you an example program that uses named pipes, here are a couple of special rules concerning their use:

- If a process tries to open a named pipe for reading only and no process currently has it open for writing, the reader will wait until a process opens it for writing, unless O_NONBLOCK or O_NDELAY is set, in which case "open ( )" succeeds immediately.
- If a process tries to open a named pipe for writing only and no process currently has it open for reading, the writer will wait until a process opens it for reading, unless O_NONBLOCK or O_NDELAY is set, in which case "open ( )" fails immediately.
- Named pipes will not work across a network.

The next example uses two programs, "reader" and "writer", to demonstrate the use of named pipes, and it works like this:

- A single reader process that creates a named pipe called "aPipe" is executed. It then reads and displays NULL-terminated lines from the pipe until the pipe is closed by all of the writing processes.
- One or more writer processes are executed, each of which opens the named pipe called "aPipe" and sends three messages to it. If the pipe does not exist when a writer tries to open it, the writer retries every second until it succeeds. When all of a writer's messages are sent, the writer closes the pipe and exits.

Following are some sample output and then the source code for each file:

Sample Output

```
$ reader & writer & writer &    ...start 1 reader, 2 writers.
[1] 4698                        ...reader process.
[2] 4699                        ...first writer process.
[3] 4700                        ...second writer process.
Hello from PID 4699
Hello from PID 4700
Hello from PID 4699
Hello from PID 4700
Hello from PID 4699
Hello from PID 4700
[2]    Done            writer   ...first writer exits.
[3]    Done            writer   ...second writer exits.
[1]    Done            reader   ...reader exits.
$ _
```

Reader Program

```
#include <stdio.h>
#include <sys/types.h>
#include <sys/stat.h>              /* For SIFIFO */
#include <fcntl.h>
/****************************************************************************/
main ()
```

```
{
  int fd;
  char str[100];
  unlink("aPipe"); /* Remove named pipe if it already exists */
  mknod ("aPipe", S_IFIFO, 0); /* Create named pipe */
  chmod ("aPipe", 0660); /* Change its permissions */
  fd = open ("aPipe", O_RDONLY); /* Open it for reading */
    while (readLine (fd, str)) /* Display received messages */
      printf ("%s\n", str);
    close (fd); /* Close pipe */
}
/*************************************************************************/
readLine (fd, str)
int fd;
char* str;
/* Read a single NULL-terminated line into str from fd */
/* Return 0 when the end of input is reached and 1 otherwise */
{
  int n;
  do /* Read characters until NULL or end of input */
    {
      n = read (fd, str, 1); /* Read one character */
    }
  while (n > 0 && *str++ != NULL);
  return (n > 0); /* Return false if end of input */
}
```

Writer Program

```
#include <stdio.h>
#include <fcntl.h>
/*************************************************************************/
main ()
{
  int fd, messageLen, i;
  char message [100];
  /* Prepare message */
  sprintf (message, "Hello from PID %d", getpid ());
  messageLen = strlen (message) + 1;
  do /* Keep trying to open the file until successful */
    {
      fd = open ("aPipe", O_WRONLY); /* Open named pipe for writing */
      if (fd == -1) sleep (1); /* Try again in 1 second */
    }
  while (fd == -1);
  for (i = 1; i <= 3; i++) /* Send three messages */
    {
      write (fd, message, messageLen); /* Write message down pipe */
      sleep (3); /* Pause a while */
    }
  close (fd); /* Close pipe descriptor */
}
```

Sockets

Sockets are the traditional UNIX interprocess communication mechanism that allows processes to talk to each other, even if they're on different machines. It is this across-network capability that makes them so useful. For example, the **rlogin** utility, which allows a user on one machine to log into a remote host, is implemented using sockets. Other common uses of sockets include:

- printing a file on one machine from another machine
- transferring files from one machine to another machine

Process communication via sockets is based on the client–server model. One process, known as a server process, creates a socket whose name is known by other client processes. These client processes can talk to the server process via a connection to its named socket. To do so, a client process first creates an unnamed socket and then requests that it be connected to the server's named socket. A successful connection returns one file descriptor to the client and one to the server, both of which may be used for reading and writing. Note that unlike pipes, socket connections are bidirectional. Here's an illustration of the process:

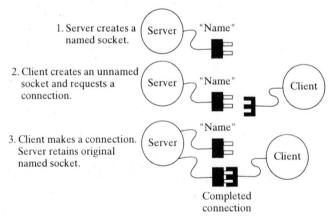

FIGURE 12.12   The socket connection

Once a socket connection is made, it's quite common for the server process to fork a child process to converse with the client while the original parent process continues to accept other client connections. A typical example of this scenario is a remote print server: The server process accepts a client that wishes to send a file for printing and then forks a child to perform the file transfer. The parent process meanwhile waits for more client print requests.

In the coming sections, we'll take a look at the following topics:

- the different kinds of sockets
- how a server creates a named socket and waits for connections
- how a client creates an unnamed socket and requests a connection from a server

- how a server and client communicate after a socket connection is made
- how a socket connection is closed
- how a server can create a child process to converse with the client

The Different Kinds of Sockets   The various kinds of sockets may be classified according to three attributes:

- the *domain*
- the *type*
- the *protocol*

Domains   The domain of a socket indicates where the server and client sockets may reside; some of the domains that are currently supported include:

- AF_UNIX (the clients and server must be on the same machine)
- AF_INET (the clients and server may be anywhere on the Internet)
- AF_NS (the clients and server may be on a XEROX network system)

AF stands for "address family." There is a similar set of constants that begin with PF, which stands for "protocol family" (e.g., PF_UNIX, PF_INET, etc.). Either set may be used, as they are equivalent. This book contains information about AF_UNIX and AF_INET sockets, but not about AF_NS sockets.

Types   The type of a socket determines the type of communication that can exist between the client and server; the two main types that are currently supported are:

- SOCK_STREAM: sequenced, reliable, based on a two-way connection, streams of bytes of variable length
- SOCK_DGRAM: like telegrams; connectionless, unreliable, fixed-length messages

Other types that are either in the planning stages or are implemented only in some domains include:

- SOCK_SEQPACKET: sequenced, reliable, based on a two-way connection, packets of bytes of a fixed length
- SOCK_RAW: provides access to internal network protocols and interfaces

This book contains information only on how to use SOCK_STREAM sockets, which are the most common. These sockets are both intuitive and easy to use.

Protocols   The protocol value specifies the low-level means by which the socket type is implemented. System calls that expect a protocol parameter accept zero as meaning "the correct protocol"; in other words, the protocol value is something that you generally won't have to worry about. Most systems support protocols other than zero only as an optional extra, so I'll use the default protocol in all of the examples in this book.

Writing Socket Programs   Any program that uses sockets must include the header files "/usr/include/sys/types.h" and "/usr/include/sys/socket.h". Additional header files must be included based on the socket domain that you wish to use. The most commonly used domains are:

Domain	Additional header files
AF_UNIX	/usr/include/sys/un.h
AF_INET	/usr/include/netinet/in.h /usr/include/arpa/inet.h /urs/include/netdb.h

Other socket domains are to be defined in "socket.h".

To clearly illustrate the way in which a program that uses sockets is written, I'll build my description of the socket-oriented system calls around a small client–server example that uses AF_UNIX sockets. Once I've shown you this example, I'll show you another example that uses AF_INET sockets. The AF_UNIX example is made up of two programs:

- "chef", the server, which creates a named socket called "recipe" and writes the recipe to any clients who request it. The recipe is a collection of NULL-terminated strings of variable length.
- "cook", the client, which connects to the named socket called "recipe" and reads the recipe from the server. It displays the recipe to standard output as it reads it and then terminates.

The "chef" server process runs in the background. Any client "cook" processes that connect to the server cause the server to fork a duplicate server to handle the recipe transfer, allowing the original server to accept other incoming connections. Here's some sample output from the "chef" and "cook" example:

```
$ chef &          ...run the server in the background.
[1] 5684
$ cook            ...run a client to display the recipe.
spam, spam, spam, spam,
spam, and spam.
$ cook            ...run another client to display the recipe.
spam, spam, spam, spam,
spam, and spam.
$ kill %1         ...kill the server.
[1] Terminated   chef
$ _
```

"Chef" and "Cook" Listing   This section contains the complete listing of the "chef" and "cook" programs. I suggest that you quickly skim through the code and then read the sections that follow for details on how they both work. I have purposely left out a great deal of error checking in the interests of space.

"CHEF" SERVER

```
1   #include <stdio.h>
2   #include <signal.h>
3   #include <sys/types.h>
4   #include <sys/socket.h>
5   #include <sys/un.h>          /* For AFUNIX sockets */
6
7   #define DEFAULT_PROTOCOL   0
8
9   /*******************************************************************/
10
11  main ()
12
13  {
14    int serverFd, clientFd, serverLen, clientLen;
15    struct sockaddr_un serverUNIXAddress;/* Server address */
16    struct sockaddr_un clientUNIXAddress; /* Client address */
17    struct sockaddr* serverSockAddrPtr; /* Ptr to server address */
18    struct sockaddr* clientSockAddrPtr; /* Ptr to client address */
19
20    /* Ignore death-of-child signals to prevent zombies */
21    signal (SIGCHLD, SIG_IGN);
22
23    serverSockAddrPtr = (struct sockaddr*) &serverUNIXAddress;
24    serverLen = sizeof (serverUNIXAddress);
25
26    clientSockAddrPtr = (struct sockaddr*) &clientUNIXAddress;
27    clientLen = sizeof (clientUNIXAddress);
28
29    /* Create a UNIX socket, bidirectional, default protocol */
30    serverFd = socket (AF_UNIX, SOCK_STREAM, DEFAULT_PROTOCOL);
31    serverUNIXAddress.sun_family = AF_UNIX; /* Set domain type */
32    strcpy (serverUNIXAddress.sun_path, "recipe"); /* Set name */
33    unlink ("recipe"); /* Remove file if it already exists */
34    bind (serverFd, serverSockAddrPtr, serverLen); /* Create file */
35    listen (serverFd, 5); /* Maximum pending connection length */
36
37    while (1) /* Loop forever */
38      {
39        /* Accept a client connection */
40        clientFd = accept (serverFd, clientSockAddrPtr, &clientLen);
41
42        if (fork () == 0) /* Create child to send receipe */
43          {
44            writeRecipe (clientFd); /* Send the recipe */
45            close (clientFd); /* Close the socket */
46            exit (/* EXIT_SUCCESS */ 0); /* Terminate */
47          }
48        else
49          close (clientFd); /* Close the client descriptor */
```

```
50      }
51  }
52
53  /*****************************************************************/
54
55  writeRecipe (fd)
56
57  int fd;
58
59  {
60    static char* line1 = "spam, spam, spam, spam,";
61    static char* line2 ="spam, and spam.";
62    write (fd, line1, strlen (line1) + 1); /* Write first line */
63    write (fd, line2, strlen (line2) + 1); /* Write second line */
64  }
```

"COOK" CLIENT

```
1   #include <stdio.h>
2   #include <signal.h>
3   #include <sys/types.h>
4   #include <sys/socket.h>
5   #include <sys/un.h>  /* For AFUNIX sockets */
6
7   #define DEFAULT_PROTOCOL   0
8
9   /*****************************************************************/
10
11  main ()
12
13  {
14    int clientFd, serverLen, result;
15    struct sockaddr_un serverUNIXAddress;
16    struct sockaddr* serverSockAddrPtr;
17
18    serverSockAddrPtr = (struct sockaddr*) &serverUNIXAddress;
19    serverLen = sizeof (serverUNIXAddress);
20
21    /* Create a UNIX socket, bidirectional, default protocol */
22    clientFd = socket (AF_UNIX, SOCK_STREAM, DEFAULT_PROTOCOL);
23    serverUNIXAddress.sun_family = AF_UNIX; /* Server domain */
24    strcpy (serverUNIXAddress.sun_path, "recipe"); /* Server name */
25
26    do /* Loop until a connection is made with the server */
27      {
28        result = connect (clientFd, serverSockAddrPtr, serverLen);
29        if (result == -1) sleep (1); /* Wait and then try again */
30      }
31    while (result == -1);
32
```

```
33   readRecipe (clientFd); /* Read the recipe */
34   close (clientFd); /* Close the socket */
35   exit (/* EXIT_SUCCESS */ 0); /* Done */
36   }
37
38   /********************************************************************/
39
40   readRecipe (fd)
41
42   int fd;
43
44   {
45     char str[200];
46
47     while (readLine (fd, str)) /* Read lines until end of input */
48        printf ("%s\n", str); /* Echo line from socket */
49   }
50
51   /********************************************************************/
52
53   readLine (fd, str)
54
55   int fd;
56   char* str;
57
58   /* Read a single NULL-terminated line */
59
60   {
61     int n;
62
63     do /* Read characters until NULL or end of input */
64        {
65          n = read (fd,str, 1); /* Read one character */
66        }
67     while (n > 0 && *str++ != NULL);
68     return (n > 0); /* Return false if end of input */
69   }
```

Analyzing the Source Code   Now that you've glanced at the program, it's time to go back and analyze it. The next few subsections cover the following topics:

- an overview of a server
- creating a server socket
- naming a server socket
- specifying the maximum number of pending connections to a server socket
- accepting connections on a server socket
- serving a client
- an overview of a client
- creating a client socket

- connecting a client socket to the server socket
- communicating via sockets

The Server   A server is the process that's responsible for creating a named socket and accepting connections to it. To accomplish this task, it must use the following system calls in the order in which they presented:

Name	Meaning
socket	creates an unnamed socket
bind	gives the socket a name
listen	specifies the maximum number of pending connections
accept	accepts a socket connection from a client

The next few subsections describe each of these system calls.

Creating a Socket: socket ( )   A process may create a socket by using "socket ( )", which works like this:

System Call: int socket (int *domain*, int *type*, int *protocol*)

"socket ( )" creates an unnamed socket of the specified domain, type, and protocol. The legal values of these parameters were described earlier in this section.
   If "socket ( )" is successful, it returns a file descriptor associated with the newly created socket; otherwise, it returns a value of −1.

The "chef" server creates its unnamed socket on line 30:

```
30 serverFd = socket (AF_UNIX, SOCK_STREAM, DEFAULT_PROTOCOL);
```

Naming a Socket: bind ( )   Once the server has created an unnamed socket, it must bind it to a name by using "bind ( )", which works like this:

System Call: int bind (int *fd*, const struct sockaddr* *address*, size_t
　　addressLen)

"bind ( )" associates the unnamed socket represented by file descriptor
fd with the socket address stored in *address*. *addressLen* must contain
the length of the address structure. The type and value of the incoming
address depend on the socket domain.

　　If the socket is in the AF_UNIX domain, a pointer to a "sock-
addr_un" structure must be cast to a "sockaddr*" and passed in as
address. This structure has two fields that should be set as follows:

FIELD	ASSIGN THE VALUE
sun_family	AF_UNIX
sun_path	the full UNIX pathname of the socket (absolute or relative)

　　If the named AF_UNIX socket already exists, an error occurs, so
it's a good idea to "unlink ( )" a name before attempting to bind to it.

　　If the socket is in the AF_INET domain, a pointer to a "sock-
addr_in" structure must be cast to a "sockaddr" and passed in as address.
This structure has four fields that should be set as follows:

FIELD	ASSIGN THE VALUE
sin_family	AF_INET
sin_port	the port number of the Internet socket
sin_addr	a structure of type "in_addr" that holds the Internet address
sin_zero	leave empty

　　For more information about Internet ports and addresses, please
consult the Internet-specific part of this section.

　　If "bind ( )" succeeds, it returns a value of 0; otherwise, it returns a
value of −1.

The "chef" server assigns the "sockaddr_un" fields and performs a "bind ()"
on lines 31 to 34:

```
31 serverUNIXAddress.sun_family = AF_UNIX; /* Set domain type */
32 strcpy (serverUNIXAddress.sun_path, "recipe"); /* Set name */
33 unlink ("recipe"); /* Remove file if it already exists */
34 bind (serverFd, serverSockAddrPtr, serverLen); /* Create file */
```

Creating a Socket Queue: listen ( )   When a server process is servicing a client connection, it's always possible that another client will also attempt a connection. The "listen ( )" system call allows a process to specify the number of pending connections that may be queued, and it works like this:

System Call: int listen (int *fd*, int *queueLength*)

"listen ( )" allows you to specify the maximum number of pending connections on a socket. If a client attempts a connection to a socket whose queue is full, it is denied.

The "chef" server listens to its named socket on line 35, where it specifies a maximum queue length of five:

```
35   listen (serverFd, 5); /* Maximum pending connection length */
```

Accepting a Client: accept ( )   Once a socket has been created, named, and its queue size has been specified, the final step is to accept connection requests from clients. To do so, the server must use "accept ( )", which works as follows:

System Call: int accept (int *fd*, struct sockaddr* *address*, int*
　　　　　addressLen)

"accept ( )" listens to the named server socket referenced by *fd* and waits until a connection request from a client is received. When this event occurs, "accept ( )" creates an unnamed socket with the same attributes as those of the original named server socket, connects it to the client's socket, and returns a new file descriptor that may be used for communication with the client. The original named server socket may be used to accept more connections.

The *address* structure is filled with the address of the client and is normally only used in conjunction with Internet connections. The *addressLen* field should be initially set to point to an integer containing the size of the structure pointed to by *address*. When a connection is made, the integer that it points to is set to the actual size, in bytes, of the resulting *address*.

If "accept ( )" succeeds, it returns a new file descriptor that may be used to talk with the client; otherwise, it returns a value of −1.

The "chef" server accepts a connection on line 40:

```
40          clientFd = accept (serverFd, clientSockAddrPtr, &clientLen),
```

Serving a Client When a client connection succeeds, the most common sequence of events is as follows:

- The server process forks.
- The parent process closes the newly formed client file descriptor and loops back to "accept ( )", ready to service new connection requests from clients.
- The child process talks to the client using "read ( )" and "write ( )". When the conversation is complete, the child process closes the client file descriptor and exits.

The "chef" server process follows this series of actions on lines 37 through 50:

```
37    while (1) /* Loop forever */
38      {
39        /* Accept a client connection */
40        clientFd = accept (serverFd, clientSockAddrPtr, &clientLen);
41
42        if (fork () == 0) /* Create child to send receipe */
43          {
44            writeRecipe (clientFd); /* Send the recipe */
45            close (clientFd); /* Close the socket */
46            exit (/*EXIT_SUCCESS */ 0); /* Terminate */
47          }
48        else
49          close (clientFd); /* Close the client descriptor */
50      }
```

Note that the server chose to ignore SIGCHLD signals on line 21 so that its children could die immediately without requiring the parent to accept their return codes. If the server had not done so, it would had to have installed a SIGCHLD handler, which would have been more tedious.

The Client Now that you've seen how a server program is written, let's take a look at the construction of a client program. A client is a process that's responsible for creating an unnamed socket and then attaching it to a named server socket. To accomplish this task, it must use the following system calls in the order in which they are presented:

Name	Meaning
socket	creates an unnamed socket
connect	attaches an unnamed client socket to a named server socket

The way that a client uses "socket ( )" to create an unnamed socket is the same as the way that the server uses it. The domain, type, and protocol of the client socket must match those of the targeted server socket. The "cook" client process creates its unnamed socket on line 22:

```
22  clientFd = socket (AF_UNIX, SOCK_STREAM, DEFAULT_PROTOCOL);
```

Making the Connection: connect ( )   To connect to a server's socket, a client process must fill a structure with the address of the server's socket and then use "connect ( )", which works like this:

System Call: int connect (int *fd*, struct sockaddr* *address*, int
         addressLen)

"connect ( )" attempts to connect to a server socket whose address is contained within a structure pointed to by *address*. If "connect ( )" successful, *fd* may be used to communicate with the server's socket. The type of structure to which *address* points must follow the same rules as those stated in the description of "bind ( )":

- If the socket is in the AF_UNIX domain, a pointer to a "sockaddr_un" structure must be cast to a ("sockaddr*") and passed in as *address*.
- If the socket is in the AF_INET domain, a pointer to a "sockaddr_in" structure must be cast to a ("sockaddr*") and passed in as *address*.

addressLen must be equal to the size of the address structure. For examples of Internet clients, see the next example of a socket and the Internet-shell program at the end of this chapter.

    If the connection is made, "connect ( )" returns a value of 0. If the server socket doesn't exist or its pending queue is currently filled, "connect ( )" returns a value of −1.

The "cook" client process calls "connect ( )" until a successful connection is made in lines 26 to 31:

```
26    do /* Loop until a connection is made with the server */
27      {
28        result = connect (clientFd, serverSockAddrPtr, serverLen);
29        if (result == -1) sleep (1); /* Wait and then try again */
30      }
31    while (result == -1);
```

Communicating Via Sockets   Once the server socket and client socket have connected, their file descriptors may be used by "write ( )" and read ( ). In the example program, the server uses "write ( )" in lines 55 to 64:

```
55 writeRecipe (fd)
56
57 int fd;
58
59 {
60      static char* line1 = "spam, spam, spam, spam,";
61      static char* line2 = "spam, and spam.";
62      write (fd, line1, strlen (line1) + 1); /* Write first line */
63      write (fd, line2, strlen (line2) + 1); /* Write second line*/
64 }
```

The client uses "read ( )" in lines 53 to 69:

```
53   readLine (fd, str)
54
55   int fd;
56   char* str;
57
58   /* Read a single NULL-terminated line */
59
60   {
61     int n;
62
63     do /* Read characters until NULL or end of input */
64       {
65         n = read (fd, str, 1); /* Read one character */
66       }
67     while (n > 0 &&*str++ != NULL);
68     return (n > 0); /* Return false if end of input */
69   }
```

The server and client should be careful to close their socket file descriptors when they are no longer needed.

Internet Sockets   The AF_UNIX sockets that you've seen so far are OK for learning about sockets, but they aren't where the action is. Most of the useful stuff involves communicating between machines on the Internet, and so the rest of this chapter is dedicated to AF_INET sockets. If you haven't already read about networking in Chapter 8, now would be a good time to do so.

An Internet socket is specified by two values: a 32-bit IP address, which specifies a single unique Internet host, and a 16-bit port number, which specifies a particular port on the host. These specifications mean that an Internet client must know not only the IP address of the server, but also the server's port number.

As I mentioned in Chapter 8, several standard port numbers are reserved for system use. For example, port 13 is always served by a process that echoes the host's time of day to any client that's interested. The first example that I present for an Internet socket allows you to connect to port 13 of any Internet host in the world and find out the "remote" time of day. It allows three kinds of Internet addresses:

- If you enter "s", it automatically means the local host.
- If you enter something that starts with a digit, it's assumed to be an A.B.C.D-format IP address and is converted into a 32-bit IP address by software.
- If you enter a string, it's assumed to be a symbolic host name and is converted into a 32-bit IP address by software.

The next subsection shows some sample output from the "Internet time" program that I just described. The third address that I entered is the IP address of "ddn.nic.mil", the national Internet database server. Notice the one-hour time difference between my local host's time and the database server host's time.

Sample Output

```
$ inettime                                    ...run the program.
Host name (q= quit, s = self): s              ...what's my time?
Self host name is csservr2
Internet Address= 129.110.42.1
The time on the target port is Fri Mar 27 17:03:50 1998
Host name (q = quit, s= self):wotan           ...what's the time on "wotan"?
Internet Address = 129.110.2.1
The time on the target port is Fri Mar 27 17:03:55 1998
Host name (q = quit, s = self): 192.112.36.5     ...what's the time at
                                              ...ddn.nic.mil.
The time on the target port is Fri Mar 27 18:02:02 1998
Host name (q = quit, s = self): q             ...quit program.
$ _
```

"Internet time" Listing This section contains the complete listing of the "Internet time" client program. I suggest that you quickly skim through the code and then read the sections that follow it for details on how it works.

```
1   #include <stdio.h>
2   #include <signal.h>
3   #include <ctype.h>
4   #include <sys/types.h>
5   #include <sys/socket.h>
6   #include <netinet/in.h>            /* For AFINET sockets */
7   #include <arpa/inet.h>
8   #include <netdb.h>
9
10  #define DAYTIME_PORT        13     /* Standard port o */
11  #define DEFAULT_PROTOCOL    0
12
```

```
13   unsigned long promptForINETAddress ();
14   unsigned long nameToAddr ();
15
16   /*****************************************************************/
17
18   main ()
19
20   {
21     int clientFd; /* Client socket file descriptor */
22     int serverLen; /* Length of server address structure */
23     int result; /* From connect () call */
24     struct sockaddr_in serverINETAddress; /* Server address */
25     struct sockaddr* serverSockAddrPtr; /* Pointer to address */
26     unsigned long inetAddress; /* 32-bit IP address */
27
28     /* Set the two server variables */
29     serverSockAddrPtr = (struct sockaddr*) &serverINETAddress;
30     serverLen = sizeof (serverINETAddress); /* Length of address */
31
32     while (1) /* Loop until break */
33       {
34         inetAddress = promptForINETAddress (); /* Get 32-bit IP */
35         if (inetAddress == 0) break; /* Done */
36         /* Start by zeroing out the entire address structure */
37         bzero ((char*)&serverINETAddress,sizeof(serverINETAddress));
38         serverINETAddress.sin_family = AF_INET; /* Use Internet */
39         serverINETAddress.sin_addr.s_addr = inetAddress; /* IP */
40         serverINETAddress.sin_port = htons (DAYTIME_PORT);
41         * Now create the client socket */
42         clientFd = socket (AF_INET, SOCK_STREAM, DEFAULT_PROTOCOL);
43         do /* Loop until a connection is made with the server */
44           {
45             result = connect (clientFd,serverSockAddrPtr,serverLen);
46             if (result == -1) sleep (1); /* Try again in 1 second */
47           }
48         while (result == -1);
49
50         readTime (clientFd); /* Read the time from the server */
51         close (clientFd); /* Close the socket */
52       }
53
54     exit (/* EXIT_SUCCESS */ 0);
55   }
56
57   /*****************************************************************/
58
59   unsigned long promptForINETAddress ()
60
61   {
62     char hostName [100]; /* Name from user: numeric or symbolic */
63     unsigned long inetAddress; /* 32-bit IP format */
```

```
 64
 65    /* Loop until "quit" or a legal name is entered */
 66    /* If quit, return 0; else return host's IP address */
 67    do
 68      {
 69        printf ("Host name (q = quit, s = self): ");
 70        scanf ("%s", hostName); /* Get name from keyboard */
 71        if (strcmp (hostName, "q") == 0) return (0); /* Quit */
 72        inetAddress = nameToAddr (hostName); /* Convert to IP */
 73        if (inetAddress == 0) printf ("Host name not found\n");
 74      }
 75    while (inetAddress == 0);
 76  }
 77
 78  /***************************************************************/
 79
 80  unsigned long nameToAddr (name)
 81
 82  char* name;
 83
 84  {
 85    char hostName [100];
 86    struct hostent* hostStruct;
 87    struct in_addr* hostNode;
 88
 89    /* Convert name into a 32-bit IP address */
 90
 91    /* If name begins with a digit, assume it's a valid numeric */
 92    /* Internet address of the form A.B.C.D and convert directly */
 93    if (isdigit (name[0])) return (inet_addr (name));
 94
 95    if (strcmp (name, "s") == 0) /* Get host name from database */
 96      {
 97        gethostname (hostName,100);
 98        printf ("Self host name is %s\n", hostName);
 99      }
100    else /* Assume name is a valid symbolic host name */
101    strcpy (hostName, name);
102
103    /* Now obtain address information from database */
104    hostStruct = gethostbyname (hostName);
105    if (hostStruct == NULL) return (0); /* Not Found */
106    /* Extract the IP Address from the hostent structure */
107    hostNode = (struct in_addr*) hostStruct->h_addr;
108    /* Display a readable version for fun */
109    printf ("Internet Address = %s\n", inet_ntoa (*hostNode));
110    return (hostNode->s_addr); /* Return IP address */
111  }
112
113  /***************************************************************/
114
```

```
115  readTime (fd)
116
117  int fd;
118
119  {
120    char str [200]; /* Line buffer */
121
122    printf ("The time on the target port is ");
123    while (readLine (fd, str)) /* Read lines until end of input */
124      printf ("%s\n", str); /* Echo line from server to user */
125  }
126
127  /*****************************************************************/
128
129  readLine (fd, str)
130
131  int fd;
132  char* str;
133
134  /* Read a single line terminated by a new line */
135
136  {
137    int n;
138
139    do /* Read characters until NULL or end of input */
140      {
141        n = read (fd, str, 1); /* Read one character */
142      }
143    while (n > 0 && *str++ != "\n');
144    return (n > 0); /* Return false if end of input */
145  }
```

Analyzing the Source Code   Now that you've had a brief look through the source code for an Internet socket, it's time to examine the interesting bits. This program focuses mostly on the client side of an Internet connection, so I'll describe that portion first.

Internet Clients   The procedure for creating an Internet client is the same as that for creating an AF_UNIX client, except for the initialization of the socket address. I mentioned earlier in this section during the discussion of "bind ( )" that an Internet-socket address structure is of the type "struct sockaddr_in" and has four fields:

- "sin_family", the domain of the socket, which should be set to AF_INET
- "sin_port", the port number, which is 13 in this case
- "sin_addr", the 32-bit IP number
- "sin_zero", which is padding and is not set

When you create the client socket, the only tricky bit is determining the server's 32-bit IP address. "promptForINETAddress ( )" [line 59] gets the host's name from the user and then invokes "nameToAddr ( )" [line 80] to convert it into an IP address. If the user enters a string starting with a digit, "inet_addr ( )" is invoked to perform the conversion. Here's how it works:

Library Call: in_addr_t inet_addr (const char* *string*)

"inet_addr ( )" returns the 32-bit IP address that corresponds to the A.B.C.D-format *string*. The IP address is in network-byte order.

"Network-byte order" is a host-neutral ordering of bytes in the IP address. This ordering is necessary, since regular byte ordering can differ from machine to machine, which would make IP addresses nonportable.

If the string doesn't start with a digit, the next step is to see if it's "s", which signifies the local host. The name of the local host is obtained by "gethostname ( )" [line 97], which works as follows:

System Call: int gethostname (char* *name*, int *nameLen*)

"gethostname ( )" sets the character array pointed to by *name* of length *nameLen* to a NULL-terminated string equal to the local host's name.

Once the symbolic name of the host is determined, the next stage is to look it up in the network-host file, "/etc/hosts". This task is performed by "gethostbyname ( )" [line 104], which works like this:

Library Call: struct hostent* gethostbyname (const char* *name*)

"gethostbyname ( )" searches the "/etc/hosts" file and returns a pointer to a hostent structure that describes the file entry associated with the string *name*.

  If *name* is not found in the "/etc/hosts" file, NULL is returned.

The "hostent" structure has several fields, but the only one we're interested in is a field of type ("struct in_addr*") called "h_addr." This field contains the host's associated IP number in a subfield called "s_addr." Before returning this IP number, the program displays a string description of the IP address by calling "inetntoa ( )" [line 109]:

Library Call: char* inet_ntoa (struct in_addr *address*)

"inet_ntoa ( )" takes a structure of type "in_addr" as its argument and returns a pointer to a string that describes the address in the format A.B.C.D.

The final 32-bit address is then returned by line 110. Once the IP address "inetAddress" has been determined, the client's socket address fields are filled by lines 37 to 40.

```
37      bzero ((char*)&serverINETAddress,sizeof(serverINETAddress));
38      serverINETAddress.sin_family = AF_INET; /* Use Internet */
39      serverINETAddress.sin_addr.s_addr = inetAddress; /* IP */
40      serverINETAddress.sin_port = htons (DAYTIME_PORT);
```

"bzero ( )" clears the socket address structure's contents before its fields are assigned:

Library Call: void bzero (void* *buffer*, size_t *length*)

"bzero ( )" fills the array *buffer* of size *length* with zeroes (ASCII NULL).

The "bzero ( )" call had its origins in the Berkeley version of UNIX. System V's equivalent is "memset ( )":

Library Call: void memset (void* *buffer*, int *value*, size_t *length*)

"memset ( )" fills the array *buffer* of size *length* with the value of *value*.

Like the IP address, the port number is also converted to a network-byte ordering by "htons ( )", which works like this:

Library Call: in_addr_t htonl (in_addr_t *hostLong*)
      in_port_t htons (in_port_t *hostShort*)
      in_addr_t ntohl (in_addr_t *networkLong*)
      in_port_t ntohs (in_port_t *networkShort*)

Each of these functions performs a conversion between a host-format number and a network-format number. For example, "htonl ( )" returns the network-format equivalent of the host-format unsigned long *hostLong*, and "ntohs ( )" returns the host-format equivalent of the net-work-format unsigned short *networkShort.*

The final step is to create the client socket and attempt the connection. The code for this task is almost the same as that for AF_UNIX sockets:

```
42        clientFd = socket (AF_INET, SOCK_STREAM, DEFAULT_PROTOCOL);
43        do /* Loop until a connection is made with the server */
44          {
45            result = connect (clientFd,serverSockAddrPtr,serverLen);
46            if (result == -1) sleep (1); /* Try again in 1 second */
47          }
48        while (result == -1);
```

The rest of the program contains nothing new. Now it's time to look at how an Internet server is built.

Internet Servers   Constructing an Internet server is actually pretty easy. The "sin_family", "sin_port", and "sin_zero" fields of the socket-address structure should be filled in as they were in the client example. The only difference is that the "s_addr" field should be set to the network-byte-ordered value of the constant "INADDR_ANY", which means "accept any incoming client requests." The follow-ing example of how to create a server socket address is a slightly modified version of some code taken from the Internet shell program that ends this chapter:

```
int serverFd; /* Server socket */
struct sockaddr_in serverINETAddress; /* Server Internet address */
struct sockaddr* serverSockAddrPtr; /* Pointer to server address */
struct sockaddr_in clientINETAddress; /* Client Internet address */
struct sockaddr* clientSockAddrPtr; /* Pointer to client address */
int port = 13; /* Set to the port that you wish to serve */
```

```
int serverLen; /* Length of address structure */
serverFd = socket (AF_INET, SOCK_STREAM, DEFAULT_PROTOCOL); /* Create */
serverLen = sizeof (serverINETAddress); /* Length of structure */
bzero ((char*) &serverINETAddress, serverLen); /* Clear structure */
serverINETAddress.sin_family = AF_INET; /* Internet domain */
serverINETAddress.sin_addr.s_addr = htonl (INADDR_ANY); /* Accept all */
serverINETAddress.sin_port = htons (port); /* Server port number */
```

When the address is created, the socket is bound to the address, and its queue size is specified in the usual way:

```
serverSockAddrPtr = (struct sockaddr*) &serverINETAddress;
bind (serverFd, serverSockAddrPtr, serverLen);
listen (serverFd, 5);
```

The final step is to accept client connections. When a successful connection is made, the client socket address is filled with the client's IP address and a new file descriptor is returned:

```
clientLen = sizeof (clientINETAddress);
clientSockAddrPtr = (struct sockaddr*) clientINETAddress;
clientFd = accept (serverFd, clientSockAddrPtr, &clientLen);
```

As you can see, an Internet server's code is very similar to that of an AF_UNIX server. The final example in this chapter is the Internet shell.

Shared Memory

Sharing a segment of memory is a straightforward and intuitive method of allowing two processes on the same machine to share data. The process that allocates the shared memory segment gets an ID number back from the call, assuming that the creation succeeds. Other processes can then use this ID number to access the shared memory segment.

Accessing a shared memory segment is the fasted form of IPC, since no data has to be copied or sent anywhere else. However, because there is only one copy of the data, if more than one process is updating the data, the processes must synchronize their actions to prevent corruption of the data.

Some of the common system calls used to allocate and use shared memory segments in System V–based versions of UNIX are:

- "shmget ( )", which allocates a shared memory segment and returns the segment ID number
- "shmat ( )", which attaches a shared memory segment to the virtual address space of the calling process
- "shmdt ( )", which detaches an attached segmenet from the address space
- "shmctl ( )", which allows you to modify attributes associated with the shared memory segment (e.g., access permissions)

Upon a successful call to "shmget ( )", a shared memory segment exists and can be accessed with the ID number returned in the call. Note that for any other process to use the same segment, it must also know this ID number. The ID number can be made available to other processes via another IPC mechanism, or a specific ID number can be passed to "shmget ( )" to force the use of a specific known ID number, with the understanding that the call will fail if that ID number has already been used by another shared memory segment.

Once you have obtained a valid ID number for a shared memory segment, a call to "shmat ( )" will return a pointer to the address in the local process' virtual memory space where the shared memory segment has been attached. You can then use that pointer to index into the block of memory just as you would for any other block of memory. (This process does presume that you know the format of the data contained in the shared memory segment.)

If and when you finish using the shared memory segment, you can release (detach) it with a call to "shmdt ( )", into which you pass the pointer, not the ID number of the shared memory segment.

When the last process to have the shared memory segment attached (which is not necessarily the process that created it) detaches it, the space allocated to the segment is released.

Semaphores

A *semaphore* is not a communication mechanism like what we've seen with pipes, sockets, and shared memory. No actual data is sent with a semaphore. A semaphore is a counter that describes the availability of a resource; this resource could be a shared memory segment, for example.

A semaphore is created and assigned a value that denotes how many concurrent uses of a resource are allowed. Each time a process wants to use a certain resource, it checks the semaphore to see if the resource is available. If the value of the semaphore is greater than zero, then the resource is available. The process allocates "a unit" of the resource, and the semaphore is decremented by one unit. If the value of the semaphore is zero, the process sleeps until the semaphore value is greater than zero—in other words, until another process has finished its use of the resource.

You can use semaphores to lock something exclusively by creating a semaphore with a value of one unit; as soon as one process uses it, the semaphore's value is zero. This type of semaphore is known as a *binary semaphore*. Semaphores can also be used to set a maximum number of concurrent uses of a particular resource.

System V's semaphore is a bit more complex than what I've just described. Semaphores are actually managed as a list, or *set*, of semaphores rather than individually. This condition provides a method of defining multiple semaphores for a complex locking mechanism, but requires unnecessary overhead when you only want one semaphore. Semaphore-related system calls include:

- "semget( )", which creates a set (an array) of semaphores
- "semop ( )", which manipulates a semaphore set
- "semctl ( )", which modifies attributes of a semaphore set

THE INTERNET SHELL

Have you ever wondered what the inside of a shell looks like? Well, here's a great opportunity to learn how they work and to obtain some source code that could help you to create your own shell. I designed the Internet shell to be a lot like the standard UNIX shells in the sense that it provides piping and background-processing facilities, but I also added some Internet-specific abilities that the other shells lack.

Restrictions

In order to pack the functionality of the Internet shell into a reasonable size, there are a few restrictions on it:

- All tokens must be separated by whitespace (tabs or spaces). This restriction means that, for example, instead of typing "ls; date", you must type "ls ; date". This restriction makes the lexical analyzer very simple.
- Filename substitution (globbing) is not supported. This restriction means that the standard "*", "?", and "[]" metacharacters are not understood.

The features that are eliminated by these restrictions are nice to have in an everyday shell, but their implementation wouldn't have taught you anything significant about how shells work.

Command Syntax

The syntax of an Internet shell command is very similar to that of the standard UNIX shells and is formally described below using BNF notation. Note that the redirection symbols "<" and ">" are escaped by a "\" character to prevent ambiguity. See the appendix for a discussion of BNF.

```
<internetShellcommand> = <sequence> [ & ]
<sequence> = <pipeline> { ; <pipeline> }*
<pipeline> = <simple> { | <simple> }
<simple> = { <token> }* { <redirection>}*
<redirection> = <fileRedirection> | <socketRedirection>
<fileRedirection> = \> <file> | >> <file> | \< <file>
<socketRedirection> = <clientRedirection> | <serverRedirection>
<clientRedirection> = @\>c <socket> | @\<c <socket>
<serverDirection> = @\>s <socket> | @\<s <socket>
<token> = a string of characters
<file> = a valid UNIX pathname
<socket> = either a UNIX pathname (UNIX domain socket) or
           an Internet socket name of the form hostname.port#
```

Starting the Internet Shell

I named the Internet-shell executable "ish". The Internet shell prompt is a question mark.

When "ish" is started, it inherits the $PATH environment variable from the shell that invokes it. The value of $PATH may be changed by using the *setenv* built-in command that is described shortly.

To exit the Internet shell, press *Control*-D on a line of its own.

Built-In Commands

The Internet shell executes most commands by creating a child shell that exec's the specified utility while the parent shell waits for the child. However, some commands are built into the shell and are executed directly. Here is a list of the built-ins commands:

Built-in command	Function
echo {*token*}*	echoes tokens to the terminal
cd *path*	changes the shell's working directory to *path*
getenv *name*	displays the value of the environment variable *name*
setenv *name value*	sets the value of the environment variable *name* to *value*

Built-in commands may be redirected. Before I describe the construction and operation of the Internet shell, let's take a look at a few examples of both regular commands and Internet-specific commands.

Some Examples of Regular Commands

Here are some examples that illustrate the sequencing, redirection, and piping capabilities of the Internet shell:

```
$ ish                              ...start shell.
Internet Shell.
? ls                               ...simple command.
ish.c        ish.cs        ish.van        who.socket   who.sort
? ls | wc                          ...pipe.
      5        5        41
? who | sort > who.sort &          ...pipe + redirect + background.
[4356]                             ...PID of background process.
? cat who.sort                     ...show that redirection worked.
glass     ttyp2                    May 28 18:33 (bridge05.utdalla)
posey     ttyp0                    May 22 10:19 (blackfoot.utdall)
posey     ttyp1                    May 22 10:19 (blackfoot.utdall)
? date ; whoami                    ...sequence of commands.
Thu Mar 26 18:36:24 CDT 1998
glass
? echo hi there                    ...execute a built-in command.
hi there
? getenv PATH                      ...look at $PATH environment variable.
::.:/usr/local/bin:/usr/ucb:/usr/bin:/bin:/usr/etc
? mail glass < who.sort            ...input redirection works too.
? ^D                               ...exit shell.
$ _
```

Some Examples of the Internet Shell

The Internet shell becomes pretty interesting when you examine its socket features. Here's an example that uses a UNIX domain socket to communicate information:

```
$ ish                          ...start the Internet shell.
Internet Shell.
? who @>s who.sck &            ...server sends output to socket "who.sck".
[2678]
? ls                           ...execute a command for fun.
ish.c        ish.van          who.sock    who.sort
ish.cs       who.sck          who.socket
? sort @<c who.sck            ...client reads input from socket "who.sck".
glass     ttyp2   May 28 18:33 (bridge05.utdalla)
posey     ttyp0   May 22 10:19 (blackfoot.utdall)
posey     ttyp1   May 22 10:19 (blackfoot.utdall)
veerasam  ttyp3   May 28 18:39 (129.110.70.139)
? ^D                           ...quit shell.
$ _
```

The really fun stuff happens when you introduce Internet sockets. The first shell in the next example was run on a host called "csservr2", and the second shell was run on a host called "vanguard":

```
$ ish                          ...run Internet shell on "csservr2".
Internet Shell.
? who @>s 5000 &               ...background server sends output to port 5000.
[7221]
? ^D                           ...quit shell.
$ rlogin vanguard              ...login to "vanguard" host.
% ish                          ...run Internet shell on "vanguard".
Internet Shell.
? sort @<c csservr2.5000        ...client reads input from "csservr2" port 5000.
IP address = 129.110.42.1   ...echoed by Internet shell.
glass     ttyp2   May 28 18:42 (bridge05.utdalla)      ...output from
posey     ttyp0   May 22 10:19 (blackfoot.utdall)      ..."who" on
posey     ttyp1   May 22 10:19 (blackfoot.utdall)      ..."csservr2"!
veerasam  ttyp3   May 28 18:39 (129.110.70.139)
? ^D                           ...quit shell.
% ^D                           ...logout from "vanguard".
logout
$ _                            ...back to l4p4csservr2".
```

Here's an illustration of the socket connection for this example:

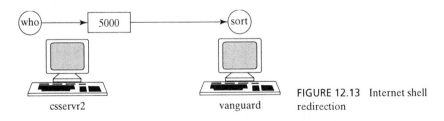

FIGURE 12.13 Internet shell redirection

The next example is even more interesting. The first shell uses one socket to talk to the second shell, and the second shell uses another socket to talk to the third:

```
$ ish                            ...start shell on "csservr2".
Internet Shell.
? who @>s 5001 &                 ...background server sends output to port 5001.
[2001]
? ^D                             ...quit shell.
$ rlogin vanguard                ...login to "vanguard".
% ish                            ...start shell on "vanguard".
Internet Shell.
? sort @<c csservr2.5001 @>s 5002 &      ...background process reads
[3756]                                   ...input from port 5001 on
                                         ..."csservr2" and sends it to
                                         ...local port 5002.
IP address = 129.110.42.1                ...echoed by shell.
? ^D                             ...quit shell.
% ^D                             ...logout of "vanguard".
logout
$ ish                            ...start another shell on "csservr2".
Internet Shell.
? cat @<c vanguard.5002          ...read input from port 5002 on "vanguard".
IP address = 129.110.43.128   ...echoed by the shell.
glass ttyp2 May 28 18:42 (bridge05.utdalla)
posey ttyp0 May 22 10:19 (blackfoot.utdall)
posey ttyp1 May 22 10:19 (blackfoot.utdall)
veerasam ttyp3 May 28 18:39 (129.110.70.139)
? ^D                             ...quit shell.
$ _
```

Here's an illustration of the two socket connections for this example:

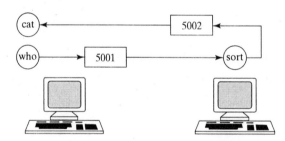

FIGURE 12.14   More Internet shell redirection

How It Works

The operation of the Internet shell can be broken down into several main sections:

- the main command loop
- parsing
- executing built-in commands
- executing pipelines
- executing sequences
- background processing
- dealing with signals

- performing file redirection
- performing socket redirection

Each operation will now be described, together with code fragments and diagrams when necessary. Before you continue reading, I suggest that you glance through the source code listing at the end of this chapter to familiarize yourself with the overall layout of the Internet shell.

The Main Command Loop

When the shell starts, it initializes a signal handler to catch keyboard interrupts and resets an error flag. It then enters "commandLoop ( )" [line 167], which prompts the user for a line of input, parses it, and then executes the command. This function loops until the user presses *Control*-D, at which point the shell terminates. The next few subsections describe the parsing and execution process.

Parsing

In order to check the command-line for errors easily, the line is first broken down into separate tokens by "tokenize ( )" [line 321], which is located in the lexical-analyzer section of the source code. "tokenize ( )" is called by the "commandLoop ( )" routine [line 167], and it fills the global "tokens" array with pointers to each individual token. For example, if the input line was "ls -l," "tokens"[0] would point to the string "ls" and "tokens"[1] would point to the string "-l". Once the line is parsed, the global token pointer "tIndex" is set to zero [line 350] in preparation for the parsing process.

The parsing is performed in a top-down fashion. The main parser, "parse Sequence ( )" [line 194], is called from the "commandLoop ( )" function. This function parses each pipeline in the sequence by invoking "parsePipeline ( )", and then records the information that "parsePipeline ( )" returns. Finally, it checks to see whether the sequence is to be executed in the background or not.

Similarly, "parsePipeline ( )" [line 222] parses each simple command in the pipeline by calling "parseSimple ( )", and then records the information that "parseSimple ( )" returns.

"parseSimple ( )" [line 242] records the tokens in the simple command and then processes any trailing metacharacters such as ">", ">>", and "@>".

The information that each of these parsing functions gathers is stored in structures for later use by the execution routines. A "struct" sequence [line 75] can hold the details of up to five (MAX_PIPES) pipelines, together with a flag indicating whether or not the sequence is to be executed in the background. Each pipeline is recorded in a "struct pipeline" [line 67], which can record the details of up to five (MAX_SIMPLE) simple commands. Finally, a "struct simple" [line 52] can the hold up to 100 (MAX_TOKENS) tokens, together with several fields that record information related to I/O redirection.

If a command is parsed with no errors, the local variable "sequence" [line 182] is equal to a "struct" sequence, which holds the analyzed version of the command.

Please note that although I could have used pointers to return structures more efficiently, I chose to keep the program as simple as I could in order to focus on the UNIX-specific aspects.

Executing a Command Sequence

The main command loop executes a successfully parsed command by invoking "executeSequence ( )" [line 444]. This routine does one of two things:

- If the command is to be executed in the background, it creates a child process to execute the pipelines in sequence; the original parent shell does not wait for the child. Before executing the pipeline, the child restores its original interrupt handler and places itself into a new process group to make it immune from hang-ups and other signals. This action ensures that a background process will continue to execute even when the shell is terminated and the user logs out.
- If the command is to be executed in the foreground, the parent shell executes the pipelines in sequence.

In both cases, "executePipeline ( )" [line 472] is used to execute each pipeline component of the command sequence.

Executing Pipelines

"executePipeline ( )" [line 472] performs one of two actions:

- If the pipeline is a simple built-in command, it executes the simple command directly, without creating a child process. This distinction is very important. For example, the built-in command *cd* executes "chdir ( )" to change the shell's current working directory. If a child shell were created to execute this built-in command, the original parent shell's working directory would be unaffected, which would be incorrect.
- If the pipeline is more than a simple built-in command, it creates a child shell to execute the pipeline; the original parent shell waits for the child to complete. Notice that the parent waits for a specific PID by calling "waitForPid ( )" [line 503]. This step occurs because the parent shell might have created some previous children to execute background processes and it would be incorrect for the parent to resume when one of these background processes terminated. If the pipeline contains only one simple command, then no pipes need to be created and "executeSimple ( )" [line 569] is invoked. Otherwise, "executePipes ( )" [line 516] which connects each command by its own pipe, is invoked.

"executePipes ( )" is a fairly complicated routine. If the pipeline contains n simple commands, then "executePipes ( )" creates n child processes, one for each command, and $n - 1$ pipes to connect the children. Each child reconnects its standard input and/or output channels to the appropriate pipe and then closes all of the original pipe file descriptors. Each child then executes its associated simple command. Meanwhile, the original process that invoked "executePipes ( )" waits for all of its children to terminate.

Executing a Simple Command

"executeSimple ( )" [line 569] redirects the standard input and/or output channels as necessary and then executes either "executeBuiltIn ( )" [line 635] or "execute

Primitive ( )" [line 596], depending on the category of the command. "builtIn ( )" [line624] returns true if a token is the name of a built-in command.

If the command is a built-in command, it's possible that the command is being executed directly by the shell. To prevent the shell's I/O channels from being altered by redirection, the original standard input and output channels are recorded and restored later.

"executePrimitive ( )" [line 596] simply execs the command using "execvp ( )". Fortunately (but not coincidentally), "p->token" is already in the form required by "execvp ( )". Built-in functions are executed by "executeBuiltIn ( )" [line 635] using a simple switch statement.

Redirection

"redirect ( )" [line 761] performs all of the preprocessing necessary for both file and socket redirection. The basic technique for redirecting the standard I/O channels is the same as the one I described earlier in this chapter.

If file redirection is required, "dupFd ( )" [line 806] is invoked to create the file with the appropriate mode and to duplicate the standard file descriptor.

If socket redirection is required, either "server ( )" [line 950] or "client ( )" [line 879] is invoked to create the appropriate type of socket connection. These functions manipulate both UNIX-domain and Internet-domain sockets in the same way as the earlier examples of sockets do.

Extensions

I think that it could be a lot of fun and fairly educational to add some new features to the Internet shell. If you're interested, please see the "Projects" section at the end of this chapter for some suggestions.

Internet Shell Source Code Listing

```
 1  #include <stdio.h>
 2  #include <stdlib.h>
 3  #include <string.h>
 4  #include <signal.h>
 5  #include <ctype.h>
 6  #include <sys/types.h>
 7  #include <fcntl.h>
 8  #include <sys/ioctl.h>
 9  #include <sys/socket.h>
10  #include <sys/un.h>
11  #include <netinet/in.h>
12  #include <arpa/inet.h>
13  #include <netdb.h>
14
15
16  /* Macros */
17  #define MAX_STRING_LENGTH       200
18  #define MAX_TOKENS              100
```

```
19  #define MAX_TOKEN_LENGTH        30
20  #define MAX_SIMPLE              5
21  #define MAX_PIPES               5
22  #define NOT_FOUND               -1
23  #define REGULAR                 -1
24  #define DEFAULT_PERMISSION      0660
25  #define DEFAULT_PROTOCOL        0
26  #define DEFAULT_QUEUE_LENGTH    5
27  #define SOCKET_SLEEP            1
28
29
30  /* Enumerators */
31  enum { FALSE, TRUE };
32  enum metacharacterEnum
33  {
34        SEMICOLON, BACKGROUND, END_OF_LINE, REDIRECT_OUTPUT,
35        REDIRECT_INPUT, APPEND_OUTPUT, PIPE,
36        REDIRECT_OUTPUT_SERVER, REDIRECT_OUTPUT_CLIENT,
37        REDIRECT_INPUT_SERVER, REDIRECT_INPUT_CLIENT
38  };
39  enum builtInEnum { ECHO_BUILTIN, SETENV, GETENV, CD };
40  enum descriptorEnum { STDIN, STDOUT, STDERR };
41  enum pipeEnum { READ, WRITE };
42  enum IOEnum
43    {
44      NO_REDIRECT, FILE_REDIRECT,
45      SERVER_REDIRECT, CLIENT_REDIRECT
46    };
47  enum socketEnum { CLIENT, SERVER };
48  enum { INPUT_SOCKET, OUTPUT_SOCKET };
49
50
51  /* Every simple command has one of these associated with it */
52  struct simple
53    {
54        char* token [MAX_TOKENS]; /* The tokens of the command */
55        int count; /* The number of tokens */
56        int outputRedirect; /* Set to an IOEnum */
57        int inputRedirect; /* Set to an IOEnum */
58        int append; /* Set to true for append mode */
59        char *outputFile; /* Name of output file, or NULL if none */
60        char *inputFile; /* Name of input file, or NULL if none */
61        char *outputSocket; /* Name of output socket, or NULL if none */
62        char *inputSocket; /* Name of input socket, or NULL if none */
63    };
64
65
66  /* Every pipeline has one of these associated with it */
67  struct pipeline
68    {
69        struct simple simple [MAX_SIMPLE]; /* Commands in pipe */
```

```
70          int count; /* The number of simple commands */
71      };
72
73
74  /* Every command sequence has one of these associated with it */
75  struct sequence
76      {
77          struct pipeline pipeline [MAX_PIPES]; /* Pipes in sequence */
78          int count; /* The number of pipes */
79          int background; /* True if this is a background sequence */
80      };
81
82
83  /* Prototypes */
84  struct sequence parseSequence ();
85  struct pipeline parsePipeline ();
86  struct simple parseSimple ();
87  char *nextToken ();
88  char *peekToken ();
89  char *lastToken ();
90  char* getToken ();
91
92
93  /* Globals */
94  char* metacharacters [] = { ";", "&", "\n", ">", "<", ">>",
95  "|", "@>s", "@>c", "@<s", "@<c", " " };
96  char* builtIns [] = { "echo", "setenv", "getenv", "cd", " " };
97  char line [MAX_STRING_LENGTH]; /* The current line */
98  char tokens [MAX_TOKENS][MAX_TOKEN_LENGTH]; /* Tokens in line */
99  int tokenCount; /* The number of tokens in the current line */
100  int tIndex; /* Index into line: used by lexical analyzer */
101  int errorFlag; /* Set to true when an error occurs */
102
103
104  /* Some forward declarations */
105  void (*originalQuitHandler) ();
106  void quitHandler ();
107
108
109  /* Externals */
110  char **environ; /* Pointer to the environment */
111
112  /*******************************************************************/
113
114  main (argc, argv)
115
116  int argc;
117  char* argv [];
118
119  {
120      initialize (); /* Initialize some globals */
```

```
121      commandLoop (); /* Accept and process commands */
122      return (/* EXIT_SUCCESS */ 0);
123  }
124
125  /*****************************************************************/
126
127  initialize ()
128
129  {
130      printf ("Internet Shell.\n"); /* Introduction */
131      /* Set the Control-C handler to catch keyboard interrupts */
132      originalQuitHandler = signal (SIGINT, quitHandler);
133  }
134
135  /*****************************************************************/
136
137  void quitHandler ()
138
139  {
140      /* Control-C handler */
141      printf ("\n");
142      displayPrompt ();
143  }
144
145  /*****************************************************************/
146
147  error (str)
148
149  char* str;
150
151  {
152      /* Display str as an error to the standard error channel */
153      fprintf (stderr, "%s", str);
154      errorFlag = TRUE; /* Set error flag */
155  }
156
157  /*****************************************************************/
158
159  displayPrompt ()
160
161  {
162  printf ("? ");
163  }
164
165  /*****************************************************************/
166
167  commandLoop ()
168
169  {
170  struct sequence sequence;
171
```

```
172 /* Accept and process commands until a Control-D occurs */
173 while (TRUE)
174 {
175         displayPrompt ();
176         if (gets (line) == NULL) break; /* Get a line of input */
177         tokenize (); /* Break the input line into tokens */
178         errorFlag = FALSE; /* Reset the error flag */
179
180         if (tokenCount > 1) /* Process any non-empty line */
181            {
182              sequence = parseSequence (); /* Parse the line */
183              /* If no errors occurred during the parsing, */
184              /* execute the command */
185              if (!errorFlag) executeSequence (&sequence);
186            }
187         }
188 }
189
190 /*******************************************************************/
191 /*                    PARSER ROUTINES                            */
192 /*******************************************************************/
193
194 struct sequence parseSequence ()
195
196 {
197     struct sequence q;
198
199     /* Parse a command sequence and return structure description */
200     q.count = 0; /* Number of pipes in the sequence */
201     q.background = FALSE; /* Default is not in background */
202
203     while (TRUE) /* Loop until no semicolon delimiter is found */
204        {
205          q.pipeline[q.count++] = parsePipeline (); /* Parse */
206          if (peekCode () != SEMICOLON) break;
207          nextToken (); /* Flush semicolon delimiter */
208        }
209
210 if (peekCode () == BACKGROUND) /* Sequence is in background */
211        {
212          q.background = TRUE;
213          nextToken (); /* Flush ampersand */
214        }
215
216 getToken (END_OF_LINE); /* Check that end of line is reached */
217 return (q);
218 }
219
220 /***************************************************************/
221
222     struct pipeline parsePipeline ()
```

```
223
224          {
225      struct pipeline p;
226
227      /* Parse a pipeline and return a structure description of it */
228      p.count = 0; /* The number of simple commands in the pipeline */
229
230      while (TRUE) /* Loop until no pipe delimiter is found */
231          {
232            p.simple[p.count++] = parseSimple (); /* Parse command */
233            if (peekCode () != PIPE) break;
234            nextToken (); /* Flush pipe delimiter */
235          }
236
237 return (p);
238 }
239
240 /****************************************************************/
241
242      struct simple parseSimple ()
243
244 {
245      struct simple s;
246      int code;
247      int done;
248
249      /* Parse a simple command and return a structure description */
250      s.count = 0; /* The number of tokens in the simple command */
251      s.outputFile = s.inputFile = NULL;
252      s.inputSocket = s.outputSocket = NULL;
253      s.outputRedirect = s.inputRedirect = NO_REDIRECT; /* Defaults */
254      s.append = FALSE;
255
256      while (peekCode () == REGULAR) /* Store all regular tokens */
257      s.token[s.count++] = nextToken ();
258
259      s.token[s.count] = NULL; /* NULL-terminate token list */
260      done = FALSE;
261
262      /* Parse special metacharacters that follow, like > and >> */
263      do
264      {
265          code = peekCode ();/* Peek at next token */
266
267          switch (code)
268            {
269                case REDIRECT_INPUT: /* < */
270                    nextToken ();
271                    s.inputFile = getToken (REGULAR);
272                    s.inputRedirect = FILE_REDIRECT;
273                    break;
```

```
274
275                 case REDIRECT_OUTPUT: /* > */
276                 case APPEND_OUTPUT: /* >> */
277                     nextToken ();
278                     s.outputFile = getToken (REGULAR);
279                     s.outputRedirect = FILE_REDIRECT;
280                     s.append = (code == APPEND_OUTPUT);
281                     break;
282
283                 case REDIRECT_OUTPUT_SERVER: /* @>s */
284                     nextToken ();
285                     s.outputSocket = getToken (REGULAR);
286                     s.outputRedirect = SERVER_REDIRECT;
287                     break;
288
289                 case REDIRECT_OUTPUT_CLIENT: /* @>c */
290                     nextToken ();
291                     s.outputSocket = getToken (REGULAR);
292                     s.outputRedirect = CLIENT_REDIRECT;
293                     break;
294
295                 case REDIRECT_INPUT_SERVER: /* @<s */
296                     nextToken ();
297                     s.inputSocket = getToken (REGULAR);
298                     s.inputRedirect = SERVER_REDIRECT;
299                     break;
300
301                 case REDIRECT_INPUT_CLIENT: /* @<c */
302                     nextToken ();
303                     s.inputSocket = getToken (REGULAR);
304                     s.inputRedirect = CLIENT_REDIRECT;
305                     break;
306
307             default:
308                 done = TRUE;
309                 break;
310             }
311         }
312     while (!done);
313
314     return (s);
315 }
316
317 /****************************************************************/
318 /*                LEXICAL ANALYZER ROUTINES                   */
319 /****************************************************************/
320
321 tokenize ()
322
323 {
324     char* ptr = line; /* Point to the input buffer */
```

```
325      char token [MAX_TOKEN_LENGTH]; /* Holds the current token */
326      char* tptr; /* Pointer to current character */
327
328      tIndex = 0; /* Global: points to the current token */
329
330      /* Break the current line of input into tokens */
331      while (TRUE)
332      {
333        tptr = token;
334        while (*ptr == ' ') ++ptr; /* Skip leading spaces */
335        if (*ptr == NULL) break; /* End of line */
336
337        do
338        {
339          *tptr++ = *ptr++;
340        }
341        while (*ptr != ' ' && *ptr != NULL);
342
343        *tptr = NULL;
344        strcpy (tokens[tIndex++], token); /* Store the token */
345      }
346
347      /* Place an end-of-line token at the end of the token list */
348      strcpy (tokens[tIndex++], "\n");
349      tokenCount = tIndex; /* Remember total token count */
350      tIndex = 0; /* Reset token index to start of token list */
351    }
352
353 /****************************************************************/
354
355 char* nextToken ()
356
357  {
358      return (tokens[tIndex++]); /* Return next token in list */
359  }
360
361 /****************************************************************/
362
363 char *lastToken ()
364
365  {
366      return (tokens[tIndex - 1]); /* Return previous token in list */
367  }
368
369 /****************************************************************/
370
371 peekCode ()
372
373  {
374      /* Return a peek at code of the next token in the list */
375      return (tokenCode (peekToken ()));
```

```
376  }
377
378  /*************************************************************/
379
380  char* peekToken ()
381
382  {
383      /* Return a peek at the next token in the list */
384      return (tokens[tIndex]);
385  }
386
387  /*************************************************************/
388
389  char *getToken (code)
390
391  int code;
392
393  {
394      char str [MAX_STRING_LENGTH];
395
396      /* Generate error if the code of the next token is not code */
397      /* Otherwise return the token */
398      if (peekCode () != code)
399        {
400          sprintf (str, "Expected %s\n", metacharacters[code]);
401          error (str);
402          return (NULL);
403        }
404      else
405          return (nextToken ());
406  }
407
408  /*************************************************************/
409
410  tokenCode (token)
411
412  char* token;
413
414  {
415          /* Return the index of token in the metacharacter array */
416          return (findString (metacharacters, token));
417  }
418
419  /*************************************************************/
420
421  findString (strs, str)
422
423  char* strs [];
424  char* str;
425
426  {
```

```
427     int i = 0;
428
429     /* Return the index of str in the string array strs */
430     /* or NOT_FOUND if it isn't there */
431     while (strcmp (strs[i], "") != 0)
432       if (strcmp (strs[i], str) == 0)
433         return (i);
434       else
435         ++i;
436
437     return (NOT_FOUND); /* Not found */
438 }
439
440 /****************************************************************/
441 /*                COMMAND EXECUTION ROUTINES                  */
442 /****************************************************************/
443
444 executeSequence (p)
445
446 struct sequence* p;
447
448 {
449     int i, result;
450
451     /* Execute a sequence of statments (possibly just one) */
452     if (p->background) /* Execute in background */
453       {
454         if (fork () == 0)
455           {
456             printf ("[%d]\n", getpid ()); /* Display child PID */
457             /* Child process */
458             signal (SIGQUIT, originalQuitHandler); /* Oldhandler */
459             setpgid (0, getpid ()); /* Change process group */
460             for (i = 0; i < p->count; i++) /* Execute pipelines */
461               executePipeline (&p->pipeline[i]);
462                 exit (/* EXIT_SUCCESS */ 0);
463           }
464       }
465     else /* Execute in foreground */
466     for (i = 0; i < p->count; i++) /* Execute each pipeline */
467     executePipeline (&p->pipeline[i]);
468 }
469
470 /****************************************************************/
471
472 executePipeline (p)
473
474 struct pipeline *p;
475
476 {
477   int pid, processGroup, result;
```

```
478
479    /* Execute every simple command in pipeline (possibly one) */
480    if (p->count == 1 && builtIn (p->simple[0].token[0]))
481      executeSimple (&p->simple[0]); /* Execute it directly */
482    else
483      {
484        if ((pid = fork ()) == 0)
485          {
486            /* Child shell executes the simple commands */
487            if (p->count == 1)
488              executeSimple (&p->simple[0]); /* Execute command */
489            else
490              executePipes (p); /* Execute more than one command */
491            exit ( /* EXIT_SUCCESS */ 0);
492          }
493        else            .
494          {
495            /* Parent shell waits for child to complete */
496            waitForPID (pid);
497          }
498      }
499 }
500
501 /********************************************************************/
502
503 waitForPID (pid)
504
505 int pid;
506
507 {
508   int status;
509
510   /* Return when the child process with PID pid terminates */
511   while (wait (&status) != pid);
512 }
513
514 /********************************************************************/
515
516 executePipes (p)
517
518 struct pipeline *p;
519
520 {
521   int pipes, status, i;
522   int pipefd [MAX_PIPES][2];
523
524   /* Execute two or more simple commands connected by pipes */
525   pipes = p->count - 1; /* Number of pipes to build */
526   for (i = 0; i < pipes; i++) /* Build the pipes */
527     pipe (pipefd[i]);
528   for (i = 0; i < p->count; i++) /* Build one process per pipe */
```

```
529        {
530          if (fork () != 0) continue;
531          /* Child shell */
532          /* First, connect stdin to pipe if not the first command */
533          if (i != 0) dup2 (pipefd[i-1][READ], STDIN);
534          /* Second, connect stdout to pipe if not the last command */
535          if (i != p->count - 1) dup2 (pipefd[i][WRITE], STDOUT);
536          /* Third, close all of the pipes' file descriptors */
537          closeAllPipes (pipefd, pipes);
538          /* Last, execute the simple command */
539          executeSimple (&p->simple[i]);
540          exit (/* EXIT_SUCCESS */0);
541        }
542
543      /* The parent shell comes here after forking the children */
544      closeAllPipes (pipefd, pipes);
545      for (i = 0; i < p->count; i++) /* Wait for children to finish */
546        wait (&status);
547 }
548
549 /*******************************************************************/
550
551 closeAllPipes (pipefd, pipes)
552
553 int pipefd [][2];
554 int pipes;
555
556 {
557    int i;
558
559    /* Close every pipe's file descriptors */
560    for (i = 0; i < pipes; i++)
561      {
562        close (pipefd[i][READ]);
563        close (pipefd[i][WRITE]);
564      }
565 }
566
567 /*******************************************************************/
568
569 executeSimple (p)
570
571 struct simple* p;
572
573 {
574    int copyStdin, copyStdout;
575
576    /* Execute a simple command */
577    if (builtIn (p->token[0])) /* Built-in */
578      {
579          /* The parent shell is executing this, so remember */
```

```
580          /* stdin and stdout in case of built-in redirection */
581          copyStdin = dup (STDIN);
582          copyStdout = dup (STDOUT);
583          if (redirect (p)) executeBuiltIn (p); /* Execute built-in */
584          /* Restore stdin and stdout */
585          dup2 (copyStdin, STDIN);
586          dup2 (copyStdout, STDOUT);
587          close (copyStdin);
588          close (copyStdout);
589       }
590    else if (redirect (p)) /* Redirect if necessary */
591       executePrimitive (p); /* Execute primitive command */
592 }
593
594 /*******************************************************************/
595
596 executePrimitive (p)
597
598 struct simple* p;
599
600 {
601    /* Execute a command by exec'ing */
602    if (execvp (p->token[0], p->token) == -1)
603      {
604        perror ("ish");
605        exit (/* EXIT_FAILURE */ 1);
606      }
607 }
608
609 /*******************************************************************/
610 /*                       BUILT-IN COMMANDS                        */
611 /*******************************************************************/
612
613 builtInCode (token)
614
615 char* token;
616
617 {
618    /* Return the index of token in the builtIns array */
619    return (findString (builtIns, token));
620 }
621
622 /*******************************************************************/
623
624 builtIn (token)
625
626 char* token;
627
628 {
629    /* Return true if token is a built-in */
630    return (builtInCode (token) != NOT_FOUND);
```

```
631 }
632
633 /********************************************************************/
634
635 executeBuiltIn (p)
636
637 struct simple* p;
638
639 {
640    /* Execute a single built-in command */
641    switch (builtInCode (p->token[0]))
642      {
643        case CD:
644           executeCd (p);
645           break;
646
647        case ECHO_BUILTIN:
648           executeEcho (p);
649           break;
650
651        case GETENV:
652           executeGetenv (p);
653           break;
654
655        case SETENV:
656           executeSetenv (p);
657           break;
658      }
659 }
660
661 /********************************************************************/
662
663 executeEcho (p)
664
665 struct simple* p;
666
667 {
668    int i;
669
670    /* Echo the tokens in this command */
671    for (i = 1; i < p->count; i++)
672      printf ("%s ", p->token[i]);
673
674    printf ("\n");
675 }
676
677 /********************************************************************/
678
679 executeGetenv (p)
680
681 struct simple* p;
```

```
682
683 {
684   char* value;
685
686   /* Echo the value of an environment variable */
687   if (p->count != 2)
688     {
689       error ("Usage: getenv variable\n");
690       return;
691     }
692
693   value = getenv (p->token[1]);
694
695   if (value == NULL)
696     printf ("Environment variable is not currently set\n");
697   else
698     printf ("%s\n", value);
699 }
700
701 /*****************************************************************/
702
703 executeSetenv (p)
704
705 struct simple* p;
706
707 {
708   /* Set the value of an environment variable */
709   if (p->count != 3)
710 error ("Usage: setenv variable value\n");
711   else
712 setenv (p->token[1], p->token[2]);
713 }
714
715 /*****************************************************************/
716
717 setenv (envName, newValue)
718
719 char* envName;
720 char* newValue;
721
722 {
723   int i = 0;
724   char newStr [MAX_STRING_LENGTH];
725   int len;
726
727   /* Set the environment variable envName to newValue */
728   sprintf (newStr, "%s=%s", envName, newValue);
729   len = strlen (envName) + 1;
730
731   while (environ[i] != NULL)
732     {
```

```
733          if (strncmp (environ[i], newStr, len) == 0) break;
734          ++i;
735      }
736
737    if (environ[i] == NULL) environ[i+1] = NULL;
738
739    environ[i] = (char*) malloc (strlen (newStr) + 1);
740    strcpy (environ[i], newStr);
741 }
742
743 /*****************************************************************/
744
745 executeCd (p)
746
747 struct simple* p;
748
749 {
750    /* Change directory */
751    if (p->count != 2)
752      error ("Usage: cd path\n");
753    else if (chdir (p->token[1]) == -1)
754      perror ("ish");
755 }
756
757 /*****************************************************************/
758 /*                      REDIRECTION                            */
759 /*****************************************************************/
760
761 redirect (p)
762
763 struct simple *p;
764
765 {
766    int mask;
767
768    /* Perform input redirection */
769    switch (p->inputRedirect)
770      {
771        case FILE_REDIRECT: /* Redirect from a file */
772          if (!dupFd (p->inputFile, O_RDONLY, STDIN)) return(FALSE);
773          break;
774
775        case SERVER_REDIRECT: /* Redirect from a server socket */
776          if (!server (p->inputSocket, INPUT_SOCKET)) return(FALSE);
777          break;
778
779        case CLIENT_REDIRECT: /* Redirect from a client socket */
780          if (!client (p->inputSocket, INPUT_SOCKET)) return(FALSE);
781          break;
782      }
```

```
783
784   /* Perform output redirection */
785   switch (p->outputRedirect)
786     {
787       case FILE_REDIRECT: /* Redirect to a file */
788         mask = O_CREAT | O_WRONLY | (p->append?O_APPEND:O_TRUNC);
789         if (!dupFd (p->outputFile, mask, STDOUT)) return (FALSE);
790         break;
791
792       case SERVER_REDIRECT: /* Redirect to a server socket */
793         if (!server(p->outputSocket,OUTPUT_SOCKET)) return(FALSE);
794       break;
795
796       case CLIENT_REDIRECT: /* Redirect to a client socket */
797         if (!client(p->outputSocket,OUTPUT_SOCKET)) return(FALSE);
798         break;
799     }
800
801   return (TRUE); /* If I got here, then everything went OK */
802 }
803
804 /********************************************************************/
805
806 dupFd (name, mask, stdFd)
807
808 char* name;
809 int mask, stdFd;
810
811 {
812   int fd;
813
814   /* Duplicate a new file descriptor over stdin/stdout */
815   fd = open (name, mask, DEFAULT_PERMISSION);
816
817   if (fd == -1)
818     {
819       error ("Cannot redirect\n");
820       return (FALSE);
821     }
822
823   dup2 (fd, stdFd); /* Copy over standard file descriptor */
824   close (fd); /* Close other one */
825   return (TRUE);
826 }
827
828 /********************************************************************/
829 /*                    SOCKET MANAGEMENT                          */
830 /********************************************************************/
831
832 internetAddress (name)
```

```
833
834 char* name;
835
836 {
837   /* If name contains a digit, assume it's an internet address */
838   return (strpbrk (name, "01234567890") != NULL);
839 }
840
841 /*****************************************************************/
842
843 socketRedirect (type)
844
845 int type;
846
847 {
848   return (type == SERVER_REDIRECT || type == CLIENT_REDIRECT);
849 }
850
851 /*****************************************************************/
852
853 getHostAndPort (str, name, port)
854
855 char *str, *name;
856 int* port;
857
858 {
859   char *tok1, *tok2;
860
861   /* Decode name and port number from input string of the form */
862   /* NAME.PORT */
863   tok1 = strtok (str, ".");
864   tok2 = strtok (NULL, ".");
865   if (tok2 == NULL) /* Name missing, so assume local host */
866     {
867       strcpy (name, "");
868       sscanf (tok1, "%d", port);
869     }
870   else
871     {
872       strcpy (name, tok1);
873       sscanf (tok2, "%d", port);
874     }
875 }
876
877 /*****************************************************************/
878
879 client (name, type)
880
881 char* name;
882 int type;
883
```

```
884 {
885   int clientFd, result, internet, domain, serverLen, port;
886   char hostName [100];
887   struct sockaddr_un serverUNIXAddress;
888   struct sockaddr_in serverINETAddress;
889   struct sockaddr* serverSockAddrPtr;
890   struct hostent* hostStruct;
891   struct in_addr* hostNode;
892
893   /* Open a client socket with specified name and type */
894   internet = internetAddress (name); /* Internet socket? */
895   domain = internet ? AF_INET : AF_UNIX; /* Pick domain */
896   /* Create client socket */
897   clientFd = socket (domain, SOCK_STREAM, DEFAULT_PROTOCOL);
898
899   if (clientFd == -1)
900     {
901       perror ("ish");
902       return (FALSE);
903     }
904
905   if (internet) /* Internet socket */
906     {
907       getHostAndPort (name, hostName, &port); /* Get name, port */
908       if (hostName[0] == NULL) gethostname (hostName, 100);
909       serverINETAddress.sin_family = AF_INET; /* Internet */
910       hostStruct = gethostbyname (hostName); /* Find host */
911
912       if (hostStruct == NULL)
913         {
914           perror ("ish");
915           return (FALSE);
916         }
917
918       hostNode = (struct in_addr*) hostStruct->h_addr;
919       printf ("IP address = %s\n", inet_ntoa (*hostNode));
920       serverINETAddress.sin_addr = *hostNode; /* Set IP address */
921       serverINETAddress.sin_port = port; /* Set port */
922       serverSockAddrPtr = (struct sockaddr*) &serverINETAddress;
923       serverLen = sizeof (serverINETAddress);
924     }
925   else /* UNIX domain socket */
926     {
927       serverUNIXAddress.sun_family = AF_UNIX; /* Domain */
928       strcpy (serverUNIXAddress.sun_path, name); /* File name */
929       serverSockAddrPtr = (struct sockaddr*) &serverUNIXAddress;
930       serverLen = sizeof (serverUNIXAddress);
931     }
932
933   do /* Connect to server */
934     {
```

```
935           result = connect (clientFd, serverSockAddrPtr, serverLen);
936           if (result == -1) sleep (SOCKET_SLEEP); /* Try again soon */
937        }
938     while (result == -1);
939
940     /* Perform redirection */
941     if (type == OUTPUT_SOCKET) dup2 (clientFd, STDOUT);
942     if (type == INPUT_SOCKET) dup2 (clientFd, STDIN);
943     close (clientFd); /* Close original client file descriptor */
944
945     return (TRUE);
946  }
947
948  /*****************************************************************/
949
950  server (name, type)
951
952  char* name;
953  int type;
954
955  {
956    int serverFd, clientFd, serverLen, clientLen;
957    int domain, internet, port;
958    struct sockaddr_un serverUNIXAddress;
959    struct sockaddr_un clientUNIXAddress;
960    struct sockaddr_in serverINETAddress;
961    struct sockaddr_in clientINETAddress;
962    struct sockaddr* serverSockAddrPtr;
963    struct sockaddr* clientSockAddrPtr;
964
965    /* Prepare a server socket */
966    internet = internetAddress (name); /* Internet? */
967    domain = internet ? AF_INET : AF_UNIX; /* Pick domain */
968    /* Create the server socket*/
969    serverFd = socket (domain, SOCK_STREAM, DEFAULT_PROTOCOL);
970
971    if (serverFd == -1)
972       {
973         perror ("ish");
974         return (FALSE);
975       }
976
977    if (internet) /* Internet socket */
978       {
979         sscanf (name, "%d", &port); /* Get port number */
980         /* Fill in server socket address fields */
981         serverLen = sizeof (serverINETAddress);
982         bzero ((char*) &serverINETAddress, serverLen);
983         serverINETAddress.sin_family = AF_INET; /* Domain */
984         serverINETAddress.sin_addr.s_addr = htonl (INADDR_ANY);
985         serverINETAddress.sin_port = htons (port); /* Port */
```

```
986        serverSockAddrPtr = (struct sockaddr*) &serverINETAddress;
987      }
988    else /* UNIX domain socket */
989      {
990        serverUNIXAddress.sun_family = AF_UNIX; /* Domain */
991        strcpy (serverUNIXAddress.sun_path,name); /* Filename */
992        serverSockAddrPtr = (struct sockaddr*) &serverUNIXAddress;
993        serverLen = sizeof (serverUNIXAddress);
994        unlink (name); /* Delete socket if it already exists */
995      }
996
997    /* Bind to socket address */
998    if (bind (serverFd, serverSockAddrPtr, serverLen) == -1)
999      {
1000       perror ("ish");
1001       return (FALSE);
1002     }
1003
1004   /* Set max pending connection queue length */
1005   if (listen (serverFd, DEFAULT_QUEUE_LENGTH) == -1)
1006     {
1007       perror ("ish");
1008       return (FALSE);
1009     }
1010
1011   if (internet) /* Internet socket */
1012     {
1013       clientLen = sizeof (clientINETAddress);
1014       clientSockAddrPtr = (struct sockaddr*) &clientINETAddress;
1015     }
1016   else /* UNIX domain socket */
1017     {
1018       clientLen = sizeof (clientUNIXAddress);
1019       clientSockAddrPtr = (struct sockaddr*) &clientUNIXAddress;
1020     }
1021
1022   /* Accept a connection */
1023   clientFd = accept (serverFd, clientSockAddrPtr, &clientLen);
1024
1025   close (serverFd); /* Close original server socket */
1026
1027   if (clientFd == -1)
1028     {
1029       perror ("ish");
1030       return (FALSE);
1031     }
1032
1033   /* Perform redirection */
1034   if (type == OUTPUT_SOCKET) dup2 (clientFd, STDOUT);
1035   if (type == INPUT_SOCKET) dup2 (clientFd, STDIN);
1036   close (clientFd); /* Close original client socket */
```

```
1037
1038    return (TRUE);
1039 }
1040
```

CHAPTER REVIEW

Checklist

In this chapter, I described:

- all of the common file-management system calls
- the system calls for duplicating, terminating, and differentiating processes
- how a parent may wait for its children
- the terms *orphan* and *zombie*
- threaded processes
- how signals may be trapped and ignored
- the way to kill processes
- how processes may be suspended and resumed
- IPC mechanisms: unnamed pipes, named pipes, shared memory, and semaphores
- the client/server paradigm
- UNIX domain and Internet domain sockets
- the design and operation of an Internet shell

Quiz

1. How can you tell when you've reached the end of a file?
2. What is a file descriptor?
3. What's the quickest way to move to the end of a file?
4. Describe the way that shells implement I/O redirection.
5. What is an orphaned process?
6. How is a task run in two processes different from a task run in two threads?
7. Under what circumstances do zombies accumulate?
8. How can a parent process find out how its children died?
9. What's the difference between "execv ( )" and "execvp ( )"?
10. Why is the name of the system call "kill ( )" a misnomer?
11. How can you protect critical code?
12. What is the purpose of process groups?
13. What happens when a writer tries to overflow a pipe?
14. How can you create a named pipe?
15. Describe the client/server paradigm.
16. Describe the stages that a client and a server go through to establish a connection.

Exercises

1. **Process Trees**

   Write a program that takes a single integer argument *n* from the command-line and creates a binary tree of processes of depth *n*. When the tree is created, each process should display the phrase "I am process x", where x is the number of the process, and then terminate. The nodes of the process tree should be numbered according to a breadth-first traversal. For example, if the user enters the command:

```
$ tree 4   ...build a tree of depth 4.
```

then the process tree would look like:
and the output would be:

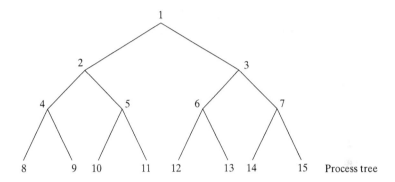

Process tree

```
I am process 1
I am process 2
...
I am process 15
```

Make sure that the original parent process does not terminate until all of its children have died. This requirement is so that you can terminate the parent and its children from your terminal by pressing *Control-C*. [level: *medium*]

2. **Circular Pipes**

   Write a program that creates a ring of three processes connected by pipes. The first process should prompt the user for a string and then send it to the second process. The second process should reverse the string and send it to the third process. The third process should convert the string to uppercase and send it back to the first process. When the first process gets the processed string, it should display it to the terminal. When this procedure is done, all three processes should terminate. Here's an illustration of the process ring:

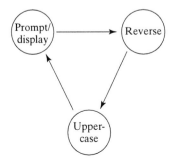

Process ring

Here's an example of the program in action:

```
$ ring                       ...run the program.
Please enter a string: ole
Processed string is: ELO
$ _
```

[level: *medium*]

3. Rewrite the "ghoul" exercise of Chapter 4 using the language of C. [level: *medium*]
4. Write a program that uses "setuid ( )" to allow a user to access a file that he/she could not normally access. [level: *medium*]

Projects

Rock, Paper, Scissors: Part 1   Write a suite of programs that run in parallel and interact to play the "Rock, Paper, Scissors" game. In this game, two players secretly choose one item out of the set of rock, paper, and scissors. They then reveal their choice. A referee decides who wins as follows:

- Paper beats rock (by covering it).
- Rock beats scissors (by blunting it).
- Scissors beats paper (by cutting it).
- Matching choices are a draw.

The winning player gets a point. In a draw, no points are awarded. Your program should simulate such a game, allowing the user to choose how many iterations are performed, observe the game, and see the final score. Here's an example of a game:

```
$ play 3 ...play three iterations.
Paper, Scissors, Rock: 3 iterations
Player 1: ready
Player 2: ready
Go Players [1]
 Player 1: Scissors
 Player 2: Rock
Player 2 wins
Go Players [2]
 Player 1: Paper
 Player 2: Rock
Player 1 wins
Go Players [3]
 Player 1: Paper
 Player 2: Paper
Players draw.
Final score:
 Player 1: 1
 Player 2: 1
Players Draw
$ _
```

You should write three programs that operate as follows:

1. One program is the main program, which fork/execs one referee process and two player processes. It then waits until all three terminate. It should check that the

command-line parameter that specifies the number of turns is legal and pass it to the referee process as a parameter of "exec ( )".

2. One program is a referee program, which plays the role of the server. This program should prepare a socket and then listen for both players to send the string "READY", which means that they're ready to make a choice. It should then tell each player to make a choice by sending them both the string "GO". Their responses are then read and their scores are calculated and updated. This process should be repeated until all of the turns have been taken, at which point the referee should send both players the string "STOP", which causes them to terminate.

3. One program is a player program, which plays the role of the client. This program is executed twice by the main program and should start by connecting to the referee's socket. It should then send the "READY" message. When it receives the "GO" message back from the referee, it should make a choice and send it as a string to the referee. When it receives the string "STOP", it should kill itself.

These programs will almost certainly share some functions. To do a good job, create a make file that separately compiles these common functions and links them into the executables that use them. Don't avoid sending strings by encoding them as one-byte numbers—that aspect is part of this problem. [level: *medium*]

Rock, **Paper**, **Scissors**: **Part 2**   Rewrite Part 1 using unnamed pipes instead of sockets. Which program do you think was easier to write? Which is easier to understand? [level: *medium*]

Rock, **Paper**, **Scissors**: **Part 3**   Rewrite Part 1 to allow the players to reside on different machines on the Internet. Each component of the game should be able to start separately. An example session of the game is as follows: [level: *hard*]

```
...execute this command on "vanguard".
$ referee 5000              ...use local port 5000.
...execute this command on "csservr2".
$ player vanguard.5000       ...player is on a remote port.
...execute this command on "wotan".
$ player vanguard.5000       ...player is on a remote port.
```

Enhancements for the Internet Shell   The Internet shell is ripe for enhancements. Here is a list of features that would be challenging to add:

- The ability to supply an Internet address of the form A.B.C.D. This feature would be easy to add, as my first example of the Internet shell can already do so. [level: *easy*]
- Job control features like *fg*, *bg*, and *jobs*. [level: *medium*]
- Filename substitution using "*", "?", and "[]" metacharacters. [level: *hard*]
- A two-way socket feature that connects the standard input and output channels of either the keyboard or a specified process to an Internet socket. This feature would allow you to connect to standard services without the aid of telnet. [level: *hard*]
- A simple built-in programming language. [level: *medium*]
- The ability to refer to any Internet address symbolically. For example, it would be nice to be able to redirect to "vanguard.utdallas.edu.3000". [level: *medium*]

CHAPTER 1 3

UNIX Internals

Motivation

The UNIX operating system was one of the most well-designed operating systems of its time. Furthermore, many of the basic underlying operating-system concepts embedded in UNIX will continue to be used in some form or fashion for a long time to come. For example, the way in which UNIX shares CPUs between competing processes is used in many other operating systems, such as Microsoft Windows NT. Knowledge of how the system works can aid in designing high-performance UNIX applications. For example, knowledge of the internals of the virtual-memory system can help you arrange data structures so that the amount of information transferred between main and secondary memory is minimized. In summary, knowledge of UNIX internals is useful for two reasons: It is a source of reusable information that may help you in designing other similar systems, and it can help you design high-performance UNIX applications.

Prerequisites

You should already have read Chapter 12. It also helps to have a good knowledge of data structures, pointers, and linked lists.

Objectives

In this chapter, I describe the mechanisms that UNIX uses to support processes, memory management, input/output, and the file system. I also explain the main kernel data structures and algorithms.

Presentation

The information in this chapter is presented in the form of several sections, each of which describes a portion of the UNIX system.

INTRODUCTION

The UNIX system is a fairly complex thing, and it's getting more complex as time goes by. In order to understand it well, it's necessary to break the system down into manageable portions and to tackle each portion in a layered fashion. Here's a description of each section of this chapter:

- "Kernel Basics": Discusses system calls and interrupts.
- "The File System": Describes how the directory hierarchy, regular files, peripherals, and multiple file systems are managed.
- "Process Management": Explains how processes share the CPU and memory. It also describes the implementation of signals.
- "Input/Output": Describes how processes access files. Special attention is given to terminal I/O.
- "Interprocess Communication" (IPC): Explains the mechanisms that allow processes to communicate with each other, even if they're on different machines.

There are some differences between the ways that the BSD and System V designers implemented portions of these subsystems. Any major differences in approach are pointed out at the appropriate time.

KERNEL BASICS

The UNIX kernel is the part of the UNIX operating system that contains the code for:

- sharing the CPU and RAM between competing processes
- processing all system calls
- handling peripherals

The kernel is a program that is loaded from disk into RAM when the computer is first turned on. It always stays in RAM, and it runs until the system is turned off or crashes. Although it's mostly written in C, some parts of the kernel are written in assembly language for efficiency reasons. User programs make use of the kernel via the system call interface.

Kernel Subsystems

The kernel facilities may be divided into several subsystems:

- memory management
- process management
- interprocess communication (IPC)
- input/output
- file management

These subsystems interact in a fairly hierarchical way. Here's an illustration of the layering:

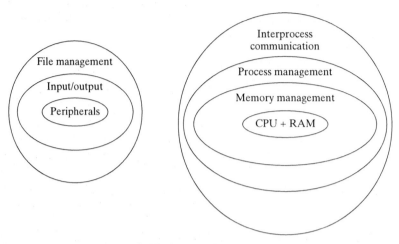

FIGURE 13.1   UNIX subsystems

Processes and Files

The UNIX kernel supports the concepts of processes and files. Processes are the "life forms" that live in the computer and make decisions. Files are containers of information that processes read and write. In addition, processes may talk to each other via several different kinds of interprocess-communication mechanisms, including signals, pipes, and sockets. Here's an illustration of what I mean when I say that the UNIX kernel supports processes and files:

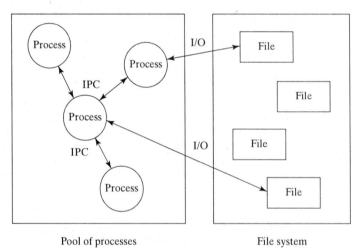

Pool of processes   File system

FIGURE 13.2   UNIX supports processes and files

Talking to the Kernel

Processes access kernel facilities via the system call interface, and peripherals (special files) communicate with the kernel via hardware interrupts. System calls and hardware interrupts are the only ways that the outside world can talk to the kernel, as illustrated by the following diagram:

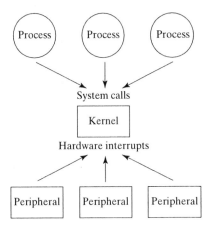

FIGURE 13.3   Talking to the kernel

Since systems calls and hardware interrupts are obviously very important, I'll begin the discussion of UNIX internals with a description of each mechanism.

System Calls

System calls are the programmer's functional interface to the kernel. They are subroutines that reside inside the UNIX kernel and support basic system functions such as the ones listed in the table below:

Function	System Call
open a file	open
close a file	close
perform I/O	read/write
send a signal	kill
create a pipe	pipe
create a socket	socket
duplicate a process	fork
overlay a process	exec
terminate a process	exit

System calls may be loosely grouped into three main categories, as illustrated in the following diagram:

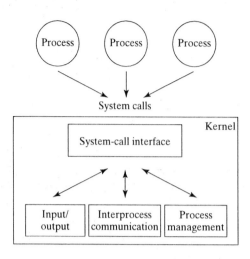

FIGURE 13.4   Major system call subsystems

User Mode and Kernel Mode

The kernel contains several data structures that are essential to the functioning of the system. Examples of these structures include:

- the *process table,* which contains one entry for every process in the system
- the *open-file table,* which contains at least one entry for every open file in the system

These data structures reside in the kernel's memory space, which is protected from user processes by a memory-management system that I'll describe to you later. Therefore, user processes cannot accidentally corrupt these important kernel data structures. System call routines are different from regular functions because they *can* directly manipulate kernel data structures, albeit in a carefully controlled manner.

When a user process is running, it operates in a special machine mode called *user mode.* This mode prevents a process from executing certain privileged machine instructions, including those that would allow it to access the kernel data structures. The other machine mode is called *kernel mode.* A kernel-mode process may execute any machine instruction.

The only way for a user process to enter kernel mode is to execute a system call. Every system call is allocated a code number, starting from 1. For example, the "open ()" system call might be allocated code number 1, and "close ()" might be allocated code number 2. When a process invokes a system call, the C runtime library version of the system call places the system call parameters and the system call code number into some machine registers and then executes a *trap* machine instruction. The trap instruction flips the machine into kernel mode and uses the system call code number as an index into a *system call vector table* located in low kernel memory. The system call vector table is an array of pointers to the kernel code for each system call. The code corresponding to the indexed function executes in kernel mode, modifying kernel data structures as necessary, and then performs a special "return" instruction that flips the machine back into user mode and returns to the user process' code.

When I was first learning about UNIX, I didn't understand why this approach was taken. Why not just use a client/server model with a kernel server process that services system requests from client user processes? This system avoids the need of user processes to execute kernel code directly. However, the reason is pure and simple: speed. In current architectures, the overhead of swapping between processes is too great to make the client/server approach practical. However, it's interesting to note that some of the modern microkernel systems are taking the latter approach.

From a programmer's standpoint, using a system call is easy; you call the C function with the correct parameters, and the function returns when complete. If an error occurs, the function returns a value of −1 and the global variable "errno" is set to indicate the cause of the error. Here's a diagram that illustrates the flow of control during a system call:

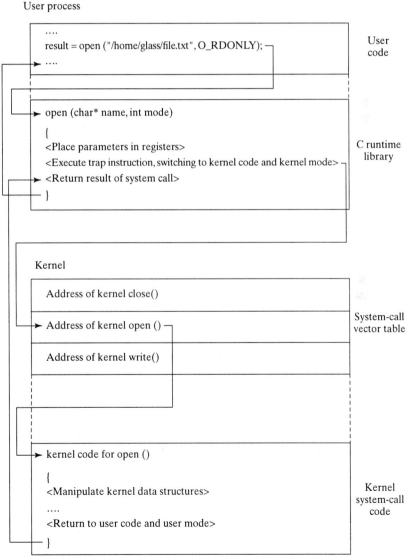

FIGURE 13.5   User mode and kernel mode

Synchronous vs. Asynchronous Processing

When a process performs a system call, it cannot usually be preempted. This condition means that the scheduler will not assign the CPU to another process during the operation of a system call. However, some system calls request I/O operations from a device, which can take a while to complete. To avoid leaving the CPU idle during the wait for I/O completion, the kernel sends the waiting process to sleep and only wakes it up again when a hardware interrupt signaling I/O completion is received. The scheduler does not allocate a sleeping process any CPU time and thereby allocates the CPU to other processes while the hardware device is servicing the I/O request.

An interesting consequence of the way that UNIX handles "read ()" and "write ()" is that user processes experience synchronous execution of system calls, whereas the kernel experiences asynchronous behavior:

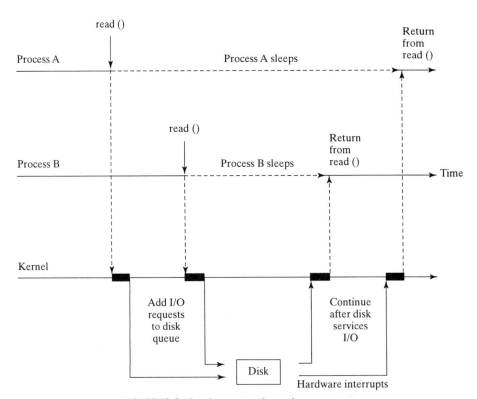

FIGURE 13.6 Synchronous and asynchronous events

Interrupts Interrupts are the way that hardware devices notify the kernel that they would like some attention. In the same way that processes compete for CPU time, hardware devices compete for interrupt processing. Devices are allocated an interrupt priority based on their relative importance, as illustrated in

Figure 13.7. For example, interrupts from the system clock have a higher priority than those from the keyboard.

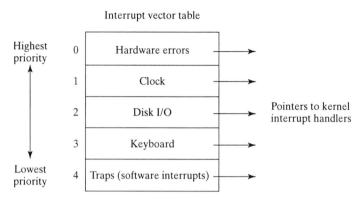

FIGURE 13.7   Interrupts have priorities

When an interrupt occurs, the current process is suspended and the kernel determines the source of the interrupt. It then examines its interrupt vector table, located in low kernel memory, to find the location of the code that processes the interrupt. This "interrupt handler" code is then executed. When the interrupt handler completes, the current process is resumed. This process is depicted in Figure 13.8.

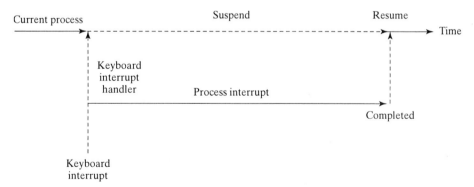

FIGURE 13.8   Interrupt processing

Interrupting Interrupts

Interrupt processing may itself be interrupted! If an interrupt of a higher priority than the current interrupt arrives, a sequence of events similar to those that occurred when the first interrupt arrived occurs, and the handler of the interrupt of lower priority is suspended until the interrupt of higher priority completes.

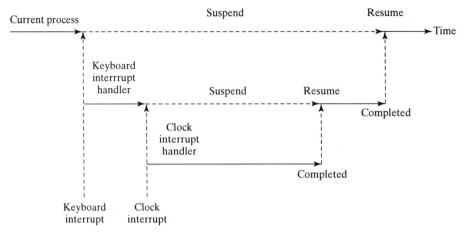

FIGURE 13.9 Interrupts may be interrupted

If an interrupt is being processed and another interrupt of an equal or lower priority occurs, the incoming interrupt is ignored and discarded. Interrupt handlers are therefore designed to be very fast, as the quicker they execute, the less likely it is that other interrupts will be lost.

Disk interrupts are of lower priority than clock interrupts

```
                                    ┌──────┐
                                    │ Disk │
                                    └──────┘

Kernel                              Processed              Ignored
                                                                    Time

                                    ┌───────┐
                                    │ Clock │
                                    └───────┘
```

Clock interrupts are processed with a high priority

FIGURE 13.10 Interrupts may be ignored

Most machines have instructions that allow a program to ignore all interrupts below a certain priority level. Critical sections of kernel code protect themselves from interrupts by temporarily invoking such instructions. Here's some pseudocode that does just that:

```
...
<disable all but the interrupts of highest priority>
<enter critical section of code>
```

```
...
...
<leave critical section of code>
<reenable all interrupts>
...
```

The "Input/Output" section later in this chapter describes the way that peripherals use the kernel interrupt facilities to perform efficient I/O.

THE FILE SYSTEM

UNIX uses files for long-term storage and RAM for short-term storage. Programs, data, and text are all stored in files. Files are usually stored on hard disks, but can also be stored on other media, such as tape and floppy disks. UNIX files are organized by a hierarchy of labels, commonly known as a *directory structure*. The files referenced by these labels may be of three kinds:

- *Regular files*, which contain a sequence of bytes that generally corresponds to code or data. They may be referenced via the standard I/O system calls.
- *Directory files*, which are stored on disk in a special format and form the backbone of the file system. They may be referenced only via directory-specific system calls.
- *Special files*, which correspond to peripherals such as printers and disks, and interprocess-communication mechanisms such as pipes and sockets. They may be referenced via the standard I/O system calls.

Conceptually, a UNIX file is a linear sequence of bytes. The UNIX kernel does not support any higher order of file structure, such as records and/or fields. This situation is evident if you consider the "lseek ()" system call, which allows you to position the file pointer only in terms of a byte offset. Older operating systems tended to support record structures, so UNIX was fairly unusual in this regard.

Let's begin our study of the UNIX file system by looking at the hardware architecture of the most common file medium: a disk.

Disk Architecture

Here's a diagram of a typical disk architecture:

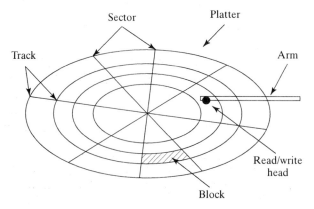

FIGURE 13.11   Disk architecture

A disk is split up in two ways: It's sliced up like a pizza into areas called *sectors* and further subdivided into concentric rings called *tracks*. The individual areas bounded by the intersection of sectors and tracks are called *blocks*, and such a block is the basic unit of disk storage. A typical disk block can hold 4K bytes. A single read/write head travels up and down a stationary arm, accessing information as the disk rotates and its surface passes underneath. A special chip called a *disk controller* moves the read/write head in response to instructions from the disk device driver, which is a special piece of software located in the UNIX kernel.

There are several variations of this simple disk architecture. Many disk drives actually contain several platters, stacked one upon the other. In these systems, a collection of tracks with the same index number is called a *cylinder*. In most multiplatter systems, the disk arms are connected to each other so that the read/write heads all move synchronously, rather like a comb moving through hair. The read/write heads of such disk systems therefore move through cylinders of media. Furthermore, some sophisticated disk drives have separately controllable read/write heads.

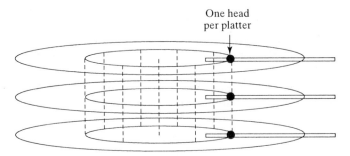

FIGURE 13.12   A multiplatter architecture

Notice that the blocks on the outside track of a disk are larger than the blocks on the inside track, due to the way that a disk is partitioned. If a disk always rotates at the same speed, it means that the density of data on outer blocks is less than it could be, thus wasting potential storage. Some of the latest disk drive designs attempt to keep the data density constant throughout the disk surface by increasing the num-

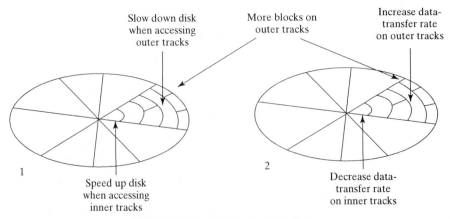

FIGURE 13.13   Disk-storage techniques

ber of blocks on the outer tracks and then either slowing down the disk rotation or increasing the data transfer rate as the head moves toward the outside of the disk.

Interleaving

When a sequence of contiguously numbered blocks is read, there's a latency delay between each block due to the overhead of the communication between the disk controller and the device driver. Logically contiguous blocks are therefore spaced apart on the surface of the disk so that by the time that the latency delay is over, the head is positioned over the correct area. The spacing between blocks due to this delay effect is called the *interleave factor*. Here are a couple of pictures that illustrate two different interleave factors:

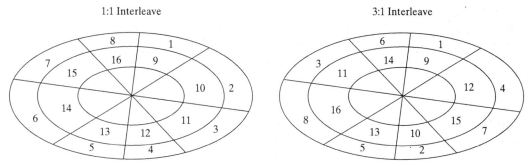

FIGURE 13.14   Disk interleaving

Storing a File

Assuming a 4K block size, a single 9K UNIX file requires three blocks of storage: one to hold the first 4K, one to hold the next 4K, and the last to hold the remaining 1K.[1] The loss of storage due to the underuse of the last 4K block is called *fragmentation*. A file's blocks are rarely contiguous and tend to be scattered all over a disk:

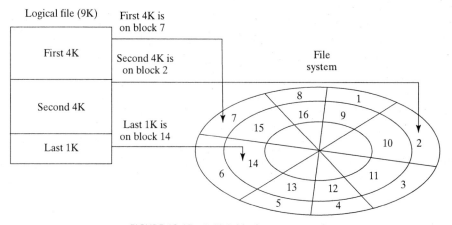

FIGURE 13.15   A file's blocks are scattered

---

[1] Some file systems remedy this situation by allocating a disk block to contain the last segments of data files. Thus, one disk block can contain fragments from different files.

Block I/O

I/O is always done in terms of blocks. If you issue a "read ()" system call to read the first byte of data from a file, the device driver issues an I/O request to the disk controller to read the first 4K block into a kernel buffer and then copies the first byte from the buffer to your process. More information about I/O buffering is presented later in this chapter.

Most disk controllers handle one block of I/O request at a time. When a disk controller completes the current block of I/O request, it issues a hardware interrupt back to the device driver to signal completion. At this point, the device driver usually makes the next block of I/O request. Figure 13.16 is a diagram that illustrates the sequence of events that might occur during a "read ()" of a 9K file.

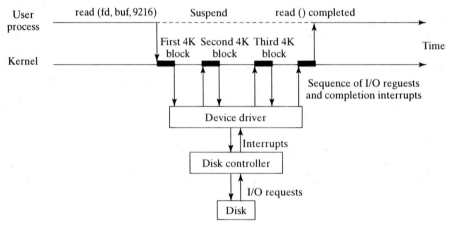

FIGURE 13.16 Block I/O

Inodes

UNIX uses a structure called an *inode,* which stands for "index node," to store information about each file. The inode of a regular or directory file contains the locations of its disk blocks, and the inode of a special file contains information that allows the peripheral to be identified. An inode also holds other information associated with a file, such as its permission flags, owner, group, and last modification time. An inode is a structure of fixed size containing pointers to disk blocks and additional indirect pointers (for large files). Every inode in a particular file system is allocated a unique inode number and every file has exactly one inode. All of the inodes associated with the files on a disk are stored in a special area at the start of the disk called the *inode list.*

Inode Contents

Here's a list of the file information contained within each inode:

- the type of the file: regular, directory, block special, character special, etc.
- file permissions

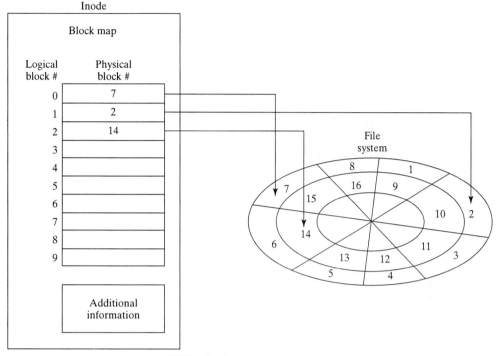

FIGURE 13.17 Every file has an inode

- the owner and group IDs
- a hard-link count (described later in this chapter)
- the last modification and access times
- if it's a regular or directory file, the location of the blocks
- if it's a special file, the major and minor device numbers (described later in this chapter)
- if it's a symbolic link, the value of the symbolic link

In other words, an inode contains all of the information that you see when you perform an "ls -l" command, except for the filename.

The Block Map

Only the locations of the first 10 blocks of a file are stored directly in the inode. Most UNIX files are less than 40K in size, so this storage is sufficient for a majority of cases. A scheme of indirect access is used for addressing larger files. In this scheme, a single user block is used to hold the location of up to 1024 user blocks. When used in this manner, a block is called an *indirect block*. Its location is stored in the inode and is used to address the next 1024 blocks. This approach allows files up to four megabytes of space in which to be addressed. (See Figure 13.18)

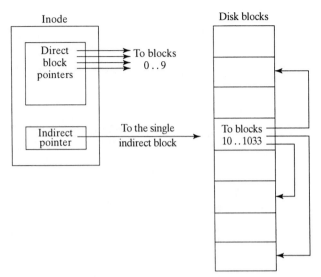

FIGURE 13.18   The single-indirect block

For files greater than four megabytes in size, a similar double-indirect scheme is used. A user block is used to hold the location of up to 1024 indirect blocks, each of which points to a maximum of 1024 user blocks. The inode holds the location of the double-indirect user block. (See Figure 13.19.)

Note that as the file gets larger, the amount of indirection required to access a particular block increases. This overhead is minimized by buffering the contents of the inode and commonly referenced indirect blocks in RAM. The buffering mechanism is described later in this chapter.

Layout of the File System

The first logical block of a disk is termed the *boot block*, and it contains some executable code that is used when UNIX is first activated. See Chapter 14 for more information. The second logical block is known as the *superblock*, and it contains information concerning the disk itself. Following this block is a set of blocks that is of fixed size and is called the *inode list*. The inode list holds all of the inodes associated with the files on the disk. Each block in the inode list can normally hold about

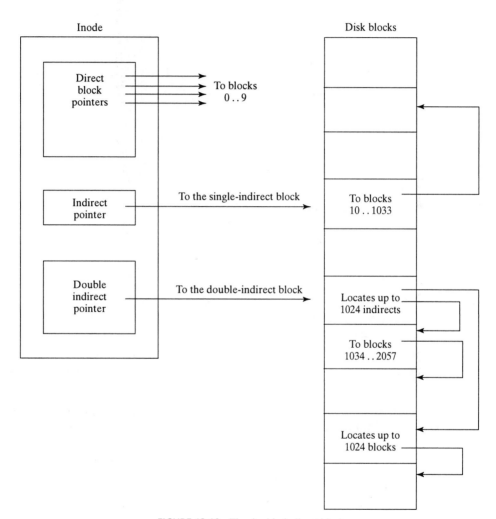

FIGURE 13.19   The double-indirect block

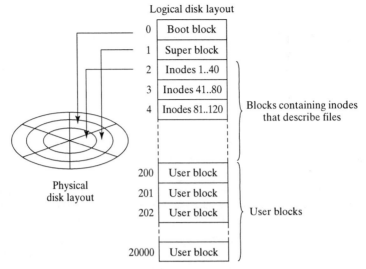

FIGURE 13.20 Usage of disk blocks

40 inodes, although this number varies with different versions of UNIX. The remaining blocks on the disk are available for storing file blocks and contain both directories and user files. (See Figure 13.20.)

The Superblock

The superblock contains information pertaining to the entire file system. It includes a bitmap of free blocks, which is a linear sequence of bits, one per disk block. A "1" indicates that the corresponding block is free, and a "0" means that it's being used.

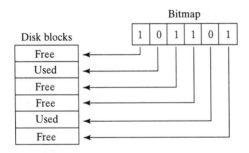

FIGURE 13.21 The free-block bitmap

The information in the superblock includes the following items:

- the total number of blocks in the file system
- the number of inodes in the inode free list
- the size of a block in bytes
- the number of free blocks
- the number of used blocks

Bad Blocks

A disk always contains several blocks that for one reason or another are not fit for use. The utility that creates a new file system, described in Chapter 14, creates a single "worst nightmare" file that is made up of all of the bad blocks in the disk and that records the locations of all of these blocks in inode #1. This file prevents the blocks from being allocated to other files.

Directories

Inode #2 contains the location of the block(s) containing the root directory. A UNIX directory contains a list of associations between filenames and inode numbers. When a directory is created, it is automatically allocated entries for "..", its parent directory, and ".", itself. Since a pair made up of a filename and an inode number effectively links a name to a file, these associations are termed *hard links*. Since a filename is stored in a directory block, it is not stored in the file's inode. In fact, it wouldn't make any sense to store the name in the inode, as the file may have more than one name. Because of this observation, it's more accurate to think of the directory hierarchy as being a hierarchy of *file labels*, rather than a hierarchy of *files*.

All UNIX systems allow a filename to be at least 14 characters long, and most support names up to 255 characters in length.

Here's an illustration of the root inode corresponding to a simple root directory. The inode numbers associated with each filename are shown as subscripts:

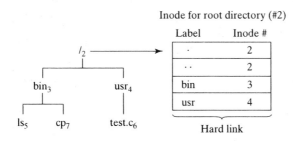

FIGURE 13.22   The root directory is associated with inode #2

Translating Pathnames into Inode Numbers

System calls such as "open ()" must obtain a file's inode from its pathname. They perform the translation as follows:

1. The inode from which to start the pathname search is located. If the pathname is absolute, the search starts from inode #2. If the pathname is relative, the search starts from the inode corresponding to the process' current working directory. See the "Process Management" section of this chapter for more information.

2. The components of the pathname are then processed from left to right. Every component except the last should correspond to either a directory or a symbolic link. Let's call the inode from which the pathname search is started the *current inode*.

3. If the current inode corresponds to a directory, the current pathname component is looked for in the directory corresponding to the current inode. If it's not found, an error occurs; otherwise, the value of the current inode's number becomes the inode number associated with the located pathname component.

4. If the current inode corresponds to a symbolic link, the pathname up to and including the current path component is replaced by the contents of the symbolic link, and the pathname is reprocessed.

5. The inode corresponding to the final pathname component is the inode of the file referenced by the entire pathname.

To illustrate this algorithm, I'll list the steps required to translate the pathname "/usr/test.c" into an inode number. Figure 13.23 contains the disk layout that I assume during the translation process. It indicates the translation path with bold lines and the final destination with a circle.

Sample Pathname-to-Inode Translation

Here's the logic that the kernel uses to translate the pathname "/usr/test.c" into an inode number:

1. The pathname is absolute, so the current inode number is 2.

2. The directory corresponding to inode #2 is searched for the pathname component "usr". The matching entry is found, and the current inode number is set to 4.

3. The directory corresponding to inode #4 is searched for the pathname component "test.c". The matching entry is found, and the current inode number is set to 6.

4. "test.c" is the final pathname component, so the algorithm returns inode #6.

As you can see, the translation bounces between inodes and directory blocks until the pathname is fully processed.

Mounting File Systems

When UNIX is started, the directory hierarchy corresponds to the file system located on a single disk called the *root device*. UNIX allows you to create file systems on other devices and attach them to the original directory hierarchy using a mechanism termed *mounting*. The **mount** utility allows a super-user to splice the root directory of a file system into the existing directory hierarchy. The hierarchy of a large UNIX system is typically spread over many devices, each containing a subtree of the total hierarchy. For example, the "/usr" subtree is commonly stored on a device other than the root device. Nonroot file systems are usually mounted automatically at boot time.

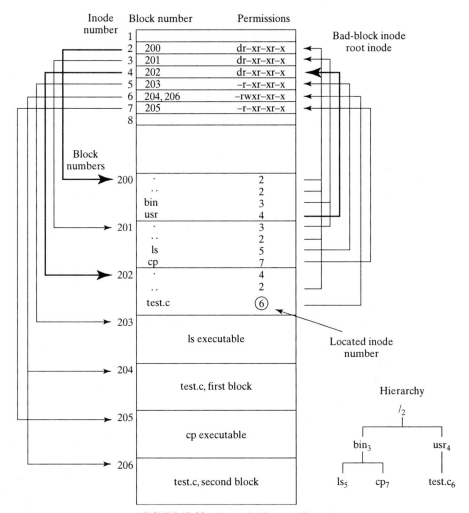

FIGURE 13.23   A sample directory layout

See Chapter 14 for more details. For example, assume that a file system is stored on a floppy disk in the "/dev/flp" device. To attach it to the "/mnt" subdirectory of the main hierarchy, you'd execute the command:

```
$ mount /dev/flp /mnt
```

Here's a diagram that illustrates the effect of this command:

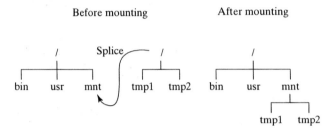

FIGURE 13.24   Mounting directories

File systems may be detached from the main hierarchy by using the **umount** utility. The following commands would detach the file system stored in "/dev/flp":

```
$ umount /dev/flp
```

or

```
$ umount /mnt
```

File-System I/O

For details about the kernel implementation of file-system I/O, refer to the "Input/Output" section later in this chapter.

PROCESS MANAGEMENT

In this section, I describe the way that the kernel shares the CPU and RAM among competing processes. The area of the kernel that shares the CPU is called the *scheduler*, and the area of the kernel that shares RAM is called the *memory manager*. This section also contains information about process-oriented system calls, including "exec ()", "fork ()", and "exit ()". For the sake of simplicity, we will not concern ourselves with *kernel threads* (threads that run in kernel mode), since most application programmers do not have an occasion to use them. However, be aware that just as a user application can run multithreaded tasks, some kernel modules (like device drivers) may also run in multiple threads. This factor introduces most of the same complexities discussed in the previous chapter.

Executable Files

When the source code of a program is compiled, it is stored in a special format on disk. The first few bytes of the file are known as the *magic number* and are used by the kernel to identify the type of the executable file. For example, if the first two bytes of the file are the characters "#!", the kernel knows that the executable file contains shell text and invokes a shell to execute the text. Another sequence identifies the file as being a regular load image containing machine code and data. This kind of file is divided into several sections containing code or data, with a separate header for each section. The headers are used by the kernel for preparing the memory management system described shortly. Here's an illustration of a typical executable file:

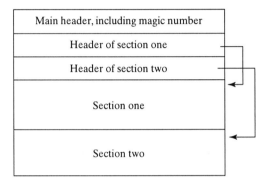

FIGURE 13.25   Layout of an executable file

The First Processes

UNIX runs a program by creating a process and then associating it with a named executable file. Surprisingly enough, there's no system call that allows you to tell UNIX, "Create a new process to run program X"; instead, you must duplicate an existing process and then associate the newly created child process with the executable file "X".

The first process, with process ID (PID) 0, is created by UNIX during boot time. This process immediately fork and execs twice, creating two processes with PIDs 1 and 2. In System V UNIX, the names of these first few processes are:

PID	Name
0	sched
1	init
2	pageout

The purpose of these processes is described later in this chapter. All other processes in the system are descendants of the "init" process. For more information concerning the boot sequence, see Chapter 14.

Kernel Processes and User Processes

Most processes execute in user mode except when they make a system call, at which point they flip temporarily into kernel mode. However, the "sched" daemon (PID 0) and "pageout" daemon (PID 2) processes execute permanently in kernel mode due to their importance and are termed *kernel processes*. In contrast to that of user processes, their code is linked directly into the kernel and does not reside in a separate executable file. In addition, kernel processes are never preempted.

The Process Hierarchy

When a process duplicates by using "fork ()", the original process is known as the parent of the child process. The "init" process (PID 1) is the process from which all user processes are descended. Parent and child processes are therefore related in a hierarchy, with the "init" process as the root process. Here's an illustration of a process hierarchy involving four processes:

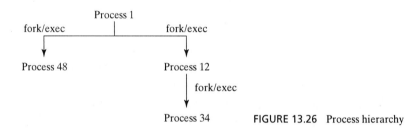

FIGURE 13.26   Process hierarchy

Process States

Every process in the system can be in one of six states. The six possible states are as follows:

- *Running*, which means that the process is currently using the CPU.
- *Runnable*, which means that the process can make use of the CPU as soon as it becomes available.
- *Sleeping*, which means that the process is waiting for an event to occur. For example, if a process executes a "read ()" system call, it sleeps until the I/O request completes.
- *Suspended*, which means that the process has been "frozen" by a signal such as SIGSTOP. It will resume only when sent a SIGCONT signal. For example, a *Control*-Z from the keyboard suspends all of the processes in the foreground job.
- *Idle*, which means that the process is being created by a "fork ()" system call and is not yet runnable.
- *Zombified*, which means that the process has terminated but has not yet returned its exit code to its parent. A process remains a zombie until its parent accepts its return code using the "wait ()" system call.

Here's a diagram that illustrates the possible state changes that can occur during the lifetime of a process:

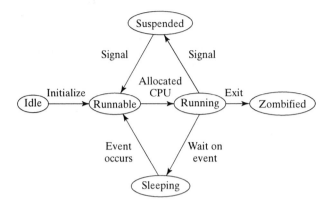

FIGURE 13.27   Process states

Process Composition

Every process is composed of several different pieces:

- a *code area*, which contains the executable (text) portion of a process
- a *data area*, which is used by a process to contain static data
- a *stack area*, which is used by a process to store temporary data
- a *user area*, which holds housekeeping information about a process
- *page tables*, which are used by the memory management system

The uses of the first three areas should be familiar to you, and I'm going to leave a discussion of page tables until later. The next subsection contains a description of the user area.

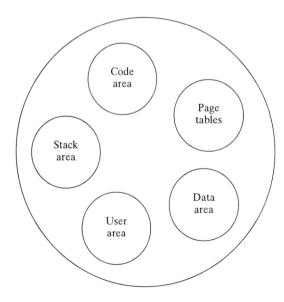

FIGURE 13.28   Process composition

The User Area

Every process in the system has some associated "housekeeping" information that is used by the kernel for process management. This information is stored in a data structure called a *user area*. Every process has its own user area. User areas are created in the kernel's data region and are only accessible by the kernel; user processes may not access their user areas. Fields within a process' user area include:

- a record of how the process should react to each kind of signal
- a record of the process' open file descriptors
- a record of how much CPU time the process has used recently

The contents of a user area are described in more detail later in this chapter.

The Process Table

There is a single kernel data structure of fixed size called the *process table* that contains one entry for every process in the system. The process table is created in the kernel's data region and is accessible only by the kernel. Each entry contains the following information about each process:

- its process ID (PID) and parent process ID (PPID)
- its real and effective user ID (UID) and group ID (GID)
- its state (running, runnable, sleeping, suspended, idle, or zombified)
- the location of its code, data, stack, and user areas
- a list of all pending signals

Here's the process table that would result from the small process hierarchy that I illustrated earlier in this chapter. It assumes that the process with PID 48 is currently waiting for I/O completion:

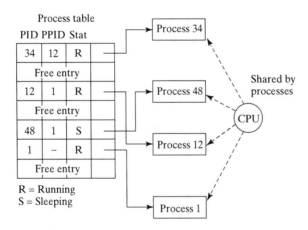

FIGURE 13.29   Process table

The Scheduler

The kernel is responsible for sharing CPU time between competing processes. A section of the kernel code called the *scheduler* performs this duty and maintains a special data structure called a *multilevel priority queue* that allows it to schedule processes efficiently. A priority queue is a linked list of the runnable processes that have similar priorities. The way that the kernel calculates a process' priority is discussed later in this chapter.

Processes are allocated CPU time in proportion to their importance. CPU time is allocated in units of fixed size called *time quantums*. On most systems, each time quantum is tenth of a second. Here's an illustration of the queues in relation to the process table, based on the small process hierarchy illustrated earlier in this chapter:

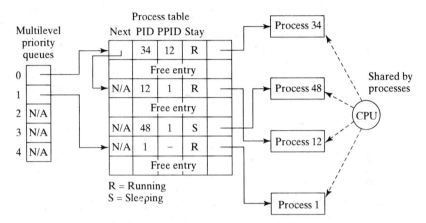

FIGURE 13.30   The process table and priority queues

Scheduling Rules

Here are the rules that describe the way in which the scheduler works:

- Every second, the scheduler calculates the priorities of all of the runnable processes in the system and organizes them into several priority queues. The queues are stratified based on the process' priority values.
- Every tenth of a second, the scheduler selects the process of highest priority in the priority queues and allocates it the CPU (unless the currently running process is in kernel mode).
- If a process is still runnable at the end of its time quantum, it's placed at the end of its priority queue.
- If a process sleeps on an event during its time quantum, the scheduler immediately selects another process to run and allocates it the CPU.
- If a process returns from a system call during its time quantum and a process of higher priority is ready to run, the process of lower priority is preempted by the process of higher priority.
- Every hardware clock interrupt, which typically occurs 100 times a second, the process' clock-tick count is incremented. Every fourth tick, the scheduler recalculates the process' priority value. This operation tends to reduce a process' priority during its time quantum.

The formula for calculating a process' priority may be stated roughly as follows:

$$priority = (Recent\ CPU\ usage)/constant + base\ priority + nice\ setting$$

base priority is the threshold priority and the *nice setting* is the value set by the "nice()" system call. This formula ensures that a process' priority diminishes if it uses a lot of CPU time in a particular "window" of time. It also ensures that processes that have a high nice setting will have a lower priority. A spin-off of this formula is that interactive processes tend to have a good response time; as an interactive process waits for a user to press a key, it uses no CPU time, and therefore, its priority level rises rapidly.

The act of switching from one process to another is termed a *context switch*. To "freeze" a process, the kernel saves its program counter, stack pointer, and other important details into the process' user area. To "thaw" a process, the kernel reinstates this information from the process' user area.

The result of these rules is that during every second, processes in the non-empty queue of the highest priority are allocated the CPU in a round-robin fashion. At the end of each second, the processes are repositioned in the queues, depending on their new priorities, and the round-robin allocation repeats. Here are some illustrations of the scheduling rules in action:

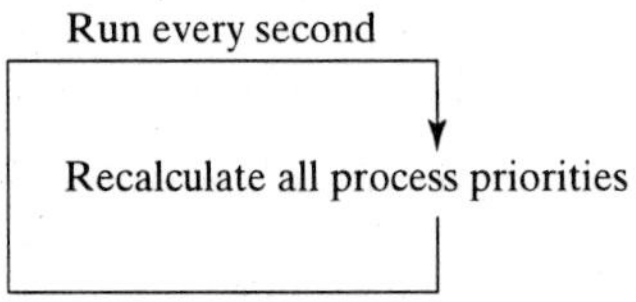

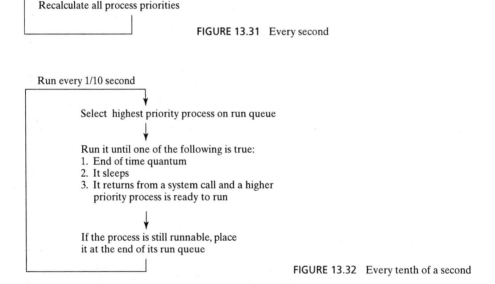

FIGURE 13.31 Every second

FIGURE 13.32 Every tenth of a second

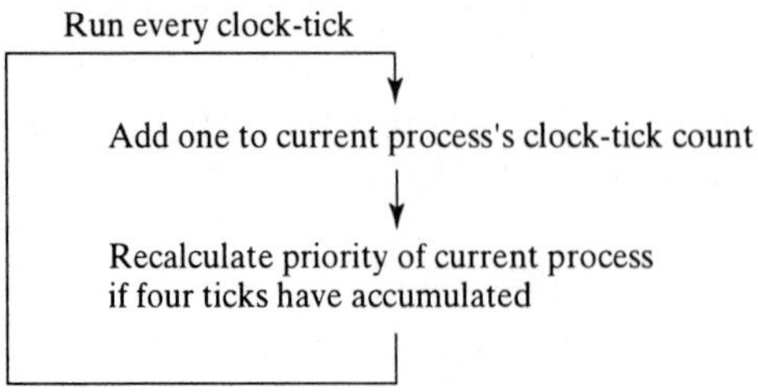

FIGURE 13.33 Every clock tick

Memory Management

In addition to scheduling, the kernel is responsible for sharing RAM between processes in a secure and efficient manner. The next few sections describe the UNIX memory management system.[2]

Memory Pages

The UNIX memory management system allows processes that are bigger than the total RAM capacity to execute. In order to achieve this capability, it divides RAM, code, data, and stack areas into chunks of memory of a fixed size called *pages*. This process is analogous to the way in which a disk is divided up into blocks of a fixed size. The size of a memory page is typically set to be equal to the size of a disk block. The reason for this relationship will soon become evident. Only the pages of a process that are currently being accessed or were recently accessed are stored in RAM pages; the rest are stored on disk.

Page Tables and Regions

The code, data, and stack areas of a process do not have to reside in logically contiguous memory. For example, the compiler might generate a program whose code, data, and stack occupy the following logical areas of address space:

Section	Logical Address
code	0K..15K
data	64K..72K
stack	64K..72K

Each area of contiguous logical address space is termed a *region*, and therefore, most processes have three regions. Also, the pages of a region do not have to be stored contiguously in RAM; every region has an associated data structure called a *page table* that records the location of each of its pages. A process' page tables are created in the kernel's data region and are only accessible by the kernel. The locations of a process' page tables are stored in the process' user area. A page table in the memory management system is analogous to an inode in the file system, as each tracks the location of individual storage units.

Figure 13.34 is an illustration of the relationship among the process table, user areas, and page tables.

---

[2] Memory management implementations vary with versions of UNIX. The algorithm described here is BSD centric.

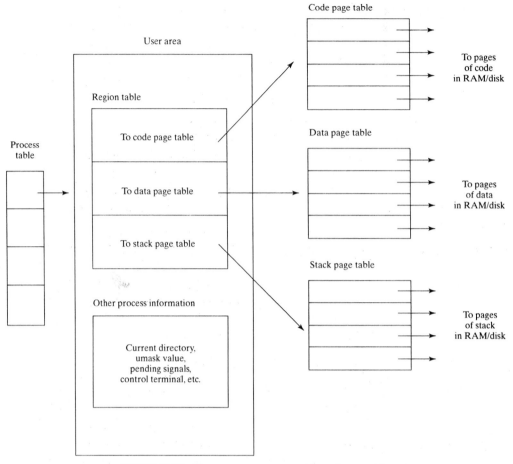

FIGURE 13.34   The user areas, process table, and page tables

The RAM Table

The memory manager allocates pages of RAM to a process only when it needs them. A single kernel data structure of a fixed size called the *RAM table* records information about each page of RAM, such as whether the page is currently being used and whether it's "locked" into memory. Locked pages are never transferred to disk; for example, all of the pages that contain the UNIX kernel are locked.

Loading an Executable: "exec ()"

When a process performs an "exec ()", the kernel allocates page tables for the process' code, data, and stack regions. At this point, all of the code and initialized data reside on disk in the executable file, and so the code and data page table entries are set to contain the locations of their corresponding disk blocks. These locations are extracted from the executable file's inode and header. When the process accesses one of these pages for the first time, its corresponding block is copied from disk into RAM and the page table entry is updated with the physical RAM page number.

The stack and uninitialized data regions do not have a corresponding disk location. The kernel therefore marks their corresponding page table entries as *zeroed*. When a zeroed page is accessed for the first time, the kernel allocates a page of RAM and fills it with zeroes *without* loading anything from disk. It then updates the page table entry with the physical RAM page number.

Assuming that the first eight pages of RAM were originally free, here's an illustration of a process' memory layout immediately after an "exec ()":

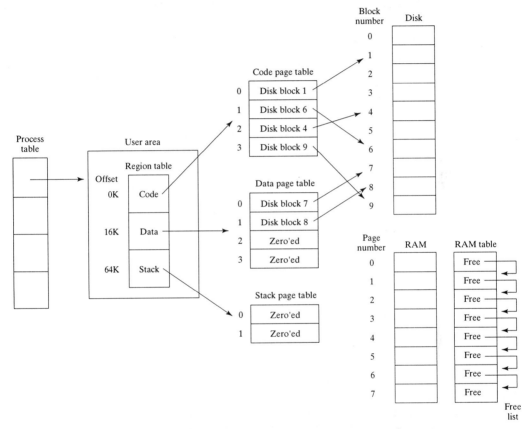

FIGURE 13.35 Memory layout immediately after an "exec ()"

Address Translation

All of the logical addresses that travel down the hardware address bus from a process must be mapped to a physical address using the information contained in the process' region and page tables. This translation process is aided by a special piece of hardware called a *memory management unit* (MMU). Assuming that every page of RAM is 4K and that all addresses are 32-bit values, the memory management unit works as follows:

- When a process is scheduled, several hardware-specific registers in the MMU are set to point to the process' region and page tables. The MMU uses these registers to access these data structures during the address translation process.

- When an address appears on the hardware address bus, the MMU is activated and starts the translation process. I'll call the incoming address "ADDR".
- The MMU then determines which region the incoming address ADDR lies within: either the code, data, or stack region.
- The MMU then subtracts the starting virtual address (SVA) of the region from the incoming address ADDR. This procedure yields the offset of the incoming address from the start of the region (OSR).
- The OSR is then split into two pieces. The most significant 20 bits correspond to the region page number of the incoming address (RPN), and the least significant 12 bits are equal to the offset within this region page (ORP).
- The MMU then consults the region's page table to determine the current location of the logical page RPN. If the page is currently in RAM, the incoming logical address is translated into a physical address by replacing the logical page number by the physical RAM number. If the page is not in RAM, the MMU gives up trying to translate the logical address, generates a page-validity interrupt, and then processes other incoming logical addresses.
- When UNIX receives a page validity interrupt, it issues an I/O request that loads the page from disk into a free page of RAM. When the page is loaded, the appropriate page table entry is updated with the RAM page number, and the address translation is restarted.

Illustration of MMU Algorithm

Here's an illustration of the MMU-mapping algorithm:

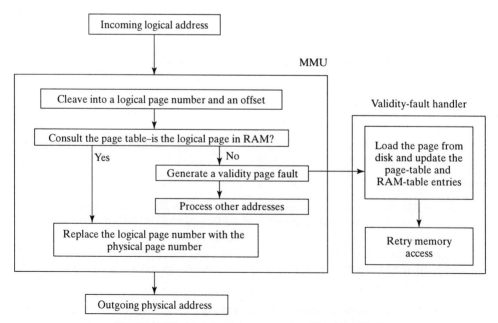

FIGURE 13.36 Memory management algorithm (simplified)

The MMU and the Page Table

Each page table entry contains a number of fields that are used by various facets of the memory-management system. Some of these fields are set automatically by the MMU under certain circumstances:

- The *modified bit* is set when a process writes to the page.
- The *referenced bit* is set when a process reads from or writes to the page.

Some of the other fields are automatically used by the MMU when translating an incoming logical address:

- If the valid bit is set, the MMU replaces the logical page number of the incoming address with the *physical page number* field.
- If the valid bit is not set, the MMU generates a page fault.
- If the *copy-on-write bit* is set and a process attempts to modify the page, the MMU generates a page fault regardless of the state of the valid bit.

The Memory Layout After the First Instruction

An "exec ()" causes the first instruction of the executable to be fetched from memory, which in turn causes the MMU to fault in the first page. The address of the first instruction is stored in the executable's header and tends to be a low memory address. In Figure 13.37, I assumed that the first instruction was located at logical address 0 and that page 0 of the code region was paged into page 0 of physical RAM.

The Memory Layout After Many Instructions   When a process continues to execute after an "exec ()", it tends to fault in more of its code, data, and stack pages. The diagram in Figure 13.38 illustrates a situation in which all of the physical pages of RAM have been filled by a single process. This situation can never happen in a real UNIX system, as the kernel occupies low RAM addresses and several other daemon processes will always occupy portions of high RAM addresses, but it does show how the page tables of a process gradually get filled in with RAM addresses.

The Page Daemon

The diagram in Figure 13.38 illustrated a situation in which all of the physical pages of RAM were filled. If a process tried to fault in another one of its pages, the system could save one or more of the RAM pages onto disk to make room for the incoming page. In practice, it works out much better if the memory management system always keeps a certain number of RAM pages free for pages that wish to fault in.

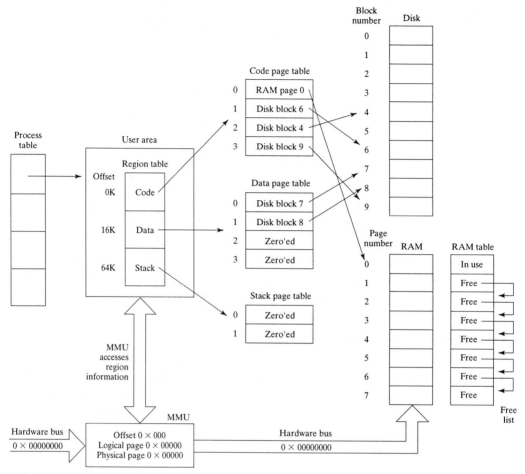

FIGURE 13.37 Memory layout after the first instruction executes

The minimum number of pages that it tries to keep free is called the *low water mark*. When the number of free pages drops below this level, the memory management system wakes up a process called the *page daemon*, sometimes called the *page stealer*, to free up some RAM pages. The page daemon uses an algorithm that is described shortly to save pages to a special area of disk called the *swap space* until the number of free pages rises above a *high water mark*. It then goes to sleep until it's needed again.

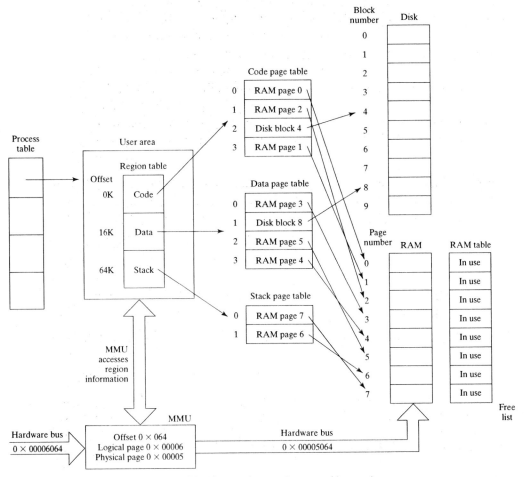

FIGURE 13.38   Memory layout after several instructions

Swap Space

Swap space is a special contiguous area of disk set aside for the efficient transfer of pages to and from RAM. Although it can reside on the root device, it is often allocated on a separate disk so that regular file access and paging can occur simultaneously. The swap space is supported by a special kernel data structure called the *swap map* that is used to track the usage of its blocks. The swap map is used to find free contiguous chunks of blocks in the swap space, and is updated whenever swap space is allocated or deallocated. When two neighboring chunks of swap space become free, the swap map automatically combines them into a single, larger chunk of free space.

The Page Daemon Algorithm

Every page table entry includes three fields called the *modified bit*, the *referenced bit*, and the *age*. Whenever a process accesses a particular page, its referenced bit is set and its age is set to zero. The page daemon uses these two fields in order to free the pages that have been least recently used. It cycles through every page table in the system, performing the following operation:

- If the referenced bit of a page is set, it resets it and sets the age field to zero; otherwise, it increments the age field.

The age fields of pages that are currently being accessed will hardly increase at all, as they're continually being reset back to zero; however, the age fields of pages that are inactive will continue to grow. When the age field reaches a certain system-dependent value, the page daemon attempts to free the page using the following rules:

- If the page has never been paged out to the swap device, the page is placed on a list of pages to be paged out and its RAM table entry is marked as "ready to page out."
- If the page has been paged out before and hasn't been modified since, its valid bit is reset and its RAM table entry is immediately marked as "free" and placed on the free page list.
- If the page has been paged out before and has been modified since, it's placed on the list of pages to be paged out, its RAM table entry is marked as "ready to page out," and its previous swap space area is deallocated.

When the list of pages to page out reaches a certain size, the kernel locates a suitable chunk of swap space by consulting the swap map and then schedules the pages to be written to swap space. When a page is written, its valid bit is reset and its RAM table entry is marked as "free" and placed on the free list.

The result of this algorithm is that the least recently used pages are gradually paged to swap space until the number of free pages rises above the preset high-water mark.

The Memory Layout After Some Page Outs

The following diagram illustrates the state of the example process' memory map after code page 1, data page 0, and stack page 1 were paged to swap space:

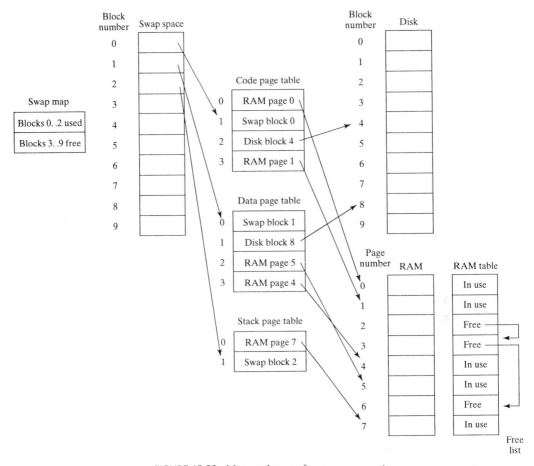

FIGURE 13.39   Memory layout after some page outs

Accessing a Page That's Stored in Swap Space

When the MMU attempts to access a page whose valid bit is not set, it generates a page fault. Before requesting that the page is read from disk, the kernel checks to see if the page is still in RAM, having been freed by the page daemon but not yet overwritten by another page. It can do this quickly because it maintains a hash table that maps disk block addresses onto RAM page numbers. If it finds that the page is still cached in RAM, it simply updates the page table entry and sets the valid bit. If the page is not found in RAM, one of two cases is possible:

- If the page has never been loaded into RAM, the kernel requests that the page is loaded in from the executable file.
- If the page is stored in swap space, the kernel requests that the page is loaded in from the swap device.

One consequence of this algorithm is that a page is only loaded once from the executable file; from then on, it spends the rest of its lifetime travelling between RAM and swap space. This aspect is illustrated by the following diagram:

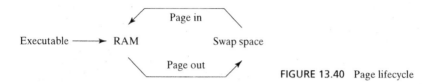

FIGURE 13.40   Page lifecycle

Duplicating a Process: "fork ()"

When a process forks, the child process must be allocated a copy of its parent's code, data, and stack areas. Unfortunately, a process often immediately follows a "fork ()" by an "exec ()", thereby deallocating its previous memory areas. To avoid any unnecessary and costly copying suggested by these two observations, the kernel processes a "fork ()" in a crafty way:

- It sets the region entry of the child's code to point to the page table of the parent's code and increments a reference count associated with the page table to indicate that it's being shared.

- It creates a data page table and a stack page table for the child that are duplicates of those of the parent and sets the copy-on-write bit for every page-table entry of both processes' data and stack tables. If the parent's page table entry points into RAM, the child's page table entry is set to point to the same location and a reference count associated with the RAM page is incremented to indicate that it's being shared. Similarly, if a parent's page table entry points into swap space, the child's page table entry is set to point to the same location and a reference count associated with the swap space location is incremented to indicate that it's being shared.

The copy-on-write flag is used by UNIX to process shared RAM and swap pages in a special way that is described shortly. Figure 13.41 is an illustration of the parent and child memory maps immediately following a "fork ()" command. The small numbers next to the region tables, RAM table, and swap table are reference counts maintained by the kernel.

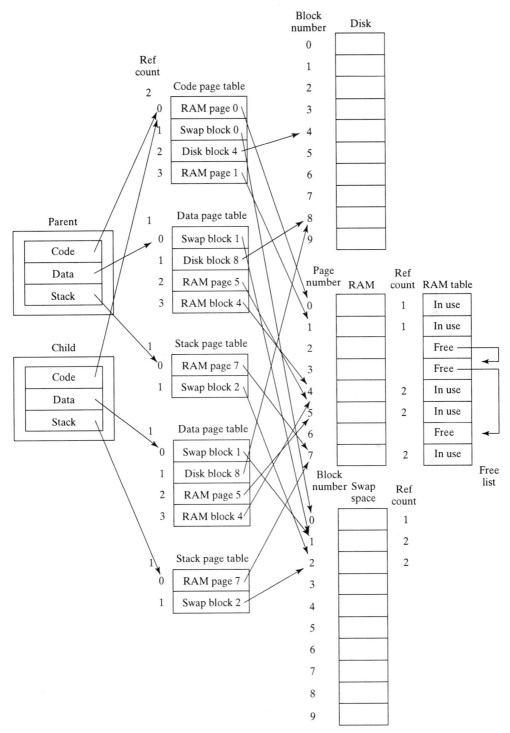

FIGURE 13.41   Layout after a "fork ()" command

Processing References to Shared RAM and Swap Pages

Shared pages are processed by UNIX as follows:

- If a process reads a shared RAM page, nothing special happens at all.
- If the page daemon decides to page out a shared RAM page, the page's reference count is decremented and a copy of the page is transferred to swap space. The process whose page was transferred has its page table entry updated to reflect the transfer, but the other processes that share the same page still reference the RAM page. If the reference count of the RAM page is still nonzero after it's decremented, the RAM page is not added to the free list.
- If a process accesses a shared swap page, it's paged in from swap space and the process whose page was transferred has its page table entry updated to reflect the page-in. The other processes that share the same swap page still reference the swap space.
- If a process attempts to modify a page whose copy-on-write bit is set, the MMU automatically generates a page fault. The page fault handler looks to see if the RAM page's reference count is greater than unity; if it is, it means that a process is writing to a shared page. In this situation, the fault handler copies the page into another page of RAM and updates the child's page table entry to point to the new copy. The child's page table entry's copy-on-write bit is reset. It then decrements the original RAM page's reference count and resets its copy-on-write bit if the count dropped to unity. If a process attempts to modify a copy-on-write page and its reference count is equal to unity, the fault handler allows the process to use the physical page and resets the copy-on-write flag, but also disassociates the page from its current swap copy. This action is taken because it's possible that another process related by a "fork ()" is also sharing the same swap copy.

Thrashing and Swapping

If a large number of processes are running at the same time, it's possible that the rate of page faulting causes most of the CPU time to be spent transferring pages to and from swap space. This situation is called *thrashing*, and it results in poor system performance. When the memory management system detects thrashing, it wakes up the "sched" process, which chooses processes to deactivate and transfer to disk. It selects processes based on their priority and memory usage, marks them as "swapped," and pages all of their RAM pages to swap space. The "sched" process continues to swap processes to swap space until thrashing stops, at which point it goes back to sleep. Once a predetermined time period has elapsed, a swapped process is marked as "ready to run," and its pages are faulted back into RAM in the normal manner.

Terminating A Process: exit ()

When a process terminates, the following events occur:

- Its exit code is placed in its process table entry.
- Its file descriptors are closed.
- The reference count of each of its regions is decremented.

- If the reference count of a region drops to zero, the reference counts of all of its RAM pages and swap pages (if appropriate) are decremented.
- Any RAM or swap pages that have a reference count of zero are deallocated.

Its process table entry is deallocated only when its parent accepts its termination code via a "wait ()" command.

Signals

Signals inform processes of asynchronous events. The data structures that support signals are stored in the process table and the user areas. Every process has three pieces of information associated with signal handling:

- an array of entries, called the *signal-handler array*, in its user area that describes what it should do when it receives a particular type of signal
- an array of bits in its process table entry called the *pending signal bitmap*, one per type of signal, that records whether a particular type of signal has arrived for processing
- a process group ID, which is used when distributing signals

Figure 13.42 is a diagram of these signal-related kernel data structures. I'll describe the implementation of signals by describing the implementation of the system calls that are related to signals.

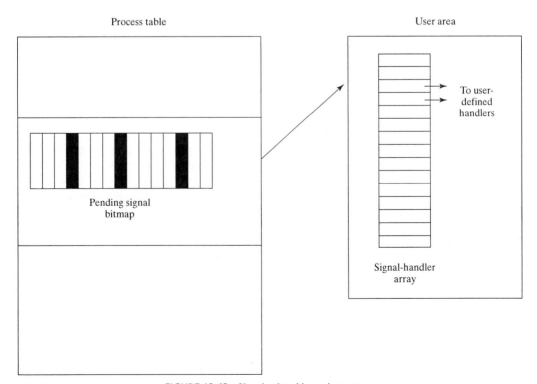

FIGURE 13.42   Signal-related kernel structures

setpgrp ()   "setpgrp ()" sets the calling process' process-group number to its own PID, thereby placing it in its own unique process group. A forked process inherits its parent's process group. "setpgrp ()" works by changing the entry of the process group number in the system-wide process table. The process group number is used by "kill ()", as you'll see later.

signal ()   "signal ()" sets the way that a process responds to a particular type of signal. There are three options for this response: ignore the signal, perform the default kernel action, or execute a user-installed signal-handler. The entries in the signal-handler array are set as follows:

- If the signal is to be ignored, the entry is set to 1.
- If the signal is to cause the default action, the entry is set to 0.
- If the signal is to be processed using a user-installed handler, the entry is set to the address of the handler.

When a signal is sent to a process, the kernel sets the appropriate bit in the receiving process' signal bitmap. If the receiving process is sleeping at an interruptible priority, it is awakened so that it may process the signal. The kernel checks a process' signal bitmap for pending signals whenever the process returns from kernel mode to user mode (e.g., when returning from a system call) or when the process enters or leaves a sleep state. Therefore, note that a signal is hardly ever processed immediately; the receiving process deals with pending signals only when it's scheduled to do so. This condition makes signals a relatively poor mechanism for real-time applications. Also, note that the pending signal bitmap does not keep a count of how many of a particular type of signal are pending. This factor means that if, for example, three SIGINT signals arrive in close succession, it's possible that only one of them will be noticed.

Signals After a "fork ()" or an "exec ()" Command   A forked process inherits the contents of its parent's signal-handler array. When a process execs, the signals that were originally ignored continue to be ignored and all others are set to their default setting. In other words, all entries equal to 1 are unchanged, and all others are set to 0.

Processing a Signal   When the kernel detects that a process has a pending signal, it either ignores it, performs the default action, or invokes a user-installed handler. To invoke the handler, it appends a new stack frame to the process' stack and modifies the process' program counter to make the receiving process act as if it had called the signal handler from its current program location. When the kernel returns the process to user mode, the process executes the handler and then returns from the function back to the previous program location. The "death of a child" signal (SIGCHLD) is processed slightly differently, as you'll see when I describe the "wait ()" system call.

exit ()   When a process terminates, it leaves its exit code in a field in its process-table entry, and the process is marked as a zombie process. This exit code is obtainable by the parent process via the "wait ()" system call. The kernel always informs a parent process that one of its children has died by sending it a "death of child" (SIGCHLD) signal.

wait ()   "wait ()" returns only under one of two conditions: Either the calling process has no children, in which case it returns an error code, or one of the calling process' children has terminated, in which case it returns the child process' PID and exit code. The way that the kernel processes a "wait ()" system call may be split up into a three-step algorithm:

1. If a process calls "wait ()" and doesn't have any children, "wait ()" returns an error code.
2. If a process calls "wait ()" and one or more of its children is already a zombie, the kernel picks a child at random, removes it from the process table, and returns its PID and exit code.
3. If a process calls "wait ()" and none of its children is a zombie, the "wait ()" call goes to sleep. It is awakened by the kernel when *any* signals are received, at which point it resumes from Step 1.

Although this algorithm would work as it stands, there's one small problem: If a process chose to ignore SIGCHLD signals, all of its children would remain zombies, which could clog up the process table. To avoid this problem, the kernel treats the ignoring of the SIGCHLD signal as a special case. If a SIGCHLD signal is received and the signal is ignored, the kernel immediately removes all of the parent's zombie children from the process table and then allows the "wait ()" system call to proceed as normal. When the "wait ()" call resumes, it doesn't find any zombie children, and so it goes back to sleep. Eventually, when the last child's death signal is ignored, the "wait ()" system call returns with an error code to signify that the calling process has no child processes.

kill ()   "kill ()" makes use of the fields of the real user ID and process-group ID in the process table. For example, when the following line of code is executed, the kernel sets the bit in the pending-signal bitmap corresponding to SIGINT in every process table entry whose process group ID matches that of the calling process:

```
kill (0, SIGINT);
```

UNIX uses this facility to distribute the signals triggered by *Control*-C and *Control*-Z to all of the processes in the control terminal's process group.

INPUT/OUTPUT

In this section, I'll describe the data structures and algorithms that the UNIX kernel uses to support I/O-related system calls. Specifically, I'll look at the UNIX implementation of these calls in relation to three main categories of files:

- *regular* files
- *directory* files
- *special* files (i.e., peripherals, pipes, and sockets)

I/O Objects

I like to think of files as being special kinds of objects that have I/O capabilities. UNIX I/O objects may be arranged according to the following hierarchy:

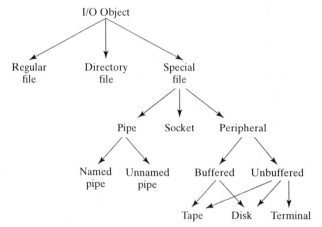

FIGURE 13.43 The I/O object hierarchy

I/O System Calls

As I described in Chapter 12, the I/O system calls may be applied in a uniform way to all I/O objects. A few exceptions exist; for example, you can't use "lseek ()" on a pipe or a socket. Here's a list of the system calls that are described in this section:

- sync
- open
- read
- write
- lseek
- close
- dup
- unlink
- ioctl
- mknod/mkdir
- link
- mount
- umount

I/O Buffering

The kernel avoids unnecessary device I/O by buffering most I/O in a system-wide data structure of fixed-size call the *buffer pool*. The buffer pool is a collection of buffers that are used for caching file blocks in RAM.

When a process reads from a block for the very first time, the block is copied from the file into the buffer pool and then copied from there into the process' data space. Subsequent reads from the same block are serviced directly from RAM. Similarly, if a process writes to a block that isn't in the buffer pool, the block is copied from the file into the pool and then the buffered copy is modified. If the block is already in the pool, the buffered version is modified without any need for physical I/O. Several hash lists based on the block's device and block number are maintained for the buffers in the pool so that the kernel can quickly locate a buffered block.

When a process accesses a buffer during an I/O system call, the buffer is allocated, or locked, to prevent other processes from using it. If another process attempts to access an allocated buffer, it is put to sleep by the kernel until the buffer is freed. When UNIX is booted, all buffers in the pool are marked as *free* and placed in the *buffer freelist.*

When the kernel services a process' I/O system call and needs to copy a block from an I/O object into the buffer pool, several steps are required. First, the kernel selects the first buffer in the buffer freelist and marks it as allocated. Then it removes the buffer from the buffer freelist and issues an asynchronous read request to the appropriate device driver. Finally, the kernel puts the process to sleep. When the read request has been serviced, the process is awakened and the kernel continues to execute the system call. If the buffer freelist is empty, the process is put to sleep until a free buffer becomes available. If the block is already buffered, the kernel simply allocates the existing buffer. When the system call is finished with the buffer, it is freed and placed on the end of the buffer freelist. This scheme ensures that the least recently used buffer is selected each time a new buffer is required.

It's tempting to think that the kernel copies all of a file's modified buffered blocks back to disk when the file is closed; however, it doesn't. Instead, the kernel sets a "delayed-write" flag in a buffer's header whenever it is modified by a "write ()". The buffered block is only physically written to disk when another process attempts to remove it from the buffer freelist due to the algorithm described in the previous paragraph. This scheme delays physical I/O until the last possible moment. Figure 13.44 is an illustration of buffering in action.

sync ()   "sync ()" causes the kernel to flush all of the delayed-write buffers to disk. On systems on which the System V daemon "fsflush" is not present, system administrators arrange for the "sync" utility, which invokes "sync ()", to run regularly. This procedure ensures that the contents of the disk are kept up to date. If "fsflush" runs on the system, it handles this function.

Regular File I/O

The next few sections describe the implementation of *regular file I/O*, including the implementations of "open ()", "read ()", "write ()", "lseek ()", "close ()", "dup ()", and "unlink ()".

open ()   Let's take a look at what happens when a process opens an existing regular file for read-only access. Later, we'll examine the way that the kernel creates

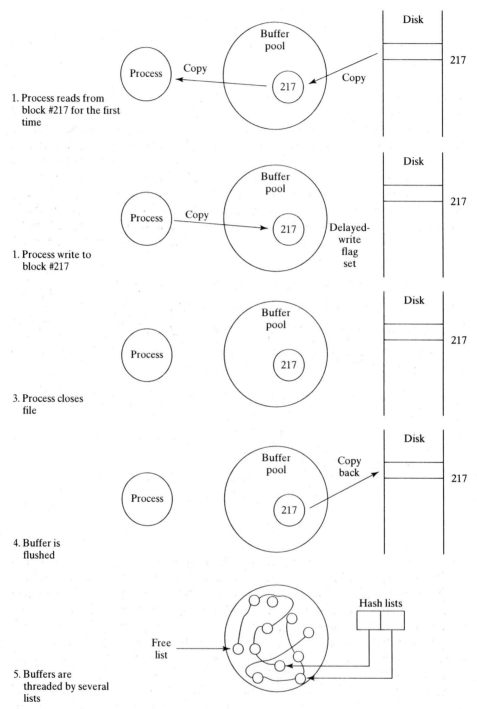

FIGURE 13.44 Buffering in action

a new file. Assume that the process is the first process to open the file since the system was last rebooted and that it executes the following code:

```
fd = open ("/home/glass/sample.txt", O_RDONLY);
```

The kernel begins by translating the filename into an inode number, using the algorithm described earlier in this chapter. If the inode of the file is not found, an error code is returned. Otherwise, the kernel allocates an entry in a system-wide data structure of fixed size called the *active-inode table* and copies the inode from disk into this entry. The kernel also stores several other values, which are described later, in this entry. The kernel caches active inodes and recently used inodes in this table to avoid unnecessary disk access.

Next, the kernel allocates an entry in another system-wide data structure of fixed-size called the *open-file table*. It fills this entry with several useful values, including:

- a pointer to the new entry in the active-inode table
- the read/write permission flags specified in the "open ()" system call
- the process' current file position, set to 0 by default

Finally, the kernel allocates an entry in the per-process file descriptor array, points this entry to the new entry in the open-file table, and returns the index of this file descriptor entry as the return value of "open ()". Following is an illustration of the process and kernel data structures that result from this example.

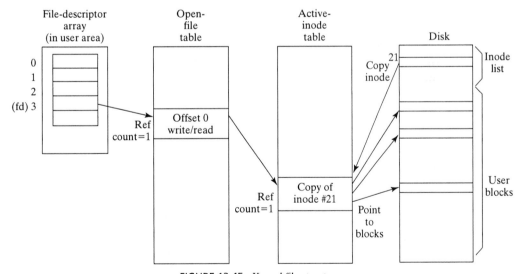

FIGURE 13.45   Kernel file structures

If a process opens a nonexistent file and specifies the "O_CREAT" option, the kernel creates the named file. To do so, it allocates a free inode from the file system's inode list, sets the fields within it to indicate that the file is empty, and then adds a hard link to the appropriate directory file. Recall that a hard link is an entry consisting of a filename and its associated inode number.

Now that you've seen the way that the kernel handles an "open ()" system call, I'll describe the "read ()", "write ()", "lseek ()", and "close ()" system calls. For simplicity, assume that the example file is being accessed by just one process. I'll describe the kernel support for multiple users of the same file later in this chapter.

read ()   Let's see what happens when the example process executes the following sequence of "read ()" system calls:

```
read (fd, buf1, 100);    /* read 100 bytes into buffer buf1 */
read (fd, buf2, 200);    /* read 200 bytes into buffer buf2 */
read (fd, buf3, 5000);   /* read 5000 bytes into buffer buf3 */
```

Here's the sequence of events that would occur during the execution of the example:

- The data requested by the first "read ()" resides in the first block of the file. The kernel determines that the block is not in the buffer pool, and so copies it from disk into a free buffer. It then copies the first hundred bytes from the buffer into **buf1**. Finally, the file position stored in the open file table is updated to its new value of 100.
- The data requested by the second "read ()" also resides in the first block of the file. The kernel finds that the block is already in the buffer pool, and so copies the next 200 bytes from the buffer into **buf2**. It then updates the file position to 300.
- The data requested by the third read resides partly in the first block of the file and partly in the second block. The kernel transfers the remainder of the first block (3796 bytes) from the buffer pool into **buf3**. It then copies the second block from disk into a free buffer in the pool and copies the remaining data (1204 bytes) from the buffer pool into **buf3**. Finally, it updates the file position to 5300.

Note that a single read may cause more than one block to be copied from disk into the buffer pool. If a process reads from a block that does not have an allocated user block (see Chapter 12 for a discussion of sparse files), then "read ()" doesn't buffer anything, but instead treats the block as if it were filled with ASCII NULL (0/) characters.

write ()   The example process now executes the following series of "write ()" system calls:

```
write (fd, buf4, 100);       /* write 100 bytes from buffer buf4 */
write (fd, buf5, 4000);      /* write 4000 bytes from buffer buf5 */
```

Recall that the current value of the file position is 5300, which is situated near the start of the file's second block. Recall also that this block is currently buffered, courtesy of the last "read ()". Here's the sequence of events that would occur during the execution of our example:

- The data to be overwritten by the first "write ()" resides entirely in the second block. This block is already in the buffer pool, and so 100 bytes of **buf4** are copied into the appropriate bytes of the buffered second block.
- The data to be overwritten by the second "write ()" resides partly in the second block and partly in the third block. The kernel copies the first 3792 bytes of **buf5** into the remaining 3792 bytes of the buffered second block. Then it copies the third block from the file into a free buffer. Finally, it copies the remaining 208 bytes of **buf5** into the first 208 bytes of the buffered third block.

lseek ()   The implementation of "lseek ()" is trivial. The kernel simply changes the value of the descriptor's associated file position, located in the open file table. Note that no physical I/O is necessary. Here's a diagram that illustrates the result of the following code:

```
lseek (fd, 3000, SEEK_SET);
```

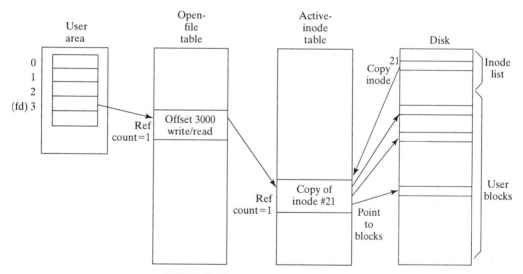

FIGURE 13.46   lseek changes the file offset

close ()   When a file descriptor is closed and it's the only one associated with a particular file, the kernel copies the file's inode back to disk and then marks the corresponding open file table and active inode table entries as *free*. When a process terminates, the kernel automatically closes all of its file descriptors.

As I mentioned earlier, the kernel has special mechanisms to support multiple file descriptors associated with the same file. To implement these mechanisms, the kernel keeps a *reference count* field for each open file table entry and each active inode entry. When a file is opened for the first time, both of these counts are set to one. There are three ways that a file can be shared by several file descriptors:

1. The file is explicitly opened more than once, either by the same process or by different processes.

2. The file descriptor is duplicated by dup (), dup2 (), or fcntl ().

3. A process forks, which causes all of its file descriptor entries to be duplicated.

When a file descriptor is created by the first method, the kernel creates a new open file table entry that points to the same active inode, and increments the reference count field in the file's active inode:

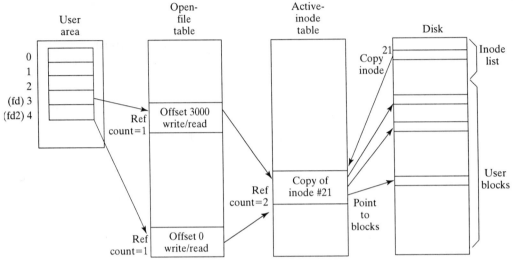

FIGURE 13.47 Open creates a new open file table entry

When a file descriptor is created by either of the latter two methods, the kernel sets the new file descriptor to point to the same open file table entry as the original file descriptor, and increments the reference count field in the descriptor's open file table entry.

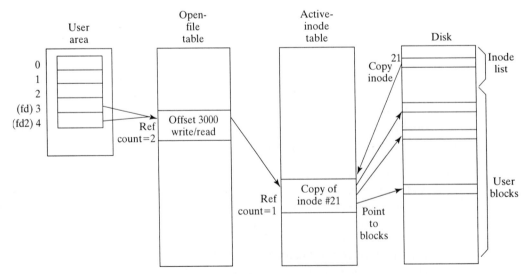

FIGURE 13.48 Duplicating a file descriptor

The algorithm for "close ()" handles the reference count fields as follows: when a file descriptor is closed, the kernel decrements the reference count field in its associated open file table. If the open file table reference count remains greater than zero, nothing else occurs. If the reference count drops to zero, the open file table entry is marked as free and the reference count field in the file's active inode is decremented. If the active inode reference count remains greater than zero, nothing else happens. If the reference count drops to zero, the inode is copied back to disk and the active inode entry is marked as free.

dup ()   The implementation of "dup ()" is simple; it copies the specified file descriptor into the next free entry in the file-descriptor array and increments the corresponding reference count for the open-file table.

unlink ()   "unlink ()" removes a hard link from a directory and decrements its associated inode's hard-link count. If the hard-link count drops to zero, the file's inode and user blocks are deallocated when the last process that is using it exits. Notice that this procedure means that a process may unlink a file and continue to access it until the process exits.

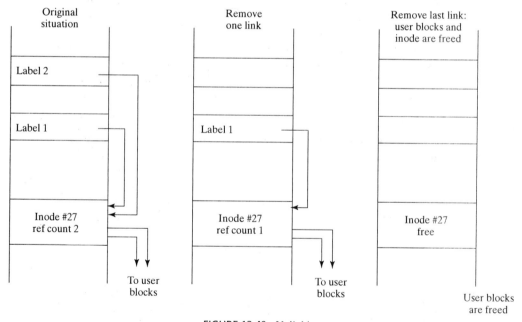

FIGURE 13.49   Unlinking

Directory File I/O

Directory files are different from regular files in a few ways:

- They may be created only by using "mknod ()" or "mkdir()".
- They may be read only by using "getdents ()".
- They may be modified only by using "link ()".

These conditions ensure the integrity of the directory hierarchy. Directory files may be opened just like regular files. Let's take a look at the implementation of "mknod ()" and "link ()".

mknod ()   "mknod ()" creates a directory, named pipe, or special file. In every case, the system call starts by allocating a new inode on disk, setting its type field accordingly, and adding it via a hard link into the directory hierarchy. If a directory is being created,[3] a user block is associated with the inode and filled with the default "." and ".." entries. If a special file is being created, the appropriate major and minor device numbers are stored in the inode; more on this type of file is described later.

link ()   "link ()" adds a hard link into a directory. Here's an example of the use of "link ()":

```
link ("/home/glass/file1.c", "/home/glass/file2.c");
```

In this example, the kernel would find the inode number of the source filename "/home/glass/file1.c" and then associate it with the label "file2.c" in the destination directory "/home/glass." It would then increment the inode's hard-link count. Only a super-user may link directories; this restriction exists to prevent unwary users from creating circular directory structures.

Mounting File Systems

The kernel maintains a single system-wide data structure of fixed size called the *mount table* that allows multiple file systems to be accessed via a single directory hierarchy. The "mount ()" and "umount ()" system calls modify this table and are executable only by a super-user.

mount ()   When a file system is mounted using "mount ()", an entry containing the following fields is added to the mount table:

- the number of the device that contains the newly mounted file system
- a pointer to the root inode of the newly mounted file system
- a pointer to the inode of the mount point
- a pointer to the filesystem-specific mount data structure of the newly mounted file system

The directory associated with the mount point becomes synonymous with the root node of the newly mounted file system, and its previous contents become inaccessible to processes until the file system is later unmounted. To enable the correct translation of pathnames that cross mount points, the active inode of the mount directory is marked as a *mount point* and is set to point to the associated mount table entry. For example, Figure 13.50 is a diagram showing the effect of the following system call, which mounts the file system contained on the "/dev/da0" device onto the "/mnt" directory:

---

[3] In many versions of UNIX, "mkdir()" is preferred when creating a directory.

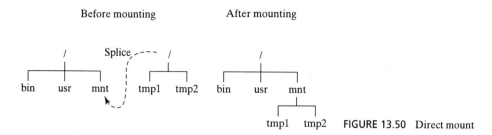

FIGURE 13.50   Direct mount

```
mount ("/dev/da0", "/mnt", 0);
```

Translation of Filenames

The name translation algorithm uses the contents of the mount table when translating pathnames that cross mount points. This event can occur when moving up or down the directory hierarchy. For example, consider the following example:

```
$ cd /mnt/tmp1
$ cd ../../bin
```

The first cd command crosses from the root device to the "/dev/da0" device, and the second cd command crosses back across to the root device. Here's how the algorithm incorporates mounted file systems into the translation process:

- When an inode that is a mount point is encountered during the translation process, a pointer to the root inode of the mounted file system is returned instead. For example, when the "/mnt" portion of "/mnt/dir1" is translated, a pointer to the root node of the mounted file system is returned. This pointer is used as the starting point for the rest of the pathname translation.
- When a ".." pathname component is encountered, the kernel checks to see whether a mount point is about to be crossed. If the current inode pointer of the translation process points to a root node and ".." also points to a root node, then a crossing point has been reached. It replaces the pointer to the current inode of the translation process with a pointer to the inode of the mount point in the parent file system, which it finds by scanning the mount table for the entry corresponding to the device number of the current inode.

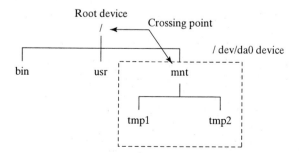

FIGURE 13.51   Crossing point

umount ()   When unmounting a file system, there are several things that the kernel must do:

- It checks that there are no open files in the file system about to be unmounted. It can do so by scanning the active inode table for entries that contain the file system's device number. If any active inodes are found, the system call fails.
- It flushes the superblock, delayed-write blocks, and buffered inodes back to the file system.
- It removes the mount table entry and removes the "mount point" mark from the mount point directory.

Special File I/O

Most special files correspond to peripherals such as printers, terminals, and disk drives, so for the rest of this section I'll use the terms *special file* and *peripheral* synonymously.

Every peripheral in the system has an associated *device driver*, which is a custom-crafted piece of software that contains all of the peripheral-specific code. For example, a tape drive's device driver contains the code for rewinding and retensioning the tape. All instances of a particular kind of peripheral may be controlled by a single device driver. In other words, three tape drives of the same type can share a single device driver. The device drivers for every peripheral in the system must be linked into the kernel when the kernel is configured by the system administrator. For more information, consult Chapter 14.

Device Interface   A peripheral's device driver supplies the peripheral's *interface*, which can come in two flavors:

- *block oriented*, which means that I/O is buffered and that physical I/O is performed on a block-by-block basis. Disk drives and tape drives have a block-oriented interface.
- *character oriented*, which means that I/O is unbuffered and that physical I/O occurs on a character-by-character basis. A character-oriented interface is sometimes known as a *raw interface*. All peripherals, including disk drives and tape drives, usually have a raw interface.

A peripheral's device driver sometimes contains both kinds of interfaces. The kind of interface that you choose depends on how you're going to access the device. When performing random access and repeated access to a common set of blocks, it makes good sense to access the peripheral via its block-oriented interface. However, if you're going to access the blocks in a single linear sequence, as you would when making a backup tape, it makes more sense to access the peripheral via its character-oriented interface. This interface avoids the overhead of the kernel's internal buffering mechanism and sometimes allows the kernel to use the hardware's DMA (Direct Memory Access) capabilities.

Switch tables   All UNIX device drivers must follow a predefined format, which includes a set of standard entry points for functions that open, close, and access the peripheral. Block-oriented device drivers also contain an entry point called *strategy* that is used by the kernel for performing block-oriented I/O to the physical device. The entry points of each block-oriented interface and each character-oriented interface are stored in system-wide tables called the *block device switch table* and the *character device switch table*. These tables are stored as arrays of pointers to functions and are created automatically when UNIX is configured. One dimension of the array is indexed by a peripheral's major number, and the other dimension is indexed by a function code. Here's an illustration of a small sample switch table:

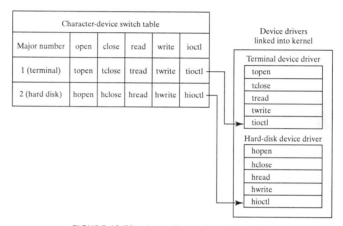

FIGURE 13.52   A small sample switch table

Figure 13.53 illustrates the kernel data structures that might be formed after the following bit of code is executed

```
fd = open ("/dev/tty2", O_RDWR);
```

"lseek ()", "chmod ()", and "stat ()" work the same way for special files as they do for regular files. "open ()", "read ()", "write ()", and "close ()" work slightly differently and make use of the block and character switch tables. In each case, their operation may be split into a peripheral-independent part and a peripheral-dependent part. The next subsections contain a description of each system call.

open ()   When a process opens a file, the kernel can tell if it's a peripheral by examining the "type" field of the file's inode. If the field indicates a block-oriented or character-oriented device, it reads the major and minor numbers to determine the class of the device and the instance of the device that is being opened.

When processing "open ()", the kernel performs peripheral-independent actions, followed by peripheral-dependent actions. The peripheral-independent part of "open ()" works just like "open ()" for a regular file: The file's inode is cached in the active inode table and an open-file table entry is created. The peripheral-dependent

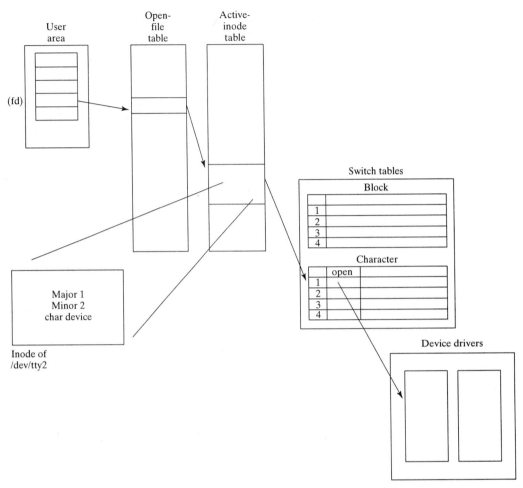

FIGURE 13.53 Special file access

part of "open ()" invokes the device driver's "open ()" routine. For example, a tape driver's "open ()" routine usually retensions and rewinds the tape, whereas a terminal driver's "open ()" routine sets the device's baud rate and default terminal settings.

read () When reading from a character-oriented device, "read ()" invokes the "read" function in the device driver to perform the physical I/O.

When reading from a block-oriented device, "read ()" makes use of the standard I/O buffering mechanism. If a block needs to be physically copied from the device to the buffer pool, the "strategy" function in the device driver is invoked. This function combines both read and write capabilities.

write () When writing to a character-oriented device, "write ()" executes the "write" function in the device driver to perform the physical I/O.

When writing to a block-oriented device, "write ()" uses the I/O buffering system. When a delayed-write eventually takes place, the device's "strategy" function is used to perform the physical I/O.

close ()   The kernel closes a peripheral in the same way as it closes a regular file, except when the process that performs the "close ()" is the last process that was accessing the device. In this special case, the device driver's "close ()" routine is executed, followed by the series of actions for closing a regular file.

The kernel cannot determine that a special file has been closed by its last user by simply examining the active inode's reference count, as a single device may be accessed via more than one inode. Such a situation occurs if one process accesses a device via its block-oriented interface and another accesses the same file via its character-oriented interface. In this case, the active inode list must be searched for other inodes associated with the same physical device.

ioctl ()   "ioctl ()" controls device-specific features via a file descriptor. It simply passes on its arguments to the "*ioctl*" entry point of the device driver. Examples of device-specific operations include setting a terminal's baud rate, selecting a printer's font, and rewinding a tape drive.

Terminal I/O

Although terminals are a kind of peripheral, terminal device drivers are interesting and different enough that I'm devoting a separate section here for their discussion. The main difference between terminal device drivers and other device drivers is that they must support several different kinds of preprocessing and postprocessing on their input and output, respectively. Each variety of processing is termed a *line discipline*. A terminal's line discipline can be set using "ioctl ()". Most terminal drivers support the following three common line disciplines:

- *Raw mode*, which performs no special processing at all. Characters entered at the keyboard are made available to the reading process based on the "ioctl ()" parameters. Key sequences such as *Control*-C do not generate any kind of special action and are passed as regular ASCII characters. For example, *Control*-C would be read as the character with ASCII value 3. Raw mode is used by applications such as editors that prefer to do all of their own character processing.
- *Cbreak mode*, which only processes some key sequences specially. For example, flow control via *Control*-S and *Control*-Q remains active. Similarly, *Control*-C generates an interrupt signal for every process in the foreground job. As with raw mode, all other characters are available to the reading process based on the "ioctl ()" parameters.
- *Cooked mode* (sometimes known as *canonical mode*), which performs full preprocessing and postprocessing. In this mode, the delete and backspace keys take on their special meanings, together with the less common word-erase and line-erase characters. Input is made available to a reading process only when the *Enter* key is pressed. Similarly, tabs have a special meaning when output and are expanded by the line discipline to the correct number of spaces. A new-line character is expanded into a carriage return/new-line pair.

Terminal Data Structures   The main data structures that the kernel uses to implement line disciplines are:

- *C-lists*, which are linked lists of character arrays of a fixed size. It uses these structures to buffer the preprocessed input, the postprocessed input, and the output associated with each terminal.
- *Tty structures*, which contain the state of a terminal, including pointers to its clists, the currently selected line discipline, a list of the characters that are to be processed specially, and the options set by "ioctl ()". There is one tty structure per terminal.

Here's an illustration of a tty structure and its associated clists:

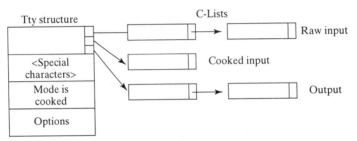

FIGURE 13.54   The tty structure and C-lists

Reading from a Terminal   When a key is pressed, the keyboard interrupt handler performs the following operations, depending on the mode of the terminal:

- *raw mode*: the character is copied onto the end of the raw clist and the process waiting on the read is awakened so that it may read from the raw clist. When the process awakens, all characters on the raw clist are moved into the process' address space.
- *cbreak mode*: if the character is a flow control or break character, it is processed specially; otherwise, the character is copied onto the end of the raw clist and the process waiting on the read is awakened. When the process awakens, all characters on the raw clist are moved into the process' address space.
- *cooked mode*: if the character is a flow control or break character, it is processed specially; otherwise, the character is copied onto the end of the raw clist. If the character is a carriage return, the contents of the raw clist are moved onto the end of the cooked input clist and the process waiting on the read is awakened. When the process awakens, the special characters such as backspace and delete in the cooked input clist are processed, and then the post-processed contents are copied into the process' address space.

ioctl ( ) allows you to specify conditions that must be satisfied before a reading process is awakened. Conditions include the number of characters in the raw clist and an elapsed time since the last read ( ). If two or more processes try to read from the same terminal, it's up to them to synchronize; otherwise, the input will be shared indiscriminately between the competing processes. Signals generated by special characters in cbreak and cooked modes go to the processes associated with the *control terminal*. For more information about control terminals, consult Chapter 12.

Writing to a Terminal   When a process writes to a terminal, any special characters are processed according to the currently selected line discipline and then placed onto the end of the terminal's output clist. The terminal driver invokes hardware interrupts to output the contents of this list to the screen. If the output clist becomes full, the writing process is sent to sleep until some of the output drains to the screen.

Streams

When a stream is created with the open ( ) system call, a *stream head* is created. The stream head provides the system call interface to the user application and contains the data structures that represent the stream. It handles subsequent calls to read ( ), write ( ), getmsg ( ), or putmsg ( ) by sending data to, or receiving data from the first module in the stream.

The stream head, all modules, and the stream driver run in kernel mode. Stream drivers may be inserted into the stream from user mode. This is done by "pushing" it onto the stream. A new module pushed onto a stream goes on top of any existing modules (i.e. connected to the stream head). The module list is a LIFO (last in first out) stack. This is usually done when a driver is installed into the kernel. Modules, like traditional device drivers, execute in kernel mode and are linked into the kernel when the kernel is built.

Some newer terminal drivers are implemented with STREAMS rather than the *clist* mechanism described above.

INTERPROCESS COMMUNICATION

In this section, I describe the data structures and algorithms that the UNIX kernel uses to support pipes and sockets.

Pipes

The implementation of pipes differs significantly between System V and BSD, so I'll begin by describing System V pipes, introduced in System V Release 3.

System V.3 pipes   There are two kinds of pipes in System V: *named* pipes and *unnamed* pipes. Named pipes are created by "pipe ()", and unnamed pipes are created by using "mknod ()". Data written to a pipe is stored in the file system. When either kind of pipe is created, the kernel allocates an inode, two open file entries, and two file descriptors. Originally, the inode describes an empty file. If the pipe is named, a hard link is made from the specified directory to the pipe's inode; otherwise, no hard link is created and the pipe remains anonymous.

Pipe Data Structures   The kernel maintains the current "write" position and current "read" position of each pipe in its inode, rather than in the open file table entry. This set-up ensures that each byte in the pipe is read by exactly one process. It also keeps track of the number of processes reading from the pipe and writing to the pipe. As you'll soon see, it needs both of these counts in order to process a "close ()" properly.

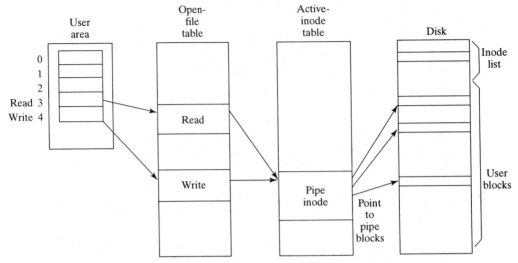

FIGURE 13.55   System V.3 pipes are stored in the file system

Writing to a Pipe   When data is written to a pipe, the kernel allocates disk blocks and increments the current "write" position as necessary until the last direct block has been allocated. For reasons of simplicity and efficiency, a pipe is never allocated indirect blocks, thereby limiting the size of a pipe to about 40K, depending on the file system's block size. If a "write" to a pipe would overflow its storage capacity, the writer process writes as much as it can to the pipe and then sleeps until some of the data is drained by reader processes. If a writer tries to write past the end of the last direct block, the write position "wraps around" to the beginning of the file, starting at offset 0. Thus, the direct blocks are treated like a circular buffer. Although it might seem that using the file system for implementing pipes would be slow, remember that disk blocks are buffered in the buffer pool, and so most pipe I/O is buffered in RAM.

Reading from a pipe   As data is read from a pipe, its current read position is updated accordingly. The kernel ensures that the read position never overtakes the write position. If a process attempts to read from an empty pipe, it is sent to sleep until output becomes available.

Closing a pipe   When a pipe's file descriptor is closed, the kernel does some special processing:

- It updates the count of the pipe's reader and writer processes.
- If the writer count drops to zero and there are processes trying to read from the pipe, they return from "read ()" with an error condition.
- If the reader count drops to zero and there are processes trying to write to the pipe, they are sent a signal.
- If the reader and writer counts drop to zero, all of the pipe's blocks are deallocated and the inode's current write and read positions are reset. If the pipe is unnamed, the inode is also deallocated.

System V.4 pipes   Beginning with System V Release 4, pipes are implemented using STREAMS.

BSD pipes   BSD pipes are implemented in terms of sockets. The write and read file descriptors are each connected to an anonymous socket's endpoint within the UNIX system domain.

Sockets

A complete description of the implementation of sockets would be rather lengthy, as it would require an explanation of the workings of Internet addressing, routing, and communication. For this reason, I supply only a brief overview of the socket system in terms of its memory management and interface to the Internet protocols. For a more in-depth discussion of sockets, see Chapter 12 of this book and [13].

Memory Management   When data is transferred between socket endpoints, the data is buffered using a dynamic memory-allocation system that uses data packets of a fixed size called *mbufs*. Each *mbuf* is 128 bytes long, broken down as follows:

- a 112-byte buffer
- a field that records the size of the data in the buffer
- a field that records the offset of the data in the buffer

Routines that read buffers can strip off protocol headers simply by adjusting the data size and offset fields, rather than having to shift the valid data in memory. The *mbuf* memory manager is relatively efficient, and several other kernel routines use it for non-socket-related uses.

Sockets and the Open File Table   When a socket is created using "socket ()", the system creates a socket structure that records all of the information pertaining to the socket, including the following fields:

- the socket domain
- the socket protocol
- a pointer to the socket's *mbuf* lists

In order to tie the file descriptor system to the socket system, the kernel keeps a pointer from the socket's open file table entry to its associated socket structure. This structure is accessed when performing socket I/O. A diagram of this arrangement is shown in Figure 13.56.

Writing to a Socket   When data is written to a socket using "write ()", the data is placed onto the output *mbuf* list for transmission by the protocol module.

Reading from a Socket   When data arrives at the protocol module, it is placed onto the input *mbuf* list for consumption by the process. When the process performs a "read ()", the data is transferred from the input *mbuf* list into the process' address space.

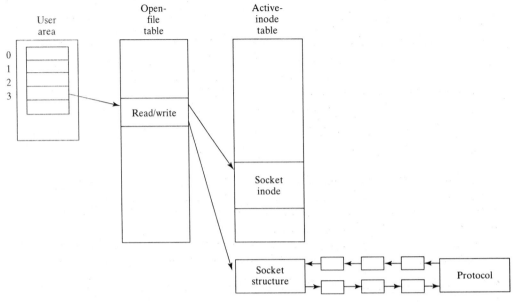

FIGURE 13.56   Berkeley sockets

CHAPTER REVIEW

Checklist

In this chapter, I described:

- the layering of kernel subsystems
- the difference between user mode and kernel mode
- the implementation of system calls and interrupt handlers
- the physical and logical layout of the file system
- inodes
- the algorithm that the kernel uses for translating pathnames into inode numbers
- the process hierarchy
- the six process states
- how the scheduler decides to allocate the CPU
- memory management and the MMU
- the I/O subsystem, including buffering
- interprocess communication via pipes and sockets

Quiz

1. Why does the kernel maintain multiple priority queues?
2. Why do system calls make use of kernel mode?
3. What happens when an interrupt interrupts another interrupt?

4. How do modern disk designs attempt to increase total storage capacity?

5. Where is the name of a file stored?

6. What information does the superblock contain?

7. How does UNIX avoid using bad blocks?

8. Why is inode #2 special?

9. What is the meaning of the term "magic number"?

10. What is the meaning of the term "context switch"?

11. What information is stored in a process' user area?

12. If a signal is sent to a process that is suspended, where is the signal stored?

13. Describe an overview of the memory mapping that the MMU performs.

14. What does the page daemon do?

15. How does UNIX copy a parent's data to its child?

16. What is the meaning of the term "delayed write"?

17. What is the purpose of the open file table?

18. What is the use of the I/O switch tables?

19. Why does the UNIX terminal driver use c—lists?

20. What is the main implementation difference between BSD pipes and System V pipes?

Exercises

1. An interrupt of low priority may be lost if it occurs during the servicing of an interrupt of higher priority. How do you think the systems software deals with lost interrupts? [level: *hard*]

2. The superblock contains a lot of important information. Suggest some ways to minimize disruption to the file system in the case that the superblock gets corrupted. [level: *medium*]

3. When very small files are created, some disk space is lost due to the minimum unit size for allocation. This wasted space is called *internal fragmentation.* Suggest some ways to minimize internal fragmentation. [level: *medium*]

4. Delayed writing normally causes a modified buffer to be flushed when its RAM is needed, not when its file is closed. An alternative method is to flush modified buffers when disk traffic is low, thereby making the best use of the idle time. Critique this strategy. [level: *medium*]

Projects

1. If you know object-oriented techniques, design a basic object-oriented kernel for which system services are provided by a collection of system objects. How does the design of your kernel differ from that of the UNIX kernel? [level: *hard*]

2. Investigate some other operating systems such as Mach, Plan 9, and Windows NT. How do they compare to UNIX? [level: *medium*]

C H A P T E R   1 4

System Administration

Motivation

Several administrative duties must be performed on a UNIX system to keep it running smoothly. Without them, files may be irrecoverably lost, utilities may become out of date, and the system may run slower than its potential speed. Many UNIX installations are large enough that they warrant a full-time system administrator. Smaller UNIX installations, such as my home system, do not. Regardless of whether or not you're destined to perform administrative duties, this chapter contains valuable information on how to oversee a UNIX installation.

Prerequisites

In order to understand this chapter, you should have read Chapters 1 and 2. It also helps if you've read Chapters 3 and 8.

Objectives

In this chapter, I describe the main tasks that a system administrator must perform in order to keep a UNIX system running smoothly.

Presentation

The information presented in this section is in the form of several small, self-contained subsections.

Utilities

This section mentions the following utilities, listed in alphabetical order:

ac	getty	newfs
accton	halt	pac
config	ifconfig	reboot
cron	last	route
df	mkfs	shutdown
du	mknod	su
fsck	netstat	

INTRODUCTION

The tasks that a system administrator must perform in order to keep a UNIX system running properly include the following:

- starting and stopping the system
- maintaining and backing up the file system
- maintaining user accounts
- installing software (both operating system and application software)
- installing and configuring peripherals
- managing the interface to the network
- automating repetitive tasks
- performing system accounting
- configuring the kernel
- checking system security

Almost all of these tasks require the administrator to be in super-user mode, as they access and modify privileged information. If you don't have access to the super-user password, you'll just have to use your imagination as to how these events are managed on your system. Even in this case, however, being aware of these functions increases your overall understanding of how UNIX works.

To cover each of these topics in depth would require an entire book devoted to the subject, so this chapter simply presents an overview of system administration. For more detailed information, I highly recommend the *UNIX System Administration Handbook* [16].

BECOMING A SUPER-USER

The *super-user* is a special user ID of 0 that has permission to do practically anything on a UNIX system. Because of this ability, you can see how important it is for not "just anyone" to have this access, especially anyone with any malicious intentions. Most administration tasks require that you have super-user powers, and there are two ways to access these powers if they have been granted to you:

- Log in as "root", the username of the super-user.
- Use the **su** utility, described in Chapter 7, to create a child shell owned by "root".

Although the first method is very direct, there are some dangers associated with it. If you log in as "root", every single command that you execute will have super-user privileges, even the ones with errors in them. Imagine typing "rm -r * .bak" in the super-user directory instead of "rm -r *.bak" whilst in the "/" directory! Because of this problem, I strongly recommend that you always use the second method. Log into UNIX as a regular user, and only become a super-user when you need to.

Another advantage of the second method is that the **su** utility keeps a log of who uses it and when. In an environment with more than one system administrator, it is sometimes hard to make sure that the super-user password is given only to those who really need it. Having a log to examine helps you see who is using root privileges.

STARTING UNIX

Depending on the origin of your version of UNIX, there are two ways in which a UNIX system can run. Berkeley-UNIX-based systems usually run in one of two modes:

- *Single-user mode,* which means that a single user may log in from the system console and execute commands from a shell. In this mode, the system runs very few system daemons and is generally used for system maintenance, back-ups, and kernel reconfiguration only.
- *Multiuser mode,* which means that many users may log in from different terminals. This mode has active system daemons and is the default operational mode for most systems.

System V–based versions of UNIX run at various *run levels.* Run levels describe what runs on the system, much like singler-user and multiuser modes in BSD, but they provide more granularity in options than their BSD counterparts. Typically, systems have eight run levels, 0–6 and "s" for single-user mode. Each run level can have its own specific boot scripts and can be configured to suit your local needs. For example, you might configure run level 3 to be everything your system normally runs in operational mode except the database application of your company's product. This configuration would allow you to do database maintenance on the database while allowing the rest of the system to be used by the employees.

Some machines allow you to choose the mode by toggling a front-panel switch; other machines enter multiuser mode by default, unless the boot sequence is interrupted by a *Control*-C. The only way to tell what your own system does is to read the manual.

When you turn on the computer, the following sequence of events occurs:

1. The hardware performs diagnostic self-tests.
2. The UNIX kernel is loaded from the root device.
3. The kernel starts running and initializes itself.
4. The kernel starts "init", the first user-mode process.

"init" starts by checking the consistency of the file system using **fsck**, which is described later in this chapter. If single-user mode was chosen, "init" then creates a Bourne shell associated with the system console. If multiuser mode was chosen, "init" performs the following actions:

- It executes the system's *boot scripts,* which perform initialization tasks such as starting the mail daemon and clearing the "/tmp" directory.
- It creates a "getty" process for every terminal in the "/etc/ttytab" file. "/etc/ttytab" contains one line of information for every terminal on the system, including its baud rate and pathname.

The names of the boot scripts vary with different versions of UNIX. BSD-based systems typically run "/etc/rc" to start the standard UNIX daemons and "/etc/rc.local" to start locally maintained services. System V divides the boot files into a more complex set of files, grouping them by subsystem (e.g., networking, disk, etc.). These files are stored in the "/etc/rc.d" directory. A "getty" process listens for activity on its associated terminal and replaces itself by a "login" process if it detects that someone's trying to log in. The "login" program prompts the person for a user-name and a password, checks them against the entries in the "/etc/passwd" file, and replaces itself with the user's start-up program if the password is correct. The start-up program is usually a shell.

When a user logs out, "init" receives a SIGCHLD signal from the dying shell. When this event happens, "init" removes the user from the "/etc/utmp" file, which contains a list of all of the current users. Then it appends an entry to the "/var/adm/wtmp" file, which contains a list of all of the recent logins and logouts. Finally, "init" creates a new "getty" process for the freed terminal.

The behavior of "init" may be modified by sending it a signal:

- SIGHUP causes "init" to rescan the "/etc/ttytab" file and create "getty" processes for all of the terminals in the file that need them. It also kills "getty" processes that don't have an associated terminal. This facility allows you to add and remove terminals without rebooting the system.
- SIGTERM causes "init" to take UNIX to single-user mode.
- SIGTSTP tells "init" not to create a new "getty" process when a user logs out. This signal allows the system to phase out terminals gradually .

"init" is vital to the functioning of UNIX, as it's responsible for creating and maintaining login shells. If "init" dies for any reason, the system reboots automatically.

STOPPING THE SYSTEM

A modern computer prefers to run all of the time; turning it on and off causes it stress. However, there are some circumstances for which it's a good idea to turn it off. For example, if a storm is coming, you should disconnect your computer from its power source to avoid high-voltage surges. UNIX should not be shut down directly; instead, you should use one of the **shutdown**, **halt**, or **reboot** utilities.

shutdown can be used to either halt UNIX, place it into single-user mode, or place it into multiuser mode. It emits warning messages prior to the shutdown so that users may log out before the system changes state.

Utility: **shutdown** -hkrn *time* [*message*]

shutdown shuts down the system in a graceful way. The shutdown time may be specified in one of three ways:

- *now*: the system is shut down immediately.
- *+minutes*: the system is shut down in the specified number of minutes.
- *hours:minutes*: the system is shut down at the specified time, expressed in a 24-hour format.

The specified warning message, or a default one if none is specified, is displayed periodically as the time of shutdown approaches. Logins are disabled five minutes prior to shutdown.

When the shutdown time arrives, **shutdown** executes **sync** and then sends "init" a SIGTERM signal; this signal causes "init" to take UNIX to single-user mode. The **-h** option causes **shutdown** to execute **halt** instead of sending the signal. The **-r** option causes **shutdown** to execute **reboot** instead of sending the signal. The **-n** option prevents **shutdown** from performing its default sync. The **-k** option is funny; it causes **shutdown** to behave as if were going to shut down the system, but when the shutdown time arrives, it does nothing. "k" stands for "just kidding"!

halt causes an immediate system shutdown with no warning messages:

Utility: **halt**

halt performs a sync and then halts the CPU. It appends a record of the shutdown to the "/var/adm/wtmp" log file.

reboot may be used to force the system to reboot:

Utility: **reboot** -q

reboot terminates all user processes, performs a sync, loads the UNIX kernel from disk, initializes the system, and then takes UNIX to multi-user mode. A record of the reboot is appended to the "/var/adm/wtmp" log file. To perform a quick reboot, use the **-q** option. This option instructs reboot not to bother to kill the current processes before rebooting.

MAINTAINING THE FILE SYSTEM

This section describes the administrative tasks related to the file system:

- ensuring the integrity of the file system
- checking disk usage

- assigning quotas
- creating new file systems

File System Integrity

One of the first things that "init" does is to run a utility called **fsck** to check the integrity of the file system. **fsck** works like this:

Utility: **fsck** -p [*fileSystem*]*

fsck (file system check) scans the specified file system(s) and checks it/them for consistency. The kind of constistency errors that can exist include:

- A block is marked as free in the bitmap, but is also referenced from an inode.
- A block is marked as used in the bitmap, but is never referenced from an inode.
- More than one inode refers to the same block.
- An invalid block number.
- An inode's link count is incorrect.
- A used inode is not referenced from any directory.

    For information about inodes, see Chapter 13.
    If the **-p** option is used, **fsck** automatically corrects any errors that it finds. Without the **-p** option, it prompts the user for confirmation of any corrections that it suggests. If **fsck** finds a block that is used, but is not associated with a named file, it connects it to a file whose name is equal to the block's inode number in the "/lost + found" directory.
    If no file systems are specified, **fsck** checks the standard file systems listed in "/etc/fstab."

Fortunately, **fsck** is very good at correcting errors, which means that you'll probably never have the joy of patching disk errors by hand, as was done in "the good old days."

Disk Usage

As I just mentioned, disk errors are uncommon and are generally corrected automatically. Problems with disk usage, on the other hand, are very common. Many users treat the file system as if it's infinitely large and create huge numbers of files without much thought. When I taught UNIX at the University of Texas at Dallas, the disks would invariably fill up on the last day of the semester, just as everyone was trying to complete their projects. Students would try to save their work from **vi**, and **vi** would respond with a "disk full" message. When they quit from **vi,** they would find that their file had been deleted.

To avoid running out of disk space, it's wise to run a shell script from **cron** that periodically runs the **df** utility to check the available disk space. **df** works like this:

Utility: **df** [*fileSystem*]*

df displays a table of used and available disk space, in kilobytes, on the specified mounted file systems. If no file system is specified, all mounted file systems are described.

Here's an example of **df** in action:

```
$ df                        ...list information about all file systems.
Filesystem     kbytes       used      avail     capacity     Mounted on
/dev/sd3a       16415      10767      4006        73%          /
/dev/sd3g      201631     125513     55954        69%          /usr
/dev/sd3d       60015      34773     19240        64%          /export
$ df /dev/sd3a              ...list information about a specific file system.
Filesystem     kbytes       used      avail     capacity     Mounted on
/dev/sd3a       16415      10767      4006        73%          /
$ _
```

If **df** reports that a disk is greater than 95% full, your script could detect this situation and send you some warning mail. Even better, your script could then run the **du** utility to determine which users are using the most disk space and then automatically send them mail suggesting that they remove some files. **du** works like this:

Utility: **du** -s [*fileName*]*

du displays the number of kilobytes (BSD) or 512-byte blocks (System V) that are allocated to each of the specified filenames. If a filename refers to a directory, its files are recursively described. When used with the **-s** option, **du** displays only the grand total for each file. If no filenames are specified, the current directory is scanned.

In the next example, I used **du** to find out how many kilobytes my current directory and all of its files were using up. I then obtained a file-by-file breakdown of the disk usage:

```
$ du -s .   ...obtain a grand total of the usage of the current directory.
9291     .
```

```
$ du     .   ...obtain a file-by-file listing.
91          ./proj/fall.89
158         ./proj/summer.89/proj4
159         ./proj/summer.89
181         ./proj/spring.90/proj2
21          ./proj/spring.90/proj1
204         ./proj/spring.90
455         ./proj
...             ...other files were listed here.
38          ./sys5
859         ./sys6
9291        .
$ _
```

Assigning Quotas

Some systems allow a system administrator to set disk quotas for individual users. You may specify the maximum number of files and the maximum number of blocks that a particular user is allowed to create. It's fairly complicated to add quotas, and doing so may involve reconfiguring the kernel, updating the "/etc/rc" file, modifying the "/etc/fstab" file, and creating a quota control file. Quotas are implemented differently in different versions of UNIX, so I suggest that you consult your system's documentation to find out more.

Creating New File Systems

If you buy a new disk drive, you must perform the following tasks before your file system can use it:

1. Format the media.
2. Create a new file system on the media.
3. Mount the disk into the root hierarchy.

The manufacturer of the device may supply you with a formatting utility. If it does, use this utility to perform Step 1. If your version of UNIX has a **format** command, this command may also work. This step is system specific, so again, you should consult your system's documentation about formatting the media.

Next, create a file system on the media using **mkfs** or **newfs**. Here's a description of **mkfs**:

Utility: **mkfs** *specialFile* [*sectorCount*]

mkfs creates a new file system on the specified special file. A new file system consists of a superblock, an inode list, a root directory, and a "lost+found" directory. The file system is built to be *sectorCount* sectors in size. Only a super-user can use this command.

Because it's unlikely that you'll know the correct value of *sectorCount* without looking it up in the manufacturer's handbook, the **newfs** utility (available on most, but
not all versions of UNIX) was designed as a user-friendly front end to **mkfs**:

Utility: **newfs** *specialFile deviceType*

newfs invokes **mkfs** after looking up the *deviceType*'s sector count from
the "/etc/disktab" file, which contains information about standard device
characteristics.

Note that **newfs** can work only if geometric information about the media is listed in
the "/etc/disktab" file. Once the file system is created, it may be connected to the
root file system by using the **mount** utility described in Chapter 7.

Backing Up File Systems

Making a backup copy of file-system information is the most important and most
frequently overlooked task that a system administrator should do. It's frustrating to
spend time doing it, since you believe you'll never need the backup media. But just
like buying insurance on your car, you should do it because if you ever do need it, it
will be a big problem if you don't have it. The procedure and utilities for backing up
the file system are described in Chapter 7.

MAINTAINING USER ACCOUNTS

One of a system administrator's most common tasks is to add a new user to the system. To do this task, you must:

- add a new entry to the password file.
- add a new entry to the group file.
- create a home directory for the user.
- provide the user with some appropriate start-up files.

The Password File

Every user of the system has an entry in the password file (usually "/etc/passwd") in
the following format:

```
username:password:userId:groupId:personal:homedir:startup
```

The meanings of the fields in this entry are as follows:

Field	Meaning
username	the user's login name
password	the encrypted version of the user's password
userId	the unique integer allocated to the user
groupId	the unique integer corresponding to the user's group
personal	the description of the user that is displayed by the **finger** utility
homedir	the home directory of the user
startup	the program that is run for the user at login

Because the password field is an encrypted value, putting any single character in that field is equivalent to disallowing logins on that account. Since there is no string you could type that would encrypt into the text "*", for example, nothing that could be typed would match when encrypted and compared against such a password field. Here's a snippet from a real-life password file:

```
$ head -5 /etc/passwd        ...look at the first five lines.
root:rcfsmtio:0:0:Operator:/:/bin/csh
daemon:*:1:1::/:
sync:*:1:1::/:/bin/sync
sys:*:2:2::/:/bin/csh
bin:*:3:3::/bin:
$ _
```

I used **grep** to find my own entry:

```
$ grep glass /etc/passwd     ...find my line.
glass:dorbnla:496:62:Graham Glass:/home/glass:/bin/ksh
$ _
```

The Group File

To add a new user, you must decide which group the user is in and then search the group file to find its associated group ID. As an example, I'll show you how to add a new user called "simon" into the "cs4395" group.

Every group in the system has an entry in the group file (usually "/etc/group") in the following format:

```
groupname:groupPassword:groupId:users
```

The meanings of the fields in this field are as follows:

Field	Meaning
groupname	the name of the group
groupPassword	the encrypted password for the group (not used, and often filled with an "*")
groupId	the unique integer corresponding to the group
users	a list of the users in the group, separated by commas

Here's a snippet from a real-life "/etc/group" file:

```
$ head -5 /etc/group              ...look at the start of a group file.
cs4395:*:91:glass
cs5381:*:92:glass
wheel:*:0:posey,aicklen,shrid,dth,moore,lippke,rsd,garner
daemon:*:1:daemon
sys:*:3:
$ _
```

As you can see, the "cs4395" group has an associated group ID number of 91. To add "simon" as a new user, I allocated to him the unique user ID number 10, a group ID number of 91, and left his password field empty. Here's what his entry looked like:

```
simon::101:91:Simon Pritchard:/home/simon:/bin/ksh
```

Once the entry was added to the password file, I added "simon" onto the end of the "cs4395" list in the "/etc/group" file, created his home directory, and gave him some default start-up files, such as ".kshrc" and ".profile". I copied these files from a directory called "/usr/template" that I made to keep the default versions of user start-up files.

```
$ mkdir /home/simon                       ...create home directory.
$ cp /usr/template/.* /home/simon         ...copy startup files.
$ chown simon /home/simon /home/simon/.*  ... set owner.
$ chgrp cs4395 /home/simon /home/simon/.* ...set group.
$ _
```

Finally, I logged in as "simon" and used **passwd** to change his password to a sensible default value.

To delete a user, simply reverse these actions: Delete the user's password entry, group file entry, and home directory.

INSTALLING SOFTWARE

Installing new software or updates to existing software is an important task of a system administrator. However, the details can vary greatly from site to site. If you maintain a large site with many NFS (Network File System) servers, you might install an application on a server so that workstations can access it from a central location. A more expensive piece of software might be installed only on the machines where it is needed. Similarly, at a smaller site, even a less expensive application might be installed only on a few machines as well.

The long-time tradition in UNIX environments was to install local software in the "/usr/local" directory. That location made it obvious that the software did not come with the UNIX distribution. Over time, UNIX vendors have modified the name of the "standard" directory that they use for application software (e.g., Sun uses "/opt" for optional software, AIX uses "/usr/lpp" for licensed program products, etc.). You may use one or more of these locations, but it is important to maintain some logic to the structure so that you (and others) can find what you're looking for.

There are two philosophical ways to install software. One is to create a directory for it and put *everything* it needs (except, perhaps, system files) under that directory. For example, if I create an application called "pianoman", I might write installation tools for it that assume it will be installed in "/opt/pianoman". If the user chooses to install it in "/usr/local/pianoman" instead, he or she should be able to do so. The other philosophy is to put only software in such a central directory and to put any needed configuration, header, or library files in a more centralized location for those types of files. The example here might be that the software required to build the application may live in "/usr/local/pianoman", but when it is installed on the system, the executable is copied to "/usr/local/bin/pianoman" and the library it uses is copied to "/usr/local/lib/pianolib.a". This method has advantages and disadvantages. The major advantage is that the user community does not have to add another directory to their $PATH definition, since the binary is in a "known" location ("/usr/local/bin") that is already in their path. The major disadvantage is that you have files spread out in many other places besides "/usr/local/pianoman", in this example.

How you choose to install software may depend on the default method that the developer of the software has chosen. Any good installation tool (script or program) should allow you to change the default location for the installation. While it is easier to go with the defaults if they fit into your environment in a reasonable fashion, you are free to configure the installation to better match your local environment. Any software that hard-codes the installation location is poorly designed.

The **tar** and **cpio** commands are some of the most popular methods of creating an installation image for a UNIX system. The advantage here is that these commands already exist on most versions of UNIX. A shell script that uses **tar** and other standard UNIX commands to install software can be run on most types of UNIX systems without requiring other software. Some UNIX vendors provide their own improved software installation tools (e.g., HP-UX has **swinstall,** AIX has **installp**). While these tools are generally better than generic UNIX commands, their disadvantage is that you lock yourself into one architecture if you use them. Of course, you can write install instructions for each tool, but doing so is more work than writing only one installation method for all UNIX platforms that your application supports. The best choice of an installation method depends greatly on the target customers, their platforms, and their comfort level with UNIX tools.

You, as the UNIX system administrator, will encounter just about all possibilities and will need to know how best to integrate the applications into your local environment.

PERIPHERAL DEVICES

Let's assume that you've just bought a new device and you wish to connect it to your system. How do you install it? In addition, if it's a terminal, which terminal-specific files must be updated? This section presents an overview of device installation and a list of the terminal-related files.

Installing a Device

For the system to be able to "talk to" a new device, the hardware must be connected and the software must be installed or activated. Some systems require new device drivers be loaded into the kernel and the kernel rebuilt, and others may use dynamically loadable device drivers for which the driver will be loaded into the kernel when the device is accessed. The basic steps of device installation are as follows:

1. Install the device driver if it isn't currently in the kernel and loadable device drivers are not used.
2. Determine the device's major and minor numbers.
3. Use **mknod** to associate a filename in "/dev" with the new device.

Once the device driver is installed and the major and minor numbers are known, you must use **mknod** to create the special file:

Utility: **mknod** *fileName* [c] [b] *majorNumber minorNumber*
      mknod *fileName* p

mknod creates the special file *fileName* in the file system. The first form of **mknod** allows a super-user to create either a character-oriented (c) or block-oriented (b) special file with the specified major and minor numbers. The major number identifies the class of the device, and the minor number identifies the instance of the device. The second form of **mknod** creates a named pipe and may be used by anyone.

In the following example, I installed the 13th instance of a terminal whose major number was 1:

```
$ mknod /dev/tty12 c 1 12        ...note that the 13th instance is index 12
$ _
```

The "c" indicated that the terminal was a character-oriented device. In the next example, I installed the first instance of a disk drive whose major number was 2:

```
$ mknod /dev/dk1 b 2 0          ...note that the 1st instance is index 0.
$ _
```

The "b" indicated that the terminal was a block-oriented device.

Major and minor numbers are the fourth and fifth fields, respectively, in an "ls -l" listing. In the following example, I obtained a long listing of the "/dev" directory:

```
$ ls -l /dev             ...get a long listing of the device directory.
crw--w--w-  1     root  1,  0 Feb 13 14:21 /dev/tty0
crw--w--w-  1     root  1,  1 Feb 13 14:27 /dev/tty1
brw--w--w-  1     root  2,  0 Feb 13 14:29 /dev/dk0
crw--w--w-  1     root  3,  0 Feb 13 14:27 /dev/rmt0
...
$ _
```

Terminal Files

Several files contain terminal-specific information. Here's a list of them, together with a brief description of the function of each:

Name	Description
/etc/termcap or /etc/terminfo	An encoded list of every standard terminal's capabilities and control codes. The UNIX editors use the value of the environment variable $TERM to index into this file and fetch your terminal's characteristics.
/etc/ttys	A list of every terminal on the system, together with the program that should be associated with it when the system is initialized (usually "getty"). If the terminal's type is constant and known, this information is also included.
/etc/gettytab	A list of baud-rate information that is used by "getty" when deciding how to listen to a login terminal.

THE NETWORK INTERFACE

An important aspect of system administration is getting a UNIX machine connected to the local network so that other machines and all users can communicate with it. Some of the basic concepts and tools used to do so were discussed in Chapter 8. Because the details vary so greatly with different versions of UNIX, we'll just hit the main points here. For a detailed view, I strongly recommend [16].

Unless you are experimenting with wireless networking, some kind of network cable will have to be connected to your UNIX computer in order for it to talk to the network. Your machine will have to have an IP address and hostname assigned to it, and the rest of the network will need to be made aware of this name and address (by updating the local host table or DNS database).

Most systems use the **ifconfig** command to configure the network interface. The typical way to activate a network interface is:

```
$ ifconfig il0 194.27.1.14 up
```

This command causes the interface called "il0" (this designation is a device name somewhere in the "/dev" directory hierarchy) to be assigned the IP address 194.27.1.14 and configured to be up. Other IP attributes can also be configured with **ifconfig.** While you can issue this command by hand at a terminal, it is usually found in boot scripts that initialize all network interfaces. When you add a network interface, you'll have to add the appropriate configuration command to the appropriate boot file.

For your UNIX machine to communicate with any other computer that is not directly connected to the same network cable (segment), routing information on your machine will need to be specified. The **route** command is used to specify routers that provide a path to other networks. Generally, you only have to make sure that a "default" route is established. A packet will be sent to this router when the destination is not on the local network. The packet is sent to the default router with the assumption that upstream routers will know how to get to the destination.

You can look at your current route table by using the **netstat** command with the "-r" argument:

```
$ netstat -r
Routing tables
Destination      Gateway        Flags   Refs      Use   If
194.27.1.0       194.27.1.1     U       1        16611  il1
default          194.21.1.1     UG      0       231142  il0
```

This machine knows about two routers, 194.21.1.1 being the default path. Any address not on the local network and not on the 194.27.1 network will be sent to 194.21.1.1 for routing to its destination.

AUTOMATING TASKS

There are several system tasks that are fairly simple, but tedious, to perform. For example:

- adding a user account
- deleting a user account
- checking for full disks
- generating reports of logins and logouts
- performing incremental backups
- system accounting
- removing old "core" files
- killing zombie processes

One of the powers of UNIX is its facility that allows you easily to write simple shell scripts or C programs to automate tasks that you perform by hand. I recommend that you automate as many of these chores as you can. Tasks that must be executed on a periodic basis can be scheduled by the **cron** utility. The **cron** utility works slightly differently on different versions of UNIX, but in general, it allows you to schedule a program to run anywhere from once every minute to once every year. Any messages generated by the program are sent via e-mail to the user who registered the program to be run.

For example, a simple script to see if any of your filesystems are at 95% capacity or greater might be:

```
#!/bin/sh
#
df | egrep "9[56789]%|100%"
```

If this script is registered by "root" with **cron** to be run every hour until a filesystem is at 95% capacity or greater, nothing (visible) happens. The script is run every hour, but no output is generated. When a filesystem reaches 95% capacity, the search pattern specified to the **egrep** command will be satisfied by the line from **df** about the offending filesystem, so the script will generate a line of output. This line will be e-mailed to "root", so within one hour of the filesystem hitting 95% capacity, you'll know about it.

Many system administrators swap useful scripts at weekly meetings. Web pages devoted to system administration may also provide templates or examples of some of these tasks.

ACCOUNTING

The UNIX accounting facilities allow you to track the activity of its subsystems. Each subsystem keeps a record of its own history in a special file, as follows:

- *Process management:* A record of the user ID, memory usage, and CPU usage of every process is appended to the "/usr/adm/acct" file. The **sa** utility may be used to report on the information in this file. Process accounting is toggled by the **accton** utility.

- *Connections:* A record of the login time, user ID, and logout time of every connection is appended to the "/usr/adm/wtmp" file. The **ac** and **last** utilities may be used to report on the information in this file. Connection accounting is enabled by the presence of the "/usr/adm/wtmp" file.

- *Printer usage:* Every printer records information about its print jobs in the "/usr/adm" directory. The **pac** utility can generate reports from this information. Printer accounting is toggled by an entry in the "/etc/printcap" file.

- Other subsystems such as **uucp** and **quota** also produce log files.

Different subsystems generate files that are converted into reports by utilities and shell scripts. The system administrator is responsible for maintaining accounting records for the target subsystems and for purging and/or archiving the accounting files periodically.

CONFIGURING THE KERNEL

The UNIX kernel is a program written mostly in C, with a few sections in assembly language. When you purchase a UNIX system, the manufacturer includes several pieces of software related to the kernel:

- a generic executable kernel
- a library of object modules that correspond to the parts of the kernel that never change
- a library of C modules that correspond to the parts of the kernel that may be changed
- a configuration file that describes the current kernel setup
- a **config** utility that allows you to recompile the kernel when the configuration file is changed

The kernel configuration files are kept in either the "/usr/conf" (BSD) or the "/usr/src/uts/cf" (System V) directories. The facets of the kernel that may be changed include the following:

- the device drivers
- the maximum number of open files, c-lists, quotas, and processes
- the size of the I/O buffer pool and system page tables
- some important networking information
- the physical addresses of devices
- the name of the machine
- the time zone of the machine

To recompile a new kernel, you must follow a multistep process:

1. Edit the configuration file and change the parameters to their new values.
2. Run the **config** utility, which creates some header files, some C source code, and a makefile.
3. Run the **make** utility, passing it the name of the makefile created by **config. make** recompiles the newly created source code and links it with the unchanging portion of the kernel to produce a new executable.
4. Rename the old UNIX kernel.
5. Rename the new UNIX kernel to take the place of the old one.
6. Reboot the system.

SECURITY ISSUES

Security is another topic for which it would be possible to devote an entire book to a thorough discussion. I can heartily recommend [27] and [29] as well as the security chapter in [16] for more information.

As you are no doubt aware, UNIX systems are not 100% secure. No computer connected to any network can be. With the explosion of Internet connectivity, the problems have grown as well.

UNIX was not originally designed with security in mind. The original UNIX environments were places where everyone trusted each other and there was no need for security measures. Most UNIX systems are quite secure these days, but this security has happened only after years of locating weaknesses and fixing them.

While there are many aspects to UNIX security, the ones with which every user has experience are passwords and file permissions. These mechanisms are tough for a regular user to break, but not so hard for experienced hackers to do so. The best that a system administrator can do is to read about as many of the known security loopholes as possible and adopt strategies to stop them all. To give you an idea of what you're up against, here are a couple of common password-nabbing techniques:

- If you have a regular account and desire a super-user account, you begin by obtaining a copy of the one-way encryption algorithm that is used by the UNIX **passwd** utility. You also buy an electronic dictionary. Next, you copy the "/etc/passwd" file to your home PC and compare the encrypted versions of every word in the dictionary against the encrypted root password. If one of the dictionary entries matches, you've cracked the password! Other common passwords to test for include names and words spelled backward. This brute-force technique is very powerful and may be defended against by asking everyone to pick non-English, nonbackward, nontrivial passwords.

- A scheming user can use the command overloading technique described earlier to trick a super-user into executing the wrong version of **su.** To use this Trojan-horse technique, set $PATH so that the shell looks in your own "bin" directory before the standard "bin" directories. Next, write a shell script called **su** that pretends to offer a super-user a login, but really stores the super-user password in a safe place once the super-user types it in, displays "wrong password", and then erases itself. When this script is prepared, call a super-user and tell him/her that there's a nasty problem with your terminal that requires super-user powers to fix. When the administrator types "su" to enter super-user mode, *your* **su** script executes instead of the standard **su** utility, and the super-user password is captured. The super-user sees the "wrong password" message and tries **su** again. This time, it succeeds, as your Trojan horse script has already erased itself. The super-user password is now yours! The way to defeat this technique is never to execute commands using a relative pathname when you're at an unfamiliar terminal. In other words, execute "/bin/su" instead of just "su".

The best ways to improve your knowledge of cunning schemes is to network with other system administrators and to read specialized books on system administration [16].

CHAPTER REVIEW

Checklist

In this chapter, I described:

- the main system administration tasks
- how to access super-user powers
- how to start and stop UNIX

- the difference between single-user and multiuser modes
- some useful disk-utilization utilities
- installing software
- how to create a new file system
- how to add and delete user accounts
- an overview of how a device is installed
- configuration of a network interface
- the process of creating a new kernel
- some common security problems

Quiz

1. Under which situations is it appropriate to shut down a UNIX system?
2. What does a "getty" process do?
3. Why is it better to use **su** to become a super-user than simply to login as "root?"
4. How can you put UNIX into single-user mode?
5. When is the file system checked for integrity?
6. Which files must be modified when you add a new user?
7. What does the **ifconfig** command do?
8. Which UNIX subsystems generate accounting records?
9. Which kernel parameters may be modified?
10. Describe the Trojan horse technique for capturing a super-user password.

Exercises

1. Use **du** to examine your disk usage. Write a script that prints out the full pathnames of your files that are over a specified size. [level: *medium*]
2. Obtain a floppy disk, format it, create a file system on it, mount it, and copy some files onto it. You'll almost certainly need a system administrator to help you through this process. [level: *medium*]
3. Try using **cpio** and **tar** to transfer some files to and from a floppy disk. Which of these utilities do you prefer? Why? [level: *easy*]

Project

Ask your system administrator what he/she believes to be the strengths and weaknesses of UNIX from a system administrator's standpoint. Are these issues being addressed by current UNIX releases or in other operating systems? [level: *medium*]

CHAPTER 15

The Future

Motivation

Operating systems continue to develop and improve as software and hardware technology expands. Although old, stagnant systems will inevitably hang around for quite a while, systems that incorporate the best concepts and philosophies will eventually replace them. UNIX is almost 30 years old, and is beginning to show its age in terms of its internal architecture. Knowledge of operating system trends will help you to understand the changes that will occur in UNIX over the next few years, as well as allowing you to place the role of UNIX in perspective.

Prerequisites

This chapter has no prerequisites, although it may help to have read Chapter 13.

Objectives

In this chapter, I'll describe the latest trends in operating system evolution that are influencing the evolution of UNIX. I will also provide a quick survey of the major versions of UNIX that are in wide use today.

Presentation

The first half of the chapter examines topics that are changing the face of UNIX. The second half shows examples of these influences.

INTRODUCTION

To set the scene for this chapter, let's look at the latest trends in software and hardware:

- object-oriented programming
- distributed and parallel processing
- the move from 32-bit to 64-bit systems
- high-bandwidth communication systems

These trends represent an exciting and interesting future for UNIX and computing in general. In order to take advantage of these changes, the software that is UNIX will have to adapt, as well as the hardware platforms upon which it runs.

CURRENT AND NEAR-FUTURE INFLUENCES ON UNIX

Many current topics in computer science and improvements in hardware will have a profound effect on the future directions of UNIX systems. Some of these issues have already exerted influence and continue to do so. Some are only now coming into view.

Object-Oriented Programming

Objects have been responsible for much buzz in the computer industry for many years now. The most popular object-oriented languages in use in UNIX environments today are C++ and Java. In many situations, an objected-oriented paradigm can greatly increase the development productivity and manageability of software projects. Used simply because they are cool, objects can actually cause trouble.

Let's take a quick look at object-oriented programming, but please realize that this glance is an extreme oversimplification. Entire volumes have been written on objects and the philosophy behind their use; to hope to do any more than whet your appetite in a few paragraphs would be foolhardy.

What is an Object?   An *object* is an abstraction, a way to describe the purpose and use of data. In traditional procedural programming, you defined data structures and then performed operations on that data. Your program had to "know" which data was applicable to which functions and which operations could be performed on the data.

The idea behind object orientation is that rather than simply to perform procedural operations on data, you conceptually enclose the data in an object. Within this object, you can define a set of functions, or *methods*, that can operate on the specific data maintained in the object. By sending a message to the object, another entity can request that the object execute one of its functions, but it cannot directly access the data. This structure protects the data from any kind of random modification that might happen because the modifying code thinks it "knows" the format of the data, but there is a bug in the code or the data format has changed.

How Objects Are Used   Besides any specific methods defined for any object, two other methods are always defined. Each object must have a way to be created and deleted. In most object-oriented languages, these methods are called *constructors* and *destructors.*

A constructor is the special method that is executed when a new instantiation of the object is created. In C++, this process occurs when the "new ()" function is called on the object type. The constructor creates and initializes any data used by the object.

A destructor, as you might have guessed, does the opposite of a constructor. A destructor is a special method that cleans up when the object is being deleted. Any terminal processing is performed, and all resources that have been allocated are freed. In C++, this process occurs when the "delete ()" function is called on the object.

So What Good Is All This?   For an oversimplified example, consider a printer that you can have on-line (printing) or off-line (not accepting data to print). The printer might have a byte that defines whether it is on-line or off-line (1 for on-line, 0 for off-line). You might write a program that sets the value 2 in that byte. What would the printer do? It depends on the printer, but perhaps a 2 means "explode!" However, if you wrote a *printer object* in software that encapsulated the printer-status byte and defined "printer-on ()" and "printer-off ()" methods, then you couldn't set a value of 2 in that byte. You could only call "printer-on ()" to set it to 1 or "printer-off ()" to set it to 0.

Objects, therefore, help you specifically describe which operations can be performed and which data can be affected and prevent the changing of data in ways that don't make sense.

Inheritance   You can also created new objects based on old objects. If I had a new printer that had another status variable besides the on-line/off-line variable, I could *inherit* the attributes of the original printer object and add any new methods in my new code. Then I would have a new, more sophisticated printer object, but I would not have had to rewrite all of the same code that the two printers had in common.

Parallel, Distributed, and Multiprocessor Systems

Historically, a computer had a single CPU, sat on a desk (or in a computer room), and processed data that was entered into it. As networks proliferate, computers are connected together to share data and cooperate in their processing. As microprocessor technology has advanced, more than one processor can be put into a single computer.

Parallel Processing   If a problem can be divided into separate and unrelated parts, those parts can be run separately. This way, the problem is solved faster than if each part were run on a single computer sequentially. This procedure is known as *parallel processing* (doing more than one task in parallel). Processing can be done in parallel either by different computers or by different processors inside the same computer, as we will see shortly.

True parallel processing is an extremely difficult goal to achieve. Many tasks have some kind of relationship to one another and cannot easily be separated. Object-oriented programming helps in this respect, since the processing for a single object can be separated out from that of the others. If multiple users log on to a system for which each user's shell process can be assigned to a different processor, a lot of processing power is provided to multiple users in a very easy way. But to divide a single application program into semiunrelated pieces that can run independently is a challenging task. An even more challenging task is to write a compiler that can *automatically* determine which parts of a program are unrelated and break up the code during compilation so that the various pieces can be assigned to different processors.

Distributed Systems   One way in which to execute separated tasks in parallel is to execute them on different computers at the same time. One centralized program can distribute parts out to different computers and collect the result as they finish. Some overhead is involved in managing the separation and communication, but if the tasks are reasonably complex, the parallel execution will cause the total elapsed time to be much shorter than if each task were run sequentially on the same computer.

This type of architecture is often referred to as a *shared-nothing architecture* because each processor does not share any resources with the others. Each system has its own memory, its own disk, and its own data path to the network. While it is possible for processes on different computers to share blocks of memory (as two processes running on the same computer can), quite a bit of overhead is involved, since the sharing happens over a network.

Multiprocessor Systems   Another way to run separate processes in parallel is to run them on the same computer. If the machine has a single CPU, then it has to split its time across the various processes, which results in no gain (in fact, it results in a loss due to the overhead of multiple processes) over traditional single-processes programming. However, if the computer has more than one CPU, the separate processes can each be assigned to their own processor.

Multiple processes running on the same computer do share disk resources. They may also more easily share segments of memory via operating system methods for shared-memory access. Therefore, this type of architecture may sometimes be called *shared-memory* or *shared-resource architecture.*

Sequent was one of the first UNIX vendors to provide a multiprocessor system specifically designed to allow parallel programs to be written and executed in multiple processors. Today, many UNIX platforms are available in multiprocessor architectures. All of the same complexities involved in parallel programming apply here; the extra complexity of distributing the processes to different computers is avoided.

As CPU speeds continue to increase, the advantage of multiprocessors isn't as obvious for the "typical" user. However, there will always be applications that need the throughput speed that parallel programming offers.

The Year 2000

You have to have been living under a rock not to have heard about "the Y2K problem." Any electronic equipment that keeps track of dates with years as two-digit values will have a problem after 11:59:59 on December 31, 1999. Applications running on UNIX machines will be no different.

What Is It *Really?*   Most people you hear talking about the Year-2000 problem do not describe it correctly. The common belief is that computers will not "understand" dates past 1999. This presumption is not really true. The problem is that we, people, insist on specifying years in two digits. We believe that it will be obvious to anyone, either from the context or simply because we're talking about *this* year, which century we mean. With a person who can reason, this assumption usually works. However, a computer is different.

So far, all computer programs have been written in the 20th century. Therefore, programmers who deal with two-digit dates assume that the other two digits are "19". We're rapidly approaching a point where this assumption is no longer valid. It would be "the computer's fault" if the system itself could not represent a year value of 2000, but actually, almost all computers can. The problem is the assumption made by the application programmer.

Two-Digit Years   Consider the UNIX command **cal**. This command is used to print out a calendar for a particular month or year. For example, the command "cal 6 1998" prints a calendar for June 1998:

```
$ cal 6 1998
      June 1998
Su Mo Tu We Th Fr Sa
    1  2  3  4  5  6
 7  8  9 10 11 12 13
14 15 16 17 18 19 20
21 22 23 24 25 26 27
28 29 30

$ _
```

However, notice what happens if I assume I can use a two-digit year:

```
$ cal 6 98
      June   98
Su Mo Tu We Th Fr Sa
             1  2
 3  4  5  6  7  8  9
10 11 12 13 14 15 16
17 18 19 20 21 22 23
24 25 26 27 28 29 30

$ _
```

This calendar doesn't look right, does it? It is. This is a calendar for June in the year 98 A. D.! Is this the fault of **cal** or my fault? Of course, it's my fault, **cal** did exactly what I asked it to do.

Take the example of a 105-year-old man. If you are looking at an insurance form he filled out, you might read his birthday on the form as 06/06/93. Would you assume he was 105 or would you assume this form applied to a 5-year-old child? Of course, if he's sitting with you at the time, you will have enough context to figure it out. However, a computer would not be able to come to this conclusion. There is not enough information there for a computer to do anything but assume the date is from the current century, and it would therefore assume he was 5 years old.

The solution is for software to store and display four-digit dates.[1] Short-cuts that allow two-digit-date specifications are fine as long as the user is aware that they're using a shortcut and that there is little possibility for ambiguity. Sometimes the assumption that is made won't work. In those instances, there must be way to specify the full date.

Years Since 1900   Another manifestation of the problem will be programs and functions that return a value specifying the number of years since 1900. For a date in the 20th century, this type of program or function returns a two-digit value. But in the year 2000, a function that returns a value specifying the number of years since 1900 will return a value of 100. If your application assumes that it can simply print "19" followed by the value returned, you'll start printing values such as "19100" for dates!

Again, this problem will occur due to misuse of the function, not really a fault of the system. This problem is even easier to fix, since you technically should be adding the return value to 1900 and then printing the result. If you do so, it will work just fine.

UNIX in 2000   UNIX itself doesn't really have a problem in the year 2000. UNIX dates are stored as 32-bit integer values representing the number of seconds past midnight on January 1, 1970. Therefore, the value of 12:00:01 AM on January 1, 2000 is simply an integer that is two larger than the value that was represented at 11:59:59 PM on December 31, 1999.

Application programs that use dates can and do have a problem because of the way that they use and store values for the year. But UNIX itself will cruise along through New Year's Eve and New Year's Day in the year 2000 and not even know there's any problem.

UNIX in 2038   However (there's always a "however," isn't there?), this is not to say that UNIX will never have a problem. Astute readers will realize that even a 32-bit value has a limit. In the year 2038, the UNIX date value will roll over to zero; all 32 bits of the value will be "1" and when that value is incremented, all bits will be "0" again. At that point, all UNIX machines will believe it is January 1, 1970 again.

The good news is that we still have almost 40 years to prepare for this problem. With the advent of 64-bit systems, it seems safe to assume that this problem will be fixed long before we get there. (Not that a 64-bit system is *required,* but it will make the fix easier.) I feel confident in saying that if what we're using for operating systems in 2038 is even called UNIX, this problem won't be part of it.

64-Bit Systems

The first small computers were eight-bit systems. That is, the *bus* that connected the CPU to the memory had an 8-bit data path. Memory words were 8-bits long. Most

---

[1] If you're *really* thinking ahead, you might use five-digit dates, but I suppose it would be reasonable to assume that your code won't still be in use 8000 years from now!

memory addressing was 16 bits long (since eight-bits can represent only 256 different values). But combining two memory words to make an address reference was complicated to do in hardware.

Later, 16-bit systems, which allowed more data across the bus at one time, were introduced. A 16-bit value that is all ones (the maximum) is 65,536 or 64K. At the time, people really thought that 64K of memory would be enough for anything!

When 32-bit systems finally came about, four gigabytes of memory was addressable. Again, more data could be sent across a 32-bit bus. Everyone thought that this value would be the limit. After all, why wouldn't four gigabytes of addressable disk or memory be enough?

Now we're seeing 64-bit systems. A wider bus path allows more data to travel across the bus, so throughput is faster. Addressing is simplified because a 64-bit address can be stored in a single word of memory. This ability makes it easier to increase the 32-bit limit of four gigabytes for memory and disk addresses. If I were now to say that 64-bit architectures will surely be where we'll stop, I'll be wrong later, of course, so I won't say it!

Internet Addressing: IPv6

The current implementation of the Internet Protocol (IP), version 4, implements 32-bit addresses. However, with the growth of the Internet, this amount is quickly becoming insufficient to support all of the machines that people are connecting to the Internet. Like telephones, we are finding more uses for and more devices requiring IP addresses. Many printers also have their own IP addresses, and some laptops have multiple IP addresses for use in different locations.

In the early 1990s, it became clear that a new generation of IP that allowed for many more addresses would be necessary. Work began to define IPng (IP next generation), and a formal proposal for version 6 of IP was released in 1995.

IPv6 is a superset of IPv4 and allows addresses to be 128 bits long. The fact that IPv6 is a superset of IPv4 allows existing IPv4 machines to coexist on a network with IPv6 machines. This coexistence is necessary because the Internet is far too large to coordinate a "cut-over" to a new protocol at any moment in time. A smooth transition to a new addressing scheme requires the ability to evolve to it gradually rather than to require that we all wake up one day using the newer protocol.

IP packets of both versions specify a version in the first four bits of the packet. Therefore, a computer that speaks IPv6 can still recognize and handle an IPv4 packet. This feature allows the two to interoperate on the same network. Older machines can be upgraded to IPv6 as implementations become available or as system administrators have the opportunity to upgrade without requiring it all to happen simultaneously.

IPv6 is not currently in wide use. Some details of the standard are still being worked out, and vendors are implementing and testing the new protocol. However, over the next few years, IPv6 will be deployed across the Internet. If all goes well, users likely will not even notice.

High-Bandwidth Networks

In the early days of the Ethernet standard, one megabit per second was fast. Today, a rate of 100 megabits per second is not unusual in a local network. With fiber optics and other digital media, more data can be pushed through a network than ever before.

Because of the boom in Internet usage from web browsing, much more data is being sent than ever before. E-mail messages are small compared to the images, video, and sound that make up today's web pages. Fortunately, network bandwidth is increasing as fast as disk capacity and CPU speed. As usual, as we find newer, faster, bigger ways to do anything, we also find things to do with them. Remember when no one could imagine needing more than 64K of memory?

Fault-Tolerant Systems

As corporations rely more and more on computer systems, downtime becomes a bigger and bigger problem. In certain situations (e.g., with routers in the telephone network), almost any downtime is unacceptable.

Traditionally, the solution here has been to have *hot backup systems*. These systems run in parallel to the production system, updating the same data and shadowing activity. In the event that the production system crashes, the duplicate system can take over its function almost immediately while engineers fix the first system.

Fault-tolerant systems try to accomplish this task within a single system. A system with duplicate CPUs, memory, and devices can use the backup resource if the primary resource fails.

A few companies, Tandem being the best known, have been active in researching and providing fault-tolerant UNIX systems. Although hardware components are more reliable than they were a decade ago, some applications will always require as close to 100% uptime as is possible to achieve.

A SURVEY OF CURRENT POPULAR VERSIONS OF UNIX

Although UNIX had its start in a computer lab in Bell Laboratories, it has had a long, and sometimes convoluted, evolution since then. An in-depth discussion of how UNIX got to this point is beyond the scope of this book, but [22] gives an excellent view of the rich history of UNIX.

Part of the UNIX lore is the competition between Berkeley UNIX (BSD) and System III—and later, System V—UNIX as it continued at AT&T. For many years, the UNIX world was divided into these two camps. Most implementations of UNIX were based on one of these two types. The differences revolved mainly around kernel architecture and low-level operating-system algorithms (e.g., BSD and System V used radically different memory management algorithms). On the surface, where most users spent their time, the differences were subtle when they were noticeable at all.

When Sun Microsystems and AT&T joined forces to bring the BSD and System V worlds together, System V Release 4 and Solaris were born. SVR4 blended the best of both worlds.[2] With BSD lovers having most of their favorite capabilities in SVR4-based versions of UNIX, the "UNIX wars" began to subside.

---

[2] "Best" being an objective term, of course. You certainly can find people who will argue this point to this day. The *intent* was to merge the best of both versions.

The Open Software Foundation (OSF) was soon formed by a few companies (most notably HP and DEC) to come up with their own version of UNIX. This coalition was an attempt to prevent AT&T and Sun from completely dominating the perceived ownership, and therefore the future direction, of UNIX. As SVR4-based systems proved to meet customer needs and AT&T and Sun did not completely dominate UNIX, as many had feared they would do, this UNIX war also subsided, and OSF took its place in history.

Today, while there are still some BSD-centric versions of UNIX, the major differences are related to hardware platforms and performance. Other differences are mainly cosmetic. The basic UNIX system and interfaces are largely the same from one version to another (but just different enough to give you trouble from time to time). Vendors that supply their own distribution of UNIX add their own "value-added" commands and capabilities that they feel their customers demand. Porting software from one version to another, depending on the depth of operating system function the application might use, is still not trivial, but it also isn't the huge task that it was in the past.

Currently, there are at least 50 different versions of UNIX in existence. Most of these versions are targeted to specific applications (e.g., real-time computing), specific low-volume hardware (e.g., UNICOS, that runs on Cray Research supercomputers), or research based on previous work with UNIX. When you examine the "mainstream" versions of UNIX that are easily available on workstations or hardware for small servers, you wind up with about nine major versions of UNIX. The next set of alphabetically ordered subsections is not an exhaustive list, but it contains most of the versions that you are likely to run into in an average UNIX environment. All of these versions of UNIX provide facilities (in varying implementations) discussed in previous chapters of this book (e.g., the X Window System, TCP/IP networking, most "standard" UNIX commands) unless otherwise noted.

AIX

AIX (Advanced Interactive eXecutive) is IBM's implementation of UNIX and runs on their RISC System/6000 workstation and server platforms. It is based on System V UNIX with SVR4 and BSD extensions. RS/6000 platforms offer multiprocessor systems as well as 64-bit systems.

If you have used other IBM systems in the past, parts of AIX will seem more familiar to you than other versions of UNIX will. AIX has more verbose error messages than do other versions of UNIX. Most of these messages are indexed with error codes to direct you to more information in a manual. While at first this process, seems cumbersome, especially compared to the terse nature of the original versions of UNIX, it does prove helpful at times.

More information on AIX is available on the web at the URL http://www.rs6000.ibm.com/software.

Digital UNIX

Digital Equipment Corporation (DEC) has made several forays into the UNIX world. Their original UNIX offering, BSD-based Ultrix, never had much more than a cult following. Ultrix ran on DEC's VAX hardware line, and at the time, if you had a VAX and wanted to run BSD UNIX, you simply ran BSD UNIX straight from Berkeley. When the Open Software Foundation was formed, DEC contributed some of the best parts of Ultrix to what eventually became OSF/1.

DEC distributed OSF/1 for a while, but as the OSF movement lost its momentum, they rolled it all into what is now Digital UNIX. Based on SVR4, Digital UNIX is a 64-bit operating system and runs DEC's Alpha platform.

As I write this text, Compaq has just acquired DEC. It remains to be seen how, if at all, this change will affect DEC's UNIX offering. For more information on Digital UNIX, see http://www.unix.digital.com.

FreeBSD

FreeBSD, as you might guess, is a free implementation of the Berkeley Standard Distribution version of UNIX. It is one of several free versions of UNIX available today. FreeBSD runs on PC-compatible hardware (386, 486, Pentium CPUs, and most standard PC bus architectures).

Programmers all over the world contribute code to the FreeBSD Project to fix and improve code in FreeBSD. The web site for FreeBSD provides information about the contributors and how to participate.

FreeBSD can be downloaded from the Internet (but it's big) or can be obtained on CD-ROM for only a media charge. For more information about FreeBSD, see http://www.freebsd.org.

HP-UX

The Hewlett-Packard Company's contribution to UNIX is known as HP-UX, and it runs on their PA-RISC hardware platform. HP-UX is based on System V UNIX with SVR4 and BSD enhancements.

HP-UX is a 64-bit version of UNIX and conforms to all of the popular UNIX standards. It is currently the number-one or number-two vendor-supplied version of UNIX, depending on whose statistics you read. For a company that wasn't involved at the beginning of the evolution of UNIX, HP has done a nice job of adopting "the UNIX philosophy" and staying true to it in their development of HP-UX.

For more information on HP-UX, go to http://www.hp.com/go/hpux.

IRIX

Silicon Graphics, Inc. has traditionally set the standard in high-speed, high-resolution graphics hardware. Their version of UNIX, known as IRIX, has always seemed to trail somewhat behind the other vendors' versions. It was System V–based in the days when most versions of UNIX were BSD based, so compatibility in mixed environments was problematical. Back then, you bought an SGI UNIX platform because you wanted an incredible graphics workstation. (When the little girl in *Jurassic Park* walks up to the workstation in the computer room and says, "It's a UNIX box!", it's an SGI box.)

In the past few years, as the world has standardized on SVR4 and IRIX releases have stabilized, IRIX has become a real competitor all by itself (even outside of the fact that SGI still makes one of the best graphics platforms). IRIX now includes most of the best features of SVR4 as well as of BSD UNIX and is a 64-bit platform.

For more information on IRIX, go to SGI's website at http://www.sgi.com.

Linux

Linux is another of the free versions of UNIX for PC architectures. In addition, it has also been ported to DEC's Alpha, Sun's SPARC, and Motorola's Power PC platforms. It was originally written by Linus Torvalds, a student at the University of Helsinki at the time, to conform to the POSIX standard, probably the most dominant UNIX specification. He started it as a hobby, but as Linus felt that the world needed an unencumbered version of UNIX that could be freely distributed without worries about licensing restrictions, he continued and completed his project. Today, developers around the world contribute new code and fixes for Linux.

Linux is loosely based on SVR4. I say "loosely" because it didn't actually start with System V source code, since Linus wrote the code from scratch. In fact, the Linux web site calls it a "UNIX-like" operating system rather than calling it a "UNIX" operating system, but it mimics UNIX so well that only a kernel hacker would be able to tell the difference. New code and fixes are developed by the Free Software Foundation's GNU Project (the same place that gave the world the GNU Emacs editor).

Since Linux was written from scratch and contains no source code belonging to AT&T, the University of California at Berkeley, or anyone else, it can be distributed with the source code. This aspect is probably the greatest advantage that Linux has over most other versions of UNIX. If you want to learn about its internal workings or modify it to suit your own specific purposes, the option is there.

Linux can be redistributed and even sold, so long as the source code remains available. Several companies have made it their business to sell and support their own distributions of Linux. You can often find the Red Hat or Slackware distributions of Linux in your local computer store.

For more information on Linux itself, see http://www.linux.org.

NetBSD

NetBSD is often confused with FreeBSD. They truly are two separate projects, but with similar goals: to provide a free implementation of BSD UNIX.

The NetBSD project is, as with Linux and FreeBSD, a collaborative effort among developers all over the world to maintain and improve the operating system. NetBSD is also called a UNIX-like operating system, but is based on code from 4.4BSD Lite, a subset of the BSD code from Berkeley. Like Linux, NetBSD is also distributed with source code.

NetBSD runs on many different platforms, including PCs, DEC Alphas and Vaxes, HP 9000s, Macintoshes, and Sun SPARC workstations. For more information about NetBSD, visit its web site at http://www.netbsd.org.

SCO Unixware

The Santa Cruz Operation has been in the UNIX business for a long time. For years, SCO UNIX on PCs was the choice for small UNIX shops that couldn't afford higher priced workstations.

Over the years, SCO moved towards a standard AT&T-based distribution of UNIX. During a period in their history, AT&T called their distribution Unixware. In 1995, when SCO acquired UNIX Systems Laboratories, the group that owned the UNIX trademark, it also acquired the Unixware name.

SCO also offers a free license for SCO Unixware to individuals for personal, noncommercial uses. Media is available for a nominal production fee. For more information on SCO Unixware, see http://www.sco.com.

Solaris

Sun Microsystems, Inc. is probably credited with starting the modern UNIX revolution. In the early 1980s, most distributions came directly from AT&T or the University of California at Berkeley and ran on whatever hardware you had that those versions supported. However, a handful of small companies were springing up that took various versions of these base distributions and tried to make a business out of selling and supporting UNIX systems, most based on the Motorola 68000 CPU.

SunOS ran on the MC68010 and MC68020 early on. Eventually, Sun decided that they could better serve their customers if they also designed hardware specifically to run UNIX, as Motorola had not designed the 68000 family with UNIX in mind. Sun emerged from the pack as the early leader in developing and improving UNIX systems and is arguably still the leader. (HP and IBM would probably argue the point.)

Solaris is the current point in the evolution of Sun's UNIX. The original SunOS was based on BSD UNIX, which was because several of the founders of Sun came from Berkeley—most notably Bill Joy, author of the **vi** editor. Sun made a leap from SunOS to Solaris when it entered into a partnership with AT&T to standardize around System V. Solaris, of course, includes all of the best features of BSD and SunOS to which Sun's customers had become accustomed.

Solaris runs on Sun's SPARC platform family, as well as on Intel (PC) architectures. For more information on Solaris, see http://www.sun.com/solaris.

CHAPTER REVIEW

Checklist

In this chapter, I described:

- object-oriented programming
- parallel, distributed, and multiprocessor systems
- multiprocessing systems
- the Year 2000 problem
- 64-bit architectures

- high-bandwidth networking
- fault-tolerant systems
- various versions of UNIX

Quiz

1. Which versions of UNIX are free?
2. Is the Y2K problem solvable? Is it solvable before 1/1/00? Should I even write "1/1/00?"
3. How is data associated with an object different than traditional data in a computer program?

Projects

1. Determine the last date and time in the year 2038 that UNIX will be able to represent. [level: *medium*]
2. Download one of the free versions of UNIX from the Internet and install it. [level: *medium*]

Appendix

REGULAR EXPRESSIONS

Regular expressions are character sequences that describe a family of matching strings. They are accepted as arguments to many UNIX utilities, such as **grep**, **egrep**, **awk**, **sed**, and **vi**. Note that the filename-substitution wildcards used by the shells are *not* examples of regular expressions, as they use different matching rules.

Regular expressions are formed out of a sequence of normal character and special characters. Here is a list of special characters, sometimes called *metacharacters*, together with their respective meanings:

Metacharacter	Meaning
.	Matches any single character.
[]	Matches any of the single characters enclosed in brackets. A hyphen may be used to represent a range of characters. If the first character after the "[" is a "^", then any character *not* enclosed in brackets is matched. The "*", "^", "$", and "\" metacharacters lose their special meaning when used inside brackets.
*	May follow any character, and denotes zero or more occurrences of the character that precedes it.
^	Matches the beginning of a line only.
$	Matches the end of a line only.
\	The meaning of any metacharacter may be inhibited by preceding it with a "\".

A regular expression matches the longest pattern that it can. For example, when the pattern "y.*ba" is searched for in the string "yabadabadoo", the match occurs against the substring "yabadaba" and not "yaba". The next page contains some examples of regular expressions in action.

To illustrate the use of these metacharacters, here is a piece of text, followed by the lines of text that would match various regular expressions. The portion of each line that satisfies the regular expression is italicized.

Text

```
Well you know it's your bedtime,
So turn off the light,
Say all your prayers and then,
Oh you sleepy young heads dream of wonderful things,
Beautiful mermaids will swim through the sea,
And you will be swimming there too.
```

Patterns

Pattern	Lines That Match
the	So turn off *the* light, Say all your prayers and *the*n, Beautiful mermaids will swim through *the* sea, And you will be swimming *the*re too.
.nd	Say all your prayers *and* then, Oh you sleepy young heads dream of w*ond*erful things, *And* you will be swimming there too.
^.nd	*And* you will be swimming there too.
sw.*ng	And you will be *swimming* there too.
[A-D]	*B*eautiful mermaids will swim through the sea, *A*nd you will be swimming there too.
\.	And you will be swimming there too*.* (The "." is italicized.)
a.	S*ay* all your prayers and then, Oh you sleepy young he*ad*s dream of wonderful things, Be*au*tiful mermaids will swim through the sea,
a.$	Beautiful mermaids will swim through the se*a,*
[a-m]nd	Say all your prayers *and* then,
[^a-m]nd	Oh you sleepy young heads dream of w*ond*erful things, *And* you will be swimming there too.

Extended Regular Expressions

Some utilities, such as **egrep**, support an extended set of metacharacters, which are described below:

Metacharacter	Meaning
+	Matches one or more occurrences of the single preceding character.
?	Matches zero or one occurrence(s) of the single preceding character.
| (pipe symbol)	If you place a pipe symbol between two regular expressions, a string that matches either expression will be accepted. In other words, a "|" acts like a logical "or" operator.
()	If you place a regular expression in parentheses, you may use the "*", "+", or "?" metacharacters to operate on the entire expression, rather than on just a single character.

Here are some examples of full regular expressions, using the example file from the previous page:

Pattern	Lines That Match
s .*w	Oh you *sleepy young heads dream of* wonderful things, Beautiful mermaids *will sw*im through the sea, And you will be *sw*imming there too.
s .+w	Oh you *sleepy young heads dream of* wonderful things, Beautiful mermaids *will sw*im through the sea,
off|will	So turn *off* the light, Beautiful mermaids *will* swim through the sea, And you *will* be swimming there too.
im*ing	And you will be sw*imming* there too.
im?ing	No matches.

MODIFIED-FOR-UNIX BACKUS–NAUR NOTATION

The syntax of the UNIX utilities and system calls in this book are presented in a modified version of a language known as Backus–Naur Form, or BNF for short. In a BNF description, the following sequences have special meanings:

Sequence	Meaning
[*strings*]	*strings* may appear zero or one time.
{ *strings* }*	*strings* may appear zero or more times.
{ *strings* }+	*strings* may appear one or more times.
string1 | *string2*	*string1* or *string2* may appear.
-*optionlist*	Zero or more options may follow a dash.

The final sequence is the UNIX-oriented modification, which allows me to avoid placing large numbers of brackets around command-line options. To indicate a "[", "{", "|", or "-" without its special meaning, I precede it with a "\" character.

Some variations of commands depend on which option you choose. I indicate this situation by supplying a separate syntax description for each variation. For example, take a look at the syntax description of the **at** utility:

Utility: **at** -csm *time* [*date* [, *year*]][+*increment*][*script*]
     at -r { *jobId*}+
     at -l { *jobId*}*

The first version of the **at** utility is selected by any combination of the command-line options "-c", "-s", and "-m". These options must then be followed by a time and an optional date specifier. The optional date specifier may be followed by an optional year specifier. Additionally, an increment and/or script name may be specified.

The second version of **at** is selected by an "-r" option and may be followed by one or more job ID numbers.

The third version of **at** is selected by a "-l" option and may be followed by zero or more job ID numbers.

SYSTEM CALLS: AN ALPHABETICAL CROSS-REFERENCE

Here is a list of references to each system call. The page number of the description of the system call is in boldface.

Name	Synopsis	Examples
accept	accepts a connection request from a client socket	463, **468**, 469, 479, 507
alarm	sets a process "alarm clock"	**442**, 444
bind	binds a socket to a name	463, **467**, 479, 507
chdir	changes a process' current working directory	**431**, 432
chmod	changes a file's permission settings	**415**, 457, 458
chown	changes a file's owner and/or group	**414**
close	closes a file	387, 394, 400, **401**, 408, 416, 418, 436, 439, 455, 456, 458, 463, 465, 469, 473, 498, 499, 503, 506, 507
connect	connects to a named server socket	464, **470**, 473, 478, 506
dup	duplicates a file descriptor	**415**, 416, 499
dup2	similar to "dup"	**415**, 416, 439, 456, 498, 499, 503, 506, 507
execl	replaces the calling process' code, data, and stack from an executable file	**430**
execlp	similar to "execl"	**430**, 431, 456
execv	similar to "execl"	**430**
execvp	similar to "execl"	**430**, 435, 439, 446, 499
exit	terminates a process	395, 406, 408, **427**, 428, 430, 436, 447, 451, 452, 463, 465, 469, 473, 496, 497, 498, 499
fchmod	similar to "chmod"	**415**
fchown	similar to "chown"	**414**
fcntl	gives access to miscellaneous file characteristics	387, **417**, 418
fork	duplicates a process	**424**, 425, 426, 428, 429, 434, 436, 446, 447, 450, 451, 452, 455, 456, 469, 496, 497, 498
fstat	similar to "stat"	**411**
ftruncate	similar to "truncate"	**420**
getdents	obtains directory entries	408, **412**, 436
getegid	returns a process's effective group ID number	**433**

Name	Synopsis	Examples
geteuid	returns a process's effective user ID number	**433**
getgid	returns a process's real group ID number	**433**
gethostname	returns the name of the host	474, **476**, 505
getpgid	returns a process' process-group ID number	**450**
getpid	returns a process' ID number	**425**, 426, 430, 450, 451, 496
getppid	returns a parent process' ID number	**425**, 426, 430
getuid	returns a process' real user ID number	**433**
ioctl	controls a device	**418**
kill	sends a signal to a specified process or group of processes	**445**, 447, 448
lchown	changes a link's owner and/or group	**414**
link	creates a hard link	**418**, 419
listen	sets the maximum number of pending socket connections	463, **468**, 479, 507
lseek	moves to a particular offset in a file	387, 394, **399**, 400, 408, 417, 436
lstat	returns status information about a link	**411**
mknod	creates a special file	**419**, 457, 458
nice	changes a process' priority	**432**, 433
open	opens/creates a file	386, 387, 393, **396**, 397, 400, 408, 416, 417, 436, 439, 458, 503
pause	suspends the calling process and returns when a signal is received	**443**, 444, 451
pipe	creates an unnamed pipe	**454**, 455, 456, 497
read	reads bytes from a file into a buffer	387, 393, 394, **397**, 398, 400, 455, 458, 465, 471, 475
setegid	sets a process' effective group ID number	**434**
seteuid	sets a process' effective user ID number	**434**
setgid	sets a process' real and effective group ID number	**434**
setpgid	sets a process' process-group ID number	**450**, 451, 452, 496
setuid	sets a process' real and effective user ID numbers	**434**
signal	specifies the action that will be taken when a particular signal arrives	**443**, 444, 446, 451, 452, 463, 490, 496
socket	creates an unnamed socket	463, 464, **465**, 470, 473, 478, 479, 505, 506
stat	returns status information about a file	407, **411**, 412, 435
sync	schedules all file buffers to be flushed to disk	**420**
truncate	truncates a file	**420**, 421
unlink	removes a file	394, **401**, 402, 458, 463, 467, 507
wait	waits for a child process	**429**, 430, 436, 447, 452, 497, 498
write	writes bytes from a buffer to a file	387, 393, 394, **398**, 399, 400, 416, 417, 418, 455, 458, 464, 471

Bibliography

Here's a list of the texts that I refer to in this book. The number that precedes the title of each text is the index number that I use in my references. I've included the ISBN and edition numbers just in case they're useful to you.

1. *A Practical Guide to the UNIX System*, 2d. ed., Sobell, ISBN 0-8053-0243-3
2. *Advanced UNIX Programming*, Rochkind, ISBN 0-13-011800-1
3. *C Programming in the Berkeley UNIX Environment*, Kernighan, ISBN 0-13-109760-1
4. *DOS\UNIX—Becoming a Super User*, Seyer and Mills, ISBN 0-13-218645-4
5. *The Design of the UNIX Operating System*, Bach, ISBN 0-13-201799-7
6. *The Korn Shell*, Bolsky and Korn, ISBN 0-13-516972-0
7. *The UNIX C Shell Field Guide*, Anderson and Anderson, ISBN 0-13-937468-X
8. *The UNIX Operating System*, 2d. ed., Christian, ISBN 0-471-84782-8
9. *The UNIX Programming Environment*, Kernighan and Pike, ISBN 0-13-937681-X
10. *The X Window System Programming and Applications With Xt*, Young, ISBN 0-13-497074-8
11. *Tricks of the UNIX Masters*, Sage, ISBN 0-672-22449-6
12. *UNIX Communications*, The Waite Group, ISBN 0-672-22511-5
13. *UNIX Network Programming*, Stevens, ISBN 0-13-949876-1
14. *UNIX Papers*, The Waite Group, ISBN 0-672-22578-6
15. *UNIX RefGuide*, McNulty Development, Inc., ISBN 0-13-938957-0
16. *UNIX System Administration Handbook*, Nemeth, Snyder, Seebass and Hein, ISBN 0-13-151051-7
17. *UNIX System Architecture*, Andleigh, ISBN 0-13-949843-5
18. *4.3 BSD UNIX Operating System*, Leffler, McKusick, Karels and Quarterman, ISBN 0-201-06196-1
19. *UNIX Desktop Guide to EMACS*, Roberts, ISBN 0-672-30171-7
20. *Advanced Programming in the UNIX Environment*, Stevens, ISBN 0-201-56316-7
21. *UNIX Internals—The New Frontiers*, Vahalia, ISBN 0-13-101908-2
22. *A Quarter Century of UNIX*, Salus, ISBN 0-201-54777-5
23. *Perl 5 by Example*, Medinets, ISBN 0-7897-0866-3
24. *X Window System User's Guide—OSF/Motif Edition*, Quercia and O'Reilly, ISBN 0-937175-61-7

25. *OSF/Motif User's Guide*, Open Software Foundation, ISBN 0-13-643131-3

26. *Motif Reference Manual*, Ferguson, ISBN 1-56592-038-4

27. *Practical UNIX Security*, Garfinkel and Spafford, ISBN 0-937175-72-2

28. *Programming Perl*, Wall and Schwartz, ISBN 0-937175-64-1

29. *UNIX System Security*, Curry, ISBN 0-201-56327-4

30. *Firewalls and Internet Security*, Cheswick and Bellovin, ISBN 0-201-63357-4

Index